THE ENEMY IS WITHIN

BIBLICAL INTERPRETATION SERIES

VOLUME 67

THE ENEMY IS WITHIN

A Jungian Psychoanalytic Approach to the Book of Judith

BY

HELEN EFTHIMIADIS-KEITH

BRILL ACADEMIC PUBLISHERS, INC.
BOSTON • LEIDEN
2004

Library of Congress Cataloging-in-Publication Data

Efthimiadis-Keith, Helen.
The enemy is within: a Jungian psychoanalytic approach to the book of Judith/by Helen Efthimiadis-Keith.
p. cm. — (Biblical interpretation series; v. 67)
Includes bibliographical references and index.
ISBN 0-391-04214-9
1. Bible. O.T. Judith—Criticism, interpretation, etc. 2. Bible. O.T. Judith—Pschology.
3. Jungian psychology. I. Title. II. Series.

BS1735.52.E38 2004
229'.246'019—dc22 2004045611

The following diagrams, appearing within on the pages indicated,
The Anthropos and Shadow *Quaternios*, p. 73
The Paradise *Quaternio*, p. 74
The Lapis *Quaternio*, p. 74
The Vertical Arrangement of Jung's *Quaternio*, p. 76
The Uroboric Arrangement of Jung's *Quaternio*, pp. 76, 396
The *Quaternio* Equation, p. 76,

are taken and adapted from C. G. Jung, *Aion: Researches into the Phenomenology of the Self. The Collected Works of C. G. Jung*; trans. R. F. C. Hull, 2d ed. London: Routledge & Kegan Paul, © 1968, and are used with permission.

The financial assistance of the National Research Foundation (RSA) and the University of the North towards the doctoral dissertation on which this book is based is hereby gratefully acknowledged. Opinions expressed and conclusions arrived at in this publication are those of the author and are not necessarily attributable to the National Research Foundation (RSA) or the University of the North.

ISSN 0928-0731
ISBN 0-391-04214-9

PRINTED IN THE UNITED STATES OF AMERICA

In loving memory of the best parents
that I could ever have had

Varvara & Neofytos M. Efthimiadis
(R.I.P.)

CONTENTS

PREFACE

First and foremost, my thanks, appreciation, and adoration go to my Lord and Saviour, Jesus Christ, my best Friend in all creation for His continued, unstinting support, inspiration, encouragement and the way that He has led me on my particular path of individuation towards the Father through the Blessed Holy Spirit. Soli Deo Gloria.

Without Prof. J. Cook, my promoter, and Prof. M. J. Oosthuizen, my co-promoter, this study would not have reached its completion. Their advice on all aspects of this dissertation has been invaluable. Their insightful direction has afforded better clarity to my work in times when I was unsure of the way ahead. They have gone beyond the call of duty in their work as promoters. Thank-you gentlemen. I am forever grateful to you.

The University of the North has helped me financially twice in times of need, and twice granted me study leave to complete various sections of my work. In particular, I wish to express my gratitude to my colleagues in Biblical Sciences at the former Faculty of Theology and Religious Studies for assisting me with my workload when particular deadlines in respect of this thesis had to be met. I wish to express my undying gratitude to Mr. WES Thema, Ms. N. Machethe, Dr. K. D. Payle and my colleagues at Student Development & Support Services and the Academic Development Unit for making it possible for me to take the academic vacations and study leave for my work on at least two occasions. You are all wonderful and I am privileged to know you. Thank you.

My beloved husband, soul mate, and friend, Jerry Keith, has been an invaluable sounding board for many of my ideas, and he has unselfishly sacrificed time with me to enable me to work on my dissertation. He has taken so many household chores off me and cooked nutritionally balanced food so that I could complete my studies in good health. Honey, you are a one-in-a-million angel. Thank you too for assisting me so expertly with editing the final draft of my work and printing it.

Without my parents Varvara and Neofytos, where would I be? Both have supported me with prayer, love, and encouragement. Both have really suffered with me in this great trial. Dad always said that he would find peace and rest once I had completed my thesis. That opportunity was never granted him whilst he was still on earth. I hope he is proud of me now that he is in eternal glory. You are the best parents I could ever have asked for. Thank-you for all you are and all you have done for me.

My best friends, Lianne Barnard, Beryl Judd, Ladan Shaker, Thora and Andy Sapiro, Ron Pitts, Linda Roome, Lynn and Candice Pearmain, Kenny Payle, and Arda Spijker-Harris have been absolutely wonderful in their support, encouragement, and intellectual appraisal of my work at various stages. In particular, Ms. Judd's professional language editing of the first draft of my dissertation has been superb. Whatever mistakes there may be in the final draft are there through no fault of her own. You are the best friends anyone can have.

Thora and Andy Sapiro, our friends and house-church leaders, have been phenomenal. Their prayers, encouragement, and counsel have been invaluable to me and us. Andy tirelessly fixed an ailing computer and twice saved me from losing all my work. Bless you, dear saints and friends!

My feline children—ten stunning creatures of superb beauty and individuality—have always come to encourage me whilst I have been typing, reading, etc. Their subtle calls for attention, unmistakable love, and crazy antics have often kept me grounded and provided great comic relief in times of stress. Miau!

LIST OF ABBREVIATIONS

א*	Codex Sinaiticus, original, fourth century A.D.
A/LXXA	Codex Alexandrinus, fifth century A.D.
A.D.	*Anno Domini*
Absol.	Absolute
BC	Before Christ
BHS	*Biblia Hebraica Stuttgartensia* (1990. Deutsche Bibelgesellschaft Stuttgart. LLS)
c.	*Circa*
cf.	Compare
cont.	Continued
Ed./eds	Editor/editors
e.g.	For example
ESL	Enhanced Strong's Lexicon (LRS)
i.a.	Inter alia
i.e.	Id est
ibid.	Ibidem
KJV	King James Version (1769. Cambridge: Cambridge. LLS)
KJVA	King James Version Apocrypha (1995. Oak Harbor, WA: LRS)
LLS	Logos Library Services 2.1.
LRS	Logos Research Systems Inc. (1995)
LXX	Septuaginta (1979. Deutsche Bibelgesellschaft Stuttgart. LLS)
LXX^{B}	Codex Vaticanus, fourth century A.D.
LXX^{N}	Codex Basiliano-Vaticanus, eighth–ninth century A.D.
LXX^{S}	Codex Sinaiticus, fourth century A.D.
Ms/s	Manuscript/s
n.	Footnote
NEB	New English Bible
OTE	Old Testament Essays
op. cit.	Opere citato
p./pp.	Page/pages
RAPC	1957 RSV Apocrypha (as per Online Bible Millennium Edition 2.1
RSV	Revised Standard Version (as per BibleDatabase 4.0.3)
Transl.	Translation/translated (by)
viz.	Videlicet
vs.	Versus

LIST OF DIAGRAMS

LIST OF TABLES

CHAPTER ONE

INTRODUCTION

When I began studying the Book of Judith, I discovered a certain paucity of research on this book relative to the seemingly endless stream of literature available on other Old Testament books that I had studied (e.g., Psalms, Exodus, Ruth, Deuteronomy, Proverbs). There also seemed to be a large gap between studies of the past and studies of more recent times, with few significant works appearing between the second half of the seventeenth century and the second half of the nineteenth century. Arguably, the most important works of this time are: Capellus's *Commentarii et Notae Criticae in Lib. Judith* (1689), Fritzsche's *Die Bücher Tobi und Judith erklärt* (1853), Volkmar's "Judith" (in *Handbuch der Einleitung in die Apokryphen I*, 1860), Ball's "Judith" (in Wace's *The Holy Bible Apocrypha*, 1888), and Gaster's "Judith" (in *Encyclopaedia Biblica*, 1894).[1] Analyses of *Judith*[2] had roughly three main emphases: historical, nonhistorical (e.g., literary-critical, art criticism) and a combination of these. The 'historical' analyses emphasised the historicity of the book—either refuting or supporting it in various ways—while the nonhistorical approaches were concerned with, inter alia, the structure of the book, its narrative aspects, and the way it had been represented in world literature or artistic form. Notably, the nonhistorical approaches were a more recent trend, represented primarily by Alonso Schökel's *Narrative Structures in the Book of Judith* (1975), Toni Craven's seminal dissertation, *Artistry and Faith in the Book of Judith* (1983a), Margarita Stocker's 1998 monograph, *Judith: Sexual Warrior. Women and Power in Western Culture*, as well as a number of essays published in volumes such as "*No-one*

[1] I have tried repeatedly and in vain to obtain copies of these and other works (e.g., Steinmetzer's *Neue Untersuchung über die Geschichtlichkeit der Judith-erzählung*, 1907). Hence, I refer to them here, exclude them from my bibliography, and reluctantly rely on authors such as Moore (1985), Enslin (1972), and Pfeiffer (1949) for the content of their work.

[2] '*Judith*' (italicised) refers to the Apocryphal Book of Judith, while 'Judith' (no italics) refers to the heroine of the book.

Spoke Ill of Her" (VanderKam [ed.] 1992) and *A Feminist Companion to Esther, Judith and Susanna* (Brenner [ed.] 1995). It soon became apparent that many of the essays were published two or three times over, under different or the same titles (see chapter 3, especially sections D and E). The combination approaches commented upon the historical situation that gave rise to the Book of Judith and proceeded to discuss its value as a literary work of art and provide commentary on the entire book or sections of it. These works—even the commentaries—were not overly concerned with the historicity of the book or its historical situation per se. Such is the work of, inter alia, Enslin (*The Book of Judith*, 1972), Moore (*Judith. A New Translation with Introduction and Commentary*, 1985), Lacocque (*The Feminine Unconventional. Four Subversive Figures in Israel's Tradition*, 1990), and Craghan (*Esther, Judith, Tobit, Jonah, Ruth*, 1982a).

Although this did not appear to be a 'modern' problem, I became keenly conscious of the dispute that raged between those who tried to prove *Judith's* historicity and those who disparaged it altogether. It perturbed me that those who clung to *Judith's* historicity did so primarily because they believed that, as the 'Word of God', *Judith* had to comply with exact historical facts in order for it to be true, while those of the latter persuasion seemed to regard the book as 'pure fiction' precisely because it did not correspond with historical 'truth'.[3]

Moreover, many of those who held onto *Judith* as the 'Word of God' often tried to defend the seemingly dual character of the heroine who is at once a woman of great piety and one of great lies and deception—"the saint who murdered for her people" as someone once called her. Naturally, members of the opposing faction often found the character of this 'murdering saint' most reprehensible and totally unfit for the moral instruction of the faithful (and of women in particular, I dare add). The latter added the heroine's dual nature to their list of reasons for rejecting the book in its entirety.

I was further intrigued by the way in which some rejected the book's value on account of its supposedly lopsided structure. According to these critics, the first section of the book, chapters 1–7, were completely superfluous to the 'real story' recorded in *Judith* 8–16. Even those who were not entirely biased against *Judith* 1–7 tended to ignore it in their commentary upon the text (e.g., Craghan 1982b).

[3] For a similar opinion, see Pfeiffer 1949:291.

I could not believe that the great Holofernes and the battles he fought for his king and god, Nebuchadnezzar, were there merely for the show, a rather bad artistic whim of the book's author.

In my opinion, the positions described above did serious violence to the text and message of *Judith*, failing to appreciate it on a textual level and beyond because of their narrowly defined concepts of artistic 'balance', morality, historicity, and truth. For me, the book was perfectly balanced, and its heroine true to life *because of* her so-called 'duality'. Moreover, I believe that truth cannot be related to historical correspondence on a one-to-one basis. On a personal level, something need not reflect so-called 'objective' reality for it to be true *for me* and, to extend the argument, a book does not need to reflect exact historical occurrences for it to have played a significant psychological role[4] in the circles of those who produced it. The Book of Daniel in the Old Testament is just such a case. It purports to have occurred during the reign of Nebuchadnezzar, whereas, in fact, its contents clearly indicate a Hellenistic background. *Daniel* may be regarded as 'underground literature' that was written with the purpose of encouraging the faithful during the hazardous time of Antiochus IV Epiphanes. Many commentators have made similar claims for *Judith*, as we shall see later (see e.g., Lacocque 1990:47).

Be that as it may, modern authors such as Moore (1985:52) have rightly emphasised the importance of distinguishing the period of *Judith's* setting from that of its composition in order to overcome the problem of conflicting historical elements (e.g., Persian vs. Hellenistic) that are scattered throughout the book. Others, such as Steinmetzer, have pointed to the textual evolution of the book. Yet others (e.g., Craven—see below) have regarded them as deliberate signs of the book's fictionality. While the thinking of modern scholars certainly represents an improvement on that of the past, such comments, quickly made, do not, in my opinion, offer an in-depth, holistic solution to the problem at hand. They do not respond to why these historical inconsistencies should be present beyond the possible evolution of the text or the difference between the context and setting of the book. They do not account for the intrinsic value that these often

[4] As will be seen in chapter 2, Jung regards the psyche—particularly the unconscious psyche—as the matrix of all things and of all beings. Thus, to speak of the psychological role of an event/figure, etc. is to speak of the way it has affected all spheres of life.

confusing and contradictory elements may have. Why are these elements there beyond the textual evolution of the text? Why did the author (deliberately) include these elements and not others? What is their functional value? What could they possibly have meant to those who read/heard them in their totality (the so-called first audience of the completed book)?

The same type of questions may be asked with regard to the other problem areas: What was the function and meaning of the book's clearly bipartite structure? Why is it divided in this fashion beyond, for example, the possible evolution of the text? Why is the heroine imbued with such a dual nature? What possible meaning did this character hold for the book's first audience? What hopes and dreams did she personify? Why is Achior there beyond providing a kind of connecting bridge between the two sections of the book, as Moore (op. cit., 59) has suggested?

In an attempt to answer these questions, I set about finding an approach to the text that would integrate the presence of these 'inconsistencies' in situation, structure, and character with their psychological value. I needed to find a way that would accommodate my 'liberal' approach towards historicity/truth and maintain the essential integrity (validity) that I felt both the book and its heroine possessed. In other words, I was looking for a method that would permit me to integrate the book's structure and content within a more holistic approach to truth.

Owing to my long-standing interest in psychoanalytic theory, I had already begun to study the works of Freud and Jung—the men who are generally regarded as the fathers of modern psychoanalytic practice—at approximately the same time that all these questions about *Judith* were taking shape in my head. To my great excitement, I discovered that while some of the works on *Judith* briefly referred to possible psychoanalytic or archetypal interpretations of the book and its heroine (e.g., Coote 1975:21–26 and Bal 1995:253–285), no one had ever applied psychoanalytic categories to this book on a larger scale. Hence, I began investigating the viability of applying such theories to *Judith*. As a result, I published my first psychoanalytic reading of the book (written in 1998) according to the Freudian concept of castration (cf. Efthimiadis-Keith 1999a:211–228). Having done so, I applied myself to the works of Freud's student—and, some would argue, his successor—Carl Gustav Jung. While the theories of these two men bear some affinity, they are also characterised by important differences, not only regarding their subject matter—the psyche—per se, but also the way in which they conduct their research, their approach to therapy, and their writing styles.[5] Despite myself, I found that I was soon drawn to Jung's narrative, mystical (and, some would say, 'unscientific') approach. To my mind, the fact that Jung took seriously the study and function of (supposedly) 'irrational' myths/dreams/legends in the formation of the human psyche made his approach a far more conducive medium for interpreting *Judith* than Freud's biological determinism. To my mind, the workings of the unconscious psyche as revealed by Jung's studies accurately reflected the 'chaos' and 'irrationality' of which others had accused *Judith* (cf. Efthimiadis-Keith 1999b:156–158). Moreover, his dictum that something is true if it is *psychologically* true echoed my own thinking and presented me with the holistic interpretative framework that I was looking for.

The more I studied Jung's theories, the more I began to see the importance of both Holofernes and the first section of *Judith*, and the more I began to regard *Judith* as a national dream depicting the individuation (maturation) process of the Judaean/Jewish nation at the time reflected by the book's main events, namely the battles between Judas Maccabeus and Nicanor (c. 165 and 161 B.C.; see Efthimiadis-Keith 1999b:164–167). I published my preliminary thoughts on the subject in an article entitled *The Dream of Judith: a Jungian Psychoanalytic Approach* (op. cit., 151–169) and continued studying *Judith*, Jung, and the manifold applications of his work to various types of biblical and secular literature. This book is the result of these studies.

A. *Research Problem and History of Research:* Judith's *Historicity, its Structural Unity, and the Characters Judith and Achior*

Most, if not all, of the works I have studied on *Judith* identify at least two of the following points as problematic and deal with them in different ways—sometimes toiling laboriously over an issue, and at other times glancing them over and voicing assent or dissent with other scholars:

[5] As it is not the purpose of my thesis to compare the works of these two men, I refer the reader to Brown (1961:42–50) for a succinct summary of the differences between them. I will refer to such by means of footnotes where necessary throughout the course of my work.

- The glaring historical, geographical, and chronological anachronisms found in *Judith*
- The historical identification of the book's main characters and events
- The date, place, and compositional evolution of *Judith*
- The book's religious background
- The theology of *Judith*
- The canonicity of the book
- The purpose of Judith
- The book's division into two neat units (1–7; 8–16) and the relation between them
- The seemingly dual nature of Judith's character; her deed, and the way it was accomplished
- The role of God in the book
- The relation between Holofernes and Nebuchadnezzar (why Holofernes is punished if Nebuchadnezzar is the main instigator)
- The role of Achior
- The relation between Judith and other biblical/extrabiblical works
- The book's genre

When comparing commentaries and works of the past with those of more recent times, it soon becomes evident that there is little consensus regarding the explication of these points. With the exception (perhaps) of the book's theology, the role of God in the book, and the relation between *Judith* and other biblical/extrabiblical works, the above have become contentious issues in the history of *Judith* studies. Amongst these, the historicity and date of *Judith*, the historical identification of its main characters and events, the bipartite division of the book, the character of its heroine, and (recently) the role of Achior have undoubtedly elicited the keenest interest and, sometimes, the fiercest debate. In this section, I should like to address these issues in the following order: the historicity and date of *Judith*, its structural unity and style, the nature of Judith and the function of Achior.

a. *The Historicity and Date of the Book of Judith*

The Book of Judith purports to be a historical documentation of events. Like so many other historical documents it begins with a time indicator, "In the twelfth year of the reign of Nebuchadnezzar"[6]

[6] English quotations of the Old Testament Apocrypha are taken from *The Revised Standard Version Apocrypha* (RAPC) of the Online Bible unless otherwise stated.

(1:1), and contains many such indicators throughout (cf. e.g., 1:13, 16; 3:10, 7:20, and 15:11). It contains genealogies (6:15 and 8:1) and the names of well-known historical figures, places, and nations such as Nebuchadnezzar, Jerusalem, Nineveh, Azotus, and Assyria. It also has a quite plausible plot—despite some rather improbable details such as Judith's living age (16:23) and her extended periods of fasting (8:6). Nevertheless, as I have indicated at the outset of this chapter, *Judith* is also replete with various types of inconsistencies and outright contradictions that seriously undermine the self-professed historical nature of its diction. In this subsection, I should like to investigate how these contradictory elements have been interpreted throughout the history of *Judith* studies, and I should like to do so by situating the various approaches within at least some of the many anachronisms/inconsistencies present in this book.

Historical and Geographical Anachronisms/Inconsistencies

A quick perusal of the story reveals that *Judith* abounds with the kind of historical, geographical, and chronological anachronisms that haunt its very first verse:

> 1:1 Ἔτους δωδεκάτου τῆς βασιλέωας Ναβουχοδονοσορ,
> ὅς ἐβασίλευσεν Ἀσσυρίων ἐν Νινευη τῇ πόλει τῇ μεγάλῃ,
> ἐν ταῖς ἡμέραις Αρφαξαδ, ὃς ἐβασίλευσεν Μήδων ἐν Ἐκβατάνοις[7]

Nebuchadnezzar is said to have ruled over the Assyrians in Nineveh, in the days of Arphaxad, king of the Medes. As is well known, however, Nebuchadnezzar was a Babylonian king and Nineveh was destroyed in 612 B.C., seven or eight years before the 'real' Nebuchadnezzar became king. There is also no record—secular or biblical—of a Median king named Arphaxad (Moore, op. cit., 46), and Ecbatana (a great city indeed) was 'conquered' by Cyrus in 550 B.C. and not by Nebuchadnezzar as *Judith* 1:14 claims (Pfeiffer, op. cit., 293). Furthermore, Holofernes, Nebuchadnezzar's general, reportedly led 120,000 infantry and 12,000 cavalry from Nineveh to Northern Cilicia—a distance of some 300 miles—in just three days, after which they cut through Libya (Put) in Africa and Lydia (Lud) in Asia Minor, only to find themselves crossing the Euphrates and going west through Mesopotamia to arrive at Cilicia and Japheth facing

[7] All quotations from the Greek text of *Judith* are taken from *Septuaginta*, Deutsche Bibelgesellschaft Stuttgart, 1979, as per Logos Library Services (LLS) 2.1.

Arabia (2:21, 23–25; Efthimiadis-Keith 1999a:216, n. 13 and 1999b: 156–157; Moore, op. cit., 47)! Possibly the worst problem of all is the location of Bethuliah—the local setting of the book. This site is completely unknown either historically or biblically!

Yet another historical problem relates to the period in which the narrative of *Judith* is *set*—there is evidence for both a pre-exilic and a postexilic setting. Some of the material in this book reflects at least a general pre-exilic setting:

- The LXX text refers to the twelfth,[8] seventeenth, and eighteenth years of Nebuchadnezzar's reign (593, 588, and 587 B.C., respectively; ibid.).
- According to the first section of *Judith* (1–7), Nebuchadnezzar had not yet destroyed the temple in Jerusalem.
- One may perhaps and with great caution add to this that Assyria is assumed to be the dominant world power throughout *Judith*. This was indeed the case until the death of Ashurbanipal in 625 B.C. Furthermore, Steinmetzer has argued that the campaigns of *Judith* 1–3 "are historically demonstrable during the reign of Ashurbanipal" (in Pfeiffer, op. cit.). Note too that, according to Herodotus, Ecbatana was fortified by Deioces in approximately 700 B.C. (ibid. n. 8; cf. 1:2).
- There are many parallels between *Judith* and the account of Sennacherib's attack in II Kings 18 (especially verse 13ff.) and 19.
- In my opinion, however, references to Assyria need not be taken seriously as affecting the book's setting per se. Aside from the fact that very little of the action takes place in 'Assyria', the latter is obviously a pseudonym for another world power as attested to by the naming of Nebuchadnezzar as its king. The 'Assyrian' references may rather be taken as vestiges of *Judith's* compilation history—if one believes that *Judith* was compiled in various stages, that is—or, simply, as deliberate and pseudonymous.[9]

Nevertheless, the overall ambience of the book reflects the postexilic era. Herein we can discern two, and perhaps even three, different postexilic settings:

[8] According to *Jeremiah* 32:1, the twelfth year of Nebuchadnezzar's reign (1:1) would have coincided with the fourth year of Zedekiah, Judah's last pre-exilic king.

[9] One may argue that the same applies to the Book of Daniel and that I am

i) *Persian Era* (sixth–fourth century B.C.)

- The book assumes the Jews' return from the Babylonian exile in 538 B.C. (4:3; 5:18–19; cf. also the cessation of idolatry in 8:18f), and indicates that the Medo-Persian Empire (550–525 B.C.; cf. 1:1–4) is at the height of its power (Pfeiffer, op. cit., 293).
- Certain words and phrases denote a Persian influence: Judith, Holofernes, Bagoas and Joakim are names commonly used in the Persian period (Moore, op. cit., 50); 'preparing earth and water' (2:7) is a Persian practice denoting submission (Enslin 1972:67, n. 7); and κιδάρις, ἀκινάκης (in LXX *hapax legomenon*), and σατράπης are Persian loan words for 'turban', 'sword', and 'governor', in *Judith* 4:15, 5:2 and 13:6.
- Cyrus captured Ecbatana in 550 B.C. (Pfeiffer, op. cit.; cf. 1:13–15).
- Holofernes and Bagoas are the names of a general of Artaxerxes III and his eunuch (Nickelsburg 1981:108). In addition, the events of *Judith* 1–7 find many parallels in Artaxerxes' campaigns against Phoenicia, Syria, and Egypt in 353 B.C. and the Revolt of the Satraps during the time of Artaxerxes II (ibid.).
- The appellation "God of Heaven" strongly suggests a Persian setting (Moore, op. cit.).

ii) *Early Maccabean Era* (168–135 B.C.)[10]

- The main events of *Judith* correspond strongly with the events that occurred in the Maccabean period[11] (Table 1, below, is adapted from Efthimiadis-Keith 1999b:165–166).

therefore making a false distinction in this regard. In Daniel, however, most if not all of the action takes place in "Babylon"; and Babylon is correctly affiliated to King Nebuchadnezzar. Thus, even though Babylon is as pseudonymous in Daniel as "Assyria" is in *Judith*, Daniel's "Babylon" may indeed be regarded as the book's setting while *Judith's* "Assyria" may not.

[10] The Early Maccabean era refers to the events surrounding the Maccabean-Hasmonean Revolt under Mattathias and Judas (168 and 168–160 B.C.), and the High Priestly reigns of Jonathan (160–142 B.C.) and Simon (142–135 B.C.). The Hasmonean Era refers to the era hereafter, i.e., from the inception of the Hasmonean State proper under John Hyrcanus (135–104) to its fall under Aristobulus II. For a concise history of each era, see Newsome 1992:36–50 and 50–66, respectively.

[11] This seems to be the broad consensus of most modern scholars. Cf. e.g., Harrington 1999:29.

Table 1. A Comparison Between *Judith* and the Events Relating to the War Between Judas Maccabeus and Nicanor in 161 B.C.

Judith	***Maccabean History***
A heathen king (the 'Assyrian' Nebuchadnezzar) sends out his general (Holofernes) to punish the Judaeans (at Bethuliah) for defying him (i.e., rebelling against him).	Alcimus, a High Priest deposed by Judas Maccabeus, incites Demetrius I against the Judaeans, claiming future instability for the kingdom if Judas and his band are allowed to continue. Demetrius sends his general, Nicanor, against Judas Maccabeus (161 B.C.; cf. Pfeiffer, op. cit., 16–17; Schäfer 1995:49).
The citizens are terrified for Jerusalem and its temple, for the "sacred vessels and the altar and the temple had [just/recently] been consecrated after their profanation" (4:3)	Nicanor demands of the High Priest to surrender Judas, threatening to raze the temple if his demands are not met. The priests are greatly afraid and pray "so now, O holy One, Lord of all holiness, keep undefiled for ever this house that has been so recently purified." (II Maccabees 14:36)
The Judaeans' desperation mounts, but Judith saves the day by going down to the Assyrian camp with her maid and decapitating Holofernes. (She strikes twice at his neck with his own sword). Judith and her maid return to Bethuliah, where they mount the head of Holofernes up on a wall for all, especially the Assyrian army, to see.	Judah and his compatriots decapitate Nicanor. (Nicanor led two campaigns against Judas in 166 and 161 B.C., cf. Schäfer, op. cit., 46 and 49). Nicanor's head and right hand are displayed outside Jerusalem (I Maccabees 7:47; cf. Newsome 1992: 43).
The Judaeans, under Judith's leadership, pretend to go out against the Assyrians. When the Assyrians see this, they attempt to awaken Holofernes, but scatter and flee upon discovering his decapitation.	When Nicanor's army see that he had fallen—he was the first to fall—they throw down their arms and flee (I Maccabees 7:44).
The Judaeans pursue and loot the fleeing army and return to Bethuliah/Jerusalem where God and Judith are praised for the victory.	The Judaeans pursue Nicanor's army a day's journey and seize the booty and plunder (I Maccabees 7:45). Note that people "out of all the villages of Judea round about" partake in this event as in *Judith* 14:4 and 15:5–6.
The Judaeans rejoice and celebrate. They have peace during Judith's lifetime and beyond following the defeat of this enemy.	The Judaeans rejoice and celebrate. "So the land of Judah had rest for a few days" (I Maccabees 7:50).

- There is a very strong possibility that *Judith's* Nebuchadnezzar is symbolic of Antiochus IV Epiphanes as is indeed the case in Daniel (so too Nickelsburg, op. cit.; Moore, op. cit., 51; and Pfeiffer, op. cit., 294).
- *Judith* is not so much concerned with the rebuilding of the temple but with the consecration of its altar, vessels, and the Temple itself after their profanation (cf. 4:3, above and, more especially 4:12, 8:21, and 9:8). The only profanation of the altar occurred under Antiochus IV.
- In *Judith* 4:6ff., the book further attests to the sweeping powers of the High Priest, who acts as both military and civil governor. Jonathan (160–142 B.C.) was the first High Priest to be officially appointed in both these capacities (Schäfer, op. cit., 53). Note too the supremacy of the Jerusalem γερουσία over other councils in *Judith* 4:6, 8; and 11:14. The heightened powers of the High Priest are also a feature of the Hasmonean Rule.

iii) *The Hasmonean Era (135–63 B.C.)*

- We have already noted the sweeping powers of the High Priest who acts both as military and civil governor (στρατηγός and μεριδάρχης).
- Moore (op. cit.) has suggested that *Judith* appears to treat certain Palestinian cities as though they formed part of the Judaean territory, whereas these cities were independent of Israel until the time of John Hyrcanus I. This is the case with, for example, Azotus (2:28) and Scythopolis (3:10), which did not become part of Judaean territory until they were devastated and conquered, respectively, by John Hyrcanus I, who also destroyed the Samaritan Temple at Mount Gerizim and the city of Shechem itself (cf. Gowan 1986:130). In fact, many have suggested that Bethuliah *is* the city of Shechem.

[According to *Judith*, Bethuliah lies south of the Esdraelon plain (3:10; 4:6); it lies directly between the Assyrian attack and Jerusalem, near Bethomasthaim and Dothan (4:6; 11:9); it is a walled town in the hill country of Samaria (cf. 6:11); it is surrounded by mountains (7:12–13); it overlooks a valley (10:10); and it has a nearby spring (10:10–11). Thus, the text would seem to place the otherwise unknown city of Bethuliah within the territory of Samaria. Taking their cue from these and other clues, scholars have suggested a number of sites, with the overwhelming consensus falling on Shechem—an opinion with which I agree].

- *Judith* displays an open and friendly attitude towards Samaria and its territories—something that, according to Moore (op. cit.), could perhaps only have been possible after they had been conquered and integrated into the Judaean state.

  I am not quite convinced that Moore's assumption—one cannot call it anything else—is correct. If anything, those conquered would surely harbour resentment against their new lords. Furthermore, I think that the inclusion of these cities in the Judaean state has less to do with *Judith's* setting than with the dating of the book.
- Judith's life span of 105 years (16:23a–b) is exactly the same as the duration of what I have called the early Maccabean and the Hasmonean periods (168–63 B.C.).

  Once again, I do not believe that this may be taken as a reference to *Judith*'s setting. I would prefer to see *Judith* 16:23a–b as an indication of the book's recension.

Over and above its divergent settings, *Judith* also contains many outright contradictions with regard to what seems to be an overall postexilic setting. For example, *Judith* 4:3 relates that the Jews had just returned from exile, gathered again in Judaea and rededicated the temple. However, Achior's account of Israel's history (cf. 5:5–21), which includes the destruction of the temple in 586 B.C., does not even mention the name of the king responsible for the exile, namely, Nebuchadnezzar (cf. especially 5:18–19), while the first section of the story itself would have us believe that 'Nebuchadnezzar' had not yet destroyed the temple in Jerusalem. Similarly, the interchange between Judith and Holofernes in chapters 10–13 indicates that he (through Holofernes) had not yet ravaged Jerusalem (cf. especially 11:19)!

Various Attempts to Deal with Judith's *Historical and Geographical Anachronisms/Inconsistencies*

In light of the above, throughout the history of *Judith* studies, scholars have adopted essentially six different attitudes with regard to both the book as a whole and the various inconsistencies and contradictions it entails. Some have clung to the belief that *Judith* must and does reflect historical truth. By contrast, others have regarded the book as a religious allegory, i.e., as fictional, and some have discarded the book altogether. Some have located its inconsistencies within its presumed recension history, while others have seen them as the storyteller's deliberate attempts to mask the identity of the main characters involved. More artistically minded individuals have located them within what they regard as the storyteller's artistic license or flair. Yet others simply believe that the storyteller may just have been confused:

i) Clement of Rome, Tertullian, Clement of Alexandria, Origen, and Jerome, amongst others, have accepted *Judith* "as a record of historical events" (cf. Pfeiffer, op. cit., 291–292). Notably, with the exception of O. Wolff (1861), this has been the opinion of mostly Catholic scholars prior to the Reformation (ibid.).
ii) The advent of the Reformation saw the first doubts concerning the historicity of *Judith* emerge. Martin Luther, for example, regarded it as a religious allegory. This has been a popular view since then, with scholars such as Ewald (1852) and Graetz (1866) acknowledging a small kernel of historical truth within the allegory. Others such as Bauer (1796) and Bertholdt (1815) have regarded the book as fiction proper (op. cit., 292), while Capellus (1689) has dismissed it as "'a most silly fable, invented by a most inept, injudicious, impudent, and clownish Hellenist'" (Enslin, op. cit., 49).
iii) In recent times, however, Catholic scholars have advanced theories such as "textual corruption and successive interpolations" to account for the obvious anachronisms and inconsistencies that I have outlined above (Pfeiffer, op. cit., 291). The latter, that has gained a much wider following than the former, is known as 'the evolving text theory'. It is best represented by the work of Franz Steinmetzer (1907). According to Steinmetzer (in Moore, op. cit., 52), the events contained in the 'original' story took place during the reign of the Assyrian king Ashurbanipal (seventh century B.C.), while the second edition was set in the days of the Persian king Cyrus (sixth century B.C.); the third phase saw the addition of events from the time of Artaxerxes I, Longimanus (fifth century B.C.), and the final edition was adapted to events occurring during the time of Antiochus IV Epiphanes (second century B.C.).
iv) Then there are the proponents of the pseudonym theory who believe that *Judith* reflects historical data in disguised form. They attempt to equate the main characters and events of *Judith* with certain verifiable historical data. This belief is represented primarily by the historical reconstructions of Volkmar (1860), Gaster (1894), and Ball (1900; in Moore, op. cit., 53):

The Cast	Volkmar	Gaster	Ball
Nebuchadnezzar	Emperor Trajan	Pompey	Antiochus IV Epiphanes
Assyrians	Syrians		Syrians
Nineveh	Rome or Antioch	Rome	Antioch
Arphaxad	Arsaces, a Parthian king	Mithridates	Arsaces
Medes	Parthians		Parthians
Ecbatana	Nisibis		
Holofernes	Lusius Quietus, a Roman general	Scarus	Nicanor, a general under Antiochus IV and Demetrius I
Judith	The Judaeans		Judas Maccabeus
Joakim		Onias, a pharisee	Alcimus, a Hellenist
The Time	117 A.D.	63 A.D.	The Hasmonean Period

v) Some scholars believe that the storyteller deliberately confused historical, geographical, and chronological events. Pfeiffer (op. cit., 291) writes, somewhat undecidedly:

> From a purely historical point of view it is much simpler to assume that the original author, like the authors of the Books of Daniel and Esther, had only the foggiest notions of the length of the period from Nebuchadnezzar to Alexander, when Jewish history was almost a blank; and regarded Nebuchadnezzar and Cyrus as almost contemporaries—unless he blundered deliberately to show that his story was fiction.

Craven (1983a:73–74, italics mine), on the other hand, is firmly convinced:

> The Book of Judith simply does not yield literal or even allegorical data. Instead, its opening details seem to be *a playful manipulation of* both historical and geographical *facts and inventions*. . . . The historical and geographical absurdities point not to ineptitude on the part of the author, but rather to skilfulness in focusing attention on something other than a historical recitation.

Similarly, Moore (op. cit., 48, 78–79) advances that the many anachronisms are deliberately constructed, and locates them within the overall ironic stance of the author.

vi) Some scholars are of the opinion that the storyteller wrote in a much later period than the events described and therefore confused historical and geographical facts from previous periods. Pfeiffer (op. cit., 297) himself seems to be confused when he writes, just six pages after the previous quotation from his book:

> Taking the book as we have it . . . our objective conclusion must be that the original author wrote historical fiction. His knowledge of past history and of the geography of Western Asia (outside of Palestine) was so limited that he committed numerous errors.

I have the following to offer in criticism and/or praise of the responses to *Judith's* historical and nonhistorical data that I have outlined above:

i) I believe that all these historical/geographical inconsistencies—of which there are many more than I have listed—point to the fact that *Judith* is in no way intended to be a historical document in the strict sense of the term, and that it is therefore a fruitless and senseless endeavour to try and make it so. It is indeed a work of 'fiction'.

ii) Hence, it is utterly foolish to try to fight for the historicity of the events and characters in this book. Those who attempt to do so seem to be motivated by a narrow sense of historicity and truth with regard to what they perceive as the Word of God. They seem to be of the opinion that for *Judith* to be the Word of God, for it to be 'truth', it *must* reflect historical events accurately. Notwithstanding the emotional ladenness that it carries *as* the Word of God, perhaps it is the book's outward show of historical detail that has lured more than one of these scholars to even consider such a highly untenable position. Whatever their motivation, they violate the book's integrity, as I would define it, i.e., by its functionality. Moreover, they do violence to the Word of God—if such they believe it to be—which, in my opinion, does not have to be precisely historical to be inspirationally functional in matters of faith and deed (see e.g., Daniel).

iii) A similar criticism applies to those who have outrightly rejected the book. They too are far too narrow in their outlook on historicity, and blind to the fact that something need not be historically accurate for it to be psychologically *functional* within any given historical situation. To prove my point, I should like to refer to the way in which the story of Judith has inspired countless people who found themselves in similar straits of desperation to take action on behalf of themselves and/or their nation/political-religious grouping. Margarita Stocker's brilliant monograph, *Judith: Sexual Warrior. Women and Power in Western Culture* (1998), bears ample documentation of the powerful effect which this book has had in 'real' modern history. For example, she documents cases where the book and/or artistic renditions thereof—particularly Judith's beheading of Holofernes—has inspired deeds of valour or treachery—depending on one's partisan perspective—by both men and women, noble and plebeian alike, amongst both 'sides' in the French Revolution and the Reformation (cf. Stocker 1998: 67–134, especially 87–119). *Judith* may not reflect 'real' historical facts per se, but no-one can deny its real historical outcomes in the face of, for example, the justification given by Juan de Mariana (a Jesuit zealot) for godly tyrannicide of Protestant monarchs based from the first on this book (op. cit., 87), and Charlotte Corday's murder of the demagogue Citoyen Marat during the Terror phase of the French Revolution (op. cit., 111–114 in particular). The latter, inspired by *Judith*, gained access to Marat by pretending to inform against his enemies, the Girondins in Caen. Not fearing a woman and wishing to indulge his fancy for female pulchritude, Marat, like Holofernes, allowed Corday to enter his quarters. As he was seated customarily in his slipper-bath—to treat a painful skin disease—he could offer little or no resistance when Corday pulled out a knife and stabbed him "efficiently and mortally" in the lung (op. cit., 113). The irony of the situation is that he was—at that very time—noting down the names of his enemies and exulting in their imminent decapitation. As Stocker (op. cit., 114) aptly concludes, "The Judithic character of the scene [Corday] underwrote this irony of his 'headtaking'". Corday went on to be both canonised and villainised, just as Judith herself was exulted and villainised in former and subsequent eras (op. cit., 114–117). Her act became the subject of visual representation and psychological motivation/inspiration even as Judith's did (op. cit., 117–119). Clearly then, a document need not be historically accurate in order for it to be historically functional and psychologically motivational in any given situation. Thus, to discard the Book of Judith on account of its historical and other inconsistencies is to have a very narrow view of what is historically functional and, hence, true. In my opinion, this too destroys the integrity of the book (as defined in terms of its functionality).

iv) While presenting rather attractive reconstructions and 'saving' the historicity of *Judith*, the theories of Volkmar, Gaster, and Ball are fraught with problems, not least of which is the fact that they are unable to sustain a complete correspondence between the Judithic characters/events and the historical characters/events they are said to represent. This certainly is the main criticism levelled against Gaster's reconstruction. Furthermore, there are anomalies and contradictions within a single 'cast'. For example, Ball identifies Judith as Judas Maccabeus and then equates the faithful Joakim with Alcimus, Judas' sworn enemy (cf. Pfeiffer, op. cit., 16)! Last but not least, Volkmar's dating (117 A.D.) post-dates by more than a quarter of a century the first Christian allusion to *Judith*, that of Clement I of Rome—"pure hallucination" as Zeitlin (1972:27) puts it.[12]

v) The evolving text theory is an equally attractive approach, and takes seriously the rugged contours of *Judith's* text. It helps to explain many of the book's inconsistencies and shows up the 'seams' of its (seemingly) various interpolations for what they are. However, I am not entirely sure that it takes the narrative seriously as a narrative nor, in fact, that it considers it as a whole. It also fails, in my mind, to consider the very real possibility that this is a single narrative piece written at a single point in time—a theory that I will advance below.

vi) The more recent approaches of scholars such as Moore and Craven are highly representative of the modern trend that seeks to understand the book from a literary or advocacy point of view. They are far more creative in that they take the narrative more seriously as a narrative by recognising the author's creative licence. As such, they take the dynamics of the text into account and are freed from the kind of fruitless 'strictly historical' investigation in which the first two approaches engage. Even so, they fail to explain the presence of these inconsistencies beyond appealing to structural considerations and the storyteller's poetic licence.

[Advocacy approaches such as that of Narito (1992) and Schuller (1992) deal with the functionality of the book in the *modern* era.

---

[12] Similarly, Pfeiffer (op. cit., 295): "It rests on hallucinations . . ."

In this they are highly commendable and point further to the fact that a book—this book—need not be historically accurate for it to be functionally inspiring. They seek, inter alia, to derive models of liberation from the book for the women in their communities—a very necessary activity even in the most 'liberal' of nations. Nevertheless, they rarely consider the book's functionality in the era that it reflects or in which it was written. Why was Judith portrayed in such a 'feminist' manner at that time? What purpose did such a portrayal serve?]

vii) Lastly, to assert that the storyteller was simply confused is, in my opinion, to avoid dealing honestly with the text at a scholarly level. It may seem an entirely plausible argument, but to say that the author was confused and leave it at that speaks of a certain hastiness or laziness that may not be permitted in the field of scholarly endeavour. One should at the very least speculate as to what brought this confusion about—was it, for example, the dire situation the author found herself/himself in?—and one should definitely probe further into its possible functionality.

From a psychoanalytic standpoint, the inconsistencies and anachronisms of the book may easily be accommodated within the workings of the unconscious psyche, which communicates with us in the form of 'irrational' dreams, myths, visions, and the like. This is what I have referred to as the book's mythopoeic qualities elsewhere (cf. also Efthimiadis-Keith op. cit., 156–158).

Judith's Date/Compilation

While the dating of *Judith* does not form the main emphasis of my work, it is nevertheless important to me in light of my proposed Jungian analysis. As I will indicate briefly later, Jung is adamant that dream interpretation cannot take place outside the context of both the dream and the dreaming subject. Therefore, if I am to treat *Judith* as a national dream reflecting the individuation of the Jewish nation at the time in which it was written, I will need to establish the date of its writing before proceeding with my analysis. In so doing, I should like to examine both the internal and the external evidence at hand. For the sake of brevity I will merely refer to the historical situations to which I believe the 'evidence' alludes.

Internal Evidence

The surface structure of the text itself provides us with a number of clues regarding its possible date of composition:

1. The Book of Judith reflects a political-religious crisis in which the faithful are threatened by the onslaught of a foreign nation. The latter seeks to impose its own religion/religious beliefs upon them. This crisis is aimed at both Judaea and Samaria (cf. e.g., 2:7–10, 12; 2:6; 3:9–10) even though it is centred on Jerusalem and, more specifically, the Jerusalemite temple that had apparently just been consecrated or "consecrated after their profanation" (cf. 4:3).

As many scholars have correctly observed, this kind of crisis is most easily accommodated within the Hellenistic period of Jewish history. During this time, increasing Hellenisation foisted upon the ordinary people by the upper echelons of society—and particularly the ruling party—proved to be a constant threat (cf. particularly the reigns of Jason, Menelaus, Alcimus, Jonathan, John Hyrcanus, and Alexander Jannaeus); three Jewish High Priests orchestrated the persecution of their own 'dissident' people, i.e., those who would not comply with their Hellenisation programmes (e.g., Menelaus, Alcimus, and Jannaeus); Antiochus IV Epiphanes proscribed Judaism and desecrated the Jerusalemite temple by turning it into a shrine for Zeus Baal Shamayim and offering swine's blood there on an altar erected to Zeus. The temple was subsequently reconsecrated by Judas Maccabeus and his men on 25 Kislev 164 B.C.

2. Certain cities in Samaria seem to be included within the Judaean territory (cf. 2:28, 3:10, and 4:4), and the author seems to have a more inclusive attitude towards Samaria and its territories. Two situations seem possible here, with the second having the highest degree of correlation with the text of *Judith*:

- The reign of Jonathan (160–142 B.C.): Demetrius I officially ceded three Samaritan toparchies to Judaea (c. 146–145 B.C.).
- The reign of John Hyrcanus I (135–104 B.C.): Hyrcanus captured many Samaritan cities, adding them to Judaean territory. He destroyed the Samaritan temple on Mt. Gerizim and the city of Samaria itself, the latter in c. 107 B.C.

3. Bethuliah seems to be located in Samaria, and is the port through which Holofernes hopes to gain access to Jerusalem—he has apparently already passed through Arabian territory (2:25). In fact, as

previously noted, many have argued that Bethuliah *is* the city of Shechem:

- The reign of Alexander Jannaeus (104–78 B.C.): Demetrius III marched towards Alexander's forces through Galilee and into Samaria, adding dissident Jews to his ranks (cf. 3:6). He clashed with Alexander's forces in a bloody battle near Shechem (c. 88 B.C.). Alexander had just made his way up from a nearly fatal foray into Arabia at this time.
- The reign of John Hyrcanus I (135–104 B.C.): Hyrcanus conquered and destroyed Shechem (107 B.C.) and the nearby temple on Mt. Gerizim.

4. Judith decapitates Holofernes and hangs his head on the wall of Bethuliah. She is received as a great heroine and the people sing, dance, and play tumbrels in her honour.

- As previously noted, the main events of *Judith* find numerous parallels in the story of Judas Maccabeus' defeat of Nicanor in 161 B.C.
- The reign of Simon (142–135 B.C.): having made the Jewish people independent of Seleucid rule, Simon enters the Akra (in Jerusalem) "with praise and palm branches, and with harps and cymbals and stringed instruments, and with hymns and songs, because a great enemy had been crushed and removed from Israel" (I Maccabees 13:51).

5. Judith is said to have lived for 105 years (16:23a–b)—the same number of years as the Maccabean-Hasmonean period (168–63 B.C.).

External Evidence

1. There are many correspondences between the Book of Judith and I and II Maccabees in terms of both style and content.[13] Some of these have already been indicated and/or alluded to in my comparison between *Judith* and the second war of Judas with Nicanor, above (cf. also Zeitlin op. cit., 28–31).

It is possible that the author of *Judith* knew and utilised both of these works. I Maccabees, which details events from the rise of

[13] For a detailed comparison between I and II Maccabees see Pfeiffer, op. cit., 472–483.

Antiochus IV to the end of John Hyrcanus' reign (175–104 B.C.) is dated at c. 104–63 B.C. (cf. e.g., Nickelsburg, op. cit., 117; Pfeiffer, op. cit., 491; Harrington, op. cit., 123). II Maccabees, which details events from 176 B.C. to the second war between Judas Maccabeus and Nicanor (161 B.C.) has been accorded various dates of composition ranging from the time of Alexander Jannaeus (Nickelsburg, op. cit., 121), to c. 160–161 B.C. or even the early first century B.C. (Harrington, op. cit., 139), to 41–44 A.D. (Zeitlin, op. cit., 30)—the last date being the latest of all the commentaries I have consulted. The 'mean difference' between these views—if one may indeed be permitted to adduce such 'evidence'—is c. 102 B.C., which falls within the reign of Alexander Jannaeus, the last great king of the Hasmonean kingdom.

2. The first Christian allusion to *Judith* is the first epistle to the Corinthians by Clement of Rome (cf. Zeitlin, op. cit., 26–27). Clement died at the end of the first or the beginning of the second century A.D. Hence, *Judith* must have been written well before then.

If we study both the internal and the external evidence carefully, we can posit a date for *Judith* at the end of the reign of John Hyrcanus[14] or the latter part of the reign of Alexander Jannaeus[15]—that is if we ignore the 'fact' that Judith's lifetime of 105 years corresponds exactly to the chronological duration of the Maccabean-Hasmonean era (168–63 B.C.). However, this 'fact'—*Judith* 16:23a–b—cannot be ignored. How, then, do we account for it? Is it indeed a gloss as Moore (op. cit., 260) opines, or is it an indication of the book's date of composition? I agree with Moore and regard it as a gloss. In that case, I propose that *Judith* was composed in the early first century

[14] For a further point of correspondence, note that Antiochus VII besieged Hyrcanus in Jerusalem and starved him and its inhabitants out. Similarly, Holofernes besieges Bethuliah and almost drives its citizens out by thirst.

[15] For further comparison, note that Nebuchadnezzar wreaks revenge upon 'disobedient nations' and treats his enemies harshly, spreading fear wherever he goes. He boasts that the blood of his enemies will fill every brook and valley and cover every high mountain. Similarly, Jannaeus wreaks terrible revenge upon dissident Jews and cruelly mistreats his opponents. He spills blood wherever he goes. At one point he even has 800 Jewish opponents crucified and murders their wives and children before them while they are hanging on the cross.

B.C. (soon after Demetrius III's attack on Jannaeus) and that it was 'reviewed'—for want of a better word—in the late first century B.C. shortly after Pompey's attack on Jerusalem in 63 B.C. As I propose to test this hypothesis against my analysis in chapter 5, I should like to end my deliberations on the date of *Judith* here. However, before considering the structural unity and style of the Book of Judith, I offer the reader a tabulation of modern commentators' opinions on the subject at hand for the sake of comparison (Table 2).

Table 2. The Date and Setting of *Judith* According to Various Authors

Author	Date of Composition	Historical Situation Reflected in *Judith*
Pfeiffer 1949	c. 150 B.C. (p. 297)	The war for political independence ended in 141 B.C. (p. 15)
Enslin 1972	". . . well prior to the end of the first Christian century" (p. 46)	
Zeitlin 1972	Late Hasmonean or early Roman period (p. 28)	One of the many invasions of Judaea between 161 B.C. (Judas' victory over Nicanor) and the time of Agrippa I (40 A.D.). Zeitlin emphasises Judas' second war with Nicanor as the basis for the book (p. 28).
Craghan 1982a	c. 150 B.C. (p. 73)	The persecutions of Antiochus Epiphanes to c. 150 B.C. (p. 74)
Lacocque 1990	second century B.C. (pp. 38, 42)	Hellenisation and persecutions of Antiochus Epiphanes (Cf. n. 12, p. 39)
Newsome 1992	c. 150 B.C. (p. 219)	Seleucid period (p. 220)
Schuller 1992	End of second or beginning of first century B.C. (p. 307)	Maccabean wars (p. 307)
Elder 1994	During Hasmonean dynasty (142–63 B.C.) (p. 455)	Hasmonean period (p. 455)

Table 2 (*cont.*)

Author	Date of Composition	Historical Situation Reflected in *Judith*
Koester 1995	Unspecified, second century B.C. implied (p. 259)	Maccabean period implied (p. 259)
Moore 1985	Toward the end of John Hyrcanus' reign (135–104 B.C.) or the beginning of the reign of Alexander Jannaeus (103–78 B.C.) (p. 67)	The political situation after 107 B.C. (see below) (pp. 69–70)
Harrington 1999	Prefers not to provide a date vis-à-vis the fictitious nature of the book. (p. 29)	The book is set in the sixth century B.C. but does not reflect any known historical situation. (p. 28)

b. *The Structural Unity and Style of the Book of Judith*

As previously indicated, certain scholars have found fault with *Judith's* style or compositional structure. For example, Pfeiffer (op. cit., 299) laments the "turgid style" of the book. His comments, quoted at length below, cover many of the complaints levelled against *Judith* in this regard:

> The Hebrew style of the lost original work is fairly good, although at times more prolix (cf. 4:9–12) and bombastic than that of the Book of Esther . . . The chief literary defect of the book is the lack of simplicity: the gorgeous Oriental *mise en scène*, the turgid style, the patent exaggerations, the stately pomp and ceremony throughout, unrelieved by a sense of humor, give to the book a baroque rather than a classic appearance. A comparison of the story of Judith's deed in prose (12:10–13:10) or in verse (16:6–9) with the similar assassination of a foe by Jael, as sung in Deborah's ode (Judg. 5:24–27) or told in simple prose (Judg. 4:17–22), is a contrast between the extravagantly ornate and the superbly natural, between sophistication and unadorned reality, between conscious and unconscious art.

Despite these "literary blemishes", which he claims are "more or less characteristic of the period of Hebrew literature in which the book was written", Pfeiffer (ibid.) nevertheless regards *Judith* as "a good example of an ancient short story".

Others seem particularly concerned about the so-called imbalance between the first and second sections of the book, namely, *Judith* 1–7 and 8–16. Alonso Schökel (1975a:3, my italics), for example, comments that:

> *The main character enters the stage late, almost too late* . . . More than one exegete, evaluating this fact, finds in the story *a lack of proportion*, namely that *the extension of the first part* (1–7) *is not justified by the narrative function it fulfils.*

While the second sentence in the above quotation does not reflect his own position (for which see below), it certainly reflects that of Dancy, whom Alonso Schökel (ibid.) quotes at length. According to Dancy (1972, in Alonso Schökel, op. cit.), the first part is "duller in thought and flatter in style". It fails to provide a historical setting with the "economy" and "accuracy a modern reader looks for". Rather, it has "few merits", being spoiled dramatically by "tedious descriptions . . . and confusions" and "stylistically by exaggerations (e.g., 1:16) and empty rhetoric (e.g., 2:5–13)".

Consequently, it is not surprising to find that many *Judith* scholars disregard the first section when analysing the book—even though they may not entirely disparage it and may even accord it some merit. This seems to be the position of Craghan (op. cit., 67) who states the following with regard to the first seven chapters:

> The first seven chapters of the book are not simply a boring catalogue of Assyrian successes and non-Assyrian failures. They serve to demonstrate the might of the Assyrians and thus underline the depth of faith required to counteract such might. In so doing, they set the stage for the appearance of Judith in [chapter] 8.

He then proceeds to a more lengthy analysis of *Judith* 8–16 (op. cit., 75–126), while offering only a brief résumé of the former chapters (Craghan, op. cit., 67–69). Similarly, Alonso Schökel (op. cit., 4) postulates that this "'lack of proportion' . . . construes the character of Holofernes, and prepares and introduces the dramatic irony which is substantial to the story. . . . The author is building for his heroine a magnificent pedestal, which to reach high has to spread wide". Nevertheless, he is still disappointed because the first section "lacks vividness" (op. cit., 5).

Contrary to Alonso Schökel's "feeling of delusion" (ibid.) about the first seven chapters of *Judith*, other scholars have correctly acclaimed its intrinsic validity and close thematic relationship to chapters 8–16 and have pointed out its well-defined structure. Undoubtedly, the most complete work in this regard—and the best, in my opinion—is that of Toni Craven, reflected in both her article published in *Semeia* 8 (1977:75–101) and her doctoral thesis published in 1983. Through her "[l]iterary/rhetorical" study of the book, Craven shows that the narrative of *Judith* is indeed both "balanced and proportioned" (op. cit., 75), with repetition and chiastic structure governing both sections (op. cit., 81, 88). Furthermore, she shows how fear or its denial in the first section contrasts with Judith's beauty in the second (op. cit., 83–84, 91); that both sections deal with the struggle for sovereignty—*Judith* 1–7 introduces the struggle, while 8–16 resolves it (op. cit., 85, 91); and that both Judith and Holofernes act out "a 'commission' not explicitly ordered from on high"—Judith to deliver the nation, and Holofernes to acclaim Nebuchadnezzar as God (3:8; op. cit., 93). There are thus definite, intentional connections between the two sections, on the level of both thematics and vocabulary.

Craven presents the following structures for *Judith* 1–7 and 8–16:[16]

<u>Section I (*Judith* 1–7)</u>

1. Introduction to Nebuchadnezzar and his campaign against Arphaxad (1:1–16)
2. Nebuchadnezzar commissions Holofernes to take vengeance on the disobedient vassal nations (2:1–13)
3. Development

   A The campaign against the disobedient nations; the people surrender (2:14–3:10)
   B Israel hears and is "greatly terrified"; Joakim orders war preparations (4:1–15)
   C Holofernes talks with Achior; Achior is expelled from the Assyrian camp (5:1–6:11)
   C' Achior is received into Bethuliah; he talks with the people of Israel (6:12–21)
   B' Holofernes orders war preparations; Israel sees and is "greatly terrified" (7:1–5)
   A' The campaign against Bethulia; the people want to surrender (7:6–32).

[16] For a very different, and I believe erroneous, subdivision of *Judith*, see Van Henten's (1994:33–48) views, taken up in chapter 3.

Section II (*Judith* 8–16)[17]

Aa Introduction to Judith (8:1–8)[18]
Bb Judith plans to save Israel (8:9–10:9a)
Cc Judith and her maid leave Bethulia (10:9b–10)
D Judith overcomes Holofernes (10:11–13:10a)
Cc' Judith and her maid return to Bethulia (13:10b–11)
Bb' Judith plans the destruction of Israel's enemy (13:12–16:20)
Aa' Conclusion about Judith (16:21–25)

From a Jungian point of view, one may say that the very structure of the book (a palindrome in both sections) reflects the concept of individuation: a palindrome is another form of a mandala, the symbol of wholeness/individuation. The fact that the second section of *Judith* shows a clear central point (D) around which this structure 'revolves' further indicates that this is the turning point in the individuation drama which *Judith* is. Moreover, the character of Achior bridges and connects these two sections (similarly Moore, op. cit., 59). As we shall see in chapter 5, he represents a shadow component of the psyche without which this individuation drama could not have taken place. There is thus nothing at all haphazard or dull about the compositional structure of this book. To the contrary, *Judith* is expertly structured and perfectly balanced (a mandala symbolizes balance, one outcome of the individuation/maturation process).

Furthermore, as I will demonstrate in the course of the forthcoming analysis (chapter 5), the author's style is far from "tedious" or "turgid". To the contrary, I find it exciting and dramatic. For one thing, *Judith's* author is a genius with words. Rarely have I come across an Old Testament book that makes such extensive use of synonyms, exquisite hyperbole and dramatic irony—to name but three of its excellent stylistic features—to convey its point of view (see Alonso Schökel, op. cit., 8–11; Kikawada 1975:38–39; and Moore, op. cit., 78–85 on the book's outstanding use of irony). Over and above that, it is rich in the type of dream imagery that would gladden any Jungian's heart. It expertly intertwines diverse images and

[17] I have slightly modified the labelling of each subsection here to facilitate easy referencing: Craven's "A" is indicated as "Aa" to distinguish it from "A" in Section I and so forth. "D" has remained as such owing to the fact that there is no subsection "D" in the first section.

[18] Craven's structure has (8:1–18) here, but this is surely a mistake if one considers the scope of "B" (8:9–10:9a) and the story itself.

archetypal energies to narrate its tale of deception, victory and intrigue: an evil enemy, a brilliant deceiver, huge armies, a seductive heroine, a 'holy' city, war, passion, sacrifice and religion. There is certainly nothing "tedious" or "turgid" about that.

c. *The Characters Judith and Achior*

Judith

Judith is a highly ambiguous, ironic character whose nature has often been hotly debated throughout the history of *Judith* studies. On the one hand:

- She has a sixteen-tier genealogy that roots her in the history of Israel [Jacob] and identifies her potential to act as judge [Gideon], prophet [Elijah, Nathaniel], ambassador [Joseph], and priest [Merari] (8:1; Levine 1989:565. Cf. also Van Henten 1995:241, 242; Alonso Schökel, op. cit., 10).
- She is a wealthy, beautiful, pious, chaste, blameless, wise, generous, and God-fearing widow who lives fasting before God (cf. e.g., 8:4–8, 28–31; 10:19, 23; 11:20–21; 16:23, 25).
- She is an expert in intercessory prayer (cf. 9:2–14).
- Her faith and courage exceeds that of the Bethulian elders and fellow-citizens.
- She has "a profound understanding of the effects which compromise and surrender will have for Israel . . . [She] reminds the leaders . . . that slavery is apostasy . . . Her words describe a faith that exceeds the limits of reason; she perceives quite clearly that to God alone belongs the right to test" (Craven, op. cit., 85). Thus, she has a better understanding of both the complexities of the situation at hand (cf. Kolenkow 1975:41–42) and the nature of God than the religious leaders of her people.
- She is very community-orientated and self-sacrificial in her community service—a true liberator of her people (cf. Craghan, op. cit., 65–67; Coote, op. cit., 21, 22; and Van Henten, op. cit., 238–242 especially).
- As a result of her self-sacrifice, death is transformed into life and social transformation is effected for a number of characters, including Achior and her unnamed stewardess (cf. Levine, op. cit., 566–567; Craghan, op. cit., 106, 116, 118; Craven, op. cit., 94, Dundes 1975:29; Kikawada, op. cit., 39; Lacocque, op. cit., 47).

On the other hand, and in sharp contrast to the above—as some would have it:

- Judith does not hesitate to request God's assistance in deceiving Holofernes (9:10, 13).
- She is a master at using 'feminine wiles' (beauty, flattering speech, and sexuality) to deceive and murder (symbolically castrate) Holofernes (10:23–13:8; Lacocque, op. cit., 36; Dundes, op. cit., 28).
- She easily transgresses gender boundaries in liberating her people (cf. e.g., Levine, op. cit., 561, 566).

It is this juxtaposition *and* combination of godliness vs. carnality, chastity vs. 'immorality', truth vs. deception, strength vs. weakness, masculinity vs. femininity—this duality of character and deed—that has made it easy for *Judith* commentators to depict its heroine both as a 'virginal saint' and a voracious femme fatale. Most of them—mostly men until recent times—have focused on one 'side' of the composite duality that is Judith, depending on their perceptions of womanhood and the needs or circumstances of their times. For example, Bissel (1886 in Moore op. cit., 64), undoubtedly motivated by Victorian, patriarchal concerns regarding women, writes,

> [Judith's] character, moreover, is not simply objectionable from a literary point of view, but even more from a moral standpoint. . . . Her way is strewn with deception from first to last, and yet she is represented as taking God into her counsels and as having his special blessing in her enterprise. . . . she assents to [Holofernes'] request to take part in a carousal at his tent and to spend a night in his embrace . . . it would seem a mere matter of chance that Judith escaped an impure connection with Holofernes . . . that she would have been willing even to yield her body . . . [to accomplish] her purpose. That God by his providence interposed to prevent such a crime, cannot relieve her of the odium attaching to her conduct. . . . And she exposes herself . . . to sin, simply for the present purpose of gaining the confidence of a weak slave of his passions that she may put him to death. . . . there are elements of moral turpitude in the character of Judith.

Likewise, Shumaker (1975:33, author's italics), writing almost a century later, voices a similar though less acrimonious opinion:

> As I read *Judith*, a scruple is raised by her lying. I should have preferred her to speak in such a way as to invite misinterpretation. Is her heroism in some degree compromised, or is it not, by her assurance to Holofernes that if he does as she says he will "not fail to attain his ends" and that not only men but animals and birds will owe their

> lives to his power so long as the dynasty of Nebuchadnezzar reigns? For me, the answer must be a reluctant "Yes" . . .

Contrary to the above, Clement of Rome, who wrote at a time when Christians were suffering pagan persecution, was able to seize upon her bravery and comment as follows:

> Many women have received power through the grace of God and have performed many deeds of valor. The blessed Judith, when her city was besieged, *asked the elders to allow her to go out into the camp of the strangers* [sic]. So she gave herself up to danger, and went forth for love of her country and her people in the siege, and the Lord delivered over Holofernes by the hand of a woman (I Clement 55:45).

Similarly, at a time when sexual temptation was more of a threat to the celibate clergy than was religious persecution, Church Fathers such as Tertullian (c. 160–230 A.D.), Methodius of Tyre (third century A.D.), and Ambrose of Milan (339–97) were able to overlook Judith's patent sexuality and "unconventional sexual behaviour" (Brenner 1995:14) and praise her for her self-imposed celibacy (cf. Moore, op. cit.).

The debate regarding Judith's character continues into the modern era with scholars like Dundes (see above) decrying Judith for her deception, while feminists like Levine (op. cit., 561) praise her for transgressing social and gender boundaries, and still others can extol her as an "alternative leader" (Van Henten, op. cit., 238) who is "morally superior to the subverted male figures" because she "manages" to save herself (Brenner, op. cit., 12).

There are, in fact, almost as many interpretations of this character as there are commentators/interpreters. For example, Montley (1978, in Moore, op. cit., 65; cf. also Lacocque, op. cit., 37) regards her as the archetypal androgyne: warrior, seductress, and femme fatale. Similarly, Coote (op. cit., 21–26) regards her as the epitome of the "faithful wife" paradigm in which a woman, disguised as a man, switches sex roles and saves her enslaved husband. Others, such as Craghan (op. cit., 79 especially), Kolenkow (op. cit., 40–41), and Narito (1992), focus upon Judith as a model of liberation. Similarly, as we have seen, Van Henten (1994 and 1995) regards her as an "alternative leader" in the style of Moses, in particular, and many other prophetic/liberative Old Testament figures. Yet others, such as Levine (1989 and 1992) and Lacocque (op. cit., 41), focus on Judith's subversive potential as an unconventional female figure (cf. also White 1989 and 1992), with authors such as Moore (1989:586) and Lacocque (op. cit.) suggesting that it is this subversive, near 'feminist' aspect of Judith which cost the book its canonicity (cf. also Dundes op. cit., 29—Judith "usurps" the male role). Still others, (notably Alonso Schökel, op. cit., 14–15), prefer to see her as the 'weak woman/widow' through whom God saved Israel—and this despite acknowledging her strength of character, wisdom, and prophetic status (op. cit., 10, 14). By contrast, many highlight her strength over and against the weakness of the male characters in the tale (cf. Brenner op. cit.; Craven op. cit., 85ff; and Lacocque, op. cit., 33), with Dundes (op. cit., 28) suggesting that *Judith* typifies the perennial battle of the sexes.

The visual depiction of Judith has been equally varied and has often alternated between the two aspects of her 'dual' nature. Once again, the 'interpreters' have been mostly male. Note, for example, the differences between the chaste, pensive look that Botticeli (1445–1510) gives her; her cruel, smug appearance in the painting by Lucas Cranach the Elder (1472–1552); the sexual, yet somehow innocent depiction of Judith holding Holofernes' head by Massys (1509–1575); the disinterested, almost emotionless Judith of Cristoforo Allori (1577–1621); the almost gaudy, prostitute-like depiction of Kremser-Schmidt's (1718–1801)[19] triumphant Judith; and the downright vampish, evil looks she is given by Gustav Klimt (cf. Bade 1979:33) and Franz von Stuck (cf. op. cit., 6). These interpretations contrast starkly with Artemesia Gentileschi's depictions of Judith. The faces of Judith and her maidservant in *Judith Slaying Holofernes* (1620; Bal, op. cit., 268), for example, "[radiate] a contained and serious, almost organized passion that enhances the sense of efficacy of the work being done" (op. cit., 269). In similar vein, Gentileschi's *Judith and her Maid Servant Leaving the Enemy Camp* (1613–14; op. cit., 275) shows the women with heads turned back in an attentive pose—aware of "the precise moment of greatest danger" (op. cit., 276), intently listening to sounds (and perhaps looking at sights) outside the pre-established frame of the painting, but also moving forward. Likewise, the women in *Judith and her Maid Servant with the Head of Holofernes* (1625; op. cit., 279) look beyond the frame. In this painting, Holofernes' sword cov-

[19] Cf. Sölle et al. 1994:206–219 for these and other portrayals of Judith. Cf. also Stone 1992:73–94.

ers Judith's genitalia (even though she is fully dressed), and Judith wears a heavy-duty, military type of shoe (op. cit., 277). Her left hand is raised across her body, signalling the leader, signalling attention, warning, directing. It "foretells the cautious actions to follow, which will bring complete success to Judith's self-assigned mission" and directs the gaze of the viewer "outside the bedroom, as if it were dismissed as indiscreet" (op. cit., 278). There is no vampishness in any of these paintings, no emphasis on Judith's sexuality, no pristine innocence, no distanced, disinterested parties; there are just two "working women" (as Bal calls them; op. cit., 277) going about their business attentively, intently aware of the importance of their mission and its dangers.

What, then, is one to make of the often-contradictory manner in which this highly complex figure has been depicted? In my opinion, there are at least two factors at play here. Firstly, from a Western point of view, Judith is indeed a heady mixture of dualities. Western binary thinking tends to translate her textual depiction into either one of its components, favouring either her 'innocent' or her 'vampish' side. Secondly, as I have repeatedly pointed out, most interpreters of *Judith*—commentators and artists alike—have been male until recent times. As males subject to castration anxiety—the fear of losing one's essential power or manhood to a woman in particular—they have been terrified by Judith's castrating potential (cf. Efthimiadis-Keith 1999a: 216–219; and Bal, op. cit., 257–258) and produced Judith figures of a vampish, disinterested, or downright evil type. By contrast, and in reaction to these views, many women have emphasised the subversive and liberating potential of this woman from a feminist point of view. In essence, however, they have sanctified the very castrating potential that their male counterparts have demonised. Strangely, their views often succumb to the very Western binarism and the patriarchal vision of women that they purport to eschew. For me, the best interpretation of Judith is found in the paintings of Artemesia Gentileschi. It is remarkable how Gentileschi manages to eschew the very patriarchal concerns of her peers and present Judith in a way that emphasises her determination, mission, and bravery without necessarily focusing upon the male-female dilemma that has so fascinated them. In other words, Gentileschi's paintings do not depict Holofernes' decapitation as the victory of a woman (or two women) over a man. They do not engage the "perennial battle of the sexes" because they see what many others do not:

this is not necessarily a story about women disempowering men; it is the story of two women, two people, offering dedicated, sacrificial service to their nation.

Having read that, it may surprise the reader to find me applying Jungian theories to this character, as Jung's views have often been regarded as irredeemably patriarchal or sexist in nature. The controversy in this regard has centred around Jung's proposal of contrasexual soul images: the anima (female) for the male psyche and the animus (male) for its female counterpart. Personally, I find nothing inherently sexist about this concept. (Even if I did, I would certainly not have to put it to sexist use). Rather, I see in Jung's concept of the anima a potential framework within which to investigate (and appreciate) this highly acclaimed and defamed 'murdering saint'. According to Jung, the anima is one of the most powerful archetypes of the collective unconscious. In this view, Judith is in full possession of the undivided nature with which all archetypes are invested, so that the good abides with the bad, the innocent with the vampish, and so forth in an undifferentiated state. The assimilation of this archetype constitutes a vital step in the individuation process of any male psyche. It brings the male into greater unity with himself and the world around him. It is my contention that Judith is just such an anima figure and that her duality stems from this very 'fact'. Furthermore, as I have previously argued, one aspect of the Judithic dream warns that the nation, which is typically male, will never achieve inner peace or transcend its current level of individuation unless it permits the integrated anima free reign in its current state (cf. Efthimiadis-Keith 1999b:164, 167–168). This is an aspect that I hope to explore further in my current study. I will also explore the possibility that Judith represents the national ego at an advanced stage in the individuation process. The ego is yet another Jungian archetype. It too possesses a dual nature within which Judith's duality may be investigated. Thus, in my opinion, Jung's psychoanalytic studies provide us with a potentially valuable framework within which to study this highly complex character and to achieve a far more comprehensive, holistic understanding of her function within Judaean society at the time of the book's composition.

Achior

Few commentators have focused upon the role and function of Achior in *Judith*, despite the fact that he is "a crucial character for uniting both sections of the book" (Moore, 1985:59), "a splendid study in contrasts and an effective foil for several of the book's characters" (ibid.), and the only secondary character in *Judith* whose role is developed (Roitman 1989:551). In fact, the only detailed study of this character is that of Roitman (op. cit., 540–549 and 1992:31–46). Shortly, Roitman (1989:552) shows that "there is an especially intriguing structural relationship and a subtle complementarity between Achior and Judith" in terms of their respective functions. He traces these similarities/complementarities through five stages in each character's development (see op. cit., 557–558 for the complete table as well as chapter 5F) and correctly concludes that Achior is "a kind of double or 'alter ego'" for Judith (op. cit., 558–559).

Roitman's study on Achior is excellent, and one which has echoed and extended my thinking in many ways. In my opinion, however, it is incomplete in that it does not treat the psychological function of this character. Achior is indeed Judith's alter ego but, as I hope to show in my study, he is also an aspect of the Jewish nation's *shadow* archetype, an acceptable portion of the nation's hidden psyche which becomes reintegrated with its consciousness and assists in its individuation process. It is my belief that submitting Achior's character to Jungian analysis will further reveal the psychological importance of this character and raise him to a higher level than the one that he has normally been accorded. It will reveal that Achior's character is on a par with that of Judith in importance—not a surprising conclusion seeing that he is indeed her "alter ego" (alias *shadow*) as Roitman has shown.

B. *Essential Hypothesis and Methodological Approach Underlying the Current Study*

a. *The Essential Hypothesis of the Current Study*

The essential hypothesis of the current study may be stated as follows:

1. *Judith* was composed in the early first century B.C., soon after Demetrius III's attack on Jannaeus, and 'reviewed' in the late first century B.C., shortly after Pompey's attack on Jerusalem in 63 B.C.

2. The book's historical/geographical anachronisms and inconsistencies are a deliberate feature of this text. They constitute what I have called its mythopoeic qualities (cf. point 6 below).

3. The duality of Judith may be understood in terms of Jung's concept of the anima and/or the ego.

4. Far from being a peripheral character that merely joins the two sections of the book, the character of Achior is central to *Judith*, and may be understood as a positive shadow element of the national ego that requires reintegration into the conscious psyche.

5. There is nothing haphazard about the composition of the book. Each of its two sections (*Judith* 1–7 and 8–16) is a palindrome that is reminiscent of the symbol of individuation, the mandala.

6. *Judith* possesses mythopoeic qualities which, when viewed through the lens of Jungian psychoanalytic theory, facilitate its understanding as a dream of and for the Jewish nation. As such, the book may be seen as a communication from the unconscious psyche that (i) reflects the nation's state of individuation and (ii) functions as a 'big dream'. Such dreams are usually given to community leaders and "[hold] important portents, warnings, etc. for the community as a whole" (Efthimiadis-Keith 1999b:167).

7. Following on from this, the characters in the book may be seen as representing both the diverse personalities present within and without Judaean society during the first century B.C., *and* as reflections of the archetypal energies underlying these aspects.

8. In this sense, the *enemy is within*, because the inimical Gentile characters may be seen as unconscious manifestations of the (female and/or male) 'dreamer' or 'dreamers'.

Having said that, it becomes necessary for me to outline briefly Jung's psychoanalytic theory, its general application to the Bible and secular literature, and the particular way in which I will apply it to *Judith*.

b. *A Brief Résumé of Jungian Theory*

According to Jung, the human psyche embraces both the conscious and the unconscious, the personal and the collective aspects of a person's being. The conscious psyche is based upon a deeper layer, the *personal unconscious*, and an even deeper layer, the *collective unconscious* (Jung 1940:52). The former contains the sum total of our (individual) life-experiences, subliminal perceptions, repressed memories and images, and "contents that are not yet ripe for consciousness" (Jung 1956b:76). The latter consists of our universal ancestral memories and patterns of behaviour—including the animal stage of our existence—that Jung calls *archetypes* (Jung 1940:53; 1953a:177–179; and 1956b:75. Cf. also Jung 1959a:279 and 1959b:7).

Favourable conditions may imbue the contents of the unconscious psyche with sufficient psychic energy or libido[20] for them to cross the threshold of consciousness and begin to communicate with us through semiconscious activities such as slips of the tongue, sudden mood swings, emotional outbursts, dreams, myths, fantasies, and the like. When this happens, we must pay close attention to the unconscious message that they bring and integrate those parts which have resurfaced into our ego consciousness. In this way, we shall achieve greater psychic wholeness and progress to the next level in our individuation process. Should we choose to ignore these messages, we suppress the contents underlying them, imbue them with negative psychic energy, and facilitate their destructive potential in our lives. For Jung, the integration of both the archetypal shadow (our hidden side) and the anima/animus (our contrasexual aspects) form the acme of this process in that they entail the resolution of psychic aspects that we perceive as opposites to our conscious ego.

For Jung, fantasies, visions, and, particularly, dreams form the primary vehicle of unconscious communication (cf. also Jung 1953a: 176–177). He consequently believes that careful consideration and amplification of an analysand's dream or vision material allows both analyst and analysand to 'decode' the messages of the latter's unconscious. This enables the analysand to integrate the unconscious elements that have surfaced into her/his consciousness and so attain a higher level of individuation which, in turn, effects a higher level of social integration for her/him. Accordingly, Jung places great emphasis on the interpretation of a patient's dreams and visions during therapy, carefully noting both the context and the content of the unconscious communication.

Having recorded and collected a patient's dreams (Jung 1940:43), Jung subjects the dream/vision/fantasy (henceforth "dream") material to two successive types of analysis. The first he calls '*objective analysis*', by which he relates the dream contents to the world outside the dreamer. In the second method, which he calls '*subjective analysis*', he relates the dream contents to the dreamer herself/himself, so that the underlying memory complexes may be reunited with

[20] Jung's concept of libido should not be confused with the more popular, Freudian, concept. For Freud, libido was a broadly defined sexual energy, whereas for Jung it represents psychic energy as such.

her/him. Once the dream symbols begin to represent the images of the collective unconscious, Jung 'amplifies' certain images by using both the analysand's own interpretations and "numerous parallels from the psychology of primitive and historical symbolism". This yields the richest possible meanings and also helps the analysand to integrate relevant aspects from the collective unconscious (cf. Jung 1956a:91, 93–95).

Jung has further emphasised that myths, fables, and legends, the other well-known expressions of the unconscious psyche, have much in common with the dream world (cf. Jung 1940:54–56). Like dreams, they too may reflect the process of individuation/psychological maturation of the ego—alias the hero.[21] On the basis of the collective unconscious, I believe that these forms of unconscious communication may also reflect what I should like to call 'national dreams' (cf. also Efthimiadis-Keith 1999b:154). In other words, I believe that myths, fables, and legends may reflect the psychological exigencies *within the nation from which they stem* (so too Jung and Jacoby in Jacoby 1992:66–67). Therefore, they are good indicators of the state of individuation or self-becoming (cf. Jung 1953a:173) that a particular nation has achieved at the time of their composition.

c. *Literary Applications of Jungian Thought*

Jung addressed the question of psychology-and-literature in three particular essays: "On the Relations between Analytical Psychology and Literature/On the Relation of Analytical Psychology to Poetry";[22] "Psychology and Literature" (1930/1950);[23] and " 'Ulysses': a Monologue" (1932). The second of these presents the clearest portrayal of Jung's thinking in this regard. According to Jung, the psychologist's task with regard to literature is intimately tied with her/his mandate to investigate the human psyche from which all sciences, arts, and

[21] As I will show in chapter 2, Jung did not consider the fact that the process and its outcomes may be different for heroines/female characters. That is why 'hero' and not 'heroine/hero' is used here.

[22] This essay, taken from Jung's 1922 Zurich lecture, was originally published in *The British Journal of Medical Psychology*, in 1923. It was subsequently reprinted in *The Collected Works of C. G. Jung*, volume 15, in 1966. The essay is known by both titles.

[23] As far as I have been able to determine, this essay first appeared in *Modern Man in Search of a Soul* (Jung 1933: 175–199). See Aniela Jaffe's "Chronology of C. G. Jung" in Sugg 1992:xv–xix, particularly xvii.

culture flow (op. cit., 86). This entails two separate and distinct tasks (ibid.):

i) Explaining the psychological structure of a work of art.
ii) Investigating the factors that make someone artistically creative.

As Jacoby (op. cit., 65) rightly observes, Jung's position establishes "a clear-cut dividing line between the psychological and aesthetic consideration of literature". This division is also carried through in Jung's distinction between "visionary" and "psychological" works of art. The former, drawing upon the primordial experiences of humankind, are full of mythical allusion at a deep level (op. cit., 96–97) and require keen psychological elucidation. The latter deal with "the stuff of human fate in general" (op. cit., 88) and require no further psychological elucidation on account of the fact that their characters are already presented in a psychological light. It is important to note that visionary works of art are not necessarily those that literary critics of past and/or present times have acclaimed. As Jung has said, literary critics and psychologists may differ widely both in their appreciation of the material before them and in the way which they explicate it. The former have a greater appreciation for a work's aesthetic value and analyse it as such, while the latter value works that teach them more about the workings of the human psyche and the functions of the archetypes.

It is evident that Jung's point of view does not constitute any specific method of analysis. As he has said, it merely outlines general ways in which "a psychological approach to poetry [read: all artistic forms] might be *oriented* . . ." (op. cit., 85, my italics). In fact, Jung has never established a school of Jungian literary criticism, nor did he ever intend to. Rather, the *how* of Jungian literary criticism has been developed in the last six or seven decades by Jungian and non-Jungian critics/psychoanalysts whose work shows varying degrees of commitment to Jung and his work. Sugg (1992a:1–2) has identified three such groups of 'Jungian critics': the "shared affinities" group, the myth critics, and the demonstrably Jungian literary critics:

i) As their name indicates, the "shared affinities" group share certain affinities with Jungian psychology, such as 'mythical vision' (Drew 1992:9–20) and a belief in archetypes (cf. Russo 1997:240–254; Kerbelker 1997). They nevertheless do not acknowledge outright the validity of his work, with critics like Baird (cf. e.g., 1992:38–52) scrupulously honouring the boundaries of literary criticism, and carefully distinguishing it from psychology (Sugg, op. cit., 2).

ii) Myth critics see myth as a mode of apprehending (thinking about and imagining) the world, and consequently believe that literature is informed by "a mythic vision . . . as carrying a significance of archetypal and collective importance" (op. cit., 3.). The work of Northrop Frye (cf. Wright 1998:63–66, Frye 1992:21–37) and Joseph Campbell (cf. e.g., 1992:75–82) constitutes some of the finest in this category.

iii) Contrary to the first two groups, the demonstrably Jungian critics acknowledge a strong Jungian influence upon their work (Sugg, op. cit., 4). The proponents of this group include Mario Jacoby (1992:59–74), James Hillman (1992:129–138), Michael Atkinson (1992a:83–102, 1992b:328–342), Annis Pratt (1992a:153–166, 1992b:367–375), and Terrence Dawson (1997:255–280). They "identify an important aspect of their critical approach to literature as Jungian. They . . . have demonstrated the usefulness of a serious study of both Jung's psychology and the history and practice of approaches to literature that stem from it" (Sugg, op. cit., 5). Many have even applied his theories to their lives. "Typically, such critics begin to work in both directions . . . using literature to clarify psychology as well as the other way round" (ibid.).

Naturally, these groups are not rigidly defined entities. Certain works/critics tread the boundaries between two or more groups. Northrop Frye, for example, may be categorised with the first group, though belonging more properly to the second. Similarly, my approach, which I shall explain below, straddles the second and third categories, but finds its home more properly in the third. This is not surprising, as Terrence Dawson's methodological approach, which I will apply to *Judith* in conjunction with Jung's dream analysis, may be classified almost exclusively under the demonstrably Jungian banner. I should like to outline his theory briefly below before proceeding to the specific way in which I shall apply it.

Drawing upon Jung's concept of the dream ego—the one personality in a dream who best represents the dreamer's unconscious personality (op. cit., 257)—Dawson suggests that there may be a vast difference between the *obvious* and the *effective* protagonist of the tale (see chapter 4 for his application of these principles to *Pamela*). The latter is the character who has undergone the most change in the course of the tale and the one to whom all its deep-structure events may be related (ibid.). The effective protagonist of a tale may be a relatively minor figure. Alternatively, the effective protagonist may indeed be the obvious heroine/hero of the tale.

For Dawson, the effective protagonist is the proper subject of psychoanalytic investigation. The first step of analysis entails identifying this character. This is done by examining which character has undergone the most psychological change and seeing whether, in fact, all the events in the story may be related to her/him. Should this indeed be the case, then the critic may safely assume that s/he has correctly identified the effective protagonist. The critic should then identify the dilemma that confronts the effective protagonist at the outset and describe the way this character deals with the challenges implicit in the dilemma (op. cit., 257). As a second step, the critic may then test the results of her/his findings against what is known of the tale's author and her/his times (op. cit., 263). In the third step, which acts as a further check for the findings of the analysis, the effective protagonist's stage of consciousness may be tested against Jung's five stages of consciousness (op. cit., 267, 274). This step, in combination with the second, then establishes the tale's dominant psychological concern (vis-à-vis that of the effective protagonist) and the level of individuation or self-awareness evidenced in it. Dawson finally takes his essay one step further by applying Jung's five stages of consciousness to the dominant concerns of the various phases in literary history as such.

As can be seen from the above, there are many affinities between Jung's dream analysis and Dawson's methodological approach. Not least of these is the fact that Dawson bases his concept of the effective protagonist on Jung's concept of the dream ego. Furthermore, Dawson's subsequent stages of analysis clearly relate to Jung's objective and subjective modes of analysis, but in reverse order, to an extent. As shown below, while Dawson's first step (1) relates to Jung's subjective mode of analysis (b), and his second step (2) relates to Jung's objective mode of analysis (a), his third step (3) relates to Jung's first *and* second steps (b) in that it extrapolates the findings of these two steps onto the textual world in order to determine the text's dominant psychological concern:

Dawson	**Jung**
1) Identify the effective protagonist and the dilemma confronting her/him.	a) Relate the dream images to the dreamer's external world—an objective analysis.
2) Test the results of the findings against what is known of the tale's author and her/his times.	b) Relate the dream images, which represent the dilemma facing the dreamer, to the dreamer's internal world and conduct a subjective analysis.
3) Identify the text's dominant psychological concern.	

d. *The Methodological Approach of the Current Study*

In this book, I propose to analyse *Judith*—a clearly fictitious myth or folk legend—as a dream of or for the Jewish nation in order to reveal what I believe to be *a* depiction of the nation's level of individuation at the time of the book's composition. As I have stated elsewhere, this will also assist me to clarify the contentious issues surrounding the historical/geographical inconsistencies of the book, the dual nature of its heroine, and the character of Achior. In my analysis I propose to merge Dawson's approach to literary texts with Jung's method of dream interpretation in the following way:

i) I will apply Jungian psychological categories to each character in order to establish the identity of the effective protagonist. Seeing that *Judith* has a definite bipartite structure, and Jung dictates that dream images should be analysed in the order of their appearance, I will analyse all the characters found in *Judith* 1–7 before analysing those appearing in *Judith* 8–16. I will identify the effective protagonist of the first section and establish her/his level of individuation before proceeding to the identification of the same in the second. Then, when this process has been completed for both sections, I will be in a better position to identify the effective protagonist of the entire tale and to analyse her/his state of individuation. This, in turn, will identify the 'main dream ego' of the Judithic dream and facilitate a subjective analysis of this material.

ii) The results of this extensive analysis will then be extrapolated to the historical events taking place at the time of the book's composition. This will both constitute the objective analysis and enable me to check my own theory concerning the book's dating against the subjective analysis previously completed.

iii) This, in turn, will assist me to identify the text's dominant psychological concern, and comment meaningfully on the function of *Judith* as an individuation drama as well as the psychological function/validity of its inconsistencies and bipartite structure, its heroine, and the role of Achior.

Having briefly delineated the broader aspects of my methodological approach, I should like to make some brief comments before going on to chapter 2. Firstly, for the sake of brevity, I shall refrain from laborious discussions of the possible amplifications of the imagery found in *Judith*. Rather, I should like to take these up briefly and where necessary within the course of my analysis and not in a separate section/subsection. In other words, I shall take up various aspects of amplification within the course of identifying the effective protagonist and the ensuing subjective analysis. Secondly, as *Judith* is a biblical text and not a person, amplification will be achieved by means of intertextual parallels with other biblical material known to me. This, I believe, is commensurate to Jung's mode of amplification by means of "numerous parallels from the psychology of primitive and historical symbolism" (cf. Jung 1956a:91 and 93–95). Thirdly, I find it strange that Jung, who was so concerned with the individual psyche, began his dream interpretation by examining the external forces to which his patient's dream images referred. To me, it makes more sense to establish internal connections before analysing the external ones. I therefore find Dawson's methodology far more appealing, in that he first establishes the identity of the effective protagonist (internal connection) before proceeding to the external context.

CHAPTER TWO

INDIVIDUATION, DREAM ANALYSIS, AND OTHER BASIC JUNGIAN CONCEPTS: AN OVERVIEW AND EVALUATION

This chapter aims at providing the reader with a thorough understanding of Jung's concept of individuation and his theory regarding dream interpretation, which form the theoretical basis of my study.

A. *Basic Jungian Concepts Relevant to the Individuation Process*

a. *The Conscious and Unconscious Psyche*

Although Jung was not the first to introduce the concept of the unconscious,[1] his documentation of its existence and elucidation of its processes is, arguably, the most important single contribution to the field of psychology and the understanding of the human race.[2] Jung (1940:4) contends that the sum total of a person's psyche consists neither of her/his conscious ego personality nor her/his persona; that people are defined neither by their own conscious understanding of themselves nor by the persona/'mask'[3] that they put on before the outside world. The latter, being "the ideal picture of a man as he should be" (Jung 1956b:194), is a (necessary) mechanism of protection and adaptation to the outside world. One often finds, however, that the "genuine self-sacrifice" necessary for the construction of such a persona "drives the ego straight into identification with the persona", so that there are people who really think that

[1] This is so by his own admission. For a brief synopsis of the historical development of thought on the unconscious, see Jung 1940:52 and 1959a:276–277.

[2] Crediting Jung with documenting the existence of the unconscious in no way minimises Freud's fundamental contribution to our understanding of the unconscious. Freud was the first to construct a systematic, scientific investigation of the manifestations of the unconscious psyche (see Jacobi 1942:20, n. 1).

[3] The word 'persona' stems from the masks worn by actors in ancient Greece, for example.

they are who they pretend to be—an extremely soulless position, not at all tolerated by the unconscious (Jung 1953a:193). Jung's experience has led him to argue for a psychological layer deeper than consciousness and the related persona,[4] namely, the unconscious. This layer of the psyche is itself divided into two layers: the personal and the collective unconscious.

Being more superficial, the personal unconscious rests on the deeper, inborn layer, the collective unconscious (op. cit., 52) and consists chiefly of "the *feeling-toned complexes*" (op. cit., 53, Jung's italics). That is, it consists of the sum total of a person's life-experiences, repressed images and memories, subliminal perceptions, and "contents that are not yet ripe for consciousness" (Jung 1956b:76). These are "integral components of the individual personality" that could therefore just as well be conscious (Jung 1959b:7). Over and against this, the impersonal collective unconscious consists of universal ancestral memories deriving from universal experience—including the residues of man's animal ancestry (Jung 1956b:109) and patterns of behaviour that Jung calls primordial images or archetypes. Being universal, these archetypes are "the same everywhere and in all individuals" (Jung 1940:53). They are, nevertheless, "as much feelings as thoughts" (Jung 1956b:76).

The personal unconscious thus constitutes a person's private psychic life (ibid.), while the collective unconscious constitutes the psychic life of humanity as a whole, establishing a bond between every person on earth and all those ancestral beings who have gone before, as well as those who are to follow (cf. Jung 1953a:177–179 and 1959a:279). The content-group of the collective unconscious "forms, as it were, an omnipresent, unchanging, and everywhere identical *quality or substrate of the psyche* per se" (Jung 1959a:7, Jung's italics).

The unconscious psyche is by far the largest and deepest aspect of the human psyche. According to Jung (1959b:4), the contents of the unconscious fall into three groups: contents that are temporarily subliminal and can thus be reproduced voluntarily (memory); unconscious contents that cannot be reproduced voluntarily; and contents that are not capable of consciousness at all (i.e., those which have not yet irrupted into consciousness, or those that never will). Being possessed of hidden contents that may or may never cross the

[4] For the relationship between the ego, the persona and the unconscious psyche see Jung 1953a:193–197.

threshold of consciousness, the unconscious is by far the most influential aspect of the psyche. By the same token, it is also the most dangerous, for one never knows when a hidden content may spontaneously break through the threshold of consciousness and upset its precarious balance. This spontaneous intervention of the unconscious contents often proves to be particularly disturbing to our (rational) consciousness because of their irrational and unpredictable nature. The problem is heightened all the more by the fact that the unconscious never sleeps. "It seems to be always at work, for even when asleep we dream" (Jung 1953a:177). It is thus not as harmless as people think. It is, in fact, the precondition upon which consciousness is based, upon which it depends, and from which it has evolved (cf. Jung 1959a:281 and 1964:23–25 and Jacobi, op. cit., 23–24). That is why the unconscious psyche holds as much sway over the conscious psyche as it does, making its presence felt in sudden mood swings, slips of the tongue, actions or thoughts in which we do not quite recognise ourselves to be the conscious subject ("I don't know quite what got into me", we say later), emotional outbursts, and fantasies and dreams, for example (cf. Jung 1953a:176–177). It is in these unguarded moments that we realise that we are being controlled by an 'other' and that this 'other' lives and moves within ourselves, nay, drives us, with a 'mind', 'will', passion, energy, and instinct[5] or purpose of its own (see Jung 1956b:44). It is in these moments that the unconscious shows its autonomy and ascendancy over the conscious mind; and it is in these selfsame moments that we realise, with hindsight, that it does not live in us, i.e., it is not under our control, but that we are under its control, and that it is far more powerful than we thought. It is then too, particularly after we have seen the results of such unconscious, irrational moments, that we realise that the unconscious psyche is far more 'dangerous' than we thought (see Jung 1959a:282). The realisation and concomitant fear that we are not as 'together' as we thought then usually leads us, erroneously, either to suppress the unconscious contents which have thus surfaced, or to allow unconsciousness to take over our conscious mind. That the unconscious is able to assert its autonomy by taking over the role of the conscious ego is shown not only

[5] Here 'instinct' is used in the sense of 'drive' as with Freud (cf. Brown, op. cit., 9 for an explanation of the Freudian 'drive' theory).

in extreme (psychotic) cases, but "*above all* in affective states" (Jung, op. cit., 278, my italics).[6] It does not take much, as Jung says, "to reverse the relation between the ego and the unconscious", even in so-called 'normal' people. "[L]ove, hatred, joy, or sadness is often strong enough" (Jung 1940:9). It is at such points that all sorts of neuroses and psychoses may develop (Jung 1956b:35). In these cases, one behaves "more or less like a primitive" (ibid.); otherwise sound people may be seized by strange ideas; and even whole groups of people may succumb to such "mental epidemics" as have plagued us, for example, in the last world war (cf. Jung 1940:9 and 1964:85).

Here we have touched upon another important facet of the conscious and unconscious psyche: though the conscious mind is rational, as opposed to the irrationality of the unconscious, both must have a central 'consciousness'—an ego, a 'personality', or an "I"—through which they 'think' and act. As Jung (1959a:283) puts it, the autonomy and efficacy of the unconscious in affecting the conscious thoughts, plans, wishes, and desires of a human being "suggest the existence of a consciousness in the unconscious" (ibid.). This means that we have to postulate an acting, thinking subject, for "no consciousness can exist without a subject", i.e., an ego to which its contents are related (ibid., Jung's italics):

> Consciousness needs a centre, an ego to which something is conscious. We know of no other kind of consciousness, nor can we imagine a consciousness without an ego. There can be no consciousness when there is no one to say: '*I* am conscious'.

That central 'consciousness' is for the conscious mind the ego, and for the unconscious mind, the Self (see the relevant section below).

b. *The Ego*

Jung (1959b:3) describes the ego as "the subject of all personal acts of consciousness". He claims that it rests upon both a somatic basis (inferred from "the totality of endosomatic perceptions"),[7] as well as

[6] "Affects usually occur where adaptation is weakest, and at the same time they reveal the reason for its weakness, namely, a certain degree of inferiority and the existence of a lower level of personality" (Jung 1959b:9).

[7] The ego's somatic basis is inferred from the totality of endosomatic perceptions that are produced by endosomatic stimuli. A considerable proportion of these occur unconsciously, i.e., subliminally, and few possess the energy to cross the threshold

a psychic basis that comprises "the *total field of consciousness*" and "the *sum total of unconscious contents*" (op. cit., 4, Jung's italics).[8] As both its psychic and somatic bases consist of conscious and unconscious elements, the ego stands "between the two spheres [consciousness and unconsciousness], which not only supplement but also complement or compensate each other.[9] That is, the dividing line that marks them off from each other in our ego can be displaced in both directions" (Jacobi, op. cit., 20). It follows, then, that the smaller the sphere of consciousness the greater the sphere of the unconscious.

Taking the above into consideration, we conclude that the ego is a complex factor composed of elements that are both the same everywhere and yet infinitely varied as affects "clarity, emotional colouring and scope" (Jung, op. cit., 6). It is unique, individual, and able to retain its stability up to a point. At the same time, its stability is rather relative (and fragile) owing to the "far-reaching changes of personality" (developmental or pathological) that are sometimes brought about by the interaction of its components (ibid.).

Being that through which the environment is encountered, "the ego is the subject of all successful attempts at adaptation" and a portrait of the conscious personality (ibid., cf. also op. cit., 5).

of consciousness and become perceptions precisely because of their very elementary or basic nature (Jung 1959b:4).

[8] Having said that, it is important to note that while the ego 'rests' on the total field of consciousness *it does not consist of it*. Were that the case, the ego would be "indistinguishable from the field of consciousness as a whole" (Jung 1959b:4). As a matter of (Jungian) fact, the ego is only the latter's point of reference, "grounded on and limited by the somatic factor described above" (ibid.).

[9] [This footnote is my own addition and does not form part of the Jacobi quotation into which it has been inserted]. The compensatory nature of the conscious-unconscious relation is particularly evident at times when the unconscious psyche is in control as, for example, when we dream (cf. Jung 1956b:114–120). So it is that a man who looks down upon his brother may dream of him as a great statesman or hero (Jung 1953a:179); or a person who thinks too much of herself/himself may see herself/himself descending or taking a fall (from a high place). This type of "compensatory criticism exercised by the unconscious" (ibid.) is vital in that it not only compensates mood, but offers a "*mental corrective*" too (Jung 1956b:114, Jung's italics). It may, as is the case with the dream of falling, even attempt to warn the dreamer. In this way, the unconscious exercises a regulatory effect on the conscious mind and attempts to "maintain the psychic equilibrium" by "always stress[ing] the other side" (ibid.). The compensatory relation between consciousness and the unconscious mind is also evident, inter alia, in the existence of two different attitudes in one person, so that a conscious, extraverted attitude is compensated by an unconscious, introverted one (cf. Jung's parable to this effect, op. cit., 66–68).

In myths and various other literary works, the ego is represented by the hero or main protagonist (see Hillman 1992:135, 136).

c. *The Self*

Given that the ego rests upon both conscious and unconscious bases, it follows that the total personality of a human being does not coincide with the ego, i.e., the conscious personality (Jung, op. cit., 5). Jung calls that total personality the Self, and describes it as a "quantity that is *supraordinate to the conscious ego*"[10] (Jung 1953a:177, my italics). For him, the Self is "an inclusive term that embraces our whole living organism" (op. cit., 192). In other words, it embraces both the conscious and the unconscious psyche. This means that the ego and Self are not to be confused. While both are subjects or centres in their own right—the ego of consciousness, and the Self of unconsciousness (and the psyche as a whole)—they are not interchangeable. In fact, the ego relates to the Self as a subordinated part to a whole (op. cit., 177), as an object upon which the subject acts.[11] In contrast to the ego's 'limitation' to the conscious mind (cf. ibid.), the Self is 'limitless'. Embracing both the conscious and the unconscious psyche, it simultaneously contains "the deposit and totality of all past life", *and* is "a point of departure, the fertile soil from which all future life will spring" (op. cit., 192).

Given the above, it is not surprising to find that:

> the most prevalent literary and mythical representations of the Self are the babe and the wise old man . . . since it is that nuclear source of energy within us at birth (or re-born in self-discovery), which, if we integrate our lives, comes to the fullness of its wisdom in our maturity (Atkinson 1992a:92).

In terms of the individuation process, the Self is the archetype of meaning or wholeness. It is both that which urges the individual on

[10] "There is little hope of our ever being able to reach even approximate consciousness of the Self, since however much we may make conscious there will always exist an indeterminable amount of unconscious material which belongs to the totality of the self. Hence the self will always remain a supraordinate quantity" (Jung 1953a:177).

[11] While the ego has free will or free choice inside the field of consciousness, "it finds its limits outside the field of consciousness in the subjective inner world, where it comes into conflict with the facts of the self . . . so the self acts upon the ego like an objective occurrence which free will can do little to alter" (Jung 1959b:5–6).

through this vital process of maturing and becoming all that s/he is ("that near divinity which each human being has the potential to become" [ibid.]) and the goal that s/he hopes to attain. In other words, the Self is simultaneously that which drives the process of individuation and its highest goal. It is "[t]he innermost archetype" (Samuels 1985:31) and, as Jung (op. cit., 238) observes, "It may equally be called the 'God within us'". Hence, from a Christian point of view, it comes as no surprise that Jung regards Christ as *the* Western symbol of the Self (Jung 1959b:36–71; cf. also 1953b: 345–431).

d. *The Archetypes*

While the Self occupies a central place in the process of individuation, as both its initiator and goal, there are many other archetypes[12] that relate to the selfsame process. The ones most commonly experienced are the shadow, the animal, the wise old man, the anima, the animus, the mother, and the child, as well as "an indefinite number of archetypes representative of situation" (Jung 1956b:120). Nevertheless, the most important of these are the shadow, the animus, and the anima, as they are the ones "which have the most frequent and the most disturbing influence on the ego"[13] (Jung 1959b:8, cf. also Atkinson, op. cit., 85).

A General Overview of Archetypes

The Nature and Expression of Archetypes

We have previously observed that, whereas the contents of the personal unconscious constitute a person's private psychic life and are "chiefly the *feeling-toned complexes*" (Jung 1940:53), the contents of the collective unconscious are the so-called *archetypes*. These "dominants" or "primordial figures of the unconscious" (op. cit., 23) constitute,

[12] For a very insightful developmental history of the term from Philo, to Augustine, to Lévy-Bruhl, see Jung 1959a:4–5. Cf. also Samuels (op. cit., 23) for Jung's indebtedness to Kant and, particularly, Schopenhauer in this regard.

[13] Accordingly, this subsection will focus on these three archetypes alone—an emphasis that is more germane to my overall purpose, i.e., interpreting the main cast of *Judith* as personified archetypes. Other types will be discussed in the ensuing analysis of the book as the need arises.

among others, patterns, modes of thought, and behaviour that are "common to the whole of humanity" (op. cit., 50). In this regard, archetypes "correspond to the concept of the 'pattern of behaviour' in biology" (Jung 1956a:158). Thus, they function similarly under similar circumstances regardless of time and place, and produce the same ideas and symbolic material in people of diverse traditions, nationalities, and social and educational backgrounds (ibid.; see also 1940:50). Being ideas—or rather, the possibility thereof—that have been "stamped on the human brain for aeons" (Jung 1956b:76, 79), they rise up and seize people under conducive circumstances, compelling them to reshape traditional concepts in their own likeness (cf., e.g., the case of Robert Mayer and his conception of energy conservation; op. cit., 77–78). In this way, the archetypes form the "blueprint" upon which "the greatest and best thoughts of man shape themselves" (op. cit., 79).

Just as the psyche contains the blueprints for all of mankind's greatest thoughts, so too does it contain "all the images that have ever given rise to myths" (Jung 1959a:7), legends, fairytales, the dogmas of world religions, esoteric teachings, and tribal lore. The images and symbols[14] encountered in these forms of archetypal expression are "historical formula[e]" or "conscious elaboration[s]" (op. cit., 5); they are not to be confused with the archetype itself (cf. Jacoby 1992:62–63). Rather, these archetypal expressions transform the immediate psychic experience of the archetype into a slightly more palpable—and palatable!—(conscious) form. It is this transformation, then, that makes the archetype more accessible to the heart and conscious thought of one who encounters the form and allows herself/

[14] An image or symbol is not to be confused with a sign. A symbol is "a term, a name, or even a picture that may be familiar in daily life, yet that possesses specific *connotations in addition to its conventional and obvious meaning*. It implies something vague, unknown, or hidden from us. . . . It has a *wider 'unconscious' aspect* that is *never precisely* defined or fully *explained*" (Jung 1964:20–21, my italics). Nor can it be. By contrast, a sign denotes nothing more than the object to which it is attached. As examples, looking at the disc of the sun may raise all sorts of unconscious connections to a divine "sun god", whereas the acronym "UN" refers to nothing more than what it is—an acronym for "United Nations" (ibid.). Here I must disagree a little with Jung. It is well known that even the barking of a dog may subconsciously raise all sorts of unconscious associations (cf. Jung's own example to this effect, op. cit., 36). Similarly, "UN" may raise archetypal ideas such as peace and brotherhood, etc., though these associations may admittedly not be as immediately accessible as the sun–sun god association (by virtue of the latter's long and elaborate symbolism and history, if nothing else).

himself (and/or her/his instincts) to be touched—indeed, overpowered—by its mysterious, beckoning, numinous presence (cf. Jung 1956a:158).[15] Unfortunately, and by the same token, images (particularly dogmatic or religious ones) tend simultaneously to safeguard us from the immediate and direct experience of the archetype they represent (Jung 1959a:8).[16] Generally, and perhaps as a rule, the more grandiose and comprehensive such an image is, i.e., the more it has been submitted to conscious elaboration, "*so much farther is it removed from our experience*" (Jung 1940:56). We can feel our way into it, as it were, but the original experience is lost.

In summary, the form or expression of an archetype is not to be confused with the archetype itself: the archetype has no form, i.e., it has "not yet been subjected to conscious elaboration" (op. cit., 54; cf. also Jung 1964:67–69, Samuels, op. cit., 25).

Two Classes of Archetypes

There are two main classes of archetype: those that can be personified and those that speak of transformation. Personified archetypes include the shadow, the anima and animus, the wise old man, the mother, the maid, the trickster, and the child (see Fontana 1993:13–17), while archetypes of transformation represent a situation, place, or means (e.g., ways, animals, plants) by which a rite of passage or some type of change (whether 'good' or 'bad') is effected (Jung 1940:89), e.g., journeys, death, rebirth, etc. (on the last see Jung 1959a:113–150). Both archetype classes have a characteristically "eternal and compelling" nature (Engelsman 1994:16) that causes them, under certain circumstances, to emerge spontaneously and effortlessly from the depths of the collective unconscious. Once they have crossed the threshold of consciousness—against which act the entire arsenal of the conscious mind is powerless—they attract, fascinate, convince,

[15] "The archetype . . . has a characteristically numinous effect, so that the subject is gripped by it as though by an instinct" (Jung 1956a:158).

[16] Cf., e.g., the vision of Brother Klaus. Originally, this vision of God so terrified him and so changed his countenance, that everyone who saw him became scared too. It was only after years of conscious elaboration—reading the vision through the illustrated work of a German mystic—and association with another, mandala-like vision that Brother Klaus was able to assimilate the almost iconoclastic and heretical vision with the currently accepted doctrine of the Trinity, thus making it more palatable to his conscious psyche and saving himself from dementia or the death of a heretic. For more details, see Jung 1959a:9–12.

overpower, and, in fact, so possess an individual that either great thoughts or great neuroses arise—it all depends on how and how well they are assimilated by or into the conscious mind. Naturally, while interpreting archetypes and assimilating them into the conscious mind is vital for greater psychic integration and personal growth, the process can be a long and laborious one. The reason for this is that they are not allegories or signs that can be "exhaustively interpreted" (Jung 1940:89). Rather, they are genuine symbols in so far as they are "ambiguous, full of intimations, and, in the final analysis, inexhaustible" (ibid.).

The Unity, Repression, and Projection of Archetypes

Being symbolic in nature and "pleromatic" of character (Jung, op. cit., 89), archetypes are also characteristically ambivalent or polysemous. In other words, they can never be limited to any single point of reference, because each archetype primordially combines both the positive and the negative aspects of itself within itself (cf. Jung 1956b:80, Samuels, op. cit., 30–31). However, consciousness, whose either/or mentality prevents it from doing otherwise, "splinters the unity of the archetype by seeing its various aspects as separate and unrelated entities" (Engelsman, op. cit., 17). So it is, for example, that the composite great mother archetype has been splintered into a good and a bad goddess. It is then that the less palatable form of the archetype is either repressed or projected onto another person and/or situation. An arrogant, self-centred person, for example, may repress her/his negative attitudes and project them onto a person in her/his environment who has the traits to make that specific attachment possible. The latter may then begin to take on the form of a sadist or a demon in the former's eyes. In similar vein, a person with low self-esteem may project all that is good in herself/himself upon someone else out of a sense of nullity or self-punishment, etc. S/he may then begin to view the person onto whom these attributes are projected as a god or saviour. Thus, it is not only the negative side of an archetype that can be repressed or projected.

As may be deduced from the above, repression and projection have a very negative effect on the so-called 'subject'. Repression places the subject more firmly than ever under the archetype's ironclad control, giving it free reign to haunt her/him in the form of neuroses, for example (cf. Jung 1940:27). Likewise, the overvaluations and prejudices that result from projection slowly create walls and barriers between the individual and her/his environment, bringing about neuroses, isolation, and broken relationships (Jung 1956b: 106). This occurs because the archetypes are part of "the unconscious [psyche which] *is* life, and . . . if life is repressed it will live against us" (ibid., my italics). The only way to break such a projection is to trace "the mysterious feeling [that X is a demon or god] . . . back to a definite entity in the unconscious" (Jung, op. cit., 106, 107) and deal with it. It is thus vital to come to terms with these archetypes as they make their appearance during dreams, visions, fantasies, analysis, and active imagination. That, according to Jung, is the way of individuation, which I will discuss below.

The Shadow, the Anima, and the Animus

As I have previously mentioned, the shadow, the anima, and the animus belong to the class of archetypes that are immediately experienced in personified form. Hence, they "come upon the scene as active personalities" in the process of individuation and may easily disrupt it (Jung 1940:88, 89).

The Shadow

Essentially—from a conscious point of view, that is—"the shadow is an inferior component of the personality" (Jung 1956b:63–64) whose "nature can in large measure be inferred from the contents of the personal unconscious" (Jung 1959b:8). In other words, it is an archetype whose nature is manifest chiefly in the emotional disturbances that affect the conscious state (Jung 1940:20). It is thus the archetype whose contents can be made conscious with the least difficulty (Jung 1959b:10). By the same token, it is the one that is most easily experienced (op. cit., 8) and so one that is often either projected or repressed.[17]

[17] Although the shadow is an essential part of the human psyche, we often repress it during the earlier years of life in order to seem more acceptable to our parents, and particularly to gain their love (cf. Fontana, op. cit., 16). This type of repression often continues throughout life, with the aim of appearing more acceptable to one's peers or society in general. It thus contributes to the constitution of the mask we wear, i.e., to the creation of our persona. By repressing the shadow, we not only give it the power to act against us and 'bedevil' our lives at the most inopportune moments, as it were, but we open the gates of projection whereby we project those undesired parts of our particular psyche onto others who then become the scapegoats for our faults (cf. ibid.). The recent Holocaust provides ample, gruesome, examples of what happens as a result.

One may say of the shadow that it is that which we fear, despise, and cannot accept in ourselves (Samuels, op. cit., 31), "the self-willed, self-seeking part of human nature" (Fontana, op. cit., 16), or, as Jung would have it, "the will to power" (Jung 1956b:43).[18] An encounter with the shadow means an encounter with that powerful world of instincts that underlie and threaten to destroy our carefully constructed persona (cf. Jung 1940:69). As such, it represents "a moral problem that challenges the whole ego-personality" (Jung 1959b:8). Nevertheless, becoming conscious of it and so "recognizing the dark aspects of the personality as present and real . . . is the essential condition for any kind of self-knowledge" (ibid.). This is something we all know, no matter how much we fear it; as Jung (1956b:40, my italics) says, "A dim premonition tells us that *we cannot be whole without this negative side*".

According to Jung (1940:21), the shadow manifests as a masculine figure in men's dreams and (presumably, although Jung does not specify, to the best of my knowledge) as a feminine figure in women's dreams.

The Anima/Animus

As we have mentioned above, the shadow is an archetype whose "nature is manifest chiefly in the emotional disturbances which affect the conscious state". Nevertheless, it is not alone in creating disturbances of this nature (cf. Jung 1940:20–22). Two other, very powerful archetype personalities come into play here, viz., the anima in men and the animus in women.

[It should be noted that Jung was less than straightforward in his statements about the animus. He merely *assumed* that the animus functioned in the same way as the anima. This assumption has been spelled out in more definite terms by strict adherents like Von Franz (see below) and severely criticised by (notably feminist) others such as June Singer, Naomi Goldenberg, and Annis Pratt. I do not believe that Jung's assumption is correct, as I will show in my evaluation of his work. In this subsection, however, I will merely delineate his views and those of his staunch adherents].

[18] Briefly, "the will to power" refers to humankind's instinct for self-preservation (cf. Jung 1956b:41). For a thorough discussion of this instinct and how it relates to (Adlerian) psychoanalytic practice see Jung, op. cit., 39–50.

According to Jung, the anima is the personification of a man's unconscious, just as the animus is the personification of a woman's unconscious (cf. Gelpi 1992:105–106 for this specific formulation of Jung's views). Given the compensatory relation between consciousness and unconsciousness, the anima manifests as a woman in man, just as the animus manifests as a man in woman. So it is, Jung claims, that in times of emotional weakness a man is overtaken by moods, irrationality, and waspish, devaluative comments, while a woman puts forth her opinions as unshakeable, unassailable truths or principles—with both sets of reactions based on "equally unconscious prior assumptions" (Jung 1953a:207; cf. also Jung op. cit., 194–195 and 206–207; Von Franz 1964:177–179).

Being personifications of the unconscious, the anima and animus have both a personal and an impersonal basis—both a personal and a collective 'history' and development. On a personal level, the man's anima is shaped primarily by his perceptions of his mother—his mother-imago; just as a woman's animus is shaped primarily by her perceptions of her father—her father imago (cf. Jung 1959b:13). These parental imagos—shaped, in turn, by "parental influences *plus* the specific reactions of the child" (Jung 1953a:186, my italics)—become receptacles for the universal, inborn image of woman in man, and of man in woman (cf. Jung 1959b:14; Fontana, op. cit., 13, 14). As a child grows up, the parental images are increasingly shut off from consciousness and may thus easily assume a negative aspect. Parental influence wanes, and other women/men take up their positions "as the most immediate environmental influence" in the life of an adult woman/man (cf. Jung 1953a:188). In other words, women and men other than the parents become the receptacles for an adult's corresponding soul-image, i.e., for the corresponding female/male imago, the anima/animus or soul-image (cf. Jung, op. cit., 189 and 197 for the equation of these terms). This means that both the personal and impersonal soul-image may be projected onto other women/men in an adult's 'environment', causing phenomena such as (among others) love at first sight[19] and intense, unqualified distrust upon meeting someone for the first time.

[19] According to Jung (1953a:189), "the imago of woman (the soul-image) becomes a receptacle for [a man's suppressed contrasexual demands or feminine traits], which is why a man, in his love-choice, is strongly tempted to win the woman who best corresponds to his own unconscious femininity—a woman, in short, who can unhesitatingly receive the projection of his soul".

A further characteristic of the anima and animus, as symbols of the collective unconscious, is that they have both a positive and a negative aspect, and thus manifest themselves in either positive or negative ways. On a personal level, their characteristic manifestations (described above) provide ample evidence of their negative aspects that seem hell-bent on destroying the relationships and/or the self-confidence of the person they come to possess. In myths, fantasies, legends, dreams, and the like, these negative aspects find their manifestations in femme fatales, sirens, uncaring lovers, or Bluebeards, wicked or evil personalities that try to waylay the heroine/hero and lead her/him to destruction.

On the more positive side, the anima assists a man to find the right marriage partner, to excavate facts hidden in his unconscious which cannot be reached via the conscious mind alone, and, most importantly, tunes a man's mind into "the right inner values . . . thereby opening the way into more profound inner depths" (Von Franz, op. cit., 180). In this guise, the anima "takes on the role of guide, or mediator, to the world within and to the Self" (op. cit., 183, 185). According to Von Franz (op. cit., 185, my italics):

> This positive function occurs when a man takes seriously the feelings, moods, expectations, and fantasies sent by his anima and when he fixes them in some form—for example, in writing, painting, sculpture, musical composition, or dancing.

Even more important is that he regards these fantasies and expectations as "absolutely real", and submits them to intellectual and ethical scrutiny "with an evaluating feeling reaction" (ibid.).

Similarly—for Von Franz (op. cit., 193), that is—a woman's animus "too can build a bridge to the Self through his creative activity". According to her (op. cit., 192, my italics):

> the conscious attention a woman has to give her animus problem takes much time and involves a lot of suffering. But if she realises who and what her animus is and what he does to her, and if she faces these realities instead of allowing herself to be possessed, her animus can turn into an invaluable inner companion who endows her with the masculine qualities of initiative, courage, objectivity, and spiritual wisdom.

In myths, legends, fairytales, and so forth, the more positive anima may appear (inter alia) as a princess locked up in an enchanted castle, a wise woman who helps the hero, or as Wisdom, while the positive animus may appear (inter alia) as prince charming, the knight in shining armour, or "the adventurer who becomes a prince or overcomes the forces of evil" (Fontana, op. cit., 12).

Finally, being symbols of unity, both the anima and animus show a fourfold development.[20] Thus, at the first stage, the purely instinctual, sensual anima is symbolised by Eve; Faust's Helen symbolises the second, romantic, aesthetic, but still sexual stage of the anima; the third stage of spiritual devotion is symbolised by the Virgin Mary; and Wisdom (Sophia, or Sapienta, or even the Shunamite) represents the fourth and final stage, "transcending even the most holy and the most pure" (Von Franz, op. cit., 185). Similarly, the first stage of the animus entails the personification of a mere physical power (e.g., Tarzan); the second stage is represented by the romantic man of initiative and planned action (e.g., the poet Shelley, or a war hero, hunter, etc.); the 'word' bearer (e.g., Lloyd George) represents the third stage; and the incarnation of meaning, the wise guide of spiritual truth (Jesus? or often as projected upon Gandhi) represents the fourth and final stage of the animus development (op. cit., 192). It is at this fourth and highest level that the animus, like the anima, "becomes . . . a mediator of the religious experience whereby life acquires new meaning" (ibid.).

B. *Individuation: the Five Stages of the Process, the Role of Dream Interpretation, and the Mythical, Gnostic-Alchemical Precursors of Individuation*

a. *The Psychological Process of Individuation*

The Five Stages of Individuation

According to Jung (1953a:174), individuation is "a process of psychological development that fulfils the individual qualities given [a human being]; . . . it is a process by which man becomes the definite, unique being he in fact is". In other words, it is a (life-long) psychological process that drives a human being to become the 'individual'—the unique, indivisible unit or 'whole' person (cf. Jung 1940:3)—that s/he potentially is.[21] As Monick (1991:34, my italics) has put it,

[20] Four is the number of totality or wholeness, and is often found in symbolic manifestations of the Self (Jung 1959b:194, 223–226).

[21] I think it is sufficiently clear by now that Jung regarded the psyche as a

individuation is "the *urge* in all human beings to *differentiate* themselves from collective or traditional patterns of self-understanding, and to make a journey peculiarly theirs, deeply personal, essentially mythic". In essence, this 'mythic journey' entails a gradual withdrawal of projections via integrating the dilemma/s (the unacceptable elements) inherent in each (cf. Dawson, op. cit., 267), and coming to terms with the opposite(s) within oneself (within one's own psyche). According to Jung, the following steps or stages are involved in each withdrawal:

1. *Complete identification with societal norms and expectations*
   A person (or even a group of people) at this level is completely at one with the society of which s/he forms a part. Such people have no concept of themselves as distinct from the group; their thinking and actions are consequently determined entirely by their group's/society's expectations.
2. *Separation from the 'other'*
   This is a long and sometimes painful process whereby "a person explores his or her identity, usually by way of a dialectic with different facets of the 'other'" (ibid.). These 'others' may be authority figures or those representing 'difference'. For example, if one is a male teenager, one might explore one's identity vis-à-vis young women of one's age group, or older men within one's societal group. This is the first step of conscious differentiation from the group or 'herd'.
3. *The differentiation of moral properties*
   At this stage, a person attempts to ascertain and establish her/his own moral or ethical code by "testing the collective morality of his or her society" (ibid.).
4. *Realisation of social reality and individual consciousness*
   Here the collective norms and expectations of a person's society/group lose their '*mana*', and the world is seen as it is. The 'projection' is broken and the person is freed to become who s/he really is. Most often, as a result of the world losing its '*mana*', a

dynamic (rather than static) entity that consists of an interplay of forces (often instinctual) and of opposition between conflicting forces (cf. Samuels, op. cit., 8–9). Such oppositional 'forces' may be attributed to the interaction between the conscious and unconscious contents of the psyche that remain in opposition unless merged into a new dialogic relationship by the transcendent function (see below).

person may experience various degrees of alienation, thus necessitating the fifth stage, outlined briefly below.

5. *Individual identity or self-realisation*
   A person who has reached this stage of consciousness begins to question her/his innate tendencies, particularly those that s/he is unaware of and that are revealed "through a searching analysis of [her/his] dreams and waking fantasies" (ibid.). With this stage the process comes full circle as the person is prepared to re-enter society, to reintegrate with it, being wholly conscious of her/his own identity (nature, function, limitations). This is entirely different from the first stage in which the person was un-conscious of her/his identity apart from that of her/his group.

It should be noted that:

- The five stages of individuation are not 'fixed' or exclusive entities. One does not exit completely from the first stage before entering the second, and so forth. Furthermore, "[d]ifferent parts of oneself very often 'inhabit' different stages" (ibid.). One might, for instance, have completely extricated oneself from one's group expectations regarding spirituality, but not regarding the role that one plays within the home or in society. Similarly, someone who lives in and functions primarily out of the first stage has some kind of consciousness about the fourth (op. cit., 268).
- Each stage corresponds to a different and greater level of consciousness or conscious adaptation to the world around us.
- Successful adaptation hinges on one's definition of the world (stage 4), which, in turn, hinges on one's understanding of oneself in it (see stages 2 and 3). Without some form of self-understanding (conscious differentiation from the 'herd'), one cannot see the world for what it is relative to oneself (see e.g., stage 3).
- The goal of the individuation process is not complete extrication from society, even though the initial separation is necessary (stage 2). The goal of the process is reintegration into society (stage 5), regardless of how arduous this task may seem. As Jung (1953a: 173–174) has said, individuation is the very opposite of egoistic individualism:

> Individualism means deliberately stressing and giving prominence to some supposed peculiarity rather than to collective considerations and obligations. But individuation means precisely the better and more complete fulfillment of the collective qualities of the human being . . .

Paradoxically, as we have already seen, achieving a greater union with one's fellow human beings requires "disengag[ing] the ego from all its entanglements from collectivity and the collective unconscious" (Monick, op. cit., 227). It also requires "detachment from the world of objective reality as the center of existing . . . [and] from the ego as the center of interest and the discovery of a different center" (Drew, op. cit., 18).

Assimilating Opposites

Individuation, or allowing oneself to succumb to the instinct of individuation (cf. Monick, op. cit., 34), is not an easy task. In fact, as we will see from the ensuing subsections, it is an arduous task, an ἆθλον proper, a true labour in the magnitude of the Twelve Labours/Tasks of Hercules (and a rather apt portrayal of book-writing). It takes courage, perseverance, and resilience as it entails the assimilation of potentially (ego-) destabilising opposites at almost every turn. These opposites include one's shadow components (the negative or hidden parts of oneself, one's instincts) and one's contrasexual image, the anima/animus (op. cit., 26; cf. also 219, 226, 238).[22] Taking his cue from the historical antecedents of this psychological process (i.e., from Gnosticism and the subsequent alchemical doctrines), Jung has called this archetypal union of the opposites the *hieros gamos*, or 'holy (whole -y) marriage' (cf. Jung 1940:28).[23] For Monick (op. cit., 34–38), as for Jung, the *hieros gamos* establishes one firmly in one's own (male sexual) identity[24] with the result that one's consciousness is broadened; one is more at peace with oneself and can therefore relate to others in a more compassionate, wholesome way.

Braving the Unconscious: Going Down to the Water's Edge

As we may deduce from the above, Jung regards individuation as an inborn instinct: note the words "drive" and "urge" that are used

[22] While an assimilation of the male contrasexual image may be inferred from Jung's writings, it is never explicitly stated. For the critical problem this 'omission' raises, see the evaluation pp. 78–92 below.

[23] For a detailed exposition on this matter that contains one of Jung's fascinating conflations of Gnostic quaternities with alchemical doctrines see Jung 1959b: 184–221 and 222–265.

[24] Neither Monick nor Jung ever fully develops what the *hieros gamos* would mean for women. In fact, Jung focuses almost exclusively on male individuation, while this is the sole concern of Monick's work; hence the gender specification in parenthesis.

to characterise this process. This means that the potential for individuation is innate and may therefore begin at any time. It does, however, seem to be a more frequently occurring phenomenon from the middle years of life onwards. This is usually the time when a crisis compels one to re-examine one's life, identity, and values (cf. Monick, op. cit., 32–38). Essentially, individuation 'begins' when one recognises that one's carefully constructed persona is not all there is to oneself; when one is willing to overcome the fear of encountering what one does not know, to go down to the water's edge (a popular Jungian metaphor)[25]—that deep pool of the unconscious—and face the image of oneself that appears there.

In most myths and in many literary works, the call to the individuation process or 'hero's quest' "begins with a perception of a lack, an imbalance" (Atkinson, op. cit., 90). The hero is called "from the ordinary world of experience into the realm of the mysterious, where he battles various foes, conquers or converts them, and gains a boon, his 'inheritance,' a life-restoring elixir with which he recrosses the threshold and with which, after some readjustment, he transforms the world or his vision of it" (op. cit., 98). In ordinary life, however, the 'call' to individuation begins most frequently with a change in circumstance and/or an inner change that alerts us to the fact that we are not all that we purport to be. A crisis, an affliction, or some monumental (psychic) event bring us to the realisation that there is another side to ourselves (the monster/enemy of myth), one that has been hidden or suppressed or, simply, one that has lain dormant, waiting for the right opportunity to rise to consciousness and challenge our precious (persona-based) identity anew. In Jungian terms, a certain situation in life has lent enough psychic energy—libido—to an unconscious content for it to cross the threshold of consciousness and challenge the authority of the ego-personality. As the risen content is most often a characteristic or attribute opposite or contrary to that of ego-consciousness, the ego is torn between the emerging content (e.g., sensuality) and the one by which it has customarily functioned (e.g., intellectualism or spirituality). The ego may then choose one or the other, or it may become strong enough to protect the intermediary product/attitude that has developed in the

[25] Water is often a symbol of the unconscious (Jung 1956b:99), as it is both fascinating and dangerous.

tension between opposites. The first option leads to the further splitting of the person's psyche, while the second leads to the benefits of the transcendent function (cf. Samuels, op. cit., 58–59) that bridges "the yawning gulf between conscious and unconscious" (Jung 1956b:90). By facilitating the 'dialogue' between previously opposite psychic contents, the transcendent function "mediates between a person and the *possibility* of change by providing, not an *answer*, but a *choice*" (Samuels, op. cit., 59, my italics in the first instance). Should the ego take the opportunity offered in this way, "[a] new attitude is available for conscious living and, at the same time, ego-consciousness itself is strengthened" (ibid.). This, in turn, provides "the starting point for a new dynamic" whereby the new 'mediatory product' is "once again challenged from within" (op. cit., 60) leading to ever heightened forms of ego-differentiation and community-identification.

Setting Aside the Persona and Encountering the Shadow

As can be expected from the preceding subsections, the first thing one encounters when going down to the water's edge is one's own shadow; for the first thing one sees in the water is one's own face (Jung 1940:69). The water is a far-from-flattering mirror. Unlike the mirror of the wicked witch/queen,[26] it shows us the truth about ourselves; it shows us our true selves stripped of the persona we have so elaborately fashioned. We see now that the shadow, whom we had projected onto the 'devil' or others, and whom we had relegated to a realm outside of ourselves, is within us; it is part of ourselves. The immense moral problem that this realisation presents us with is "the first test of courage on the inner way" (ibid.)—enough to frighten off the most stalwart. And yet, becoming conscious of the shadow—"recognizing the dark aspects of the personality as present and real"—is "the essential condition for any kind of self-knowledge" (Jung 1959b:8).

The encounter with the shadow meets with considerable resistance because of the discomfort it brings. In the first place, it shows us that we are not the masters that we thought we were; that we are "the

[26] One cannot help but recall the mirror of the wicked witch in this regard. According to my childhood memory, whenever she cried out, "Mirror, mirror, on the wall, who's the fairest one of all"? the mirror would answer, "*You* are, my queen".

object of factors" (gods, 'makers' of things), who have unconsciously controlled us for years (Jung 1940:72). In the second place, it opens our conscious minds up to the uncomfortable world of instincts, "that formidable dynamism lurking in the background" (Jung 1956b:40). Nevertheless, if we choose to persevere, and to assimilate the contents of our shadow-side into our consciousness, we find that it bestows upon us its healing wholeness. For, in assimilating the shadow, we embrace the possibility of being in full possession of our personality (Jung 1956b:35–36); and in so doing we empower ourselves to overcome in those moments when unconscious elements resurface and strike us at the point of our greatest sensitivity (ibid.).

Assimilating the Anima/Animus

If we continue gazing intently into the water, we soon observe many types of not-so-harmless living beings looming up from its depths. If we are male, we will see the nixie, for example. The nixie is "an early stage, still on the level of instinct, of a magical feminine being" that Jung has called the anima (Jung 1940:73). With her we enter "the realm of the gods or of metaphysics, for everything in which the anima appears takes on the quality of the numen—that is, becomes unconditional, dangerous, taboo, magical" (op. cit., 77). Having a moral range which runs the whole gamut from virgin to harlot (op. cit., 23), she represents the fear that those who encounter and assimilate her will succumb to all sorts of gross, hidden immorality and unspeakable evil. Consequently, the anima is "the most convincing foundation for the prejudice against dealing with the unconscious" (op. cit., 77). She is, however, by no means 'bad'. Being spirit and being life, she wishes life upon all who find her and, in that sense, "wishes [them both] good *and* bad" (ibid., Jung's italics).

Jung (op. cit., 79–80, my italics) writes as follows concerning the assimilation of the anima:

> If coming to terms with the shadow is the companion-piece to the individual's development, then that with the anima is the masterpiece. For the relation with the anima is again a test of courage and—more than that—a test by fire of all a man's spiritual and moral forces. We must never forget, in the case of the anima, that it is a question of psychic facts which have never before been in man's psychological possession; that hitherto were always to be found outside his consciousness in every possible form of projection [upon various female figures from childhood onwards].

For, when the anima is dissolved as an autonomous complex, she is no longer projected onto others, but she can deliver her power, her *mana*, to the person who has dealt with her (assimilated her contents) successfully. She then becomes an invaluable bridge to the unconscious (Jung 1953a:227, my italics):

> [With] the conquest of the anima as autonomous complex, and her transformation into a function of relationship between the conscious and the unconscious . . . it becomes possible to disengage the ego from all its entanglements from collectivity and the collective unconscious.

The anima then "forfeits the daemonic power of an autonomous complex" (ibid.), is depotentiated, and becomes a psychological function of an intuitive nature. She becomes 'the little bird' that tells you things, with dreams being her primary means of communication.

According to Jung (1940:23), "The figure of the animus . . . is equally paradoxical . . . running the whole gamut from utter banality to supreme mystery". It elicits the same fear of the unconscious. This view is also followed by staunch Jungians, who assume that assimilating the unconscious contents of the animus is as important to a woman as the assimilation of the anima's contents is to a man (cf. Von Franz, op. cit., 194 quoted above), and this despite the fact that that Jung did not delve into a woman's incorporation of the animus in any acceptable manner. As I have previously mentioned, Jung concentrated almost exclusively on the benefit that incorporating the anima held for males and assumed that incorporating the animus would be of equal benefit to women. This assumption will be dealt with in my evaluation of Jung's work, below.

Dangers Inherent to Assimilating Unconscious Contents

We have seen that, according to Jungians, there are obvious benefits to assimilating unconscious contents such as the shadow and the anima/animus. There are also certain inherent dangers that need to be addressed:

Positive/Negative Ego-inflation

When an archetype gathers enough libido to enter the sphere of consciousness and is subsequently assimilated into that consciousness, the ego-consciousness takes on its erstwhile *mana* or magical power. This, unfortunately, entails a subtle psychic danger, in that identification with the surfaced unconscious content may cause an ego-inflation (introjection) that can destroy everything that was gained by coming to terms with that content in the first place (Jung 1953a:228). This inflation may be positive or negative, since "exaggeration . . . loss of free will, delusion, and enthusiasm in good and evil alike" (Jung 1956b:80) are associated with inflation and indeed result from the archetypal effect on the conscious mind. One who has assimilated the risen shadow contents may, for example, suffer from 'positive inflation' and become extremely sure of herself/himself. Such a person believes herself/himself to have glimpsed, nay, appropriated, the truth and becomes an obnoxious loudmouthed type who tries to convince everyone of the rightness of her/his action and the validity of its results. "Come, join me! Become like me! Mine is the only way!" s/he would gush. By contrast, another person may become negatively inflated, regarding herself/himself as the very embodiment of all evil. This person may subsequently withdraw from social contact with others out of guilt, shame, or even fear of contaminating them too! The resultant alienation that introjection brings is both inevitable and understandable (ibid.).

Alternatively, a person who is consciously dealing with her/his psyche may also project her/his discoveries about herself/himself onto someone else; projection being the flip side of the introjection entailed in inflation. More specifically, such a person would project or transfer the rejected part of the activated archetype/content onto someone other than herself/himself, almost always her/his analyst. Projection onto the analyst or other 'helper'/authority figure (teacher, pastor, doctor, spouse) is known as transference (see Perry 1997: 141–155, especially 143). Jung (op. cit., 74–75) has identified three stages of transference:

1) The projection of superficial unconscious contents (doctor seen as possible lover)
2) The projection of personal memories (doctor appears as father/mother of the good or bad kind)
3) The projection of impersonal (collective) unconscious contents. Here one finds the occurrence of primordial images "belonging . . . to the domain of . . . the secrets of the mental history of mankind" (op. cit., 75). This is the most advanced stage of transference.

The person so endowed (e.g., projected upon) becomes the embodiment of the positive or negative characteristics of the surfaced archetype that have been projected upon her/him. The alienation that such a projection achieves—primarily for the projecting subject—is as understandable and inevitable as that which introjection causes.

Enantiodromia

Now, when an idea so seizes the conscious mind that it concentrates the greatest sum of psychic energy upon itself, "the ego [as a rule] is drawn into it so powerfully" that the resultant identification "imperils the psychic equilibrium" (op. cit., 82). It is then that the psychic rule of *enantiodromia* threatens (op. cit., 83); psychic energy is withdrawn and everything turns into its opposite. In this way, 'introjecting' and 'projecting' subjects alike soon turn into the very opposite of what they have become during the period of assimilation. Similarly, energy is withdrawn from the object of projection/transference, and s/he seems to become the opposite of what s/he was perceived to be. In this way, hero-doctors soon become villains in the eyes of their patients.

Should *enantiodromia* set in, the subject is forced to go through the trauma of assimilating other components of the same introjected/projected content all over again in order to achieve psychic balance—a process that may take a much longer time the second or even third and fourth time around. To give a fairly simple example, an alcoholic becomes attached to a nondrinking love-interest and loses the need to drink. Sooner or later, however, the initial excitement is lost as the anima/animus projection loses libido, and the person reverts to a worse form of alcoholism than before. It is then far more difficult for that person to overcome her/his alcoholism than before.

According to Jung (1956a:82), the only way to escape falling into the trap inherent to *enantiodromia* is to "be firmly rooted in [one's] ego-function" and to keep a level head through each stage of individuation. What he means by this is that a person must be able to differentiate that which s/he is from that which s/he is not; "he must fulfil his duty to life" and be a viable member of the community in every respect, or else "[a]ll that he neglects in this respect falls into the unconscious and reinforces its position" (ibid.) placing her/him within the dangerous reaches of being swallowed up by it. Thus,

> [t]he only person who escapes the grim law of *enantiodromia* is the man who knows how to separate himself from the unconscious, not by repressing it—for then it simply attacks him from the rear—but by putting it clearly before him as *that which he is not* (Jung, op. cit., his italics except for *enantiodromia*).

In other words, s/he "must learn to differentiate what is ego and what is non-ego, i.e., collective psyche. In this way . . . [her/his] energy . . . has come into its proper sphere" (ibid.) and s/he avoids the twin dangers of projection and introjection described above.

b. *Dreams: Their Interpretation and Role in the Individuation Process*

Given that individuation involves the integration of various unconscious contents/archetypes into one's consciousness, and that dreams/fantasies are expressions of the (personal and collective) unconscious that guides the individuation process according to the machinations of the Self, it follows that one can trace the stages of someone's individuation by studying her/his dreams/fantasies (henceforth, 'dreams'). It is for this reason that Jung encouraged his patients to keep a written record of their dreams and, moreover, to interact actively with them and amplify them as much as they could. Such a recording of dreams brought various recurring themes and motifs out into the light of consciousness, and so enabled both analyst and analysand to discern the leading of the unconscious and the stage of individuation that the analysand had attained (cf. Jacoby, op. cit., 63).

Before examining Jung's method of dream interpretation, I should briefly like to turn to some of his more important points on the nature, content, and function of dreams.

The Nature, Content, and Function of Dreams

In our dreams, events often occur in illogical sequence, known faces—even our own—often carry different characteristics to the ones we are consciously familiar with, and the most fantastic, baffling creatures, events, and symbols manifest their presence (cf. Jung 1940:4–6). In this, dreams are excellent examples of the 'illogical' or 'irrational' behaviour of the unconscious—and many of us tend to disregard them for that very reason. According to Jung, however, these baffling contents may reflect past, present, or future situations, aspirations, attitudes, and hopes, or they may stand in *compensation* to the state of the conscious mind, as the unconscious often does (cf. op. cit., 100; Jung 1956a:114). The people we dream about may reflect actual known persons or they may represent forgotten—'lost'—and/or repressed aspects of our own psyche that are crying out for conscious integration. They may also represent all four aspects of our personality—the ego, shadow, anima/animus, and Self (Atkinson, op. cit., 85) as well as other personated archetypes, such as the trickster and the wise old man/woman (the guide along the way). In other words, they may reflect the contents of both the personal and the collective unconscious.

To give a hypothetical example: I dream that my friend, Raymond, is trying to cut off my head. The dream figure 'Raymond' may refer either to Raymond himself or to an aspect of Raymond that I too possess. Seeing that Raymond is cutting off my head, the dream may be warning me that the actual man is about to/wishes to disempower me in some way, or that the Raymond element in me is doing so/wishes to do so. It may also be telling me that the actual Raymond or the Raymond elements in me are not as harmless as I thought. That is, if my conscious attitude towards Raymond was positive, and the unconscious knew better, it could compensate by showing me the danger in our relationship: he is trying to decapitate me! Depending on how I myself figure in the dream, I would have to work out which aspect of my life/psyche the real Raymond is having a negative effect upon, for example, and why. I would subsequently look within myself and explore which aspects within my own psyche the Raymond-in-me might want to eliminate and why; or whether, in fact, he wishes to atomise my entire being! Seeing that I, the dreaming subject, am female, and the dream figure is a dangerous, decapitating male, he would more than likely represent a very malevolent animus. I would then have to examine my relationship to the male soul-image within me and the power that it has over me. I may discover that I have to modify my conscious behaviour to outsmart the animus and prevent him from taking control of my life, wrecking my female-male relationships, and so forth. The interpretation of my dream would depend on the entire range of circumstances engaging me during that period of my life, and the place of that particular dream within the sequence of dreams at that time. Naturally, I would also have to examine or "amplify" the symbolism of the decapitator, the decapitating object, the location of the decapitation, and all other aspects of the dream; but that need not detain us now. Suffice it to say that these two aspects of the dream analysis—investigating my relationship to both the external and internal Raymond—refer to 'objective' and 'subjective' modes of dream analysis, elucidated below.

The 'Objective' and 'Subjective' Analysis of Dreams

Essentially, after recording and collecting the analysand's dreams (Jung 1940:43), Jung follows two successive modes of dream interpretation: objective and subjective analysis. During objective analysis, dream contents are interpreted according to their relation to the external world, the world outside the dreamer—the 'real' Raymond in my hypothetical dream. Subsequently, the contents of the dream are related to the dreamer herself/himself, so that the underlying memory complexes are regarded as the patient's own tendencies or components and are thereby reunited with her/him. Jung moves to this subjective, synthetic mode of analysis once the reductive-objective analysis yields nothing new and the dream symbols begin to represent the images of the collective unconscious. He employs both the patient's own associations with and interpretations of the dream's contents as well as "numerous parallels from the psychology of primitive and historical symbolism" to amplify certain images occurring in the patient's dreams in order to yield the richest possible meanings (cf. Jung 1956a:91, 93–95). The reason for doing so rests on the collective base of all symbols. As Jacoby (op. cit., 64) says:

> The parallels taken from myths, fairy tales, and religious history are a kind of philogenetic association; they stem from a collective memory on which, in the final analysis, our entire culture is based.

Together, these two forms of dream analysis assist the patient to integrate the 'lost' or repressed contents that the dream material represents. The conscious integration of such unconscious contents leads, in turn, to the extension of consciousness and to the gradual diminishing of "the dominant influence of the unconscious" (Jung 1953a:219)—the dissolution of autonomous complexes. The resultant personality change—a change in "the general attitude" (ibid.)—helps the analysand to be in full possession of her/his own personality (Jung 1956a:36) *and* to achieve greater integration with society as a whole (Jung 1953a:173–174). This "important change" is the "transcendent function" (op. cit., 219) to which I have referred above (cf. also Hall 1989:18, 26, 27, 71–79).

Here we have touched upon both the vehicle and the goal of the individuation process. For, dreams are the *via regia* to the unconscious (Jung 1956b:34); and the dissolution of autonomous complexes engenders the transformation which is the goal of both psychological analysis and the individuation process (cf. Jung 1953a:212).

c. *The Mythical, Gnostic-Alchemical Precursors of the Individuation Process*

The preceding subsections have often referred to the similarity of dreams and myths. We have seen, for example, that Jung and his followers attribute both dream symbols and those found in myths to the symbol-making capacity of the collective psyche. We have further observed that Monick (op. cit., 34) has described the individuation process as a "deeply personal, essentially mythic" journey, and this is not in vain. As Jung, Drew, Henderson, and others have shown, myths reveal psychic facts; they are ancient man's expression of direct symbolic experience (Drew, op. cit., 11, 12), stories that manifest the "fundamental truth[s] of the human condition" (Hinz and Teunissen 1992:140) and depict in fictive form the ego/hero's struggle to free herself/himself from the grasp of the unconscious/monster and become the person s/he potentially is (cf. e.g., Jung, op. cit., 169–170, 1940:54–56, and Henderson 1964:109, 120, 126). I should here like to outline briefly Jung's thinking regarding the significance of the hero's quest—or "whale-dragon myths" as Frobenius called them (Jacobi 1959:179)—and Gnostic-alchemical *quaternios* for the individuation process, particularly as he often utilises these in the amplification of dreams and the interpretation of other unconscious symbols.

The Hero's Quest

Jung regarded the hero's quest as the mythopoeic counterpart of the individuation process. It became "the informing principle that [he], with some help from Frobenius, perceived in myth, folklore, and literature" (Frye, op. cit., 26; cf. also Jung 1956b:109–110).

The heroic quests of the world share the same essential structural elements despite "innumerable variations" in content (Frye, op. cit.). Essentially, a lack or some kind of imbalance sets the hero on his[27] quest to a foreign country or up a difficult mountain to find assistance or gain power to solve the initial problem. The hero sets off on his quest, and arrives at his point of destination after passing many tests and/or overcoming numerous monsters. He is often accompanied by a shadowy companion who seems to be his double, and

[27] I deliberately refer to the male hero. Female quests are different; see my discussion of Pratt's research in my evaluation of Jung's theories, below.

is offered advice by various deities and/or other magical creatures/people with magical powers (e.g., a magician, patron deity, old woman, or faithful animal). His troubles are not over when he arrives at his destination, as he usually has to liberate a maiden and/or untold treasure from a dragon or other monster. He does so, with a little help from his magical friends, and returns to a hero's welcome in the maiden's land and/or his own. He marries the maiden—usually as a reward for his bravery—and becomes a powerful leader who transforms his world and/or his vision of it (cf. op. cit., 26–27 and Henderson, op. cit., 110). Alternatively, the hero is sometimes swallowed by the dragon he battles, but returns after slaying it from within, with the rest following.

Psychologically speaking, the movement from the ordinary to the extraordinary or supernatural world (the foreign country/the monster's belly) signifies a movement from the familiar world of consciousness to the unfamiliar terrain of the unconscious. According to Jung, the unconscious is also signified by the water elements in the story (the sea in which the monster lives/the lake by which the dragon sleeps). The monsters or giants that the hero battles along the way are representative of his inner shadow (the shadow-elements of his life), while the guides or helpers (magical or otherwise) symbolise the Self, "the whole psyche, the larger and more comprehensive identity that supplies the personal strength that the personal ego lacks" (op. cit., 112). The defeat of the dragon symbolises the freeing of psychic energy attached to the mother, while the resultant liberation of the maiden symbolises the requirement "to liberate the anima as that inner component of the psyche that is necessary for any true creative achievement" (op. cit., 126). Naturally, the hero's wedding to the maiden then depicts the integration of the anima. The treasure gained and the transformation that follows indicate the value of overcoming the (collective) unconscious/the devouring mother, and the benefits of the psyche's transcendent function.

In some myths, the hero is unsuccessful in his battle against the dragon. This symbolises identification with the collective unconscious, the maternal consciousness, and a failed cycle of individuation.

The Night Sea Journey

The night sea journey is an elaboration of the swallowing/devouring motif illustrated above. This "whale-dragon myth" follows the basic outline of the Old Testament *Jonah* narrative:

A hero is devoured by a water monster in the West. The animal travels with him to the East (sea journey), usually in the night time. While in the monster's belly, the hero lights a fire and, feeling hungry, cuts himself a piece of the heart. The endangered monster soon glides to land and the hero escapes by cutting the animal open from within and slipping out. Sometimes his hair has fallen out because the heat was so intense in the monster's belly. Often, the hero simultaneously frees all those previously swallowed by the monster (Jacobi op. cit., 180–181).

The night sea journey depicts both the perils of being swallowed by the unconscious (the maternal sea monster) and also the necessity thereof. As in the hero's quest, it represents the transformation that victory over the unconscious brings: the hero cuts open the monster's belly and stands again on dry land—achieves greater consciousness. The fact that he liberates others, whom the monster had also swallowed, indicates his transformative effect on society: those who had previously given in to the unconscious and had been devoured by it, i.e., those who did not successfully complete a particular cycle of the individuation process, are brought to consciousness by his brave encounter with the collective unconscious.

Jung, Alchemical Symbolism, and Gnostic Quaternios

Jung has invested a vast amount of energy into researching the Gnostic and alchemical teachings (see Jung 1953b and 1959b) that he regards as precursors to the individuation process. Here I should like to focus upon his development of the Naasene (Gnostic) 'Moses' and 'Paradise' *Quaternios* (Jung 1959b:184–221) into a system of four connected *quaternios* depicting the fall of the *Anthropos* or Original Man into *physis* and his subsequent (consequent?) rise to spirituality.

The Moses, *Anthropos*, and Shadow *Quaternios*

On a mathematical level, the *quaternio* is "a system of co-ordinates" that Gnostics used for dividing up and arranging a "chaotic multiplicity" of beliefs and feelings (op. cit., 242). It is a three-dimensional diamond-shaped configuration consisting of two contrasting pairs of opposites situated around the middle horizontal axis, which forms a square. For Jung, the *quaternio* represents the conjunction of the (pairs of) opposites (op. cit., 194) and depicts "the fourfold basis of wholeness" (op. cit., 159). The Naasenes often used *quaternios* to depict complex thoughts and feelings. For example, they believed that all things derived from a triad that consisted, firstly, of 'the blessed nature' of the Higher Adam/*Anthropos*; secondly, of the mortal nature of the lower man/the Lower Adam; and thirdly, of 'the kingless race begotten from above', to which Miriam, Moses' sister (who also acts as his anima and mother; op. cit., 210), Jethro, Moses' father-in-law (a physical and spiritual father, the latter by virtue of his priesthood), Zipporah, and Moses himself belong (op. cit., 209).

By virtue of the triadic scheme, the four characters mentioned above are related to both the Higher and the Lower Adam. The latter corresponds to the ordinary or somatic man, while the former corresponds to that originally perfect, hermaphroditic One, the *Anthropos* or *Protanthropos*. Moses (as culture hero/lawgiver) and Zipporah (as the Higher Mother—daughter of a king and priest) relate to Jethro (the spiritual man—'the wise old man') and Miriam (the prophetess and mother-anima) even as the ordinary man and woman relate to Moses (the carnal man) and Zipporah (the foreign woman).

Furthermore, when reviewing the lives of the four biblical characters in the *quaternio*, we see that they have a 'higher' and a 'lower' or 'darker' side which correspond to the *Anthropos* and Lower Adam respectively. This means that the four persons in the *quaternio* leave room for "the extension of the ordinary man's psychic structure downwards, towards the sub-human, the dark and evil side represented by the shadow" (op. cit., 228)—something not fully developed in this type of Gnostic thinking. In terms of the Lower Adam, then, Jethro is a heathen High Priest and a stranger to the tribes of Yahweh; Miriam becomes leprous (negative) for speaking out against Moses; and Moses, the carnal man (*vs.* the culture hero/lawgiver), represents his own shadow by marrying an Ethiopian woman (cf. Jung op. cit., 210 and 227–229). This latter senarius, that Jung himself added in order to express mankind's more chthonic—subordinate—psyche (cf. op. cit., 255–257) is the so-called Shadow *Quaternio*. It reaches its nadir not in the Lower Adam, "but in his dark, theriomorphic prefiguration—the serpent who was created before man, or the Gnostic *Naas*" (op. cit., 230, Jung's italics). The two sides of the characters described above yield the following *quaternios*, Diagrams 1 and 2:[28]

[28] Diagrams 1 and 2 are facsimiles of those by Jung (1959b:231).

Diagram 1. The *Anthropos Quaternio*.

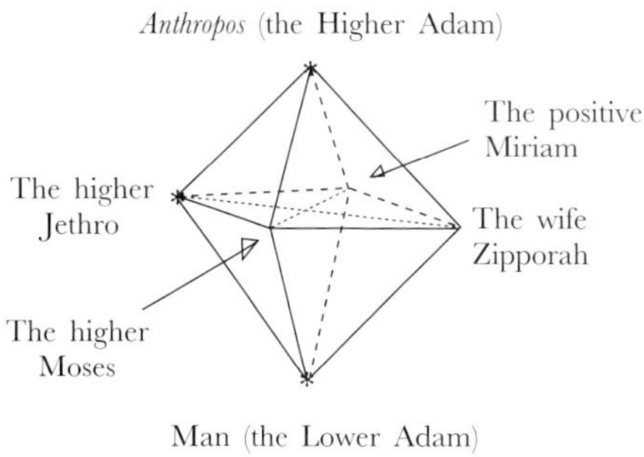

Diagram 2. The Shadow *Quaternio*.

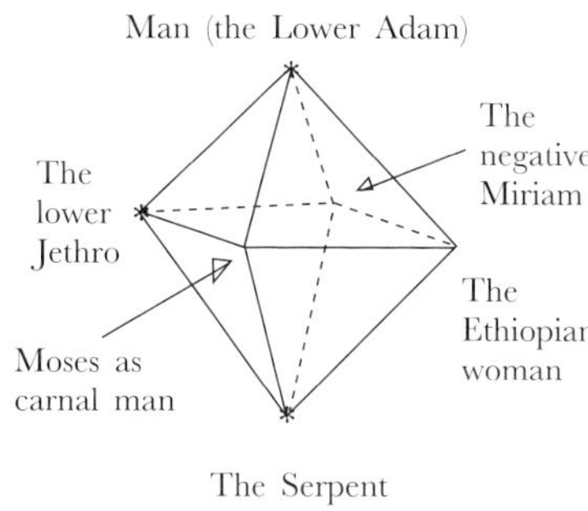

The *Anthropos*, or higher man, corresponds to the lower man as the latter corresponds to the serpent, making the serpent either the forerunner of man, or "a distant copy"—twice removed—of the *Anthropos*. According to Jung (op. cit., 230, 232–233), this is corroborated by the fact that the snake is an allegory of both the devil and Christ; being simultaneously symbolic of the lower (animal), darker side of man and of wisdom and spirituality. Since the shadow remains hidden for most people, the snake also corresponds to that which is totally unconscious and incapable of consciousness in man (cf. op. cit., 232–234).

The Paradise and *Lapis Quaternios*

In alchemy, the snake is symbolic of *Mercurius non vulgi* (bracketed with Hermes, the god of revelation). The *Serpens Mercurii* is "a chthonic spirit who dwells in matter, more especially in the bit of original chaos hidden in creation, the *Massa confusa* or *globossa*" (op. cit., 234, Jung's italics). It reminded the Naasenes of the tempter in the Garden of Eden. For them, the Garden of Eden (Paradise) with its four rivers, the Pison, Gihon, Hiddekel, and Euphrates, formed yet another *quaternio* (see diagram 3 below), parallel with and of a similar meaning to the Moses *Quaternio*.

The snake's connection with the tree, a symbol of "the development and phases of the transformation process", makes it a symbol of transformation both in Genesis and in Gnostic-alchemical texts (op. cit., 235). Furthermore, through its relation to Paradise, tree and earth, the snake represents an "evolutionary regression" from the animal kingdom to plants and inorganic nature, "epitomized in alchemy by the secret of matter, the *lapis*" (ibid., Jung's italics), which was also the name of the arcane matter or *prima materia*.

The *lapis*, the nadir of the Paradise *Quaternio*, was thought of as a living being and the *filius macrocosmi*. As such, it is not only an allegory, but also a direct parallel of Christ and the Higher Adam, making it a further counterpart of the *Anthropos*. It was also thought of as a unity which consists of the four elements (water, earth, wind, and fire) or which has to be made up from them in the alchemical process. In their turn, the four elements "represent an unfolding of the unknowable inchoate state, or chaos" (op. cit., 237). This is the *prima materia*, the primary substance or *arcanum*, held to be co-eternal with God. It is round (*massa globossa, rotundum*), like the world and the *anima mundi*, the world-soul; "it is in fact the world-soul and the world-substance in one" (ibid.). It is "the stone that has a spirit", described as primal water, primal fire, or as pneuma, primal earth or "the little body of our wisdom" (op. cit., 238). Together, these considerations yield the following *quaternios*, diagrams 3 and 4:[29]

Diagram 3. The Paradise *Quaternio*.

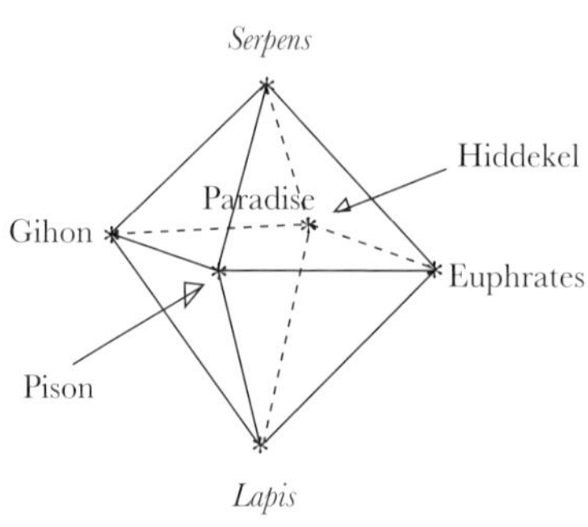

Diagram 4. The *Lapis Quaternio*.

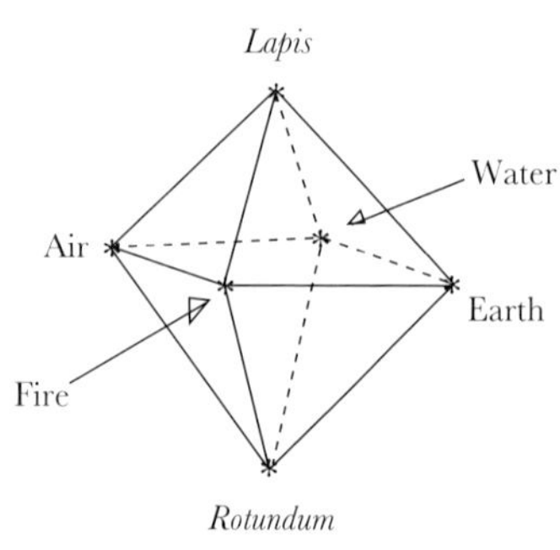

According to alchemical teachings, the four elements making up the *lapis* merely co-exist in chaotic form—they are not united. They are even mutually hostile and will not unite of their own accord, but have to be combined through the alchemical procedure. This image

[29] Diagrams 3 and 4 are facsimiles of Jung's Paradise and *Lapis quaternios* (op. cit., 236, 238).

serves to illustrate "the splitting up or unfolding of the original unity into the multiplicity of the visible world" (op. cit., 237). This too is the case of the Original Man, that hermaphroditic One from whom the two sexes, man and woman, came. According to the old view, the form of the Original Man is round as is the soul (op. cit., 239), which establishes the connection between the Original Man and the *rotundum* (op. cit., 238–242).

Quaternities and the Individuation Process

It is clear from the foregoing that we are constantly dealing with the transformation of one substance: the *Anthropos*, who originates from the arcanum, falls into *physis*, losing its original androgyny and encountering the tensions of the ordinary man who has her/his darker psyche founded in the serpent. The serpent, however, also foreshadows the possibility of a transformation towards light and wisdom, as well as a healing of the original rift (fall from grace = fall into *physis*) so that man may once again rise to her/his transcendent self (see the direction of the arrows in diagram 6, below), though now in a more conscious form (the snake introduces the original Edenic couple to consciousness). This, in short, is nothing but a mystical analogy (parallel) to the psychic process of individuation: loosening the bonds of unconsciousness, i.e., becoming more conscious and becoming whole. Jung has chosen to illustrate the sequence of this process in terms of two diagrams, one vertical and one uroboric, and one diagrammatic equation (see diagrams 5–7, below).[30] The diagrams clearly demonstrate the tensions and polarities encountered in the individuation process, while the equation focuses more upon the way in which the transformation occurs.

The vertical arrangement (diagram 5) highlights the point of greatest polarity between opposites, i.e., the double significance of the serpent which occupies the centre of the system; while the uroboric arrangement (diagram 6) shows that there are two major tensions: the greater one between the *Anthropos-rotundum* and the serpent, and the lesser one between ordinary man and the *lapis* (as expressed by the distance of the points in question from one another). Diagram 6 also shows that the lowest point of descent is the serpent, and that the *lapis*, though decidedly of a material nature, is also a spiritual

[30] Diagrams 7, 8, and 9 are facsimiles of those by Jung (op. cit., 247, 248, and 259, respectively).

Diagram 5. The Vertical Arrangement of Jung's *Quaternios*.

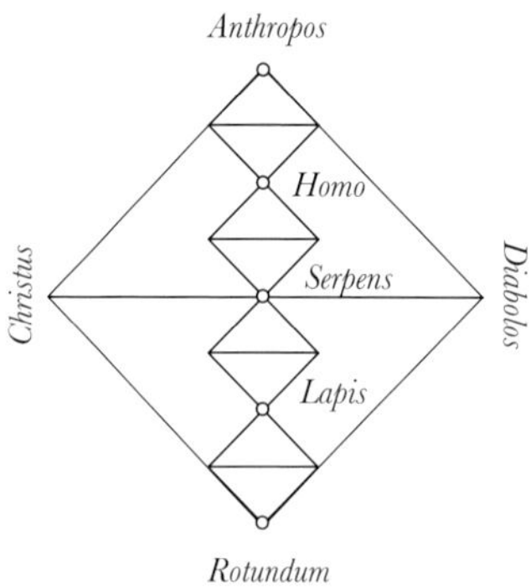

Diagram 6. The *Uroboric* Arrangement of Jung's *Quaternios*.

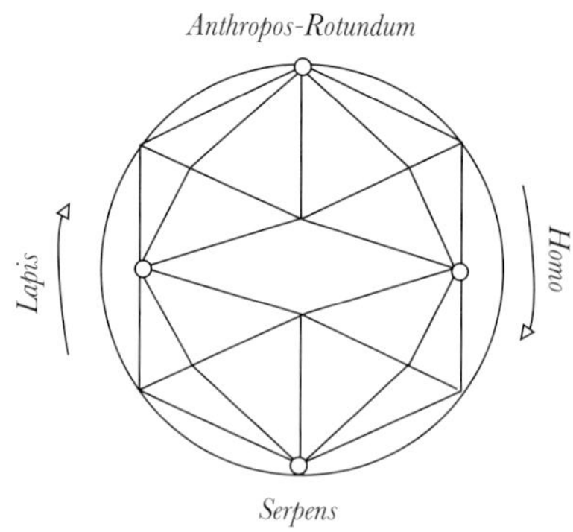

symbol (it is situated on the ascending path). The *rotundum* connotes a transcendent entity (op. cit., 249) and the loftiest plane attainable.

Diagrams 5 and 6 teach us that the snake, the symbol of transformation, is integral to the individuation process, for without it there cannot be a rise to a higher or even transcendent plane. When we recall that the snake is also a symbol of that which is unconscious in mankind, the shadow, then we see that there can be no individuation without encountering the serpent, i.e., without experiencing the shadow and raising it to consciousness. This, however, requires us to make the dreaded descent into the unconscious, i.e., to sacrifice the 'flesh' or die to it, to use a Christian idiom (see op. cit., 173–179).

Jung rightly sees fit to express the four *quaternios* involved in the form of a diagrammatic equation that deals with the continual transformation process described above (op. cit., 259):

Diagram 7. Jung's *Quaternio* Equation.

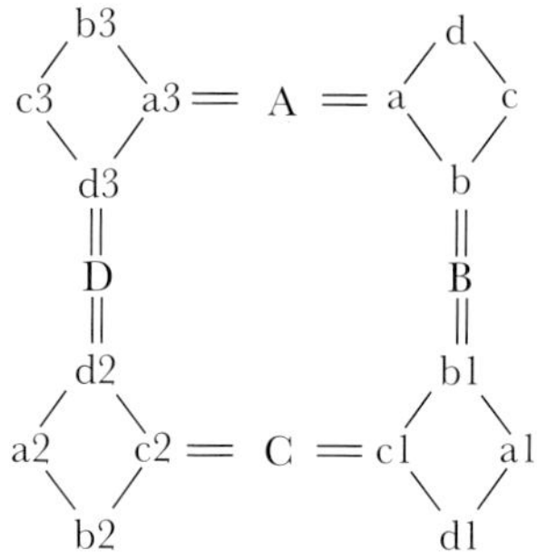

In Jung's equation, A stands for the initial state (the *Anthropos*) and for the end state, while B, C, and D stand for successive intermediate states. The small letters, a, b, c, and d, denote the formations that split off from each state. Since we are dealing with the transformation of one and the same substance, it, and its respective states of transformation, will always produce its like. Thus, A will always produce a, etc. (Jung, op. cit., 258). From a, the process advances by contingence to b, which then produces B. B produces b1 which becomes c1 and in turn produces C. C produces c2 which becomes d2 and produces D. D produces d3 which becomes a3, once again producing A, which represents both the beginning and the end of the transformation process. Jung describes the process of transforming D into a3 as "a kind of *enantiodromia*" (my italics) by virtue of the fact that D is at that point of contingency furthest removed from A (ibid.). The formula is thus again being depicted 'uroborically', i.e., as moving clockwise from left to right and towards greater consciousness or conscious differentiation (ibid.). According to Jung (ibid.), the quaternity represents "a psychic fact" which can be brought into relationship with the four orienting functions of consciousness: thinking, feeling, intuition, and sensation. Usually only one of these functions is highly differentiated. It is Jung's thesis that at least two of the other functions become more differentiated as a person matures (moves into higher consciousness) and advances in the individuation process. The fourfold split indicates that the psychic processes "have been subjected to discrimination by the four orienting functions of consciousness. Only the production of these four aspects makes a total description possible" (op. cit., 259).

The formula reproduces exactly all the essential features of the symbolic individuation process and hints at the higher plane that is reached through transformation and integration. As is evident, the process consists of totality unfolding into four parts four times, which means that it becomes conscious (ibid.). In other words, the *Anthropos* (A) descends to *physis* (C—the serpent) via the shadow (B) and is transformed through the ordering process symbolised by the *lapis* (D) to rise again to its original state (A), which has meanwhile been transformed from an unconscious state to a conscious one (op. cit., 259–260).

The formula represents a symbol of that dynamic process which is the self, while the four transformations represent "a process of restoration or rejuvenation taking place . . . inside the self" (op. cit., 259). And, as Jung seems to suggest, this constant rejuvenation may well be the secret of existence, which points again to the absolute necessity of not stunting the individuation process by resisting these transformations in whatever guise they may be presented to us.

C. *An Evaluation*

In this section, I should like to examine Jung's theories more closely, and to evaluate them more critically. To this end, I discuss what I consider as 'negative' and 'positive', with the "religious function" being placed between them as it is neither positive nor negative.

a. *'Negative' Criticism*

Logic and Unconscious Argument

Offering criticism on Jungian thought is very difficult indeed, not only because of its esoteric, subjective nature, but also because of the way that Jung writes. His writing truly reflects the chaotic mode of unconscious communication—and this is not at all a derogatory judgement! As John Freeman (1964:13–14) says in his 'Introduction' to *Man and His Symbols*, Jung and his colleagues seem to eschew the kind of "algebraic" method of argument that proceeds "from assumed premises to incontestably deduced conclusions". He continues:

> It is not that they ignore logic, but they appear all the time to be arguing to the unconscious as well as to the conscious. Their dialectical method is itself symbolic and often devious. They convince not by means of the narrowly focused spotlight of the syllogism, but by skirting, by repetition, by presenting a recurring view of the same subject seen each time from a slightly different angle—until suddenly the reader who has never been aware of a single, conclusive moment of proof finds that he has unknowingly embraced and taken into himself some wider truth.

Indeed, so persuasive is the sheer magnetic force of his argument, that I have often found myself simply carried along in near hypnotic fashion. In many cases it was only upon consciously distancing myself from this or that essay that I found myself able to offer logical criticism to his work; so esoteric and entrancing is it. I asked, "What is the logic in it"? and "Why *should* there be any logic in it"? simultaneously. I found that Jung's mode of argumentation challenged the fundamental assumption of academic writing—the strict logic of conscious thinking—and opened up the joyful, though often frustrating, possibility of writing 'unconsciously' within the academic sphere too. I use the word 'too' because my experience of God often defies conscious categories—because it transcends them—and just as often receives the same kind of criticism that Jungian thought does. Undoubtedly, it is this integration of the unconscious with academia that has elicited much of the criticism levelled at Jung's work—and at him personally. As Samuels (op. cit., 5) wisely notes, "for those who demand what they consider to be the highest scientific standards, Jungian psychology will always be wanting . . ."

The Existence and the Nature of Archetypes and the Unconscious Psyche

The most problematic aspect of Jungian thought, to my mind, concerns the archetypes. Although I am not going to focus specifically upon developments in Jungian 'schools' (the Classical, Archetypal, and Developmental Schools)[31] with regard to these and other aspects for practical reasons, I will naturally incorporate material from the propounders of these schools into my evaluation.

According to Jung:

i) The existence of archetypes is proved by the remarkably similar patterns of recurring symbols that are found in the dreams, etc. of peoples from widely divergent times and cultures (cf. Samuels, op. cit., 24).
ii) These archetypes reflect universal human forms of experience and behaviour (what I have called 'memories') that are expressed as "*images* and situations that have a tremendous impact on the individual" (op. cit., 29, my italics).
iii) They stem from and form the contents of the collective unconscious.
iv) They are unchanging.
v) They are transcendent dominants that exert their power over unsuspecting human objects; they thus act as subjects upon an individual who experiences the full force of both their imaginal and emotional potency in awe.
vi) The collective unconscious is made up of the collective ancestral memories of mankind (including the animal phase).

[31] These groups reflect Samuels's (op. cit., 15–19) classification of post-Jungian Jungian analysts. For a more thorough examination of these three schools see Hart (1997:89–100), Adams (1997:101–118), and Solomon (1997:119–140), respectively.

To my mind, there is a certain discrepancy between the nature of the archetypes expressed in points i), ii), iv), and v) and their location in the unconscious psyche of mankind, as expressed in points iii) and vi). Points ii) and vi) lead to the inevitable conclusion that the archetypes are essentially inherited (though not innate) human memories—forms of experience and behaviour that we have inherited[32] from all the way back to our (supposed) animal ancestors. In other words, it would be fair to postulate that there were no archetypes at some point in time, and that forms of experience and behaviour only developed into recurrent, established patterns ('archetypes') along with human development as humans, learned, practised, and transmitted them to succeeding, evolving generations over the ages. Archetypes are what they are—if they are at all—*because of us*, and this, for me, holds the potential that they can and will change or develop as long as humankind continues to do so (see, e.g., Gelpi, op. cit., 113). Whence their transcendence and unchanging nature?

Even if one were to hold that archetypes reflect and incorporate future human developments (memories) within themselves, this still does not render them either unchanging or transcendent, for they still consist of and are dependent upon future human development (memories). The only way to conceive of the archetypes as transcendent would be to regard them as part of a God-given individuation process, as part of a plan for human development which *God* established in the genes of humankind—however that humankind began. Even then, they cannot be regarded as unchanging, for it is a well-known fact that when one entity acts upon another, both subject and object undergo transformation—albeit to lesser or greater extent.

In terms of the existence and nature of the archetypes, I prefer the view of Samuels's so-called Archetypal School above that of the Classical Jungian School that tries to preserve Jung's ideas without critical emendation. According to James Hillman (in Adams, op. cit., 103), the founder of the Archetypal School,[33] the distinction between

[32] "Archetypes are a *collective inheritance of general, abstract forms* that structure the personal acquisition of particular, concrete contents" (Adams, op. cit., 102, my italics).

[33] James Hillman and a number of other Jungians founded the Archetypal School in Zurich in the late 1960s and early 1970s. This 'school' arose, inter alia, "in reac-

'archetype' and 'archetypal image' is untenable (so too Goldenberg 1977:63–64). All that human beings ever encounter physically are images or phenomena; there are no archetypes as such, only images that may be archetypal (Adams, op. cit.). In other words, there is no archetype category; the archetypal is "*a perspectival operation that an individual may perform on any image*" (ibid., my italics). While I regard Hillman's physical focus as biased and restrictive, I tend to agree that the "archetypal" is "archetypal" only by virtue of the perceiving subject. As Hillman says, all that is required is 'capitalisation'. Capitalising "the Sweat-Drenched Warrior" renders that image "archetypal" from *my* perspective. The archetypal value accorded the capitalised image makes it wholly different from its noncapitalised counterpart, "the sweat-drenched warrior" (cf. op. cit., 102–103). In this I agree, but I would like to propose a modification to Hillman's assertion that there is no archetype 'category'. I propose that there are various, manifold, archetype 'categories' in existence, and that each of these is highly individualised in the sense that it is related to a specific human being or cultural-ethnic group alone. An individual's/particular group's archetype 'category' would then consist of the images, behaviours, and experiences (memories) that that specific individual/group has invested with archetypal (typical, valuable) qualities. It follows then that the contents of this category would vary and evolve along with that particular individual's/group's development. Some memories may fall in and out of archetypal status at various times, while others may undergo changes according to changing societal climates, and so forth.

In contrast to Jung, I regard archetypes as dynamic, ever-changing, personal valuations that individual human beings/groups accord to various 'memories' at various times. I do, however, agree that they may and do affect the behaviour, emotions, and psyche of human beings, that they may be projected or repressed with detrimental consequences, and that they must be assimilated into a person's/group's conscious attitude so that that person/group may develop into her/his full potential. Furthermore, I believe that while the weight of a particular archetype (or, rather, archetypal image) may give it a 'transcendent' power in the individual's life at a given

tion against what they regarded as unnecessarily metaphysical assumptions in Jung" (Adams, op. cit., 103).

moment, I do not regard the archetypes as transcendent in the 'objective' and 'unchanging' sense that Jung does. I believe that they may both influence and be influenced by the human being/s in whose (personal/collective) psyche they 'exist'.

Lastly, I too believe that there is both a conscious and an unconscious aspect to the human psyche; that the latter is more powerful than we would like to acknowledge, and that it may indeed be 'divided' into a personal and a collective unconscious. However, I would prefer to view the collective psyche as a series of interconnected *Zeitgeisten*, each of which is never fully replaced, but rather incorporated into its historical successors.

While Jung's archetype theory may be applauded for accentuating the common bond that connects all human beings, it is not free of the manifest difficulties that I have outlined above. In the next subsection I wish to highlight the problem areas within Jung's theory concerning the anima/animus. These are of particular interest to me as a woman in that they present certain stereotypical views of women (and men) that have become reified over the years.

The Anima/Animus and Gender Stereotyping

In contrast to his anti-Semitic and racist views (cf. Friedman 1998:385–401 and the response to his article by Segal 1999:461–467), Jung's blatant sexism has often gone unnoticed (or, perhaps has been forgiven) because of his emphasis on 'the feminine' (so too Goldenberg, op. cit., 57–58; cf. also Pratt 1992a:155). According to Jung, a man can only develop to his full potential if he willingly integrates the female contrasexual image, the anima, into his consciousness. Jung's 'disciples' have often assumed that this applies equally to a woman integrating her contrasexual image, the animus (see the quotations by Von Franz noted previously). However, a closer examination of Jung's statements regarding woman, her psyche, and her animus reveal that this is not so. In fact, Jung never developed the animus theory to the same extent as the anima theory.

According to Goldenberg (op. cit., 59–60), the reason for this discrepancy lies in the fact that Jung merely *assumed* that the soul-image in women was male because the one in men was female, rendering "further development [of the animus theory] . . . impossible because he was forcing a mirror image [to the anima] where there was none". Goldenberg's assertion may well be correct in certain respects. I, personally, find nothing objectionable in the theory of contrasexual soul images. I suggest that the underdevelopment of Jung's animus theory rests upon his own ambivalence towards women and his realisation that the inferiority that he ascribed to the male soul-image reflects negatively on the conscious aspects of the male gender too. In short, I suggest that Jung 'abandoned ship', as it were, on account of his own sexism, and his feelings regarding the superiority of the masculine which clashed with what he subsequently postulated about the activity of the animus. I should, however, like to make the following qualification to Goldenberg's views: there are male and female contrasexual images, but the animus does not play the same role in women's individuation as the anima does in men. My suggestion is based partly on Pratt's research, outlined below, and partly on my own personal observations.

In her essay entitled *Spinning among Fields: Jung, Frye, Levi-Strauss, and Feminist Archetypal Theory*, Pratt (op. cit., 153–156) outlines what I would regard as one of the most important psychological discoveries concerning women. She (op. cit., 160) reports that, when she began exploring women's individuation in literature, she expected to find a dual god or powerful male figure where Jung had found the dual mother—that frighteningly disarming conflation of shadow and anima in the collective unconscious, the dragon of the hero's quest (cf. op. cit., 159). To her surprise, Pratt found that, whereas male figures achieve rebirth by encountering the dual mother, "the woman hero often encounters a 'horrible husband' who stops her dead in her tracks . . . dragging her into masochistic compliance with social standards" (op. cit., 161).[34] In confronting him, "the female character falls into madness, determines to commit suicide, or lapses into a zombielike state that precludes further development" (ibid.). Pratt (op. cit., 160–161) further observes that similar results occur when women encounter "erotic, godlike figures" as they are "often natural, antisocial, and above all antimarital". This suggests to her, and

[34] According to Dawson (op. cit., 265), Pamela, the heroine of Richardson's novel by the same name (published 1740), played a great role in propagating a depiction of the heroine as a woman with a horrible husband. She served as a model (prototype?) "for innumerable later images of women whose strength of character can be boiled down to their ability to bear with an intolerable husband and make themselves useful by their good deeds. Such women became stock types of Victorian fiction, especially in novels by women", and "provided a pattern of behavior that was to be enormously detrimental to the personal fulfilment of several generations of women". For Dawson's "Jungian" analysis of Richardson's book see chapter 4.

with quite some justification, I believe, that these male figures represent not the animus but the shadow, which for women is "socially conformist [*vs.* the antisocial aspects of the male shadow], incorporating women's self-loathing for their deviations from social norms, specifically the norms of femininity" (op. cit., 161). That is why they often punish themselves for "any erotic feelings that spring from authentic, self-ish, desire", devalue their sexuality, and loathe their own bodies (ibid.).

In conjunction with the above, Pratt (op. cit., 163) also discovered that women's successful quests were facilitated by "a powerful integrative mother-figure". These mother figures are encountered at the nadir of women's quests, even as the dual mother is encountered at the nadir of men's quests; they assist women to overcome their 'horrible husband' shadows and achieve "a deeper and more holistic sense of the feminine" (op. cit., 162). Typically, however, this integration estranges a woman from society, as opposed to the male journey that leads the quester back into society where he is welcomed as a hero. In this case, the women's journey of rebirth is structured after the archetypal pattern of the Demeter-Kore myth, and as we know, Demeter was never admitted to Olympus even though she saved her daughter from the jaws of Hades (op. cit., 159).

We see, then, that while man's individuation is depicted as a struggle against the 'other' (an *agon* of Herculean proportions, we are told) by which he achieves 'hero status' (see ibid. and op. cit., 163), woman's successful individuation is dependant upon fusion with a "being similar to herself, which empowers even as it exiles her from the social community" (op. cit., 163). This, to my mind, offers the following correctives to Goldenberg's thesis:

i) There *is* a male contrasexual image in women. This image may, for all intents and purposes, be called the 'animus'.
ii) This 'animus' figure in women corresponds to the shadow figure in men. It follows, then, that the animus function in women does not equal the anima function in men. In men the anima is integrative, whereas in women the animus is disintegrative in terms of both the personality and society at large.
iii) Because women achieve individuation, albeit accompanied by societal alienation, through fusion with a female goddess-like being, *vs.* men's *agon* with the dual mother, women and men's psyches *are* different. Jung recognised this in his later career (cf. Jung

1953a:207): he believed that the Demeter-Kore narrative is so specifically feminine that it has no import for the male personality and that it, along with other feminine archetypes, is "probably only accessible to and definitive of women" (Pratt op. cit., 155, cf. also 162). This is a point of celebration, not condemnation, for the following reason.

iv) In individuation, it is one's embrace of the feminine that counts. Whether one is male or female, the female aspect must be accepted and ultimately embraced for successful individuation—even if it first takes on the guise of 'the enemy' in men's individuation quests.

In short, I do not believe that the concept of contrasexual psychological images is inherently sexist. Rather, I believe that Jung's sexism lies in the *associations* he makes with these images. In *Aion*, for example, Jung identifies anima and animus with Eros and Logos, respectively, claiming that:

> Woman is compensated by a masculine element and *therefore her unconscious has, so to speak, a masculine imprint.* This results in a considerable difference between men and women, and accordingly, I have called the male projection-making factor in women the animus, *which means mind or spirit.* The animus corresponds to the paternal Logos just as the anima corresponds to the maternal Eros . . . I use Eros and Logos as conceptual aids to describe *the fact that woman's consciousness is characterized more by the connective quality of Eros than by the discrimination and cognition associated with Logos.* In men, Eros, the function of relationship is usually less developed than Logos. In women, on the other hand, *Eros is an expression of their true nature, while their Logos is often a regrettable accident.* It gives rise to misunderstandings and annoying interpretations in the family circle and among friends. This is because it consists of *opinions* instead of reflections, and by opinions I mean *a priori* assumptions that lay claim to absolute truth (Jung 1959a:14–15, my italics in the first six instances).

This is a highly sexist and patriarchal image of woman, no matter how it is veiled in abstract, philosophical nomenclature: men are associated with Logos, women with Eros (similarly, Pratt, op. cit., 155). With men, Eros is present but underdeveloped, but with women Logos is "a regrettable accident"! If Eros and Logos are necessary functions of human existence, as Jung seems to suggest, then women are only half human at best. The assumed inferiority of women even extends to their animus and their ability to create (and understand?) traditional symbols. Women are said to have a contrasexual soul-image that is 'masculine' but nevertheless "irritating" because it spews out "opinions" and not logical "reflections" (cf. also Jung 1953a:207). The animus is thus an inferior Logos function. Furthermore, the female is limited in her symbol-making ability, a rather strange notion given that the animus is part of the symbol-making collective unconscious psyche:

> . . . traditional symbolism is chiefly a product of the masculine psyche and is, therefore not a suitable object of imitation for woman. *Exempla sunt otiosa* (Jung 1940:95, his italics).

In short, the pristine male image is tarnished and limited because it is 'housed' in a female vessel! Jung (1953a:209) further claims that the manifestation of the animus is plural *vs.* the 'unipersonality' of the anima due to woman's more exclusively personal consciousness. This, to me, seems rather contradictory—a well-known characteristic of Jungian writing—unless one is to assume that the animus has superior manifestations because it is a male image, albeit a tarnished one. The male soul-image supersedes the female despite its inferiority vis-à-vis consciousness.

To further the insult, Jung believes that coming to terms with the peculiarities of the animus is the same as coming to terms with the anima, "only here *the woman must learn to criticize and hold her opinions at a distance*" (ibid., my italics). She must try to discover the primordial images behind these opinions and not try to repress them. A woman who represses the animus is "*always in danger of losing her femininity*, her adapted feminine persona" (ibid., my italics). In other words, a man must battle, conquer, and assimilate his contrasexual image in order to achieve conscious differentiation and establish himself in his masculinity, while a woman must simply receive and accept her animus—while holding her opinions at a distance—for fear of losing her femininity! A woman's consciousness is made to depend on Jung's ambivalence towards women, a tarnished male (soul) image, and the patriarchal society's expectations of women!

Seeing that Jung regarded the unconscious as the 'mother' of consciousness, and the collective, archetype-driven layer of the latter as the most powerful 'actor' in the psyche, it is surprising to find the following statement: "An inferior consciousness cannot *eo ipso* be ascribed to women; it is merely different from masculine consciousness" (op. cit., 206). To this he adds that what may be consciously differentiated for women may not be so for men and *vice versa*. The gender-biased statement that follows vitiates the concessionary quality of this one. Woman, says Jung (ibid.), concentrates more on personal relationships while relegating the "wide fields of commerce . . . technology and science . . . to the penumbra of consciousness". This kind of ambivalence and contradiction is typical of Jung's argument concerning women and female-male relationships.

The same equivocation towards women is evident in Jung's assertions concerning the "omnipresent and ageless image" of woman in man. Note how he describes the anima in traditionally polarised patriarchal terms:

> It belongs to him, this *perilous image of woman*; she stands for the loyalty which in the interest of life he must sometimes forgo; she is the much-needed compensation, for the risks, struggles, sacrifices that all end in disappointment; she is the solace for all the bitterness of life. And at the same time she is *the great illusionist, the seductress*, who draws him into life with her Maya—and not only into life's reasonable, but into its frightful paradoxes and ambivalences. . . . Because she is *his greatest danger* she demands from a man his greatest, and if he has it in him she will receive it (Jung 1959a:13, my italics).

> [As long as a man remains unconscious of his anima, she is projected upon a real woman, his fantasy equipping her] with all the fascinating qualities peculiar to the anima. Her moral range is rather wide: she embraces the degraded woman and the *femme inspiratrice*, Faust's Gretchen, and the Virgin (Jung 1940:23, my italics).

Woman the possession of man, woman the nurturer, the devourer, the virgin, and the whore—patriarchal images of women are projected so successfully onto the anima, the female soul-image of man, that one is amazed that Jung could regard the assimilation of this baffling creature as beneficial to man at all.

In summary, Jung's theories concerning the anima and animus reveal an unyielding, blatant sexism—whether we regard him as being a man of his time or not! Far from fostering integration, Jung's anima/animus theory furthers alienation between the sexes (cf. also Pratt, op. cit., 156). It furthers gender-stereotyped notions of what 'masculine' and 'feminine' are, supporting the status quo by enshrining these stereotypes in "mystification". This guards against change on a social level "where women are [still, often] at a huge disadvantage" (Goldenberg, op. cit., 60). Such stereotypical images of womanhood are harmful to men and women alike. As Polly Young-Eisendrath (1997a:227–228, my italics) astutely observes, "When people insist on a strong division between the sexes, and assume that women are naturally more relational than men, *they risk losing parts of themselves forever*".

Jung's Interpretation of Dream Symbolism

I experience only one difficulty with Jung's interpretation of dream (and other) symbolism. Firstly, Jung constantly emphasises the point that one cannot assign specific meanings to dream symbols, but that one must interpret them according to the (dream) context in which they are found (cf., e.g., Jung, op. cit., 98–99). He is thus not in favour of 'dream books' that equate this or that image to this or that psychic phenomenon, event, premonition, and the like. However, he repeatedly regards water as "the commonest symbol of the unconscious" (op. cit., 68; cf. also Jung 1956a:99). I am not aware of a single instance where he applies a different, contextual, interpretation to water. I am also not aware of his interpreting different bodies of water differently. He thus generalises in his interpretation of all water bodies, not taking seriously the specific form in which the unconscious images appear. The same applies to his interpretation of movement within dreams. Downward movement is almost always interpreted as regression, while downward movement to bodies of water is always interpreted as 'going down to the unconscious'. Similarly, a female figure in a man's dreams is almost always interpreted as (an aspect of) his anima, while a violent man in a woman's dreams is said to represent her animus.

With regard to the interpretation of dream symbolism, I find myself in agreement with Hillman's Archetypal School once again. According to Hillman, it is unwise to reduce various plural images of water to the singular 'water' and then to an abstract concept such as 'the unconscious' (Adams, op. cit., 108). Over and against Jung's 'hermeneutic' approach, Hillman proposes (and practices) a more 'imaginal' psychology that takes seriously the specificity of the concretised images (ibid.). For him, "[t]he descriptive qualities that they [water images] exhibit are so incredibly diverse as to be potentially infinite—as are the metaphorical implications" (op. cit., 109). I believe that the same principle applies to the 'interpretation' of movement and all other dream symbols, including 'anima' and 'animus' figures. Should the context not support the interpretation of a female figure in a man's dreams as his anima, for example, then other possibilities must be sought by means of metaphorical amplification.

b. *The 'Religious Function'*

In the preceding subsections, we have encountered in rather veiled terms what Jung has termed the 'religious function' of the psyche (cf. Ulanov 1997:299–313, especially 296–305), for example, in a quotation by Von Franz regarding the fourth and highest level of anima/animus development. Here, it is said, the animus (like the anima) "becomes . . . a mediator of the religious experience whereby life acquires new meaning" (Von Franz, op. cit., 192). This may seem like a wonderful notion, and indeed it is in many respects, but I am not as enthusiastic about it as Raine (1992:168–169) seems to be:

> It was Jung who restored to us in the West the key to the long-closed door of the inner worlds and their symbolic language—the door to our own inner universe, trapped as we were in the prison of prevailing materialist ideologies and a religious iconography located, in Jung's words, 'all outside' . . . [He has] made possible again the inner adventure, yet freed from the trammels of religion . . .

It is true that Jung has "restored the key to the long-closed door of the inner worlds" for many Westerners who have lost faith in their religious—predominantly Christian—tradition. To my mind, however, it would be a fallacy to attribute to Jung a return to the inner worlds "freed from the trammels of religion" (ibid.). To the contrary, it is a well-known fact that Jung encouraged his patients to get in touch with the symbols of their religious tradition as keys to their psychological development. Perhaps I have misunderstood 'religion' in Raine's statement above, but I cannot see how the inner experience, mediated by the world's esoteric teachings and religions, can be accomplished without 'religion'. If that 'religion' refers to God—and not just in the psychological sense of the Self—then I would venture that this is impossible. If, on the other hand, 'religion' refers to reified religious beliefs, then I would agree with Raine's sentiment: ossified religion that has lost its connection to the living God cannot offer anyone what Jung has called "inner meaning"; it cannot help them along the path of individuation, but will rather hinder them because there is no longer any living memory of the divine in it. This is something that Jung himself has pointed out.

My chief concern with Jung's concept regarding the religious function of the psyche is precisely that it may lead to the kind of misunderstanding that I feel Raine expresses. I fear that it may lead people further away from God than many already are, positing as it does a type of humanistic spirituality as an acceptable substitute to real interaction with the Divine. This is where I also have a problem with Jung's concept of the Self. As we have seen, he regards it as the "god within us" (contra Ulanov, op. cit., 299–301). While I do not understand Jung to be reducing the Divine to an aspect of the psyche (so too ibid.), it is my fear that his writings may be misconstrued to refer to the sort of "I am God" teachings advanced by many New Age cults today. Having said that, I simultaneously fear that I am wrong and that Jung's writings may indeed be read in this manner; this is the ambivalence I experience. To suggest that we are 'god' would be at complete variance with biblical revelation and should be avoided at all costs. The reader may decide.

c. *Positive Contributions*

Self-Knowledge Leads to the Acceptance of 'Others'

To my mind, Jung's most important contribution lies in the area of self-knowledge, self-awareness, and the important role this plays in social awareness and respect for others. In this sense, Jung's documentation of the unconscious and his elucidation of its processes have been of monumental importance. Taking the unconscious and its processes seriously, actively participating in the images it presents to us as they appear (i.e., not forcing or repressing them) is the first step in self-awareness. It is part of being gentle with ourselves and so extending that gentleness to others.

Perhaps the most important aspect of self-awareness is recognising the 'other' in us. As Jung has pointed out, there are at least two 'others' in us, our shadow side and our contrasexual soul image. Not repressing these 'others' within ourselves is the first step to eliminating the desire to 'rule' or 'oppress' 'others' in our external environment.

Jung's concept of the collective unconscious further assists us to see the 'other' in ourselves. It shows us the common thread uniting all human beings, irrespective of race, creed, gender, and other differences that we have converted into dividing factors.

A Re-Appreciation of Ancient Symbols

Jung has often said that modern man has generally lost the ability to relate to symbols as once was the case. He avers that the 'primitive' peoples of today are good examples of the way that all mankind once responded to the symbols of the unconscious. Conscious differentiation and the loss of religion have led to a breakdown in modern mankind's ability to interpret the symbols of the unconscious as manifest in dreams, myths, fantastic visions, and religion. Sensing the incredible loss of soul that this has brought about, Jung has made it his "particular endeavor . . . to make consciousness receptive to symbols in order to strike a possible chord of meaningful experience" (Jacoby, op. cit., 63). In this respect, he has taught us to come to terms with our own unconscious psyche by insisting upon our need to appreciate and interpret the symbols of our dream world and waking fantasies. He has thus put us back in touch with our own imagination (op. cit., 64–65; cf. also Raine, op. cit., 168) that essentially springs from unblocked communication with the unconscious (cf. Atkinson, op. cit., 90).

Jung has also given us back our mythological history, thereby connecting us with the symbolic experience of our predecessors. He has given us the tools with which to explore the meaning of these ancient expressions of direct, symbolic experience (cf. Drew, op. cit., 11). Understanding the psychological meaning of these myths not only puts us in touch with our roots, but also shows us that we are not alone. The heroes of old have walked this path before us and survived; we can too (cf. Jung 1953a:169–170, and Hinz and Teunissen, op. cit., 140).

A New Perception of Knowledge

In pointing us inward, Jung has once again made possible the perception of knowledge as experience. I say 'once again' because others before and after him have pointed in the same direction, albeit with different motives or underlying assumptions, desired effects, and so forth. Jung's focus on knowledge as experience and his insistence on gaining knowledge through experience *vs.* the dryness of academic, textbook knowledge, is echoed, for example, in Jesus' recorded complaints against the Pharisees of his day: they knew the letter of the law, but not the spirit thereof. They had textbook knowledge of God and His precepts, as it were, but no real authoritative experience. In Raine's words:

> Jung understood 'knowledge' . . . [as do] all who enter into the realms of the imagination as the thing itself and not book-learning about those living regions (Raine, op. cit., 171).

Furthermore, Jung's thought and his perception of knowledge facilitate a different, more integrated mode of academic writing. It allows for the inclusion of a personal, 'subjective' dimension (cf. e.g., Hambidge 1989:138) that was previously eschewed and even demonised in favour of 'scientific objectivity'.

A More Creative Approach to Secular/Biblical Literary Texts

Jung's emphasis on experiencing symbols and archetypes allows the reader/analyst of a particular text to experience what s/he is analysing, to allow significance to flow in both directions. The text—whether secular or biblical—is no longer merely an object to be acted upon, it is a subject that may act upon the reader/analyst through its symbols, archetypes, and images. Furthermore, Jungian thought rejoices in intertextuality through amplification—something particularly germane to biblical texts (such as *Judith*) with their rampant intertextuality. It also exalts in poly-valency, recognising that a number of different and even opposing 'meanings' may be discovered in a single symbol, archetype, or image. It thus allows us to read our texts—whether biblical or secular—and the oppositions inherent to their imagery in a far more creative, experiential manner. In so doing, it allows us to experience and reconcile the opposites within ourselves.

CHAPTER THREE

AN EVALUATIVE SURVEY OF CURRENT *JUDITH* ANALYSES

As Craven (1977:75) correctly observes, *Judith* studies were long dominated almost exclusively by historical concerns. Literary, advocacy (mostly feminist), and iconographic studies of the book and the art it has generated are a relatively new field. To my mind, the most recent works have been inspired primarily by Craven's seminal doctoral thesis, *Artistry and Faith in the Book of Judith* (Craven 1983a), even though her literary-rhetorical approach was preceded by the work of scholars like Steinmann (1953), Haag (1963), Dancy (1972), Alonso Schökel, and those who responded to his "Narrative Structures in the Book of Judith" (in Alonso Schökel 1975).[1]

The works that I have been able to access fall primarily into the 'new field' of *Judith* studies, and may be divided into five categories: commentaries, various types of literary/advocacy analyses, essays/articles on particular aspects of the book, comparative studies, and iconographic studies. There is also a sixth category of works that focus on a broad range of subjects relating to *Judith*, without it forming their central focus. Such is the work of Aschkenasy (1986), for example, which traces the development of female characters in Hebrew literature from biblical to modern times. These six categories are primarily informed by five methodological approaches: historical criticism, literary analysis, advocacy, rhetorical criticism, comparative/intertextual analysis, and iconographic studies (I refer here to studies of extant artworks inspired by *Judith*). These approaches often overlap so that we find Craven (1983b:49–61), for example, employing an intertextual reading of *Judith, Esther*, and *Ruth*, with a decidedly feminist agenda. Likewise, the five categories dealing with *Judith*

[1] Steinmann's *Lecture de Judith* (1953), Haag's *Studien zum Buche Judith: Seine theologische Bedeutung und literarische Eigenart* (1963), and Dancy's *The Shorter Books of the Apocrypha* (1972) preceded Alonso Schökel's narrative study of *Judith* (Alonso Schökel 1975a:1, n. 1). I have unfortunately been unable to procure copies of these works.

per se sometimes overlap, so that Kikawada (1975) could be placed equally under both 'literary analyses' and 'essays/articles on particular aspects of *Judith*'.

Seeing that I am adding a new category to *Judith* studies—i.e., psychoanalytic, Jungian, literary criticism/analysis—I shall document the main insights presented in the fifty-odd monographs, articles, and essays that I have been able to access *by category* and indicate their significance for my own study. In order to facilitate swift referencing, I have arranged these works in six tables at the end of this chapter (Tables 4–9).

A. *Commentaries*

Here we find works of varying lengths and different foci [Table 4]. Some, such as those of Moore (1985) and Enslin (1972), employ primarily historical-critical tools to present the introductory aspects of *Judith* before providing verse-by-verse or pericope-by-pericope commentary on the entire book. Others devote chapters of varying length to *Judith*, with some consisting of merely a few paragraphs (Koester 1995, Newsome 1992), and others of entire subsections (Pfeiffer 1949, Otzen 2002). The majority of works in this category attempt to deal with *Judith* as a whole, while Craghan (1982a) and Elder (1994) focus only on chapters 8–16. Whereas many of these works do not espouse a specific methodological approach, others show a distinctly feminist orientation (Schuller 1992, Elder 1994, and even Lacocque 1990, who regards *Judith* as a 'feminist tractate').[2] In this section, I should like to pay particular attention to the more important works of Enslin, Moore, and Otzen. The views of the other commentators regarding *Judith's* date and place of composition, genre, and purpose are tabulated along with those of Enslin, Moore, and Otzen in Table 3 for comparison.

[2] Lacocque's work may be better classified under 'literary analyses' as it does not purport to be a commentary per se. I have, nevertheless, decided to place it here because Lacocque treats the historical aspects of *Judith* with a fair measure of depth in the course of his analysis. Cf. e.g., his treatment of *Judith*'s historical anachronisms (Lacocque 1990:31–32) which he, like Moore, regards as an intentional part of the author's ironic stance (ibid.).

a. *Enslin 1972*

Enslin's commentary begins with an introduction by Solomon Zeitlin (op. cit., 1–37), which deals primarily with issues such as *Judith's* genre, its date and place of composition, and its textual recension. Zeitlin's introduction also provides a brief summary of *Judith* and *Esther*, after which it draws parallels between the two books (including their view of God and the temple, the character of the two heroines, and the purpose of the books, op. cit., 13–15). It then discusses the Apocryphal Supplements to *Esther* (op. cit., 15–21), and provides reasons for the canonical inclusion/exclusion of *Esther/Judith* (op. cit., 21–24, 24–26. See also Moore 1989/1992 in this regard).

Briefly, Zeitlin (op. cit., 1) regards *Judith* as a "very well constructed [highly imaginative] . . . popular Jewish novelette" that was written "to instruct the people and to inflame the Judaeans' patriotism" (ibid.). According to him, the original Hebrew version of the book was composed in Antioch (op. cit., 32) during the late Hasmonean or early Roman periods (op. cit., 28); it "reflects the war of Nicanor against the Judaeans" (op. cit., 29–30); and 'neutralises' the more secular *Esther* (op. cit., 14; cf. also 13–15). Zeitlin believes that *Judith* was excluded from the Hebrew canon for the following reasons (op. cit., 24–26): the Ammonite Achior's conversion contradicts the Pentateuchal laws; Achior was only circumcised upon his conversion—he was not baptised as was required during the Second Commonwealth;[3] *Judith* was written in the Diaspora after the time of Antiochus Epiphanes, and thus after the Persian period—the rabbis did not believe books written after the Persian period to be inspired, nor were any books written in the Diaspora included in the Hebrew canon.

Enslin (op. cit., 38), on the other hand, regards *Judith* as "a romantic story" that borrows "many colourful details" from earlier biblical, historical, and traditional sources. Contrary to Zeitlin, Enslin believes that the book was "written by a Jew in Hebrew and *not improbably in Palestine*" (op. cit., 42, my italics). He does not grant as much detail to the introductory issues of the book, but provides

[3] During the Second Commonwealth, many sages encouraged widespread proselytisation that included the 'accursed' Ammonites (cf. Deuteronomy 23:4). Nevertheless, the practice of allowing Ammonite proselytes was later curtailed by the opinion of Rabbi Joshua at Javneh (Zeitlin, op. cit., 25).

valuable information on the ancient reception of *Judith* in Josephus, Philo, Origen, Clement, and Jerome (op. cit., 43–48), as well as references to the book in patristic sources (op. cit., 48–49). After his extensive commentary, Enslin closes with an appendix on "Judith the Widow" (op. cit., 180–181), a Midrash of *Judith* entitled יהודית מעשה (op. cit., 182–190), and "The Latin Rendering of Judith" (op. cit., 191–216).

b. *Moore 1985*

Moore's commentary is far more thorough, detailed, and balanced than that of Enslin. It takes serious note of the literary aspects of *Judith* in subsections such as "The So-called Imbalance of the Narrative" (Moore 1985:56–60), "The Heroine's Character" (op. cit., 64–66), "Irony: The Key to the Book" (op. cit., 78–85),[4] "Style and Syntax" (op. cit., 86), and "The Canonicity of Judith" (op. cit., 86–91).[5] To be fair, however, it must be mentioned that his commentary was published some thirteen years after Enslin's, thus giving him access to the literary analyses of *Judith* that began springing up in greater concentration from the early 1970s (e.g., Alonso Schökel 1975a, Craven 1977 and 1983a).[6] Even so, Moore treats the historical-critical issues that Zeitlin and Enslin address more thoroughly. His work is also more accessible to the modern reader because of his simpler academic style and the many illustrations and maps that he provides.

Shortly, Moore attributes the many anachronisms and historical/geographical impossibilities found in *Judith* to its author's ironic stance (cf. op. cit., 47–48, 78–79). He maintains that the book was "probably composed in the Hasmonean period, most likely either toward the end of the reign of John Hyrcanus I (135–104 B.C.) or at the beginning of the reign of Alexander Jannaeus (103–78 B.C.)" (op. cit., 67). Regarding the place of composition, Moore (op. cit., 70) suggests, contrary to Zeitlin, that "the author of Judith was a Palestinian Jew, probably an early Pharisee".

---

[4] For a detailed study of the book's irony, see especially Kikawada 1975:38–39. Cf. also Alonso Schökel 1975a and Lacocque 1990.

[5] For a comparison between his views on the canonicity of the book as expressed here with those expressed in his 1992 article, see chapter 3 d.

[6] See n. 1, above, for literary analyses published before 1975.

For me, the most valuable aspects of Moore's work lie in his scholarly presentation of evidence for and against the historicity of *Judith* (op. cit., 38–49), his detailed discussion of the so-called pseudonym theories of Gaster, Ball, and Volkmar (op. cit., 52–56), his presentation of previous thinking regarding Judith's duality, and his deep understanding of the profound irony in the book. Thanks to his work and that of Pfeiffer, I have been able to access the important aspects of many earlier works regarding *Judith's* historicity and the nature of its heroine, something which I would otherwise not have been able to do. Unlike Enslin (op. cit., 182–190), Moore also provides a number of interesting *Judith* Midrashim (op. cit., 103–108) that provide a greater scope of comparison with the extant text.

c. *Otzen 2002*

Otzen is one of the modern scholars who prefers to deal with the text of *Judith* (Otzen 2002:68–153) prior to dealing with its historical-critical aspects. From the outset, he regards *Judith* as the meeting place between two strong traditions: the salvation of the chosen people (a rescue/deliverance story) and the clever and heroic woman (op. cit., 68). He acknowledges the numerous biblical and non-biblical sources that have influenced it (op. cit., 68–80), and deals creatively with Judith's geographical and historical anachronisms (op. cit., 81–93) as well as various other 'thorny issues' such as *Judith's* deception and sexuality (op. cit., 98–113). Otzen then provides a succinct account of some of the most important feminist and narrative approaches to *Judith* (op. cit., 114–123), after which he finally addresses the historical-critical aspects of the book (op. cit., 124–142).

Like Moore, Otzen regards Judith's historical-geographical irregularities as a deliberate artifice and an aspect of the book's ideology by which the author elevates the struggle between Nebuchadnezzar/Holofernes and God/the Jewish people/Judith to "the eternal struggle between good and evil" (op. cit., 90). For him, this theological transcendentalisation (a term he borrows from Zenger, 1981) lends *Judith* a parabolic quality that is "not a long way" from apocalyptic conceptions (op. cit., 92).

Contrary to my belief and that of many other modern scholars, Otzen advances the theory that Bethulia symbolises Jerusalem (op. cit., 94) and advocates that Judith is written in the Maccabean period from the perspective of the rededication of the temple in

165 B.C. (op. cit., 96). For him, the dilemma presented by Judith's deceitful and seductive dealings with Holofernes finds resolution in its theological function, i.e., the presentation of Yahweh as the acting subject, who hardens his enemy's heart by the hand of a woman (op. cit., 104). While Otzen examines Judith's character in detail, Achior is merely regarded as a pagan witness to the power of Israel's God (op. cit., 107–109), a Graecised form of Tobit's (Semitic) Ahikar (op. cit., 108).

Otzen further defends the integrity of the book in accordance with a theological structure (op. cit. 70. Similarly Zenger 1981. See also Van Henten 1994/1995.):

1. Nebuchadnezzar demonstrates that he is God (*Judith* 1–3)
2. Who is God—Nebuchadnezzar or Yahweh? (*Judith* 4–7)
3. Yahweh demonstrates that he is God (*Judith* 8–16)

While this structure is theologically justifiable, it does not deal with the textual intricacies of *Judith*. I therefore find for Craven's structure (see chapter 1) rather than the one presented here.

Finally, Otzen does non-Danish speaking persons a great favour by discussing in detail an essay by H. J. L. Jensen, "Juditbogen" (in T. Engberg-Pedersen and N. P. Lemche eds. 1990. *Tradition og nybrud. Jǿodommen i hellenistusk tid.* Forum for bibelsk eksegese, 2. Copenhagen: Museum Tusculanum, 153–89). The article is otherwise not available in English.

The works of Enslin, Moore, and Otzen have been invaluable to my understanding of the text, its dating, its relation to *Esther*, and its broader intertextuality.[7] I only wish I had Otzen's book at hand while I was writing my doctoral thesis in 1999.

I now invite the reader to compare the works of various scholars in this category as reflected in the table below.

B. *Literary Analyses*

These texts have been classified as literary analyses [Table 5] because of their predominantly literary concerns with or approach to *Judith*. The main works included in this category are those by Craven (1983a)

[7] For further comparison between *Judith* and *Esther*, see Craven 1983b and Craghan 1982b. Cf. also Koester 1995 and Newsome 1992.

Table 3. Judith's Date and Place of Composition, its Historical Situation, Genre, and Purpose According to Various Commentaries

AUTHOR	DATE AND PLACE OF COMPOSITION	HISTORICAL SITUATION REFLECTED N *JUDITH*	GENRE	PURPOSE
Pfeiffer 1949	Palestine, c. 150 B.C. (p. 297).	The war for political independence ended in 141 (p. 15).	Historical fiction; a good short story (p. 297).	To inflame people's patriotism (p. 297).
Enslin 1972	Palestine, ". . . well prior to the end of the first Christian century" (pp. 42 and 46).	—	A romantic story (p. 38).	
Zeitlin 1972	Antioch, late Hasmonean or early Roman period (pp. 32 and 28).	One of the many invasions of Judaea between 161 B.C. (Judas' victory over Nicanor) and the time of Agrippa I (40 A.D.). Zeitlin emphasises Judas' second war with Nicanor as the basis for the book (p. 28).	A well-constructed, imaginative popular Jewish novelette (p. 1).	To instruct the people and fuel the flames of patriotism (p. 1).
Craghan 1982a	Palestine, c. 150 B.C. (p. 73).	The persecutions of Antiochus Epiphanes to c. 150 B.C. (p. 74).	A historical novel; a story of how the weak triumph with God's help pp. 72, 65).	Challenges the ancient and modern faith-community to action —a model of human liberation (pp. 66–67 and 72–73).
Moore 1985	Palestine, toward the end of John Hyrcanus' reign (135–104 B.C.) or the beginning of the reign of Alexander Jannaeus (103–78 B.C.), (p. 67).	The political situation after 107 B.C. see below, (pp. 69–70).	A folktale (pp. 76 and 78).	Encouragement, advancing Pharisaic theology and presenting a model for behaviour (all implied) (p. 78).

Table 3 (*cont.*)

AUTHOR	DATE AND PLACE OF COMPOSITION	HISTORICAL SITUATION REFLECTED N *JUDITH*	GENRE	PURPOSE
Lacocque 1990	Second century A.D. (pp. 38 and 42).	Hellenisation and persecutions of Antiochus Epiphanes (cf. n. 12, p. 39).	Displays features of a Greek romance, with ties to Greek tragedy, polemical literature (pp. 45, 46).	To subvert conformist and exclusivist Judaism religiously and politically (pp. 39–41 and 44–47).
Newsome 1992	c. 150 B.C. (by Jewish author, unspecified, location), (p. 219).	Seleucid period (p. 220).	Short story framed in the style of a Hellenistic novella (p. 219).	To encourage Jews to resist Seleucid forces and remain faithful to Torah (p. 220).
Schuller 1992	End of second or beginning of first entury B.C. (p. 307).	Maccabean wars (p. 307).	A 'story' (pp. 307, 308).	Judith as model of faith, wisdom, prayer, piety, and action (pp. 309–310).
Elder 1994	Palestine; during Hasmonean dynasty (142–63 B.C.E.), (p. 455).	Hasmonean period (p. 455).	A fictional story of a heroic saviour in Israel (p. 467)	(Puts story to feminist use to challenge stereotypes).
Koester 1995	Unspecified, second century B.C. implied (p. 259).	Maccabean period implied (p. 259).	A story focusing on the victory of female power (p. 258).	To encourage faithfulness to Law under most adverse circumstances (p. 259).
Otzen 2002	Jerusalem; during the Maccabean era, from the perspective of the temple's rededication in 165 B.C. (p. 96).	Maccabean period (pp. 96 and 105).	Parabolic story combining traditions: rescue story with powerful woman, intertwined with apocalyptic concepts (pp. 68 and 92).	To show the ascendancy of YHWH, law-piety, and the centrality of Jerusalem—implied throughout (see e.g., pp. 77, 102, and 105).

and Alonso Schökel (1975), which apply rhetorical-critical and narratological theory, respectively, to the book. The works of Coote 1975 et al. listed under Alonso Schökel 1975 respond to the latter, pointing out the strengths and weaknesses of his analysis (e.g., Shumaker 1975). They sometimes address an issue in greater detail (e.g., Kikawada 1975), or address an issue that he did not (e.g., Coote 1975, Peterson 1975). They will therefore be discussed with Alonso Schökel's work, below.

a. *Craven 1977/1983a*

Craven's seminal dissertation, which enlarges upon and bears the same title as her 1977 article, *Artistry and Faith in the Book of Judith*, was published in 1983. Seeing that both her monograph and her article deal with the same topic, I will restrict my discussion to the former, pointing out similarities and differences only where necessary by way of references to both works.

Craven's "literary/rhetorical" approach to *Judith* (cf. Craven 1983a: 44–46, 1977:75) entails an in-depth study of the book's external and internal structure that is as detailed as it is important. I will only outline the contours of her study here, as I have already adopted the external structure she proposes, and will incorporate her insights into my analysis in chapter 5.

Craven begins by providing the reader with a methodological orientation (Craven, op. cit., 11–46) in which she acknowledges the influence of Robert Lowth and James Muilenburg upon her work, and in which she outlines what she calls "The Rules of My Game". This is followed by chapters that deal with the external design and internal structural patterns in *Judith*, respectively (op. cit., 47–64, 65–112; cf. also Craven 1977:81, 88 and 89 for the external structure of *Judith* 1–7, 8–16, and 81–85, 85–91 for the internal structure of these sections). It is found that repetition governs both external and internal design (Craven 1983a:53, 65).

The most valuable contribution of Craven's work is the presentation of conclusive proof that "The Book of Judith is a self-defined literary unit of sixteen chapters" (op. cit., 47). She disproves the (then) commonly held assertion that the book is structurally unbalanced by pointing out the essential symmetries between Section I (chapters 1–7) and Section II (chapters 8–16). These include:

a) "Expressed identities" or "correspondences between the [two sections] in which two parallel passages of similar meaning share at least one set of equivalent or identical terms" (op. cit., 53), e.g.:

- The first act of the leading character (Nebuchadnezzar and Judith, respectively) is to send for others—1:7 and 8:10.
- Both leading characters call a gathering of their own and announce their plan—2:2 and 8:10, 34.
- They both claim to execute this plan by their own 'hand'—2:12 and 8:33.
- Feasts for honoured guests are held in both sections—6:21 and 12:10.
- Worship is explicitly urged—3:8 and 8:17.

b) "Expressed antitheses . . . in which two parallel passages in direct opposition to each other share at least one set of equivalent or identical terms" (op. cit., 54), e.g.:

- Holofernes and Judith carry out opposing plans—2:2 and 8:16. (see also Lundbom 1975 and Levine 1995)
- Fear and trembling falls both on the rebel nations and on Holofernes' army—2:28 and 15:2.

c) "Implied antithetical correspondences . . . in which implicitly parallel elements . . . are sharply contrasted with each other" (op. cit., 54–55), e.g.:

- Holofernes and Judith, the executors of Nebuchadnezzar and God's plans, respectively, are sexual opposites.
- They employ strikingly dissimilar weapons—military might on the one hand, and beauty and wisdom on the other.
- The central opposition concerns the identity of the true God—is it Yahweh or Nebuchadnezzar?

d) "Artificial identities" in which "the correspondences are artificially implied by sets of skilfully matched components" (op. cit., 55–56):

- A prose introduction opens each section of the narrative—1:1–6 and 8:1–8.
- Both plan-executors make food preparations—2:18 and 10:5.
- A specified and implied three-day period precedes the enactment of both plans—2:21 and 12:10.

Craven ends her dissertation by investigating Judith's often iconoclastic use of tradition and convention in the liberation of the Judaean peoples (op. cit., 113–124)—an aspect of her study which she also takes up in her 1983 article "Tradition and Convention in the Book of Judith" (Craven 1983b:49–61).

Craven's study has already proved invaluable to my understanding of *Judith* in that her analysis of the book's external structure has bolstered my view of *Judith* as an individuation narrative drama/dream. As I have previously argued, the palindrome structure that she has discerned in both sections of the book reflects the pattern of the mandala—the symbol of individuation that Rollins (1983:29) has labelled a "cryptogram of the self". Furthermore, the parallels she draws between 'the principal characters' will assist greatly in my interpretation of them as aspects of the Judaean/Jewish national psyche (see also Lundbom 1975 and Roitman 1992 in this regard).

b. *Alonso Schökel 1975a and the Responses to his Work in Alonso Schökel 1975*

In his paper entitled "Narrative Structures in the Book of Judith", Alonso Schökel discusses the composition (1975a:3–7), irony (op. cit., 8–11), dénouement (op. cit., 12–13), characters (op. cit., 13–17), and function (op. cit., 17–19) of *Judith*. Seven academics from various disciplines are given the opportunity to comment upon his work (Alonso Schökel 1975:21–42), and this is followed by the minutes of colloquy in which further discussions take place (Wuellner 1975:45–69).

Alonso Schökel's most insightful contributions consist of the following:

i) The necessity of chapters 1–7: he states, inter alia, that the narrative's "lack of proportion . . . constitutes the character of Holofernes, and prepares and introduces the dramatic irony which is substantial to the story" (Alonso Schökel 1975a:4). Nevertheless, he feels that it "lacks vividness" (op. cit., 5).
ii) His analysis of the irony inherent in the book and, particularly, in Judith's words to Holofernes (op. cit., 8–11, especially 9–10).
iii) His analysis of Judith as the personification of Israel (op. cit., 15).
iv) The parallels he draws between *Judith's* characters and events and those of other biblical passages. For example, Judith is compared (very briefly) to Jael, Deborah, Miriam, the wise woman of Abel Beth-Maacah, David confronting Goliath, and Moses (op. cit., 15, 16). This aspect of his work in particular will be of

> great value to the 'amplification' that I will conduct in the course of identifying the effective protagonist (chapter 5).[8]

The responses to his work are very interesting indeed. Here, I should like to review those of Coote, Dundes, Lundbom, and Peterson, as they will be the most useful to my own study. I refer the reader to Table 5, below, for a brief summary of the contents of the remaining contributions, viz. those of Kikawada, Kolenkow, and Shumaker.

Mary Coote's *response* is of great interest to me as she interprets *Judith* according to mythological categories that have a strong psychoanalytical underpinning (see also Elder 1994). According to her, in its "basic pattern and motifs the story of Judith strongly resembles a type of traditional rescue story in which a female hero assumes the role of the hero and saves a male figure (or social group) from captivity" (Coote, op. cit., 21). The folk tale type to which this corresponds is AT 888, The Faithful Wife: Enslaved Husband is Rescued by his Wife in Disguise as a man. It contains four elements clearly found in *Judith* (cf. op. cit., 21–25) and offers many parallels with the anima archetype that holds the potential both to 'save' and to 'destroy' the masculine psyche:

1. Enslaved husband (besieged Bethulians).
2. Chaste wife (Judith's chastity is repeatedly emphasised).
3. Wife in disguise wins captor's favour and secures release of prisoner (Judith takes off her widow's attire, bathes and perfumes herself, puts on festive clothing, and goes down to Holofernes' camp. There she wins his favour—and everyone else's—deceives, and decapitates him, thus setting her people free from his oppression).
4. Recognition (Judith is highly praised by all the Bethulians and receives special commendation from Jerusalem's High Priest).

This article will prove very useful to me in my understanding of Judith as a possible national manifestation of the Judaean/Jewish anima and ego at the time of *Judith's* composition (chapter 5).

Dundes's response points out the basic oppositions governing *Judith*. He regards the book as an exemplar of "the perennial battle of the sexes" (Dundes 1975:28), adding that, "[t]his is very much a woman's

[8] For a more in-depth investigation of these and other parallels see the works discussed in below pp. 118–22.

story inasmuch as a woman successfully resists a man's attempt to violate her. The man is appropriately punished for his sexual desire. In this light, decapitation could well be symbolic castration" (ibid.). On the basis of this contention, Dundes proceeds to accentuate sexual allusions in the book pertaining to the landscape, the proposed attack on the Bethulians, and so forth (ibid.). While I think that Dundes's conception of *Judith* as "a woman's story" is highly overstated, his work is very significant in terms of the sexual allusions and oppositions he highlights. (It will be remembered that archetypes have both a positive and a negative pole that the human mind often regards as oppositional).

In his response to Alonso Schökel, Peterson challenges the former's focus on main characters as the determinants of function in *Judith*. He identifies the various crowds (e.g. the Assyrian army, the Bethulians) as characters in their own right and summarises their function as follows (Peterson 1975:35):

1. They act as a foil for Judith (7:19–32).
2. They, along with individuals in the story, provide examples for the Jewish reader to follow or shun. In this way they contribute to the didactic purpose of the story.
3. They symbolically portray the Jewish theology of moral and physical separation from the Gentiles. This same separation is shown by other elements in the story, such as the dietary laws (12:1–3), and the ritual of purification (12:7–9).

Since crowds are often indicative of the collective unconscious and/or weaker aspects of consciousness, Peterson's delineation of their function in *Judith* could shed important light on the function of the unconscious or weaker elements of consciousness in both *Judith* and the human psyche. More particularly, with regard to the unconscious, integrating his insights into the analysis will facilitate my understanding of the shadow elements of the psyche because many of the 'crowds' he discusses belong to Holofernes who will be identified as a shadow content. Furthermore, Peterson's work also indicates that so-called minor characters may not be disregarded in the analysis of this work, something which is very important for a "Jungian" analysis, as Dawson has shown us.

Lundbom investigates, inter alia, the relevance of Achior's speech and the points of comparison between the strategies that Judith and Holofernes employ. He also briefly alludes to parallels with the Book of Ruth.[9] In the first instance, Lundbom argues for "a totally Jewish audience" for Achior's speech in *Judith* 5 (Lundbom 1975:37). He does not regard Achior as a typical proselyte (*contra* Alonso Schökel 1975a:5), and finds confirmation for this view in *Judith* 11:20–23 which, he maintains, "relates what must be the main point of the story, viz. a pagan general is led into reliance upon Israel's God: 'your God shall be my God' (cf. Ruth 1:6)". This, he concludes, "is Judith's great accomplishment. Where Achior failed she succeeded" (ibid.). Secondly, Lundbom sees the "various ironies" underscoring the interchange between Judith and Holofernes as "merely another way of stating the book's theology" (ibid.). He points out, for example, that both march directly to the heart of the enemy camp, dress festively in victorious anticipation, and praise each other's wisdom. On the basis that "Judith in the end wins out," he concludes that "Judith overcame her opponent with the very strategy that he was using to overcome her (and her people). His end was thus fitting" (ibid.). This, he believes, is a "more subtle expression" of the theology of II Maccabees in which "the author repeatedly tells us about punishment that befits the crime" (ibid.).

While I hardly think that bringing a pagan general into reliance upon Israel's God is the main point of the story, or that this is a justifiable interpretation of *Judith* 11:20–23—Holofernes was not someone to be trusted as the text itself establishes (cf. e.g., his dealings with the coastal nations in 2:28–3:8)—the points of comparison between Judith and Holofernes which Lundbom raises will be used as a check against my own contention that *all* the characters in *Judith* may be seen as manifestations of the Judaean/Jewish soul. Furthermore, his analysis of the relevance of Achior's speech will assist in my interpretation of this character as a vital aspect of the Judaean/Jewish psyche, as it inadvertently underlines Dawson's contention that all characters in a narrative are of psychological importance. Lundbom's allusion to Ruth will also prove helpful in the intended 'amplification'.

In summary, the works categorised as "literary analyses" provide valuable information as to the psychological and mythical aspects of *Judith*, its various structural and literary aspects, and the depiction of its characters.

[9] For more detailed comparisons between *Judith* and *Ruth*, see Craghan 1982b and Craven 1983b. See also Lacocque 1990.

C. *Essays/Articles on Particular Aspects of* Judith

The material in this section [Table 6] focuses on a particular aspect of the Book of Judith, e.g., Judith's prayer (Craven 1995) or the canonicity of the book (Moore 1992). A variety of methodological approaches are used, with feminist hermeneutics informing two of the six essays/articles. It will be noted that three of the articles presented here have been published (at least) twice in different years—strangely enough, three years apart in each case (e.g., Roitman 1992 = Roitman 1989, and Levine 1995 = Levine 1992 and 1989). I will therefore refer to the first publication of each in my evaluation below, unless an author's later article constitutes a significant revision of an earlier one.

a. *Craven 1995*

In an article entitled "Judith Prays for Help",[10] Craven (1995) offers commentary on *Judith* 9:1–14. She identifies the various occasions when the Bethulians offer prayer to God and notes the following concerning Judith, "a woman of habitual and daily prayer" (Craven 1995:209):

- Judith prays before every action in the story (ibid.).
- Judith's nightly purification and prayer habit provide the ruse for her escape once she has slain Holofernes (op. cit., 210).
- Judith's personal lament in *Judith* 9 is embedded in her plan to save Israel (*Judith* 8:9–10:8), a narrative section that underscores the importance of hearing and being heard by its "concentrated uses of the verb 'hear'" (ibid.).

After proffering certain comments regarding the canonical status, date, and purpose of *Judith* (op. cit., 210–211), Craven concludes that "the petitions of Judith's prayer . . . are fundamental to the plot and success of the entire narrative. . . . [It] effects deliverance . . . because . . . [of her] unswerving belief that God is with the people whether they are delivered or destroyed. Theology makes this prayer great. . . . In her prayer and in the book as a whole, Judith serves

[10] The full title is "Judith Prays for Help (Judith 9:1–14); Prayer from Alexander to Constantine: A Critical Anthology".

as an example that covenant, not deliverance, counts most" (op. cit., 211). Craven's article is well written but does not nearly match the scope suggested in the full title (n. 10). Nevertheless, it will prove useful in the analysis of Judith as the 'true' Jewish soul—the one who upholds the covenant at all (personal) cost.

b. *Levine 1989 and 1992/1995*

Levine's "Sacrifice and Salvation: Otherness and Domestication in the Book of Judith", published in 1992 and 1995, is essentially an elaboration of an article that she published in 1989, namely, "Character Construction and Community Formation in the Book of Judith". I will therefore restrict myself to discussing her 1992 article.

In "Sacrifice and Salvation", Levine (1992:17–30) explores how Judith, the metaphoric representation of the Israelite community,[11] muddles gender roles and threatens societal norms through her characterisation, while simultaneously being 'domesticated' by the text.[12] For example, Levine shows how Judith's 'otherness', her independence, public action, and sexual activity relativises the normative cultural constructions of her community and thus threatens the *status quo*, while the threat which she represents is subverted by her reinscription into Jewish society and its norms at the end of the story (op. cit., 17–18). She also notes how Judith's return to Bethuliah brings to the forefront the threat she poses, in that "she offers those previously marginal to or excluded from the power base . . . roles in society and cult" (op. cit., 24): she transforms the women into active agents (ibid.), her action causes the Ammonite Achior's conversion and integration into Jewish society, and she frees her stewardess (op. cit., 25). In other words, Judith transforms both her own life and the lives of those around her.[13] Nevertheless, for Levine, the inherent threat to societal norm is subverted in that the women eventually return to their homes, Judith's own transformation is temporal, and the stewardess is given neither voice nor name (op. cit., 24–25). In the end, Judith's sacrifice is contained, and her return to

[11] Cf. also Alonso Schökel 1975a for a similar interpretation of Judith vis-à-vis the Israelite community.

[12] For this aspect of Judith cf. also Van Henten 1994/1995 who, *contra* Levine, does not seem to think that Judith is 'domesticated' by the text.

[13] Regarding the transformative potential of Judith, and the transformation that she and Achior go through, see Roitman 1992.

private life ends the inversion of gender roles and reinforces the *status quo* (op. cit., 27).

In my opinion, Levine's article points clearly to the threat posed by the anima and the ambivalence surrounding her integration. It also demonstrates the power of the anima in transforming the society/person who encounters her.

c. *Moore 1989/1992*

In this article, Moore (1989:579–587) investigates the reasons for the exclusion of *Judith* and the inclusion of *Esther* in the Hebrew canon—a "very puzzling" fact when one considers the religious nature of the former and the rather secular nature of the latter (op. cit., 579). Moore rejects "the old scholarly answer", i.e., that the 'Council of Jamnia' closed the canon in 90 A.D. and excluded all Apocryphal books including *Judith* (op. cit., 580). Instead, he cites the current consensus which severely downplays, if not negates, the so-called council's role (op. cit., 581) in favour of "an extended, three-stage, *dynamic* process engaged in by the Jewish community, whereby, first, the Law . . . then the Prophets . . . and, lastly, the Writings . . . were canonized" (op. cit., 582, Moore's italics). Taking the possible early closure of the Writings into account—possibly in the first or the second century B.C. (op. cit., 583–584)—Moore suggests that *Judith's* date of composition may be the principal reason for its canonical exclusion (op. cit., 584). He observes that *Judith* and Daniel reflect the same period in history, and contends that *Judith* was excluded from the canon because it was patently not written during the late exilic/early postexilic period—something which would not have been so easy to say of Daniel. Taking the similarities between *Judith's* story line and the wars of Nicanor into account, as well as the book's 'friendly' attitude towards Bethuliah (= Samaria), Moore concludes that the book was more than likely written during the reign of John Hyrcanus I (135–104 B.C.), possibly after 107 B.C. when he annexed and integrated Samaritan territory into Judah (op. cit., 585). He ends the article by suggesting some more reason's for *Judith's* exclusion, i.e., its questionable veracity, its 'pro-feminist' stance, the dubious character of Judith, and its heady mixture of four emotionally laden subjects: "God, power, sex, and death" (op. cit., 586–587).

Moore's article adds little to the views he expressed in his 1985 commentary. While I will not focus on the canonicity of *Judith* at all, and I have placed the date of *Judith* "soon after Demetrius III's attack on Jannaeus" in 88 B.C., Moore's contribution may well act as a checkpoint for this date during my 'objective analysis' of *Judith* in chapter 5.

d. *Narito 1992*

Narito's "The Book of Judith" forms part of a 1992 publication by the Asian Women's Resource Centre for Culture and Theology entitled *Women of Courage: Asian Women Reading the Bible*. In her contribution, Narito (1992:53–62) notes that *Judith* presents a challenge to "the machismo" of male (Catholic) biblical interpreters (op. cit., 53–54). She maintains that "Judith is a critique to the Hebrew patriarchal structure that blocked the independence and leadership of women" (op. cit., 55), and that Judith had the "qualities needed in the struggle for genuine peace and liberation" (op. cit., 57): vision of a nation free from all oppression, standpoint for the oppressed, and method—"well-planned strategies and tactics to achieve her vision" (ibid.). For Narito, "[t]he book of Judith also spells out the empowerment of powerless women for peace-building, defined here as the struggle for freedom and liberation and the building of a new society of love, truth, justice and peace" (ibid.).

Narito's exposition of *Judith* in terms of liberation and women's empowerment is very topical in the present era. It emphasises the liberative potential of free women in society and, as such, may be used to underscore the importance that the anima holds for men in particular and society in general.

e. *Roitman 1989/1992*

According to Roitman (1989:551), the Ammonite Achior constitutes "one of the book's greatest mysteries" not least because of his familiarity with sacred history that gets him expelled from Holofernes' camp, his willingness to suffer on behalf of Israel's faith (cf. *Judith* 5–6), and his counter-Torah conversion to Judaism (*Judith* 14). In his article, Roitman agrees with Moore (1985:59) that "Achior is a crucial character for uniting both sections of the book". He regards Moore's insight as "[a]n important breakthrough" in the study of this oft-neglected character (Roitman, op. cit., 552), and then sets upon the most enlightening study of Achior that I have encountered.

Roitman's article proves that "there is an especially intriguing structural relationship and a subtle complementarity between Achior and Judith" (ibid.) in terms of their respective functions. He traces these similarities/complementarities through five stages in each character's development (see op. cit., 557–558 for the complete table and chapter 5):

1. Opposite roles and location (op. cit., 552–553), e.g.: man/woman; Ammonite/Israelite; Pagan/Jew; Holofernes' encampment/ Bethuliah.
2. Parallel roles and location (op. cit., 553–554), e.g.: both deliver a speech, which utilises the history of the Jews to teach spiritual lessons upon which suggestions/advice/recommendations are made.
3. Change of places (op. cit., 554), e.g.: Achior is expelled from Holofernes' camp/Judith leaves Bethuliah voluntarily.
4. Change of roles in terms of function and reactions, and speech (op. cit., 555–556), e.g.: Achior's truthful advice earns the ire of Holofernes and his people, whereas Judith's misleading advice earns the praise and approval of the same.
5. Meeting and transformation of the characters (op. cit., 556–557) Achior meets with Judith and is transformed into a civilian and a Jew/Judith meets with Achior and is transformed into a pious and secluded widow.

For Roitman, these parallels show that Achior is "a kind of double or 'alter ego'" for Judith (op. cit., 558–559). As previously indicated, his study will form an integral part of my own analysis in which I interpret Achior as a depiction of the positive aspects of the Jewish shadow in *Judith.*

f. *Bruns 1956*

In a brief article, Bruns (1956:19–22) puts forth his thesis that the genealogy of Judith in chapter 8 may indeed reflect "the actual lineage of a famous woman of Leontopolis" (op. cit., 19) and that this supports an Egyptian origin for the Book of Judith as a whole. In this he contradicts Steinmann's belief that the said genealogy is fictitious, created to mock the pseudo-aristocrats and their love for pedigree (which they did not have, ibid.). Allowing 25 years per generation and placing *Judith* at 146 B.C., Bruns traces the beginning of the genealogy to the fifth century B.C., the time when the Jewish colony of the Elephantine community was founded. He overcomes the problem of the last three names (Salamiel, Sarasadai, Israel)—which designate Judith as a Simeonite, a Samaritan—by saying that many generations could have come between Nathanael, the fourth last name, and Salamiel, on account of the fact that the Jews who entered Egypt under harsh conditions could hardly be expected to carry their genealogies with them (op. cit., 20). In order to prove his thesis further, Bruns (op. cit., 20–21) offers the contention that Judith's genealogy reflects the onomastic change from pre-exilic names to those found amongst the Jews (from Elephantine and Palestine) who settled in Leontopolis in the second and first centuries B.C. Taking into account the parallels between Judith and Jael, and the fact that the ruins of Leontopolis have been known throughout the centuries as the 'Mound of the Jewess' or the 'Mound of Judith' (op. cit., 21–22), Bruns contends that *Judith* 8 represents the genealogy of the actual woman "who was, perhaps, responsible for the preservation of the Elephantine version of [the Jael] story and also, perhaps, for the idea of revising it" (op. cit., 22).

While I do not necessarily agree with his findings, Bruns's thesis provides historical backup for the imitations of Judith during the French Revolution and at other times of modern history (see the discussion of Stocker's work, below) and demonstrates that archetypal figures may well be based on solid historical grounding.

D. *Comparative/Intertextual Analyses*

The material in this category [Table 7] draws parallels between Judith and other biblical/extra-biblical characters, passages, and genres. Owing to the high preponderance of sources in this category, I have thought it wise to divide the said material into subcategories for discussion. This yields five essential subcategories or sets of comparison: Judith/Moses/Miriam, Judith/Deborah/Jael, Judith/Esther/Ruth, Judith/Delilah, and *Judith*/miscellania. For the purposes of my study, the value of the texts represented here lies precisely in their capacity to elucidate at least some of the rich intertext informing *Judith*. They will assist me to 'amplify' the 'dream symbols' of this Apocryphal book (chapter 5). In the case of articles/essays that have been published on two or more separate occasions, I will review the article/essay with the latest date of publication.

a. *Judith/Moses/Miriam: Van Henten 1994/1995 and Skehan 1963*

Van Henten 1994/1995

Van Henten (1995) begins his article "Judith as Alternative Leader: A Rereading of Judith 7–13" by establishing *Judith* 7–13 as a literary unit (op. cit., 225–232), with chapter 7 providing both the context and the starting point for Judith's performance (op. cit., 228). He then proceeds to read these chapters intertextually with the Massah and Meribah episodes in Exodus 17:1–7; Numbers 20:2–13, and Deuteronomy 33:8–11 (op. cit., 232–238) to show how the text of *Judith* underscores Judith's role as an alternative leader to Moses (op. cit., 238–245).[14] Van Henten appeals particularly to the testing motif in both the *Judith* and the Exodus stories to show how the positive and negative aspects of Moses' leadership are split between Judith and the Judaean elders respectively. Pointing to the fact that "Judith is not the regular leader of the people" (op. cit., 241), he argues that her independent, charismatic leadership bears the blessing of YHWH and "links up with the image of a 'judge'" (op. cit., 242)—a link corroborated by the similarities between *Judith* 16 and the Song of Deborah in the Book of Judges.

Having established Judith as a leader alternative to Moses, Van Henten turns his attention to the gender dynamics of the story. He concludes that *Judith's* "significant adaptation of . . . androcentric patterns [in the 'Moses' intertexts he has established] . . . seem to justify reading parts of the narrative of Judith as F [female] voices within a dominant male framework" (op. cit., 252).

Van Henten's division of *Judith* obviously contradicts that of most scholars, such as Craven, Moore, and myself, who regard *Judith* 1–7 as a separate unit. While it is not my intention to discuss this issue at this point—it would take me too far afield of the scope of this chapter—I should like to say that I regard his view as erroneous in that it is based primarily on extratextual concerns, with weak textual motivation. Be that as it may, Van Henten's parallels between Judith and Moses will prove invaluable both in terms of the 'amplification' of images in chapter 5 and in terms of understanding Judith

[14] For Exodus parallels see also Skehan 1963, Lacocque 1990, Otzen 2002, Craghan 1982a, and Alonso Schökel 1975a.

as a narrative manifestation of the national ego, composed of various facets of Israel's psychological history, of which Moses is a part.

Skehan 1963
In "The Hand of Judith," Skehan (1963:94–110) investigates the specific relevance of the hand in *Judith*. He does so on the analogy of Wisdom 11:1 and Daniel 9:10—where 'hand' has no necessary meaning of its own, and concludes that 'hand' is relevant to the translation of *Judith* 9:9, 13:14, and 15:10 alone (op. cit., 94–95). In order to discover the reason behind the seemingly 'superfluous use of χείρ' in the remaining passages, Skehan focuses upon Judith's prayer in chapter 9 and the canticle of *Judith* 16:1–12 that reflects directly the events of the prose narrative (op. cit., 95–96). Noting the occurrence of Exodus motifs and the theme of the woman's hand in both passages, as well as the parallels between Judith's canticle and that associated with Miriam in Exodus 15:1–19, he proceeds to draw out detailed comparisons between the events in *Judith* and those in Exodus (op. cit., 96–98, 98–102). Skehan concludes that in both the poetic and the prose sections of *Judith*, "what is done by Judith's hand is . . . a revival in some sense of what was done by God's at the Exodus" (op. cit., 103).

The rest of Skehan's article (op. cit., 103–110) justifies this conclusion through many parallels with other biblical passages and draws a clear line of comparison between the 'hand' of God, the 'hand' of Moses, and the 'hand' of Judith. After working through Skehan's article, one may conclude that the author of *Judith* used the phrase 'by the hand of Judith' and other related phrases to draw clear and deliberate parallels between Judith and Moses insofar as both are shown to be the weak, lowly agents of YHWH (in contrast to their foes, that is) who by His strength brings about the deliverance of His people through His willing and trusting agents. This, of course, corroborates to a certain extent Van Henten's view of Judith as an alternative leader to Moses.

b. *Judith/Deborah/Jael: White 1989/1992 and Van Dijk-Hemmes 1986*

White 1989/1992
White (1992:5) maintains that "the comparison [of Judith] to Jael and Deborah is neither superficial nor coincidental." She then depicts

what she calls "exact similarities" (ibid.) in the structure and plot (op. cit., 5–6), characters (op. cit., 6–10), and other elements of the two stories, especially the victory songs (op. cit., 11–13).[15] White concludes that "the author of the book of Judith used the specific story of Jael and Deborah as the model for his story" (op. cit., 13), and that "[t]his modelling technique is a good example of the use of earlier biblical literature in the literature of the second-temple period", demonstrating "the high esteem in which it [*Judith*] was held at the time" (op. cit., 14).

Van Dijk-Hemmes 1986

Van Dijk-Hemmes (1986:123–147) traces the parallels between Mary (New Testament), Jael, and Judith in respect of the phrase 'blessed amongst women' that is used of each of these three women. The phrase leads her to believe that they each represented the ideal of womanhood in certain periods of Israel's ancient history (op. cit., 123). She then explores the meaning of this phrase for each woman, from Jael (op. cit., 124–136) through Judith (op. cit., 137–142) to Mary (op. cit., 142–146), and concludes as follows (op. cit., 146): the phrase 'blessed amongst women' as conferred upon Jael, Judith, and Mary seems to indicate 'blessing above [other] women', as each of these women are given an exemplary role to play in their respective stories and have fired popular imagination accordingly. Van Dijk-Hemmes makes the important observation that the seductive role accorded to Jael in Judges 4 is 'censured' in Judith and completely abolished in Mary, thus transforming the activity and sensuality of Jael and Judith to the passivity and asensuality of Mary (op. cit., 147).

c. *Judith/Esther/Ruth: Craven 1983b and Craghan 1982b*

Craven 1983b

Craven (1983b:49–61) draws some interesting parallels between Judith, Esther, and Ruth in terms of the way that each woman maintains tradition by both upholding and contravening the societal norms and

[15] Cf. also Ackerman 1998 and Meredith 1989 for the relation of Judith to Judges women and a comparison between Judith and Delilah.

practices of the covenant community. For example, she points out that each of these women acts resolutely—without any promise or assurance from God—to move the plots of their respective stories "from tragedy to triumph" (op. cit., 50). They each emerge as victorious subjects within an androcentric world "because they use well the human resources available to them" (ibid.). She concludes as follows (op. cit., 60–61):

> Judith and her canonical sisters Esther and Ruth conserve ancient religious truths and preserve the life of the covenant community in ways suitable to their times. . . . In Ruth and Judith, women bind together for mutual support. . . . In Esther and Judith, political concerns motivate sexual involvements. . . . Ruth, Esther, and Judith teach that certain conventions may be forced to give way so that tradition can be faithfully preserved. No unalterable set of prescriptions regarding appropriate female behaviour forbids their participation in the process of modifying tradition. And no small debt is owed these women of scripture for their part in the hermeneutical process of continuity and change.

Craghan 1982b

Craghan's comparison of Esther, *Judith*, and Ruth proceeds from the premise that each presents a different paradigm for human liberation that moves from the shattering of orientation—i.e., disorientation—to reorientation. The books are compared on the grounds of six common themes:

1. The setting of liberation (Craghan 1982b:11–12)
2. Lamentation (op. cit., 12–13)
3. The emergence of the leader (op. cit., 13–14)
4. Banqueting and empowerment/disempowerment (op. cit., 14–15)
5. The sexual element (op. cit., 15–16)
6. Communal concern (op. cit., 16–18)

Craghan (op. cit., 18) concludes that Esther, *Judith*, and Ruth, exhibit a drive for the common good of the people, to the extent that even the most private actions have "public and hence communal impact". The reader may choose any one of these three paradigms as befits the time that s/he lives in. Not to choose any is, according to Craghan, "unforgivable," as these three books teach that to be human is to be engaged in human liberation (ibid.). This is a very similar contention to that made in his commentary (Craghan 1982a; see above).

d. *Judith/Delilah: Meredith 1989*

Meredith (1989:63–78) explores the similarities between the Judith-Holofernes and Samson-Delilah stories, focusing on the notion of betrayal. She is particularly interested in the diverse reception that these texts have enjoyed, and in their reflection of and contribution to "the cultural ideology that women's sexuality is dangerous to men" (op. cit., 63). Drawing upon deconstruction, reader-response criticism, feminist criticism, and narrative theory—particularly Bal's concept of focalisation—she sets out to prove that "it is not only the 'negatively' interpreted stories [like Delilah's] that contain anti-woman ideologies. Rather, *the interpretations which are 'positive' toward women are equally capable of representing women's sexuality as dangerous to men*" (op. cit., 64, my italics). She notes that with many interpreters 'betrayal' has become a structural element that causes them to interpret Delilah's story in terms of the story of Samson's wife (Judges 14:16–18)—despite obvious and important differences (op. cit., 67, 69–73). Her analysis shows that Delilah did not betray Samson at all as "she divulges the entire [Philistine] plan [to capture/destroy Samson], not merely her part in it" from the outset (op. cit., 70). Meredith (op. cit., 72) correctly suggests that "the story is at least as much about Samson's pride and pretensions to immortality as it is about Delilah's harm to him". Contrary to the Delilah story, Judith's betrayal of Holofernes constitutes "true betrayal" (op. cit., 73)—Judith deliberately lies and uses her charm to deceive and kill Holofernes (op. cit., 74). Despite this, interpretation often casts Delilah as a villainness and Judith as a heroine. Meredith (op. cit., 74) suggests that the reason for this lies in the different way that each woman has been focalised in the text (op. cit. 76). For example, Judith is symbolically identified with the Jews, she is beautiful, her piety and character are beyond reproach, and she is a wise, chaste widow—that is why, says Meredith, she can still remain the heroine of the story. By contrast, we are told very little about Delilah, except that she is a Philistine and definitely not chaste (op. cit., 75). As Meredith (ibid.) avers, "This double standard—that she [Judith] must be beautiful and sexual and yet chaste and untouched—reflects profound male ambivalence toward women's sexuality: that it is simultaneously desirable and dangerous". Meredith's article contributes not only towards my intended 'amplification' (chapter 5), but also towards a better understanding of the so-called negative anima.

e. *Judith/Miscellania: Caponigro 1992 and Nelson 1991*

Caponigro 1992

In "Judith, Holding the Tale of Herodotus", Caponigro (1992:47–60) explores the possibility that the author of *Judith* was familiar with Herodotus' *Histories* and that she modelled the book (in part) on Herodotus' account of the Persian invasions of Greece in the fifth century B.C. He believes that this accounts for the anachronisms of the first section (op. cit., 56):

> [The] problem spots in the first half of Judith . . . are more or less solved or explicated when they are considered to be adaptations of Herodotian material . . . once the connection has been established. . . . it is possible to re-read Judith with a new appreciation of how well the Auctrix understood Herodotus' narrative art, and how wisely she adapted it to her own ends.

Nelson 1991

Nelson compares the work of an anonymous poet on Judith, with Cynewulf's poems on Juliana and Elene. She provides an interesting introduction (Nelson 1991:1–8) to the three poems and the way that each portrays the heroine as possessing the female virtues considered cardinal in the Anglo-Saxon world. Beginning with Judith (op. cit., 9–52), and moving on to Juliana (op. cit., 53–112) and Elene (op. cit., 113–206), Nelson provides the original Old English version for each poem on even-numbered pages and a parallel translation on odd-numbered pages. Each poem is then followed by an 'afterword' in which the poem is discussed and analysed. Of interest to the author (Nelson) is the way that each 'saint' deals with and overcomes the temptation facing her.

E. *Iconographic Studies*

It will be noted that every author represented in this section [Table 8] approaches artistic renditions of Judith or scenes from *Judith* from a predominantly feminist perspective.

a. *Stocker 1998*

Stocker's monograph is the most exhaustive of the works represented here. It not only traces the progression of literary/artistic renditions of Judith/Judithic scenes from the Middle Ages onwards, but also provides fascinating evidence of the way in which Judith acted as a model for action in diverse historical-political situations. Stocker's *Judith: Sexual Warrior. Women and Power in Western Culture* is an extraordinary contribution to *Judith* studies, and certainly gives one renewed appreciation for this 'murderous saint'. To think that there were actual men and women, nobles and paupers, who were not only inspired by Judith but deliberately took on her 'persona' to perform deeds of valour and liberation or to legitimise their reigns, certainly fans a legitimate desire to see this Apocryphal book reinstated to its rightful place as scripture—i.e., as a model for human behaviour.

b. *Bal 1995*

In "Head-Hunting: 'Judith' on the Cutting Edge of Knowledge", Bal (1995:253–285) goes "in search of the missing head through the history of western culture" (op. cit., 254) in order to analyse "today's culture [of which *Judith* is a part] as the messy, by no means straightforward product of the past" (op. cit., 253). In her search, Bal uses artistic portrayals of Judith as a topos for epistemology, for attaining knowledge about power and gender in society. Beginning with Michelangelo da Caravaggio's severed *Medusa's Head*, Bal notes how Judith and the Medusa have often been juxtaposed or even confused because, in psychoanalytic theory, beheading symbolises castration (op. cit., 257). The association of Judith with this ultimate femme fatale image is clearly seen in the striking similarities between Golzius' sixteenth-century print of Judith with Holofernes' head and Cellini's *Perseus*, itself inspired by Donatello's *Judith* (op. cit., 257–258). Bal traces the way that beheading is figured in many paintings covering that topic and the 'murder scene' in *Judith*, focusing on Caravaggio's representation of a dispassionate Judith severing the head of a tragic hero, Holofernes (op. cit., 258–264, 268), and Artemesia Gentileschi's 1620 portrayal of a rather masculine Judith slaying a feminised Holofernes with the active assistance of her stewardess (op. cit., 265–274). She shows how the killing powers that men attribute to women—their fear of castration by a woman, (and so) of becoming a woman—are borne out in and perpetuated by the paintings she discusses.

c. *Sölle et al. 1994*

The chapter entitled "Judith, Saviour of her People" (Sölle et al. 1994:206–219) forms part of a rich volume that displays and comments upon the "great women of the Bible in art and literature"—the title of this volume. Included among these women are, inter alia, Eve and Lillith (op. cit., 10–31), Tamar (op. cit., 88–96), the Witch of Endor (op. cit., 176–183), and Bathsheba (op. cit., 184–193). Each chapter contains (excerpts from) the relevant biblical text, Sölle's commentary to the biblical material, a host of beautiful artistic reproductions, and Kirchberger's contributions under "Extra-biblical Materials". The latter is divided into "Ancient and Medieval Sources" and "Post-Medieval Literature".

In her commentary on *Judith*, Sölle (op. cit., 213) speaks highly of a "new type of woman" who emerges in postexilic Israel, an Esther and a Judith who, following and extending upon the biblical tradition of "strong and courageous heroines", become the rescuers of their people. She notes how Judith put personal concerns aside and used lust in the interest of her people. This, she seems to suggest, is a gender reversal of the rape that usually accompanies war, one that was sanctioned not only by 'the Bible', but by the early Church, which links Judith and other famous biblical women allegorically to Christ. While Sölle's commentary adds little to the academic score of biblical knowledge, Kirchberger's discussion of extra-biblical material reflecting *Judith* (op. cit., 215, 216, 218) provides valuable intertexts for interpretation and an interesting array of rabbinic, medieval, and sixteenth-twentieth-century responses to the book. The chapter on *Judith* also includes excellent reproductions of several visual renditions of the book. Amongst them one finds a bronze statue of Judith decapitating Holofernes by Donatello, paintings by Boticelli, Michaelangelo, Artemisia Gentileschi, Kremser-Schmidt, Massys, Mantegna, Lucas Cranach the Elder, Solimeno and Cristoforo Allori, as well as various miniatures and Codex/Bible illustrations.

d. *Stone 1992*

Stone (1992:73–94) examines the representations of *Judith* in art from the early Middle Ages until the modern period, with particular emphasis on the representation of the Judith-Holofernes scene. According to Stone, artistic renditions figure Judith in four chief ways (op. cit., 74):

1. A Christian religious presentation beginning in the early Middle Ages
2. A national-patriotic way—in Italian art from the Renaissance period onwards
3. A national-religious way—in Jewish art from the Renaissance on
4. The feminine-emotional way—in modern art.

Likewise, these renditions may be divided into four main types:

A. Narrative descriptions of the entire story represented on a single page or part of a page, e.g., the ninth-century Carolingian Bible (earliest example), the Greek tenth-century Leo Bible, a fifteenth-century Jewish manuscript from Germany (op. cit., 75–78).
B. Epitomized representations of Judith decapitating Holofernes, with or without her servant, e.g., the eleventh-century Codex Barberini, Donatello's bronze sculpture (op. cit., 78–79).
C. The expanded or detailed representation over a number of pages, e.g., the Velislaus Bible, the Pamplona Bible (op. cit., 79–81).
D. Symbolic appearance of Judith the heroine in painting or sculpture, with the sword of victory in her hand, e.g., the eleventh-century Italian Bible, Ghiberti's bronze *Gates of the Garden of Eden* (op. cit., 81–83).

Throughout these categories and depictions, Judith is often represented alongside figures such as Jael, Judas Maccabeus, David, Mordecai, and Esther. She is often related to Christ or the Virgin crushing Satan (op. cit., 80, 82), and the Prague Haggadah associates her with the Passover story. At times, Judith even replaces "meaningful symbols like the crown of the Torah over the Ark of the Torah" amongst European Jewry of the fifteenth-sixteenth centuries A.D.—particularly in Italy (op. cit., 83). From this point on a "Great Transformation" takes place which represents Judith and Holofernes amongst other famous couples, such as Adam and Eve, with the woman shown as carrying out a betrayal of the "beloved" (ibid.), e.g., Caravaggio and Allori's seventeenth-century paintings of a decapitating Judith. Interestingly enough, this development of Judith has only taken place in Christian art. "In Jewish art, Judith never ceased being the figure of faithfulness to her people and of heroism and sacrifice for them. She continued as a heroine of the Feast of Hanukkah beyond the candelabra" (op. cit., 84). This is also true of modern Jewish art, like Leonard Baskin's 1981 representation of Judith as Hanukkah in *Chosen Days*.

The iconographic studies featured here give credence to Jung's assertion that archetypes have a dual nature that is often split in the mind of human beings. The paintings that these authors discuss give us a clear, mostly vivid, visual representation of this phenomenon by representing Judith as both 'pure virgin' and femme fatale—as well as a host of combinations of these two archetypal opposites. These artistic renditions and their interpretations will certainly assist my analysis of *Judith* by elucidating relevant passages.

F. *Works Featuring* Judith *as an Aspect of their Study*

I will deal very briefly with the works categorised under this section [Table 9] as they merely include *Judith* as an aspect of their study; *Judith* is not a main focus of these works. Here we find primarily what one could call comparative or intertextual studies. So it is that Ackerman (1998), Phipps (1992:31–47), Fontaine (1988:84–102), and Williams (1982:71–78) discuss Judith within the overarching framework of Judges women, biblical female saviours/assertive women, the trickster goddesses of the ancient Near East, and 'aggressive warrior women', respectively. While these works focus primarily on biblical figures of comparison, Aschkenasy (1986) discusses Judith within the far wider scope of the literary representation of women in Jewish literature, from the Bible, through Rabbinic sources, down to the modern era. Here she investigates, in depth, the oppositional representation of woman as deadly seductress/formidable giver of life in its various guises; the connection created between women, sex, and evil; the oppression of women; and the main strategies that women have developed to overcome the strictures of their actual and mythical roles in androcentric culture. Aschkenasy's is a very valuable study for those who wish to understand the diverse, contradictory representations of womanhood and of Judith as well as the reasons behind them. It also gives insight into the powerful appeal of the anima figure, albeit indirectly.

The remaining two works in this category, namely, Hudson and Jacot (1991) and Bade (1979), include *Judith* as part of their respective psychoanalytical and iconographic studies. In *The Way Men Think*, Hudson and Jacot explore the psychobiological effects of mother-separation upon men. These include (not always) insensitivity, emotional handicaps, misogyny, and the fear of castration, which is none other than men's fear of losing their manhood and becoming women. Conrad Meit's sixteenth-century carving of Judith with Holofernes' head is discussed as a visual depiction of men's fear of women and their castrating power (Hudson and Jacot 1991:46–49). Bade (1979) follows a rather similar theme, and includes copies of various artists' renditions of Judith in his study of the femme fatale in art.

G. *Summary*

My survey has shown that *Judith* studies fall into six categories that are informed primarily by five main methodological orientations, viz. historical criticism, literary analysis, advocacy, rhetorical criticism, comparative/intertextual analysis, and iconographic studies. Given the nature of the Book of Judith/its story, it is not surprising to find that fourteen of the forty-eight monographs/articles/essays are informed specifically by feminist hermeneutics. The highest incidence of this is found in the iconographic studies, all of which approach their subject matter from a feminist point of view. The category with the highest number of contributions is comparative/intertextual studies. This too comes as no surprise as *Judith* offers the (biblical) reader a panegyric of almost every Old Testament female/male figure of note, as well as a rich motif—intertext spanning the entire Old Testament. Further to the summary:

- *Judith* studies have been dominated primarily by the historical-critical approach until fairly recently.
- Despite the fact that there is currently a resurgence of interest in *Judith* studies and, moreover, in applying diverse forms of modern literary and other theory to the book, no-one—besides myself (Efthimiadis-Keith 1999a and 1999b)—has ever applied a psychoanalytic approach to the book per se. The only psychoanalytic studies that I have encountered are those of Bal (1995:253–285) and Hudson and Jacot (1991:145–160), both of which have applied primarily Freudian categories to the iconography of *Judith*.
- Many recent works are not in-depth studies of the *entire* book—most are articles/essays.
- Many of the recent articles/essays have been published over and over again in various anthologies.

- Only one article, that of Roitman 1989/1992, has attempted to deal with the function of Achior in a meaningful manner.
- The more recent studies, which I have surveyed here, are concerned neither with the historicity of the book nor the function of its anachronisms/inconsistencies beyond attributing the latter to the book's ironic stance and/or the author's whim. The same applies to the so-called duality of Judith that is mentioned but not sufficiently dealt with, perhaps because duality as such is not a modern issue, i.e., the modern mind does not find it offensive or problematic but 'natural'—a normal fact of everyday life.
- While most modern scholarship acknowledges the necessity of both 'parts' or sections of *Judith*, and the structural integrity of the text as we have it today, none of them deal with the function of its bipartite structure beyond the narratological validity of Section I (*Judith* 1–7) as a background/antithesis to the events that take place in Section II (*Judith* 8–16).

This means that there are some serious 'gaps' in current *Judith* studies vis-à-vis an in-depth analysis of the book as a whole, a psychoanalytic approach to its contents, a detailed understanding of the function of Achior, Judith's duality, the book's anachronisms/inconsistencies, and its structure. There is thus a lacuna in *Judith* studies that needs to be filled by using a holistic approach to the various problems that the book presents. As I have already indicated, I believe that this lacuna may be filled (at least partially) by a specifically Jungian psychoanalytic approach that combines Jungian theory with Dawson's method of discerning a narrative's effective protagonist. I will apply my mind to this matter in chapter 4. Before doing so, however, I should like to state that, while not overtly informed by psychoanalytical—let alone Jungian—principles, the literature surveyed in this chapter will provide very useful background for my analysis (chapter 5) in that it presents, inter alia:

- Glimpses into the ancient reception of *Judith.*
- Possibilities for establishing the historical setting/date of composition for the book.
- Insightful analyses of the characters involved.
- Knowledge that will contribute to the discussion of the *Judith* characters as archetypes.
- A rich storehouse of intertextual possibilities for *Judith* both within and without the biblical text.

- A profound understanding of the book's external structure and its internal structural relationships—in the case of Craven's monograph, in particular.
- Valuable commentary on the book as a whole.
- Dramatic visual material to accompany the analysis where necessary.

Table 4. *Commentaries*

CATEGORY	METHODOLOGICAL ORIENTATION(S)	WORKS	SUBJECT/MAIN INSIGHT/ SPECIAL FEATURES
Commentaries	Address introductory issues (such as composition, date, historicity); verse for verse or pericope for pericope commentary on the entire book (historical criticism).	Moore 1985	More sensitive to literary aspects of *Judith*; uses modern authors e.g. Craven, Alonso-Schökel; anachronisms linked to ironical stance of author.
		Enslin 1972	Includes introduction by Zeitlin that deals with most of the introductory issues.
	Devote chapters of varying length to the study of *Judith*; briefly address introductory issues and provide commentary on the book in a fashion similar to that of standard commentaries.	Otzen 2002	Deals creatively with inconsistencies. Discusses much intertextual material. Deals thoroughly with Jensen's article, otherwise unavailable in English.
		Koester 1995: 258–259	Relation: *Judith* and Esther; Judith as example of Hasidic piety.
		Elder 1994: 455–469	(Specifically feminist orientation) Transformation of the *Judith* mythos—objectification of Judith denies her subjectivity; artworks; Judith as *femme fatale* and military strategist.
		Newsome 1992: 219–220	Subversive nature of Judith; Bethuliah as Shechem; relation: Judith, Esther, and Susanna.
		Schuller 1992: 306–310	(Specifically feminist orientation) *Judith* as androcentrically orientated book; use of *Judith* in Latin-American/Western context(s); relation: God and Judith.
		Lacocque 1990: 31–47	Anachronisms due to irony; relation: Judith, David, Ruth, and Exodus; *Judith* as subversive political literature; *Judith* as feminist tractate.
		Craghan 1982a: 65–126	Liberative purpose of *Judith*; weakness *vs.* strength; Exodus motifs; reversal of fortunes; challenges posed to modern society.
		Pfeiffer 1949: 285–302	Historicity and date; religious teaching; the characters have psychological validity.

Table 5. *Literary Analyses*

CATEGORY	METHODOLOGICAL ORIENTATION(S)	WORKS	SUBJECT/MAIN INSIGHT/ SPECIAL FEATURES
Literaray Analyses	Rhetorical Criticism; Structural Analysis	Craven 1983a (based on Craven 1977:75–101)	Micro- and macrostructure of *Judith*; Judith and Holofernes act out unsolicited missions.
	Narratology	Alonso Schökel 1975a: 1–20	Literary composition; irony; Judith as Israel and Wisdom; Exodus motifs; eschatological aspects.
	Comparative: Folk Tale	Coote 1975:21–26	*Judith* as Faithful Wife folk tale; Judith as female warrior; *Judith* as patriarchal fantasy.
	Close Reading	Dundes 1975:27–29	Basic oppositions governing *Judith; Judith* as exemplar of the battle of the sexes.
	Rhetorical Criticism	Kikawada 1975: 38–39	Various forms of irony; irony in *Judith*.
	Close Reading	Kolenkow 1975 40–42	Eschatological aspects of *Judith; Judith* as model for and affirmation of success, of human action in a perilous time.
	Rhetorical Criticism	Lundbom 36–37	Parallels: Judith/Holofernes, Achior, Ruth.
	Close Reading	Peterson 34–35	The importance and function of 'crowds' (e.g. Bethulians, Assyrian army) in *Judith*.
	Close Reading	Shumaker 1975: 30–33	Importance of paying attention to "historical" detail and Hebrew nuances; Judith as redeemer-widow

Table 6. *Essays on Particular Aspects*

CATEGORY	METHODOLOGICAL ORIENTATION(S)	WORKS	SUBJECT/MAIN INSIGHT/ SPECIAL FEATURES
Essays on Particular Aspects	Textual Study	Craven 1995: 208–212	The prayer of *Judith* 9.
	Feminist Hermeneutics	Levine 1995: 208–223 (= Levine 1992: 17–30 and Levine 1989:561–578)	Metaphorisation and subversion of Judith; parallels: Manasseh, Judith/Holofernes, Judith's maid/Bagoas, Judith/Achior; Judith as priest and warrior; sacrifice and salvation challenge to status quo; social reversal; public *vs.* private spheres; sexual/phallic imagery; Judith as widow; the line of Simeon.
	Canonical Criticism	Moore 1992:61–72 (= Moore 1989: 579–587)	Canonical issues; relation: *Judith* and Esther.
	Liberation Struggle Study	Narito 1992:53–62	Liberation in *Judith* against the background of "valiant Filipina women."
	Close Reading	Roitman 1992: 31–46 (= Roitman 1989: 550–560)	The function and meaning of Achior in *Judith*; parallels: Judith/Achior, plus transformation of both.
	Textual Study	Bruns 1956:19–22	The genealogy of Judith.

Table 7. *Comprative/Intertextual Studies*

CATEGORY	METHODOLOGICAL ORIENTATION(S)	WORKS	SUBJECT/MAIN INSIGHT/ SPECIAL FEATURES
Comparative/Intertextual Studies	Feminist Hermeneutics and Reader Response	Van Henten 1995: 224–252 (= 1994:33–48)	*Judith* 7–13 as remake of Exod 17, Num 20, and Deut 33; parallels: Judith/Moses, *Judith*/Exodus; *Judith* as parody to male leadership; Judith's priestly and Simeonite connections; Judith as judge and prophet (possible contrast to Hasmonean leadership).
	Intertextual Study	Caponigro 1992:47–60	Parallels: *Judith*/Herodotus' account of Persian invasions of Greece in fifth century B.C.
	Feminist Hermeneutics; Structural and Rhetorical Criticism	White 1992:5–16 (= White 1989:570–578)	Parallels: Judges 4–5/*Judith* (structure, characterisation, plot, hymns, etc.); sexuality and death.
	Poetic Literary Study	Nelson 1991	Parallels poetry re: Judith, Juliana, Elene; elements of interrogation, torture, victory of the 'saint' (includes Old English text and modern translation).
	Feminist Hermeneutics; Intertextual Study	Craven 1989	Parallels: Judith/other women who lied for their faith.
	Russian Formalism combined with Reader Response and Ideological Criticism	Meredith 1989: 64–78	Parallels: *Judith*/Samson and Delilah in terms of sexuality, betrayal, and death.
	Feminist Hermeneutics	Van Dijk-Hemmes 1986:123–147	Parallels: Jael/Judith/Mary (NT) in terms of phrase (title?) "Mother in Israel" and being blessed of God.
	Intertextual, Feminist Study	Craven 1983b:49–61	Parallel: Judith/Esther/Ruth—women who conserve tradition and further the faith through their unconventional behaviour.
	Thematic Comparison/ Intertextual Study	Craghan 1982b:11–19	Parallels: Esther/*Judith*/Ruth (banqueting; liberation; lamentation; sexuality; communal concern; emergence of leader).
	Intertextual	Skehan 1963	Parallels: Judith/Moses, *Judith*/Exodus; analysis of use of Hebrew phrase "by the hand of."

Table 8. *Iconogaphic Studies*

CATEGORY	METHODOLOGICAL ORIENTATION(S)	WORKS	SUBJECT/MAIN INSIGHT/ SPECIAL FEATURES
Iconographic Studies	Feminist Hermeneutics; Art Criticism; Historiography	Stocker 1998	Traces development of literary, historical, political, and artistic renditions of the *Judith* story throughout modern history.
	Feminist Hermeneutics plus Lacanian and Freudian Psychoanalytic Criticism	Bal 1995:253–287	*Judith* as topos for epistemology; depictions of decapitation in various artistic renditions of *Judith.*
	Feminist Hermeneutics; Art Criticism	Sölle et al. 1994	Artistic and literary renditions of *Judith*; conversion of Judith to *femme fatale* in more modern works.
	Feminist Hermeneutics; Art Criticism	Stone 1992:73–94	Representations of Judith and Holofernes in art.

Table 9. Works Featuring *Judith* as an Aspect of their Study

CATEGORY	METHODOLOGICAL ORIENTATION(S)	WORKS	SUBJECT/MAIN INSIGHT/ SPECIAL FEATURES
Works Featuring Judith as an Aspect of Their Study	Feminist and Comparative; with Narrative Aspects	Ackerman 1998	Judith related to women in the Book of Judges and Biblical Israel (various roles in society investigated at the hand of Judges women: warrior, dancer, seductress, queen, mother, barren woman, etc.).
	Intertextual Study	Phipps 1992: 31–46	Various women saviours in the Biblical tradition; cf. especially parallel: Judith/Miriam.
	Psychoanalytic Presentation	Hudson and Jacot 1991:46–49	Conrad Meit's carving of Judith with Holofernes' head (early 16th century) as example of men's fear of women and of castration at woman's hand.
	Comparative Study	Aschkenasy 1986	Comparative study of woman in Jewish literature from the Bible to modern age: deadly seductress and formidable giver of life; evil, sex and women; woman as mother; woman and oppression; main strategies devised by women to overcome their mythical and actual roles in Jewish androcentric culture.
	Comparative Study	Williams 1982:71–78	Deborah, Jael, Judith as aggressive warrior women.
	Art Criticism	Bade 1979	Judith as *femme fatale* in art.

CHAPTER FOUR

METHODOLOGICAL CONSIDERATIONS: JUNG, LITERATURE, AND THE INTERPRETATION OF *JUDITH*

In this chapter, I should like to expand on the methodological issues that I raised in chapter 1. Owing to the fact that my work is not primarily concerned with methodological issues per se, I shall eschew protracted discussions of specific ways in which Jung's theories have been applied to biblical/secular literature. Instead, I shall concentrate on Jung's views regarding psychology-and-literature, the potential these hold for the study of *Judith*, and my own methodological approach to the text.

A. *The Application of Jungian Theory to biblical/Secular Literary Texts: General Considerations with a Focus on Terrence Dawson*

a. *Jung on the Relationship between Psychology and Literature*

As I pointed out in the introduction, Jung addressed the question of psychology-and-literature in three particular essays: "On the Relations between Analytical Psychology and Literature"/"On the Relation of Analytical Psychology to Poetry"; (1930/1950); and "'Ulysses': A Monologue" (1932). All these essays have been published in *The Collected Works*, volume 15 (Jung 1966). I should like to focus on the second of these essays (Jung 1966:84–105) as it presents, to my mind, the clearest portrayal of Jung's thinking concerning the topic at hand. It is a more refined endeavour than the first essay (op. cit., 65–83), while "'Ulysses': A Monologue" (op. cit., 109–134) presents his psychological evaluation of James Joyce's controversial *Ulysses*.

In "Psychology and Literature", Jung sets out to elucidate "points of view by which a psychological approach to poetry [read: all artistic forms] might be *oriented* in a general way" (op. cit., 85, my italics). For him, the work of the psychologist consists of investigating the psyche, which is "the womb of all arts and sciences" (op. cit.,

86). This entails two separate and distinct tasks in terms of art/literature (henceforth 'art', 'the work', or 'literature'):

i) Explaining the psychological structure of a work of art.
ii) Investigating the factors that make someone artistically creative (ibid.).

In this, Jung modifies his earlier views, which had identified the creative process alone as the proper subject of a psychological approach to art (op. cit., 65–66), and establishes "a clear-cut dividing line between the psychological and aesthetic consideration of literature" (Jacoby, op. cit., 65).

According to Jung (op. cit., 88–89; cf. also 72–77), there are also two types of literary works: the psychological and the visionary. The former intentionally shows its characters in a psychological light whereas the latter does not. The latter therefore requires further psychological elucidation whereas the former does not:

> An exciting narrative that is quite devoid of psychological intentions is what interests the psychologist most of all. Such a tale is constructed against the background of unspoken psychological assumptions, and the more unconscious the author is of them, the more this background reveals itself in unalloyed purity to the discerning [psychologist's] eye (op. cit., 88).

Psychological literature deals with "the stuff of human fate in general"—emotions, experiences, passions, sufferings—that the author has "raised from the commonplace to the level of poetic experience" (op. cit., 89) with such conviction that it affords the reader new insight into life's everyday matters. Whereas the raw material of this type of literature is drawn from human consciousness, the raw material of visionary literature is drawn from mankind's collective unconscious, where the primordial experiences of humankind reside. As a result (op. cit., 90):

> [t]he experience that furnishes the material for artistic expression is no longer familiar. It is something strange that derives from the hinterland of man's mind, as if it had emerged from the abyss of prehuman ages, or from a superhuman world of contrasting light and darkness. . . . [T]he primordial experiences rend from top to bottom the curtain upon which is painted the picture of an ordered world, and allow a glimpse into the unfathomable abyss of the unborn and of things yet to be.

Contrary to the Freudian view, Jung believes that such works cannot be traced back or reduced to "some highly personal circumstances" (op. cit., 92) that influenced the author. Such an approach would soon turn art into neurosis, as Jung explains (ibid.), and it would divert the critic's attention from the psychology of the work to the psychology of its author (op. cit., 93, cf. also 67–69). It consequently does not take seriously the primordial experience upon which such visionary work is founded, dismissing it as "'lively fantasy' or 'poetic licence'" (op. cit., 93–94). Such "vision", avers Jung, "is not symptomatic of something else" (op. cit., 94). It is rather "a true symbol—that is, an expression for something real and unknown" (ibid.)—and shows that its author is "in touch with the night-side of life", much like a seer and a prophet (op. cit., 95). It should therefore come as no surprise that the author turns to mythological themes and figures to lend suitable expression to her/his experience. This, as Jung says, is not to be regarded as second-hand material in any way.

> On the contrary, the primordial experience is the source of his creativeness, but it is so dark and amorphous that it requires the related mythological imagery to give it form. In itself it is wordless and imageless, for it is a vision seen 'as in a glass, darkly'. It is nothing but a tremendous intuition striving for expression . . .
>
> The psychologist can do little to elucidate this variegated spectacle [of images] except provide comparative material and a terminology for its discussion. Thus, what appears in the vision is the imagery of the collective unconscious (op. cit., 96–97).

Given that the unconscious often compensates for the one-sidedness of consciousness, we may then ask a very important question: in what relation does the artist's work stand to the conscious attitude of her/his time, and could this relation also be regarded as compensatory (op. cit., 98)? Should the latter indeed be the case, the collective unconscious has become "a living experience" (ibid.). It is brought to bear "upon the conscious outlook of an age", manifesting itself in "a creative act which is of importance for *a whole epoch*" (ibid., my italics). Such a work of art may then "truthfully be called *a message to generations of men*" (ibid., my italics; cf. also op. cit., 66 and 83).

The artist who produces a visionary work "is not a person endowed with free will" (op. cit., 101); one who seeks her/his own ends. Consequently s/he may not realise the importance of her/his work vis-à-vis the society or epoch in which s/he lives (op. cit., 103, 104).

Rather, this artist is someone who is given over to the collective unconscious and who consequently allows art to achieve *its* ends in and through her/him. S/he is thus "the instrument of a collective creative power" (op. cit., 66; cf. also 130), and 'unconsciously' chooses to use those archetypal ideas that are best suited to coping with the conscious conditions of her/his time. The result is that her/his work "represents a process of *self-regulation in the life of nations and epochs*" (op. cit., 83, my italics).

> As a human being he may have moods and a personal will and aims, but as an artist he is a 'man' in a higher sense—he is 'collective man', a vehicle and moulder of the unconscious life of mankind. That is his office, and it is sometimes so heavy a burden that he is fated to sacrifice happiness and everything that makes life worth living for the ordinary human being (op. cit., 101).

Such an artist becomes "an especially interesting specimen for the critical analysis of the psychologist", and her/his art explains her/his psyche rather than the reverse (op. cit., 102):

> The creative process has a feminine quality, and the creative work arises from unconscious depths. . . . Whenever the creative force predominates, life is ruled and shaped by the unconscious rather than by the conscious will, and the ego is swept along on an underground current, becoming little more than a helpless observer of events. *The progress of the work becomes the poet's fate and determines his psychology. It is not Goethe that creates* Faust, *but* Faust *that creates Goethe* (op. cit., 103, my italics in both instances).

According to Jung, such a 'visionary artist' is caught in the tension between her/his ordinary desires and the creative process, resulting in her/his suffering for her/himself, her/his world, and the general spirit of her/his age, which is the "the very thing that opens his consciousness to those compensatory images and ideas that arise from the unconscious" (Jacoby, op. cit., 68).

Jung counted the *Shepherd of Hermas*, Dante's *Divina Commedia*, Goethe's *Faust* (Part II), Blake's drawings and poems, Hoffmann's images in *The Golden Pot*, and James Joyce's *Ulysses* amongst such visionary works. The last he honoured with the accolade of "a work of the greatest significance in spite of or perhaps because of its nihilistic tendencies" (Jung, op. cit., 91, n. 7).

b. *Jung's Answer to Job*

It is difficult to classify, categorise, or describe aptly Jung's monumental "Answer to Job"[1]—his only full-fledged 'commentary' on a biblical book. This twenty-part essay is, in the first instance, not a literary one. It is a deeply personal, very visceral psychological response to "the divine darkness which is unveiled in the Book of Job"—"a purely subjective reaction", as Jung himself has termed it—that might "act as a voice for many who feel the same way as I do, and . . . give expression to the shattering emotion which the unvarnished spectacle of divine savagery and ruthlessness produces in us" (Jung 1958:365–366 and 1986:309). Perhaps it is because of its very subjectivity and strange circumstance of origin that Jung found this alone of all his works "totally satisfying" (Rollins 1999:50). It came to him, he says, "as if accompanied by the great music of a Bach or a Handel", as if a "spirit" had seized him by the scruff of the neck and compelled him to do its will (ibid.). In this sense, then, it is an essay that must be experienced first and 'criticised' later. While this may be a difficult concept for some who have become accustomed to the 'sound reasonable arguments' of various historical or literary persuasions on this and other biblical texts, it certainly presents a novel and honest way of dealing with a very difficult text.

The title, "Answer to Job", is rather misleading. The content of the essay is not limited to Job alone, but incorporates Jung's understanding of a wide range of biblical topics, from the suffering of Job to the visions of Ezekiel, the relationship of the female Wisdom figure to God, the incarnation of God in Christ, Paul's experiences, and even the 1950 Papal Bull on the Assumption of Mary. These seemingly incompatible topics are moulded into a tight relationship by means of Jung's concept of the psyche and provide him with a startling but fresh 'answer' to Job's sufferings.

According to Jung, one may glean a startling harvest from God's dealings with Job as to the nature of God, man, and the problem of evil. He proposes, for example, that God did not consult His omniscience when he listened to Satan's voice; He was aware of

[1] Jung's "Answer to Job" was first published in 1952 and subsequently included in *The Collected Works*, volume 11, aptly entitled *Psychology and Religion: West and East*. Excerpts of this work may be found in Storr's 1986 edition of *Jung: Selected Writings* (Jung 1986:310–321, 321–329, 343–345).

Job's faithfulness but put him through untold and unnecessary misery because of the mere *possibility* that Job might be serving him for gain. God's "experiment" with "a powerless creature" shows that this God cared little for the ethical mores He expected his creatures to uphold (Jung 1958:370). This, in turn shows that God is an inner "antinomy" (op. cit., 369) the (self-) doubting, negative side of which He projects upon Job (op. cit., 380). His treatment of Job also shows that this God had very little self-awareness and that He was unconscious of Himself to a large degree (cf. op. cit., 371, 375, 378)—living in an unconscious state.

According to Jung, Job's insistence on bringing his case before God, "even without the hope of a hearing", creates "the very obstacle that force[s] God to reveal his true nature" (Jung 1986:312). Job effectively compels God to look at His own shadow-side, the Satan (op. cit., 315, 317) that He had hidden so deep in His bosom, and the only one who is able to influence Him sufficiently to transgress His own penal code. By confronting Yahweh with His own capriciousness and ruthless cruelty, Job brings about a change in His behaviour, and "stands morally higher than Yahweh" (op. cit., 309).

Jung (1958:367–377) further avers that Job gains a new understanding of God along these lines, but wisely gives no indication of it. Instead, he allows his demand for justice to be silenced by Yahweh's harangue on omnipotence, designed to convince no one other than Satan and Himself of His almighty power (op. cit., 378–379). This harangue shows that something has begun to stir in God's consciousness and that self-reflection has begun on the basis of Job's "moral victory" over God. This is when Jung announces his most startling 'revelation'. Job's 'victory' shows God that Job has a higher level of consciousness than Himself and that makes Him aware of the error of His ways. This creates in God the twofold desire to become man and to provide Job with some restitution, some 'answer'. "In this respect the creature has surpassed the creator" (Jung 1986:309).

God's desire to become man is prefigured in Ezekiel's visions of the Man (the Self) and the title "Son of Man" accorded to Ezekiel and Enoch (Jung 1966:383, 419–428). This desire, claims Jung, is fulfilled as God begins to remember His female counterpart and co-creatrix Sophia (op. cit., 386–399). It is His anamnesis of her that allows the birth of Christ and the news of God's goodwill towards mankind. Christ's new concept of God as a good and loving God represents God's desire to become 'good' and atone for His actions towards Job (cf. op. cit., 397–412). Eventually, this leads to a split in the antinomy, the original duality of God, whereby all that is evil is projected onto Satan and mankind, and all that is good is accorded to God (op. cit., 410, 454–455). This is the split, according to Jung, which is responsible for the giant *enantiodromaic* movement expressed in the Book of Revelation (cf. op. cit., 433–434, 435–452): the good God turns to mass destruction and few survive, while Satan, the one who truly deserves the punishment for sin, doubt, and evil, is never totally destroyed but locked up in his eternal abode forever.

Having thus expounded on the dual nature of God according to his reading of Job, Jung proceeds to examine the doctrine of Mary's bodily assumption (cf. op. cit., 461–470). Mary is hailed as the embodiment of Sophia, the female aspect of God. Jung believes that the elevation of Mary's bodily assumption to the level of a Catholic dogma (Pope Pius XII, November 1950) is "the most important religious event since the Reformation" in that it adds a fourth figure to the trinity, making it a quaternity (Jung 1986:321). This, then, unites all the conflicting aspects of God in a *hieros gamos* of the first degree and allows the goodness of God to be expressed concretely to those on earth once again.

c. *Jungian Approaches to biblical/Secular Literary Texts: General Considerations*

As can be seen from his discussion of psychology-and-literature, and his reading of Job, Jung had very little interest in the aesthetic value of literary texts/works of art (cf. Jung 1966:65, 66; Raine 1992:168). Rather, as an analytical psychologist, he was more concerned with the process of artistic creation (Jung, op. cit.), the psychological structure of artworks (Jung, op. cit., 86), the role of existential archetypes (cf. Frye 1992:35) and the exposition of "the basic experience" of human beings (Baird 1992:42, my italics). He has combined these last two aspects expertly in his reading of Job, which is, in many ways, typical of the way in which he reads other texts (e.g., the myth of Hiawatha). The result is a disturbingly frank account, which treats the God in Job as though He were any other subject of analysis, prone to unfulfilled dreams, projections, inconsistencies, dualities, personal growth (individuation), and the like. While I as a Christian cannot possibly agree with his findings, I am nevertheless amazed by the way in which he has applied his own psychoanalytic categories to this text.

Be that as it may, Jung did not found a school of literary criticism at any time, and there is no concrete Jungian method of reading texts. This aspect of literary/Jungian studies was later developed by both Jungian and non-Jungian critics and psychoanalysts whose work shows varying degrees of commitment to Jung and his work. These critics have identified the following general areas as suitable for Jungian psycho-literary activity: the text, the author, and the reader. This means that they have investigated, among others:

- The main archetypes, myths, symbols, and other expressions of the unconscious that form a particular text's/genre's psychological structure
- The way the text relates to (compensates/does not compensate) the conscious attitude of the time in which it was produced
- The text's psychological value for its readers
- The psychological relation between the author and her/his work
- The psychological relation between text and reader, and author and reader
- The psychology of reading
- The psychoanalytic profile of the characters
- The text's literary features (genre, etc.) as products of the author's/human psyche
- Language and psychology

Similarly, for scholars in the biblical field, the following issues have become representative of "the effective agenda that psychological biblical criticism has adopted to date" (Rollins, op. cit., 84–87):

1. Psychological interpretation of specific genres such as myth, legend, and apocalypse (cf. also op. cit., 116–121).
2. Psychological analysis of biblical personalities. This approach, popular in the first half of the twentieth century, presumed to deal with the 'actual' biblical personalities behind the biblical characters and thus became "the leading cause of estrangement between psychology and biblical studies" (op. cit., 85; cf. also 128–130 and Zeligs 1974).
3. Analysis of psychodynamic factors in biblical narrative and character. This approach analyses the literary constructs informing a narrative and attempts to identify one (or all) of the following: the psychodynamic aspects that make a story work, the origins of defining Western myths, and positive or negative models of human

behaviour. In the last instance, the characters are treated in their literary, non-historical capacity (cf. Rollins, op. cit., 123–127, 128–129. Cf. also Kille 1995:40–54).

4. Religious phenomena in biblical culture and cultus (cf. Rollins, op. cit., 121–123). "This ranges from research on totemic meals, circumcision, Eucharist, baptism, and women's religion, to prophetic inspiration and utterance and other psycho-spiritual experiential phenomena" which some have classified as "parapsychological" (op. cit., 85).
5. Dreams and dreaming. This is, essentially, a subdivision of the previous category. Nevertheless, it has received sufficient attention to stand on its own (cf. Watt 1995:55–70).
6. Psychological hermeneutics per se (cf. Rollins 1995:9–39).
7. Exegetical commentary from a psychological perspective. This category represents commentaries on entire Bible books that have been written from a psychological perspective.
8. Linguistics—"'patterns of the mind'" manifested "in language systems and speaking everywhere" (Rollins 1999:86).
9. Archaeology—using psychological categories to analyse artefacts.
10. Biblical psychology (cf. also op. cit., 139–144).
11. The use of the Bible in pastoral psychology and counselling (cf. also op. cit., 177–181).
12. The Bible's contribution to contemporary psychological theory and models of humanity.

The aspects that I am most interested in—perhaps because of my own psyche and/or stage of individuation—relate to a text's use of archetypes, its compensatory aspects, its psychological structure, its (possible) depiction of the individuation process, its mythopoeic qualities, and the psychology of its characters. I have been most intrigued by four works in particular, namely, the monographs by Engelsman and Edinger, Russo's reading of Homer's Odysseus according to the trickster archetype, and Terrence Dawson's theories regarding the effective protagonist. I should like very briefly to discuss these works and indicate their importance for/influence upon my own, before proceeding to my own methodological interpretation. I have chosen to discuss Dawson's theories in a separate section, as his work, in combination with Jung's method of dream analysis, has been the most formative for my own methodological approach.

d. *The Work of Engelsman, Russo, and Edinger*

Engelsman 1994: Sophia and Feminine Images in Religion
In her monograph *The Feminine Dimension of the Divine. A Study of Sophia and Feminine Images in Religion*, Engelsman marries the then-available research on Sophia with the psychoanalytical approaches of Jung and Freud—primarily the former—in order to "open up aspects of theology that have been hidden" (op. cit., 7). She contends that Western Judaeo-Christian religious tradition has repressed the feminine principle of the divine in favour of the masculine one, citing clear examples of the repression of Sophia in the Old and the New Testaments (op. cit., 74–94, 106–118) and Philo (op. cit., 95–105). She also traces the way in which this repressed feminine image has returned in the form of the Mariology of the Roman Catholic Church, only to be repressed again. According to Engelsman, Mary's repression as a feminine symbol takes place on at least two levels:

i) Her hypostatisation as *the* virgin, *the* submissive woman, and so forth puts her beyond the reach of ordinary women.
ii) The Catholic Church has allowed only the positive aspects of her feminine archetype to resurface, once again putting her beyond the reach of ordinary women who are not only good.

This excellent monograph constitutes my first exposure (1995) to Jung's theories and their application to biblical texts (see my paper entitled "Sexual Politics and the Power of Wisdom", Efthimiadis 1995:1–25). Engelsman's study is thorough, clear, and sufficiently detailed, bearing lucid testimony to the way in which Jungian theory may facilitate a better understanding of various biblical texts, theological constructs, and phenomena. It has thrown light on the complex nature of the Wisdom figure in Proverbs, Ecclesiasticus, and the Wisdom of Solomon, demonstrating that all her (Sophia's) contradictory aspects are an essential part of the anima archetype. It has also helped to clarify the relation between the 'Strange/Foreign Woman' and Sophia, by analysing the two (three?) figures as complementary but split-off aspects of the Great Mother archetype of which the anima is a part. In terms of the current study, Engelsman's work has doubtlessly influenced my understanding of Judith not only as an anima figure, but also as an expression of Sophia herself. The latter is something that I hope to take up, albeit in a very limited manner, in the ensuing analysis of *Judith*.

Russo 1997: Homer's Odysseus as Trickster

In "A Jungian Analysis of Homer's Odysseus", Russo (1997:240–254) sets out to analyse Homer's Odysseus according to the trickster archetype. This figure is symbolic of a rather archaic or animal level of undifferentiated consciousness that is prone to "intense expressions of libido, gluttony, and physical abuse" (Russo, op. cit., 243; cf. also Jung 1959a:260). It contains the "unsocialised, infantile, and unacceptable aspects of the self" (Russo, op. cit., 242) and is closely related to the shadow (cf. Jung, op. cit., 270). S/he is both the subject and often the object of silly pranks, as well as the master of disguise and shape changing. This latter aspect speaks to the transformative capability of this archetype, which allows her/him to change situations and so possibly bring 'salvation' and meaning (cf. op. cit., 263).

Russo (op. cit., 247–248) demonstrates that Homer's Odysseus displays many characteristics of the trickster archetype and traces these through his lineage to his great-grandfather, Hermes. The latter is a well-known trickster. He is also the patron deity of travellers, crossroads, traders, and interpreters, and of transactions and interchange, in which Odysseus engages many a time. Strangely enough, however, Hermes is not presented as Odysseus' patron deity and help. Rather, his patron is Athena, the goddess of *metis*—clever wisdom or "cunning intelligence" (op. cit., 247). Given this 'modification', Russo believes that 'Homer' consciously substituted the 'good goddess' Athena for the highly ambivalent Hermes in order to play down the 'original' Odysseus' negative traits and associations, and so "elevate him to epic standards" (op. cit., 250).

Russo's work not only allows "the archetype underneath the mortal hero" (op. cit., 252) to emerge, but clearly shows how archetypes/archetypal images may be modified to suit the needs of the author who uses them and/or the age in which s/he writes.

While my own preliminary study (Efthimiadis-Keith 1999b:151–169) did not unearth any archetypal "tricksters" lurking in the text of *Judith*, Russo's work brought home to me, with greater force, the transformative abilities of the shadow archetype and confirmed my suspicion that the author of a particular story is not the blind instrument of the (collective) unconscious as Jung assumes. Homer's conscious modification of the traditional trickster archetype in the way that he portrays Odysseus is a clear indication of that. These important aspects of Russo's work have assisted me to formulate a more informed view of the character Achior, about whom I was completely uncertain when I compiled my preliminary study (to the extent that I did not deal with him at all). They have facilitated my understanding of the way in which the author of *Judith* has split the shadow archetype into its negative and positive components through the characters of Holofernes and Achior, respectively.

Edinger 1986: Individuation Symbolism in the Old Testament

In fifteen chapters that deal with various subjects ranging from "Beginnings" (Edinger 1986:15–24) to "Messiah: The Self Realized" (op. cit., 147–161), Edinger demonstrates that the Bible is full of individuation symbolism. For example, he shows that the three kings of the united monarchy may be seen as representations of successive stages of ego development. Saul is said to represent the first stage of "ego-kingship in which the ego inevitably identifies with the archetypal authority granted it" (op. cit., 81–82). This identification results in inflation that ultimately causes him the loss of both his kingship and his sanity. David represents the second stage of ego development in which identification with unconscious contents and the resultant inflation have been overcome (op. cit., 82). Furthermore, David's story is characterised by many pairings in which he has ample opportunity to deal with 'the other' (op. cit., 84). This "reminds us of the fact that consciousness is a product of the number two. Number one is the ego; number two is the unconscious, the other, which generates awareness of the opposites; and number three is the consciousness that grows out of the conflict between one and two. David as king number two manifests the symbolic implications of that number" (ibid.). Similarly, Solomon, the third king, manifests the symbolic implications of the number three—"the consciousness that grows out of the conflict between one and two" (ibid.). This, Edinger intimates, is depicted in the glory of his reign and the wisdom symbolism connected to him. The Messiah, the symbol of the Self who is otherwise known as 'the Son of David', is then interpretable as "a product or consequence of the second-stage ego" (op. cit., 91–92). His double parentage—he is the son of both God and David—"suggests that the Self consciously realized (Messiah) is begotten by *both* the original Self [i.e., God] and the ego [i.e., David]" (op. cit., 150, his italics).

Edinger's monograph (*The Bible and the Psyche: Individuation Symbolism in the Old Testament*) is an excellent depiction of the interdependence of Scripture and psychology (see, e.g., his interpretation of the Messiah).

As a study on individuation, his work has been invaluable for my own, which seeks to understand *Judith*, inter alia as an individuation drama. It has given me great insight into both the Bible and the process of individuation. It has also helped me to form a clearer understanding of the causes and results of inflation, which I shall apply to the characters of Holofernes and Nebuchadnezzar in chapter 5.

e. *Terrence Dawson's Effective Protagonist*

In his essay entitled "Jung, Literature, and Literary Criticism", Dawson (op. cit., 256–257) focuses his attention upon the first best-seller of English literature, Samuel Richardson's *Pamela.* This book is presented in the form of letters or journal entries that concern Pamela's hardships as a fifteen-year-old maidservant in the house of Mr. B. After his mother's death, Mr. B. imposes himself on Pamela at every opportunity with increasing violence even though he appeared to be the 'perfect gentleman' in former times. Dawson makes the astute observation that Pamela may not be the story's protagonist from a psychological point of view. Drawing upon Jung's concept of the dream ego—the one personality in a dream who best represents the dreamer's unconscious personality (op. cit., 257)—Dawson suggests that a psychoanalytic reading should focus on the text's *effective protagonist.* This is the person who undergoes the most change in the story and to whom all the events in the narrative may be related (ibid.). In the case of *Pamela,* Mr. B. is the effective protagonist (op. cit., 259). Throughout the story, Pamela unwittingly but directly challenges his views of society, especially his idea that high-society women are loose and immoral. By refusing to succumb to his advances, Pamela forces Mr. B. to change from the arrogant ladies' man of high society to her husband, despite his sister's protestations (op. cit., 260). He even accepts responsibility for his illegitimate daughter towards the end of the story because Pamela takes her in. In other words, Pamela's refusal to become his mistress forces him to come to terms with the values she represents, her view on relationships, his view on women, his identification with both his status and his shadow side after his mother's death, and his role in society (cf. op. cit., 261–263). It is clear, then, that Pamela represents both the Eros principle with which Mr. B. is unacquainted and his anima—note the intensity with which he pursues her. Her constant refusal leads him to a (slightly) higher plane of consciousness or individuation even though he only partially integrates his unconscious shadow contents; he never deals with the harm he had brought upon Pamela while he pursued her. By contrast, Pamela remains the same throughout, undergoing a change only in marital and societal status. Furthermore, it is Mr. B., and not Pamela, who makes the important decisions in the story. Mr. B. is therefore the story's effective protagonist, and not Pamela who may be described as the 'obvious heroine'. The surface structure concerning Pamela's experiences may then be seen as a projection of the story's deeper structure, i.e., the events viewed in relation to Mr. B. (cf. op. cit., 257). These, in turn, reflect a dilemma confronting the effective protagonist at the outset (for which see below) and describe the way this character deals with the challenges implicit in the dilemma (ibid.).

Having concluded his textual analysis, Dawson proceeds to test his findings against what is known about *Pamela's* author, Samuel Richardson. The question is whether we can identify Mr. B. with Richardson (op. cit., 263). Dawson believes that we can, but cautions that we must specify the nature of any parallels that we may adduce, as the effective protagonist does not reflect the totality of Richardson's character, but only certain aspects of his unconscious personality (op. cit., 264).

Richardson was reportedly commissioned to compose a 'letter writer' that would assist young ladies in elegant correspondence. Nevertheless, he became so absorbed by what a young maidservant might write to her parents concerning her work hardships that he soon abandoned the letter writer and completed the 500-page manuscript in two months, at night, after returning home from a hard day's work at a printer's (ibid.). As Dawson observes, Richardson's absorption in the subject-matter of *Pamela* and his speedy completion of the story reflects the process of active imagination, whereby the analysand seeks to integrate unconscious contents through consciously entering into and participating in waking visions. His fascination with 'Pamela'—akin to Mr. B.'s—represents a clear case of anima possession in both Richardson and his effective protagonist. Given that Mr. B. is able neither to differentiate nor integrate his shadow tendencies throughout the course of *Pamela* (cf. op. cit., 261), we may adduce that this was an issue which Richardson himself had not dealt with at the time. The fact that Mr. B.'s inability to integrate his shadow elements causes domestic squabbles in *Pamela: Part Two*, and that the same issues are raised again in *Clarissa*, corroborates this assumption, i.e., that Richardson himself remained largely unconscious of his shadow side (op. cit., 265). Mr. B. may thus be seen as a personification of Richardson's unconscious personality (his dream ego, as it were), with the former's good and bad sides representing the latter's persona and shadow side respectively. The entire story may then be regarded as "a projected representation of a dilemma facing . . . Richardson at the time of writing" (ibid.; cf. further op. cit., 265–266). This dilemma naturally contributes towards the text's dominant psychological concern, a subject that Dawson addresses in the next part of his essay ("Toward a Theory of Literary Consciousness"; op. cit., 266–275).

According to Dawson, the text's dominant psychological concern is intimately connected to the self-awareness of the effective protagonist on the one hand, and the dilemma facing the author on the other. The correlation of these factors is to be expected as the effective protagonist symbolises the author's dominant unconscious personality. For Dawson, determining the effective protagonist's level of self-awareness may be achieved by relating her/his psychological profile/activities to Jung's five stages of consciousness (op. cit., 267, 274).

Having submitted Mr. B.'s character to this further step of analysis, Dawson avers that *Pamela's* chief psychological concern lies between Stages 3 and 4, i.e., between moral or ethical dilemma (the differentiation of moral properties) and social reality/individual consciousness (the realisation of social reality and individual consciousness), respectively. In other words, no definite 'ego' has as yet been formed (op. cit., 269). This corroborates Dawson's previous findings that Mr. B.'s dilemma stems from his inability to differentiate and integrate his shadow elements, differentiation of shadow tendencies being the first step towards the conscious awareness of one's own individual identity. Thus, it may confidently be said that "[t]he novel illustrates a phase in the evolution of consciousness immediately prior to the differentiation of the shadow as separate from the 'ego'" (op. cit., 265).

In his third and final section ("Toward a Psychological History of Literature"), Dawson applies Jung's five stages of consciousness to the dominant concerns of the various phases in literary history as such. He points out the following correspondences (op. cit., 270–273. Please note: Dawson's name for each stage is accompanied by the name I accorded it in chapter 2):

1. Identity in itself (Complete identification with societal norms and expectations)—"oral traditions and very early myths" (op. cit., 270).
2. Identity in relation to an other/others (Separation from the 'other')—specific adaptations of oral culture such as *The Iliad.*

   Moral or ethical dilemma (The differentiation of moral properties)—Greek tragedies, but more especially the literature of the late Middle Ages and the Renaissance, e.g., Augustine's Confessions, Dante's Divine Comedy.
3. Social reality/individual consciousness (Realisation of social reality and individual consciousness)—Literature concerned with the exploration of both social reality and individual consciousness is a relatively recent phenomenon, making its advent "from about the third quarter of the seventeenth century when the collective projection represented by the Christian 'worldview' gradually began to break apart. . . . The apparently conflicting aspects of this fourth stage are perhaps best illustrated by the works of French philosopher Jean Jacques Rousseau" (op. cit., 271).
4. Individual identity (Individual identity or self-realisation)—this stage has not been reached as yet.

Based on the above, he avers that modern literature, which is predominantly concerned with the exploration of both social reality and individual consciousness, may be placed at the fourth level of consciousness.

Dawson completes his essay with an erudite assessment of "Jungian" literary criticism. He asserts that this mode of literary analysis is over-dependent on archetypal images without making any distinction between the kinds of archetypal imagery found in a text (op. cit., 274). In order to overcome this lack of distinction, Dawson advocates that archetypal material should also be related to the five stages of consciousness (ibid.) and that specific Jungian archetypal images be differentiated further. For example, Jung referred to *the* shadow by which he designates both the totality of the unconscious and the hidden aspects of oneself. These need to be differentiated in analysis. Furthermore, Jungian criticism should also differentiate between the collective and the personal aspects of the archetype. As he points out, there is a radical difference between the collective shadow figures found in literature written prior to the eighteenth century and the personal shadow in post-Enlightenment works (ibid.).

Dawson's essay takes seriously the strengths and weaknesses of "Jungian" literary criticism and applies the insights gained beyond the analysis of literary texts to considerations of the author's relation to the text, the text's dominant psychological concern, and the history of literature itself. By beginning with the textual analysis and only then proceeding to test his findings against what is known of the author and her/his times, he avoids the trap of turning art into a neurosis, as Jung has termed it (cf. Jung 1966:92). This, in combination with his interest in the identity of the effective protagonist, the text's deep structure, and its dominant psychological concern, constitutes a vital contribution to "Jungian" literary criticism, and offers a well-argued corrective to a blind application of Jungian concepts to literary texts.

Next to Jung's method of dream analysis, Dawson's work has undoubtedly had the greatest impact on my own. Together, they form the dominant methodological thrust of my own approach.

B. *Jung and* Judith: *The Methodological Approach of the Current Study*

As indicated above, Dawson's approach rests upon the identification of the effective protagonist. Schematically his method may be represented as follows:

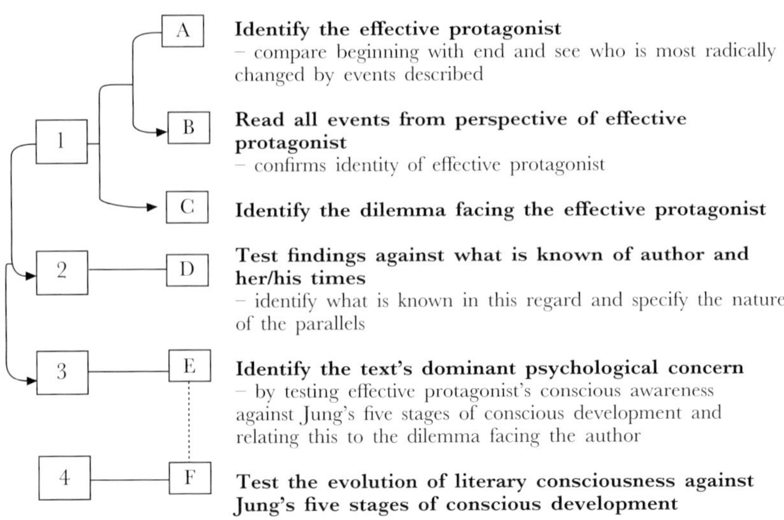

Diagram 8. Dawson's Method of Jungian Analysis[2]

[2] Block F is effectively an addendum to Dawson's essay, in that it does not form

Dawson's method of analysing literary texts bears many affinities with Jung's method of analysing dreams. Not least of these is the fact that he bases his concept of the effective protagonist on Jung's concept of the dream ego. Furthermore, having identified the effective protagonist (Block A), Dawson's first step (Block 1) consists of reading all the events in the story from the perspective of this character (Block B), and identifying the dilemma facing her/him (Block C). This step clearly relates to Jung's subjective mode of analysis (Block S, below), which analyses the dream images as complexes relating to the dreamer herself/himself. Similarly, Dawson's second step (Block 2), which tests the findings of Step 1 according to what is known of the author and her/his times (Block D), corresponds to Jung's objective mode of analysis (Block O, below) which relates the dream images to the dreamer's external world.[3] Dawson's third step (Block 3/E) corresponds in part to both modes of Jungian dream analysis in that discerning the text's dominant psychological concern is dependant upon the effective protagonist's self-awareness (subjective analysis) on the one hand, and the dilemma facing the author on the other (objective analysis).

Taking the above into consideration, we see that Dawson reverses the order of Jungian dream analysis in his first two steps—he conducts the subjective analysis before proceeding to the 'objective' one—and then extrapolates the results of both onto the level of the text in order to determine its dominant psychological concern:

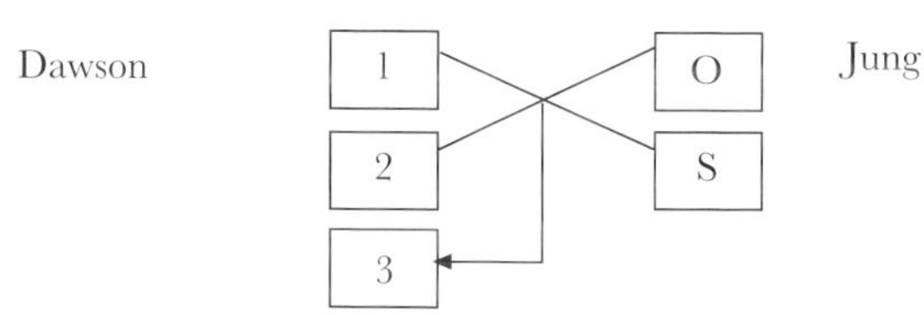

Diagram 9. The Relation between the Theories of Dawson and Jung

an integral part of his "Jungian" reading of *Pamela*. (This is depicted by the dotted line connecting it to Block E to which it is related on account of Jung's stages of conscious development). Hence, it will not be taken into consideration in the discussion below.

[3] Dawson never mentions Jung's modes of analysis that I have referred to here, nor does he ever relate his work to them. It is I who have drawn the correlation.

In my opinion, Dawson's 'reversal' of Jung's method makes far better methodological sense when dealing with texts in general, because it begins with what we have immediately in front of us, i.e., the text with its (discernable) effective protagonist, and only then moves to factors outside the text such as the author and her/his times. This reflects the same basic route that I followed in my preliminary analysis of *Judith* (Efthimiadis-Keith 1999b). His reversal makes even greater methodological sense when dealing with a text like *Judith* whose author is completely unknown and whose date of composition is unclear. Even so, these two factors—the lack of clarity regarding authorship and date of composition—make it difficult to test the results of the analysis (Blocks A–C) against what is known of the author (Block D) *before* identifying the text's dominant psychological concern (Block E). I therefore propose to alter Dawson's method slightly in order to take these factors into account:

a) I will examine the effective protagonist's level of conscious awareness during my analysis of each character in *Judith* (see below). The ensuing subjective analysis will then enable me to conduct an interim situational analysis:
   i) Draw some (albeit tentative) broad conclusions concerning the author of the text—or, at least, the socioreligious circle to which s/he belonged—and the times in which s/he lived by extrapolating my findings to a hypothetical external environment.
   ii) Test my own theories regarding the date of *Judith* against the results.

The above will, in turn, enable me to:
c) Conduct the objective analysis.
d) Identify the text's dominant psychological concern.

Having concluded the subjective and objective analyses of the Judithic dream, I should then like to test my hypothesis that *Judith* is an individuation drama against the results of these analyses and the patterns of individuation that Jung discerned in Gnostic-mythological material. I will subsequently be in a better position to deliberate about the psychological function of *Judith* at this time and at the time during which the gloss (16:23) was added (possibly after Pompey's attack on Jerusalem in 63 B.C.). This, in turn, will assist me to determine the psychological function of *Judith's* inconsistencies, its bipartite structure, and the characters Judith and Achior—something that is sorely lacking in the approaches that I have discussed in chapter

1. I will then proceed to evaluate the analysis and the conclusions drawn.

Combining Dawson's approach to texts with Jung's approach to dreams will necessarily entail the amplification of dream images as an integral part of the subjective analysis. However, for the sake of brevity, I shall refrain from a detailed discussion of such things. Rather, I should prefer to take up this part of Jung's subjective analysis within the course of identifying the effective protagonist and not in a separate section. As *Judith* is a biblical text and not a person, amplification will then be achieved by means of intertextual parallels with other biblical material known to me.

My proposed modification of Dawson's method may be represented as follows:

A SUBJECTIVE ANALYSIS

Seeing that *Judith* has a definite bipartite structure, and Jung dictates that dream images should be analysed in the order of their appearance, I will:

α1 Apply Jungian psychological categories to each character found in Section I (*Judith* 1–7) in order of their appearance, so as to determine the effective protagonist of this section.

α2 Determine the dilemma facing him (there are only male characters in Section I).

α3 Summarise and conclude on the findings of α1 and α2.

α4 Apply Jungian psychological categories to each character found in Section II (*Judith* 8–16) in order of their appearance, so as to determine the effective protagonist of this section.

α5 Determine the dilemma facing her/him.

α6 Summarise and conclude on the findings of α4 and α5.

α7 Identify the effective protagonist of the entire tale, or "the Judithic dream" (as I have come to call *Judith*).

α8 Conduct a subjective analysis of the material from her/his point of view.

β **AN INTERIM SITUATIONAL ANALYSIS**

β1 Extrapolate findings onto hypothetical context

β2 Test my own hypothesis regarding the date of Judith

Γ **AN OBJECTIVE ANALYSIS**

Δ **THE RELATION BETWEEN THE SUBJECTIVE AND OBJECTIVE ANALYSES—THE TEXT'S DOMINANT PSYCHOLOGICAL CONCERN**

E ***JUDITH* AS AN INDIVIDUATION DRAMA**

Z **THE PSYCHOLOGICAL FUNCTION OF *JUDITH'S* 'IRREGULARITIES'**

H **AN EVALUATION OF THE COMPLETED ANALYSIS**

CHAPTER FIVE

THE ENEMY IS WITHIN—A JUNGIAN PSYCHOANALYTIC PERSPECTIVE ON *JUDITH*

In this chapter, I should like to analyse *Judith* as a national dream depicting the Jewish nation's stage of individuation at the time in which the book was written (c. 88 B.C.). This implies that *Judith* will be regarded as an unconscious communication stemming from the national Jewish psyche or soul. Seeing *Judith* as a picture of the national soul is justified by Jung's theory concerning dreams and various elements of the book itself:

- As we have seen, dreams are the principal mode of unconscious communication. They share their 'irrational' nature with other unconscious expressions such as myths, fables, and legends. While dreams/myths usually reflect the dreamer's/hero's unconscious psyche and state of individuation, there are also what Jung calls the 'big dreams', which hold important portents for the dreamer's nation/tribe. It is therefore possible for certain myths/fables/legends to reflect the unconscious world of the nation from which they stem.
- *Judith*, a clearly fictitious myth or legend, is just such an unconscious communication (cf. Efthimiadis-Keith 1999b:154). It is filled with the kind of 'irrationality' and 'duality' that one finds in dreams: historical and geographical anachronisms, military forces of exaggerated magnitude, improbable journeys, intense emotional ladenness, and an 'improbable' but powerful heroine who is imbued with a duality that has proved disconcerting to many of her ancient and modern commentators. (She is both a pious, chaste, wise 'saint' and a deceptive murderer who does not hesitate to lie and to use her sexuality to decapitate Holofernes). The combination of these elements is what I have referred to as *Judith's* mythopoeic qualities.
- Furthermore, the book clearly deals with a national crisis and Judith may easily be regarded as a female personification of the nation itself—not least because her name means "Jewess." (The

Bible often characterises the nation as female in its relation to YHWH. Cf., e.g. Ezekiel 16).

- We have also seen that *Judith* is an individuation drama. This is evident both in the structure of the book and in the adventures of its heroine which closely follow the pattern of the hero's quest and the night sea journey—*the* myth(s) of individuation, according to Jung.

Judith may thus justifiably be seen as a dream reflecting the Jewish nation's stage of individuation at the time in which it was written. Viewing *Judith* in this way and subjecting it to Jung's method of dream analysis in conjunction with Dawson's method of identifying a text's effective protagonist allows me to interpret the text and each character in it on a number of different interactive levels:

a) According to the objective mode of analysis, Judaean characters refer to Judaean people, while Gentile characters refer to Gentile people. (As we have seen, this is the premise upon which the pseudonym theories are based).
b) According to the subjective mode of analysis, each character—whether Judaean or not—represents an aspect of the Jewish psyche. Furthermore, each character represents someone within Judaean society at the time in which the book was written. This means that each character may be analysed both as a person and as a psychological content of the collective Jewish psyche. This, in turn, means that the psychological functionality of any particular character and her/his individuation is dependent not only on what s/he does and says, but also on the totality of psychic processes pertaining to consciousness/the unconscious. Furthermore, these processes are defined by the subjective position of 'the Judaean nation' as the subject of the dream. Thus, for example, Achior's eviction from the Assyrian camp is defined not only by the anger he causes Holofernes, but also by the Judaeans' conscious connection to the Self.
c) Following on from point a), the book reflects the external struggle(s) of the Judaean nation at the time in which it was written.
d) Following on from point b), *Judith* reflects the internal struggle(s) facing the Judaean nation at the time in which the book was written. *Judith* therefore represents both the struggle(s) between various Jewish factions/sectors *and* those within the collective Jewish

psyche as a whole. In this sense, then, 'the enemy is within' because the inimical Gentile characters are unconscious manifestations of the Jewish psyche just as much as the book's Judaean characters are.

e) While each character represents an aspect of the Jewish psyche, Dawson's research indicates that it is a tale's effective protagonist who carries the dominant unconscious personality of the dreamer. Therefore, in order to determine the nation's state of individuation as per the Book of Judith, I must first identify its effective protagonist and establish her/his stage of individuation and the dilemma facing her/him. The subjective analysis of the Judithic dream will then be focalised through her/him.

Seeing that *Judith* has two distinct (but not completely separate) parts, *Judith* 1–7 (Section I) and *Judith* 8–16 (Section II), I will attempt to determine the effective protagonist of each of these sections and analyse the dilemma that s/he faces before attempting to do the same for the entire story. Maintaining the bipartite structure of the book will assist me to manage its contents. I should further like to follow Jung's injunction of noting when and how each character or aspect of the 'dream' is introduced. I will therefore analyse each character/group of characters in the order of their appearance both as people and as psychological/archetypal contents. For practical reasons, I will refer only to the most important intertextual associations in my analysis of the characters and the events involved and I will eschew discussions of minute details, focusing only on those that I regard as the most vital for my interpretation of the text. Naturally, this process will be informed by the workings of my own unconscious psyche as much as by the knowledge of such parallels that I may consciously possess. Thus, the parallels drawn will also reflect my own psychic needs—as indeed the entire book does. The personal aspect of this work will be explored in chapter 6.

I believe that my work will not only demonstrate that Jungian theory can provide a holistic lens through which to view all aspects of the text, but also prove *Judith's* essential integrity as defined by the function of all the diverse elements present in it. In other words, I believe that my analysis will demonstrate that the inconsistencies in *Judith*, its bipartite structure, the duality of Judith, and the character of Achior are intentional (deliberate), integral aspects of the text, which contribute to the book's functionality at the time in which it was written and beyond.

I begin with a brief résumé of *Judith* as a point of orientation. Thereafter I will follow the contours of the analysis as sketched in chapter 4. The evaluation will follow in chapter 6.

A. Judith: *A Concise Summary of the Basic Story*[1]

The story of *Judith* begins in the twelfth year of Nebuchadnezzar, king of Assyria, in the days of Arphaxad, king of the Medes who reigned in Ecbatane (1:1–2). Arphaxad's high and mighty towered walls are torn down and his city is destroyed by the military power of Nebuchadnezzar's forces in the seventeenth year of the latter's reign. Nebuchadnezzar obliterates Arphaxad's forces, takes command of his towers and puts his people to the sword (1:14). Thereafter, at the end of chapter 1, he goes home to feast with his troops (1:16).

Chapter 2, set in the eighteenth year of Nebuchadnezzar's reign, begins with "talk" in his house to the effect that he should avenge himself on those nations who had disparaged him in the previous chapter. He had sent word that they should join him in his foray against Arphaxad but they had refused, "for they were not afraid of him, but looked upon him as only one man" (1:11; 2:1). Nebuchadnezzar summons his chieftains and relates "his secret plan" after which it is decided that, "every one who had not obeyed his command should be destroyed" (2:3). Thereupon the Assyrian king summons Holofernes, his chief general, and mandates him to annihilate all those who will not yield themselves to him and to keep captive for their day of judgment those who do (2:5–11). Holofernes' obedience is recorded from the time that he leaves Nebuchadnezzar's presence to prepare for war (2:14) to the point where the Judaeans hear of the carnage that follows in his wake (4:1). Temples and places of worship are torn down, fields are burned, people are killed, the towns are pillaged, and the very best men are drafted into an ever-burgeoning Assyrian war machine. The most interesting aspect of this carnage is Holofernes' seemingly self-proclaimed mandate "to

[1] The present outline follows largely the contours presented at various points throughout my 1999a and 1999b articles. I do, however, include the involvement of Achior, Judith's trusted stewardess, and Bagoas, which I had omitted then owing to the spatial constraints of an article.

destroy all the gods of the land, so that all nations should worship Nebuchadnezzar only, and all their tongues and tribes should call upon him as god" (3:8).

Having heard of what Holofernes had done amongst the Gentiles and how he had destroyed all their holy places, the Judaeans become gripped with fear for Jerusalem and its temple as they had just returned from captivity and consecrated those items that had been defiled (4:1–3). They alert other key cities in their province, take possession of the high mountains, fortify the towns in them, and gather provisions for war (4:4–5). Upon the command of Joachim, the high priest, those in Bethuliah, Bethomasthaim, and others near the plain of Esdraelon take control of the mountain passes by which entry might be gained into Judaea (4:6–8). The whole community then humbles itself before God and cries out for protection and salvation (4:9–15). As the story progresses, the Bethulians' cries reach a fever pitch of desperation in accordance with the increasing threat that Holofernes and his forces pose (cf. 6:14–21; 7:19–29). Being citizens of the city closest to his marauding forces, they are first to come under attack. Holofernes cuts off the fountain from which the Bethulians draw water (7:16–17) and his allies encamp right around them, blocking every way of escape (7:18–19). Seized by fear, they cry out to God again, yet without faith. They despair, believing that they have sinned against God and that God has delivered them into the Assyrians' hands (7:25, 28). They blame Ozias, their governor, for having encouraged 'rebellion' against the Assyrians and command him to hand them over to their enemy so that they may live as Holofernes' slaves rather than perish (7:24–29). Ozias persuades the people to wait five more days. Should God not bring about deliverance within the specified period, he will do as they say (7:30–32). So ends what has commonly been regarded as the first section of *Judith*, chapters 1–7.

Returning to the Assyrian camp, we find Holofernes rather indignant at the Judaeans' battle preparations. He calls his military leaders together and inquires of them concerning this 'insolent' nation (cf. 5:1–4). Achior, "the leader of all the Ammonites" (5:5), steps forward and offers Holofernes a relatively accurate historical account of the Jewish nation from the time of Abraham to the temple's destruction (5:5–21). Achior's account, intended to dissuade Holofernes from attacking the Jews without first ascertaining their guilt before YHWH (5:20–21), elicits the ire of all those present (5:22–24). He is evicted from the Assyrian camp and left tied at the bottom of Bethuliah's mountain (6:10–11, 13). Holofernes promises that Achior would see the destruction of the Jews first before experiencing their fate for himself (cf. 6:1–9). Achior is subsequently 'rescued' by the Bethulians who honour him with a banquet for the information he imparts regarding Holofernes' plans (6:14–17, 19–20). They pray to God in all earnest for deliverance once again (6:18, 20).

The second section of the book (*Judith* 8–16) begins with an introduction to its eponymous heroine, Judith. Judith is depicted as a highly religious, God-fearing, beautiful, wise, and chaste widow who has lived in a tent above her house since her husband's rather ignominious death three years previously (Manasseh, we are told, died of heat stroke whilst overseeing the binding of sheaves during the harvest. Cf. 8:1–8). Upon hearing "the wicked words spoken by the people against the ruler" and what Ozias had purposed, she summons the elders of her people and chastises them for the way in which they are testing God through their five-day ultimatum (8:9–12). She teaches them that God is sovereign even as His will is sovereign (8:13–16), and encourages them to "wait for his deliverance" for none in their age had worshipped foreign gods (8:17–20). She also encourages them to stand firm for their brethren's sake and to realise that if their city, Bethuliah, is taken then the whole country will be destroyed—including the temple (8:21–23). As a final point of persuasion, she asks them to recall the sufferings of Abraham, Isaac, and Jacob, urging that they (the Bethulians) should continue waiting upon God for His deliverance as they had not been tested to the extent that these patriarchs had (8:25–27). Instead of merely praying for rain on the people's behalf, as Ozias requests (8:28–31), Judith embarks on a secretive course of action, declaring that the Lord will deliver the enemy into her hand within the specified five-day period (8:32–34). Not knowing her plans, Ozias and the elders/magistrates bid her to go with their blessing and return to their wards (8:35–36).

After an extensive prayer for empowerment (9:1–14) in which she likens herself to Dinah's avengers, Judith bathes, perfumes herself, and discards her widow's attire (10:1–4). Dressed to kill—she "made herself very beautiful, to entice the eyes of all men who might see her" (10:4)—she obtains the leaders' admiration and blessing and sets off to the enemy camp. Her trusted housekeeper accompanies her, carrying a bag of 'kosher' food that Judith had packed, as the people of Bethuliah look on in amazement (cf. 10:5–10). Upon arriving at the Assyrian camp, Judith and her maid are encountered by a group of Assyrian soldiers. Judith declares her allegiance to Holofernes and proclaims that she has come "to give . . . a true report" that would help the Assyrian general to become master of the entire hill country without the loss of a single soul amongst his forces (cf. 10:11–13). The soldiers, and indeed everyone in the camp, marvel at her beauty. They counsel her not to fear but to speak plainly to their lord, who would 'treat her well' (10:14–16). Thereupon no less than a hundred soldiers escort her to Holofernes' tent (cf. 10:17–20). Having been admitted into Holofernes' presence, she falls before him in mock subservience. She declares that she has fled the Judaeans who have sinned against YHWH and would most certainly be destroyed. She has therefore come to assist her 'lord' who will surely succeed if he follows her words (10:23–11:19). Holofernes is overjoyed. He grants her request to eat her own 'kosher' food and to exit the camp each evening for prayer (and bathing), little knowing that this is (or will become) part of her plan for his demise (cf. 11:20–12:9).

The crucial scene takes place four days later when Holofernes, dumb-struck and overcome with lust, 'vows' to seduce Judith, fearing that she would mock him should he fail to do so (12:11–12, 16). He commands his eunuch, Bagoas, to invite Judith to a private banquet (12:10), with the intent of taking advantage of her once all the servants leave. When the servants exit the tent, however, the tables are soon turned. Judith takes advantage of his drunken stupor, prays to God for assistance, and severs his head by striking it twice with his own sword (cf. 12:20; 13:1–10). She escapes—undetected—under the pretext of her prayer habit and returns to Bethuliah where all its citizens valorise her (13:10–20). She commands that the dreaded Holofernes' head be mounted on a pole outside the city. After establishing battle plans for the final destruction of the Assyrians (14:1–4), she commands that Achior be summoned to verify the identity of the severed head (14:5). He does so by fainting when he sees it (14:6). When he comes to, he falls at Judith's feet and asks her to recount all her deeds to him (14:7–8). The people rejoice and Achior converts to Judaism after being circumcised (14:9–10).

When the Assyrians see the Judaeans coming down the mountain in (mock) attack, they send Bagoas to rouse their lord. He soon discovers what has happened, and Holofernes' men flee in terror as a result (14:12–15:3). Judith commands her countrymen to pursue, which they do, routing many and taking great booty (cf. 14:2–5; 15:4–11). After receiving the highest praise from the High Priest and all the people (especially the women who welcome her as a great battle victor, cf. 15:8–12), Judith sings an extensive praise/victory song to YHWH (16:1–17). She falls down before her real Lord in worship (cf. 16:18 and 10:23) and dedicates her share of the spoils to YHWH (16:19). She then returns to her tent (16:21). The text tells us that she lived to the ripe old age of 105, that she refused all suitors, set her handmaid free, and distributed her goods amongst the poor (16:22–23). It even testifies that the Judaeans lived in peace thereafter, for no one dared attack them while Judith yet lived (16:25). So the story ends.

B. *Identifying the Effective Protagonist in* Judith

In this section, I shall attempt to discern the effective protagonist of *Judith* according to Dawson's categories and the methodology that I have proposed in chapter 4. Before proceeding with the analysis proper, I should first like to make the following points concerning the text and translations that I will utilise throughout:

i) As previously indicated, all quotations from the Greek text of *Judith* and other Hebrew Testament books are taken from the LLS *Septuaginta*, just as all quotations from the Hebrew text of the Hebrew Testament are taken from the LLS' BHS. Similarly, English translations of the Hebrew/Greek Testaments are taken from the BibleDatabase RSV, while all English translations of the Apocrypha are taken from the 1957 RSV Apocrypha (RAPC) of the Online Bible unless otherwise stated. These are *my* received texts and any form of emphasis in such verses is my own.
ii) Where necessary, I have chosen to retain the RSV/RAPC English translations in the text, while engaging with any differences that I may have in the footnotes. I have done this for a number of reasons:
    - This study is not primarily concerned with the translation of the Greek/Hebrew text, nor yet with which Greek/Hebrew text is the more 'correct' one. I am dealing with *Judith* as a part of the collective human psyche. Therefore, arguments

concerning the best or 'correct' text are superfluous because all texts of *Judith* form part of that collective psyche.
- I wish to avoid cluttering the main body of my work with arguments concerning the best translation of particular words/phrases.

iii) The 'meaning' of Greek words is derived mostly from the gloss attached to the LLS *Septuaginta*, the LLS' *Enhanced Strong's Lexicon*, and the entries in the abridged form of *Liddell and Scott's Greek-English Lexicon*. These are parenthetically referred to as 'gloss/the gloss', 'ESL', and 'Liddell and Scott', respectively. Such 'meanings' are only provided where I wish to point out the correctness/incorrectness of the RSV/RAPC and/or other translations or highlight particular aspects of a word that are relevant to my analysis. Where necessary, I have emphasised the most appropriate meanings for a particular word in its given context.

a. *Section I*—Judith *1–7*

Nebuchadnezzar

The Book of Judith begins with Nebuchadnezzar (1:1). He is the driving force behind the movement of the plot from *Judith* 1:5 to 2:13, and he profoundly influences the entire first section in so far as it is his command that seals the execution of the Western nations (1:7–12; 2:1–13). Nebuchadnezzar is presented as a haughty, power-wielding despot who attacks and obliterates the seemingly innocent kingdom of Ecbatane without provocation (cf. 1:5). His words and deeds reflect the kind of deity presupposed by many kings and rulers. They also come 'uncomfortably' close to many statements made by YHWH, the God of Israel: Nebuchadnezzar swears upon his own throne and kingdom as though there were nothing higher by which he could swear (1:12; 2:12);[2] he demands complete obedience and 'goes out in his wrath' against those who disobey him (2:6, 7, 11, 13);[3]

[2] Cf., e.g. Isa. 45:22–23 and Jer. 22:5 where YHWH swears by Himself as there is no one higher by whom to swear, and where the Israelites are required to swear by YHWH and no one else.

[3] Cf., e.g. Jer. 49:37; Isa. 10:6, 13:13; Jer. 21:5 and Zech. 8:14 where YHWH swears to destroy/punish various nations in His wrath—including Israel, in some instances.

he regards himself as the Great King, Lord of the Whole Earth (2:5);[4] and he demands libations fit for a god from his soon-to-be vanquished subjects (2:7). Similarly, the narrator refers to Nebuchadnezzar's will as a 'mystery' (2:2) and states that **συνετέλεσεν** πᾶσαν τὴν κακίαν[5] τῆς γῆς ἐκ τοῦ στόματος αὐτου ("[he] *concluded* the afflicting of the whole earth out of his own mouth"—2:2, KJVA[6]). In so doing, the narrator confirms Nebuchadnezzar's godlike attitude because YHWH's will is also referred to as a mystery (cf., e.g. Ephesians 1:9)[7] and He, too, effectively speaks into existence (cf. "*concluded*" in 2:2) His "plan"/will and/or destruction of disobedient nations including Israel (Cf., e.g. Isaiah 46:10–11; Ezekiel 23:34, 26:4, 28:10, and 39:5).[8] Finally, his gathering with his θεράποντες[9]

[4] Cf., e.g. Ps. 47:2; Mal. 1:14; Josh. 3:11 and Zech. 6:5 where others designate YHWH or YHWH designates Himself as a "great King" ("over all the earth" in many cases) and/or "Lord of all the earth".

[5] Κακία has a wide range of meanings, which KJVA does well to translate with "the afflicting". According to the gloss, the noun refers to "badness; cowardice, sloth". The *ESL* accords the following meanings to the noun, which highlight Nebuchadnezzar's malignant attitude towards "the whole earth": "1) malignity, malice, ill will, desire to injure. 2) wickedness, depravity. 2a) wickedness that is not ashamed to break laws. 3) evil, trouble".

[6] RAPC reads "and recounted fully, with his own lips, all the wickedness of the region", which does not capture the sense of the Greek verb συντέλλω.

[7] Cf. also other New Testament scriptures that speak of the mystery/mysteries of God's kingdom (e.g., Matt. 13:11), revelation in Christ (e.g., Rom. 16:25), etc.

[8] Cf. also Isa. 11:4 where the Rod of Jesse—the anointed of YHWH/His main representative here on earth—is said to smite the earth with the rod of his mouth and slay the wicked with the breath of his lips.

[9] The noun θεράπων is difficult to translate and appears to be used in various ways throughout the book. According to Liddell and Scott (their italics), the noun refers to "*an attendant, servant*, differing from δοῦλος, as implying free service". In Homer, it also refers to "*a companion in arms, comrade*, though inferior in rank, as Patroclus was the θεράπων of Achilles". The same dictionary also indicates that kings were regarded as θεράποντες of Zeus and warriors as θεράποντες of Ares. Given that the people so designated are coupled with the μεγιστᾶνες in Nebuchadnezzar's 'gathering', the use of the noun in *Judith* 2:2 may be akin to the last meaning referred to in Liddell and Scott. RAPC has "officers" here. Moore (op. cit., 131) may thus be justified in translating the noun as "ministers" in this case—though not without some degree of uncertainty. Even so, the same translation cannot be maintained throughout the book, as Moore's own various translations of this word attest: "servants" (6:6), "staff" (7:16), "ruler" (9:10!), "personal servants" (10:20), and "attendants" (10:23; 11:20; and 12:5). Given the uncertainty of meaning attached to this noun, I have preferred to translate as "officers/attendants" here and elsewhere. This, to my mind, accords sufficient 'clout' to the group thus designated within the context of *Judith* 2:2 and 7:16 *and* conveys the uncertainty to which I have referred.

(officers/attendants) and μεγιστᾶνες ("nobles"—2:2) resembles the meeting of a divine pantheon, underscoring the portrayal of this 'Assyrian' king as a divine entity.[10]

Nebuchadnezzar is thus portrayed as a cruel megalomaniac (cf. 1:15), a despot who regards himself as god, and the accomplishment of whose word is taken for granted (cf. 1:12; 2:1, 5, 12–13). He fears nothing and no one, caring for little else than the advancement of his realm and complete obedience to his name.

In psychological terms, Nebuchadnezzar represents the kind of person who has been 'positively' inflated by contact with archetypal material. His behaviour and speech bear clear testimony to this in two almost contradictory ways: he is the great, fearless despot, and yet finds it necessary to call all the nations of the earth to assist him in the destruction of a single kingdom and its relatively few allies (cf. 1:6, 7–12). While the latter action may be justifiable in an actual war situation, given the magnitude of Arphaxad's fortifications and the nations who rally to his support (1:2–7), it speaks psychologically of the fear that is involved in inflation: fear that the person one has become (the 'new you') is not real, and that one's endeavours might fail. This is the fear of *enantiodromia* intimated by the psyche and unconsciously realised by the inflated ego-consciousness. In this context, fear may also account for the fact that Nebuchadnezzar appears to require the ratification of his officers and nobles for his plans (2:2–3): despite the self-assurance that 'positive inflation' produces, a compensatory doubt arises in the unconscious and makes itself felt in consciousness so that one needs one's thoughts to be ratified. Naturally, 'positive' inflation and the fear of *enantiodromia* also make themselves felt in the need to draw everyone to oneself and to surround oneself only by those who will agree with one's ideas, plans, demeanour, etc. This may be interpreted as a need to be surrounded by approving disciples—without offering them any real discipleship, however, as the focus is upon oneself and not one's 'disciples'. (This is contrary to a highly individuated person attracting disciples for the purpose of elevating them to a position in which they may impact positively upon society). As indicated by the text, this kind of inflation is but a delusion and may quickly sideline the one who has embraced

[10] Cf. Job 1:6 and 2:1 where "the sons of God" come to present themselves before YHWH in a manner resembling that of an Ancient Near Eastern pantheon.

it: Nebuchadnezzar vanishes as an active participant in the Judithic drama/dream; he never again acts as an independent subject after his speech to Holofernes, his chief general, by whom he is replaced in the narrative. Furthermore, Nebuchadnezzar begins and ends his short Judithic career as a power-wielding despot. There is thus no change or growth in his character, depicting the stagnation that 'positive' inflation entails. (As we shall soon see, this inflation is also highly infectious: it is carried over to and continued by Holofernes who often functions as Nebuchadnezzar's chief disciple). Nebuchadnezzar's inflation is never resolved, thus placing him firmly in the realm and hence the grip of the unconscious.

Given that he is depicted as an arrogant, power-wielding despot, we may also say of him that he represents the archetype of power in the unconscious realm. Similarly, his godlike attitude and destructive activities intimate that he may well be seen as the negative Self or the Shadow, in opposition to YHWH, the positive Self.

Arphaxad

On a syntactical level, Arphaxad's introduction is sharply juxtaposed to that of Nebuchadnezzar. The introduction of both kings occurs in *Judith* 1:1, with the information concerning Nebuchadnezzar (see underlined portions below) being broken off *in medias res* to introduce Arphaxad (see boldfaced portions below). Verses 2–4 continue with Arphaxad's fortifications and only then do we hear of Nebuchadnezzar again, with verse 5 picking up where verse 1 left off:

1:1 Ἔτους δωδεκάτου τῆς βασιλείας Ναβουχοδονοσορ, ὃς
ἐβασίλευσεν Ἀσσυρίων ἐν Νινευη τῇ πόλει τῇ μεγάλῃ,
ἐν **ταῖς ἡμέραις Αρφαξαδ,** ὃς **ἐβασίλευσεν Μήδων** ἐν
Εκβατάνοις,
1:2 **καὶ ᾠκοδόμησεν [Αρφαξαδ] ἐπ᾽ Ἐκβατάνων κύκλῳ τείχη
ἐκ λίθων λελαξευμένων εἰς πλάτος πηχῶν τριῶν . . .**
1:5 καὶ ἐποίησεν πόλεμον ἐν ταῖς ἡμέραις ἐκείναις
ὁ βασιλεὺς Ναβουχοδο-νοσορ πρὸς βασιλέα Αρφαξαδ . . .

The syntactical juxtaposition, couched in the style of an anacoluthon, intimates that Arphaxad may soon find violent opposition in the form of the Assyrian king.

What we learn about the 'Median' king lends further support to the possibility of immanent conflict in that we find him severely fortifying his city, Ecbatane (1:2–4). The conflict alluded to in this way takes place in the following verses, which detail Nebuchadnezzar's campaign against Arphaxad and his victory over him (1:5, 6, 13–16). Nebuchadnezzar obliterates the latter's forces—despite the fact that Arphaxad is assisted by various other Eastern nations—and destroys his mighty walls (1:5, 6, 13–14). Finally, Nebuchadnezzar strikes Arphaxad down with "hunting spears" (καὶ κατηκόντισεν[11] αὐτὸν) in the mountains of Ragau (1:15).

Arphaxad represents the type of person who desperately attempts to shield herself/himself from the workings of the unconscious and ends up being swallowed up by it as a result. The detailed description of the height, length, and breadth of the walls and towers that Arphaxad built around his city (representative of the soul) graphically represent the intense fear that a weak consciousness experiences in the face of an immanent unconscious uprising (1:2–4). The sheer magnitude of the fortifications (walls and towers) and the narrator's intimation that these were built "so that his armies could march out in force and his infantry form their ranks" (1:4) re-enforces the hostile attitude of consciousness towards the unconscious and further reveals the fear that feeds it.

Likewise, the total annihilation of Arphaxad's forces (1:13–15) and his own destruction represent the psychological fact that a weak consciousness, which baulks at the mere possibility of unconscious 'attack' (it is not patently clear that Arphaxad fortified Ecbatane on account of Nebuchadnezzar's attack as the latter only occurs after the account of Arphaxad's fortifications), is eventually swallowed up and assimilated by the forces from which it attempted to shield itself. In this sense, then, Nebuchadnezzar and his marauding forces represent the power of the unconscious psyche and the vengeance it wreaks upon a weak, fearful consciousness. Arphaxad's death depicts the complete assimilation of a weak consciousness into the unconscious and/or the total assimilation of weak conscious contents via a loss of libido. As mountains are representative of higher states of spirituality, his death in the mountains of Ragau is symbolic of the spiritual death that assimilation to the unconscious causes the conscious psyche. Given

[11] Κατακοντίζω—"to shoot down" (the gloss). The verb (κάτα + ἀκοντίζω) more properly means "to strike down with darts" (Liddell and Scott). RAPC is therefore not incorrect in translating this phrase as "and struck him down with hunting spears". Nevertheless, Moore's (op. cit., 122) translation conveys the force of the phrase in a more powerful way: "riddled him with his javelins".

his close proximity to and easy annihilation/assimilation by Nebuchadnezzar/the unconscious, I would say that Arphaxad and his forces/allies represent a first-stage consciousness, i.e., one that is still largely swayed by the unconscious even though it has differentiated itself from the unconscious to a small degree. The syntactical juxtaposition of *Judith* 1:1–5, which effectively embeds the introduction of Arphaxad within that of Nebuchadnezzar, illustrates textually the fact that Arphaxad has only barely extricated himself from the unconscious mass/sway. It thus lends support to my interpretation of him and his forces/allies as representative of a first-stage consciousness.

Arphaxad's Eastern Helpers

In *Judith* 1:6 we read:

> καὶ **συνήντησαν πρὸς αὐτὸν** πάντες οἱ κατοικοῦντες τήν ὀρεινὴν καὶ πάντες οἱ κατοικοῦντες τὸν Εὐφράτην καὶ τὸν Τίγριν καὶ τὸν Ὑδάσπην[12] καὶ πεδία Αριωχ βασιλέως Ἐλυμαίων, καὶ **συνῆλθον** ἔθνη πολλὰ **εἰς παράταξιν** υἱῶν Χελεουδ.

The meaning of the verbs συναντάω[13] and συνέρχομαι[14] (see boldfaced portions above) makes it difficult to determine whether these nations 'met' and 'came/rallied together' to assist Nebuchadnezzar or to oppose him, as neither one entails any intrinsically positive or negative sense.[15] Nevertheless, *Judith* 1:6 is sandwiched between *Judith* 1:5 and 1:7, which inform the reader that Nebuchadnezzar attacked Arphaxad and called upon the western nations to assist him. To my mind, this indicates that the eastern nations of *Judith* 1:6 came to aid *Arphaxad* and that Nebuchadnezzar therefore had to call upon

---

[12] This possibly refers to the Choaspes (modern Kerkheh), a 200-mile-long river that flows west of Susa into the Tigris-Euphrates (Moore, op. cit., 125–126).

[13] Συναντάω—"to meet" (gloss); "1) to meet with. 1a) of events: to happen or befall" (ESL); "to meet face to face: generally, to meet together, assemble. II. to meet with. III. Of things, to happen to one" (Liddell and Scott).

[14] Συνέρχομαι—"to go together" (gloss); "1) to come together. 1a) to assemble. 1b) of conjugal cohabitation. 2) to go (depart) or come with one, to accompany one" (ESL); "to go along with or together. II. to come together, meet: to have dealings or intercourse with. 2. in hostile sense, to meet in battle, encounter . . . of a battle, to be engaged in. 3. . . . to join an expedition . . . to share thy bed. III. of things, to be joined in one, be united. IV of events, to concur, coincide, happen together." (Liddell and Scott).

[15] The Greek text reads καὶ συνῆλθον ἔθνη πολλὰ εἰς παράταξιν υἱῶν Χελεουδ, which literally translates as 'and came together many nations *to/against the battle arrangement of the sons of Chelod*'.

the western nations to assist him against the now considerably stronger opposition. The Syriac version (cf. Moore, op. cit., 121) certainly follows this interpretation by adding "to fight against" after "συνῆλθον" (they came together). I would thus agree with the New English Bible's (NEB's) reading that makes this opposition clear: "Nebuchadnezzar was opposed by" over and against that of the RAPC ("he was joined by") and that of Moore ("There rallied to him"—op. cit., 121), which indicate that the eastern nations mentioned in *Judith* 1:6 came to aid *Nebuchadnezzar*. I believe that my reading of this verse is further supported by the following:

i) Most of these Ancient Near Eastern people are located in the hilly country (ὀρεινή) and near rivers, which are traditionally representative of spirituality/consciousness and spiritual refreshment. They may therefore be associated with a certain level of Ancient Near Eastern spirituality or spiritual consciousness over and against Nebuchadnezzar and his forces who represent the unconscious forces.
ii) These nations are said to have joined the forces of the sons of "Chelod" or "Cheleoud"—a completely unknown nation or country that has elicited a fair amount of speculation/comment regarding its identity. According to Moore (op. cit., 126), the noun may refer to the Assyrians or some other group that joined them (cf. his interpretation of *Judith* 1:6 above). However, on the strength of the Syriac reading, "the Chaldeans", I prefer to see this word as a corruption of "Chaldeans"—a possibility that Moore (ibid.) also mentions, citing Barucq and other sources who concur with this viewpoint. The Babylonians, as we know, often clashed with the Assyrians and may thus justifiably be seen to oppose the 'Assyrian' Nebuchadnezzar here. Of course, the problem remains that *Judith's* Nebuchadnezzar is fighting against Ecbatane and not Babylon. To my mind, however, this lack of correlation is part of the book's 'confused factuality' that stems from its nature as an unconscious communication/dream and need not distract us unnecessarily here.
iii) Even if πρὸς αὐτὸν refers to Nebuchadnezzar and "the sons of Chelod" refers to the Assyrians, as Moore (ibid.) suggests, my interpretation of these nations' role still holds as it is still possible to read καὶ **συνήντησαν πρὸς αὐτὸν** . . . καὶ **συνῆλθον** ἔθνη πολλὰ **εἰς παράταξιν** υἱῶν Χελεουδ in a negative sense. The reason for this lies in the negative potential of *sunantavw* and *sunevrcomai* cou-

pled with the fact that both πρὸς and εἰς are used to indicate some form of opposition in *Judith*. Note particularly *Judith* 1:13, 5:20, 6:17, 7:1 and 11:

1:13 καὶ παρετάξατο ἐν τῇ δυνάμει αὐτοῦ **πρὸς** Αρφαξαδ βασιλέα . . .
5:20 καὶ νῦν, δέσποτα κύριε, εἰ μὲν ἔστιν ἀγνόημα ἐν τῷ λαῷ τούτῳ καὶ ἁμαρτάνουσιν **εἰς** τὸν θεὸν αὐτῶν . . .
6:17 . . . καὶ ὅσα ἐμεγαλορρημόνησεν Ολοφέρνης **εἰς** τὸν οἶκον Ισραηλ
7:1 Τῇ δὲ ἐπαύριον παρήγγειλεν Ολοφέρνης . . . ἀναζευγνύειν ἐπὶ Βαιτυλουα . . . καὶ **ποιεῖν πόλεμον πρὸς** τοὺς υἱοὺς Ισραηλ.
7:11 . . . μὴ πολέμει **πρὸς** αὐτοὺς καθὼς γίνεται πόλεμος παρατάξεως . . .

1:13 he led his forces against King Arphaxad . . .
5:20 Now therefore, my master and lord, if there is any unwitting error in this people and they sin against their God . . .
6:17 . . . and all that Holofernes had said so boastfully against the house of Israel.
7:1 The next day Holofernes ordered his whole army . . . to break camp and move against Bethulia . . . and make war on the Israelites.
7:11 . . . do not fight against them in battle array . . .

Thus, it is possible to regard Nebuchadnezzar and his forces as the referents of *Judith* 1:6 while simultaneously interpreting the nations' actions as hostile towards him/them.

The interesting thing about Nebuchadnezzar's foreign opposition is that they join Arphaxad's forces without either coercion or invitation. The opening and closing phrases of *Judith* 1:6, συνήντησαν πρὸς αὐτὸν and συνῆλθον ἔθνη πολλὰ εἰς παράταξιν, certainly seem to suggest this. Their willing cooperation with Arphaxad places them in stark contrast to the western nations (1:7–10) who are summoned to join Nebuchadnezzar's forces but refuse (1:11), *and* those who are forcefully conscripted into Holofernes' army at a later stage (3:6). Even so, these foreign nations have a very short-lived career in the Book of Judith. They appear as Arphaxad's unsolicited helpers against Nebuchadnezzar in *Judith* 1:6 and disappear as soon as Nebuchadnezzar's war with him is over (cf. 1:16), presumably having been destroyed along with Arphaxad.

Their uncoerced alliance with Arphaxad, their swift destruction with him, their potential as spiritual/conscious symbols, and their close proximity to the 'Assyrian' kingdom indicate that they are weak conscious contents that are both closely situated to the unconscious realm and closely constellated to the first-stage consciousness that Arphaxad represents. We may thus say of them that they represent people who have barely emerged from the unconscious mass—note their proximity to the unconscious and the textual confusion as to their allegiance. In other words, we may say that they are people who have barely emerged from Jung's first stage of consciousness (complete identification with societal norms and expectations).

The Coastal Dwellers and Other Vanquished Western Nations

Judith 1:7–10 mentions specifically by name some eighteen different 'communities' from Persia to Ethiopia—'The Coastal Dwellers and Other Vanquished Nations'—who disparaged Nebuchadnezzar's call (1:7–10). They are introduced immediately after Arphaxad's eastern helpers (1:6) and also oppose Nebuchadnezzar, albeit with greater numbers than the eastern nations of whom only five are mentioned in *Judith* 1:6. Their shared opposition intimates that they too are part of the conscious psyche, while their numerical superiority suggests a higher level of consciousness than that represented by Arphaxad and his foreign helpers. Their greater conscious level is also borne out by the greater geographical area they cover and the greater national diversity amongst them, which may indicate a higher form of conscious differentiation.

These nations' disparaging attitude (ἐφαύλισαν[16] . . . τὸ ῥῆμα Ναβουχοδονοσορ—1:11) towards the unconscious may be seen as derivative of their greater, though incomplete, conscious differentiation: unlike Arphaxad they have no fear (1:11). They therefore do not join Nebuchadnezzar in battle and extend the same disparaging attitude towards his ambassadors or envoys ("they sent back his messengers empty-handed and shamefaced"—1:11). Their attitude is typical of an immature consciousness—one that has not achieved full differentiation: arrogant, fearless, bearing no knowledge of either the strength or the stealth of the unconscious. As a result of their immaturity, they repress the rising contents of the unconscious (they send back Nebuchadnezzar's ambassadors) with catastrophic results: mass

[16] RAPC's "disregarded" is a little weak, as φαυλίζω means "to hold cheap, to depreciate, disparage" (Liddell and Scott).

destruction of that which consciousness has achieved/produced (note the words underlined below), that which feeds consciousness, and that which ensures its survival—which protects it from being subsumed into the unconscious psyche (italicised words below). This is aptly illustrated by the violent verbs describing Holofernes' actions (boldfaced below) against them. (In my opinion, the RAPC does not always reflect the utter violence of his actions and I have therefore provided footnotes indicating a particular verb's range of meaning where necessary):

2:23 καὶ **διέκοψεν** τὸ Φουδ καὶ Λουδ καὶ **ἐπρονόμευσεν** υἱοὺς πάντας Ρασσις καὶ υἱοὺς Ισμαηλ τοὺς κατὰ πρόσωπον τῆς ἐρήμου πρὸς νότον τῆς Χελεων.

2:24 καὶ παρῆλθεν τὸν Εὐφράτην καὶ διῆλθεν τὴν Μεσοποταμίαν καὶ **κατέσκαψεν**[17] πάσας τὰς πόλεις τὰς ὑψηλὰς τὰς ἐπὶ τοῦ χειμάρρου Αβρωνα ἕως τοῦ ἐλθεῖν ἐπὶ θάλασσαν.

2:25 καὶ **κατελάβετο** τὰ ὅρια τῆς Κιλικίας καὶ **κατέκοψε**[18] *πάντας τοὺς ἀντιστάντας* αὐτῷ καὶ ἦλθεν ἕως ὁρίων Ιαφεθ τὰ πρὸς νότον κατὰ πρόσωπον τῆς Ἀραβίας.

2:26 καὶ ἐκύκλωσεν πάντας τοὺς υἱοὺς Μαδιαμ καὶ **ἐνέπρησεν** τὰ σκηνώματα[19] αὐτῶν καὶ **ἐπρονόμευσεν** τὰς *μάνδρας* αὐτῶν.

2:27 καὶ κατέβη εἰς πεδίον Δαμασκοῦ ἐν ἡμέραις θερισμοῦ πυρῶν καὶ **ἐνέπρησεν** πάντας τοὺς *ἀγροὺς* αὐτῶν καὶ τὰ *ποίμνια* καὶ τὰ *βουκόλια* **ἔδωκεν εἰς ἀφανισμὸν**[20] καὶ τὰς πόλεις αὐτῶν **ἐσκύλευσεν** καὶ τὰ πεδία αὐτῶν **ἐξελίκμησεν** καὶ **ἐπάταξεν** πάντας τοὺς νεανίσκους αὐτῶν ἐν στόματι ῥομφαίας.

The natural response to this kind of unconscious attack (Nebuchadnezzar's forces) is indicated by the succeeding verses and the destruction of consciousness (the coastal and other nations) that they entail. The coastal nations' erstwhile fearlessness (cf. 1:7 and 1:11) is swiftly

[17] Κατασκάπτω—"to dig down, destroy utterly" (gloss). RAPC's "destroyed" is a little weak. Perhaps 'annihilated' would be better.

[18] Κατακόπτω—"to cut in pieces, cut up: to kill, slay" (Liddell and Scott). RAPC has "killed".

[19] Σκήνωμα—a tent, tabernacle: a habitation: in plural, soldiers' cantonments (Liddell and Scott).

[20] Ἀφανισμός—"a disappearance, destruction" (Liddell and Scott). RAPC has "destroyed". Perhaps a verb like 'obliterate' or 'wipe out' would be better. An even better translation may be 'reduced to nothing', which is more in keeping with ἔδωκεν εἰς ἀφανισμὸν.

replaced by fear as they witness the destructive force of Holofernes bearing down upon them (2:28). Fear is then followed by bargaining (3:1) and a surrender to the unconscious force (3:2–4) in the attempt to survive its onslaught. Their arrogance (cf. "disregarded the orders of Nebuchadnezzar . . . and refused to join him in the war—1:11) is thus converted to bargaining and their hostility (cf. "sent back his messengers"—1:11) to complete surrender. Note how the synonymous parallelisms in verses 2 and 3 (ABC $A^1B^1C^1$) culminate in the complete self-abnegation and surrender of verse 4 (A^2DE, where D parallels B/B^1 and E parallels C/C^1).

3:2	**Ἰδοὺ** ἡμεῖς οἱ παῖδες Ναβουχοδονοσορ βασιλέως μεγάλου	A
	παρακείμεθα ἐνώπιόν σου,	B
	χρῆσαι ἡμῖν καθὼς ἀρεστόν ἐστιν τῷ προσώπῳ σου,	C
3:3	**ἰδοὺ** αἱ ἐπαύλεις ἡμῶν καὶ πᾶς τόπος ἡμῶν	A^1
	καὶ πᾶν πεδίον πυρῶν καὶ τὰ ποίμνια καὶ τὰ βουκόλια	
	καὶ πᾶσαι αἱ μάνδραι τῶν σκηνῶν ἡμῶν	
	παράκειται πρὸ προσώπου σου,	B^1
	χρῆσαι καθὸ ἂν ἀρέσκῃ σοι,	C^1
3:4	**ἰδοὺ** καὶ αἱ πόλεις ἡμῶν καὶ οἱ κατοικοῦντες ἐν αὐταῖς	A^2
	δοῦλοι σοί εἰσιν,	D
	ἐλθὼν ἀπάντησον αὐταῖς ὡς ἔστιν ἀγαθὸν ἐν ὀφθαλμοῖς σου	E

With each ἰδού consciousness surrenders itself, its provision, and its achievements (cities) to the unconscious. Declaring themselves παῖδες Ναβουχοδονοσορ (3:2) and Holofernes' δοῦλοι, the fearful nations prostrate themselves before the latter (3:2, 3) and ask him to do as he desires (3:2, 3, and 4). They surrender to him all those things that he took by force from other vanquished nations (πόλεις, μάνδρας, ποίμνια, βουκόλια, σκηνώματα, πᾶν πεδίον πυρῶν—cf. 2:24–27) and he treats them in similar fashion (note the parallels between 3:6 and 2:24 as well as 3:8 and 2:25):

3:6	ἐφρούρωσε τὰς πόλεις τὰς ὑψηλὰς
2:24	καὶ κατέσκαψεν πάσας τὰς πόλεις τὰς ὑψηλὰς
3:8	καὶ κατέσκαψεν πάντα τὰ ὅρια αὐτῶν
2:25	καὶ κατελάβετο τὰ ὅρια τῆς Κιλικίας

The annihilation of conscious achievements and conscious resources is completed by the forced conscription of their best men into his army (3:6), the destruction of their form of worship (see boldfaced portions below) and the enforced worship of Nebuchadnezzar as God (see underlined portions below):

3:8 καὶ κατέσκαψεν πάντα τὰ ὅρια αὐτῶν καὶ **τὰ ἄλση αὐτῶν ἐξέκοψεν**, καὶ ἦν δεδομένον αὐτῷ **ἐξολεθρεῦσαι πάντας τοὺς θεοὺς τῆς γῆς**, <u>ὅπως αὐτῷ μόνῳ τῷ Ναβουχοδονοσορ λατρεύσωσι</u> πάντα τὰ ἔθνη, καὶ πᾶσαι αἱ γλῶσσαι καὶ αἱ φυλαὶ αὐτῶν <u>ἐπικαλέσωνται αὐτὸν εἰς θεόν</u>.

Thus ends the fairly brief career of these coastal nations (2:28). They were ransacked despite the fact that they surrendered totally (3:2–4) and welcomed Holofernes into their midst "with garlands and dances and tambourines" (3:7) as though he were one of their own returning victoriously from battle with the enemy. Their fate aptly illustrates the foolishness and the consequences of ignoring rising unconscious contents. It also indicates that once the wrath of the unconscious has been roused there is no placating it; it simply enters in and takes over with an even greater vengeful energy than before.

Regarding the level of consciousness/individuation achieved by these nations, we have already noted that they are of a higher consciousness than Arphaxad and his allies as people (above). We have also seen that they have achieved a greater degree of conscious differentiation as both people and contents. Nevertheless, they are swiftly destroyed because they are still too immature to realise the destructive power of repressed unconscious contents. Furthermore, Holofernes seems able to access them fairly easily, which intimates that they are still relatively close to the unconscious mass—even though they function at a higher level of consciousness than Arphaxad and his helpers. This indicates that we may place the coastal and other vanquished western nations at the second of Jung's stages of consciousness, viz. 'separation from the other.'

Nebuchadnezzar's Officers/Attendants and Nobles

Nebuchadnezzar's officers/attendants (θεράποντες) and nobles (μεγιστᾶνες) make their first and last appearance in chapter 2 after their master's destruction of the 'Median' kingdom. They seem to play a very small part in terms of the overall narrative in Section I, merely ratifying Nebuchadnezzar's plans and deciding on the fate of the disobedient nations with him (2:2–3). They represent the type of people who often gather around someone functioning out of a positive inflation. Having little or no maturity of their own, they mistake this inflation for real leadership and usually become dependent on their leader for their self- and group-identity. They function as mindless disciples, agreeing on their leader's every word. On a more archetypal level, and in accordance with Nebuchadnezzar's representation of the unconscious psyche, these men may be regarded as weaker or attendant psychological contents that have constellated themselves around the dominant power archetype in the unconscious psyche. In this sense, they are both similar to and different from Arphaxad's eastern helpers: they are to Nebuchadnezzar what the eastern nations of *Judith* 1:6 are to Arphaxad, even though they represent unconscious elements while the latter represent elements of the conscious psyche.

Holofernes

Holofernes, Nebuchadnezzar's chief general and second-in-command, makes his first, silent appearance in *Judith* 2:4 where he is commissioned by his master, Nebuchadnezzar, to wreak vengeance upon the western nations. He is to go out in Nebuchadnezzar's name and obliterate all those nations who had disobeyed him and hold for their day of judgment those who submit. He is further to command that they "prepare earth and water" for Nebuchadnezzar—a Persian form of libations offered to deity (cf. 2:5–13, especially 7, 11 and 10).

In execution of his commission, Holofernes gathers "all the commanders, generals, and officers of the Assyrian army (2:14), chooses 120,000 of the best men as well as 12,000 archers on horseback and instructs them in the order of battle (2:15–16). He then amasses countless numbers of carrier and slaughter animals (2:17), food, and an abundance of gold and silver for their provision (2:18) and sets off to cover the western lands with his forces (2:19). He is joined by a motley crew of nations, which is so numerically vast that it prompts the narrator to liken them to swarms of locusts and grains of sand (2:20):

2:20 καὶ πολὺς ὁ ἐπίμικτος ὡς ἀκρὶς συνεξῆλθον αὐτοῖς καὶ ὡς ἡ ἄμμος τῆς γῆς, οὐ γὰρ ἦν ἀριθμὸς ἀπὸ πλήθους αὐτῶν.

Leaving his master's presence, Holofernes goes on a rampage throughout the Ancient Near Eastern, destroying towns, fields, stables, temples, and peoples and leaving a trail of terror in his wake (2:19–28). He deals mercilessly even with those who submit themselves to him:

he destroys their gods and sacred groves (cf. ἄλση—3:8), declaring Nebuchadnezzar to be god alone, and drafts their best men into his ever-increasing army (3:1–8). Having rested his army for a month (3:9–10), he turns his attention to Judaea.

Upon receiving information regarding the Judaeans' war preparations (5:1) Holofernes becomes extremely angry (5:2). He calls together his foreign advisors and enquires of them concerning the identity, (military) strength, and leadership of this insolent nation who have dared to defy him in this manner (5:2–4). The answer he receives from Achior (5:5–21) incenses him so much that he has the Ammonite ruler bound and cast out to the foot of Bethuliah's mountain, there to await his hot displeasure and share the fate of the insolent nation (cf. 5:22, 6:13). Then, in the final chapter of Section I, he mobilises his army towards Bethuliah (see 7:1–7, especially verses 6–7). There, upon the recommendation of all the leaders of Esau and Moab (7:8–16), he commands that the springs supplying water to the city be blocked, in order to force the people to surrender. He also commands his armies to block off all the exit points so that those who attempt to flee may not escape and become easy prey to him (cf. 7:17–22).

On a psychological level, we may also regard Holofernes as a person who has become 'positively inflated' through the archetypal ego-conqueror function that Nebuchadnezzar has conferred upon him. He has both identified with Nebuchadnezzar's function and taken on the accompanying persona of a haughty, 'divine' potentate, effectively continuing the inflation that we discerned in Nebuchadnezzar. In terms of Nebuchadnezzar's leadership over Holofernes and the fact that he is Nebuchadnezzar's second-in-command, we may regard his inflation as belonging to that of a favourite or chief disciple who 'naturally' speaks—and even prophesies (note especially 6:4)—with her/his master's voice and feels empowered to enact various deeds in the master's name. This is confirmed by the fact that he progresses from a nonspeaking character who merely accepts his master's commandments (see 2:4–13) to one who speaks both in his master's name and of his own accord. He also makes all the decisions from the point that he leaves Nebuchadnezzar's presence (cf. 2:19.ff.). In fact, he is so empowered by the positive inflation that he even takes it upon himself to modify his master's commands in significant ways. For example, Holofernes' 'mandate' to ensure that all nations worship Nebuchadnezzar alone as god (3:8) seems to be entirely of his own making—Nebuchadnezzar certainly does not command it directly, even though he commands that his enemies prepare "earth and water" for him (note 2:5–13, especially 2:7 and n. 5). He may thus be carrying Nebuchadnezzar's mandate further than he (Nebuchadnezzar) had intended. By contrast, Holofernes never seems to ensure that Nebuchadnezzar's demand for divine libations is specifically met. His own power and arrogance increase as the story unfolds (2:20; 3:1–8, especially 6 and 8; 7:1, 16–17, 21–22ff.) and he speaks with his master's voice all the more as can be seen by comparing his words in *Judith* 5:3–4 and 6:1–9 with those in *Judith* 2:5–13. Note, for example, how he merely enquires—albeit angrily—why this insolent Judaean nation has set itself against him in *Judith* 5:3–4, thus echoing Nebuchadnezzar's "they disobeyed my orders" (2:6), how he acknowledges Nebuchadnezzar as god in *Judith* 6:2 (cf. 2:7) and as king over the whole earth (6:4)—a title that Nebuchadnezzar used in self-reference (2:5)—and how he affirms his master's conviction that none would be able to withstand his forces and that the valleys, hills, and rivers would be filled with the enemy slain (cf. 6:2–4, 9, which finds many parallels in Nebuchadnezzar's speech in 2:7–12, some of which are taken up below). However, he begins to arrogate the right of uncontested speech to himself (6:9)—a 'divine' right that has only been accorded to Nebuchadnezzar so far (6:4 and 2:13). Note especially the close parallels between *Judith* 6:4, 6:9, and 2:12 in this regard:

2:12 ὅτι ζῶν ἐγὼ καὶ τὸ κράτος τῆς βασιλείας μου,
λελάληκα καὶ ποιήσω ταῦτα ἐν χειρί μου.
6:4 . . . ἀλλὰ ἀπωλείᾳ ἀπολοῦνται,
λέγει ὁ βασιλεὺς Ναβουχοδονοσορ ὁ κύριος πάσης τῆς γῆς,
εἶπεν γάρ, οὐ ματαιωθήσεται τὰ ῥήματα τῶν λόγων αὐτοῦ.
6:9 . . . ἐλάλησα, καὶ οὐδὲν διαπεσεῖται τῶν ῥημάτων μου.

It would seem, then, that Holofernes sees himself not only as Nebuchadnezzar's 'envoy', but also as his 'replacement' that possesses equal power. As I have previously noted, Nebuchadnezzar effectively vanishes as an active participant in Section I from the time that he commissions Holofernes to go out and wreak vengeance in his name. From here on it is Holofernes' decisions and actions that most impact the outcome of Section I; there are no messages from or to Nebuchadnezzar, no 'progress reports' required, and so forth. Holofernes acts on his own. What, then, are we to make of this? In answer to this question, I should like to examine the archetypal significance of both these characters at the hand of the following considerations:

We have seen that Nebuchadnezzar and Holofernes stand in a psychological master-disciple relation. Furthermore, we have observed that while Nebuchadnezzar initially forms the driving force behind the events in this section, it is Holofernes' decisions and deeds that ultimately determine its outcome. As we have also seen, Nebuchadnezzar may indeed be regarded as an unconscious content. By virtue of his close association with the same, Holofernes too may be said to belong to the realm of the unconscious. Seeing that he is the highest in command after Nebuchadnezzar and his principal 'disciple', as it were, we would not err in regarding Holofernes as a split-off of the archetype that his master represents. Taking into account the destructive nature of both these characters, I propose that both are archetypes of power and destruction. Similarly, given Nebuchadnezzar's 'divine' attributes as indicated by parallels with YHWH, the Assyrian king should be seen as the archetypal image of the negative Self/the Shadow and Holofernes as its archetypal manifestation, i.e., the (negative) shadow. The changing depiction of Holofernes and his separation from Nebuchadnezzar indicate that he has become loosed from the deep recesses of the unconscious psyche. Similarly, his largely unhindered attacks on other nations show that he has reached and assimilated the lower stages of consciousness. This means that he has crossed the threshold of consciousness as a psychological content without acceding to consciousness himself. This is commensurate with my interpretation of him as the malignant shadow. The shadow, as we will recall, is the psychological content that is closest to the conscious threshold. When it is not integrated, it becomes malignant and poses a considerable threat to the conscious ego, as can be seen by the destruction Holofernes leaves in his wake.

Finally, we may conjecture that Holofernes' identification with Nebuchadnezzar as both archetype and person—his god and his master—accounts for his exaltation of the 'Assyrian' king as god. By hailing Nebuchadnezzar as god, Holofernes is showing his admiration for his master, while simultaneously approving himself as god via his identification. This would be wholly commensurate with the respective archetypal character of each: as the shadow, Holofernes is the archetype closest to the negative Self and, paradoxically, the archetype closest to the threshold of consciousness. Exalting the one is tantamount to exalting the other. By commanding that he be reverenced or 'worshipped' with libations (2:7), Nebuchadnezzar was effectively granting the same right/privilege to his chief general. Similarly, by explicitly instating the worship of Nebuchadnezzar, Holofernes' action was tantamount to his instating the worship of himself, both by deferral and by direct association.

Holofernes' Troops

As we have seen, Holofernes' troops are selected from the best ranks of Assyria's elite (2:14, 15). These men who trust in their own strength (2:5) constitute a vast army of 120,000 soldiers and 12,000 archers on horseback who are willingly joined by a numerically vast motley crew of nations (2:14, 20). The motley crew thus resembles Arphaxad's eastern helpers in their willingness even though the former side with the unconscious while the latter side with consciousness. In relatively few vv., Holofernes' vast army wreaks destruction throughout the Ancient Near East (cf. e.g., 2:23–3:10). As the story progresses, he swells his army by adding to them choice foot soldiers from the western nations whom he conquers (3:7; cf. 2:19 and also 2:15). They become a numberless multitude (cf. 2:20), a well-oiled war machine set to cover the whole earth under their feet and drown the mountains with the blood of Nebuchadnezzar's enemies (cf. 2:7, 8, 19 and 6:4).

The way that Holofernes' forces are described and the destruction which they wreak is reminiscent not only of the destruction that Nebuchadnezzar's forces wreaked, but also of the way that unconscious contents rise from the nether lands of the psyche and take over a consciousness that is either too weak to resist or too foolish to recognise the power of the unconscious. In this sense, they truly resemble a rising locust plague that devours the unsuspecting crop (2:20). The author's comparison of Holofernes' army to locusts and grains of sand bears further significance in that it intimates the depth of the unconscious from which these forces are drawn: in Jungian terms, locusts signify mankind's prehuman, preanimal consciousness and, according to the Pentateuch, sand signifies that from which mankind was made (Genesis 2:7). The ἐπίμικτος (the mixture of nations) which accompanies Holofernes' choice soldiers and the sheer numbers of his forces may then be said to signify the Gnostic *massa confusa* or *globossa*, the original chaos from which the world was created.

Furthermore, we see that Holofernes' army is accompanied by vast numbers of carrier and slaughter animals (2:17) as well as gold and silver (2:18). Animals are usually indicative of the presence of instinctual forces, while "gold and silver" represents the possible transformation of these unconscious (underground) forces into valuable psychic substances that can feed and transform consciousness as they come into its realm (are brought to the surface) and are assimilated by it (purified by fire). This transformation, as we have seen, is the true value of alchemical practices, according to Jung, and the medium through which the goal of individuation, i.e., maturation, is achieved.

We may conclude, then, that Holofernes' forces consist of those unconscious forces closest to the shadow archetype which he represents (they are *choice* men); hidden instinctual forces that are possibly close to the threshold of consciousness; deeper unconscious contents that stem from the preanimal consciousness of humankind; and even deeper contents that hark back to the original chaos from which the world was made. In other words, we have here what may amount to a 'total onslaught' upon consciousness. The combined elements of the unconscious attack are so powerful that, with relative ease, they obliterate lower levels of consciousness and even manage to assimilate some relatively higher conscious contents (the choice men of the coastal nations) in their ranks. Nevertheless, they also carry with them the seeds of renewal and change in the form of the gold and silver they bear.

The Judaeans

The Judaeans as a whole make their active appearance halfway through the first section of *Judith* in chapter 4. According to the text, they have recently returned from the (Babylonian) exile, gathered in Judaea, and reconsecrated the temple vessels (4:3). Hence, they are "very greatly terrified" (4:2) when they hear of the treatment that the other nations have received at Holofernes' hand. In particular, they are "alarmed" (4:2) on account of Jerusalem and the temple of their Lord God for they have heard how Holofernes had stripped the other nations' temples and razed them to the ground (4:1). They therefore alert the surrounding areas (4:4), take possession of the high mountain peaks, fortify the towns in them, and set aside provisions for war as their fields had just been reaped (4:5). Following the instruction of Joachim, the high priest, they also take possession of the mountain passes (4:6–8). The entire community—including the animals, the slaves, and the foreigners—then humble themselves before God in prayer. Donning sackcloth, they cover the altar with sackcloth, fast, and implore God in all earnest to prevent the injury of their children, their women, their cities, and their temple. In the midst of this, the priests in Jerusalem continue to offer up the required daily sacrifices, the people's vows, and their free-will offerings (4:9–12, 13–15).

The Judaeans may also be seen as elements of consciousness in accordance with our interpretation of Nebuchadnezzar–Holofernes as elements of the unconscious psyche and those who oppose them as representative of various levels of consciousness. There are, however, a number of factors that distinguish the Judaeans from the other nations at this point in the narrative:

1. Judaea is the last port of call for Holofernes' forces.
2. The Judaeans are even more scared of Holofernes and his forces than the 'heathen' nations (cf. καὶ ἐφοβήθησαν σφόδρα σφόδρα ἀπὸ προσώπου αὐτοῦ—4:2—versus ἐφοβήθησαν αὐτὸν σφόδρα—2:28).
3. They have recently returned from exile in a foreign country and are just beginning to reconstitute themselves in their community and in their worship (4:3). This, according to *Judith*, does not apply to the other nations—there is no mention of any other nation having returned from exile.
4. The Judaeans send word to their fellow-Israelites to rouse them to action (4:4) whereas the other nations send word to Holofernes in an attempt to sue for peace (3:1–5). There is no record of other nations soliciting help from anyone against Holofernes in any way.
5. Contrary to the coastal nations (cf. 3:1–5, 7), the Judaeans do not try to entreat or placate Holofernes in any way.
6. They do not wait patiently for Holofernes to arrive as the other nations had done. They begin taking control of their own territory and garrisoning their own towns and cities—something *Holofernes* did amongst some of the vanquished nations (4:4–8 versus 2:24, 25, and especially 3:6, 8).
7. The Judaeans make provision for war in every way, making use of their freshly harvested fields. By contrast, the other nations lose their fields and crops to Holofernes' fire or simply give them over to him and do not seem to have made any provision for war despite knowing of his intentions (4:5 versus especially 2:27 and 3:3).

8. The Judaeans pray for assistance and continue to serve their own God whereas the other nations do not pray and are forced to serve Nebuchadnezzar as god (note especially 4:9, 12, 15, and 14 versus 2:28–3:5 and 8).

The differences listed above reveal that we are dealing here with a much more differentiated and so higher stage of consciousness than that represented by the other nations who had opposed Nebuchadnezzar–Holofernes: the Judaeans are aware of their conscious territory and do everything in their power to maintain control over it; they seem knowledgeable about the power of the unconscious and are prepared to do battle with it; and they are also prepared *for* the battle (4:4–8). This places them above the second-stage consciousness of the other western nations whom Holofernes has already obliterated. In other words, it places them at stage 3, the differentiation of moral properties. Nevertheless, their intense fear indicates that they have not quite settled at this level. Their relative newness to this level is depicted textually by the fact that they had only recently returned from exile to a foreign country and reconstituted themselves (4:3). Psychologically speaking, we may say that they had recently been subsumed by the unconscious, survived, and reclaimed valuable conscious territory, to the extent that they have surpassed the first two stages of consciousness and acceded to the third. (This also points to their higher stage of consciousness). Perhaps their recent dealings with the unconscious, as depicted through their exile and return, account for both their greater awareness and their greater fear of it. Thus, knowledge of the unconscious brings both preparedness and fear. The result is that they cry out (note the boldfaced words below) to the positive Self (henceforth Self/God or God/the Self) with great desperation (note the italicised words below) to help them retain their territory and the new conscious strength that they have attained. In order to clear the channels between themselves and the Self they re-enforce their cries with a process of inner purging executed in terms of self-sacrifice (e.g., fasting), self-humiliation (e.g., donning sackcloth), and submission to God/the Self (e.g., prostration; note the underlined words below). As *Judith* 4:10 indicates, the entire community throughout all its strata of consciousness is involved in humbling themselves and crying out before God. Note how this verse lists the conscious strata of this stage of the Judaean consciousness in descending order: "They [the men] and their wives and their children . . . and every resident alien and hired laborer and purchased slave—they all girded themselves with sackcloth" (4:10). Note too that they employ the instinctual forces within their control (their cattle—4:10) in their attempt to access the Self and engage the unconscious. The fact that these instinctual forces are listed squarely between the upper strata of consciousness (men, women, and children) and the lower ones (strangers, hirelings, and slaves/servants) shows that these forces are important to and hence tightly in the grip of consciousness. The above, in turn, shows that the Judaeans may be/are cognisant of the instinctual nature of the unconscious attack and that they are willing to employ everything at their disposal in their intense attempt to elicit help from the Self:

4:9 καὶ **ἀνεβόησαν** πᾶς ἀνὴρ Ισραηλ πρὸς τὸν θεὸν ***ἐν ἐκτενείᾳ***
μεγάλῃ καὶ ἐταπείνωσαν τὰς ψυχὰς αὐτῶν *ἐν ἐκτενείᾳ μεγάλῃ*.[21]
4:10 αὐτοὶ καὶ αἱ γυναῖκες αὐτῶν καὶ τὰ νήπια αὐτῶν καὶ τὰ κτήνη
αὐτῶν καὶ πᾶς πάροικος καὶ μισθωτὸς καὶ ἀργυρώνητος αὐτῶν
ἐπέθεντο σάκκους ἐπὶ τὰς ὀσφύας αὐτῶν.
4:11 καὶ πᾶς ἀνὴρ Ισραηλ καὶ γυνὴ καὶ τὰ παιδία οἱ κατοικοῦντες ἐν
Ιερουσαλημ ἔπεσον κατὰ πρόσωπον τοῦ ναοῦ
καὶ ἐσποδώσαντο τὰς κεφαλὰς αὐτῶν
καὶ ἐξέτειναν τοὺς σάκκους αὐτῶν κατὰ πρόσωπον κυρίου,
4:12 καὶ τὸ θυσιαστήριον σάκκῳ περιέβαλον
καὶ **ἐβόησαν** πρὸς τὸν θεὸν Ισραηλ ὁμοθυμαδὸν ***ἐκτενῶς***
τοῦ μὴ δοῦναι εἰς διαρπαγὴν τὰ νήπια αὐτῶν καὶ τὰς γυναῖκας
εἰς προνομὴν καὶ τὰς πόλεις τῆς κληρονομίας αὐτῶν εἰς
ἀφανισμὸν καὶ τὰ ἅγια εἰς βεβήλωσιν καὶ ὀνειδισμὸν ἐπίχαρμα
τοῖς ἔθνεσιν.

Joachim (the High Priest), the Γερουσία, and the Priests in Jerusalem

As the spiritual and political leader of this newly reconstituted community, Joachim represents the highest level of consciousness available to the Judaean people at this point in the narrative. The fact that he is situated in Jerusalem, the capital city of Judaea, along with the γερουσία (Council of Elders/Sanhedrin) and the Jerusalemite priests, indicates that he is situated closest to the centre of ego-

[21] RAPC interprets the second occurrence of the phrase *ἐν ἐκτενείᾳ μεγάλῃ* in 4:9 "with much fasting". While such an interpretation may be correct, it does not reflect the contours of the Greek text. I would therefore prefer to translate "with vehemence" or "with great commitment".

consciousness. He and his leadership team may be placed at the fifth stage of individuation, i.e., individual identity or self-realisation. True to his lofty identification, it is he who commands the cities closest to the attack to guard the high, narrow mountain passes by which access could easily be gained into Judaea (4:6–7). In other words, it is he who holds the ultimate responsibility of protecting the highest element of conscious achievement—the Jerusalem temple—at the centre of ego-consciousness/Jerusalem. He is thus the most highly individuated member of *Judith's* cast that we have encountered so far. He is also the only Judaean character that acts independently (see B below), making the biblically aware reader wonder whether he will be the Lord's anointed who will deliver his people from the Assyrian foe. The overall structure of *Judith* 4 seems to suggest that this is indeed a possibility (overleaf):

A	4:1–5	The Judaeans hear, fear, send word, and garrison the cities in the mountainous areas.
B	4:6–7	**Joachim** sends word to guard the high mountain passes.
C	4:8–12	*The Judaeans* obey Joachim and the *gerousiva.* They call out to God. The entire community humble themselves before God in sackcloth. They put dust/ashes on their heads. They cry out to God for protection.
D	4:13a–b	***GOD*** hearkens to their voice and pays attention to their affliction.
C'	4:13c	The *Judaeans* fast before God.
B'	4:14–15	**Joachim** and the priests who served before the lord cover themselves in sackcloth. They offer the daily sacrifices, vows, and free-will offerings with ashes on their mitres. They cry out to God for assistance.

This chapter consists of an introductory section (A) followed by a palindrome structure (B–C–D–C'–B') to which God's action (D) is central. The author cleverly places Joachim's actions on the outer legs of the palindrome (B and B') so that they enclose the actions of the Judaeans (C and C')—protectively, as it were. This affirms his role as the protector of consciousness. It also makes him the first character to take military/political action (B) before the narrator relays God's response (D) to the reader and the last one to undertake spiritual-ritual action with his priests (B') thereafter. We note too that he is the only member of the γερουσία and the Jerusalemite priesthood to be singled out by name. Taken together, these factors corroborate Joachim's high state of consciousness and suggest that he is the one most likely to 'deliver' his people from their foe.

Joachim is further assisted by the γερουσία (Council of Elders/Sanhedrin) and the priests in Jerusalem. These two groups represent the political and spiritual leadership of Israel, respectively. The former assist Joachim in making the strategic decisions necessary to fend off the attack (4:8), while the latter assist him in his duties as the chief religious functionary of the land (4:14–15). These two groups of people may thus be said to assist him in maintaining the people's connection to both central consciousness and the Self. In psychological terms, then, the γερουσία and the priests are conscious elements that are constellated close to the central ego-consciousness, though at a little greater distance than Joachim who appears to be the leader of both (see 4:6–8 and 4:14–15.). In this sense they may be construed as the conscious counterparts of Nebuchadnezzar's officers/attendants and nobles.

The Lord YHWH

4:13 καὶ **εἰσήκουσεν** <u>κύριος</u> τῆς *φωνῆς* αὐτῶν
καὶ **εἰσεῖδεν** τὴν *θλῖψιν* αὐτῶν,
καὶ ἦν ὁ λαὸς νηστεύων ἡμέρας πλείους ἐν πάσῃ τῇ Ιουδαίᾳ καὶ Ιερουσαλημ κατὰ πρόσωπον τῶν ἁγίων <u>κυρίου παντοκράτορος</u>.

The Lord has hearkened (εἰσήκουσεν) to the Judaeans' cry—he has heard their voice (φωνή), and he has beheld—he has looked intently upon (εἰσεῖδεν)—their oppression, their affliction (θλῖψις). These two phrases (*Judith* 4:13a–b) constitute the sole ray of hope within the entire story so far—if one is identifying with the Judaeans, that is. The phrases "the Lord has heard" and "the Lord has seen" entail the turning point in the Exodus saga (cf. Exodus 3:7–9 in particular), heralding the Lord's intended and actual deliverance of His people through Moses. Although God's deliverance is not explicitly stated here, one expects it on account of the intertextual connections of these two phrases. Furthermore, as previously indicated, Joachim seems poised to take on the mantle of saviour at this point—if only by virtue of his position as military/political and spiritual leader. These verses thus infuse hope at this point both by what they *say* and by what they *don't say*, leading the reader to expect the deliverance of God's people yet again. It seems, however, that this hope is held out to the reader alone. The characters seem totally unaware of it as their continuing cries of desperation show. Furthermore, God does not express this hope in person either to the entire community or to any chosen vessel as he did in the time of Moses. These verses are merely the function of an omniscient narrator's knowledge, who cleverly holds out hope (for the reader) and despair (for the Judaeans) through the self-same verse. What, then, are we to make of these verses and the God-character in them?

On a psychological-archetypal level, the character of God in this narrative represents the 'good' or positive Self vs. Nebuchadnezzar's 'bad' or negative Self. The fact that the positive Self has heard the cries of the afflicted consciousness is a good indication that it will come to the latter's assistance. However, the fact that this positive Self has not yet communicated with anyone suggests one or all of the following:

i) None of the characters presented thus far is capable of communicating effectively with/accessing the resources and plans of the Self.
ii) The Self is not ready to be accessed.
iii) Something is amiss in the ego-Self communication.

Firstly, the fact that offerings continue to be made indicates that there is still a connection to the Self—that consciousness is still trying to access the Self by traditional means. This, however, does not seem to bring peace to the Judaean ego-consciousness as the Judaeans' cries of desperation show. Secondly, in terms of the parallels with Exodus, it is clear that the Self has heard and has therefore answered (note the parallels with Exodus above). I would therefore say that point iii obtains, i.e., that there is something amiss in the ego-Self communication. It would seem, then, that the positive Self is there and wishes to reach out (God has seen and heard—4:13) to a consciousness that is temporarily out of tune with its 'voice'. The hope of contact nevertheless remains:

a) The functionaries of the Self still exist and continue in their attempt to access it as best they know how (by offering sacrifices, praying, and crying out for deliverance).
b) The Self has heard its people's voice—despite the fact that it has not yet spoken.

Thus, the mixture of hope and despair remains, creating an almost unbearable tension that will be resolved for both the reader and the Judaeans only when God speaks and/or delivers His people through his chosen instrument.

Holofernes' Foreign Advisors and Nobles

According to *Judith* 5:2, Holofernes' foreign advisors consist of the Moabite princes/rulers (ἄρχοντες), the Ammonite generals (στρατηγοί), and the governors or viceroys of the coastal regions (σατράπες).[22] These foreign leaders represent the people geographically closest to Judaea, and it is perhaps for this reason that Holofernes calls upon them at this juncture in the narrative. Their importance seems to lie in his belief that they possess a special knowledge about Judaea that would help him understand why they (the Judaeans) alone of all Western nations have taken it upon themselves to resist him: καὶ διὰ τί κατενωτίσαντο[23] τοῦ μὴ ἐλθεῖν εἰς ἀπάντησίν μοι παρὰ πάντας τοὺς κατοικοῦντας ἐν δυσμαῖς (5:4).

Achior, the Ammonite ruler, chooses to respond, delivering a fairly accurate history of Israel and cautioning that the Judaeans should not be attacked before their standing with their God is established (5:5–21). His speech elicits the anger of all those surrounding Holofernes' tent and they determine to macerate him (καὶ εἶπαν . . . συγκόψαι[24] αὐτόν—5:22), stating indignantly that they stand fearless before the puny might of the Judaeans who would surely become a prey to be devoured by Holofernes' superior forces (5:22–24). As a result of their intervention, Holofernes readies his troops for battle (7:1–3) and Achior finds himself bound and cast at the foothill of Bethuliah, there to await his punishment once the Judaeans are destroyed (6:1–13).

Holofernes' μεγιστᾶνες (nobles) and his 'foreign advisors' are two seemingly distinct groups of influential people that surround him at

---

[22] Σατράπης—title of a Persian viceroy or governor of a province.

[23] RAPC effectively ignores the verb κατά[ν]ωτιζομαι in its translation, "And why have they alone, of all who live in the west, refused to come out and meet me?" In light of the meaning of κατά[ν]ωτιζομαι—"to carry on one's back" (gloss)—perhaps this verb should be translated as "take upon [oneself]".

[24] Given that συγκόπτω means "to beat together. 2. to knock in pieces, cut up. II. to thrash soundly, maltreat" (Liddell and Scott), RAPC's "put to death" is a little too benign. That is why I have chosen "to macerate", though Moore's "thrashing" (op. cit., 164) is just as good.

this time. Judging from the fact that the former are mentioned for the first (and last) time in *Judith* 5:22—separately from the Moabites and the coastal dwellers—I would argue that they are of 'Assyrian' stock, while the foreign advisors are from specified non-Assyrian stock, viz., Ammon, Moab, and the coastal region (5:2). The following points also seem to support this view:

a) The narrator uses the term μεγιστᾶνες in *Judith* 2:2 that describes how Nebuchadnezzar assembled his war council after returning to Assyria. There is no indication of any foreign presence there; Nebuchadnezzar's war council meeting occurs in Assyria amongst Assyrian 'leaders' of whom the μεγιστᾶνες form a part.
b) Holofernes addresses Achior and all the Moabites ἐναντίον παντὸς τοῦ δήμου ἀλλοφύλων—"in the presence of all the foreign contingents" in *Judith* 6:1. The term ἀλλοφύλων literally designates foreigners, i.e., non-Assyrian peoples.
c) Furthermore, the foreign advisors are specifically called to assist Holofernes (5:1) while the nobles seem to be present throughout the deliberations here.

On an archetypal level, these two groups of 'advisors' represent two groups of unconscious contents: the μεγιστᾶνες, by virtue of their shared nationality with Holofernes, represent those contents that are most closely constellated around the shadow archetype that he images, while the other group represent conscious contents that have been subsumed by the unconscious and, more specifically, by the shadow/power archetype, Holofernes, and his minions.

Nevertheless, unlike the choice men of *Judith* 3:6, the 'foreign advisors' seem to maintain some of their own autonomy/libido. As we have seen, Holofernes regards them as important resources of information regarding the strength of the conscious forces (the Judaeans) that he is up against. This intimates that they have not lost their conscious energy/libido altogether despite having been subsumed by the unconscious—a fact that is further borne out by the freedom that they seem to possess in *Judith* 7:8–16. In these verses, "all the leaders of the Moabites and the commanders of the coastland" join "all the chieftains of the people of Esau" in approaching Holofernes. They offer him unsolicited advice in respect of blocking the fountain at the foothill of Bethuliah so as to defeat the disobedient Judaeans by bringing thirst and famine upon them (7:11–15). The fact that Holofernes' foreign advisors participate in this action and menacingly encircle the Bethulians (7:16–18) with their forces represents the danger that former conscious contents pose to the consciousness out of which they have fallen.

(I would ask the reader to remember that all the characters in *Judith* are elements of the same 'dreamer's' psyche, i.e., that of the Jewish nation as a whole. This is the standpoint of the subjective dream analysis. In accordance with this mode of analysis, both the Judaeans and Holofernes' foreign advisors are elements of the same psyche. The difference between them lies in the fact that the former are still part of consciousness while the latter are not. Having fallen from consciousness, Holofernes' foreign advisors pose a threat to the Judaeans, who are still rooted in consciousness, and hence to the 'dreamer's' conscious psyche overall.)

Achior

Like the Judaean nation, Achior makes his first, indirect, retrospective appearance in *Judith* 1 where he is (presumably) amongst those who initially disparage Nebuchadnezzar's call (the Ammonites are specifically mentioned and he is the Ammonite leader—1:12 and 5:5). The narrative does not distinguish him by name until his first, direct appearance in *Judith* 5 where he is depicted as one of the foreign leaders/advisors whom Holofernes has summoned (5:2–4). Achior voluntarily responds to Holofernes' questions regarding the identity and military strength of the Judaeans by recounting their history from the time of Abraham to the destruction of the Jerusalem temple (5:5–21). The most remarkable aspect about his account is that it follows the Deuteronomistic view of sacred history: when the Jews obey God they are invincible; when they sin they are overcome (cf. especially 5:17–19 and also 20–21). On the basis of his account, Achior cautions Holofernes not to attack the Judaeans without having previously ascertained their acceptability before God—if they had not sinned then their God would defend them and "we shall be put to shame before the whole world" (cf. 5:21).

The fact that Achior is able to stand out amongst his group of peers but still cling to the Deuteronomistic philosophy of retribution—a philosophy that underwent a fair amount of criticism and even outright rejection in the later wisdom literature such as Job and Ecclesiastes—shows that he has reached a stage of consciousness in his personal capacity in which the 'ego' has separated itself from both the unconscious mass and its peers (stage 2) but has not quite distinguished itself from ancient norms and patterns of thought. In other words, his is a consciousness that has not quite reached or become established at the third stage of conscious awareness, viz., the differentiation of his moral properties. This is borne out by his seemingly ambiguous, midway position: he is an Ammonite—a traditional enemy of the Jews—who nevertheless shows some measure of identification with their values/moral properties by espousing their philosophy, and he uses this philosophy to warn his captor, Holofernes, thus identifying with his values/moral properties too.

To return to the text, Achior's well-intended words provoke the indignation of all present. They determine to macerate him, and declare that the Judaeans are powerless and would easily become fodder for Holofernes' (and their) forces (5:22–24). With words full of sarcasm, ire, and irony Holofernes declares that Nebuchadnezzar alone is god (6:2) and that the Judaeans have no hope of being delivered out of his hand by *their* God (6:3–4). He decrees (cf. "I have spoken and none of my words shall fail"—6:9) that they will be destroyed and that Achior, who had dared to "prophesy" in this manner (cf. 6:2), would be cast out to one of the Judaean villages on a mountain pass (6:7), there to await his own destruction once Holofernes had returned from destroying the Judaeans (cf. 6:5–9). With these words Holofernes commands that Achior be bound and taken to Bethuliah and left there at the mercy of its citizens (literally: "[to] hand him over to the men of Israel"—6:10). This is done and Achior is left at the foothill of Bethuliah (6:11–13). There he is 'retrieved', as it were, by the Bethulians who take him, untied, to their leaders (6:14–15). The whole city gathers around as he recounts "the words of the council of Holofernes, and all the words that he had spoken in the midst of the princes of Assur, and whatsoever Holofernes had spoken proudly against the house of Israel" (6:17). Thereupon the people pray (6:18) and offer him comforting praise (6:19), and Ozias, their chief magistrate, hosts a banquet for him and the elders at his own house (6:20). With this, we see the last of Achior in Section I of *Judith*.

Like the vanquished nations that we have encountered so far, Achior too may be regarded as a conscious content that has been swallowed up by the unconscious psyche despite initial resistance: he is drafted into Holofernes' army and becomes part of the unconscious realm. More specifically, he becomes swallowed up by and so a part of the unconscious shadow of the Judaean people (Holofernes has been identified as the national shadow). Nevertheless, he possesses enough psychic energy to achieve a greater consciousness (autonomy/differentiation) than that of his peers—Holofernes' foreign advisors—who had suffered a similar fate: he somehow gains enough libido to stand alone and warn Holofernes of the perils attached to attacking the Judaeans, whereas his peers always seem to speak to the Assyrian general in groups (see, e.g., 5:22 and 7:8). Typically, the unconscious reacts with great displeasure at this form of insurrection and spews him out of its mouth—much like Jonah's 'great fish' (cf. 5:22–6:14 and Jonah 1:17 and 2:10). As a result, he is separated—almost despite himself (he warns Holofernes)—from the unconscious mass (he is cast out to Bethuliah). We may thus say that he represents a part of the Judaean national shadow (see further below) that has been washed up on the shores of consciousness/Bethuliah.

For a while, this psychological shadow content, which has now begun to regain its consciousness, is alone and not altogether free from its former shackles to the unconscious (Achior is bound when he is cast out of the Assyrian camp). There is, however, a ray of hope: Achior is evicted to the foothill of Bethuliah (6:13). This indicates that he has arrived at the threshold of a potentially higher form of consciousness as a psychological content and also to a potentially higher spiritual experience/stage of consciousness as a person. The Bethulians keenly embrace him (cf. 6:14–21), proving that this erstwhile unconscious content is readily accepted into the realm of consciousness. There may be at least two interrelated reasons for Achior's easy acceptance into Bethulian society:

a) Both he and the Bethulians view the crisis through the eyes of Deuteronomistic theology, although this only becomes apparent at a later point in section I. Thus, his level of consciousness finds keen rapport with (some aspect of) their consciousness as people.
b) He comes from a nation that is intimately related to the Judaeans. He is a descendant of Lot's son, Ammon, born through an incestuous relationship with one of his daughters (the two women made their father drunk and slept with him because they believed that there was no other way to continue their father's line. Cf. Genesis 19:30–38, especially verses 32 and 38). He is thus the Judaeans' not-so-distant cousin, if you will, and an aspect of their national shadow by virtue of his shadowy, incestuous beginnings.

As we have seen, the shadow typically consists of psychological contents that are not consciously acknowledged as belonging to the conscious ego. They may therefore lose libido and be subsumed by the unconscious (in this case, Holofernes and his armies). It is thus not surprising to find that Achior comes to the light of consciousness only after his sojourn in the unconscious. My interpretation of Achior as an aspect of the Judaean national shadow is further confirmed by the Deuteronomistic injunction against including Ammonites in the Congregation of YHWH—one hides, suppresses, 'bars', and demonises that which one cannot accept about oneself, often providing 'cogent' reasons (see the italicised portions below) for doing so as is the case in Deuteronomy 23:3–4:

> No Ammonite or Moabite shall enter the assembly of the LORD; even to the tenth generation none belonging to them shall enter the assembly of the LORD for ever; *because they did not meet you with bread and with water on the way*, when you came forth out of Egypt, *and because they hired against you Balaam the son of Beʾor from Pethor of Mesopotamia, to curse you.*

The fact that the Bethulians readily accept Achior signifies that some aspect of their psyche recognises the validity and necessity of integrating this aspect/set of elements belonging to their unconscious shadow—despite the Torah injunction against doing so. From this, we deduce that their central consciousness and hence the Self, which regulates all psychic processes, has seen fit to disregard and even to reverse the earlier philosophical injunction (Deuteronomy 23:3–4)—which is nothing but a psychic communication—in light of the present crisis. We may therefore conjecture that the Self regards Achior as a content that is necessary for the growth and the individuation of the conscious subject (represented at this stage by the Bethulians), and that central consciousness recognises that the Deuteronomistic way of thinking/law is now psychologically invalid, i.e., no longer functional.

Achior's necessity for and beneficence towards the conscious realm is corroborated by the fact that he provides valuable information regarding the machinations of the unconscious (Holofernes' war plans) from which he has just emerged (6:17). For this service he is rewarded with a banquet at the chief magistrate's house (6:20), which indicates that this aspect of the national shadow has been integrated into the Bethulian society/conscious psyche to a relatively high degree (Ozias and the magistrates represent the most highly individuated elements of Bethulian society by virtue of their leadership positions).

Taking all the above into cognisance, we may say the following of Achior's rise to consciousness and his integration into higher consciousness:

a) There are four steps in his extradition from the unconscious realms, which signifies that he is completely loosed from the bounds of the unconscious (four is the number of wholeness). These steps are marked by the actions of Holofernes/Holofernes' slaves (the unconscious) towards him:

Step 1: Holofernes evicts him from his presence and so from the Assyrian camp (cf. especially 6:10–11a).
Steps 2–4: Holofernes' servants/slaves lead him out of the camp into the plain (step 2–6:11b) and through the plain to the hill country (step 3–6:11c), and then leave him near the fountains at the foothill of Bethuliah (step 4–6:11d and 13).

b) Then there are seven steps which signify his acceptance into the Bethulian community and hence his greater integration into consciousness. By contrast to his eviction from the unconscious, these steps are marked by the actions of the Bethulian community (consciousness) towards him:

Step 1: The Bethulian men come down the mountain and loose him from his bonds (6:14a).
Step 2: They take him up the mountain to Bethuliah where they place him before their princes/rulers (6:14b–c).
Step 3: The young men and women gather around him (6:16a–b).
Step 4: He is placed in the midst of the people (6:16c).
Step 5: Ozias speaks with him (6:16d—and he responds [6:17]).
Step 6: The people comfort and praise him (6:20).
Step 7: Ozias takes Achior to a banquet at his own house where they cry out to the God of Israel for help the whole night long (6:21).

As intimated in the preceding paragraph, the fellowship implied in the last step, particularly in Achior's inclusion in the prayer vigil, indicates the great measure to which Achior has been integrated into Bethulian society/consciousness. Nevertheless, we see that this integration is marked by seven steps. As seven is not a multiple of four, the number of wholeness, this signifies that his integration at this stage of consciousness is not yet complete. The reason for this is not entirely clear at this point in the narrative. It is only clarified in the second section of *Judith*. I will therefore take this matter up again in the relevant subsections of 5.B.c., particularly in my discussion of Achior.

Holofernes' Officers/Attendants and Servants

Holofernes' θεράποντες (officers/attendants) and δοῦλοι (slaves/servants) are two distinct groups. The first group is constituted of those who willingly serve him, while the second group are bond slaves. As such, both groups are obviously of lower rank than Holofernes' μεγιστᾶνες (nobles) and foreign advisors whom we have encountered previously. Holofernes' θεράποντες are mentioned twice in section I, viz. in *Judith* 6:5–6 and 7:16. These verses appear to depict them as lower ranking officers/attendants who execute Holofernes wishes (cf. especially 6:6) but who may also advise Holofernes and/or take decisions with him from time to time (see especially 7:16):

6:5 σὺ δέ, Αχιωρ μισθωτὲ τοῦ Αμμων, ὃς ἐλάλησας τοὺς λόγους τούτους ἐν ἡμέρᾳ ἀδικίας σου, οὐκ ὄψει ἔτι τὸ πρόσωπόν μου ἀπὸ τῆς ἡμέρας ταύτης, ἕως οὗ ἐκδικήσω τὸ γένος τῶν ἐξ Αἰγύπτου,

6:6 καὶ τότε διελεύσεται ὁ σίδηρος τῆς στρατιᾶς μου καὶ ὁ λαὸς τῶν θεραπόντων μου τὰς πλευράς σου, καὶ πεσῇ ἐν τοῖς τραυματίαις αὐτῶν, ὅταν ἐπιστρέψω.

7:16 καὶ ἤρεσαν οἱ λόγοι αὐτῶν ἐνώπιον Ολοφέρνου καὶ ἐνώπιον πάντων τῶν θεραπόντων αὐτοῦ, καὶ συνέταξε ποιεῖν καθὰ ἐλάλησαν.

On a psychological level, we may interpret these men in similar fashion to Nebuchadnezzar's officers/attendants, viz. as disciples who congregate around a falsely charismatic master—someone with a positive inflation as in the case of Holofernes—and as unconscious contents closely constellated around the shadow archetype.

By contrast, Holofernes' δοῦλοι are bond slaves who simply do their master's bidding. In this section (*Judith* 1–7), they are particularly responsible for binding Achior and casting him at the foothill of Bethuliah (6:10–11). When they arrive at the springs (πηγὲς) beneath Bethuliah, the Bethulians sling stones at them and they depart for their master (6:12–13).

From a psychological point of view, Holofernes' δοῦλοι signify those contents that occupy the lowest ranks of the psyche—the base instincts of mankind. They are merely unconscious contents that are in the shadow archetype's employ: they receive their directives from 'him', carry them out, and then dutifully report back to 'him'. One may thus say that the shadow archetype accords them enough libido to do 'his' bidding and then withdraws it as soon as the task is completed. This is corroborated by *Judith* 6:11–13:

i) They lead Achior out of the unconscious realms right to the conscious threshold but make no attempt to cross over the threshold (see especially the underlined portions below):

6:11 καὶ συνέλαβον αὐτὸν οἱ δοῦλοι αὐτου
καὶ ἤγαγον αὐτὸν ἔξω τῆς παρεμβολῆς εἰς τὸ πεδίον
καὶ ἀπῆραν ἐκ μέσου τῆς πεδινῆς εἰς τὴν ὀρεινὴν
καὶ παρεγένοντο ἐπὶ τὰς πηγάς, αἳ ἦσαν ὑποκάτω Βαιτυλουα.
6:13 καὶ ὑποδύσαντες ὑποκάτω τοῦ ὄρους
ἔδησαν τὸν Αχιωρ καὶ ἀφῆκαν ἐρριμμένον ὑπὸ τὴν ῥίζαν τοῦ
ὄρους καὶ ἀπῴχοντο πρὸς τὸν κύριον αὐτῶν.

This signifies that they are not endowed with sufficient libido to traverse the conscious threshold at that level and that they are therefore sucked back into the realm of the unconscious. It also signifies that their libido infusion is temporary and controlled by the archetype in whose employ they are and to 'whom' they return.

ii) The Judaeans sling stones at them (6:12) but there is no mention of retaliation on their part. This indicates that they are weak elements of the unconscious that have been accorded no more libido than that which is necessary to perform a specific task only and that they have no psychic energy with which to actively engage with consciousness.

Holofernes' servants are thus weak, unconscious contents that serve the dominant shadow archetype and derive their energy value solely from 'him'. As people, we may say of them that they, much like Nebuchadnezzar's nobles, represent those persons who have little or no identity of their own. Having a very poor self-image and enslaved by elements of their past/present or negative future expectations, they cling to one who speaks loudly enough to be heard, i.e., someone who suffers from a positive inflation like Holofernes.

The Bethulians

The Bethulians are citizens of a town/city situated on/near one of the important mountain passes by which entry might be gained into Judaea and its temple in the capital city, Jerusalem (4:6–7; 6:12). They may thus be seen as the (spiritual) guardians of central consciousness (Jerusalem) and/or the outer layers of it. As such, they seem to be situated closest to the approaching unconscious forces and therefore suffer the brunt of Holofernes' attack. We first encounter them as active characters in *Judith* 6:12 where they take up their weapons, come out of the city to the mountain top, and sling stones at Holofernes' servants who have come to deposit Achior at the bottom of the mountain. When the servants have departed, the Bethulians come down from the mountain, untie Achior, and set him before their leaders (6:14). They call a meeting of the whole town—elders, men, women, and children—where Achior relates Holofernes' plans for Bethuliah (6:16–17). Upon hearing what he has to say, they worship God and ask God to "behold their arrogance, and have pity on the humiliation[25] of our people, and look this day upon[26] the faces of those who are consecrated to thee" (6:19). They then offer much praise and comfort to the man they had just 'rescued', namely, Achior (6:20).

It would seem from the above that the Bethulians have a much better attitude towards the situation than the rest of the Judaeans, and that they are therefore conscious contents/people that have risen above the general conscious mass represented by the Judaean populace. This would place them at the fourth stage of conscious awareness, i.e., the realisation of social reality and individual consciousness. We note that:

---

[25] RAPC translates ταπείνωσις with "humiliation". According to the gloss (my italics), ταπείνωσις may refer to "humiliation, abasement, *defeat*; low estate, low condition". It is interesting that the word 'defeat' occurs here as it underlines what the reader knows about the Judaeans: they believe that they have already been defeated. See also *Judith* 7:32 for a similar use of this feminine noun, which the RAPC translates as 'great depression'.

[26] The Greek verb here is ἐπιβλέπω. The author makes clever use of compound verbs in this verse. The Bethulians ask God to look *down* upon the Assyrians' pride (κάτιδε—καθοράω) and to look *to/upon* (ἐπίβλεψον—ἐπιβλέπω) their own defeat/humiliation: καθοράω means "to look down [upon]" (gloss), while ἐπιβλέπω means "to look upon, look to, regard . . ." (Liddell and Scott). Furthermore, there is also an element of keen observation/perception in the former verb ("generally, to view, see, behold: to perceive, observe"—Liddell and Scott) that is lacking in the latter. This

i) There is no mention of fear whatsoever in the face of the attack, not even after they hear what Holofernes has planned, whereas fear pervades the Judaeans' initial reaction (cf. 4:2).
ii) They confidently take up their arms and keep the Assyrians from coming up the mountain pass by driving them off with stones. They then untie Achior and take him to their leaders.
iii) They cry out to God (ἐβόησαν) as the other Judaeans did, butnowhere do we see the kind of panic and distress evinced with the latter.
iv) They are seemingly so at ease with the situation that Ozias throws banquet for Achior and the elders at his own house where they call upon (ἐπεκαλέσαντο) God all night (6:20–21).
v) Above all, they regard themselves as those sanctified to the Lord (6:19).

They also appear to possess a very open attitude that readily accepts and assimilates the unconscious content (Achior) that has just risen to consciousness, whereas the Judaeans are very fearful of the unconscious. Perhaps the difference in the Bethulians' attitude stems from the fact that they are dealing with a single content/set of contents that has already risen to consciousness whereas the Judaeans were contending with the entire force of the rising unconscious attack in chapter 4. As a content/set of contents that has been spewed out by the unconscious and assimilated into consciousness to a greater or lesser extent, Achior does not pose a threat to consciousness—contrary to the threat posed by the vastly unconscious, unintegrated national shadow (Holofernes) and the entire force of the unconscious attack which accompanies it/him. As I have previously argued, the Bethulians and Achior both view the current situation through a Deuteronomistic lens (see especially the ensuing paragraphs). This indicates that some aspects of the Bethulian psyche are on a par with Achior's level of consciousness, despite the fact that they exist at a generally higher conscious plane than he does. Furthermore, they are also not-so-distant cousins by virtue of Achior's Ammonite blood, and Achior represents a palatable aspect of the national shadow in the current situation as I have previously shown. I would there-

implies that the Bethulians were asking God to look hard upon the Assyrian's pride, in the sense of judging them for it, but to exonerate them on account of their lack of pride/humiliation.

fore argue that the Bethulians recognise what Achior represents, and that that enables them to receive him easily into their midst. The Bethulians' acceptance of Achior is doubtlessly also facilitated by their positive self-concept as those sanctified to YHWH [point v) above], a point of self-confidence that makes them less fearful of the unconscious on account of the self-assurance it provides.

Even so, the Bethulians' level of fear soon begins to rise steeply as they behold the massive throng (cf. 7:2, 3, and 18) that comes up against them on the following day. They become exceedingly distressed (ἐταράχθησαν σφόδρα—7:4; cf. 4:2), their confidence fails, and they begin to repeat what Nebuchadnezzar and Holofernes would have them believe, thus negating the positive attitude they seem to have held previously. Note, for example how well their confessions (numbered 1. and 2.) in *Judith* 7:4 compare with Nebuchadnezzar and Holofernes' boastful predictions in *Judith* 2:7–8 and *Judith* 6:4, respectively (note particularly the similarly emphasised portions below):

7:4 οἱ δὲ υἱοὶ Ισραηλ, ὡς εἶδον αὐτῶν τὸ πλῆθος, ἐταράχθησαν σφόδρα καὶ εἶπαν ἕκαστος πρὸς τὸν πλησίον αὐτοῦ
1. Νῦν **ἐκλείξουσιν** οὗτοι <u>τὸ πρόσωπον τῆς γῆς πάσης</u>,
2. καὶ οὔτε <u>τὰ ὄρη</u> τὰ ὑψηλὰ οὔτε *αἱ φάραγγες* οὔτε οἱ βουνοὶ ὑποστήσονται τὸ βάρος αὐτῶν.

2:7 . . . ὅτι ἐξελεύσομαι ἐν θυμῷ μου ἐπ' αὐτοὺς
καὶ **καλύψω** <u>πᾶν τὸ πρόσωπον τῆς γῆς</u> ἐν τοῖς ποσὶν τῆς δυνάμεώς μου
καὶ δώσω αὐτοὺς εἰς διαρπαγὴν αὐτοῖς,

2:8 καὶ οἱ τραυματίαι αὐτῶν πληρώσουσιν *τὰς φάραγγας* αὐτῶν . . .

6:4 κατακαύσομεν γὰρ αὐτοὺς ἐν αὐτοῖς,
καὶ <u>τὰ ὄρη</u> αὐτῶν μεθυσθήσεται ἐν τῷ αἵματι αὐτῶν . . .
καὶ οὐκ ἀντιστήσεται τὸ ἴχνος τῶν ποδῶν αὐτῶν κατὰ πρόσωπον ἡμῶν, ἀλλὰ ἀπωλείᾳ ἀπολοῦνται . . .

Their expressed fear mounts to near mutiny in the subsequent verses when Holofernes blocks the springs that supply their city with water (cf. 7:8–16). 'Εβόησαν—they cried out—in *Judith* 6:18 becomes ἀνεβόησαν[27]—they cried/shouted out aloud—in *Judith* 7:19 and 23 and their hearts fail (ὠλιγοψύχησεν τὸ πνεῦμα αὐτῶν—literally: their

---

[27] Βοάω—"to cry aloud, to shout; to sound, resound". ἀναβοάω—to cry or shout aloud, utter a loud cry: to cry out something. II. to call on" (Liddell and Scott; see also *Judith* 4:9 and 5:12 for the use of this verb).

spirit became faint-hearted/discouraged; 7:19) as their enemies surround them and they have no way of escape. Their cisterns run dry, their water supplies fail, and their water intake is rationed to the extent that it is insufficient for a single day. As a result:

7:22 ...ἠθύμησεν τὰ νήπια αὐτῶν, καὶ αἱ γυναῖκες καὶ οἱ νεανίσκοι ἐξέλιπον ἀπὸ τῆς δίψης καὶ ἔπιπτον ἐν ταῖς πλατείαις τῆς πόλεως καὶ ἐν ταῖς διόδοις τῶν πυλῶν καὶ οὐκ ἦν κραταίωσις ἔτι ἐν αὐτοῖς

At this point, the Bethulians gather themselves around their leaders and decry them for inciting rebellion against "the children of Assur" (7:24). Believing that God has delivered them into the Assyrians' hands, they declare that there is no one to help them (7:25). Adjuring their leaders in the strongest terms (7:24, 28), they command them to entreat the Assyrians and to deliver the city over to them. Being raided (see προνομή—7:26) and plundered (see διαρπαγή—7:27) and becoming the Assyrians' servants (δοῦλοι) is preferable to watching their women and children die, they aver (7:26–27).

The above 'request' epitomises the height of their desperation as they are prepared to lose their freedom/national identity and become a Gentile nation's slaves rather than die. This, in essence, means that they are prepared to reverse the Exodus process by which they became a nation and to return to the realms of the unconscious as represented by Egypt/Assyria. As Nebuchadnezzar is the god of the unconscious realm, the Bethulians' desire to surrender to Holofernes also means that they are willing to serve a foreign god and to relinquish their identity as those specifically called out by YHWH. In other words, they are willing to return to bondage and the exile from which they had reportedly just emerged (4:3). Their proposed change of allegiance also indicates that their erstwhile confidence was not securely founded, that it was a façade (read: mask, persona). It shows that their way of thinking is not as firmly established at the general stage of consciousness at which they function/exist. (It will be remembered that various aspects of a person's psyche may exist at different stages of consciousness). Their thirst causes them to view themselves, their situation, and ultimately their God, in a very negative light. Above all, whereas they had once regarded themselves as the 'sanctified of the Lord' (6:19), they now believe themselves to be vile and dirty and full of sin from the days of their forefathers (7:28). Consequently, they believe that God has deliberately handed them over to their deaths (cf. πέπρακεν ἡμᾶς ὁ θεὸς—7:25) and they cry out to their leaders and to God with a loud voice:

7:25 καὶ νῦν οὐκ ἔστιν ὁ βοηθὸς ἡμῶν, ἀλλὰ **πέπρακεν ἡμᾶς ὁ θεὸς εἰς τὰς χεῖρας αὐτῶν τοῦ καταστρωθῆναι ἐναντίον αὐτῶν** ἐν δίψῃ καὶ ἀπωλείᾳ μεγάλῃ.
7:28 μαρτυρόμεθα ὑμῖν τὸν οὐρανὸν καὶ τὴν γῆν καὶ τὸν θεὸν ἡμῶν καὶ κύριον τῶν πατέρων ἡμῶν, **ὃς ἐκδικεῖ ἡμᾶς κατὰ τὰς ἁμαρτίας ἡμῶν καὶ κατὰ τὰ ἁμαρτήματα τῶν πατέρων ἡμῶν**, ἵνα μὴ ποιήσῃ κατὰ τὰ ῥήματα ταῦτα ἐν τῇ ἡμέρᾳ τῇ σήμερον.
7:29 καὶ ἐγένετο κλαυθμὸς μέγας ἐν μέσῳ τῆς ἐκκλησίας πάντων ὁμοθυμαδόν, καὶ ἐβόησαν πρὸς κύριον τὸν θεὸν φωνῇ μεγάλῃ.

We may conclude, then, that the Bethulians have fallen to the fear-full conscious state of the other Judaeans at this point—despite being braver and more faithful than they at the start. Judging from their response in *Judith* 7:23–29, we may also say that their erstwhile confidence was based on the positive aspect of Deuteronomistic theology: we are sanctified/holy unto YHWH and need not fear any harm. Their thinking/self-concept is subsequently destabilised by the encroaching unconscious forces to the extent that they embrace the negative aspect of this theology: we are sinners and doomed to our punishment. As a result, they fall into the fear and desperation of the general Judaean populace. This indicates a dangerous drop in libido that topples the Bethulians' thinking into the third stage of consciousness precariously occupied by the general Judaean populace. Moreover, the fact that they are so convinced about their sinfulness and consequent punishment shows that they are completely convinced of the validity of the Deuteronomistic theology which, in turn, intimates that their thinking is fast on its way to sinking to Achior's level of consciousness (stage 2) and beyond. (See the preceding subsection where I argued that Achior's clinging to Deuteronomistic philosophy indicates that he has not quite acceded to the third stage of consciousness, i.e., to the differentiation of [his own] moral properties). This means that they are reaching the point where they are ready to breach or discard their own values/moral properties developed at the third stage of consciousness and that they may soon sink beyond stage 2 as a nation, i.e., to the point where they are no longer distinguishable from the 'other'. Given that the 'other' is the unconscious national shadow as represented by Holofernes, this means that they are dangerously close to complete identification with their shadow—a fatal regression which forespells the uncontrollable rise of shadow elements and their complete domination of consciousness (something akin to what elicited the atrocities of the Third Reich in the twentieth century).

At this point we may retrospectively clarify something about Achior's acceptance into Bethulian society. As I have previously intimated, Achior represents the Deuteronomistic principle in its totality in that he presents both its positive and negative aspects to Holofernes and warns him to ascertain whether the Judaeans had sinned before attempting to attack them (cf. especially 5:20–21). When Achior arrives at the foothill of Bethuliah, the Bethulians are able to find rapport with the positive aspect of this philosophy in Achior and they are therefore able to receive him gladly in their midst—as though he were a long lost brother (which he was by virtue of being a descendant of Lot). When the crisis brought on by Holofernes' blocking of Bethuliah's spring really begins to bear down upon them, they switch over to the negative aspect of this philosophy and hence find rapport with the negative side of it in Achior. Achior then becomes a conductor for the tension which consciousness experiences regarding the Deuteronomistic philosophy, and the way is paved for a new interpretation of life to enter the conscious realm, resolve the tension within Achior/the Bethulian community, and facilitate the elimination of the crisis. (Resolving the tension between opposite aspects of Achior's conscious philosophy will resolve the same within the Bethulian community on account of the essential identity between the aspects of consciousness that both they and Achior represent at this point. See also the subsection on Achior in which I showed that the fate of Achior and the Bethulians was inextricably intertwined and hence represented the identity between them).

The passages discussed above indicate how easily consciousness may be stripped of certain aspects of its dominant persona/way of thinking in a time of crisis, and how easily consciousness/certain aspects of consciousness may be enticed to fall back into lower levels of consciousness and ultimately into the realm of the unconscious: the Bethulians become self-critical when the Assyrians surround them and they are ready to give in and become slaves to Holofernes/the conscious shadow after their water supplies run out. This is brought about by a loss of libido and the consequent drop of their thinking into a lower level of consciousness than the one that they generally represent. These passages also aptly describe how rising and suppressed unconscious contents attack consciousness at key points and attempt to strip it of its resources by denying it what it most needs for survival (water). In this sense, the Bethulians may be described as the points of consciousness that are the most vital for the survival of conscious integrity: if they fall, all of Judaea will fall, the centre of consciousness (Jerusalem) will fall, their highest conscious achievement (temple) will be destroyed, and they will become slaves of the unconscious. This, it seems, they are willing to do, for becoming Holofernes' slaves is tantamount to serving Nebuchadnezzar as god, and so reversing the Exodus process by which they became a nation and a people of YHWH. The author confirms this viewpoint in *Judith* 3:8, 6:21, and 7:26, where Nebuchadnezzar, YHWH, and Holofernes/the Assyrian forces are separately designated as the objects of the verb ἐπικαλέω (to call on, appeal to, adjure) in comparable circumstances:

3:8 . . . καὶ ἦν δεδομένον αὐτῷ ἐξολεθρεῦσαι πάντας τοὺς θεοὺς τῆς
γῆς, ὅπως αὐτῷ μόνῳ τῷ Ναβουχοδονοσορ λατρεύσωσι πάντα
τὰ ἔθνη, καὶ πᾶσαι αἱ γλῶσσαι καὶ αἱ φυλαὶ αὐτῶν
ἐπικαλέσωνται αὐτὸν εἰς θεόν.

6:21 καὶ παρέλαβεν αὐτὸν Οζιας ἐκ τῆς ἐκκλησίας εἰς οἶκον αὐτοῦ
καὶ ἐποίησεν πότον τοῖς πρεσβυτέροις, καὶ **ἐπεκαλέσαντο
τὸν θεὸν Ισραηλ** εἰς βοήθειαν ὅλην τὴν νύκτα ἐκείνην

7:26 καὶ νῦν **ἐπικαλέσασθε αὐτοὺς**[28] καὶ ἔκδοσθε τὴν πόλιν πᾶσαν
εἰς προνομὴν τῷ λαῷ Ολοφέρνου καὶ πάσῃ τῇ δυνάμει αὐτοῦ

Ozias and the Elders/Magistrates

Bethuliah's leadership consists of the Magistrates (ἄρχοντες)[29] Ozias ben Micah from the tribe of Simeon, Abris ben Gothoniel, and Charmis ben Melchiel. We first encounter them in *Judith* 6:14–16

[28] RAPC's "call them in" completely ignores the connection between "calling upon" God and "calling upon" the Assyrians that I have made here, i.e., that calling upon the Assyrians in this context is tantamount to hailing Nebuchadnezzar as god.

[29] Χαβρις and Χαρμις are sometimes called πρεσβυτέροι (cf. 8:10; and 10:6), whereas at other times the πρεσβυτέροι appear to be a different group of people (6:16, 21; 7:23, and possibly 13:12). It is thus not clear to whom πρεσβυτέροι refers, and hence the designation "elders/magistrates" in the subheading above.

where the Bethulians set Achior before them. Ozias is the first to question Achior before the people, which designates him as the chief magistrate (6:17; cf. also 7:30). When Achior concludes his account of Holofernes' plans, Ozias invites him to his own home where he hosts a banquet/feast (πότος) for him and the city's elders and where they call upon God for help the whole night long (6:20). As previously indicated, Ozias' gesture demonstrates the fact that Achior has found acceptance at a high level within the fourth stage of consciousness which Bethuliah represents.

We next hear of Bethuliah's leaders when its citizens decry them for rebelling against the Assyrians and so bringing upon them the unbearable lack of water that they are experiencing (7:23–25, cf. also 7:17, 20–22). The Bethulians adjure their leaders to yield their city to the Assyrians for spoil, stating that this and their foreseeable servitude would be preferable to witnessing the deaths of their women and children (7:26–28). Despite their words and their many cries (7:29) Ozias encourages them to hold out for another five days in which the Lord could once again direct his mercy towards them "for he will not forsake us utterly" (7:30). Should no help come to them within that time, then he would do as they have asked (7:31). With that he disperses the men each to his own post, upon the walls and the towers, while sending the women and children home (7:32). The author then concludes the first section of *Judith* with the sombre words "And they were greatly depressed in the city" (7:32).

As leaders of the city, these men may be construed as the organising form of consciousness at the outskirts of the central ego-consciousness. In similar vein, we may then say that Ozias is the highest form of consciousness encountered at stage 4 (Bethuliah) by virtue of his status as chief magistrate. What has been said of the Bethulians may equally be said of Ozias and his leadership team: they do not fear receiving and assimilating the unconscious content that Achior represents—presumably because he embodies the Deuteronomistic philosophy to which the people cling and/or because he represents the level of consciousness to which their people have sunk/are sinking, and/or because he is a 'foreign' element necessary to the resolution of the current crisis. Their ability to contain a mutiny outbreak also indicates that their consciousness is higher than that of the Bethulians around them. They are thus able to maintain a greater form of peace in the face of adversity.

b. *Summary and Conclusions—Section I*

Having considered all the characters who present themselves in *Judith* 1–7, I will now turn to identifying the effective protagonist of section I and making a few brief remarks as to the dilemma facing him and the way that he deals with the challenges implicit in it. Before doing so, however, I should like to summarise briefly the relations between the conscious and unconscious psyche as depicted in this first section of *Judith*.

The Battle between the Conscious and Unconscious Psyche in Judith *1–7*

The preceding analysis has been conducted from the viewpoint that *Judith* represents a national dream that erupted into Judaean consciousness at the time in which the book was written. Therefore it has portrayed the events occurring in *Judith* 1–7 as symbolic manifestations of the battle between the conscious and the unconscious psyche of the Judaean nation at that time. In accordance with this interpretation, it has been established that certain characters belong to the realms of the conscious psyche while others belong to the realms of the unconscious. More specifically, it has been established that Nebuchadnezzar, Holofernes, and their entourages represent contents of the unconscious realms while all those opposing them represent elements of consciousness. Thus, Nebuchadnezzar's/Holofernes' victories over Arphaxad, various western nations, and the coastal dwellers represent unconscious inroads into higher and higher levels of consciousness, with the perceived aim of taking control of the centre of ego-consciousness, i.e., Jerusalem, and demolishing its highest achievement, the temple. In diagram 10 below, the unconscious victories over the lower areas of consciousness are represented by circles a–c that completely subsume circles 5, 4, and 3, with circle 5 being the lowest level of consciousness and circle 1 the highest.

The analysis has further shown that Ecbatane, the coastal regions, Judaea, Bethuliah, and Jerusalem correspond to the first, second, third, fourth, and fifth stages of consciousness respectively. This means that the five circles of consciousness in diagram 10 correspond inversely to Jung's five stages of conscious awareness, so that circle 5 corresponds to the first stage and circle 1 to the fifth stage:

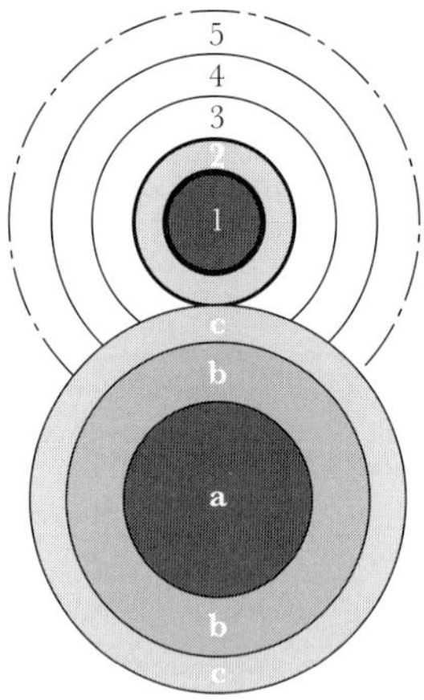

Circles 1–5 (Conscious Psyche)
1. Jerusalem ⎤ central
2. Bethuliah ⎦ consciousness
3. Judaea
4. Coastal regions (+ over vanquished nations)
5. Ecbatane + various eastern nations

Circles a–c (Unconscious Psyche)
a. Nebuchadnezzar's forces
b. Holofernes' forces + ἐπίμικτος
c. b. + choice men from 4.

Diagram 10. Schematic Representation of the Battle between the Conscious and Unconscious Forces in *Judith* 1–7.

Five Circles of Consciousness in *Judith*			**Jung's Five Stages of Conscious Awareness**
Ecbatane	5.	→	1. Complete identification with societal norms and expectations
Coastal Regions	4.	→	2. Separation from the 'other'
Judaea	3.	→	3. The differentiation of moral properties
Bethuliah	2.	→	4. Realisation of social reality and individual consciousness
Jerusalem	1.	→	5. Individual identity or self-realisation

Table 10. The Correspondence between the Five Circles of Consciousness in *Judith* and Jung's Five Stages of Conscious Awareness.

The fact that circle c merely touches upon circle 2 (Bethuliah) indicates that Holofernes' armies have reached the outer levels of central consciousness (circles 1 and 2), but have not subsumed them despite the damage caused (cf. 7:17ff.). Unfortunately, the initial resistance posed by the outer level of central consciousness is threatened as the source of conscious survival is blocked: the Bethulians' attitude changes from confidence to fear as soon as Holofernes blocks the spring supplying their city with water; their weakest elements (the infants) perish, their strongest contents (the young women and men) are debilitated, and they demand that Ozias, their leader, hand the city over to the Assyrians' marauding armies. Furthermore, their consciousness falls from the fourth stage of consciousness (circle 2) to the fear-full state represented by the Judaeans, i.e., stage 3 (circle 3), in that they lose faith in the (positive) Self. Their thinking is then fast on a regressive track to the second stage of consciousness from which Achior comes as they cling fast to the negative aspect of the Deuteronomistic code of retribution. This, as I have indicated, demonstrates that they are ready to relinquish their own hard-won values/moral properties (stage 3), and that a detrimental regression to and even beyond the second stage of consciousness—an assimilation by the shadow—is ominously imminent.

The only people who maintain a positive attitude and who seem to continue with their duties are the Bethulian leadership headed by Ozias and the very central Jerusalemite leadership headed by Joachim. These two groups of men represent the strongest level of consciousness in each of their respective domains. We may thus expect salvation to come from one of them. More especially, given that Ozias narrowly avoids buckling under the Bethulians' demands, the reader's eyes turn towards Joachim as the most probable agent through whom salvation will come. Even so, the reader cannot help noting that neither the Jerusalemite nor the Bethulian leadership teams seem able or willing to mobilise their people against Holofernes' forces. Rather, they sit back and await salvation of YHWH. This creates serious doubts in the reader's mind as to whether either one of these men—Joachim or Ozias—is capable of leading his people to salvation, which also raises doubts as to whether they are indeed the most individuated members of their communities or not. These doubts are further complicated by the weakness of the Bethulians whose position is crucial to the survival of the central ego consciousness, as we have seen. They are ready to align themselves with the shadow and the negative Self—represented by Holofernes and Nebuchadnezzar respectively—because they fear death. The cumulative result of the people's weakness and that of their leaders is that they take on a fearfully defensive position. This position is aggravated by their negative Deuteronomistic outlook which not only binds them into a dangerously passive and hopeless position at this time, but also blinds them to the fact that YHWH—the positive Self—has heard and seen (4:13), which means that He has already answered. Thus, YHWH remains the only hope for the reader (and the characters who cannot see that this is so) at the end of *Judith* 1–7, and the way is paved for a strong action-oriented representative of YHWH—a messianic figure, if you will—to enter the scene and save the day.

Identifying the Effective Protagonist in Judith *1–7*

When we compare the events at the beginning of this section with those at its end, we note the following:

1. The only people who survive both the action and the narrative are Holofernes and his entire entourage, the people of Judaea in general, Joachim and the central Judaean leadership, Achior, the Bethulians, Ozias, and the Bethulian leadership.
2. Most of these characters remain static. The only ones who change in any noteworthy manner are Holofernes, Achior, and the Bethulians:
   a) Holofernes progresses from a silent character at the outset of *Judith* 2 to one who speaks in his master's voice, carries out his master's wishes and alters them significantly. He also changes location from Nineveh and moves constantly throughout the Ancient Near East leaving carnage in his wake. Nevertheless, he starts off as an unconscious content and remains one. He destroys many conscious levels but never attains to any consciousness—despite approximating the outermost areas of central consciousness (Bethuliah).
   b) Achior changes in a number of ways. He is an Ammonite who originally resists Nebuchadnezzar but later experiences the latter's wrath through Holofernes. He is subsumed into Holofernes' army and becomes one of Holofernes' foreign military advisors. Being an originally conscious content at the second stage of consciousness (circle 4, diagram 10), he loses libido and is subsumed into the realms of the unconscious (circle b, diagram 10). Nevertheless, he seems to retain enough libido or autonomy/differentiation to dialogue with the unconscious shadow on a one-to-one basis. As a result of and despite his efforts to assist the unconscious, he is cast out of its realms to the threshold of the outer layers of central consciousness (circle 2, diagram 10). He is retrieved by conscious agents at this stage and is brought before the Bethulian leadership—the most developed conscious contents at stage 4. He is then accepted and assimilated to a relatively high degree at this stage even though his integration is incomplete.

At the end of section I, Achior is not only re-integrated into consciousness to a large extent, but he is re-integrated at a far higher entry point than the one from which he came, i.e., he has fallen from the second stage of consciousness (circle 4, diagram 10) into the unconscious and rises to the fourth stage of consciousness (circle 2, diagram 10) subsequent to his expulsion from the Assyrian camp. His sojourn in the unconscious proves most helpful to consciousness, as he is able to relay important information regarding Holofernes' plans of destruction. We may say that Achior not only changes location and conscious definition several times, but that he also changes conscious allegiance. Furthermore, he becomes a largely (though incompletely) integrated shadow content and the conductor through which consciousness experiences its tension with regard to the Deuteronomistic philosophy. As such, his presence and current state of integration also pave the way for a new interpretation of the situation that will resolve this tension and facilitate the resolution of the current crisis in the psyche of the Jewish nation as a whole.

c) The Bethulians change as regards their self-image, their image of God, and their appraisal of the situation. They also drop at least one level of consciousness in their thinking, and head dangerously towards the second stage of consciousness and beyond. Nevertheless, they remain elements of the conscious realm.

Noting the above, we may conclude that Achior is the character who has changed the most during the course of section I. Should we be able to relate all the events in this section to him, then he would undeniably be its effective protagonist. An examination of the events in section I yields the following insights with regard to Achior:

i) Nebuchadnezzar engages Arphaxad in battle and calls certain western nations to join him. Ammon is included amongst these. These nations refuse, thereby provoking his wrath. As a result, Nebuchadnezzar consults with his nobles and they decide to obliterate them. Achior is both an Ammonite and "the ruler of all the Ammonites". We may therefore justifiably conclude that he is amongst those who originally disparaged Nebuchadnezzar and triggered the ensuing carnage.

ii) Holofernes sets out against the western nations who had disobeyed his master's call. As a result Ammon is also affected and its forces (including Achior) appear to be drafted into Holofernes' army either by force or by choice—the text does not clearly indicate which applies.
iii) The Judaeans resist Holofernes, thereby eliciting his ire. He calls together his foreign advisors in an attempt to find out who the Judaeans are and what the nature of their military strength is. Achior responds and is evicted to the foothills of Bethuliah.
iv) The Bethulians retrieve Achior and decide to take him to their elders. He relays information concerning Holofernes' plans and is praised, comforted, and received into Ozias' home as a guest of honour.
v) On account of his rejection from the unconscious and his acceptance into the conscious realm, Achior too is affected by the withdrawal of libidinal energy—the blockage of the springs supplying Bethuliah with water—that plagues consciousness.
vi) Should no help be forthcoming, Ozias will give in to the Bethulians' demands and hand the city over to Holofernes. This will mean that the Bethulians will lose their hard-won identity in so far as the fourth stage of consciousness is concerned, give up their own moral properties (stage 3), sink past their differentiation from the other (stage 2), and become subsumed by the unconscious shadow. Given the fact that Achior's fate is so tightly bound up with that of the Bethulians, their regression into the unconscious will cause him to lose his new-found stage of consciousness and become an integral part of the unconscious shadow along with them, i.e., he will be destroyed with them.
vii) It is the intent of Holofernes/the unconscious to reclaim Achior and destroy him once the latter has witnessed the destruction of his new allies at the former's hand.

Given the above, we may conclude that all the events in section I may indeed be related to Achior. As he is also the character who has undergone the most change in this section, he is undeniably its effective protagonist. The obvious hero and the effective protagonist of this section are not to be confused: Achior is its effective protagonist through whom we should focalise the psychological analysis of the first section of *Judith*, while Holofernes is its obvious hero. This is a very gratifying conclusion for me personally because Achior has been sorely disregarded in the scholarly consideration of *Judith* and its characters. As we have seen in chapter 3, Roitman alone has focused sufficiently upon Achior's character and shown his importance within the *Judith* narrative.

Determining the Dilemma Facing the Effective Protagonist in Judith *1–7*

Seeing that Achior is the first section's effective protagonist, what is the dilemma facing him at the outset of this section? Which challenges are implicit in this dilemma and how does he deal with them? I believe that the answers to these questions lie within the following considerations:

a) Achior is originally a conscious content/person situated at circle 4 (diagram 10), which represents the second stage of individuation/consciousness, i.e., separation from the other (see table 10). However, he despises the unconscious and falls into its hands. This indicates that there is a certain level of instability at that stage. In my opinion, such instability occurs only as a result of one of two things: i) a lack of complete integration at a particular stage—the person/content is a 'new arrival'—or ii) a transition in progress between a particular stage and the next one. As Achior is the leader of the Ammonites, I would argue that he was indeed well established at stage 2 and that the latter applies here, i.e., that he was in the process of moving to the third stage of consciousness when the unconscious attack struck. This is corroborated by the fact that it is the third wave of this attack (circle c, diagram 10) which causes his loss of libido and subsequent fall into the unconscious.
b) The fact that he belongs to those who disparaged Nebuchadnezzar and regarded him as 'one man' reflects an immaturity or arrogance in respect of the unconscious that belongs to someone who has little or no knowledge of it or is unaware of its power. Achior's attitude towards the unconscious, and more specifically, the negative Self/Shadow, may also belong to someone who has become too sure of conscious victories over the unconscious. Someone who functions at the second stage of consciousness may simply not have encountered the unconscious enough times to remember its devastating power. Alternatively, such a person may have become positively inflated after her/his first victory over the unconscious—too sure of leaving its embrace—to fear another round

of attacks. This alternative may also apply to someone who has successfully defeated the unconscious on more than one occasion. In my opinion, this is applicable to Achior. We have already established that he was in the process of relocating to the third stage of consciousness prior to/around the time of Holofernes' attack. This means that he would have scored at least two victories over the unconscious—however tenuous they may or may not have been (stage 1–2, stage 2–3), thus making him a possible candidate for inflation and resulting in his originally disparaging attitude towards the unconscious/negative Self.

c) We have seen that Achior is the only character who addresses Holofernes/the shadow on his own, and we have interpreted this to mean that he retains more personal autonomy or libido than the other foreign advisors who appear before the Assyrian general. This infers that he has not completely lost the libidinous surge which both prompted him to move to the third stage and which resulted from it—even though the process was aborted by Holofernes' attack. This, in turn, intimates that he may have sufficient residual libido to escape the power of the shadow, which he indeed does, albeit despite himself: he 'escapes' as a result of being evicted from the Assyrian camp and the libidinal energy released through the Bethulians' prayers.

d) We have also noted that Achior is completely 'delivered' from the unconscious, as evidenced by the fact that his eviction from Holofernes' camp takes place in four steps. Having been delivered from the unconscious, Achior is taken up the path of consciousness by the Bethulians who represent psychological elements/people occupying the fourth stage of consciousness (cf. circle 2, diagram 10 and table 10). This means that he effectively 'jumps' from his fallen unconscious state straight to the stage of consciousness where realisation of social reality sets in and individual consciousness begins. Nevertheless, there are only seven steps to his integration here. This indicates that his integration at this stage is incomplete and creates the expectation that it will either be completed or aborted at a later stage in the narrative.

e) The Bethulians eagerly receive Achior in their midst because he is not an altogether foreign content (he is a distant family member through Lot) and because he reflects their conscious attitude. The dominant conscious attitude of the Bethulians is governed by the Deuteronomistic principle of retribution, a principle that Achior mediates in its totality. We have indicated that this attitude is reflective of someone who has not completely transcended the second stage of individuation, i.e., someone whose 'ego' has not sufficiently distinguished itself from older forms of societal norms and patterns of thought to form her/his own moral view of the world (stage 3).

f) Owing to his representation of both aspects of Deuteronomistic philosophy, Achior becomes a conductor for the tension that consciousness experiences regarding this philosophy vis-à-vis its interpretation of the current situation, and the way is paved for a new interpretation of life to enter the conscious realm, resolve the tension within Achior/the Bethulian community, and facilitate the elimination of the crisis, i.e., the defeat of the Assyrian/ unconscious shadow forces. Resolving the tension between opposite aspects of Achior's dominant conscious attitude will resolve the same within the Bethulian community on account of the essential identity between them. Failing that, both he and the Bethulians-Judaeans will be subsumed by the unconscious shadow/Holofernes and ultimately come to serve the negative Self *cum* destructive power archetype, Nebuchadnezzar.

Taking all the above into consideration, we may say the following concerning the dilemma which Achior faces at the outset of *Judith*: He must free himself from the force of the negative Self/Shadow *cum* power archetype that has ensnared him through the unconscious shadow so that he can establish his own moral/ethical code and come to the realisation of social reality and so to his true self.

This dilemma entails a number of interrelated and difficult challenges:

1. He must escape the clutches of the unconscious shadow completely and outgrow the inflation that caused him to disparage Nebuchadnezzar at the outset. In order to do so, he needs to separate his ego from his shadow tendencies and integrate them into his conscious psyche.
2. He must put away the ancient Deuteronomistic lore and espouse a new way of looking at life, himself, and others within the current reality.
3. He must achieve a greater connection to God/the Self.
4. He must hear and carry out God's will in the present situation so that he can become an agent of his own salvation and that of

his entire conscious psyche as well as the people with whom he is fate-fully identified.

In summary, then, Achior's dilemma involves crossing the boundaries of at least two stages of consciousness so that he may become established in the fourth: he has to regain his consciousness/conscious identity, separate his ego from his shadow (stage 2), consciously integrate his shadow tendencies, form his own moral/ethical code (stage 3), and become a fully functional member of society at stage 4. As the text indicates, this is a make or break situation. Should Achior fail to become integrally functional at the fourth stage of consciousness, he will be completely swallowed up by the unconscious shadow and his psyche will become dominated by the negative Self/power archetype represented by Nebuchadnezzar. In that case, the conscious ground that he has won will be lost, and he will become one with his unconscious shadow and the negative Self. This, as I have previously indicated, is tantamount to the complete dissolution of consciousness—he will act in union with his unconscious shadow tendencies, almost without realising it, and his original inflation will be intensified through his domination by and identification with the ego-conqueror, negative Self/power archetype. This spells disaster for both him and those around him: he will inevitably succumb to the basest of his own shadow instincts and his desire for absolute power, with the latter being expressed through the complete domination of others—under the guise of some kind of personal/national/racial superiority or attempt to rid the world of human 'vermin'/non-conformists, etc. This, of course, would be nothing but a compensation for his failure to dominate himself—his own shadow tendencies—and to conquer the desire for absolute domination of others that is born out of intense insecurity and fear and that is innate to most if not all shadow-dominations. This, as I have previously stated, is amply demonstrated by Hitler's Third Reich regime and the oppressive Apartheid system of my own South African past.

Returning to Achior, we may now examine how well he deals with the challenges implicit in the dilemma facing him. At face value, i.e., reading the story and his participation in it as is, Achior does not seem to handle these challenges very well at all:

1. Instead of separating himself from the shadow and integrating his shadow tendencies, he begins to ally himself with the unconscious from the outset, thereby letting it integrate him: he warns Holofernes

of the perils of attacking YHWH's people before ascertaining their standing before God.

2. Achior fares no better at integrating the shadow once he is out of its grasp: he merely relays Holofernes' plans to the Bethulians—who represent his (Achior's) higher shadow elements—and prays with them for deliverance. He shows little indication of accepting them apart from this, even though they seem to have accepted him.
3. While he has been accepted by the people of YHWH to a relatively high degree, Achior remains a pagan. According to the Deuteronomistic philosophy that he and the Bethulians-Judaeans have adopted, this means that he is excluded from the community *of* YHWH and that he is therefore out of community *with* YHWH—despite his possible participation in the prayer vigil.
4. Achior continues to cling to Deuteronomistic philosophy even in his ascent to higher consciousness. He joins Ozias and the elders in an all-night prayer vigil which is largely founded upon the people's Deuteronomistic perception that they have sinned and must therefore entreat God to save them from their certain doom. (Please note that neither Ozias nor the elders ever counteract the people's negative self-perception in *Judith* 1–7, which means that they too are governed by it—albeit to a lesser extent).
5. There is no indication that Achior has heard YHWH's will nor yet that he is willing to become an agent of his own salvation and that of the Bethulians who share his fate. In fact, he adopts the same passive-prayer attitude that they have espoused.

Nevertheless, Achior has indeed escaped the clutches of the Shadow and risen to the fourth stage of consciousness for which he was destined. In the very least, his willingness to assist the Bethulians—through information and prayer—shows that he has the desire to escape the shadow and integrate his own shadow tendencies, even though he may not know how. And so all is not lost, even though the first section ends on such a dreary note of desperation.

c. *Section II*—Judith *8–16*

The second section of *Judith* (chapters 8–16) is completely dominated by the actions of Judith who is unquestionably its obvious protagonist or heroine. It begins with an introduction of Judith (8:1–8) and ends with the fact that her memory outlived her lifespan and protected her people for many years beyond her physical death (16:21–25). Between these two markers lie all the 'glorious' deeds (cf. 10:8, 15:9) that this woman committed in the name of her God for the deliverance of her people, the Judaeans. The entire section turns, as it were, around Judith's decapitation of Holofernes (D in Craven's structure, chapter 1), which divides the story naturally into 'before' (Aa–Bb–Cc) and 'after' (Cc'–Bb'–Aa') scenes. I will therefore follow this section's internal subdivision where applicable—some characters appear only in Aa–Bb–Cc or Cc'–Bb'–Aa'—as I analyse the characters who present themselves in *Judith* 8–16.

Judith

When we first encounter Judith—'before' the central event(s) of section II—she is a pious, beautiful, rich, and wise widow of unassailable character (cf. καὶ οὐκ ἦν ὃς ἐπήνεγκεν αὐτῇ ῥῆμα πονηρόν—8:8a) who has dwelt in a tent above her house [see point c) below] in Bethuliah since her husband's death forty months previously (8:1–8, Aa). Upon hearing the people's "wicked words" against Ozias (8:9; they demand that he surrender their city to the enemy—7:24–28), she sends her trusted stewardess (ἅβρα)[30] to summon Chabris and Charmis, the elders of her city (8:10). They arrive seemingly without delay and Judith immediately begins to chastise them for the five-day ultimatum that they have imposed upon God (7:30). She calls them to lay down their pride by which, in effect, they were setting themselves up in the place of God (cf. 8:11). She teaches that God is sovereign, and that He is impervious to the kind of manipulation that their ultimatum entails (8:11–16). Judith encourages them to continue trusting God for salvation as none in their generation had been guilty of idolatry (8:17–20). She alerts them to the fact that, should they yield to Holofernes, they would be responsible not

[30] The word ἅβρα occurs seven times in *Judith* (8:10, 33; 10:2, 5, 17; 13:9; and 16:23) and a further eight times in other books of the LXX where it regularly translates נערה (Enslin, op. cit., 112). While some commentators derive it from ἁβρός—graceful, beautiful—many others believe it to reflect a loan word, possibly from the Aramaic/Hebrew חברה—"1) associate, fellow, companion" (ESL). Hence Enslin translates as "favorite slavegirl" here and elsewhere (cf. op. cit., 112–113). Seeing that this unnamed woman is Judith's stewardess, I prefer to translate as "trusted stewardess" or retain the Greek as "ἅβρα/*abra*."

only for their own destruction, but for that of all their 'brethren' in Judaea too (8:21–24). She further encourages them to thank God for not testing them as harshly as he had tested Abraham, Isaac, and Jacob, and to see the present difficulty as a trial born out of God's love for them rather than the punishment that they believed it to be (8:25–27). Ignoring Ozias' excuses, compliments, and his request that she pray for God to send rain (8:28–31), Judith commands that they wait for her at the city gate that night. She would then go out with her trusted stewardess and perform something that would astound generations of people and bring about God's salvation before the ultimatum expired. She would not, however, reveal what form this action would take until it had been accomplished (8:32–34). The elders bid her well and pray that God would go before her to effect the destruction of their enemies (8:35), whereupon they leave her tent and return to their stations (8:36).

As we can already see from the above, Judith is 'other' to every main character introduced to us so far. In the first place, she is 'other' concerning her gender—all the other main characters have been male. This otherness extends to her authority, the members of her gender, her piety, her character, her understanding of God's nature and His role in the situation, her sense of community, her appearance and wealth, her characterisation within the story, her location, and her genealogical heritage:

a) **Judith's Authority.** A lone widow woman summons a group of men that constitute Bethuliah's hierarchic leadership and they obey unquestioningly. They give her *carte blanche* to do as she desires. By contrast, they are unable to command the loyalty of their subjects without some sort of compromise (cf. 7:23–31). This shows that Judith commands a far higher level of authority and hence represents a higher level of consciousness than both the male leadership of Bethuliah and its people, making her the highest conscious factor in Bethuliah and the person who has achieved the highest level of consciousness. Judith thus replaces Ozias as the highest conscious factor at the fourth level of conscious awareness.

b) **Judith's Independence.** Judith is ruler over her own household and her own life, having no man over her, be he husband, son, father, or relative. The text makes sure that we understand that Manasses is *her* husband (καὶ ὁ ἀνὴρ **αὐτῆς** Μανασσης τῆς φυλῆς

αὐτῆς καὶ τῆς πατριᾶς **αὐτῆς**[31]—8:2)—she is never called *his* wife—and that he is dead (8:2–3). This clearly elevates her above him, making him her 'dependent' at a textual level. Note too that Judith has neither male nor female children. She is 'alone' and independent, albeit surrounded by man- and maidservants. The text also makes sure we comprehend that Manasses has been dead long enough—forty months—for her to overcome the grief. These factors make her the only female character encountered so far who is an independent actant. By contrast, the text always locates the actions of other women within the context of a group of people that includes (their?) men and children. Furthermore, these women are always mentioned as a 'group': *they* throng with the men to pray and cry out to God (4:10, 11), *they* thirst (7:22, 27), and the men send *them* home (7:32). They never act independently or in their individual capacities.

c) **Judith's Freedom of Movement.** Judith is also the only character—female or male—who is described as pious, wealthy, wise, and beautiful, and the only character who ventures outside the walls of Bethuliah of her own free will. Psychologically speaking, her voluntary movement outside Bethuliah indicates that she is a person who has broken out of the group—out of collective thinking, gendered expectations, and collective ideals—and that her level of individuation is higher than that of the other Bethulians. Indeed, as we shall soon see, it is higher than that of all other human characters encountered so far. Judith's voluntary freedom of movement also indicates that, as a psychological content, she has attained sufficient libido to break free from the collective unconscious of her people. In addition, her various movements are evidence of the fact that this libido is sufficiently flexible to enable her to traverse the boundaries between the psychic realms—to move in and out of Bethuliah—and engage the unconscious psyche actively should the need arise. Her wealth, servants, and unencumbered status indicate clearly that she indeed has the resources and the freedom to do so. Furthermore, her wisdom shows that she has a high form of individuation and close ties with the Self from whom all wisdom flows.

[31] The Greek could easily have omitted the second "her" (αὐτῆς). It does not do so, however. Instead, it emphasises the fact that Manasses came from her tribe and her kindred.

d) **Judith's Piety.** Judith is pious beyond the required norm—she wears sackcloth and prays constantly atop her house. She also fasts daily with the exception of days on which fasting is proscribed. According to Enslin (op. cit., 111), "the roof of a Palestinian house was frequently used for the purpose of prayer" in postexilic Judaism, and fasting was "frequently practised as a voluntary act of devotion by the uncommonly devout." It was, however, proscribed on certain days in *Megillat Taʿanit* because of the events associated with them (ibid.). Judith's super-devotion is evident in the fact that her fast is continuous—save for the days proscribed. "[Her] actions—both the constant prayer and the wearing of sackcloth—. . . [apparently] indicate that what for most was but occasional was for her regular routine" (ibid.). By contrast, the Bethulians fast and pray only in a time of crisis. Her faith and resolve to resist the attack of the enemy are unswerving, versus the Bethulians' increasing cries of desperation and their leaders' readiness to give in to their demands in the face of trouble. (See, e.g., 4:9; 5:12; and 7:19, 23 where the verb ἀναβοάω is used. Note, in this regard, that ἀναβοάω is used only for the prayer cries of the Bethulians/Judaeans. The less intensive verb βοάω—to call out (9:1, 10:1)—is used for Judith's prayer cry. Where βοάω is used for Judith's compatriots, i.e., *Judith* 4:12 and 15, it is modified by phrases indicating the great stress under which they call out to God [ὁμοθυμαδὸν ἐκτενῶς and ἐκ πάσης δυνάμεως, respectively]. The use of ἀναβοάω and βοάω as described above alludes to the high stress factor which is present in the prayers of the Bethulians/Judaeans but absent from the prayer of Judith).

Judith's piety is clearly indicative of her superlative communication with the Self—for which healthy self-abnegation and ego-sacrifice (e.g., fasting, prayer, wearing of sackcloth) is a must. It is this continual ego-sacrifice—putting the Self above the ego—which permits her to maintain an excellent relationship with the Self and to proclaim with confidence that God/the Self would indeed bring about deliverance (greater psychological integration, heightened consciousness) by her hand within the next five-day period.

e) **Judith's Integrity.** Judith alone is described as having a character that is beyond reproach (8:8a). In other words, her character is one of intense integrity, one that is achieved only as a result of the integration of unconscious contents and the resolution of opposites. This too bears testimony to the high level of individuation that she has achieved as a person.

f) **Judith's Superior Understanding of YHWH and the Current Situation.** Judith is the only character who understands the nature of God and who is able to provide a different interpretation of His role in the current situation. First and foremost, Judith is quick to ground God's actions (or lack thereof in the Bethulians' eyes) within His sovereign freedom to act or not to act on behalf of His people in the way that they envisage (cf. especially 8:15 and 17). By contrast, the Bethulians' ultimatum represents their desire to manipulate God into carrying out their need for deliverance (cf. 8:16). According to Judith, this imposition (cf. μὴ ἐνεχυράζετε[32] τὰς βουλὰς κυρίου—"do not impose conditions on the Lord our God" [Moore, op. cit., 177]; 8:16) is nothing but the highest hubris, for by it they are testing God and putting themselves above Him amongst His people (8:12). By it they also stand the chance of provoking Him to anger (8:14), because they are treating Him as a mere man who may be threatened and cajoled to bring about what they desire (8:16). Instead, God is a free agent, the Sovereign, Omnipotent Lord. "For if he does not choose to help us within these five days," says Judith, "he has power to protect us within any time he pleases, or even to destroy us in the presence of our enemies. . . . Therefore, while we wait for his deliverance, let us call upon him to help us, and he will hear our voice, if it pleases him" (ibid., 8:15 and 17). Judith's rather doubtful words of encouragement (cf. "*if* it pleases him") are based on the people's blameless record as regards idolatry (8:18, 20). This was a sin for which "our fathers were handed over to the sword, and to be plundered, and . . . suffered a great catastrophe before our enemies." (8:19). "We", however, have not committed this sin and can "therefore . . . hope that he will not disdain us or any

[32] According to the gloss, ἐνεχυράζω signifies "to take a pledge from". Similarly, Liddell and Scott render the word as "to take a pledge from one. 2. c. accus. rei, to take in pledge: Pass . . . to have one's goods seized for debt: Med. to have surety given one, τόκου for interest." The RAPC renders the phrase "ὑμεῖς δὲ μὴ ἐνεχυράζετε τὰς βουλὰς κυρίου τοῦ θεοῦ ἡμῶν" as "Do not try to bind the purposes of the Lord our God". Given the context in which this phrase occurs, Moore's "do not impose conditions on the Lord our God" is a far better translation that clearly brings out exactly what the Greek literally says: 'do not take the will/counsels of our Lord God in pledge'.

of our nation" (8:20). God is not punishing "us" for the sins of "our" fathers, she says (cf. "nor has he taken revenge upon us"—8:27; contrast 7:28). Rather, He is 'testing' "us" because we have drawn near to Him (cf. "but the Lord scourges those who draw near to him, in order to admonish them"—8:27) as he had done the patriarchs, Abraham, Isaac, and Jacob, and should be thanked for the lesser severity of "our" 'trial'/'test' (8:24–27). "We" should therefore persevere and set an example for our" countrymen, as the fate of the whole of Judaea and of the sanctuary depends upon "us" (8:21–24).

Judith's interpretation of the events significantly challenges the Bethulians' negative outlook because it vitiates their Deuteronomistically based assumption that they are suffering as a result of their sinfulness and that of their forefathers (cf. 7:28, 8:27). It redirects their attention to their erstwhile positive view of themselves, i.e., as those sanctified to the Lord (cf. 6:19), because it insists that:

a) They are blameless as regards worship (8:18–20).
b) The current situation represents a trial/test by which the Lord wishes to admonish and not punish them (8:27).

Judith's 'theology of divine testing' thus significantly challenges the ultra-Deuteronomistic approach that regards punishment as an indisputable sign of sin and blessing as a definite sign of righteousness. It replaces punishment with 'trial' and sinfulness with righteousness as it locates the origin of this trial in the righteous action of those affected, i.e., in the fact that they have drawn near to God, and in God's desire to admonish/lead people to greater maturity. In fact, by allowing for the blameless to suffer and for God to act outside the Deuteronomistic paradigm as and when He wills on behalf of His people (to admonish them), Judith's theology frees both the human characters and God from the (human) constraints that the rigid application of the Deuteronomistic principle imposes upon them. It also introduces a fine balance between what had become an absolutised interpretation of divine-human interaction and the rather thorny issue of God's freedom, with the latter correctly based on His sovereignty as Creator and Lord/King of the Universe:

The rigid, ultra-Deuteronomistic approach allows one to demand salvation of God on the basis of human righteousness or to attempt to manipulate Him to bless one because of one's presumed righteous standing with Him. This, in essence, is what underlies the Bethulian leadership's five-day ultimatum (which is endorsed by the remaining Bethulians with the exception of Judith—cf. 7:30–31). As Judith rightly points out (see especially 8:14), it represents a case of great hubris (see 8:12–14, 16), i.e., sin, which is punishable by destruction (cf. references to testing God and God's wrath in 8:12–14, and 16) according to the very Deuteronomistic principle upon which it is based. The ultimatum is a sin because it does not recognise the freedom of God and hence does not acknowledge Him as Sovereign Lord. It places the Bethulian leadership above God amongst the people (8:12) whereas only God can 'manipulate' or mould events and people according to His desires (see e.g., 8:15 and 17).

This brings me to the flip-side of this argument. The human concept of God's freedom, when taken to extremes, completely nullifies the need for human actions and/or the effect that such actions may have upon a person's life and/or that of the community. This position devalues humanity by regarding humans as puppets in the hands of an omnipotent, uncaring God who does just as He wills when He wills irrespective of the life lived by any single human being or group of humans. This is the distressing conclusion that the writer of Ecclesiastes comes to, i.e., that God's freedom is gratuitous and wholly divorced from human action (cf., e.g. Ecclesiastes 7:12–15, 23–29 and 8:6–7, 17). The concept of God's supposedly gratuitous freedom flies directly in the face of both His nature and the Deuteronomistic theology which it nullifies. This too binds God into human categories—it makes Him a mere man—just as much as it binds humanity into utter hopelessness (cf. "for God is not like man, to be threatened, nor like a human being, to be won over by pleading"; 8:16). The concept of divine testing (8:25–27) mediates skilfully between these conflicting concepts in that it allows for a symbiosis between the correct appraisal of human action—we are sinless and we are not being punished but we are being admonished—and the freedom of God to do what He wills as and when He wills on behalf of His people and to the glory of His name. (See 9:14 where Judith prays that God would assist her so that He may be glorified as the God of all power and the protector of His people, Israel). Moreover, the balanced mediation of Judith's approach becomes a source of encouragement and hope: God will help us as He wills (8:15). This is an assertion that maintains both God's beneficence towards His people and His freedom in respect of Himself. By waiting upon Him to do for "us" as He wills and by persevering in this time of trouble (cf. 8:20), "we" can encourage "our" fellow Judaeans to do the same (cf. 8:24). This will ensure that none of "us" will perish and that Jerusalem and its temple will not be destroyed (cf. 8:21–24). In other words, our correct (read: wise) response to the situation will ensure that our connection with the Self is upheld and strengthened, and that our community benefits/grows (read: enters the next phase of individuation) as a result.

In my opinion, Judith's appraisal of the situation and her understanding of the nature/role of God in it accommodates the Bethulians' righteousness, God's freedom, and the Assyrian attack in the kind of tension which is very conducive to personal growth. The reason for this is that it breaks the bonds of the traditional, collective patterns of thought, which are upheld in this case by orthodox adherence to Deuteronomistic lore, and points the way forward (to greater individuation) by presenting other means of comprehending reality. It bears clear testimony to the high stage of Judith's individuation and to her two-fold connectedness to the Self and the community from which she comes.

g) **Judith's Action- and Community Orientation.** In this time of distress, Judith alone is able to look beyond Bethuliah's immediate need—surviving the thirst (cf. 7:22, 27; and 8:28–31)—to the fate of her fellow Judaeans. By contrast, the Bethulian leadership and populace display a questionable character, caring little for their 'brethren,' as Judith calls them. In fact, Judith is the only person ever to employ the word ἀδελφός (brother), applying it both to her fellow Bethulians (7:30; 8:14, 24; 14:1) and to the Judaeans in general (8:22, 24).[33] Furthermore, she alone is willing to take the lead and actively engage the enemy on behalf of all. By contrast, the male leadership command that fortifications be made and that victuals be stored, and then wait for Holofernes'

[33] The only other occurrence of this word is found in *Judith* 8:26 and concerns Laban: μνήσθητε ὅσα ἐγένετο τῷ Ιακωβ ἐν Μεσοποταμίᾳ τῆς Συρίας ποιμαίνοντι τὰ πρόβατα Λαβαν τοῦ ἀδελφοῦ τῆς μητρὸς αὐτοῦ. This too comes from the mouth of Judith.

attack (cf., e.g., 4:4–7). Judith's strategy is to be actively on the offensive, whereas theirs is passively and hysterically defensive.

The combined factors listed in this point, the immediately preceding one, and point b) above show that Judith has reached the most advanced stage of individuation, where one is freed from the collective unconscious—from the demands, opinions, etc. of one's 'herd' or group—and so empowered to serve one's community in the most effective manner possible. As we shall soon see, this is further borne out by the fact that she has a sixteen-tier genealogy (see point j) below).

h) **Judith's Depiction in the Story.** Judith is also the character about whom the author provides the most information. She alone is described and shown as rich, beautiful, and wise—by both the narrator and, e.g., Ozias (8:4–8 and 28–29; see also 11:20), whereas what we glean about the other characters in the book is merely shown to us.[34] This too is indicative of a high level of psychological integration and, moreover, one that is recognised as such by others in her 'group': Judith wears no mask; she does as she is. The only other character who can claim such an integration between being and deed is God.

i) **Judith's Remoteness.** Judith lives in a tent above her house—literally above the other Bethulians. In addition, a certain sense of remoteness adheres to the words "At that time Judith heard about these things" (8:1) and "When Judith heard [literally: and she heard] the wicked words spoken by the people against the ruler" (8:9). It is as though Judith were not involved in any of the deliberations that had taken place up to this point—as though she were somehow set apart from or above the other Bethulians and only came to hear of the situation that they were experiencing. This kind of 'separatedness' also points to her heightened level of consciousness in that those who reach the fifth stage of consciousness often find that they are 'above' or somehow 'apart from' the rest of their fellows.

j) **Judith's Genealogy.** Judith's sixteen-tier genealogy is found in *Judith* 8:1, and is the longest genealogy in the entire book (con-

[34] I refer here to the narrative techniques of *telling*, where the narrator/author describes a character, its personality, etc., and *showing*, where the narrator/author allows the reader to discern a character's motivations, personality, etc. by way of its actions and words in the narrative.

> trast 8:1 with 6:15, the single-tier genealogies of Ozias, [Ch]abris and Charmis). This is no mean feat for a female character in an ancient Hebrew narrative! She also possesses the longest genealogy of any woman in the Hebrew Bible—Apocrypha included. Her sixteen-tier genealogy indicates that she has reached 'perfection' at her level of individuation: 16 = 4 × 4, and 4 is the 'perfect number' of individuation (see Rollins 1983:61 and Jung's *Quaternio* Equation, diagram 7). The 'perfect' depth of her ancestral roots shows that she is a person who has deep roots in the unconscious memories of her people—roots that extend to the very foundation of her culture as can be seen by the fact that Israel or Jacob is the last name in her genealogy. Similarly, she represents a conscious content that has deep, ancient roots in the unconscious psyche. This is verified by the fact that her genealogy contains names that link her to Israel's major institutional and historical traditions, viz., the priesthood (Merari), the patriarchs and the sojourn in Egypt (Joseph), the Judges (Gideon), and the prophets (Elijah; cf. Levine 1992:21). Her link to these institutions of Israel may be seen as the narrator's attempt to present her as the legitimate leader and bringer of hope in the face of the Bethulian (and Judaean) leadership's failure to resolve the current crisis of war and thirst. Her genealogy may also be read as a list of her Messianic credentials (the Messiah is a priest, prophet, judge, deliverer, etc. Cf., e.g. Isaiah 42:1–2, 52:13, 53:10–12 and Hebrews 9:1–28) to the same effect.

As we can see, the first chapter of section II establishes Judith as 'other' to all the human characters encountered so far, both as a person and as a psychological content. She is the most individuated person, the highest form of consciousness (next to God), the person/content most connected to the Self, and the person/content who is connected at the most fundamental level to the community from which she stems. She is thus the ideal hero(ine).

Having established her 'otherness,' the text then records Judith's fervent prayer for empowerment in *Judith* 9:2–14: Her prayer preparations (9:1) indicate not only the earnestness of her prayer, but also her willingness to submit her unnamed plan to the complete control of the Self.[35] She falls on her face, confirming that her position

---

[35] It is sometimes thought that Judith would not disclose her plan because she

before the Self is lowly, despite (and because of) her highly individuated nature, and she puts ashes on her head, demonstrating hereby that she purposefully sacrifices or surrenders all the thoughts/plans of her mind to the Self. Furthermore, we are told that she takes off her sackcloth: καὶ ἐγύμνωσεν ὃν ἐνεδεδύκει σάκκον (9:1c). The verb γυμνόω, which commonly means "to strip oneself (naked)", also denotes "to be stript [read: stripped] of arms, to be left defenceless" (Liddell and Scott).[36] This intimates that Judith is willing to place her entire being under the charge of the Self and all her 'weaponry' at its disposal. Clearly, hers is not the kind of lowliness and self-abnegation produced by negative inflation. Rather, it represents the humility that results from a high level of individuation and psychological integration. Similarly, the radicality of her faith indicates the kind of peace or rest that results from complete trust in the nature and operations of the Self. As this is normally achieved only by the endurance of many trials via continual submission to and communication with the Self, Judith's highly individuated nature suggests that she has indeed undergone such trials herself, even though the text gives no direct evidence of this. Judith's whole demeanour is reflective of someone who has understood suffering and hence experienced it. In my opinion, that is why she regards the current situation as a trial (cf. 8:25–27). She understands that the purpose of God/the Self is not to destroy the people of Judaea, but to bring them to a higher level of individuation through the present trial, i.e., to bring them through this leg of the *ἀγών*—in the Jungian sense—to a greater sense of community amongst themselves and a greater sense of communion with Godself.

Judith's prayer, which coincides exactly with the evening incense offering in Jerusalem (9:1), is built entirely upon an analogy between the current situation and the rape of Dinah—Jacob's daughter and

---

had none. Note, however, *Judith* 8:32–34 and 9:9, especially the phrase "δὸς ἐν χειρί μου τῆς χήρας *ὃ διενοήθην κράτος*", which RAPC correctly translates with "give to me, a widow, the strength to do what I plan".

[36] Given the meaning of γιμνόω, RAPC's translation of 9:1c, "and uncovered the sackcloth she was wearing" (so too Moore, op. cit., 189), is rather weak. Enslin (op. cit., 121) uses "laid bare", which is closer to the Greek. I would prefer to translate as "she stripped off the sackcloth which she was wearing" as this would not only be closer to the Greek, but would also convey the urgency of Judith's prayer preparation.

Simeon's sister—in Genesis 34. Addressing God as "Lord God of my father Simeon" (9:2),[37] Judith describes the onerous event of Genesis 34:2 in barely euphemistic language (cf. 9:2).[38] She extols the zeal of Simeon and his brothers for taking vengeance upon the entire community from which Shechem, the rapist, came (9:4; see especially Genesis 34:25–29). She then makes her request that God, the God who crushes battles (9:7), would crush the Assyrians through her hand as He had crushed the Shechemites through Simeon's hand (9:8–10). This request, which fervently condemns the pride and effrontery (9:7 and 8) of the Assyrian attackers, is prefixed, suffixed, and interspersed with praise to the Lord, the God of the humble, the Creator and Almighty Sovereign who slew the enemy through Simeon's hand (9:3, 4, 5–6, 9:7g, 8a, 11–12, and 14).

Judith's prayer contains a number of very striking elements (see further below). For me, the most striking of these is that it is predicated or dependent upon the use of deceit (note especially 9:13 and the boldfaced words below)—that of Shechem (9:3), Simeon (not explicitly stated, but see Genesis 34:13 below), and her own (9:10 and 13)—for its success. This may well be the 'power' she speaks of in *Judith* 9:9 (see the underlined portion in 9:9 below):

9:3 ἀνθ᾽ ὧν ἔδωκας ἄρχοντας αὐτῶν εἰς φόνον
καὶ τὴν στρωμνὴν αὐτῶν, ἣ ᾐδέσατο τὴν **ἀπάτην** αὐτῶν,
ἀπατηθεῖσαν εἰς αἷμα[39]. . .

[37] It is puzzling to find Simeon's name omitted from Judith's genealogy in *Judith* 8:1 given his importance in Judith's prayer and the fact that both she and her husband are of his lineage. It is also strange from the point of view that that Σαλαμιηλ (Shelumiel) and Σαρασαδαι (Zurishadai), who *do* appear in her genealogy, are respectively Simeon's grandson and son (Numbers 1:6; 2:12; 7:23, 41; and 10:19). Whether the author omitted his name and why is uncertain, as Mss 23 and 108 include him and two others append "ἐκ φυλῆς Συμεων" (from the tribe of Simeon) to Israel (Enslin, op. cit., 110).

[38] *Judith* 9:2 states that ἔλυσαν μήτραν παρθένου (literally: they loosed a virgin's womb), ἐγύμνωσαν μηρὸν (made bare the thigh), and ἐβεβήλωσαν μήτραν (defiled the womb).

[39] This sentence is very difficult to translate. Literally, it reads as follows: "Because of which you gave their princes/rulers over to slaughter, and their bed, which was ashamed of their deceit, they were deceived (ἀπατηθεῖσαν = Aorist Passive, third person plural of ἀπατάω) to blood." In my opinion, καὶ τὴν στρωμνὴν αὐτῶν, ἣ ᾐδέσατο τὴν ἀπάτην αὐτῶν is superfluous to the text as we have it. Omitting it would certainly make for easier reading and better continuity with the remaining portion of this verse: "You gave their rulers over to slaughter and struck down

9:9 . . . ἀπόστειλον τὴν ὀργήν σου εἰς κεφαλὰς αὐτῶν,
δὸς ἐν χειρί μου τῆς χήρας ὃ διενοήθην κράτος
9:10 πάταξον δοῦλον ἐκ χειλέων **ἀπάτης** μου ἐπ' ἄρχοντι . . .
θραῦσον αὐτῶν τὸ ἀνάστεμα ἐν χειρὶ θηλείας
9:13 καὶ δὸς λόγον μου καὶ **ἀπάτην** εἰς τραῦμα καὶ μώλωπα αὐτῶν,
οἳ κατὰ τῆς διαθήκης σου καὶ οἴκου ἡγιασμένου σου
καὶ κορυφῆς Σιων καὶ οἴκου κατασχέσεως υἱῶν σου
ἐβουλεύσαντο σκληρά.

It will be remembered that Simeon and his brothers used verbal deceit (cf. "The sons of Jacob answered Shechem and his father Hamor deceitfully"—Genesis 34:13) to cajole Shechem and the male members of his people to undergo circumcision, with the promise of intermarriage between Shechem's people and those belonging to Jacob's tribe (Genesis 34:13–17). When the Shechemites were in the throes of the resultant pain, Simeon and his brothers pounced upon them, put them to the sword, took Dinah back, and "plundered the city, because their sister had been defiled; they took their flocks and their herds, their asses, and whatever was in the city and in the field; all their wealth, all their little ones and their wives, all that was in the houses, they captured and made their prey" (Genesis 34:27–29; see further verses 25–29). This analogy indicates that Judith intends to use verbal deceit not only to kill her Shechem, i.e., the Assyrian general Holofernes, but also to plunder his goods, and to nullify the power upon which he relies and the fear with which he holds her people captive. Holofernes, as we have seen, is driven by the power archetype under whose 'spell' he has come and by which he terrorises all the western nations who had disobeyed the negative Self/Nebuchadnezzar. He is also chief of the largely instinctual force that has come upon the unfortunate western nations including

slaves with nobles, and nobles on their thrones." Nevertheless, the phrase is there and cannot be done away with so easily, even though it is clearly corrupted. There is certainly no textual evidence for its complete exclusion. However, Codices ℵ* and A omit ἀπάτην αὐτῶν—their deceit (Enslin, op. cit., 122)—yielding the following reading: καὶ τὴν στρωμνὴν αὐτῶν, ἣ ᾐδέσατο τὴν ἀπατηθεῖσαν. In this reading, ἀπατηθεῖσαν is taken as an Aorist Passive participle, feminine, accusative, and presumably refers to Dinah, "the one who was deceived". This renders the sentence in question as follows: "you gave their princes/rulers over to slaughter, and their bed—which felt ashamed for the [woman who had been] deceived—to blood/bloodshed". I tend to go along with this reading, as do Enslin (op. cit., 123) and Moore (op. cit., 189 and 191).

Judaea. This intimates that Judith's action will break the power of the unconscious instinctual forces in the people's psyche, and that she will break the 'spell'/fear of the power archetype that currently holds her people captive in the guise of the national shadow, Holofernes.

Judith's prayer is also striking in that she clearly portrays Simeon's slaying of the Shechemites as a righteous act of vengeance (note the italicised portions below) that is orchestrated *and* empowered by God (note particularly the second-person verbs that are boldfaced in the underlined portions below). By contrast, the text of Genesis 34 does not accord God any part in Simeon's act, and Jacob roundly condemns his actions and that of his brothers in Genesis 34:30:

9:2 Κύριε ὁ θεὸς τοῦ πατρός μου Συμεων, ᾧ **ἔδωκας** ἐν χειρὶ ῥομφαίαν
εἰς ἐκδίκησιν ἀλλογενῶν, οἳ ἔλυσαν μήτραν παρθένου εἰς μίασμα
καὶ ἐγύμνωσαν μηρὸν εἰς αἰσχύνην καὶ ἐβεβήλωσαν μήτραν εἰς
ὄνειδος, εἶπας γάρ Οὐχ οὕτως ἔσται, καὶ ἐποίησαν,
9:3 ἀνθ᾽ ὧν **ἔδωκας** ἄρχοντας αὐτῶν εἰς φόνον καὶ τὴν στρωμνὴν
αὐτῶν, ἣ ᾐδέσατο τὴν ἀπάτην αὐτῶν, *ἀπατηθεῖσαν* εἰς αἷμα
καὶ **ἐπάταξας** δούλους ἐπὶ δυνάσταις καὶ δυνάστας ἐπὶ
θρόνους αὐτῶν
9:4 καὶ **ἔδωκας** γυναῖκας αὐτῶν εἰς προνομὴν καὶ θυγατέρας
αὐτῶν εἰς αἰχμαλωσίαν καὶ πάντα τὰ σκῦλα αὐτῶν
εἰς διαίρεσιν υἱῶν ἠγαπημένων ὑπὸ σοῦ, *οἳ καὶ ἐζήλωσαν τὸν*
ζῆλόν σου καὶ ἐβδελύξαντο μίασμα αἵματος αὐτῶν καὶ
ἐπεκαλέσαντό σε εἰς βοηθόν,
ὁ θεὸς ὁ θεὸς ὁ ἐμός, καὶ εἰσάκουσον ἐμοῦ τῆς χήρας.
9:5 σὺ γὰρ **ἐποίησας** τὰ πρότερα ἐκείνων καὶ ἐκεῖνα καὶ τὰ μετέπειτα
καὶ τὰ νῦν καὶ τὰ ἐπερχόμενα διενοήθης, καὶ ἐγενήθησαν ἃ
ἐνενοήθης,
9:6 καὶ παρέστησαν ἃ **ἐβουλεύσω** καὶ εἶπαν Ἰδοὺ πάρεσμεν,
πᾶσαι γὰρ αἱ ὁδοί σου ἕτοιμοι, καὶ ἡ κρίσις σου ἐν προγνώσει.
Genesis 34:30 εἶπεν δὲ Ιακωβ Συμεων καὶ Λευι Μισητόν με
πεποιήκατε ὥστε πονηρόν με εἶναι πᾶσιν τοῖς κατοικοῦσιν τὴν
γῆν, ἔν τε τοῖς Χαναναίοις καὶ τοῖς Φερεζαίοις, ἐγὼ δὲ ὀλιγοστός
εἰμι ἐν ἀριθμῷ, καὶ συναχθέντες ἐπ᾽ ἐμὲ συγκόψουσίν με, καὶ
ἐκτριβήσομαι ἐγὼ καὶ ὁ οἶκός μου.

Another striking and more disturbing factor is that Judith adds the sexual violation of the Shechemite women to their 'captivity' which is mentioned in Genesis 34:29 ("They also took all the women [literally: they took their wives captive]") and, moreover, regards this as an act of God (cf. καὶ **ἔδωκας γυναῖκας αὐτῶν εἰς προνομὴν** καὶ θυγατέρας αὐτῶν εἰς αἰχμαλωσίαν[40]—9:4. See Judges 5:30 below). Here, Judith takes up the deplorable position of Sisera's mother who reportedly fantasised as follows concerning the rape of the enemy (i.e., Israelite) women (Judges 5:28–30):

Judges 5:28 From the window Sisera's mother looked out. Through the window she watched for his return, saying, 'Why is his chariot so long in coming? Why don't we hear the sound of chariot wheels?'

5:29 A reply comes from her wise women, and she repeats these words to herself:

5:30 They are dividing the captured goods [literally: the prey] they found—a woman or two for every man. There are gorgeous robes for Sisera, and colorful, beautifully embroidered robes for me.

While many feminist scholars regard this shocking disdain for other women's lives as a result of the patriarchal conspiracy to pit women against each other, I should like to view it as the desire to destroy or violate what underpins the enemy's androcentric consciousness—the 'purity' and male-controlled sexuality of its women. Of course, it may also be seen as a type of projection: we are glad that our men have the upper hand and that it is not we who are being raped but the enemy women. On a psychological level, we may also regard it as part of the author's own conscious patriarchal concerns which are coming to the fore through Judith's prayer. Alternatively, and I am grateful to Prof. Oosthuizen (the co-promoter of my doctoral thesis) for this insight, this may also be seen as another 'dark strategy'—like deception (see the discussion below)—that consciousness adopts in defence of itself and the ego. Be that as it may, to my mind, it remains an onerous, distasteful association that could foster

[40] As indicated, προνομή relates to "a foraging, foray, raid" (Liddell and Scott). Cf. also the related verb προνομεύω "to go out for foraging, to forage" (Liddell and Scott) referred to previously. When cities are 'foraged' they are robbed of all their goods. Similarly, when women are 'foraged' they are robbed of their virtue or raped. See Moore (op. cit., 189) who makes the association between 'foraging women' and raping them clear in his translation of *Judith* 9:4: "You handed over their wives for rape and their daughters for slavery . . ."

hatred and disregard for women amongst women of different national/ethnic/class backgrounds.

To return to Judith's prayer, her sanctification of Simeon's act becomes the basis for her rather surprising request, i.e., that God would grant her the same power of deception with which Simeon defeated his sisters' rapist so that she may vanquish the enemy who has come to defile God's temple (9:5–6). Judging from *Judith* 9:5–6 (above), Judith seems to regard her 'plan' (cf. 9:9) as a righteous act of salvation that has been foreordained and 'prepared' by God just as Simeon's had. In this way, Judith is clearly drawing a close analogy between herself and Simeon and between Dinah and the temple. Note in this regard that the Genesis text uses the verb μιαίνω ["1) to dye with another colour, to stain. 2) to defile, pollute, sully, contaminate, soil. 2a) to defile with sins"—ESL] to depict the rape of Dinah in Genesis 34:13. In *Judith* 9:2 and 4, Judith too refers to this act by the nominal correlate of μιαίνω, i.e., as a μίασμα ["a stain, defilement; pollute (of persons)"—Liddell and Scott]. However, she reserves the verb μιαίνω—the only occurrence of this verb in *Judith*—for what the Assyrians wish to do to the temple:

9:8 κύριος ὄνομά σοι, σὺ ῥάξον αὐτῶν τὴν ἰσχὺν ἐν δυνάμει σου
καὶ κάταξον τὸ κράτος αὐτῶν ἐν τῷ θυμῷ σου,
ἐβουλεύσαντο γὰρ **<u>βεβηλῶσαι</u> τὰ ἅγιά σου, <u>μιᾶναι</u> τὸ
σκήνωμα τῆς καταπαύσεως τοῦ ὀνόματος τῆς δόξης σου,**
καταβαλεῖν σιδήρῳ κέρας θυσιαστηρίου σου.

From the above, it is obvious that Judith uses the verb μιαίνω as a parallel to βεβηλόω ("to profane, to pollute. *Βέβηλος* allowable to tread, permitted to human use . . . of men: unhallowed, profane, unholy"—Liddell and Scott). The latter verb is used six verses earlier in reference to the 'pollution'/rape of Dinah (9:2)—the only other occurrence of this verb in *Judith* (και **ἐβεβήλωσαν** μήτραν εἰς ὄνειδος).

The restricted application of both μιαίνω/μίασμα and βεβηλόω to the 'defilement' of Dinah and the Jerusalemite temple further underscores the analogy between the rape of Dinah and the defilement of the temple. It also underscores the analogy between Judith and Simeon. Apart from their obvious gender difference, the only other difference between them is the fact that Simeon, Judith's (fore)father (8:1) and Jacob's son, avenged an act of defilement that had already been committed against a living woman, whereas Judith seeks to prevent such an act of defilement occurring against a metaphorical woman, i.e., the temple.

When we consider that Shechem is analogous to Holofernes/the Assyrians, that the latter have been identified as elements of the unconscious psyche, and that Simeon's use of deceit is applauded and adopted by Judith—a highly individuated conscious person/content—we arrive at a rather surprising conclusion: deceit/trickery is an acceptable, valuable function of consciousness and one of its chief weapons in dealing with rising unconscious contents. Moreover, the tendency towards deceit—in this case—is directly attributed to God/the Self in that Judith sees Simeon's deceitful murder of the Shechemites as an action foreordained by God. This is surprising as western binary thought would normally relate deceit to 'the dark side' and hence to Satan and the unconscious, while this may presumably not be the case in a nonbinary mode of thinking such that Judith represents here.

Finally, we note that Judith's prayer relates the Assyrian attack to an act of sexual domination, and emphasises the fact that Simeon's deception of the Shechemites culminated in their destruction upon their beds: he and his brothers killed them with a sword—a phallic symbol—as they lay in pain from the 'surgery' performed upon their chief sexual organ (cf. 9:3, quoted in Greek above). The fact that Judith identifies with Simeon suggests that her strategy will entail dismembering the enemy through the use of verbal *cum* sexual deception. This, however, is not entirely clear at this point. What *is* clear is that Judith, the character closest to God and the daughter of Jacob—the epitome of an ancient Hebrew deceiver—has deceit freely flowing in her ancestral veins. She merely asks God to (empower her to) utilise it for the sake of His temple (9:8 and 13),[41] His covenant with his people (9:13), and His reputation (9:14). That neither she

[41] Owing to the historical links between the covenant and Zion and the structural parallels between them in *Judith* 9:13 (see below), I would argue that "the house possessed by thy children" parallels "thy consecrated house" as "thy covenant" parallels "the top of Zion". This means that "the house of the possession of thy children" has the same meaning as "thy hallowed house" and therefore also refers to the temple:

9:13	... for they have planned cruel things against thy covenant,	A
	and against thy consecrated house,	B
	and against the top of Zion,	A'
	and against the house possessed by thy children.	B'

nor God have any problem with this is evident in the fact that she asks God for this power without any qualms whatsoever. Furthermore, her prayer offering coincides with the evening incense offering in Jerusalem (9:1), which signifies that God has indeed heard her prayer—inclusive of His association with deception—and that He will grant her request (see Psalm 141:2 for the idea of God-pleasing prayer being as incense rising).

Having concluded her prayer, Judith arises from her prostrate position, calls her trusted stewardess, and goes down into the house where she spent her nonfasting days (10:1–2). She bathes, perfumes, and dresses herself in the clothes that she wore while her husband lived (10:3). She also adorns herself alluringly to deceive (literally) the eyes of all men that would see her (καὶ ἐκαλλωπίσατο σφόδρα εἰς ἀπάτησιν ὀφθαλμῶν ἀνδρῶν—10:4).

Here the sexual deception merely hinted at during her prayer becomes explicit and obvious not only through her action of beautifying herself but also through its specific aim of deception. That sexual deception is to become one of her main battle strategies against Holofernes and the unconscious powers he commands is evident from the use of the noun ἀπάτησις in this verse (10:4, above). This noun is obviously related to ἀπάτη, a noun which characterises:

a) Shechem's rape of Dinah (which is typically projected upon his entire community—note the third-person plural nominal, pronominal, and verbal forms in *Judith* 9:3).
b) The object of Judith's request in *Judith* 9:10 and 13:
   9:10 πάταξον δοῦλον ἐκ χειλέων **ἀπάτης** μου ἐπ' ἄρχοντι . . .
   9:13 καὶ δὸς λόγον μου καὶ **ἀπάτην** εἰς τραῦμα καὶ μώλωπα αὐτῶν . . .

When we consider that the latter word, ἀπάτη, includes "deceit: in a less bad sense, cunning, craft: a stratagem in war" (Liddell and Scott) in its semantic range, we see that Judith indeed plans to use her 'alluring beauty'/sexuality as a war stratagem against Holofernes and his unconscious forces. Applying this knowledge retrospectively, we see that we were correct in assuming that Judith would use some form of sexuality in her battle against Holofernes (see the preceding discussion regarding deception and sexuality in her prayer to God). Moreover, we see retrospectively that her intended use of her feminine sexuality is directly associated with God in the same way that her intended use of deceptive speech is, i.e., through her belief that her act and its mode of execution are pre-ordained by God. Needless to say, this too would be a surprising association for many a western reader, although neither Judith nor God seem to regard it as strange, untoward, or sinful. To the contrary, the fact that her prayer offering coincides with the evening incense offering in Jerusalem (9:1) signifies that God has heard it—inclusive of its association of deception *and* sexuality with Him—and that He will grant her request.

Having beautified herself, Judith packs a basket of "kosher" food, gives it to her ἅβρα, and the two women set off to the city gate where Ozias and the elders are waiting for Judith's return (10:5–6; see 8:33 where Judith commands the elders to "stand at the city gate tonight" before she begins her prayer and beauty preparations). The men are completely astounded by her beauty (10:7) and pronounce a blessing upon all her endeavours to the glory of Israel (10:7–8). She commands that the gate be opened for her, which it is, and the first three subsections of *Judith* 8–16 (8:1–10:10, Aa–Cc) end with the men of Bethuliah watching her and her trusted stewardess descend the hill towards the enemy camp until they can no longer see them (10:9–10).

Judith's prayer, and particularly her identification with Simeon (his use of deception in the destruction of the Shechemites), entails the actualisation of an interesting and vital transformation that may be traced back to the conception of her secret plan in *Judith* 8. While the plan she conceived initialised the process by which she, a private woman of prayer, came out into the public sphere of men's warfare, her prayer and subsequent beautification effectively transform her from a wise woman into a vengeful, bloodthirsty man like Simeon, from a chaste widow into a beautiful, operative seductress, and from a conscious content into a 'transpsychic' one that is able to traverse the threshold of consciousness and enter the unconscious realm. The fact that she retains her feminine identity throughout, as evidenced by her intensely feminine beautification process, indicates that this transformation is temporary. Her beautification process also signifies the externalisation of her inner transformation and intimates the fact that her chosen 'weaponry' (see the interpretation of γυμνόω, above) is sexually feminine. The latter may also be inferred from the following:

i) She prays and asks God to help her both as a widow and as a female: "give to me, a widow, the strength to do what I plan" (9:9) and "crush their arrogance by the hand of a woman [literally: a female]" (9:10).

ii) She deliberately takes off the clothing of her widowhood and dresses in the clothing of her 'gladness' (RAPC: "her gayest apparel"), the clothing which she wore while her husband yet lived (10:3).
iii) She purposefully dresses to deceive or allure every man who would see her (see 10:4).

Judith's departure from her house down to the city gate (10:6) extends her outward, physical transformation (beautification) to her geographical and psychic location. Her subsequent descent to the enemy camp (10:10) then clinches her transformation from a conscious content into an unconscious one. As can be seen from the Bethulian men's reaction—they grant her request immediately (10:9)—her beauty-sexuality stratagem clearly works. It has literally opened doors for her in the realms of consciousness and is set to do so again in the realms of the unconscious.

Having entered the realm of the unconscious at the outset of the fourth and most crucial subsection of *Judith* 8–16 (D: 10:11–13:10a), Judith is encountered by an Assyrian outpost. Whereas one would expect a member of the enemy to be regarded with grave suspicion, Judith's beauty, in particular,[42] and her expressed purpose of assisting Holofernes (10:11–16) enchant these soldiers to such an extent that they detail a one-hundred-man band to escort her to Holofernes' tent (10:17).

When Judith arrives at Holofernes' tent, his attendants and officials quickly bring her into the presence of their lord (10:20–21). There, Judith falls before Holofernes in mock subservience and urges him to accept the words that she is about to speak (10:23; 11:5). True to her strategy of deceit, she promises that she will tell no lie, and that Holofernes will succeed in his purposes should he follow her advice:

11:5 . . . Δέξαι τὰ ῥήματα τῆς δούλης σου,
καὶ λαλησάτω ἡ παιδίσκη σου κατὰ πρόσωπόν σου,
οὐκ ἀναγγελῶ ψεῦδος τῷ κυρίῳ μου ἐν τῇ νυκτὶ ταύτῃ[43]

[42] Note that the men's perception of her beauty is emphasised twice in *Judith* 10:14 (my emphasis): "When the men heard her words, and *observed her face—she was in their eyes marvelously beautiful* . . ."

[43] It is interesting to note that Achior had spoken words to the same effect before Holofernes: "Let my lord now hear a word from the mouth of your servant, and

11:6 καὶ ἐὰν κατακολουθήσῃς τοῖς λόγοις τῆς παιδίσκης σου,
τελείως πρᾶγμα ποιήσει μετὰ σοῦ ὁ θεός,
καὶ οὐκ ἀποπεσεῖται ὁ κύριός μου τῶν ἐπιτηδευμάτων αὐτου

She shamelessly flatters Holofernes (11:7–8) and corroborates the verity of Achior's words (11:9–10, 11)—the only point of truth in her entire speech. She emphasises that she has fled the Judaeans because they had sinned (cf. 11:16) in their decision to consume foods dedicated to God and intended solely for priestly consumption (11:11–14). As a result, she avers, God would destroy them. God had sent her to Holofernes (note the boldfaced portions below) to do great and astonishing things with him that would excite/astound the whole earth (11:16). God would tell her when they had committed this sin (note the underlined portions below; 11:15–16). She would then lead Holofernes through Judaea to Jerusalem and set up his throne in her midst (11:18–19). As God had abandoned the Judaeans because of their sin, and specifically sent her to assist Holofernes, the Assyrian general's advance would not be resisted (italicised portion below), his victory assured, and his fame exalted (cf. 11:16–19). Note the chiastic structure (ABCC'B'A') of these verses that support the veracity of her promise to Holofernes (his unresisted success; C and C') by enclosing it within God's communication with Judith (B and B') and her supposedly God-given mission to Holofernes (A and A'), both of which are seen as God's initiative:

11:16 ὅθεν ἐγὼ ἡ δούλη σου ἐπιγνοῦσα ταῦτα πάντα
ἀπέδρων ἀπὸ προσώπου αὐτῶν,
καὶ **ἀπέστειλέν με ὁ θεὸς** ποιῆσαι μετὰ σοῦ πράγματα A
ἀφ᾽ οἷς ἐκστήσεται πᾶσα ἡ γῆ, ὅσοι ἐὰν ἀκούσωσιν αὐτά.
11:17 . . . καὶ προσεύξομαι πρὸς τὸν θεόν,
καὶ ἐρεῖ μοι πότε ἐποίησαν τὰ ἁμαρτήματα αὐτῶν. B
11:18 καὶ ἐλθοῦσα προσανοίσω σοι,
καὶ ἐξελεύσῃ σὺν πάσῃ τῇ δυνάμει σου,
καὶ οὐκ ἔστιν ὃς ἀντιστήσεταί σοι ἐξ αὐτῶν. C

I will tell you the truth about this people that dwells in the nearby mountain district. No falsehood shall come from your servant's mouth" (5:5). While he was disbelieved, even though he was telling the truth, Judith is believed even though she is blatantly lying. Obviously, Judith appealed more to Holofernes' instincts than Achior did. Other correlations between Judith and Achior will be taken up in 5.E.c.

11:19 . . . *καὶ οὐ γρύξει κύων τῇ γλώσσῃ αὐτοῦ ἀπέναντί σου,* C^1
ὅτι ταῦτα ἐλαλήθη μοι κατὰ πρόγνωσίν μου B^1
καὶ ἀπηγγέλη μοι,
καὶ ἀπεστάλην ἀναγγεῖλαί σοι. A^1

Note too that her speech, like that of Achior, is based on the very Deuteronomistic principle of retributive justice that she overturned in her speech to the Bethulian leadership (8:11c–27). It would seem that Holofernes too holds to this retributive principle and the manipulation of deity and fate that it implies, as she is easily able to deceive him. Her words are replete with irony—Judith's chief mode of verbal deceit—as she promises the victory of her "lord". Blinded to her deception by her beauty and their self-assurance/pride,[44] Holofernes and his men are overjoyed (11:20–21). Holofernes vouches for her safety (11:22–23) and readily grants her request to eat only of her own kosher food. He also foolishly grants her request to bathe at the spring outside the camp in the evenings (12:1–7a)—possibly to cleanse herself from her monthly menstruation (Holofernes waited three days to seduce Judith, the normal duration of menstruation)—without thinking that this might become a strategy for his own demise. That this would indeed be the case is indicated by Judith's constant prayer as she ascends to the said spring, i.e., that God would direct her path εἰς ἀνάστημα τῶν υἱῶν τοῦ λαοῦ αὐτοῦ[45] [τοῦ Θεοῦ] (12:8–9).

Judith's transformation and her strategy of verbal *cum* sexual deceit bear fruit on the fourth day of her sojourn in the Assyrian camp (12:10) when Holofernes, overcome with lust, sends his eunuch, Bagoas, to call her to an exclusive banquet at which he hopes to seduce her (12:11–13, cf. also 12:16). This, of course, provides Judith with the golden opportunity to utilise her sexual deceit to its climactic end, and she exalts accordingly in words full of deceit and irony:

[44] Holofernes' servants and/or the chief general himself express admiration of Judith's beauty at both the outset and conclusion of her talk with Holofernes (10:23 and 11:23a). This indicates that her beauty paved the way for her deception strategy; it both opened the door for her to address Holofernes at the outset and clinched the deception at the end of their first encounter.

[45] LXX^{BNS} has "αὐτοῦ" whereas LXX^{A} has "αὐτῆς". Moore and RAPC follow the latter, while Enslin and I follow the former: "for the elevation of the children of his people" (Enslin, op. cit., 147).

12:14 καὶ εἶπεν πρὸς αὐτὸν Ιουδιθ
Καὶ τίς εἰμι ἐγὼ ἀντεροῦσα τῷ κυρίῳ μοὺ ὅτι πᾶν,
ὃ ἔσται ἐν τοῖς ὀφθαλμοῖς αὐτοῦ ἀρεστόν, σπεύσασα ποιήσω,
καὶ ἔσται τοῦτό μοι ἀγαλλίαμα ἕως ἡμέρας θανάτου μου

Judith's ἅβρα precedes her and lays out sheepskins for her mistress before the lusty general (12:15). As Judith reclines upon the sheepskins, Holofernes' heart beats wild with ecstasy (καὶ ἐξέστη[46] ἡ καρδία Ολοφέρνου ἐπ' αὐτήν—12:16). He bids her to "drink with us" and to join "us" in εὐφροσύνη (merriment; 12:18)—an obvious sexual allusion when compared to the use of this noun in *Judith* 10:3[47]—to which she responds with characteristic deceit:

12:18 . . . Πίομαι δή, κύριε, ὅτι ἐμεγαλύνθη τὸ ζῆν μου ἐν ἐμοὶ
σήμερον παρὰ πάσας τὰς ἡμέρας τῆς γενέσεώς μου.

The textual dialogue between Judith and Holofernes ends with these words. The text then reports that Judith ate her own food and that Holofernes drank more than he had ever drunk in his entire life (12:19–20). When evening comes, Holofernes' staff leave (13:1). Judith is left alone in the tent with him and he falls onto his bed in a drunken stupor (13:2–4b). Judith quickly seizes the opportunity, prays for God to avenge His people (13:4c–5), grabs Holofernes' head by the hair (13:6–7), puts her foot to his throat (13:8a) and, using his own sword, strikes twice at his neck thereby taking off his head in true Simeonite style (13:8). She then rolls his headless corpse off the bed (13:9a) and takes the canopy off the bed poles (13:9):

---

[46] The gloss renders ἐξίστημι simply as "to change" while ESL provides a more useful range of 'meanings': "1) to throw out of position, displace. 1a) to amaze, to astonish, throw into wonderment. 1b) to be amazed, astounded. 1c) to be out of one's mind, besides one's self, insane". The semantic range provided by Liddell and Scott is similar, but adds "to put out of its place, change, alter"—a far better rendition, in my opinion, than the solitary tag "to change". Moore's translation (op. cit., 221), "Holofernes was beside himself with desire", is therefore more to the point than RAPC's "Holofernes' heart was ravished with her".

[47] The noun εὐφροσύνη occurs only three times in the book, viz. *Judith* 10:3 (in reference to Judith's dressing up as in the time when Manasseh lived), here in *Judith* 12:17 in connection with eating and the drinking of wine, i.e., in a sexually charged atmosphere, and in *Judith* 12:13 where Bagoas correctly interprets his master's wish to engage Judith in 'conversation' with these words: "drink wine and be merry with us, and become today like one of the daughters of the Assyrians who serve in the house of Nebuchadnezzar".

13:8 **καὶ ἀφεῖλεν** <u>τὴν κεφαλὴν αὐτοῦ</u> *ἀπ' αὐτου*
13:9 **καὶ ἀφεῖλε**[48] <u>τὸ κωνώπιον</u> *ἀπὸ τῶν στύλων* [τῆς στρωμνῆς]

The parallel syntactical construction of these phrases indicates that it was as easy to take Holofernes' head off his shoulders as it was to take his canopy off its post, and that there is some similarity or parallel significance between the canopy and the head. Indeed, Holofernes is the head and hence protection or power of Nebuchadnezzar's army. Ostensibly, he is therefore its most important member. His head, in turn, is *his* most important member in the current situation, and that, we know, he has already lost to Judith in a metaphorical manner. Likewise, the richly bejewelled canopy is Holofernes' nighttime protection from stinging insects with sword-like probosci. It is thus a singular irony that Judith takes off his head with his own sword and then takes his canopy for booty, as both acts signify the protection that he and his army have lost and the transference of power from him to her.

Having thus disposed of the mighty Assyrian general, Judith waits a while—no doubt to cement the sexual illusion she has created from the start—and exits Holofernes' tent (13:9c). She gives the head to her ἅβρα who stows it away in the food basket. They then exit the enemy camp under the pretext of Judith's prayer habit (13:9d–10b, cf. also 13:3), thus ending the central portion (D) of *Judith* 8–16 and bringing to fulfilment her prayer in *Judith* 9:2–14.

As we can see, Judith's transformation, initialised in the first phase of her descent from highest consciousness (from her rooftop tent to her house) and expressed primarily through her sexual strategy, has worked at every level or phase of her descent into lesser and lesser consciousness. Armed with this strategy, Judith exits her house and goes down to the city gate (phase two). There, at the outset of the third phase (from the city gate to the enemy camp), her strategy literally opens the door at the threshold of consciousness and facilitates her entry into the outer limits of the unconscious attack. Once

48 Given that the author uses ἀπαιρέω in both cases, Enslin (op. cit., 153) translates "and took his head from him . . . and took the canopy from the poles." RAPC has "and severed it [his head] from his body . . . and pulled down the canopy from the posts". Moore (op. cit., 222) also translates the verb differently in each case: "chopped off his head . . . yanked the canopy from the poles." Perhaps "yanked" or 'ripped off'—my preference—could have been used in both cases to reflect the Greek more closely.

she is in the enemy camp the deceitful aspect of her strategy comes into its own as she combines her sexuality with verbal deceit to effectively neutralise any unconscious resistance and gain access to the very heart of the unconscious attack—Holofernes' tent. Here, in the fourth phase of her descent (which again indicates completion by virtue of the number four), the symbolic transformation entailed in her prayer is actualised as her verbal *cum* sexual strategy overcomes the lords of the unconscious and deactivates (i.e., robs of its *mana*/power) its chief content, Holofernes (10:23, 11:20–21, and 23; see also 16:6 and 9). The effectiveness of her strategy is such that she is able to perform the final defeat of this formidable enemy at the very moment when she would have become completely assimilated into the unconscious—were Holofernes to have had his way with her. Fortunately for the Judaeans, Judith was prudent enough to maintain her connection with consciousness via her constant communication with the self, eating her own food, and renewing herself nightly at the fountain of conscious well-being—the spring of water at the foothills of Bethuliah. It is this communication with the Self and the continuous conscious strengthening (kosher food and water from the spring of consciousness) that empower her to escape Holofernes' clutches and prevail over him. Psychologically speaking, these activities ensure that her transformation into an unconscious content remains temporary and keeps the energy alive that enables her to return to the realm of consciousness. On a far higher level, these activities also prevent the total assimilation of consciousness per se. Thus, Judith's behaviour in the enemy camp benefits her both as a person and as a content. Moreover, it ensures the salvation of her people and the continuation of consciousness, as we shall soon see.

The central portion of section II culminates in the victory of consciousness over the unconscious. From a Jungian point of view, we may depict this portion of the tale as follows:

Firstly, consciousness defeats the unconscious on its own turf by using its own weaponry against it, i.e., by playing up to Holofernes' pride and desires (e.g., lust and domination)—two psychic elements that are very close to the instinctual drives of the unconscious forces.

Secondly, the victory is consummated at this stage by the partial integration of the highest/most powerful unconscious elements within consciousness's store of sustenance. As the defeat of the unconscious has already been dealt with in the preceding paragraph, I should like to proceed directly to the second aspect, i.e., that of assimilation or integration. This aspect is gruesomely depicted in two closely interrelated facts:

i) The moment of disarming, neutralising, and beheading the chief element of the unconscious attack takes place within the context of eating/feasting and the promise of sexual consummation (read: consumption).
ii) Holofernes' head, i.e., his power, is placed within Judith's kosher food basket or that which physically feeds her consciousness during her dealings with the unconscious field of attack.

The former indicates that the context for integration is set, while the latter is a symbolic depiction that the unconscious power or *mana* has been assimilated by Judith at this stage, and that it will become kosher for those to whom it is taken/who use it or eat of it thereafter. Note how the basket becomes the carrier of food for the survival of consciousness both from and to Bethuliah. Its contents feed Judith as she journeys from Bethuliah to the camp and during her sojourn in Holofernes' camp, and they feed the Bethulians when she exits the camp and returns to Bethuliah.

Given that (a) the chief force of the unconscious attack relates to the shadow and, more especially, to various levels of instinctual activity within the unconscious psyche, and (b) that the force of these unconscious archetypes (the instincts) often cause havoc in the lives of individuals and nations alike, the assimilation and neutralisation of Holofernes symbolically expresses the coming hope, peace, and restoration which the Judaeans experience later at a deep-seated psychic level (cf. 16:25). The cannibalistic aspect entailed in this central portion—particularly in terms of Holofernes' severed head being carried in the food basket—is by no means strange or out of place here: the conscious and the unconscious are both aspects of the same psyche, and it is only by 'eating', i.e., disempowering/assimilating aspects of the one (withdrawing libido from it—literally here), that the other can be empowered. This is the principle of compensation. As Jung has said, the unconscious is the mother or wellspring of consciousness; it is its sustenance and becomes useful to it when integrated in the fashion symbolically enacted here in *Judith*.

Furthermore, since a major portion of the attack is on the instinctual level, it is right and fitting that Holofernes' head should be placed amongst food items, as food is also symbolic of the instinctual forces. Naturally, the head on a man's shoulders also relates to the head of his penis, thus making it all the more significant that Judith took his 'head' off the (bed) 'pole' and placed it in her 'basket'. As the latter is symbolic of the womb, Judith's action of placing Holofernes' head in her food basket graphically illustrates how unhealthy unconscious instinctual forces/archetypal energies are neutralised and then mixed with healthy conscious instincts—Judith's kosher food and kosher/pure/undefiled womb—to the greater benefit of consciousness as a whole. (Cf. further Judith's return to Bethuliah and the mounting of Holofernes' head upon this city's wall, below).

To return to the text, Judith and her ἅβρα traverse the liminal space between consciousness and the unconscious attack for a second and final time (13:10b–c). They climb back up the mountain and reach the city gate of Bethuliah (13:10d–e). Still at a distance, Judith excitedly commands that the gate be opened as God has shown His power in their favour this day (subsection Cc'). The men who hear her voice rush down to the gate (subsection Bb' 13:12) and call the elders. Finding it strange that she had returned, they open the gate, light a fire and stand around her and her ἅβρα (13:13). Judith triumphantly holds up Holofernes' severed head and the canopy of his bed as she praises God for destroying His people's enemy by a woman's hand (note the boldfaced portions in 13:14–15). She declares emphatically that she had not been defiled in the process (note the underlined portions in 13:16):

13:14 ἡ δὲ εἶπεν πρὸς αὐτοὺς φωνῇ μεγάλῃ
Αἰνεῖτε τὸν θεόν, αἰνεῖτε, αἰνεῖτε τὸν θεόν,
ὃς οὐκ ἀπέστησεν τὸ ἔλεος αὐτοῦ ἀπὸ τοῦ οἴκου Ισραηλ,
ἀλλ' ἔθραυσε τοὺς ἐχθροὺς ἡμῶν διὰ χειρός μου ἐν τῇ νυκτὶ ταύτῃ.
13:15 καὶ προελοῦσα τὴν κεφαλὴν ἐκ τῆς πήρας ἔδειξεν καὶ εἶπεν αὐτοῖς Ἰδοὺ ἡ κεφαλὴ Ολοφέρνου ἀρχιστρατήγου δυνάμεως Ασσουρ, καὶ ἰδοὺ τὸ κωνώπιον, ἐν ᾧ κατέκειτο ἐν ταῖς μέθαις αὐτοῦ, **καὶ ἐπάταξεν αὐτὸν ὁ κύριος ἐν χειρὶ θηλείας,**
13:16 καὶ ζῇ κύριος, ὃς διεφύλαξέν με ἐν τῇ ὁδῷ μου, ᾗ ἐπορεύθην,
ὅτι ἠπάτησεν αὐτὸν τὸ πρόσωπόν μου εἰς ἀπώλειαν αὐτοῦ,
καὶ οὐκ ἐποίησεν ἁμάρτημα μετ' ἐμοῦ εἰς μίασμα καὶ αἰσχύνην.

Here, the nouns μίασμα and αἰσχύνη take the reader back to Judith's prayer and, specifically, to the rape of Dinah—the only other occasion where these nouns have been used together so far, and the only other occasion where we find the noun μιωασμα at all (9:2 and 4):

9:2 . . . οἳ ἔλυσαν μήτραν παρθένου εἰς ***μίασμα***
καὶ ἐγύμνωσαν μηρὸν εἰς **αἰσχύνην** . . .
9:4 . . . καὶ ἐβδελύξαντο ***μίασμα*** αἵματος αὐτῶν . . .

By using these words here, Judith—or rather, the author through her—confirms to the reader that she did not suffer at Holofernes' hands as Dinah had at Shechem's (just in case we were wondering), while simultaneously letting her people know that the 'deceit' of her face (13:16) and defeat at her hands—a *woman's* hands—in the night did not entail anything sexually untoward (cf. **διὰ χειρός μου** ἐν τῇ νυκτὶ ταύτῃ and **ἐν χειρὶ θηλείας**—13:14 and 15). Her use of the phrases διὰ χειρός μου and ἐν χειρὶ θηλείας also echoes her promise to the elders (note 8:33 which parallels 13:14 and 9:9 below) and her prayer to God (note 9:10 which parallels 13:15), thus bringing a sense of verbal closure for the Bethulian characters and the reader to these events: she has done what she has promised, and God has done as she promised He would (cf. 8:33) and as she has requested (9:9 and 10). He has delivered her and His people by destroying the enemy through her hand (cf. the parallel phrases involving θραύω in 9:10 and 13:14 below), the hand of a woman (and a widow [9:9], although her widowhood is not mentioned here):

8:33 . . . ἐπισκέψεται κύριος τὸν Ισραηλ <u>ἐν χειρί μου</u>
9:9 . . . δὸς <u>ἐν χειρί μου τῆς χήρας</u> ὃ διενοήθην κράτος
9:10 . . . *θραῦσον*-[49] *αὐτῶν τὸ ἀνάστεμα* **ἐν χειρὶ θηλείας**
13:14 . . . *ἀλλ' ἔθραυσε τοὺς ἐχθροὺς ἡμῶν* <u>διὰ χειρός μου</u> ἐν τῇ νυκτὶ ταύτῃ
13:15 . . . *καὶ ἐπάταξεν αὐτὸν ὁ κύριος* **ἐν χειρὶ θηλείας**

The people are elated by Judith's report and praise God, while Ozias once again pronounces a special blessing upon her, with their endorsement (13:17–20), as he had done before she departed for the enemy

[49] Θραύω properly means "to break in pieces, shatter" (gloss; similarly Liddell and Scott). Perhaps using the appropriate form of a phrase like "cut/bring down/crush" both here at *Judith* 9:10 and 13:14 would have captured the sense of the Greek a little better and made the parallel clearer in the RAPC translation, which reads as follows: "crush their arrogance by the hand of a woman" (9:10) and "has destroyed our enemies by my hand this very night" (13:14).

camp (cf. 10:8). Judith then commands that Holofernes' head be hung on the city wall and details a characteristically deceptive battle strategy with which finally to defeat the Assyrian army (14:1–4). She also commands that Achior be brought out to verify that the head she holds is indeed that of the man who had "despised the house of Israel" (τὸν ἐκφαυλίσαντα[50] τὸν οἶκον τοῦ Ισραηλ—14:5). This is done and Achior faints upon seeing the severed head (14:6). When the Bethulians revive him, he blesses Judith (14:7). Upon his request, she recounts the events that occurred in the enemy camp; the crowd roars with great rejoicing, and Achior converts to Judaism (14:8–10).

It is interesting that Judith and her ἅβρα leave the unconscious realm at a time in which it supposedly has the most power, viz. the night, and that they arrive at Bethuliah's city gates during the night, just before daybreak. To my mind, Judith's nightly sojourns are indicative of a number of things:

a) The unconscious has been defeated on its own turf at its time of optimal functioning, namely, the night. This attests to the thoroughness of its defeat.
b) Judith arrives to find Bethuliah in darkness, so much so that lamps have to be lit by which its inhabitants may recognise her. This symbolises that her absence has left consciousness in darkness, as it were, and that it has consequently slipped into a state of relative unconsciousness.
c) Judith's arrival at the time in which night is transformed into day signifies that:
    i) She is the bearer of consciousness who brings 'light' into the situation.
    ii) The Bethulians' situation/state of consciousness is about to change.

The last two points are further borne out by the ensuing events in which Judith is still clearly in control (subsection Bb') and during

[50] While this is the only occurrence of ἐκφαυλίζω ("to depreciate"—gloss) in *Judith*, the verb is obviously related to φαυλίζω ("to hold cheap, to depreciate, disparage"—Liddell and Scott)—the verb used to describe both the attitude of the western nations against Nebuchadnezzar and that of the Judaeans against Holofernes-Nebuchadnezzar (1:11, 11:2 and 22). Thus, the one who had come with a vast army to avenge his master's disparagement had found himself overtly disparaged by a seemingly insignificant nation and struck down by the stealth of a single woman and her ἅβρα who overtly acknowledged him, i.e., who seemed not to disparage him.

which her victory is both shared and furthered by the Bethulians with very lucrative effects. Note also the complete reversal of their situation (not to mention Achior's) and the jubilation that her victory brings about, both of which are a good indication of the new stability of consciousness that the people attain through her:

When daylight breaks—when consciousness dawns afresh—the Bethulians execute all of Judith's commands (14:11–15:3) just as Simeon's brothers seem to have executed his (cf. discussion on Genesis 34 parallels, above). It is clear that her presence, which is charged with *mana* and now conscious instinctual energy through the severed head (see above), and the visual representation of the assimilation of this *mana* on their city wall empower them to bring Judith's decapitation/symbolic castration (see above) of Holofernes to completion by routing the Assyrian forces. Encouraged by their resultant success, the Judaeans from the surrounding areas join in and drive the Assyrian forces back as far as the borders of Damascus (15:4–6). The remaining Bethulians enter and despoil the now defunct Assyrian camp to the enrichment of all (15:6–7), hereby completing the raid of unconscious resources which Judith began by taking Holofernes' head and canopy.

When this has been done, Joachim and the Jerusalem γερουσία arrive in order to view the great things that God had done through Judith and to bless her (15:8). They bless her with the highest accolades, again to the approval of the crowd (15:9–10; cf. 13:17–20). The people, who subsequently raid the enemy camp for a further thirty days, bring Holofernes' tent and all its valuables to Judith (15:11a–b). She loads them onto her chariots and leads the women (of Bethuliah?) in a triumphal victory dance as the men follow, singing praises (15:11c–13). She then leads the people in a triumphal song—much like Miriam and Moses of Exodus 15 fame[51]—extolling the greatness of God who has delivered her from her persecutors(!) and destroyed such a formidable enemy through the beauty and deception of a woman (15:14–16:17; note especially 16:2b and 5–9). When they arrive in Jerusalem, the people cleanse themselves and make sacrifice to God (16:18). Judith dedicates all the spoils from Holofernes'

[51] There are tremendous parallels between Judith's song in *Judith* 16 and "the song of the sea" in Exodus 15 as Moore (op. cit., 256–257) has indicated. Unfortunately, spatial constraints prevent me from dealing with the parallels here.

tent—including the canopy of his bed—to God. She stays with the people during their three-month festivities (16:19–20), thus ending the sixth subsection of *Judith* 8–16 (Bb'—13:12–16:20) on a high note.

Psychologically speaking, subsection Cc' and Bb' (13:10b–11 and 13:12–16:20) depict the heightened consciousness which occurs in the aftermath of a successful sortie with the unconscious. This rise to higher consciousness is symbolically represented in the actions of Judith, Achior, the Bethulians, the combined activities of the Bethulians and the Judaeans, and the blessings of the Jerusalemite leadership (Joachim, the high priest, and the *γερουσία*). In the first place, Judith not only returns to the place which she had left immediately before descending into the unconscious, but she inspires her fellow Bethulians to ascend—albeit temporarily—to higher consciousness: she ascends to Bethuliah from the Assyrian camp (13:10b–11), and from Bethuliah she leads her people to Jerusalem—the conscious centre of the entire nation—where she offers sacrifices to God at the temple in Jerusalem (15:12c–16:20). Secondly, Achior, who had arisen to consciousness from partial integration in the unconscious, becomes an integral component of consciousness: he willingly becomes a convert to Judaism and is circumcised (14:10). Thirdly, the *mana* and base instinctual energy of the unconscious attack—Holofernes' head—is consciously assimilated into the outermost areas of central consciousness (mounted on the wall of Bethuliah—14:11) where it empowers the elements inhabiting consciousness at that level to enter the realms of the unconscious attack and draw further upon and assimilate the power of its attendant elements (they push the Assyrians back and take much booty; 15:5–7, 11). Fourthly, the Bethulians' action inspires both the lower and the higher realms of consciousness (people from various Judaean cities in general and the people from Jerusalem) to enter the fray and push the unconscious attack even further back (15:5–7). Finally, the blessings heaped upon Judith in Bethuliah and Jerusalem signify that consciousness receives the integration with joy (cf. 13:18–20 and 15:8–10).

It is interesting that the Bethulians' temporary rise to the fifth stage of consciousness per se (Jerusalem) is facilitated by Judith's descent to the unconscious, which is in turn facilitated by Achior's ascent from the unconscious. Here we note that Achior's ascent as well as Judith's descent and consequent ascent have taken place in four phases (see above). We have also noted that the Bethulians'/Judaeans' actions magnify Judith's actions or bring them to completion:

a) Judith decapitates Holofernes/the chief element of the unconscious attack and takes home his/its power and his/its wealth that is represented symbolically by Holofernes' head and the bejewelled canopy above his bed.
b) The Bethulians/Judaeans 'complete' the mission by killing many of Holofernes' men and bringing home booty from the entire camp.

It would seem, then, that when consciousness is able to receive even a single element from the unconscious—Achior—the way is open for the integration of other more deeply seated and more powerful elements—such as Holofernes' head—and for the defeat of the unconscious attack. (This will be dealt with in greater detail in my discussion of Achior below). Conversely, when one is able, at a high level of consciousness—represented by Judith—to identify correctly and deal with the chief element or nature of an unconscious attack, the success of this endeavour empowers the rest of consciousness to integrate partially integrated elements (Achior), to rally the support of the whole of consciousness (the Jerusalemite leadership, the inhabitants of Jerusalem and other cities in Judaea), and to completely drive back the attack. The joy and the liberty that consciousness experiences as a result is self-explanatory: the unconscious attack is thwarted, its 'stores' are plundered to enrich consciousness, the community is empowered, and a new self-understanding is achieved—not to mention a better understanding of and connection with the Self. In this case, Judith's bravery and her 'wise' defeat of Holofernes has freed the Bethulians from their fear, united them with the other Judaeans, and taught them something concerning themselves and the nature of the positive Self that they did not understand before. In other words, she has brought about greater integrity/unity in consciousness and brought it closer to the Self. They have learned that they are able to withstand the test and that the Self is for them, not against them. They have also learned that the Self may not be manipulated or confined, and that when the Self is heeded, any attack may be overcome no matter how weak consciousness appears to be. All that is required is an abandonment of self to the Self, which/who is the source and fountain of all wisdom, power, and strength.

Having feasted with her compatriots, Judith returns to Bethuliah, the fourth stage of consciousness where she is presumably of optimal use to consciousness as a whole, and becomes famous throughout the world (or 'land') in her own lifetime (16:21). Though many desire her, she dies a widow at the age of 105, having freed her ἅβρα and distributed her goods amongst her husband's family. She is buried in the same cave as her husband, with "the house of Israel" mourning her for seven days (16:22–24). The final verse of the seventh and final subsection of *Judith* 8–16 (Aa'—16:21–25) then concludes the entire book by telling us that:

16:25 καὶ οὐκ ἦν ἔτι ὁ ἐκφοβῶν τοὺς υἱοὺς Ισραηλ ἐν ταῖς ἡμέραις Ιουδιθ καὶ μετὰ τὸ ἀποθανεῖν αὐτὴν ἡμέρας πολλάς.

In this way, it takes us back to where we began, i.e., the otherness of Judith: she remains unwedded despite many marriage offers, thereby deliberately discontinuing her husband's line. She begins as an 'outsider' by virtue of her husband's death and remains an outsider by virtue of her own will. This is a critical difference. This 'otherness' is actively underscored by Judith's choice to free her ἅβρα after her death and to distribute her own goods amongst Manasses' relatives.

Psychologically speaking, Judith's story teaches us not only the necessity of abandoning ourselves to the Self, but of clinging to the Self and to our conscious reservoirs once we find ourselves in the grip of the unconscious. These two factors, combined with her ability to use the schemes of the unconscious against itself, prevent her from being completely assimilated into the unconscious. In other words, they prevent inflation—positive or negative—from taking place while dealing with the unconscious. The fact that she is able to dedicate all the spoils of her success to the Self proves that the inflation has not been able to set in even after her success, for it is easy to fall into inflation when one is rewarded so handsomely for one's achievements on behalf of the conscious realm. The final portion of *Judith* 8–16 (16:21–25, or Aa') indicates clearly the blessedness of this state of surrender to the Self and its effects upon life as a whole: she is able to share her wealth and resist 'instinctual temptation' (remarriage), she lives to a ripe old age, and (her memory) is a guarantee for the protection of her people for many years after her death.

Manasses

We may glean much from the little that the text tells us of Manasses. In the first place, Manasses is introduced to us as Judith's husband, one who comes from her tribe and her family (8:2a), i.e., one who shares in and is dependent upon her conscious/unconscious roots (and not *vice versa*; see above).[52] Secondly, we are told that he is dead, that he died upon his bed from heat exhaustion while overseeing the binding of sheaves, and that he was buried with his ancestors in a field between Dothaim and Balamon/Belbaim (8:2b–3e). Thirdly, the text tells us that he has been dead for forty months (8:4), and that he has left Judith with much wealth (cf. "gold and silver"), male and female servants, cattle (κτήνη), and fields (8:7b). The text then records Manasses' name a further four times, always indirectly and in relation to Judith. *Judith* 10:3 records that Judith donned the clothes that she wore when he was still alive, while *Judith* 16:22–24 relates that Judith remained 'unwedded' to any man from the time of his death until she died (16:22), that she was buried in his cave (16:23), and that she distributed her goods amongst her relatives and his prior to her death (16:24).

The author of *Judith* paints a very interesting portrait of Manasses, and one that is similar to that of Achior in many respects. Manasses is someone who has reached a relatively high stage of consciousness (stage 4, Bethuliah—circle 4 in diagram 10) and has established himself fairly well there (he has servants, cattle, and fields and has amassed considerable wealth). Nevertheless, he has little or no staying power/libido. When we encounter him, we find that he is one who plants but does not reap—not only in respect of his fields, but also in respect of his wife: he dies while the sheaves are being bound, never tasting of his harvest, and he leaves Judith with everything and everyone but a child. He is thus unfruitful in many ways. I am therefore led to believe that he, like Achior, became unstable at his level of consciousness and was consequently swallowed up by the unconscious (i.e., died). Unlike Achior, however, his fall from consciousness appears to have been quite gradual as he was able to amass and leave behind considerable property and wealth before he fell into the unconscious realms forever (nothing similar is said of Achior, only that he was an Ammonite ruler). His gradual fall from consciousness may well indicate that he succumbed to inflation,

[52] The telling syntax of *Judith* 8:2a, which emphasises Manasses' dependant position on Judith, is reminiscent of the sentence reporting the death of Elimelech, Naomi's husband, in *Ruth* 1:3a. This sentence also reverses the traditional dependence of the wife upon the husband, which is depicted in *Ruth* 1:1:

despite having been well established at stage 4 (inflation often creeps upon one and is a factor at every level of individuation), and that he lost consciousness thereby.

Furthermore, Manasses is accorded no say textually: he never speaks. He also seems to be one who does not wish to get his hands dirty: he watches while others bind the sheaves, perhaps another sign of pride/inflation. He dies on his bed from heat-stroke (καὶ ὁ καύσων[53] ἦλθεν ἐπὶ τὴν κεφαλὴν αὐτοῦ καὶ ἔπεσεν ἐπὶ τὴν κλίνην αὐτοῦ καὶ ἐτελεύτησεν—8:3), giving us the impression that he is a lazy, proud, or foolish person, or a weakly developed (unstable) person/content of consciousness: he either did nothing but oversee or he did not protect himself sufficiently. Everything about him is passive. Manasses is passive when we encounter him and passive when he is taken away from our narrative memory: dead—stood around—caught heat—lay on bed—died—was buried. By contrast, Judith hears, calls, prays, acts, sacrifices, leads in worship . . . dies, is buried . . . and continues to protect her people thereafter. This indicates that Manasses has a far weaker consciousness than Judith as a person—he is dead at the outset of the action and is related to her in a textually dependent fashion. In addition, a small encounter with the unconscious (the hot east wind) produces his death (dries up his conscious awareness) and sends him to its permanent embrace (he is buried with his forefathers).

The text further relates that Manasses had died forty months prior to the events described in Section II (8:4). This period of time corresponds numerically to the forty-year wilderness wanderings of the Israelites at the end of which those who had rebelled against God died. This alerts me to the possibility that Manasses somehow rebelled against the Self as they did and was therefore divinely removed from the scene by the καύσων, the hot east 'wind' or Spirit/Self (wind = spirit = Spirit = Self/God). This reinforces my theory that he may have succumbed to inflation/sin/pride/rebellion (see above). It is as

Ruth 1:1 "וַיֵּלֶךְ אִישׁ מִבֵּית לֶחֶם יְהוּדָה לָגוּר בִּשְׂדֵי מוֹאָב [הוּא וְאִשְׁתּוֹ] [he and *his wife*]
Ruth 1:3 וַיָּמָת [אֱלִימֶלֶךְ אִישׁ נָעֳמִי] [Elimelech, *Naomi's husband*]

[53] Καύσων means "burning heat", according to the gloss, which is how the RAPC translates it. ESL has "1) burning heat. 1a) of the sun. 2) Eurus, a very dry hot, east wind, scorching and drying up everything". I prefer to use 'the (hot) east wind' for the sake of parallels with *Jonah* 4:8 (see RAPC's translations), which are discussed in this subsection.

though he were one of the 'older', sinful generation that had to be eliminated so that the remainder could enter the promised land (reach a higher state of consciousness). That this is indeed so, is demonstrated below.

The use of the καύσων (see boldfaced sections below) in situations where judgement/punishment is expressed throughout the Old Testament corroborates my thesis that there is an element of judgment about the way Manasses died. See, e.g., *Hosea* 13:15, *Jeremiah* 18:17, and *Jonah* 4:8:

Hosea 13:15 διότι οὗτος ἀνὰ μέσον ἀδελφῶν διαστελεῖ. **ἐπάξει ἄνεμον καύσωνα κύριος** ἐκ τῆς ἐρήμου ἐπ᾽ αὐτόν, **καὶ ἀναξηρανεῖ τὰς φλέβας αὐτοῦ, ἐξερημώσει τὰς πηγὰς αὐτοῦ,** αὐτὸς καταξηρανεῖ τὴν γῆν αὐτοῦ καὶ πάντα τὰ σκεύη τὰ ἐπιθυμητὰ αὐτοῦ.

Jeremiah 18:17 **ὡς ἄνεμον καύσωνα διασπερῶ αὐτοὺς** κατὰ πρόσωπον ἐχθρῶν αὐτῶν, δείξω αὐτοῖς **ἡμέραν ἀπωλείας αὐτῶν**.

Jonah 4:8 καὶ ἐγένετο ἅμα τῷ ἀνατεῖλαι τὸν ἥλιον καὶ **προσέταξεν ὁ θεὸς πνεύματι καύσωνος συγκαίοντι**, καὶ ἐπάταξεν ὁ ἥλιος ἐπὶ τὴν κεφαλὴν Ιωνα, καὶ ὠλιγοψύχησεν καὶ ἀπελέγετο τὴν ψυχὴν αὐτοῦ καὶ εἶπεν Καλόν μοι ἀποθανεῖν με ἢ ζῆν.

In all these situations, God is said to direct the καύσων as a form of judgement or punishment against his rebellious people. We may recall, e.g., that Jonah had originally rebelled against God's calling on his life. He refused to go and speak His word of redemption to the Ninevites. He foolishly sought to escape from God by boarding a ship to Tarsis. However, the ship sank and Jonah was swallowed by a big fish. When the big fish finally spat him out, he capitulated rather gracelessly and obeyed God's call. As a result of his preaching, the Ninevites repented. This however, did not please Jonah, presumably as his people and the Ninevites were sworn enemies, and he sat miserably on a heap outside the city when his work was done. In *Jonah* 4:8, *God* afflicted Jonah with the καύσων on account of his recalcitrant attitude towards the Ninevites, thus making explicit the relation between sin, God, and the καύσων. Nevertheless, Jonah survived the καύσων, because he finally repented and once again became useful to God. By contrast, the people of Israel and Judah had so incensed God by their lack of both obedience and repentance (i.e. rebellion), that he gave them over to destruction, captivity, and exile.

Comparing these passages with *Judith* 8:4 leads me to conclude that Manasses was afflicted with the καύσων and died because he had rebelled without repentance and was no longer responsive to God/the Self. Consequently, like Moses, Aaron, and the rebellious generation of the wilderness wanderings (cf. Numbers 20:7–13, 24; 14:26–35; 32:13), his rebellion barred him from 'entering the promised land', to live in the days when Israel was free from foreign oppression because of the redemption that the Lord had wrought by Judith's hand (cf. 16:25).

It is interesting to note, in terms of the preceding argument, that Manasses' death provides Judith with the means to live the life she chooses and liberates her to act as she does during the 'Assyrian' crisis: she would conceivably not have been able to deceive and kill Holofernes using her feminine sexual wiles if her husband were still alive. This confirms Manasses' association with the sinful generation of the wilderness-wandering period (above): he had to die so that others could 'inherit the land', free of the rebellion he might bring with him. It would seem, then, that Manasses was superfluous and perhaps even harmful to society as a person—as people who suffer from inflation often are—and to consciousness as a psychological content. I am therefore justifiably led to conclude that he incurred the wrath of the Self (cf. the judgement implied in dying by the καύσων), which judged him as rebellious (i.e., suffering from inflation) drawing unnecessarily upon the conscious libido, cast him out of the conscious realm, and cleverly reassigned the resultant surplus of conscious energy for assimilation into higher consciousness. This 'higher consciousness' is, of course, represented by Judith. She assimilated Manasses' libido (he left her with many servants and earthly goods over whom she had free reign) and successfully employed it when thwarting the intents of Holofernes and obliterating the force of the unconscious attack (e.g., she was able to dress alluringly and, we may imagine, very richly; see, e.g., her finery listed in 10:4). It is thus evident—on both a textual and a psychological level—that Manasses *had* to die in order for Judith and consciousness/the Bethulians/ Judaeans to overcome the shadow/Holofernes.

Finally, on an extratextual level, Manasses' death upon his bed is prefigured by the death of the Shechemites (*Judith* 9), while it also acts as a textual prefiguration of Holofernes' death on a textual level. It is interesting to note that both Shechem/the Shechemites and Holofernes/the Assyrian troops and allies die as the direct/indirect result of succumbing to 'heat'. This heat is sexual in terms of Shechem and Holofernes, which makes me think that Manasses may also represent an unstable/unhealthy instinctual influence which had to be discarded for conscious survival. Be that as it may, Manasses' link with the unconscious world underscores the absolute necessity of his physical and textual death that has been discussed above. It also underscores his complete separation from consciousness as represented by Judith—the only time they are together is in the grave, when she is finally laid to rest in his cave (16:24). In fact, Manasses' links with the unconscious almost class him with the enemy forces and set him up as a foil to Achior who was successfully redeemed from the unconscious realm. Furthermore, his negative association with the Jonah story—an individuation drama *par excellence*—and the fact that he died a largely unfruitful person despite his wealth, indicates that his was an individuation drama that was never fulfilled. The same may be said of his negative association with Moses, Aaron, and the rebellious generation of the wilderness wanderings. This sets him up as a foil to Judith, whose life reveals the very pattern of a successful individuation drama as I will show in 5.E.c. below.

Judith's Trusted Stewardess/ἅβρα

Judith's textually silent, undescribed, and nameless ἅβρα appears a total of eleven times, under the designations of ἅβρα (seven times), δούλη (three times), and παιδίσκη (once):

- We first hear of her when Judith sends her to summon the Bethulian leadership to her tent in *Judith* 8:10. The same verse also tells us that this woman is a trusted employee who oversees all that Judith has, i.e., as her trusted stewardess (my appellation for her). In my opinion, therefore, she is no ordinary slave/servant and occupies a higher status than a παιδίσκη, "a young girl, maiden; a young slave" (gloss), or a δούλη, "a born bondwoman or slave" (gloss)—even though the text uses these terms to describe her on occasion (see below). Her higher status vis-à-vis that of παιδίσκη and δούλη is further borne out by the fact that ἅβρα—Judith's favourite designation for this woman—may be derived from the Hebrew/Aramaic חברה, which ESL renders as "associate, fellow, companion".
- We next hear of her within the same context as *Judith* 8:10—Judith's admonition of the elders/magistrates—when Judith announces that she will go out with her ἅβρα to perform her secret plan (8:33).

- Having concluded her transformation/beautification process, Judith calls her ἅβρα, gives her the food basket that she has prepared (10:2 and 5), and exits Bethuliah with her (10:10; the ἅβρα is designated as παιδίσκη for the first and last time in *Judith* here at the end of subsection Cc).
- When they reach the Assyrian outpost, one hundred Assyrian soldiers 'yoke' (cf. παρέζευξαν) themselves to this ἅβρα and her mistress and escort them to Holofernes' tent (10:17).
- As a δούλη, she precedes her mistress into Holofernes' tent to lay down the sheepskins upon which she (Judith) will recline (12:15).
- During the seduction scene, Judith drinks what her δούλη has prepared (12:19).
- Judith reportedly instructs her δούλη to wait outside Holofernes' tent while she feasts with him and plots his death within. She is to wait for her there so that they may go on their daily 'prayer walk' thereafter and so escape the Assyrian camp without arousing suspicion (13:3).
- Once Judith has killed Holofernes, she hands her ἅβρα the freshly severed head, and the latter places it into their food basket as part of their escape ruse (13:9–10).
- Judith frees her ἅβρα upon her death (16:23).

The above verses seem to depict Judith's ἅβρα as an object that is acted upon in that:

a) She executes Judith's commands without question.
b) All her actions are completely centred around her mistress's deeds and needs.

Nevertheless, there is no recorded dialogue between these two women, and Judith's instructions to/concerning her are conveyed indirectly through the author's reports that:

i) Judith sent her to summon the elders (8:10).
ii) Judith had told her to wait outside Holofernes tent (13:3).
iii) Judith set her free (16:23).

There is also one occasion in which Judith reports that she will go down into the enemy camp with her ἅβρα (8:33), but again, there is no record of her direct command to this woman. On the remaining occasions, Judith's trusted stewardess simply follows her mistress (down to the Assyrian camp, to Holofernes' tent, back to Bethuliah) and seems to know what to do without any instruction from her (she takes the basket Judith gives her along with them, lays sheepskins down for her mistress to lie on, prepares drink for her, and places the head in the basket). She is thus the only female character besides Judith who is accorded any type of independent subject action whatsoever. As previously indicated, all the other women encountered so far have acted as a group. From this we deduce that while the ἅβρα is inextricably tied to her mistress in being and deed, she possesses a good measure of autonomy/libido in and of herself.

How then do we understand this unnamed, silent figure from a Jungian point of view? Given her helper function and the fact that she exists textually only when Judith does and, more particularly, when Judith is dealing with the unconscious, it is possible to regard this figure as:

a) The kind of female helper figure that women encounter on their individuation journeys.
b) Judith's shadow.
c) Judith's soul/psyche.

To my mind, the last possibility is the least plausible of the three, as the ἅβρα is clearly subordinate to Judith in the narrative and can therefore not be equated with her psyche per se. The psyche, as Jung has said, encompasses all, and all is psyche. I understand this to mean that while we may be helped by various aspects of our psyche, the psyche as a whole can never be our subordinate. By contrast, the possibility of the ἅβρα being a helper figure in the individuation drama seems very attractive because:

i) The ἅβρα has a definite helper function.
ii) Judith is the heroine and may thus be interpreted as a manifestation of the conscious ego which is going through the individuation process that the narrative describes. If Annis Pratt is correct, and women are indeed assisted by powerful goddesses/divine helper figures on their journey of individuation, then we could see the ἅβρα as a demythologised form of such a figure.
iii) The ἅβρα is released upon Judith's death, which may signify that she will now move on to help another woman in her quest for individuation.

This possibility may, nevertheless, be discounted because the text clearly depicts Judith's ἅβρα as her subordinate (cf. the use of δούλη and παιδίσκη alongside ἅβρα, and the discussion of these terms above). There is nothing remotely 'divine' or 'superordinate' about her. Even though we may regard her depiction as a trusted stewardess to be a demythologised form of her 'divine' role in a strictly monotheistic religion, the theory nevertheless fails because Judith's textual representation as a female is overshadowed by her personification of a society that is predominantly androcentric/male-identified in 'real life'. Moreover, the individuation cycle which Judith follows is wholly 'male' in that it is totally patterned after the hero's quest and the night sea journey—two models of individuation which involve fighting the unconscious in the guise of a terrible mother/goddess/(sea) monster. This, as Pratt has pointed out, is a singularly male concern. The only difference between Judith's tale of individuation and the hero's quest/night sea journey, is that the gender roles are reversed: Judith represents the ego-consciousness and Holofernes represents the great monster/unconscious. This is an issue that I will take up again in 5.E.a.

If Jung is correct about the male shadow manifesting in male guise, and I am correct about the gender reversal in Judith's very male pattern of individuation, then it would make sense for Judith to have a female shadow: Judith's female depiction in the text is offset by a female shadow. This would explain why the ἅβρα always 'shadows' Judith and only lives as long as Judith does. The only possible objection to interpreting the ἅβρα as a manifestation of Judith's shadow may be that she is found in the conscious realm, viz. Bethuliah, which, as I have previously indicated, represents the fourth stage of conscious awareness. This objection is, however, negated if we follow through to its logical conclusion the fact that Judith is the text's most highly individuated being. We have seen that encountering the shadow is the first step in the process of individuation, and that this process culminates in the individuated person's ability to relate to and contribute towards society in a very meaningful way. As we have seen, Judith contributes very meaningfully towards her society and its individuation by liberating them from the grasp of the Assyrian enemy/the unconscious Shadow. This leads me to the conclusion that she must have grappled with, conquered, and assimilated the shadow, which explains the stewardess's dependency on Judith and the fact that she is both 'companion' and 'servant' to Judith in the conscious realm: the shadow becomes a trusted companion when it is accepted and assimilated into consciousness. Once assimilated, it 'serves' the ego in that it is the first step to becoming whole. Furthermore, we have seen that the unconscious attack is depicted in the form of Holofernes who represents the national shadow element. To my mind, only someone who has integrated her/his own shadow has the ability to assist her/his nation to assimilate the national shadow. Thus, it is not surprising to find Judith drawing upon that experience in the form of her ἅβρα, who accompanies her and serves her when she is dealing with Holofernes.

Seeing the ἅβρα as Judith's integrated shadow also explains why she is depicted in a more servantlike manner the closer Judith gets to the site of the unconscious attack/the enemy camp. Paradoxically, it also explains why she comes into her own as a subject there. We have seen that she is designated as παιδίσκη while descending to the enemy camp at the end of subsection Cc (10:10) and as a δούλη once in the unconscious realm (12:19 and 13:3) even though almost all her subject-actions take place there in subsection D—see the presentation of this at the outset of this subsection (12:15, 19; 13:9–10). This, to my mind, may be interpreted as follows: as an integrated unconscious content the ἅβρα serves the highly conscious Judith in a position of absolute subordination—she is a δούλη—in the unconscious realm. However, she also 'comes into her own' there because it is the realm from which she originated. Her subordination to Judith also prefigures the later subordination of the (unintegrated, malicious) shadow elements that Holofernes and his troops represent. Regarding the ἅβρα as an integrated shadow element would then explain why she is solely involved in the story just before, during, and immediately after Judith's victory over Holofernes/the national shadow: her close association with Judith before their descent to the Assyrian camp is effectively a guarantee of Judith's successful integration of as-yet unintegrated shadow contents while she is in the unconscious realm, while her presence in the unconscious realm serves as a seal for the Bethulians' integration of the same once she has returned to consciousness with Judith. Naturally, a person's shadow is always 'attached' to that person and it never dies as it is intimately attached to her/his psyche. That is why the ἅβρα lives until Judith's death and is then set free as an unconscious content in subsection Aa'. As we are never told what happens to this woman after her 'emancipation'—only that she has been set free—we may justifiably conjecture that Judith's death releases the archetypal energy that she (the ἅβρα) represents from its particular actualisation as her shadow.

Ozias and the Elders/Magistrates

Ozias and the Bethulian elders/magistrates were the last group of characters to be introduced to us in section I and the first group of 'old' characters to make their way back into section II (13:12). They are far less active in section II than they were in section I, and even less active in the second part of section II (Cc'–Bb'–Aa') than they are in its first part (Aa–Bb–Cc):

As we have seen, Judith summons them to her tent and admonishes them over their five-day ultimatum to God (8:9–27). Once she has dismissed Ozias' excuses with her determination to act/let God act through her 'hand' on her people's behalf (cf. 8:28–31 and 32–34), they accede to her secret plan by means of a blessing (8:35):

8:35 καὶ εἶπεν Οζιας καὶ οἱ ἄρχοντες πρὸς αὐτήν
Πορεύου εἰς εἰρήνην, καὶ κύριος ὁ θεὸς ἔμπροσθέν σου
εἰς ἐκδίκησιν τῶν ἐχθρῶν ἡμῶν.

When Judith is ready to exit Bethuliah, the all-male leadership stand waiting for her at the city gates as she has instructed (10:6; cf. 8:33). They are amazed at her beauty (10:7) and pray that God would grant her favour and fulfil her plans to the glory of the Israelites and the exultation of Jerusalem (10:8). Then, towards the end of subsection Cc, they command the Bethulian gatekeepers to open the gates for her at her behest (10:7–10a). Contrary to section I, where they clearly ruled over the people and made all the important decisions affecting Bethuliah, here they are visibly ruled over by Judith. Their only real subject-action seems to be the blessing they pray over her, and even that is the result of her actions and resolve to face the enemy with no-one but her ἅβρα. Like most of the characters in section II, the actions of the Bethulian leadership centre around the person, deeds, and words of Judith.

When Judith returns from her successful foray into the unconscious (subsection Cc'), their actions become even more limited. It is interesting to note that Chabris and Charmis disappear from the scene: their names are not mentioned at all throughout the second part of section II. The Bethulian leadership also seems to cease functioning as a group. *Judith* 13:12 is the only verse in this part of section II that reports an incident involving them as a group: the Bethulians call upon the city's elders to come and see Judith and her ἅβρα. After this, the Bethulian leaders are never mentioned again either as πρεσβυτέροι (elders) or as ἄρχοντες (rulers) and Ozias becomes the only one amongst them to survive Judith's victorious return textually and as a leader (of sorts):

i) In one instance he blesses Judith highly ("you are blessed by the Most High God above all women on earth") for her bravery and the deliverance she has wrought (13:18–20).
ii) In another, he sends messengers out to inform the people in the surrounding towns of the events that had occurred and calls upon them to rout the Assyrian forces (15:4).
iii) The only other reference to Ozias occurs when Achior is called from his house at Judith's command in order to identify Holofernes' head (14:6).

It is clear, then, that the Bethulian leadership's response to the situation in the second part of section II is conditioned and governed by Judith's deeds and requests even as it was in the first part (above).

Considering all the above, we see that the actions of the Bethulian leadership are completely centred around and governed by Judith throughout section II and that she completely obscures them. This is particularly so with regard to their diminished leadership role (if they have one at all) once she appears on the scene in *Judith* 8 and the fact that they all but disappear as independent subject-agents once she returns with the coveted *mana* (Holofernes' head). This is not at all surprising given the fact that Judith operates at a far higher level of individuation than they do to start with, and that she increases in conscious power by defeating the unconscious and assimilating its *mana*. When she returns, she takes over most of their leadership functions. She becomes both a military commander and a spiritual leader:

- She details the battle plan for routing the Assyrians.
- She leads her people in worship up to the centre of ego-consciousness and the highest level of conscious awareness, i.e., Jerusalem and its temple.

Nevertheless, it must be said of the Bethulian leadership that, as with Achior, they do not hesitate to receive either the contents of the unconscious or the *mana* that Judith has secured or her leadership. This is to their credit and shows that they know and respect the power of a consciousness that is higher than their own, and that they do not stand in its way.

As for Ozias, we have already noted that he is the only member of the Bethulian leadership to survive Judith's return. This indicates that his form of consciousness is higher than that of his fellow magistrates. We have also seen that he takes over and modifies the letter-writing role of Joachim, the high priest (cf. 15:4). The latter had written to Bethuliah and Bethomasthaim to hold fast the mountain passes when Holofernes' forces had first approached (4:6–7). Here, Ozias sends messengers to Bethomasthaim, Bebai, Chobai, Cola, and every district in Israel to inform them of Judith's victory and call them to action. This, to my mind, signifies that Judith's feat has enabled Ozias to function at a slightly higher level of consciousness than he did before, as Joachim occupies a higher level of consciousness than he does by virtue of his being the military-spiritual leader of all Judaea. Nevertheless, he is a weaker content than Joachim and cannot permanently accede to his level. This is indicated by the fact that he does not remain in Jerusalem (cf. 16:20–21)—assuming that he went up there with Judith and the other Israelites—and is never heard of again once he completes his letter-writing activities.

Finally, I should like to note that there are many similarities between the Bethulian leadership and the depiction of Barak in Judges 4. In fact, the similarities between the stories of Judith's victory over the Assyrians and Deborah's victory over Sisera are many and cannot be taken up in detail at this point. Suffice it to say, however, that a cursory glance over the two stories reveals the following similarities vis-à-vis the role of the Bethulian leadership/Barak in particular:

- The male leadership do little or nothing to counteract the military onslaught of a foreign king/general that has struck fear into the hearts of their people, the Israelites (cf. *Judith* 4 and Judges 4:3 and 8).
- A woman takes the initiative to deliver God's people (cf. especially *Judith* 8:32–34 and Judges 4:9).
- The woman summons the male leadership and upbraids them/him for lack of action on God's behalf and that of His people (cf. *Judith* 8:10–27 and Judges 4:6–9).
- The woman regards the victory as her own (cf. especially *Judith* 8:32–34, Judges 4:4–9, and the phrase "by the hand of a woman/widow/female" in *Judith* 9:9, 10 and Judges 4:9).
- The men's attack on the enemy is dependant on that of the woman. They begin to attack once the woman has defeated the enemy general in Judith's case, while Barak does not mount the

attack until he has ascertained that Deborah will go with him (cf. especially *Judith* 13:1–15; 14:1–5, 11–13; 15:3b–7 and Judges 4:8–16).

- The woman has a female "accomplice" who seems as fearless as she is—the ἅβρα in Judith's case and Jael in that of Deborah.
- The woman/the woman's accomplice uses feminine wiles to destroy the enemy general (Cf. especially *Judith* 10:22–13:10a and Judges 4:17–21).
- The woman/the woman's accomplice calls the male leadership and/or her people to view the work that she has done (*Judith* 13:15–18; 14:5–10 and Judges 4:22).
- The men accompany the woman in a song that praises her and/or her accomplice and God for the victory (cf. *Judith* 16:1–17 and Judges 5:1–31).

We see, then, that the Bethulian leadership are overshadowed by Judith in very much the same way that Barak is overshadowed by Deborah (and Jael) in the Book of Judges. In both cases the men are weak and inept and almost superfluous to the story except to act as a foil for the main female character/s. As this speaks to the men's weaker consciousness vis-à-vis that of the main female character/s, it confirms my interpretation of the Bethulian leadership given above.

The Young Men/Gatekeepers of Bethuliah

The text of *Judith* makes three references to the Bethulian νεανίσκοι (young men) in section II: *Judith* 10:9, 16:4 and 6. In *Judith* 10:9 we are told that the Bethulian leadership commands them to open the gates for Judith, while the other two references occur at the outset of Judith's victory hymn. In the first of these (16:4), Judith sings of Holofernes'/the Assyrians' intent to "kill my young men with the sword," whereas in the second (16:6), she extols "For their mighty one did not fall by the hands of the young men" (16:7 in RAPC). The only reference that mentions the νεανίσκοι as independent subjects with a specific function, i.e., as gatekeepers of Bethuliah, occurs in *Judith* 10:9:[54]

[54] We also encounter the young Bethulian men three times in section I, viz. *Judith* 6:16, 7:22 and 23. They were not dealt with separately in 5.B.b. as they do not have an independent function in section I. Rather, their actions are always reported

10:9 . . . Ἐπιτάξατε ἀνοῖξαί μοι τὴν πύλην τῆς πόλεως, καὶ ἐξελεύσομαι εἰς τελείωσιν τῶν λόγων, ὧν ἐλαλήσατε μετ᾽ ἐμοῦ, καὶ συνέταξαν τοῖς νεανίσκοις ἀνοῖξαι αὐτῇ καθότι ἐλάλησεν.

This verse also makes the first reference to the functionality of these gates: the gates are opened so that Judith and her ἅβρα may exit the city to fulfil her secret plan. (I emphasise the gates' 'functionality' because we first encounter them in *Judith* 8:33 where Judith commands the elders to wait for her there, and then again in *Judith* 10:6 which reports that Judith and her ἅβρα went down to the city gates.) The next and final time that we hear of the gates functioning—and again opening—is when Judith and her ἅβρα return (13:10d–13, especially 13:13). Interestingly, this time it appears that the entire city (note the boldfaced words below) comes to open the gates for her and there is no mention that the gatekeepers are young men:

13:10 . . . καὶ προσανέβησαν τὸ ὄρος Βαιτυλουα καὶ ἤλθοσαν πρὸς τὰς πύλας αὐτῆς.

13:13 καὶ συνέδραμον **πάντες ἀπὸ μικροῦ ἕως μεγάλου αὐτῶν**,
ὅτι παράδοξον ἦν αὐτοῖς τὸ ἐλθεῖν αὐτήν,
καὶ ἤνοιξαν τὴν πύλην καὶ ὑπεδέξαντο αὐτὰς
καὶ ἅψαντες πῦρ εἰς φαῦσιν περιεκύκλωσαν αὐτάς.

Psychologically speaking, we may say that the young men of Bethuliah represent the instinctual/sexual forces of the conscious realm by virtue of their virility. It is therefore fitting that *they* should open the gates for the sexually charged Judith to exit Bethuliah and should act as gatekeepers at the threshold between consciousness and the unconscious—particularly as she has transformed herself partly into a bloodthirsty man of war *cum* sexual warrior. Once Judith returns, the sexual element is completely downplayed if not outrightly denied—her beauty is not mentioned and she vehemently denies any sexual

as part of mass action: "They called together all the elders of the city, and all their young men and their women ran to the assembly; and they set Achior in the midst of all their people" (6:16); "Their children lost heart, and the women and young men fainted from thirst and fell down in the streets of the city and in the passages through the gates; there was no strength left in them any longer. Then all the people, the young men, the women, and the children, gathered about Uzziah and the rulers of the city and cried out with a loud voice, and said before all the elders" (7:22–23).

contact with Holofernes (see 13:16). She appears, calling for the gates to be opened, and everyone runs down to meet her and to open the gates because the whole of consciousness needs the *mana* she has brought. It thus behooves the text not to mention Bethulian νεανίσκοι as a separate group again from this point onwards.

The Bethulians/Bethulian Men

Apart from the Bethulian leadership, the first group of Bethulians whom we encounter are the young men/gatekeepers whose actions we have analysed in the preceding subsection. We then encounter "the men of the city" who watch Judith descend to the enemy camp (10:10) when she exits Bethuliah. They next appear when Judith returns and seem to be the first group who hear her voice (13:12). They hurry down to the city gate from which they had watched her exit five days previously, and call the city elders (13:12). After this, everyone "both small and great" runs down together to receive Judith and her ἅβρα (13:13). Finding it strange that she should have returned, they light lamps by which to see them better. When Judith produces Holofernes' head, "[a]ll the people were greatly astonished, and bowed down and worshiped God, and said with one accord, "Blessed art thou, our God, who hast brought into contempt this day the enemies of thy people" (13:17). They also affirm Ozias' generous blessing upon Judith with the words Γένοιτο γένοιτο (cf. 13:18–20). When Achior faints at the sight of Holofernes' head, the Bethulians pick him up (14:7a) and rejoice greatly once Judith has finished recounting her dealings with Holofernes (14:9). Following Judith's plan (14:11ff), they rout the Assyrians with the assistance of their fellow Judaeans, taking much booty (14:11–15:7). Having looted their enemies' camp for a further thirty days, they offer Judith Holofernes' tent, silverware, beds, and all that was his (15:11). As Judith loads these gifts upon her wagons (15:11), the "women of Israel" run forward to bless her and rejoice with her (15:12). The men follow them as they sing and enter Jerusalem where they worship God and Judith dedicates the spoils from Holofernes' tent to God (15:13 and 16:18–20).

It is uncertain whether and to what extent the entire Bethulian community—men and women—are present and active in the events of section II, hence the heading of this subsection. The only clear-cut case involving both men and women occurs in *Judith* 15:13 when the women lead in song and dance and the men follow. Be that as it may, it is interesting to note that Judith's going out and coming in is framed by the activities of the Bethulian men: they are the last to be mentioned when she descends to the enemy camp (10:10) and the first to be mentioned when she ascends from it (13:12). The sheer irony of a lone woman going down to fight the enemy while the men watch, signifies and underscores the weakness of these men as both people and psychological contents. It also scores a point for the author who seems intent on showing up the weakness of *Judith's* male characters vis-à-vis Judith's obvious strength. The traditionally/stereotypically 'bravest' members of the Bethulian society/elements of consciousness are clearly too immobilised by fear to respond to the situation and do not possess sufficient libido to exit the realm of consciousness and face the unconscious. By contrast, Judith is fearless and faith-full, and has achieved sufficient libido by virtue of her highly individuated state to traverse the threshold of consciousness, as I have previously noted.

The Bethulian men are thus portrayed as foils to the heroine. They also represent an aspect of Judaean society that has reached the fourth stage of individuation but lacks the libido to challenge the unconscious attack and move on to the fifth stage. That they are the first to respond to Judith's voice indicates that they are aware of their lack of libido as men and as contents and that they yearn for the opportunity to gain/supplement it. As we have seen, Judith's valour gives them the libido they require in that they are subsequently able to rout the Assyrians and ascend to Jerusalem following her and the dancing women. The fact that they remain in Jerusalem for three months only (16:20) and then return to their own abodes (16:21) shows that they are unable permanently to accede to the fifth level of consciousness as yet. Nevertheless, the libido transfer remains with them and prefigures their potential to accede to the fifth stage 'in the fullness of time.'

Holofernes' Troops and Bodyguards

We have previously noted that Holofernes' troops represent the underground instinctual forces which the unconscious has amassed against consciousness. It is not surprising, then, to find that Judith dresses herself up and speaks in a way that appeals to these instinctual forces and that she achieves great success thereby. As I have previously mentioned, her beauty *cum* sexuality and verbal prowess—her wisdom, as the text calls it (cf. 8:29; 11:8 and 20)—overcome the Assyrian patrol/outpost who detail a one-hundred-man escort to accompany her to Holofernes' tent (10:10b–17, see especially verses 14–15) without ever suspecting the real reason for her presence. Her beauty and wisdom likewise overcome every member of Holofernes' army who sees her (10:18–19, 23 and 11:21), so that she is unquestioningly embraced by all, and sends the passions of Holofernes into a frenzy to his own destruction (cf. especially 12:12 and 16; also 11:23). Judith's easy access to the Assyrian camp, at a time when the Assyrian forces should have been suspicious of anything coming out of Bethuliah, proves that she appealed so strongly to their instinctual nature that they were blinded into unquestioningly accepting her story and her presence there. There is thus nothing different about the portrayal of Holofernes' troops in the first part of section II as affects their nature—they are and remain elements of the instinctual force. In fact, Judith's arrival activates and focuses their instinctual nature, channelling it into a specifically sexual mode by which they are most easily deceived.

There are, nevertheless, a number of differences in the way that Holofernes' troops are depicted in section II. Firstly, the author treated Holofernes' troops as a single mass in section I, whereas here s/he focuses primarily on two groups amongst them who have a safeguarding function: the outpost that patrols the outskirts of the camp closest to Bethuliah, and Holofernes' own bodyguards. Secondly, whereas these masses were textually silent in section I, the author permits some of them to speak in section II and describes their reactions to Judith (cf. e.g., 10:14–17 and 19). We are thus *shown* and *told* the effect that she has upon them. This renders a fuller portrayal of these men that is commensurate with their greater role in section II: they progress from speechless pawns in Holofernes' hands in section I to active elements that serve the ultimate ends of the psyche in section II (see below). Strangely, they do so by failing to perform their duties: the outpost fails to protect the camp from this most intrepid intruder because they are blinded by her beauty (10:11–17), whereas Holofernes obviates the role of his own bodyguards because of his own blindness—he commands them to allow her unhindered access to the spring (12:7) and presumably sees to it that all leave his tent so that he may seduce her (13:1). In other words, the outpost facilitate Judith's entry into the camp and even lead her to the very site of her subsequent murder of Holofernes, while Holofernes 'deactivates' his bodyguards and provides her with a way of escaping unhindered once she has slain him (cf. especially 13:3f). In this way, the Assyrian troops and Holofernes himself serve the ultimate end of the psyche, which is to deliver consciousness from the grip of the unconscious so that the conscious ego may attain a higher form of individuation and/or become stabilised at a particular level. Given the instability of the Bethulians as indicated by their wavering trust in the Self and their readiness to give themselves over to the enemy/unconscious, I would argue that the purpose of the psyche is to stabilise them at the fourth level of consciousness.

Returning to the disastrous effect that Judith has upon the entire Assyrian camp, we would not be wrong in asserting that we have here a case of unresolved group anima projection. This unresolved projection casts a 'spell' over the Assyrian troops that prevents them from seeing Judith's true agenda throughout her sojourn amongst them. The spell is finally broken in the second part of section II when Bagoas discovers the headless body of Holofernes and calls out with what must have been bitter hindsight, "The slaves have tricked us! One Hebrew woman has brought disgrace upon the house of King Nebuchadnezzar! For look, here is Holofernes lying on the ground, and his head is not on him!" (14:18). The entire camp falls into disarray and all panic and flee (cf. 15:1–5). The Bethulians and other Judaeans pursue and attack them. They drive them back as far as Damascus—the second stage of consciousness (circle 4, diagram 10)—where Holofernes stopped prior to advancing upon the coastal dwellers (cf. 2:27–28), and loot their camp of all its valuable items (15:6–7).

The attack upon and obliteration of the Assyrian forces takes place so quickly that it is almost as though it did not happen—contrast the endless verses describing Nebuchadnezzar/Holofernes' attacks on the western nations in section I to the mere fifteen verses (14:11–19 and 15:1–6) it takes to destroy Holofernes' mighty armies in section II. This scenario indicates clearly that the unconscious attack cannot thrive for long when higher consciousness fights fire with fire, or instincts with instincts as is the case here. To the contrary, it is defeated and pushed back to a far lower level of consciousness—Damascus (cf. 2:27)—from which it cannot easily gain access to the central ego-consciousness again. The speedy destruction of the Assyrian forces also indicates the disastrous effects that unresolved anima projection can have upon people: domination by the unintegrated anima

(Judith), disaster, psychological destruction (their leader is killed, they scatter, flee, and are pushed back to a far lower level of consciousness so that they lose all the ground they have gained), and a loss of all that is dear (cf., e.g., the treasures that the Assyrian army lose to Judith and her compatriots).

Holofernes

It is interesting to note that, as with most characters (all except Holofernes' bodyguards) encountered in section II so far, Holofernes' words and actions are completely centred around Judith—apart from his reclining on the couch prior to her arrival (10:21), that is.

- When Holofernes is told of Judith's presence he comes out to the entrance of the tent preceded by silver lanterns (10:22).
- When she enters and falls before him in mock subservience, he is taken by her beauty and counsels her not to fear any harm (10:23–11:4).
- He is pleased with her words and her promise of leading him up to Jerusalem where he, with her help and that of her God, will set up his throne unopposed (10:20, cf. 11:5–19).
- Once she has completed her promissory speech (11:5–19), he encourages her again (11:22) and states his intention to follow her God if she does as she has said. He further promises, "you shall live in the house of King Nebuchadnezzar and be renowned throughout the whole world" (11:23).
- He orders his servants (presumably—the Greek text simply has Καὶ ἐκέλευσεν) "to bring her in where his silver dishes were kept, and ordered them to set a table for her with some of his own food and to serve her with his own wine" (12:1).
- When Judith protests that she may not eat food that is not kosher, Holofernes is concerned about where to obtain such food for her once her supplies run out. Her response that she would not have spent her supplies "before the Lord carries out by my hand what he has determined to do" seems to allay his concerns as he does not take up this issue again (12:2–4).
- Holofernes readily grants Judith's request to exit the camp every evening to 'bathe' at the spring that once watered Bethuliah (12:6–7; cf. also 7:7–17).
- He eagerly sends his eunuch, Bagoas, to invite her to a banquet which he hosts in her 'honour'—with the explicit intent of seducing

her, of course (12:10ff.; see underlined portions below). Interestingly, he frames the failure to do so in terms of his personal shame (see boldfaced section), which yields a chiastic structure (ABB[1]A[1]):

12:11	. . . Πεῖσον δὴ πορευθεὶς τὴν γυναῖκα τὴν Εβραίαν, ἥ ἐστιν παρὰ σοί, τοῦ ἐλθεῖν πρὸς ἡμᾶς καὶ φαγεῖν καὶ πιεῖν μεθ' ἡμῶν	
12:12	ἰδοὺ γὰρ **αἰσχρὸν τῷ προσώπῳ ἡμῶν**	A
	εἰ γυναῖκα τοιαύτην παρήσομεν οὐχ ὁμιλήσαντες[55] αὐτῇ,	B
	ὅτι ἐὰν ταύτην μὴ ἐπισπασώμεθα,	B[1]
	καταγελάσεται ἡμῶν.	A[1]

• He is aroused by her beauty when she lies opposite him at the banquet. Awaiting a chance to seduce her, he becomes deliriously happy:

12:16 . . . Καὶ ἐξέστη ἡ καρδία Ολοφέρνου ἐπ' αὐτήν, καὶ ἐσαλεύθη[56] ἡ ψυχὴ αὐτοῦ, καὶ ἦν κατεπίθυμος σφόδρα τοῦ συγγενέσθαι μετ' αὐτῆς . . .

He is so overjoyed at her presence (καὶ ηὐφράνθη[57] Ολοφέρνης ἀπ' αὐτῆς) that he drinks more than he had ever drunk in his entire life (12:20). He also encourages her to do likewise, presumably that she

[55] The meaning of ὁμιλέω is, traditionally, "1) to be in company with. 2) to associate with. 3) to stay with. 4) to converse with, talk about: with one" (ESL). See, however, Liddell and Scott's third entry for this word, "III of social intercourse, to hold converse: to live familiarly with, associate with: to have dealings with. 2. absol. To be friends", which signifies that much more than mere 'conversation' is intended here. I would thus agree with Moore (op. cit., 223) that, given the nature of Holofernes and the rather veiled euphemistic use of the Greek here, this word signifies Holofernes' desire to have sexual intercourse with Judith. Cf. *Judith* 12:16, which makes this absolutely clear. Cf. also Susanna verse 54 (Theodotion Version, LRS), where the word can only refer to sexual intercourse within the context of this verse.

[56] RAPC omits translating the phrase καὶ ἐσαλεύθη ἡ ψυχὴ αὐτοῦ, probably deeming it to be another expression of Καὶ ἐξέστη ἡ καρδία Ολοφέρνου ἐπ' αὐτήν: "Holofernes' heart was ravished with her and he was moved with great desire to possess her; for he had been waiting for an opportunity to deceive her, ever since the day he first saw her" (12:16). This is a great pity as RAPC's translation loses the momentum of Holofernes' desire as a result. Σαλεύω means "to cause to rock; to move up and down [gloss]; 1) a motion produced by winds, storms, waves, etc. 1a) to agitate or shake. 1b) to cause to totter. 1c) to shake thoroughly, of a measure filled by shaking its contents together. 2) to shake down, overthrow. 2a) to cast down from one's (secure and happy) state. 2b) to move, agitate the mind, to disturb one" (ESL). Hence Moore's translation of καὶ ἐσαλεύθη ἡ ψυχὴ αὐτου "and his brain was reeling" (op. cit., 221).

[57] Εὐφραίνω—to cheer, delight, gladden (gloss); 1) to gladden, make joyful. 1a) to be glad, to be merry, to rejoice. 1b) to rejoice in, be delighted with a thing

might be willing to join him in his 'merriment' at a later stage (12:17).

- Finally, when everyone else leaves, he falls on his bed and loses his head (13:1–9b).

Holofernes undergoes some rather interesting drive changes in section II, which are similar to the changes seen in his troops, as he becomes increasingly set upon conquering Judith. He continues to speak for his master/in his master's name (11:1, 4, 22, and 23), and he is still proud, arrogant, and somewhat of a megalomaniac (cf., e.g., the ornate canopy, silver lamps, and silverware, which speak of this), but these aspects of his nature are now channelled into possessing Judith whereas they were previously channelled into exacting vengeance upon the nations who had disobeyed his master. Note particularly in this regard how his proposed sexual conquest of Judith is framed within the context of his personal honour (12:12 above): 'if I do not seduce her I will be shamed and she will laugh me to scorn.' The pride of a nation-conqueror becomes muted into the pride of conquering a woman (cf. 12:12 especially) who has come to represent that nation, just as his mandate to please Nebuchadnezzar and possess the nations for his glory is presently muted by his raging desire to possess her (cf. in this regard the troops' response to her arrival, which couples her with conquering her nation in 10:19). To this end, he tries every trick in the book: he speaks to her gently, promises her safety and position, flatters her, shows off his riches to her, and even volunteers to join her religion should she do as she has promised (11:23). It is amazing that Holofernes so eagerly accepts Judith's help in conquering the Judaeans whereas he would have none that Achior offered—particularly when Judith corroborates the verity of Achior's words. Should this very fact—her corroboration of Achior's story—not have raised some suspicion in his mind? Or, is his self-image so weak and is he consequently in such desperate need of the flattering affirmation Judith gives him that all his suspicions are allayed? Or, does Judith simply feed into his inflation without his realising it for exactly the same reason? I believe

(ESL). This verb is obviously related to the noun εὐφροσύνη in the same verse and highlights the point which I subsequently make above, i.e., that Holofernes wanted Judith to join him in drinking so that she would later be more willing to join him in 'merriment.'

that all these possibilities are appropriate in this situation, as those who suffer from inflation are often psychological weaklings who mask their insecurity and feeling of inferiority with the kind of pride and power-conqueror/'invincibility' attributes that Holofernes displays. In this sense, Holofernes has much in common with the Judges hero, Samson. Like Samson before him (Judges 16:4–21), he arrogantly believes in his invincibility, and so falls into the hands of his enemies blindly and willingly. He could have read the signs—although they were definitely not as clear as those Delilah gave Samson (note especially Judges 16:6–17 and 19)[58]—and saved himself from destruction, but he does not. It is as though he has become drunk and blind with the twin ideas of possessing Judith and the victory she promises.

What we have here, psychologically speaking, is a clear case of anima possession that is similar to and yet far more pronounced than that experienced by his troops/entourage: Judith, in the guise of the quintessential femme fatale or negative anima, mystifies Holofernes with her words, flatters him, spellbinds him with her beauty, effectively offers him her sexuality on a plate (note especially 12:14 in this context), and promises to lead him to victory—only to lead him to destruction in his own tent and by his own sword. Her beauty and her words with their simmering sexual underpinnings that are seemingly directed exclusively at him, blind him to such an extent that he readily believes her, grants her wishes freely with no indication whatsoever of suspecting foul play, and effectively disables his own bodyguards from protecting him against her (cf. 12:7). In this context, it is not remotely surprising to find that he is even willing to 'change faith', as it were, and to believe in Judith's God if she assists him to set up his throne in Jerusalem as she has promised (contrast 11:23 with 3:8 and 6:2). Such is the strength of his anima possession that he is willing to forsake his master and his 'god', Nebuchadnezzar, and become the disciple of Judith and her God. He becomes completely focused on possessing Judith/his anima. That this is a fatal flaw—the anima cannot be possessed—is evident from his resultant decapitation. (The latter, as I have previously stated, signifies the symbolic 'castration at the hand of a woman' that all

[58] For further parallels between Samson-Delilah and Holofernes-Judith see Meredith 1989 discussed in chapter 3.

men fear, i.e., their loss of power and life through succumbing to the charms of a woman).

Before proceeding to the next subsection, I should like to examine briefly the reasons for Holofernes' severe and ultimately fatal anima possession. As we have seen, a projection can only take place successfully if there is something in the person onto whom the projection is made that facilitates her/his receiving it. This 'something' may take the form of similarities and/or dissimilarities. In fact, if I read Jung correctly, the primary connection is made on the basis of dissimilarity; however, it also takes sufficient similarities to offset the primary dissimilarity if a projection is to succeed. This is something that is very evident in couples that are tremendously in love: they are fascinated by each other's differences/dissimilarities, but there are sufficient similarities to offset these and keep them together. What, then, makes Judith a suitable receptor of Holofernes' inner female image/his anima? On the one hand, we see that Judith is totally other to Holofernes and his surroundings: female vs. male, Israelite vs. 'Assyrian', deceptive vs. straightforward (Holofernes makes his intentions clear from the start, whereas she speaks in deceptive irony to mask her hidden agenda), civilian vs. military, an effigy of beauty vs. the ugliness of war, the personification of Sophia, the feminine aspect of the Self, vs. the Shadow or concretisation of the masculine aspect of the negative Self. On the other hand, there are also many similarities between them: extreme dedication to a cause, a high level of instinctuality/sexuality, a functioning on the shadow side of life (Judith's ostensible readiness to 'betray' her people corresponds with Holofernes' latent desire to be king), and a certain amount of wisdom/cunning and verbal prowess. All these facets of their similarity and difference combine in a heady mixture to make Judith a more than suitable receptor of Holofernes' inner female image/anima. It is no wonder, then, that she can grip his soul with such force that he eventually loses his head.

Holofernes' Officers/Attendants and Servants

In section II, we encounter Holofernes' θεράποντες four times exclusively within the context of Judith's arrival at Holofernes' tent. They too seem to exist solely for her, either to assist her by bringing her into their master's presence (10:20) and taking her to the tent allotted to her (12:5), or to offer exalted comment on her beauty and intelligence (10:23 and 11:20). In this way, they effectively become *her* θεράποντες and are ample indication that Judith's prayer in chapter 9 is already having the desired effect—she/God is smiting "the prince with his servant" (9:10) by her words and her beauty.

Once Judith has completed her first 'address' to Holofernes (11:5–19), both he and his officers/attendants are in awe, so much so that they regard her as the most beautiful and most intelligent woman in the world: Οὐκ ἔστιν τοιαύτη γυνὴ ἀπ' ἄκρου ἕως ἄκρου τῆς γῆς ἐν καλῷ προσώπῳ καὶ συνέσει[59] λόγων (11:21). Clearly, her weaponry is working and her strategy is so effective that it disarms everyone who encounters her and leaves Holofernes defenceless. As we have seen, it has already disarmed the patrol that guards the Assyrian camp; and it is now disarming Holofernes and his personal attendants to detrimental effect.

Regarding Holofernes' θεράποντες (officers/attendants) as persons, we may say that they too become possessed by the anima archetype which Judith represents. As they are not so tightly bound to Holofernes—they are not his bond slaves (δοῦλοι), the strength of their anima possession enables them to disconnect themselves from Holofernes—albeit temporarily—and to focus their attention almost exclusively on her—to become *her* attendants/'disciples', as it were. For the same reason, we may also say that, as elements of the unconscious, they are temporarily loosened from their connection to the shadow archetype to constellate around the far stronger anima figure that Judith represents.

By contrast, Holofernes' δοῦλοι (bond slaves) remain tightly constellated around him. We encounter them within two contexts: Judith's arrival at Holofernes' tent and Holofernes' banquet. In the first instance, they raise their master's unexpected guest to her feet (10:23), while in the second they are the sole members of the Assyrian camp to be invited to the banquet at which Holofernes hopes to seduce Judith (12:10).[60] They make haste to leave the banquet when evening

[59] Σύνεσις—a coming together, union; a quick comprehension (gloss); 1) a running together, a flowing together with 2) knowledge. 2a) understanding. 2b) the understanding, i.e., the mind so far forth as it understands (ESL); critical, apprehending the bearing of things (ESL synonyms). RAPC's "wisdom of speech" is quite a good translation of συνέσει λόγων, but I prefer Moore's more pointed rendition of this verse: "'In terms of beauty and brains there is not another woman like this from one end of the earth to the other!'" (op. cit., 207).

[60] The Greek text of *Judith* 12:10 is extremely obscure and makes it difficult to decide exactly who these δοῦλοι were. By virtue of the context, it is possible to

comes (13:1), with the patent intent to give their master a chance to 'associate' with Judith privately (cf. 12:12 in which the verb ὁμιλέω—to associate, converse with—occurs in euphemistic sense). It is evident, then, that Holofernes' δοῦλοι are simply there to do his bidding. We may therefore interpret them as we did before, i.e., as "weak, unconscious contents that serve the dominant shadow archetype" and as people of little or no self-worth who cling to those who possess the kind of false charismatic leadership that Holofernes does.

Bagoas

Bagoas is the seventh new character to be introduced to the reader in section II, the others being Judith, Manasses, Judith's ἅβρα, the Bethulian gatekeepers, the Assyrian patrol, and Holofernes' bodyguards. We first encounter Bagoas in *Judith* 12:11. This verse tells us his name, that he is an eunuch, and that he is in charge over all Holofernes' earthly goods. The same verse also tells us that Judith is under his oversight (see "persuade the Hebrew woman who is in your care"; 12:11)—for obvious reasons[61]—and presents us with his first task, i.e., to 'persuade' Judith to come to Holofernes' banquet. While Holofernes is quite direct about his purpose with the banquet, Bagoas skilfully and diplomatically interprets his words when speaking to Judith and gently 'persuades' her to attend (see 12:13 below):

- He addresses her in the third person, which softens the form of command.
- He attempts to flatter her by calling her "this beautiful maidservant".
- He turns a matter of personal shame for Holofernes into one of personal honour for Judith (note the boldfaced portions in 12:13 below).
- He minimizes the directness of Holofernes' desire by 'requesting' her (note Μὴ ὀκνησάτω in 12:13 below) to come "and become

understand this "colourless term" (Enslin, op. cit., 147) as friends or intimates who are especially invited to the banquet, or as "those regularly in attendance because of especial duties" (ibid.). I would agree with Enslin (ibid.) that the latter appears to be the "most likely" and have retained this sense by translating the word as "slaves."

[61] This verse raises the possibility that there were other women in the Assyrian camp but that we simply do not hear of them. Bagoas' relation to Judith is very similar to that between Ahasuerus' eunuch, Hagai, and Esther. Cf. particularly the parallels between *Judith* 12:11 and 15 and Esther 2:3, 8–9 and 15. For further parallels between Esther and *Judith* see the works discussed in chapter 3 E. a. and d.

today like one of the daughters of the Assyrians who serve in the house of Nebuchadnezzar", i.e., to serve Holofernes in the same way that Nebuchadnezzar's women serve him (note the underlined portion below):

12:13 . . . Μὴ ὀκνησάτω[62] δὴ ἡ παιδίσκη ἡ καλὴ αὕτη
ἐλθοῦσα πρὸς τὸν κύριόν μου
δοξασθῆναι κατὰ πρόσωπον αὐτοῦ
καὶ πίεσαι μεθ' ἡμῶν εἰς εὐφροσύνην οἶνον
καὶ γενηθῆναι ἐν τῇ ἡμέρᾳ ταύτῃ ὡς θυγάτηρ μία τῶν υἱῶν
Ασσουρ, αἳ παρεστήκασιν ἐν οἴκῳ Ναβουχοδονοσορ.

Then, once everyone has left the banquet, Bagoas bars the tent door from the outside, leaving Judith alone with his master (13:1).

We next hear of Bagoas in the aftermath of the banquet, when the Assyrian military leaders call upon him to "Waken now our lord for the slaves [i.e., the Bethulians] have been bold to come down against us to battle, that they may be utterly destroyed" (14:13). He shakes the curtain of the tent (ἔκρουσε[63] τὴν αὐλαίαν τῆς σκηνῆς) and, hearing no reply, parts the curtain to find his master dead and headless on the platform (14:14–15). The strength of the consternation this causes him is conveyed by the intensity with which his cries are reported, ("And he cried out with a loud voice and wept and groaned and shouted") and the rending of his clothing (14:16). His consternation mounts as he discovers that Judith is not in her own tent (14:17). He rushes out in a frenzy, crying out aloud to his fellows (καὶ ἐξεπήδησεν[64] εἰς τὸν λαὸν καὶ ἐβόησεν):

[62] Ὀκνέω—"to shrink, to scruple, hesitate" (gloss). While RAPC correctly captures the politeness of the request, it fails to convey its more urgent character, which is reflected in Moore's translation, "May this lovely maid *not hesitate*" (op. cit., 221, my emphasis).

[63] RAPC translates this phrase as follows: "knocked at the door of the tent." While κρούω properly means "to knock: at the door" (ESL; cf. also "to strike, smite" [gloss]), this can hardly be intended here as the object of the verb is τὴν αὐλαίαν τῆς σκηνῆς—the tent curtain. As with Moore (op. cit., 238), I would therefore prefer to render this verb as "shake": "So Bagoas went in and shook the curtain partitioning the tent . . ." (ibid.).

[64] Ἐκπηδάω means "to leap out" (gloss); "to spring out, to rush out impetuously" (ESL entry listed under εἰσπεδάω). Hence my interpretation that he rushes out in a frenzy. RAPC has "he rushed out to the people", which does not quite convey his state of frenzy.

14:18 Ἠθέτησαν οἱ δοῦλοι, ἐποίησεν αἰσχύνην μία γυνὴ τῶν Εβραίων εἰς τὸν οἶκον τοῦ βασιλέως Ναβουχοδονοσορ, ὅτι ἰδοὺ Ολοφέρνης χαμαί, καὶ ἡ κεφαλὴ οὐκ ἔστιν ἐπ᾽ αὐτῷ.

This sends everyone else into a frenzy, beginning with the Assyrian ἄρχοντες (4:19), and the rest is Judithic 'history'.

The way that Bagoas responds to Judith, his master, and his master's death tells us many things about him. We see him as a loyal steward who is intelligent enough to convey his master's rather direct wishes to Judith in the most inoffensive and yet persuasive way. We also see that he is committed both to his master and his master's cause: he does as his master wishes, and displays obvious pain upon discovering his death. His commitment to Holofernes' cause is underlined by the fact that he calls the Judaean enemy οἱ δοῦλοι (the slaves—14:18) as the Assyrian ἄρχοντες (princes/rulers) had done (14:13)—and this despite the fact that he is little more than a "slave" himself. Similarly, his reference to Holofernes' murder as an act of shame committed against Nebuchadnezzar shows his allegiance to the Assyrian potentate and his cause of which Holofernes is the champion.

Given the above, we may conjecture that there is a very strong emotional bond between Bagoas and his master: he obeys Holofernes without question and he identifies with him and all that he stands for. To my mind, his terrible consternation at Holofernes' death and the fact that he effectively ceases to exist once Holofernes dies—he is never mentioned again after that—indicate that he is somehow pathologically dependant on his master and that he relates to him with the kind of all-consuming dedication that guru devotees exhibit towards their 'masters' today. Could this be the reason for his blindness to Judith's schemes and the fact that he becomes the fourth in a line of people who fail to protect Holofernes? As we have seen, the others—the Assyrian patrol, Holofernes' θεράποντες (officers/attendants), and Holofernes' bodyguards—failed to protect their 'master'/leader from certain death because they either fell prey to Judith's verbal and sexual charms or were 'disabled' by Holofernes himself. This, however, is not the case with Bagoas. The author neither tells nor shows us his response to the sexually charged "Hebrew" female who comes to his master's tent. Perhaps the reason for this lies in the fact that Bagoas is a eunuch and does not/is not expected to desire women as other men do. If this is indeed the case, his sexual 'handicap' alone should have immunised him to Judith's charms and allowed him to use his obvious intelligence to see through her ruses and protect his master from her. This, however, does not happen, and Bagoas becomes a victim of his own commitment to Holofernes. He lets his master down by blindly accepting what/whom he accepts and doing all that he desires. Failing to see through Judith's patent flattery and her nightly ablution scheme—because he sees through Holofernes' eyes, he eagerly obeys his master—he invites her to the banquet, leaves at the appropriate time, and bars the tent from the outside. In this way, he blocks any way of escape that his master might have had—had the latter not been so drunk—and effectively seals his (Holofernes') fate. Thus, while the others are blinded by Judith's sexual and verbal prowess (the patrol and Holofernes' θεράποντες) or even by Holofernes himself (his bodyguards), Bagoas is blinded by his own loyalty to Holofernes and his cause into leaving his master defenceless and vulnerable in the hands of the highly intrepid Judith.

Furthermore, as I have previously noted, Bagoas is the only member of the instinctually based unconscious force, i.e., Holofernes and his army, that lacks sexual content by virtue of his being a eunuch. This, to my mind, makes him a weak link in the unconscious attack-force which is primarily based and dependant upon its instinctual arsenal for success. As we have seen, he is indeed the last link in the chain of Holofernes' downfall which, in my opinion, supports my interpretation of him as a weak link in the chain. Even so, his closeness to Holofernes shows that he is closely constellated to the dominant shadow archetype, which makes his role all the more pivotal: he is simultaneously the weakest link and the one closest to Holofernes. This, as the text has shown us, is foolishness on the part of the unconscious; Holofernes should have had his strongest link closest to him, and not the weakest one. However, Holofernes has a eunuch as his closest link, presumably because the latter would be unable to express his instincts towards any of the Assyrian general's women. Ironically, this very lack of instinctual content that Holofernes has chosen Bagoas for is what finally leads to his undoing—he is the one who finally fails him in the sexual war initiated by Judith.

As affects the relationship between Bagoas and his master, we also note that there are many contrasts between the two. If Bagoas is no sex, a humbly dependent servant and a man of relatively low position, Holofernes is all sex, an arrogant, powerful master, and a man of high military position. In other words, Bagoas is the opposite of his master in all respects except for being male. These contrasts and Bagoas' close ties with Holofernes indicate clearly that the former is a 'weaker' form of his master. On a psychological/archetypal level, this means that Bagoas represents the shadow of Holofernes the person. At this point, I wish to draw the reader's attention to the fact that unintegrated unconscious contents become dangerous to the conscious psyche and may cause it such a severe loss of consciousness that part or all of it becomes swallowed up in the unconscious. The fact that Bagoas fails to protect Holofernes the person from death at the hand of his anima (Judith) demonstrates this danger very well and shows that he represents an unintegrated shadow content in Holofernes' psyche. It will also be remembered that assimilating/integrating the shadow contents is the preliminary step to assimilating the anima—the latter cannot happen without the former taking place first. As we have seen, Holofernes the person falls prey to Judith, his anima; he fails to integrate her despite wanting to possess her and therefore suffers calamity at her hand. This supports my conjecture that Holofernes has not integrated his personal shadow (either fully or at all), which in turn underscores my interpretation of Bagoas as a 'weak link in the chain'.

My interpretation of Bagoas as Holofernes' shadow is further borne out by the many parallels between him and Judith's ἅβρα who has been identified as Judith's shadow:

- Both Bagoas and the ἅβρα are depicted in a helper/caretaker function in that each one is in charge of her/his superior's goods (cf. 8:10; 12:11 and 14:13).
- The critical involvement of both characters takes place before, during, and after Holofernes' failed seduction banquet.
- Even so, Bagoas has a name and is given the power of speech whereas the ἅβρα has neither name nor speech. He is sexually challenged as a eunuch, while she is textually challenged in that the author does not permit her to speak.
- Bagoas also seems to be far more dependent on Holofernes than the ἅβρα is on Judith: he is completely devastated at his master's death, and there is no indication of what happens to him after he alerts the rest of the camp to Holofernes' murder. We have also previously noted that his loyalty to and dependency on Holofernes prevent him from seeing through Judith's sexual and

> verbal ruse despite his obvious intelligence. By contrast, the ἅβρα seems to possess a greater measure of autonomy—particularly when in the unconscious realm—despite the fact that she too complies with her mistress's wishes. We note too that she is liberated once Judith dies; she does not simply disappear into the background as Bagoas does.

To my mind, these parallels between Bagoas and Judith's ἅβρα lend further support to my belief that Bagoas is tightly bonded with Holofernes. They further uphold my argument that he, unlike the ἅβρα, represents an unintegrated shadow content. This would account for his dependence on Holofernes and his disappearance from the text: he is so closely bonded to Holofernes that he loses all libido and is completely swallowed up by the unconscious once his master dies. By contrast, the ἅβρα is an integrated shadow element whose archetypal energy is simply released in the realms of consciousness once Judith dies.

Achior

Judith 14:5–10 marks the first and last appearance of Achior in section II, and so his last appearance in the entire book. These verses are located in the context of Judith's return from the Assyrian camp in general (13:11ff), and the details of her battle plan in particular (14:1–4, subsection Bb'). Having briefed the Bethulians on the next day's line of attack, Judith commands that Achior be brought to her before any of her commands are carried out (14:5). This is done and, seeing Holofernes' head in one man's hand, Achior faints: he collapses (literally, he falls on his face) and his breathing weakens (14:6). When the Bethulians revive him/pick him up (ὡς δὲ ἀνέλαβον[65] αὐτόν), he falls at Judith's feet in submission/obeisance (literally: he worshipped her face—14:7) and pronounces a blessing upon her:

> 14:7 . . . **Εὐλογημένη σὺ ἐν παντὶ σκηνώματι Ιουδα** καὶ ἐν παντὶ ἔθνει, οἵτινες ἀκούσαντες τὸ ὄνομά σου ταραχθήσονται

[65] Ἀναλαμβάνω—ordinarily "to take up" (the gloss) can either mean that they revived him in light of the previous verse, or simply that they picked him up. This verb is used in the sense of 'taking up arms' in every other verse where it occurs, i.e., in 6:12; 7:5; 14:2, 3, and 11. It is interesting to note that it may also refer to adoption into service, cf. "to take up, take into one's hands: generally to take with one. 2. to take into one's service, to adopt" (Liddell and Scott).

Achior's blessing bears marked resemblances to the blessing that Deborah pronounces on Jael in Judges 5:24 (note the boldfaced sections in 14:7 above and Judges 5:24 below), which again underscore the similarities between Deborah/Jael and Judith:

Judges 5:24 εὐλογηθείη ἐκ γυναικῶν Ιαηλ γυνὴ Χαβερ τοῦ Κιναίου, **ἐκ γυναικῶν ἐν σκηνῇ εὐλογηθείη.**

Having blessed Judith in this fashion, Achior requests that she should recount all that she had done in the preceding days (14:8). She does so and the people shout out aloud with great joy (14:9). Seeing all that the God of Israel has done Achior believes on Him completely, is circumcised, and is joined to the house of Israel "remaining so to this day" (literally "unto this day"—14:10).

When last we heard of Achior in section I (6:21), he was taken to a banquet with the city's elders at Ozias' house. This is where we find him again in section II—at Ozias' house. We may therefore say that for the duration of Judith's sojourn in the Assyrian camp Achior has continued his existence as a partially integrated psychological content, and that he has still not fully attained to the fourth stage of consciousness (represented by Bethuliah) as a person. Judith's return changes that to such an extent that Achior is converted/fully integrated at the fourth level of consciousness. In the first place, she sends people to call him so that he may "see and recognize[66] the man [Holofernes] who despised the house of Israel and sent him [Achior] to us as if to his death to us" (14:5). This intimates that Achior's recognition of Holofernes' death and, with that, the latter's ultimate powerlessness as a human being versus the absolute power of God, will be the final impetus to his complete and willing integration at stage 4 (see below). That this is indeed the case is shown by the ensuing action in *Judith* 14:6–10 and, more especially, by steps (ii) and (vii)–(ix) below. On a psychological level, each of the ten verbs of which Achior is subject in these verses has

[66] RAPC's translation aptly captures the sense of ἵνα ἰδὼν ἐπιγνοι. According to ESL ἐπγινώσκω has a clear sense of knowing and acknowledging something/someone: "to observe; to acknowledge" (gloss); "1) to become thoroughly acquainted with, to know thoroughly. 1a) to know accurately, know well. 2) to know. 2a) to recognise. 2a1) by sight, hearing, of certain signs, to perceive who a person is. 2b) to know i.e., to perceive. 2c) to know i.e., to find out, ascertain. 2d) to know i.e., to understand".

a special significance as affects his final and willing integration into the fourth stage of conscious awareness:

(i) He is willing to come out of a partially integrated position ("he came [out of Ozias' house]"—14:6).
(ii) He recognises the defeat of the unconscious and the integration of (some of) its contents/*mana* into consciousness ("when he came and saw the head of Holofernes . . . at the gathering of the people"—14:6).
(iii) He willingly drops the persona/mask/face of conscious adaptation and, in so doing, dies completely to the old life/previous level of consciousness ("he fell down on his face [read: persona], and his spirit failed him"—14:6).
(iv) He submits to the Self by falling at the feet of its highest representative, Judith (προσέπεσεν[67] τοῖς ποσὶν Ιουδιθ—14:7).
(v) He recognises the ascendancy of the Self by doing obeisance to Judith ("[he] knelt before her").
(vi) He shows his desire to communicate with the Self by blessing Judith and asking to hear of her deed: ("Blessed are you in every tent of Judah . . . Now tell me what you have done during these days"—14:7–8).
(vii) Achior hears Judith's story and gains a new understanding of/identifies with the deeds of the Self ("And when Achior saw all that the God of Israel had done, he believed firmly in God"—14:10).
(viii) He is completely convinced of the Self and "its" deeds ("he believed firmly in God"—14:10).
(ix) He willingly sacrifices the old (sexual and other?) instinctual practices that may have thwarted his integration—he is circumcised in the flesh of his foreskin (14:10).
(x) He becomes a full part of the conscious level that the Bethulians represent ("and joined the house of Israel, remaining so to this day"—14:10).

[67] Προσπίπτω—the only other use of this verb occurs in *Judith* 13:2 where Holofernes falls onto his bed in a drunken stupor after the banquet when he is left alone with Judith (ὑπελείφθη δὲ Ιουδιθ μόνη ἐν τῇ σκηνῇ, καὶ Ολοφέρνης προπεπτωκὼς ἐπὶ τὴν κλίνην αὐτοῦ, ἦν γὰρ περικεχυμένος αὐτῷ ὁ οἶνος—"So Judith was left alone in the tent, with Holofernes stretched out on his bed, for he was overcome with wine". Cf. Moore (op. cit., 222) "So Judith was left alone in the tent with Holofernes sprawled on his bed, dead drunk").

According to *Judith* 14:6–10, Achior's final and willing integration, (x), takes place in nine steps in which the recognition of the impotence of the unconscious shadow, (ii), and the ascendancy of the Self, (iv)–(viii), plays a major part. It will be remembered that the Bethulians initially integrated Achior in seven steps, which culminated in his banqueting at Ozias' house. Nine and seven up to sixteen steps. As sixteen is the square of four, which is the number of completeness, Achior's sixteen steps of total integration into the fourth stage of consciousness signify the complete success of the process here.

To return to the text, we note that Achior's recognition of Holofernes' powerlessness versus God's power and his subsequent conversion to Judaism are a prerequisite for the ensuing attack (cf. the first paragraph in this subsection: Judith commands that Achior is brought to her *before* any of her battle plans are carried out). The reason for this lies in Achior's identification with the Judaean nation and the fact that he represents their collective, Deuteronomistic, conscious attitude. Holofernes, as we may recall, had condemned Achior to await his death at Bethuliah upon Holofernes' destruction of the Bethulian/Judaean citizenry (6:5–10). This, inter alia, shows that Achior's fate is intimately tied up with that of the Judaeans' and *vice versa*. Nevertheless, Judith turns the tables on Holofernes and his entire entourage. As a result of this, Achior—whom Holofernes meant to kill once he had disposed of the Bethulians/Judaeans—finds himself staring at the severed head of his would-be executioner and the one who had "despised the house of Israel" (14:5). As I have indicated above, this functions as the final impetus to his willing and full integration at the fourth stage of consciousness as signified by his willing conversion to Judaism. The latter could not have happened without the approval of the people—see the first seven steps of his integration which are characterised by the Bethulians' actions towards him in section I and *Judith* 14:6–10. Their approval shows that they have accepted him/integrated the shadow contents that he represents to the extent that they are able. By virtue of his acceptance into the Judaean community/consciousness and his identification with them/it, Achior's conversion becomes the symbol of renewed life/thinking in the community and renewed libido in consciousness. Achior is thus symbolic of the 'new Jew' who has accepted and internalised/integrated the new life which the Self has brought/wishes to bring about through Judith.

Furthermore, Achior's conversion is preceded by the partial integration of the national shadow elements represented by Holofernes (Judith brings his severed head into the midst of the Bethulian community). His conversion, which entails the recognition of the shadow's defeat/integration, enables consciousness to come to terms with and fully integrate the same. The Bethulians' (and other Judaeans') defeat of the Assyrian army shows that this has indeed occurred, as they would have been unable to defeat the Assyrians with their previously impoverished and defeatist attitude which stemmed from their fear of the then-unintegrated national shadow/Holofernes and their Deuteronomistic self-image. As Jung has told us, integrating the shadow contents that have crossed the conscious threshold is paramount to the well-being of the psyche and the growth of the human organism, be it a person or nation. Not integrating the shadow causes fear and psychic defeat. Thus, Achior's conversion enables the Bethulians to:

i) Integrate fully the national shadow elements represented by Holofernes.
ii) Espouse a new mental attitude by which they see that God/the Self is for them and not against them (cf. 7:24–28).
iii) Become fully functional at the fourth stage of consciousness.

Similarly, Achior's conversion is facilitated by a host of events from the time of his expulsion from Holofernes' camp:

i) Achior is expelled from the camp.
ii) His retelling of Holofernes' plans and what had occurred facilitates Judith's defeat of the Assyrian general in that she is able to build upon Achior's historical account to deceive him.
iii) Judith returns bearing the unconscious *mana* in the form of Holofernes' severed head. The Bethulians' joy indicates their integration of this content.
iv) This leads them to call out Achior who subsequently becomes concerted/fully integrated into consciousness.

In turn, Achior's conversion enables the Bethulians to defeat the unconscious forces with the help of the other Judaeans, take in all its *mana*/booty, and ultimately become fully functional at the fourth level of consciousness. In this way, the interdependence of Achior, Judith, and the Bethulians is established. Should any of these characters be taken out of the 'equation', then neither Achior nor the

Bethulians would have become fully functional members of stage 4, and the consequences of Judith's victorious sojourn in the unconscious would have been hampered, which again affects the establishment/complete integration of Achior and the Bethulians at stage 4.

Holofernes' High-Ranking Officers

In section II, the author introduces us to a new component of Holofernes' "staff", namely, his ἡγουμένοι (leaders/superiors—14:3; cf. n. 48), στρατήγοι (generals/commanders—14:3 and 12), and χιλιάρχοι (commanders/tribunes—14:3; cf. n. 43). These high-ranking officers appear only once, and that is within the context of the Judaeans' attack. In what appears to reflect ascending order of rank, the Assyrian soldiers call their leaders, who call their generals, commanders, and other ἀρχόντες (princes/rulers) to inform them of the Bethulians' attack. They then call upon Bagoas to waken Holofernes in light of this:

14:12 οἱ δὲ υἱοὶ Ασσουρ ὡς εἶδον αὐτούς, διέπεμψαν ἐπὶ τοὺς ἡγουμένους αὐτῶν, οἱ δὲ ἦλθον ἐπὶ τοὺς στρατηγοὺς καὶ χιλιάρχους καὶ ἐπὶ πάντα ἄρχοντα αὐτῶν.

14:13 καὶ παρεγένοντο ἐπὶ τὴν σκηνὴν Ολοφέρνου καὶ εἶπαν τῷ ὄντι ἐπὶ πάντων τῶν αὐτοῦ Ἔγειρον δὴ τὸν κύριον ἡμῶν, ὅτι ἐτόλμησαν οἱ δοῦλοι καταβαίνειν ἐφ' ἡμᾶς εἰς πόλεμον, ἵνα ἐξολεθρευθῶσιν εἰς τέλος.

The words of these ἄρχοντες show that they have little regard for their Bethulian attackers (they derogate them as "the slaves") and that they believe that they will gain the upper hand over them (cf. "in order to be destroyed completely"). Nevertheless, when they hear Bagoas' news concerning the slaying of Holofernes, the Assyrian lords rend their clothes, become terrified (see boldfaced portion below; 14:13), cry out aloud, and become the first to flee. Their terror spreads to the rest of the camp, seemingly in descending order of rank this time, and the entire camp follows suit and flees:

14:19 <u>ὡς δὲ ἤκουσαν</u> ταῦτα τὰ ῥήματα οἱ ἄρχοντες τῆς δυνάμεως Ασσουρ, τοὺς χιτῶνας αὐτῶν διέρρηξαν, καὶ **ἐταράχθη αὐτῶν ἡ ψυχὴ σφόδρα**, καὶ ἐγένετο αὐτων κραυγὴ καὶ βοὴ μεγάλη σφόδρα ἐν μέσῳ τῆς παρεμβολῆς

The reaction of these men parallels exactly the Judaeans/Bethulians' initial and subsequent fearful reactions to the reports of Holofernes' doings in *Judith* 4:1–2 and 7:4 (see below). It also marks the first fulfilment of Achior's prophecy/blessing in *Judith* 14:7 which is taken up again in *Judith* 16:10 (see below).[68] Note that the verb ταραωσσς[69] (boldfaced portions above and below) is used in each of these verses, that it is often preceded by a verb denoting perception (see underlined portions above and below)—which is, in most cases, ἀκούω (to hear)—and that the fear/terror denoted by ταραωσσς is the result of the subject's perception.

(4:1 <u>Καὶ ἤκουσαν</u> οἱ υἱοὶ Ισραηλ οἱ κατοικοῦντες ἐν τῇ Ιουδαίᾳ πάντα, ὅσα ἐποίησεν Ολοφέρνης τοῖς ἔθνεσιν . . .)

4:2 καὶ ἐφοβήθησαν σφόδρα σφόδρα ἀπὸ προσώπου αὐτοῦ καὶ περὶ Ιερουσαλημ καὶ τοῦ ναοῦ κυρίου θεοῦ αὐτῶν **ἐταράχθησαν**.

7:4 οἱ δὲ υἱοὶ Ισραηλ, <u>ὡς εἶδον</u> αὐτῶν τὸ πλῆθος, **ἐταράχθησαν σφόδρα** . . .

14:7 . . . Εὐλογημένη σὺ ἐν παντὶ σκηνώματι Ιουδα καὶ ἐν παντὶ ἔθνει, οἵτινες <u>ἀκούσαντες</u> τὸ ὄνομά σου **ταραχθήσονται**

16:10 ἔφριξαν Πέρσαι τὴν τόλμαν αὐτῆς, καὶ Μῆδοι τὸ θράσος αὐτῆς **ἐταράχθησαν**

In a delicious twist of irony, Nebuchadnezzar's powerful army of millions flees as one man because they have heard of the deeds of a single woman, thereby corroborating the western nations' initial appraisal of Nebuchadnezzar and his army: "[they] looked upon him as only one man" (1:11).

Ironically, the Assyrian army's defeat also reverses the boastful claims made by Holofernes' μεγιστανες and Holofernes himself in *Judith* 5:23–24 and 6:3:

5:23 Οὐ γὰρ φοβηθησόμεθα ἀπὸ υἱῶν Ισραηλ, ἰδοὺ γὰρ λαὸς ἐν ᾧ οὐκ ἔστιν δύναμις οὐδὲ κράτος εἰς παράταξιν ἰσχυράν,

5:24 διὸ δὴ ἀναβησόμεθα, καὶ ἔσονται εἰς κατάβρωσιν πάσης τῆς στρατιᾶς σου, δέσποτα Ολοφέρνη

[68] It will be noted that *Judith* 16:10 refers to the Persians and the Medes as the ones who "trembled at her boldness, [and] were daunted at her daring". This is yet another of the so-called Persian elements that are usually used to 'prove' that at least *a* recension of this story occurred in the Persian period. However, as I have previously indicated, I believe that the diverse 'historical' elements found in *Judith* are indicative of the author's deliberate 'fudging' of facts, which contributes to the book's mythopoeic qualities.

[69] The verb ταράσσω is used only in the five verses indicated here (4:2; 7:4, 14:7 and 19, and 16:10).

6:3 . . . ἡμεῖς οἱ δοῦλοι αὐτοῦ πατάξομεν αὐτοὺς ὡς ἄνθρωπον ἕνα . . .

This is not the only reversal entailed in Judith's deed, which is followed by Bagoas' report thereof and the Assyrian lords' reaction to it. As we have noted, these elements combine to reverse the order of rank by which the call to waken Holofernes came (lower ranks → higher ranks → Bagoas → higher ranks → lower ranks). They also reverse the objects and subjects of fear: the Bethulians are transformed from the subjects of fear to its objects (they are the ones who—through Judith's deed—now inspire fear), while the Assyrians are transformed from the objects of fear to its subjects. As I have previously noted (see above), the 'stir' which Judith caused in the Assyrian camp began amongst the lower ranks of the Assyrian army and culminated with Holofernes and his aides etc., while the stir which Holofernes' death/Bagoas' report causes begins amongst the highest ranks of the army and fans out to include the lowest ranks. All of these reversals indicate that a major transformation has begun in the balance of power between consciousness and the unconscious. As we have seen, this transformation plays out, inter alia, in the defeat of the unconscious and the greater functionality of consciousness at the fourth stage of conscious awareness.

On a psychological level, Holofernes' 'high command' may be understood as the contents closest to the dominant shadow archetype, his choice disciples. As such, it would seem that they have imbibed Holofernes' arrogant attitude and that they too are suffering from positive inflation by their association with him. They bear a striking resemblance to their haughty leader who has adopted his master Nebuchadnezzar's pride and who suffers from a positive inflation as a result. Their reaction to Holofernes' death shows that these men are extremely dependant on Holofernes for their survival—much as Bagoas is. Even so, their higher rank and their position of authority over the rest of the army shows that they are of a higher psychological validity than Bagoas as far as the greater unconscious mass is concerned. This is indicated by the fact that the general army personnel report to them (cf. 14:12–13)—not to Bagoas—and that they flee only when they see their superiors fleeing. Bagoas however is of greater validity to Holofernes—note that he is Holofernes' personal steward and the last 'bastion' to fall in his protection. The adage "strike the shepherd and scatter the sheep" could not have been truer in respect of both Holofernes and his military elite: striking Holofernes causes the elite to flee which, in turn, causes the entire Assyrian army to do the same.

The General Judaean Populace

We first encounter the remaining Judaeans—i.e., those who are not Bethulians—in *Judith* 15:4, almost at the very end of *Judith* when the Bethulians have already won a sizeable victory over the Assyrian troops that had surrounded their city (see 15:3 and 7:17–20, especially 19 and 20). While it may seem odd that the general Judaean populace are only inspired to join the attack once Ozias writes to them and tells them to do so, their 'tardiness' is wholly commensurate with the picture of consciousness that has been presented throughout *Judith*. It speaks of the general paralysis that all of consciousness—bar Judith, of course—seems to experience in light of Holofernes' impending attack. Once they become involved, however, their contribution to consciousness's deliverance takes place in three phases (note the underlined portions below):

- The first phase begins with the towns/cities that were presumably closest to Bethuliah or those which also lay near/on the mountain passes of Judaea (cf. 15:4 and "the Israelites" in 15:5a–b).[70]
- The second phase of attack is then launched from the heart of Judaea—Jerusalem (cf. "[t]hose in Jerusalem" in 15:5c)
- The third phase involves those in Gilead and Galilee (cf. "those in Gilead and in Galilee" in 15:5e).

The result of the attack is that the Assyrians are pushed back as far as Choba in phase one, and Damascus in phase three:

15:4 καὶ ἀπέστειλεν Οζιας εἰς Βαιτομασθαιμ καὶ Βηβαι καὶ Χωβαι καὶ Κωλα καὶ εἰς πᾶν ὅριον Ισραηλ τοὺς ἀπαγγέλλοντας ὑπὲρ τῶν συντετελεσμένων καὶ ἵνα πάντες ἐπεκχυθῶσιν τοῖς πολεμίοις εἰς τὴν ἀναίρεσιν αὐτῶν.

---

[70] Note that Bethomasthaim appears twice in *Judith* (with two different spellings). In *Judith* 4:6–7 we are told that Joachim wrote to Bethuliah and Bethomesthaim (Βαιτομεσθαιμ), telling them to guard the mountain passes, while in *Judith* 15:4 Ozias writes to Bethomasthaim (Βαιτομασθαιμ), Βηβαι, Χωβαι, and Κωλα as well as all the districts of Israel to tell them the good news and encourage them to fall upon the Assyrians. The fact that these three cities are specifically named along with Bethomasthaim leads me to believe that they are the ones referred to as "the sons of Israel" in *Judith* 15:5a and that they too may have been towns/cities on the outskirts of Judaea or on mountain passes.

15:5 ὡς δὲ ἤκουσαν οἱ υἱοὶ Ισραηλ, πάντες ὁμοθυμαδὸν ἐπέπεσον ἐπ᾽ αὐτοὺς καὶ ἔκοπτον αὐτοὺς ἕως Χωβα.
ὡσαύτως δὲ καὶ οἱ ἐξ Ιερουσαλημ παρεγενήθησαν καὶ ἐκ πάσης τῆς ὀρεινῆς, ἀνήγγειλαν γὰρ αὐτοῖς τὰ γεγονότα τῇ παρεμβολῇ τῶν ἐχθρῶν αὐτῶν, καὶ οἱ ἐν Γαλααδ καὶ οἱ ἐν τῇ Γαλιλαίᾳ ὑπερεκέρασαν αὐτοὺς πληγῇ μεγάλῃ,
ἕως οὗ παρῆλθον Δαμασκὸν καὶ τὰ ὅρια αὐτῆς.

What has been said of the Bethulians may be said of the general Judaean populace too, viz. they are initially too afraid to face the Assyrians when the latter become a threat to them. Their impotence is nevertheless reversed once that of the Bethulians is reversed. This reversal, as we have seen, takes place when Judith returns with the unconscious *mana* and brings about the final integration of the psychological contents represented by Achior. It would seem as though Judith's return and the *mana* that she internalised/shared with the Bethulians, as well as the final integration of the contents represented by Achior, causes an energy/libido surge in that part of the psyche represented by the Bethulians. This libidinous surge rises to encompass the Bethulian leaders/Ozias who, in turn, inspire the towns mentioned and the "children of Israel" in them. Once the libidinous surge has reached these towns/cities, the inhabitants of central consciousness (the Jerusalemites) become involved and influence those in the outlying areas of Gilead and Galilee, i.e., those at the lower levels of consciousness. We see, then, that higher and lower levels of consciousness are able to influence one another positively to the ultimate good of consciousness as a whole once the unconscious *mana* and other unconscious (shadow) contents (Achior) have been assimilated. The combined victory of the Bethulians and the general Judaean populace over the Assyrian forces then depicts the cumulative effect that internalising unconscious contents at any level of consciousness has on the entire field of consciousness—including its centre.

Having defeated the Assyrian enemy, the other Judaeans apparently ascend to Jerusalem with Judith and the Bethulians and return to their own towns/cities once the festivities have ended. This signifies that the libidinous surge which they experienced was neither sufficient to sustain them permanently at the fifth stage of consciousness (Jerusalem) nor yet strong enough to raise them to any higher stage of consciousness than that from which they came, i.e., stage 3.

Nevertheless, as with the Bethulians, the libido remains with them as a promise of higher stages of consciousness that may still be achieved in the future.

Joachim and the Γερουσία

Whereas Joachim and the γερουσία have an independent function as the spiritual and political leaders of the Judaean nation in section I, they simply exist to provide official ratification for Judith's deeds in section II. Like most other characters in this section, they exist solely to highlight some aspect of the heroine's nature or deed. We encounter them for the first and last time in section II when they come to Bethuliah—in the midst of their peoples' attack on the Assyrian foe—"to witness the good things which the Lord had done for Israel, and to see Judith and to greet her" (15:8). When they approach her, they all bless her with one accord (εὐλόγησαν αὐτηύ πάντες ὁμοθυμαδόν—15:9):

15:9 . . . Σὺ ὕψωμα Ιερουσαλημ, σὺ γαυρίαμα μέγα τοῦ Ισραηλ,
σὺ καύχημα μέγα τοῦ γένους ἡμῶν,
15:10 ἐποίησας ταῦτα πάντα ἐν χειρί σου, ἐποίησας τὰ ἀγαθὰ μετὰ
Ισραηλ, καὶ εὐδόκησεν ἐπ' αὐτοῖς ὁ θεός εὐλογημένη γίνου
παρὰ τῷ παντοκράτορι κυρίῳ εἰς τὸν αἰῶνα χρόνον . . .

Their extremely high praise of Judith forms the acme of all other accolades that she has received from the Bethulian/Jerusalemite leadership (and Achior) so far. This can be seen when we compare the use of phrases and words such as ὕψωμα Ιερουσαλημ and γαυρίαμα in their accolade and that of the Bethulian elders, for example. Their praise of her sees the third of three phrases where ὕψωμα Ιερουσαλημ is used. These two words are always coupled together, and ὕψωμα does not occur in *Judith* outside of this coupling:

- The elders prayed that God would bless whatever she would do to the exaltation of Jerusalem (10:8).
- Judith prayed that God would direct her ways to the same end (13:4).
- Now, finally, the Jerusalemite leadership praise her for being or becoming that end through what she has done (15:9).

Similarly, this blessing sees the second of two occurrences of γαυρίαμα:

- The elders had prayed that God would bless her works to the glory of the sons of Israel (10:8).

- And now the Jerusalemite leadership praise her *as* the great glory of Israel (15:9).

Consideration of the above, particularly *Judith* 15:9 and 13:4, leads me to believe that the Jerusalemite leadership's praise of Judith establishes the fact that she has become the answer to her own prayer. The blessings that they heap on her show that this single woman has succeeded in saving her people whereas they, the male leadership of the land (along with the male leadership of Bethuliah), have failed.

As Joachim and the γερουσία are the spiritual and political leaders of the Judaean nation and so arguably the highest elements of consciousness—before Judith's appearance—it is significant that they should accord Judith such high, almost divine, praise. It means that they acknowledge her to be of a far higher form of consciousness/authority than they, which in turn means that they recognise her as the highest form of consciousness in their society, eclipsed only by God/the Self, who supersedes all conscious and other psychic hierarchies.

The understanding of Judith's level of consciousness that has been gained in this subsection corroborates my earlier findings: Judith is the highest form of consciousness beneath the Self/God. This insight necessitates that we revisit the stages of consciousness occupied by the other Judaean characters in the tale. No longer can we aver, for example, that Joachim and the γερουσία occupy the fifth stage of consciousness as we did while analysing the characters in section I. Instead, we see that Judith supersedes the consciousness of the Jerusalemite leadership just as she supersedes the conscious level of the Bethulian leadership. At which stage, then, do we locate the conscious awareness of the Bethulians and their leadership, and the Jerusalemites and the central Judaean leadership? I believe that the answer to this question lies within the following considerations:

i) The Bethulian leadership and the Bethulians occupy the fourth stage of consciousness. This was determined in our analysis of section I and nothing in our analysis of section II has indicated any finding to the contrary.
ii) Both groups of leaders have been identified as belonging to the central Judaean consciousness, with Joachim and the γερουσία constituting its innermost layer and the Bethulian leadership and the Bethulians constituting its outermost layer. This means that they may belong to the same stage of consciousness, i.e., stage 4.

iii) The general Judaean populace is placed at the third stage of conscious awareness. Once again, this was the finding of section I and our analysis of section II has not indicated anything to the contrary.
iv) Arphaxad and his forces remain at stage 1, just as the coastal people and other vanquished nations remain at stage 2, with no indications to the contrary—they do not even feature in section II.

Taking the above into cognisance, we may say that both groups of Judaean leaders belong to the fourth stage of consciousness along with the Bethulians, while the general Judaean populace belongs to the third stage of consciousness. A new hierarchy of consciousness thus develops in respect of the Judaeans, Bethulians, and their respective leaders, which replaces the one depicted in diagram 10. I have chosen to present this new hierarchy in pyramidal form (diagram 11) as this form allows for greater precision than the circular construction of diagram 10.

The general Judaean populace, Arphaxad and his forces, and the coastal dwellers and other vanquished western nations represent the lower forms of consciousness. (I remind the reader that stage 4 is the most critical stage of conscious awareness, and so the most important stage where true differentiation of the individual begins to take place. This stage may therefore be regarded as the onset of higher consciousness). As previously indicated, the Bethulians/Bethuliah and their leadership form the outermost layer of central consciousness, while the Jerusalemites/Jerusalem and the Jerusalemite leadership form the innermost layer of central consciousness. Seeing that the leadership of Bethuliah are the highest representatives at the outermost level of central consciousness, they occupy a higher place in the pyramid than the general Bethulian populace. The same applies to Joachim and the γερουσιωα who occupy a higher place in the structure than the general inhabitants of Jerusalem. Judith, who supersedes both the Bethulian and the Jerusalemite leadership, occupies the highest place accorded to humans within this structure and is superseded only by God/the Self who is the director of both consciousness and the unconscious.

In terms of Judith's conscious ascendancy over all her fellow Judaeans and her close relationship with the Self, it is interesting to note that Joachim and the γερουσία praise Judith in her personal capacity for the deeds that she has done—much as Achior had done

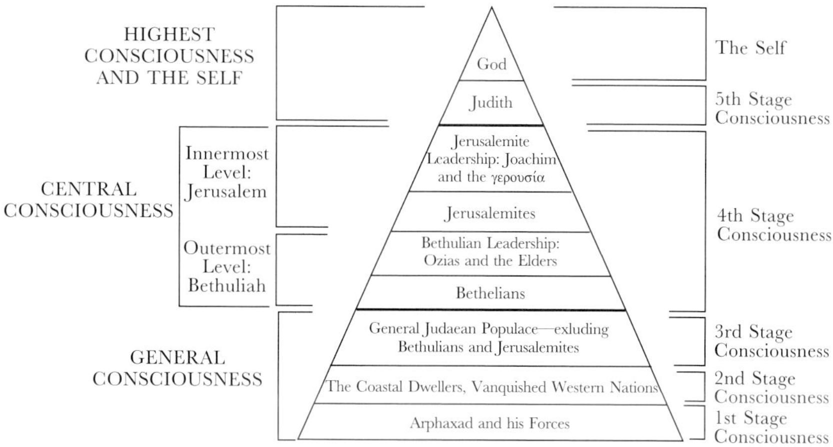

Diagram 11. The Acme of Consciousness in *Judith*

before them in *Judith* 14:7. They accord little or no part of her deed to God, but merely state that "God is well pleased with it" (15:10). By contrast, Ozias and the elders pray for God's guidance—in terms of His preceding her, granting her favour, and fulfilling her plans—once her determination to act on behalf of her people becomes clear to them (8:35) and when they see how her appearance has changed just before she exits Bethuliah (10:8). When she returns, however, Ozias hails her as one blessed above all the women of the earth (see 14:7 for an equally all-encompassing praise from Achior's lips) and then praises the creator God for guiding her "to strike the head of the leader of our enemies" (13:18). The motivation for his praise of both Judith and God seems to lie in the hope that she has brought to "the hearts of men, as they remember the power of God [forever]" (13:19). Having thus spoken, Ozias then prays "May God grant this to be a perpetual honour to you, and may he visit you with blessings, because you did not spare your own life when our nation was brought low, but have avenged our ruin, walking in the straight path before our God" (13:20). *Judith* 13:18–20 thus places praise to God in between praise to/prayer for Judith, whereas the earlier blessings in *Judith* 8:35 and *Judith* 10:8 are more focused on God and His guidance for her acts. We see, then, that the prayers and blessings of Ozias increasingly focus upon Judith and her deed while constantly upholding God's intimate involvement in her plans.

By contrast, we have already established that the Jerusalemite leadership praise Judith for her deeds and merely state that God has been pleased with them (15:10). Taking this into consideration along with Judith's nearly "divine" level of consciousness (diagram 11), we arrive at a not-unexpected conclusion: praising Judith is tantamount to praising the deity/the Self. This is further corroborated by the fact that Judith and God are the sole recipients of 'blessing' as denoted by the participial form of εὐλογέω (to bless) and its cognate adjective εὐλογητός in *Judith* (14:17 and 13:18 regarding Judith; 13:18 and 17 regarding God). Praising Judith *is* praising God. That is why she is the only object of εὐλογέω in *Judith* 15:9 and 12; and that is why there is no special praise to God in the accolades of Joachim and the γερουσία.

The fact that the nation's highest human leadership (Joachim and the γερουσία) recognises the superiority of Judith is testimony to their level of maturity as people. On a textual level, however, their recognition of Judith's ascendancy exemplifies what I have said of them at the outset of this subsection: like most other characters in section II, they exist merely to highlight the nature and deeds of Judith. In this final praise to Judith in the book by her name, the author uses their words to share with the reader and finally to reinforce in her/his mind what has been intimated from the start, i.e., Judith's near-divine nature/consciousness as seen by her high level of individuation and closeness to the Self/God.

The Dancing Women

Once Joachim and the γερουσία have blessed Judith (15:8–10), the people (men?) of Bethuliah bring her the spoils from Holofernes' tent and she heaps them onto her mules and chariots (15:11). The text subsequently records that "all the women of Israel ran together to see her, and blessed her, and made a dance among them for her" (15:12a–c). Judith takes up branches in her hands and distributes them amongst the women (15:12d–e). They all don olive wreaths and Judith leads the women in dance (15:13a–b). The men follow them, wearing their armour, bearing garlands, and singing (15:13c–d). Judith then leads them all in a worship song to YHWH until (?) they reach Jerusalem (15:14–16:18; cf. particularly 15:14 [RAPC 16:1] and 16:18).

There are two minor difficulties regarding the appearance of these women here:

(i) To what extent—if at all—the Bethulian women have been involved in the events of section II up until this point, or whether their involvement begins here where they come to celebrate Judith.
(ii) Whether women are included in the company of 'sons of Israel' who came from various Judaean locations to 'assist' the Bethulians in driving back the Assyrians (see 15:4–5). It is thus difficult to ascertain whether "all the women of Israel" refers to Bethulian women alone or includes other women from all over Judaea.

As affects point (i), we have noted that Judith's exit from and return to Bethuliah has been framed by the activities of men: they watch Judith descend to the enemy camp (10:10) and appear to be the first group of people who hear her voice upon her return (13:12). In both these cases the Greek uses the gender-specific term ἀνήρ to denote the subjects of these actions, thereby identifying them as male only (unless ἀνήρ is to be understood generically, which I doubt would be the case within the given context). Thereafter it is difficult to determine whether συνέδραμον **πάντες** ἀπὸ μικροῦ ἕως μεγάλου αὐτῶν (13:13) includes the Bethulian women or refers to the men alone. The same uncertainty applies to:

13:17 . . . ἐξέστη **πᾶς ὁ λαὸς** σφόδρα καὶ κύψαντες προσεκύνησαν τῷ θεῷ . . .
13:20 . . . εἶπαν **πᾶς ὁ λαός** Γένοιτο γένοιτο . . . [cf. also 15:10]
15:6 **οἱ δὲ λοιποὶ οἱ κατοικοῦντες Βαιτυλουα** ἐπέπεσαν τῇ παρεμβολῇ Ασσουρ καὶ ἐπρονόμευσαν αὐτοὺς καὶ ἐπλούτησαν σφόδρα.

It is also uncertain whether the Bethulian women are part of the group who hear Judith's battle plans in 14:1ff., particularly as she begins her address with Ἀκούσατε δή μου, **ἀδελφοί** (14:1). While the term ἀδελφοί may well be generic, it may also be gender-specific given the high incidence of male involvement in the ensuing battle plans. In terms of Judith's plan (cf. especially 14:1), we may ask, did the women of Bethuliah help to spike Holofernes' severed head on the wall of their city, or was this action undertaken by the Bethulian men who took up their arms immediately thereafter (14:11)? Did they participate in looting the camp with "the residue, that dwelt in Bethuliah" (15:6)? Or, does their involvement begin here in *Judith* 15:12?

As affects point (ii), it is unclear whether women accompanied the other Judaean warriors who came to assist the Bethulians in *Judith*

15:4–5. It is thus uncertain whether the phrase "all the women of Israel" (15:12) refers to Bethulian women alone or to women from other parts of Judaea too. We may then ask, did these women—whoever they may be—join "all the people" who ratified the blessing of Joachim and the γερουσία with Γένοιτο (15:10), or does λαός refer to the men alone? Did they participate in looting the Assyrian camp and bringing the spoils from Holofernes' tent to Judith (15:11)? Or, did their involvement only begin once they came out to see, bless, honour, and dance for Judith (15:12)?

While we may never be sure whether the women were involved in the comings and goings of Judith from the beginning of section II, or whether "all the women of Israel" refers to the Bethulian women or the women of Judaea as a whole, we can be sure of one thing, i.e., that their involvement here is significant for a number of reasons:

- In the first place, parallels with other Old Testament women who met a victorious warrior/warriors with song and dance are used to highlight Judith's ego-conqueror function and hence the impotence of the male leadership/their dependence upon her—they only act because she has already won the victory by slaying Holofernes/disempowering the unconscious shadow. The women's celebration of Judith finds parallels with the women's celebration of David's victory over the Philistines/the unconscious. It was this act of adulation that first provoked Saul's ire and jealousy towards David (I Samuel 18:6–9; cf. also I Samuel 21:11 and 29:5). By contrast, there is no jealousy here, and the Judaean leadership and men freely acknowledge Judith's conscious ascendancy over them (see the preceding subsection, 13:20 and 15:10)—yet another testimony to their maturity, even though they are dependant on/occupy an inferior conscious position compared to that of Judith.
- Secondly, the women's spontaneous praise/celebration of Judith is the first action accorded to a body of women throughout Judith which is independent from that of any male. The praise of these women occurs outside the influence of their menfolk, whereas the text has previously located all the other activities of women (apart from Judith) within the context of a group including men/their husbands and children. It would seem, then, that Judith's victory has raised the conscious (self-)awareness of these women as people to a place where they can act independently of their men/

families. In other words, we may say that she has enabled their conscious differentiation as people from societal norms and expectations.

- Furthermore, we see that men were involved at Judith's exit from and return to the outermost levels of central consciousness/Bethuliah, whereas women lead the procession to the innermost level of central consciousness, viz. Jerusalem (15:12–14 and 16:18 and 20). This too points to the women's heightened conscious awareness while simultaneously suggesting that they have superseded the men's consciousness here—they lead the men.
- Following on from the preceding point, this passage entails a reversal of gender roles in that the women lead and the men follow. Above all, this reversal is a cultic one as worship is involved. Furthermore, whereas the cultic participation of women appears limited to unmarried women in the Psalms (Efthimiadis-Keith 1999c:42), here it is extended to all Judaean women of diverse marital status.
- From the viewpoint of a subjective dream analysis, these women represent not only personal entities but psychological contents. This means that Judith's success has not only brought about the heightened consciousness of these women as people, but that it has also brought about the differentiation of these previously undifferentiated psychological contents in the collective Judaean psyche. Here it is indicative that these contents are portrayed in female guise. This gender specification alerts us to the possibility that the dancing women may represent anima figures in relation to the nation which, for all intents and purposes, is predominantly male from a cultic point of view. Their greater differentiation would then reflect a greater conscious integration of anima contents at a national level.

According to Jung, an integrated anima leads one closer to the Self, and this exactly occurs with these women under the leadership of Judith (cf. "and she went before all the people in the dance, leading all the women, while all the men of Israel followed"—15:13). They lead the men of Judaea in worship up to Jerusalem, the centre of consciousness and the conscious domain of the Self. In other words, they raise the conscious awareness of the cultic community to a new level, albeit only for a short while—the celebrations in Jerusalem last for three months (16:20), after which "every one returned home to his own inheritance, and

Judith went to Bethulia" (16:21). They may thus justifiably be construed as multiple anima figures.

Taking all the above into consideration, we may then say that the women's appearance in *Judith* 15:12 serves the purpose of highlighting Judith's ego-conqueror function and pointing out the importance of integrating the anima in order to gain greater access to the Self. It also serves the purpose of conveying a number of gender-related reversals that have been achieved in the wake of Judith's victory: women become independent actors which they have not been up to this point, women lead men, and women of every marital status participate in and lead worship (Judith is a widow—8:2–4—and we may assume that "all the women of Israel" consisted of both married and unmarried women, be the latter widows, betrothed, or unbetrothed). The fact that men willingly follow the women's leadership is indicative of:

i) The new maturity/greater conscious differentiation that they have achieved as both people and psychological contents.
ii) Where Holofernes' men represent raw instinct (the instinctually based unconscious force is male), the men of Bethuliah represent consciously integrated instincts, however weak—they let Judith do all 'their' work in respect of Holofernes. Their following of the women/collective anima and Judith/the national ego and anima in a worship procession indicates that these conscious instincts have been subordinated to the anima in service of the Self/God. This, in turn, shows a high degree of anima integration at a national level, which is confirmed by the survival of consciousness/the Judaean nation for many years beyond Judith's physical death.

In continuation of the last point, we note that Judith takes up branches (ἔλαβεν **θύρσους** ἐν ταῖς χερσὶν αὐτῆς—15:12) and distributes them amongst the women once they have praised her. They then crown themselves with olive wreaths (καὶ ἐστεφανώσαντο τὴν **ἐλαίαν**, αὐτὴ καὶ αἱ μετ' αὐτῆς—15:13). At face value, these actions point to the late/Hellenistic date of this narrative. They are, however, of far greater psychological import when viewed against the background of Hellenistic religion and culture:

- The θύρσος or branch is, as Enslin correctly states (op. cit., 167), "a Bacchic wand" which was carried by his devotees. It was wreathed in ivy and vine leaves and had a pinecone at the top (cf. Moore, op. cit., 246)—a rather decorative representation of the male genital organ/(stereotypically) raw sexual instinct. As is well known, the cult of Bacchus depended heavily on drink and sexuality, both of which were strong features of its various festivals. We have seen that the shadow forces of the unconscious also rely on these instinctual 'aids' in the battle against consciousness—cf. particularly the seduction scene in *Judith* 12:16–20 where Holofernes tries to make Judith drunk with wine so that she would presumably be more amenable to his sexual advances "and be made this day as one of the daughters of the Assyrians, which serve in the house of Nabuchodonosor" (12:13), i.e., be swallowed up by the unconscious psyche. Including an element from such a highly sexualised cult in the worship of YHWH indicates that the instinctual shadow contents have been so successfully incorporated/assimilated into national consciousness that they are put to the conscious service of the Self.[71]

- The same may be said of the women crowning themselves with olive wreaths. While the olive branch was a symbol of life, joy, peace, and thanksgiving in Judaean culture (cf. *Nehemiah* 8:15), wearing olive wreaths is a distinctly Greek custom, not a Jewish one. Like the θύρσος, it also points to the incorporation of unconscious shadow contents and their dedication to the Self on the one hand, and to the late/Hellenistic date of *Judith* on the other.

When considering the above points along with the fact that Judith is praised just before these 'Bacchic' activities begin, we see that Judith is celebrated not only as ego-conqueror, but also as the one who has tamed the 'uncontrollable' national shadow instincts and brought them under the control of ego-consciousness and the Self.

Furthermore, we note that a number of things occur after the women have taken up the θύρσος and the olive wreath in this way: Judith leads the people in worship up to Jerusalem (15:14–16:18) where they worship God. Once they (including women?) cleanse

[71] The word θύρσος appears once more in the LXX, again within the context of worship after a victory won over the Greeks/Hellenisers. It occurs in II Maccabees 10:7, which records that the Maccabees bore "ivy-wreathed wands [θύρσος] and beautiful branches and also fronds of palm" in honour of God "who had given success to the purifying of his own holy place", the temple.

themselves, they offer their various sacrifices to God (16:18), Judith dedicates her share of the spoils to God (16:19), and the people rejoice for three months (16:20). Worship, cleansing oneself, offering sacrifices, and dedicating things to God are very important aspects of ego-self communication. The reason for this is that they involve the elements of sacrifice and self-abnegation that produce the humility necessary for maintaining a healthy, inflation-free relationship with the Self. Thus, the fact that these actions are preceded by the women's use of the θύρσος and the olive wreaths highlights yet another important message: the instinctual shadow elements can and must be assimilated if a true and deeper connection to the Self is to be achieved.

Finally, before summarizing my findings regarding section II, I should like to close this subsection with the following remarks concerning the women's reception of Judith as hero(ine)/ego-conqueror/tamer of unruly shadow instincts:

- Firstly, the women's reception of Judith raises more parallels to the David story than the mere fact that the women celebrated her as a victorious hero(ine) in the way they did David. To mention but a few briefly:
  - Whereas David cut off the foreskins of one hundred Philistines to claim his bride (see I Samuel 18:20–30), Judith cut off the head of an enemy general in order to deliver her people, raise their level of consciousness, and bring them closer to God/the Self. David's and Judith's attacks on the enemy and their respective severances of enemy 'heads' (penile and otherwise) were thus completely differently motivated. Judith was motivated by a desire to free her people and bring them closer to God, whereas David was motivated primarily by personal gain, i.e., marrying Saul's daughter so that he could get closer to fulfilling the prophecy of becoming king (see especially I Samuel 18:26–27).
  - Unlike David (see II Samuel 11:1–5), Judith did not sit at home during a time of war, leisurely waiting for the troops to come home. She took action. She went out and fought the battle whereas David stayed at home, surveying his kingdom, violating and impregnating the trustworthy Uriah's wife. By contrast, Judith neither violated Holofernes nor was violated by him in any sexual way.

- Whereas David was punished for his sin with Bathsheba and rebuked by Nathan, a man of God (II Samuel 12:1–15), Judith is publicly praised by all—including the men of God of that time, i.e., the Bethulian and Jerusalemite leadership.
- Whereas David's sin led to many troubles within his own family and kingdom (see II Samuel 12:10–12, 14, and ensuing passages), Judith's act of valour (or the memory thereof) protected her people for many years after her death.
- Whereas David's withdrawal from battle and subsequent sin led to the death of a trustworthy foreigner in his army, i.e., Uriah the Hittite (see especially II Samuel 11:14–25), Judith's engaging herself in the task of war and her act of deliverance led to the death of the enemy and to the Ammonite Achior's conversion/entrance into the community of YHWH, Who is life.
- David tried to make one of his own men, Uriah, drunk so that he would sleep with his wife, Bathsheba, and hide the fact that he had caused her pregnancy (II Samuel 11:13). By contrast, in *Judith*, the enemy tried to make Judith drunk so that he could seduce her. Neither David nor Holofernes succeeded: Uriah refused to sleep with his wife out of loyalty to David and his troops, and Judith, as we know, turned the tables on Holofernes by letting him get drunk and then killing him. However, both David and Holofernes were motivated by their own interests and sexual satisfaction, whereas Judith acted out of loyalty to God and her people. The resemblances in the men's actions almost casts David and the enemy of God's people, Holofernes, in the same mould (see further the second paragraph, below).
- Whereas David only dreamed of going up to the house of the Lord—he was not allowed to build it because of his sin with Bathsheba—Judith actually led the people in praise and worship up to the house of the Lord. The ease with which this is reported in *Judith* gives me the distinct impression that she, despite being a woman, had the right to do so. David, as we have seen was denied that 'right' by God himself.
- It is obvious, then, that this narrative depicts Judith as being morally superior to David, who is associated with the enemy of YHWH's people by means of his dastardly shadow activities and the parallels between himself and Holofernes. By means of her moral superiority and ascension to the temple, Judith 'redeems' David and almost replaces him as the chosen king/queen of

YHWH. That Judith's story has definite messianic undertones—cf. especially the peace which her 'reign' brings about—confirms this. Through her purity and obedience to God Judith succeeded in bringing about peace whereas David's sin and disobedience led to a series of disasters culminating, perhaps, in the kingdom splitting into two.

- Secondly, Judith's defeat of Holofernes has often been likened to David's defeat of Goliath. The identification of Judith and David in this regard has been taken up graphically in Michelangelo da Caravaggio's *David with the Head of Goliath* (c. 1605–1606? Bal, op. cit., 261). This painting resembles Hendrik Golzius' print *Judith* (c. 1585. op. cit., 257), which depicts Judith holding the head of Holofernes. Even more importantly, the latter is almost an exact replica—even though gender reversal is involved—of Cellini's *Perseus*, itself inspired by Donatello's *Judith* (op. cit., 257–258). Interestingly, Caravaggio's David has distinctly feminine or, at the least, androgynous features. Judith's slaying of Holofernes has thus caused some measure of gender confusion in the art world that is certainly mirrored in her very 'manly' acts in *Judith*. This gender confusion in art is double-sided in that the Judith depicted in Golzius's print has strong manly features, with the muscles in her naked upper body being clearly defined. By contrast, Caravaggio's David has almost no visible muscle definition at all. (These are not the only paintings that depict the 'gender confusion' in *Judith*. Witness further Gentileschi's *Judith Slaying Holofernes*, discussed briefly in chapter 1. In this painting Judith's strong arms stand in great contrast to Holofernes' right arm which is bent at the elbow and almost takes on the appearance of a female upper leg, i.e., thigh to knee).[72] This reflects the 'confused' gender of Judith in the text as seen through traditionally stereotyped eyes. Moreover, this gender confusion is compounded by the fact that images of Judith holding the head of Holofernes have both inspired and been inspired by images of Perseus holding the severed head of Medusa in Cellini's sculpture. This adds the element of 'voracious female', siren, femme

[72] For a detailed discussion see my 2002 article, "Text and Interpretation: Gender and Violence in *Judith*, Scholarly Commentary and the Visual Arts from the Renaissance Onward".

fatale to Judith's image. She is thus both 'manly' and femme fatale. No wonder then that many of her early commentators and some of the later ones decried her 'otherness' and supposed immorality: she simultaneously usurped the stereotypical male ego-conqueror function and represented men's greatest fear, i.e., the femme fatale or castrating woman.

- Thirdly, the women's reception of Judith also finds parallels with the coastal dwellers' reception of Holofernes. They too received Holofernes with song and dance. Nevertheless, while the coastal dwellers' level of consciousness was foolishly welcoming the destructive energies of the as-yet-untamed unconscious, here a higher-level consciousness is welcoming the *mana*-imbued energies of the unconscious shadow as consciously integrated in both Judith and the community for which she stands. That the results are completely different therefore comes as no surprise: the coastal dwellers lose vital conscious elements and have their conscious achievements destroyed by the shadow, whereas the women's celebration of Judith enables greater connection to the Self, as indicated throughout the preceding paragraphs.

In short, then, the women's reception of Judith conjures up a wild mixture of imagery that blurs the human-made gender boundaries and points to the way that she redeems the Old Testament national hero, David. In this way, the Judithic dream begins to achieve or depicts the possibility of returning, consciously, to the image of the original *Anthropos*, who was both male and female in one. In this way, *Judith* depicts what the alchemists and Jung have called the *hieros gamos*—the conscious re-unification of psychic opposites which is, perhaps, the ultimate aim of the individuation cycle.

d. *Summary and Conclusions—Section II*

The Victory of Consciousness over the Unconscious and the Transformation of Consciousness in Judith *8–16*

In my summary of section I, I indicated that the way is paved for a strong deliverer, i.e., a heroine/hero, to appear and save YHWH's people from slavery, the worship of a foreign god, and complete destruction. From the viewpoint of my Jungian interpretation, this would mean that the psyche is in desperate need for a strong ego (-figure) to emerge and deliver consciousness from being subsumed into the unconscious. More specifically, the psyche requires a positive ego-conqueror (heroic/messianic figure) to save consciousness from identifying with its collective/national unconscious Shadow tendencies and functioning completely out of this identification. As previously indicated, such an identification would bring about the widespread destruction of consciousness in all that it has achieved and/or established. That Judith is this deliverer/ego-conqueror and the obvious protagonist/heroine of the narrative is evident from the very outset of section II (Aa—8:1–8) to its conclusion (Aa'—16:21–25):

- She takes charge of the situation from the time that she is introduced to the reader at the outset of *Judith* 8 to the time that the narrative bids her farewell at the end of *Judith* 16.
- She calls the elders and brings them to book regarding their ultimatum to God (cf. 8:10–36).
- She designs a plan of action to defeat the Assyrian enemy and she implements it—single-handedly, albeit with the help of her ἅβρα (cf. 8:33–34; 10:10[b]–13:10 and 14:1–4).
- Using the sexual-verbal deceptiveness of the femme fatale, Judith goes down to the enemy camp. She flatters Holofernes with her words and apparent 'willingness' to entertain his advances and help him gain control over Judaea, cuts off his head with his own sword, and takes it/its *mana* back to Bethuliah in her food basket (cf. 10:23–13:10ff).
- Once she and her ἅβρα return to Bethuliah, she commands that the people hang his head on the city wall and she details battle plans to crush the remaining 'Assyrian' forces, despite the presence of the Bethulian/Judaean leadership (14:1–4).
- When the enemy forces have been driven back, defeated, and looted, she leads the people in worship up to Jerusalem where they feast, celebrate, and make sacrifices to God (cf. 15:12–16:20).
- When they return to their homes she frees her ἅβρα and distributes her wealth among her relatives and those of her husband. She also chooses not to marry again despite being pursued by many suitors (16:21–24).
- As a result of her salvific acts her people are delivered from the fear of their enemies as none dared to attack them for many years after her death (16:25).

Furthermore, Judith's defeat of Holofernes effects a number of very important transformations in the interplay of characters in section

II, the Judaean community, and consciousness as a whole—not to mention the 'pagan' Achior:

- Judith transforms the absolutised form of the Deuteronomistic doctrine of retribution into a 'doctrine' of divine testing which allows good people to suffer for didactic purposes and God to be God in His dealings with His people.
- She challenges and overturns the Bethulians'/Judaeans' tyrannically negative self-image vis-à-vis their rigid view of God—both of which are based on the Deuteronomistic point of view—so that the people are able to perceive themselves as those sanctified to God once again and deepen their understanding of Him.
- Male leadership is transformed into female leadership at both military-political and spiritual-cultic levels as Judith takes charge from the outset of section II:
  - The male Bethulian and Judaean leadership are led by Judith, whereas in section I they led their respective communities.
  - The would-be conqueror of both Judith and the Judaeans is conquered by Judith as he succumbs to her charms and foolishly believes in her promise to lead him to victory through the guidance of her God.
  - Judith details the successful battle plans that bring about the complete deliverance and enrichment of her people, thereby functioning as their military leader.
  - Judith's victory leads to the heightened (self-)awareness of the Judaean women who are now able to act independently of their men/families. They become independent actants who follow Judith and lead men in worship up to Jerusalem.
- Judith, the highest conscious element—second only to YHWH—internalises and transmits the unconscious *mana*. This causes a libido surge in favour of consciousness that enables her people to integrate fully the partially integrated shadow elements (like Achior) and use the conscious-strengthening *mana* to drive off the unconscious attack. She is thus the leader of the conscious reawakening/strengthening.
- The Assyrians are transformed from the objects of fear to its subjects.
- The Bethulians/Judaeans are transformed from the subjects of fear to its objects as the Assyrians flee before their 'combined forces'.
- The seemingly innumerable, fearless, and indestructible Assyrian

army panic, scatter, and flee as one man when Bagoas announces what Judith has done. They are driven back by Judith's now fearless, but presumably still numerically fewer compatriots and completely defeated.

- Achior becomes a full member of consciousness—as seen by his willing, wholehearted conversion to Judaism—and is fully integrated at stage 4.
- Mourning is turned into joy.
- Judith's victory causes the Judaean women's freedom/conscious differentiation from societal norms and expectations, while simultaneously effecting the greater conscious differentiation/integration of these previously suppressed anima contents.
- Foreign/shadow elements are integrated into the worship of YHWH/the conscious service of the Self.
- The Bethulians are given a taste of the fifth stage of conscious awareness and become settled/fully functional at the fourth, whereas they previously seemed to be faltering at that level.
- The general Judaean populace are inspired/energised to act on behalf of consciousness as a result of Judith's deed and the way that this has been carried forward by the Bethulian community. They too are temporarily lifted to the fifth stage of conscious awareness, but return to the third stage from whence they came once the festivities in Jerusalem are over.
- The ἅβρα/positive shadow is freed upon Judith's death.
- The Judaean nation lives fearlessly and free of enemy/shadow attacks for many years after Judith's death.
- Both the Judaeans and the Bethulians are imbued with the seeds of further transformation in that they return to their various levels of consciousness with the distinct potential of ascending to higher levels of consciousness—even the fifth. I.e., they are imbued with the seeds of further transformation. This extends the transformation that Judith brings about beyond the scope of *Judith*.

As we have seen, these transformations are made possible by Judith's own internal and external transformations:

i) Her intercessory prayer (*Judith* 9) and plan of action transforms her from a woman of prayer and great piety to a bloodthirsty man of war.
ii) Her beautification process transforms her from a chaste widow to a deceitful, sexual warrior and femme fatale.

iii) Her descent to Holofernes' tent temporarily transforms her from the highest conscious ego-content and the inspiratrix (read: positive anima) of her people to the Assyrian general's negative anima and executioner.

In other words, Judith's victories are achieved as a result of her engaging/re-entering her shadow side—the 'negative' part of her that was hidden from those around her, the part that nobody expected her to display given her god-fearing nature (see 8:8). This is not at all surprising as the victory that she wins on behalf of her people and for the glorification of her God entails a battle with the national Shadow in which the latter is defeated and its *mana* integrated into her consciousness and that of the people. As I have previously indicated, this has been facilitated by the partial integration of acceptable shadow elements in the form of Achior and has, in turn, facilitated the full integration of the contents he represents. Judith's victory over the national Shadow has been accompanied by the integration of formerly suppressed anima contents (the dancing women) into Judaean consciousness, which has led to the integration of foreign/shadow elements into Judaean worship. It has also resulted in the release of Judith's shadow/ἅβρα and the distribution of her wealth (read: psychic wealth) amongst her people and those of her husband subsequent to her death.

In conclusion, we may say that Judith's self-sacrifice and commitment to her God and her people has led to the integration of previously suppressed shadow and anima contents, with the result that the nation is strengthened consciously, brought into closer communication with their God/the Self, and given the seeds for further transformation. In archetypal terms, we may therefore say that Judith represents both the ego/hero who 'slays the monster' and transforms the life of his community/strengthens its conscious functioning as well as the anima who brings the androcentric Judaic community closer to God/the Self (see further 5.E.a.).

Identifying the Effective Protagonist in Judith *8–16*

As heroes usually are, Judith is 'handsome' (beautiful), a favourite or 'son' (daughter) of (a particular) goddess/god, fearless, brave, and unwedded at the outset of the tale. Much like Theseus of old, and in response to a problem facing the community, she willingly faces many tests/challenges, risks her life in favour of her people, 'slays the monster', retrieves lost or stolen treasure, returns to her hometown, and positively influences the life of her community, which subsequently honours her with the highest accolades. This, to my mind, unquestionably qualifies her as the obvious protagonist of section II and of the narrative as a whole. However, it remains to be seen whether she is also its effective protagonist who, as Dawson has taught us, is the proper subject of a psychoanalytic textual interpretation. As previously indicated, the effective protagonist is primarily discerned by comparing the outset of the narrative to its end and determining which of the characters has undergone the most profound change during its course.

When we compare the events at the beginning of section II with those at its end, we note that most of its characters—apart from the dead Manasses, that is—undergo transformation/change of various degrees. These may be changes in function and/or level of consciousness. I have tabulated them in table 11 below. Tabulating the insights gained from my analysis of section II in this manner facilitates the separation of deep, lasting changes/transformations from minor and/or temporary ones. This, in turn, facilitates the identification of the effective protagonist as the character who has undergone the most profound change.

Table 11. Changes Occurring to and Caused by the Characters in Section II

Character	Start of Section II Aa–Bb	During Section II Cc–D–Cc'	End of Section II Bb'–Aa'	Changes
Judith	Highest conscious element and closest to the Self. Challenges Deuteronomistic assumptions re: God, the situation, and the Bethulians' self-image. Puts all her 'weaponry' at the disposal of God/the Self.	Highest conscious element, closest to Self. Undergoes temporary and partial transformation into negative anima. Reverts to highest conscious element. Is consciously strengthened by integrating the *mana* of the national shadow/power archetype (Holofernes).	Highest conscious element and closest to the Self. Sacrifices all gains to God/the Self and leads people into closer contact with God/the Self.	Challenges Deuteronomistic assumptions and leads people into closer contact with God/the Self. Temporarily transforms herself into negative anima and back into highest conscious element. Consciously strengthened by mana as indicated.
	Fearlessly takes charge of the situation.	Fearlessly in charge, even though Holofernes thinks that he is in charge. Kills Holofernes.	Triumphantly takes charge of attack plans and also stays in charge in the sense that no-one dares attack while she lives and long after her death.	Imbues community with unconscious *mana* and brings about their deliverance.
	Chaste and pious widow.	Becomes bloodthirsty man of war, deceiver, and sexual vamp.	Chaste and pious widow who refuses to marry despite having many suitors.	Affects her community's gender and power balance; sets off Achior's conversion, frees maid, bequeaths her wealth to her relatives and those of her husband. Functionally changes from and back to pious and chaste widowhood.
	fifth- stage consciousness.	fifth- stage consciousness and anima.	fifth- stage consciousness.	No change in conscious level but is strengthened consciously (*vide* above).
	Wise and speaks well (rebuke and intercession).	Wise and speaks well (deceit).	Wise and speaks well (praise).	No change except in the way that her wisdom is expressed (see bracketed items in this row).
Manasses	Dead.	Dead.	Dead.	No change at all.

Table 11 (*cont.*)

Character	Start of Section II Aa–Bb	During Section II Cc–D–Cc'	End of Section II Bb'–Aa'	Changes
῞Αβρα	Judith's stewardess/helper.	Judith's stewardess/helper.	Freed upon Judith's death.	Helps Judith to defeat shadow and so deliver people. Is freed upon Judith's death.
	Integrated shadow element.	Integrated shadow element.	Released into general psychic realm upon Judith's death.	No fundamental change in and of herself.
Ozias and the Bethulian Elders/ Magistrates	Leaders of the town/outskirts of central consciousness.	Leaders of the town/outskirts of central consciousness.	Questionable leadership roles. Judith leads them.	Undergo gender role reversal and reversal in power structure (lessened power vis-à-vis Judith's increased power).
	Essentially passive.	Essentially passive.	Elders disappear textually. No longer function as a group.	Lessened functional role vis-à-vis changes indicated above.
	Don't want Judith to do anything but pray. Bless Judith to accomplish what she wishes. Retreat to their stations.	Presumably stay at their stations to which they had previously retreated.	Ozias writes a letter to the surrounding areas as Joachim did.	Ozias' consciousness is possibly strengthened.
	Apparent libidinous dearth: fear of attack with concomitant immobilisation due to five-day ultimatum.	Presumably continue to experience libidinous dearth.	Experience libidinous surge.	Inspire other sectors of Judaean community to join the Bethulians and rout the enemy.
	fourth-stage consciousness (Bethuliah) but higher than other Bethulians by virtue of their leadership positions.	fourth-stage consciousness (Bethuliah) but higher than other Bethulians by virtue of their leadership positions.	Presumably go up to Jerusalem and return to Bethuliah. Become better integrated at the fourth stage.	Leadership is presumably better integrated at stage 4. No change in conscious level despite temporarily experiencing the fifth stage of consciousness, i.e., Jerusalem.

Young Men/ Gatekeepers of Bethuliah	Virile/sexual instinctual elements that have been made conscious.	Virile/sexual instinctual elements that have been made conscious.	Virile/sexual instinctual elements that have been made conscious.	No change.
	Presumably guard the city.	Open the gate for Judith and presumably continue guarding the city.	No function indicated. Presumably join in worship procession up to Jerusalem.	Negligible change in function.
	Fearful, libidinous dearth (presumed on basis of general Bethulian population's attitude, fear, etc.).	Fearful, libidinous dearth (presumed on basis of general Bethulian population's attitude, fear, etc.).	Libidinous surge.	Change in attitude and self-concept. Presumably help to rout enemy
	fourth-stage consciousness (Bethuliah).	fourth-stage consciousness (Bethuliah).	Go up to Jerusalem and return to Bethuliah. Become better integrated at stage 4.	No essential change except for better integration at stage 4. Temporarily experience fifth stage of consciousness, i.e., Jerusalem. Potential for further change indicated.
Bethulian Men	Presumably guard the city.	Watch Judith going down to the enemy camp and presumably continue guarding the city.	Open the gates for Judith to return.	Experience (temporary?) gender role reversal.
	Overshadowed by Judith.	Overshadowed by Judith.	Overshadowed by Judith.	No change.
	Fearful, libidinous dearth and cowardice.	Fearful, libidinous dearth and cowardice.	Libidinous surge.	Change in attitude and self-concept. Bravely rout enemy, taking much booty.
	Subjects of fear.	Subjects of fear.	Objects of fear.	Experience power role reversal.

Table 11 (*cont.*)

Character	**Start of Section II Aa–Bb**	**During Section II Cc–D–Cc'**	**End of Section II Bb'–Aa'**	**Changes**
	Presumably cultically superior to women owing to androcentric nature of Judaean society.	Uncertain. Presumably remain cultically superior to women.	Follow women in worship.	Undergo gender role reversal in cultic domain.
	fourth-stage consciousness (Bethuliah).	fourth-stage consciousness (Bethuliah).	Go up to Jerusalem and return to Bethuliah.	Become better integrated at stage 4. Temporarily experience fifth stage consciousness, i.e., Jerusalem. Potential for further change indicated.
Holofernes' Troops and Bodyguards	Unconscious instinctual elements.	Unconscious instinctual elements.	Unconscious instinctual elements	No change.
	Victor-besiegers and Holofernes' guardians.	Victor-besiegers who drop their guard as they are captivated by Judith.	Defeated—put to flight.	Experience power role reversal.
	Objects of fear.	Objects of fear.	Subjects of fear.	As above.
Holofernes	Conqueror of foreign nations and would-be conqueror of Jerusalem/Judaea. Focused on conquering Judaea through Bethuliah.	Would-be conqueror of Jerusalem/Judaea and Judith. Increasingly focused on Judith. Is murdered, conquered, and defeated by negative anima as a person.	Decapitated.	Change in focus. Experience power-role reversal and temporary anima possession that proves to be his undoing.

	Arrogant and power-conscious.	Arrogant and power-conscious. Suffers from anima possession.	Dies.	Remains arrogant, power-conscious, and arrogant, but <u>dies</u>.
	Highest element of unconscious attack. Represents Judaean national Shadow.	Highest element of unconscious attack and Judaean national Shadow. Completely deactivated/defeated and integrated by Judith.	Integrated as national Shadow by Bethulian community (which positively influences Judaean community as a whole).	Is <u>defeated and 'neutralised' in respect of consciousness</u>. He is integrated as Shadow and consciousness is strengthened as a result.
Holofernes' Officers/ Attendants and Servants	Weaker unconscious elements constellated around Shadow archetype.	Weaker unconscious elements constellated around Shadow archetype. Completely arrested by Judith's beauty and speaking prowess—i.e., experience anima possession.	Weaker unconscious elements constellated around Shadow archetype.	No change.
	Holofernes' θεράποντες.	(Quickly) become Judith's θεράποντες.	Essentially left 'headless'.	Temporary change in allegiance.
	Victor-besiegers.	Victor-besiegers, though unwittingly 'besieged' by Judith.	Defeated—put to flight as a result of Holofernes' death and Bethulian-Judaean attack.	Experience power role reversal.
Bagoas	Holofernes' 'blindly' loyal eunuch/steward.	Holofernes' 'blindly' loyal eunuch/ steward.	(Dead) Holofernes' eunuch/ steward.	No change.
	Holofernes' shadow.	Holofernes' shadow.	Holofernes' shadow.	No change.
	Part of conquering forces.	Part of conquering forces.	Part of defeated forces.	Experiences power role reversal.

Table 11 (*cont.*)

Character	Start of Section II Aa–Bb	During Section II Cc–D–Cc'	End of Section II Bb'–Aa'	Changes
Achior	Partially integrated person/shadow content at stage 4.	Partially integrated person/shadow content at stage 4.	Re-born, i.e., completely integrated and functional person/shadow content at stage 4, lays aside instinctual nature in favour of the Self.	Facilitates Judith's descent to unconscious realm, the integration of *mana* she brings back and is completely integrated at stage 4. Potential for further change indicated.
	Ammonite graciously accepted by Bethulians.	Ammonite graciously accepted by Bethulians.	Recognises ascendancy of the Self, is fully converted into Judaism.	Fully fledged member of Judaean community/content of consciousness "unto this day".
Holofernes' High-ranking Officers	Leaders of conquering forces.	Leaders of conquering forces.	Leaders of fleeing, defeated forces.	Experience power role reversal.
	Objects of fear.	Objects of fear.	Subjects of fear.	As above.
	Holofernes' disciples.	Holofernes' disciples.	The dead Holofernes' disciples.	No change.
The Other Judaeans	Subjects of fear.	Subjects of fear.	Objects of fear.	Experience power role reversals.
	Immobilised by fearful, libidinous dearth and cowardice.	Immobilised by fearful, libidinous dearth and cowardice.	Libidinous surge.	Change in attitude and self-concept. Bravely assist to rout enemy, taking much booty.

	Occupants of stage 3 consciousness.	Occupants of stage 3 consciousness. Temporarily experience fifth-stage consciousness, i.e., Jerusalem.	Rise to Jerusalem, but return to their own homes, i.e., the third stage of consciousness.	Experience a higher level of consciousness but return to their own level once the festivities end. Potential for further change indicated.
Joachim and the Γερουσία	Not present in Bethuliah. Had returned to Jerusalem.	Not present in Bethuliah. Had returned to Jerusalem.	Come only to bless Judith.	No change.
	Political-spiritual leaders of entire Judaean population.	Political-spiritual leaders of entire Judaean population.	Muted political leadership roles vis-à-vis Judith's leadership. Judith largely takes over their spiritual role.	Undergo power role reversal and gender role reversal.
	Highest conscious elements at innermost level of central consciousness. I.e., higher than the Bethulian leadership/he leaders of the outermost level of central consciousness.	Highest conscious elements at innermost level of central consciousness and higher than Bethulian leadership. Replaced by Judith as the person/element closest to the Self.	Replaced by Judith as the person/element closest to the Self and hence the highest level of consciousness, 'one step' removed from the Self.	Replaced by Judith as the person/element closest to the Self.
	Stage 4 consciousness but higher than the Bethulian leadership/the leaders of the outermost level of central consciousness.	Stage 4 consciousness but higher than the Bethulian leadership/the leaders of the outermost level of central consciousness.	Stage 4 consciousness but higher than the Bethulian leadership/the leaders of the outermost level of central consciousness.	No change. Potential for further change (?).

Table 11 (*cont.*)

Character	Start of Section II Aa–Bb	During Section II Cc–D–Cc'	End of Section II Bb'–Aa'	Changes
The dancing women	Uncertain presence. Presumably led by men in political and cultic sphere (androcentric society).	Uncertain presence. Presumably led by men in political and cultic sphere (androcentric society).	Welcome Judith as hero-conqueror. Lead men in worship up to Jerusalem.	Experience (temporary?) gender role reversal.
	Unintegrated multiple anima.	Unintegrated multiple anima.	Integrated multiple anima.	Became integrated *animas*.
	Possibly third and fourth stages of consciousness (depending on identity—Bethulians and/or Judaeans?).	Possibly third and fourth stages of consciousness (depending on identity—Bethulians and/or Judaeans?).	Follow Judith up to Jerusalem and temporarily experience fifth-stage consciousness before returning to their original conscious levels.	Temporarily accede to fifth (highest) level of consciousness. Potential for further change indicated.

As can be seen from table 11 above, most of the characters in section II experience some type of transformation and/or bring about change in the Judaean community or Assyrian army. This transformation is mostly gender- and/or power-related in that the characters experience a reversal of stereotype gender roles (e.g., Judith, the male leadership, the Bethulian men, and the dancing women) and/or a reversal in the balance of power. In the latter case, those who began the tale as objects of fear become its subjects and vice versa (e.g., the Assyrians and Bethulians), those who led become those who are led (e.g., Ozias and the Bethulian leadership, the men of Bethuliah), and those who were part of the conquering forces become part of the conquered forces (e.g., Bagoas, the high-ranking Assyrian officers, and the Assyrian troops). However, those who undergo the most profound changes (see the underlined portions in table 11 above) are those who survive the narrative and the events of section II (this was also the case in section I), viz., Judith, Ozias, the general Bethulian population, Achior, and the other Judaeans:

- Judith, who is temporarily and functionally transformed into a man of war/sexual warrior/"sexual vamp" and negative anima. She is also strengthened in consciousness by defeating Holofernes and integrating the unconscious *mana* of the national Shadow archetype that he represents. Nevertheless, she begins and ends the tale as the highest element of consciousness—second only to God himself—and as a chaste, wise, and pious widow.
- Ozias, whose consciousness appears to have been strengthened by Judith's return so that he is able to take over Joachim's letter-writing function. He and the Bethulian leadership are also presumably better integrated at the fourth stage of consciousness at the end of the tale even though their leadership functions are severely diminished upon Judith's victorious return.
- The people of Bethuliah in general (young gatekeepers, men and women) who experience a change in attitude and self-concept as a result of integrating the *mana* that Judith brings and the shadow contents represented by Achior. They are also brought closer to the Self. The male population are consequently able to drive back the forces of the unconscious and loot/assimilate its resources. As a result, they (and their leadership) are able temporarily to accede to the fifth stage of consciousness represented by Jerusalem and return to a more stable/integrated existence in Bethuliah/stage 4.

- Achior, who recognises the light of the Self (highest consciousness) through Judith and accepts the God of the Judaeans. He converts to Judaism, is circumcised/lays down his instinctual nature at the 'feet' of the Self, and becomes a full part of the community/consciousness 'unto this day'. Furthermore, he begins section II as a partially integrated shadow content and ends it as a fully integrated one. In other words, he is fully and permanently integrated as a person and as a psychological content at the fourth stage of consciousness.
- The other Judaeans who join in the battle at the behest of Ozias. They are temporarily imbued with psychic energy/libido as a result of Judith's deed and the victory of the Bethulians. In three phases of attack, they assist the Bethulians to drive off the headless Assyrian army completely. This energy surge also enables them to ascend to Jerusalem with Judith and the Bethulians. As with the Bethulians, this 'ascension' is temporary. The text indicates that they too returned home, i.e., to the third stage of consciousness whence they came.

When we consider the above, we see that Achior undergoes the most intense, permanent psychological changes, with the Bethulians following closely on his heels. This near convergence in the intensity of psychological change is not at all surprising seeing that their fates have been intimately linked since Holofernes had Achior cast out to the foothills of Bethuliah in section I (6:10–11). Be that as it may, the most radical of these changes belongs to Achior. Whilst both he and the Bethulians become fully functional at stage 4 and both experience a change in their perception of the situation, Achior is fully converted from 'paganism'/the realms of the unconscious (that which consciousness does not recognise as valid/truly a part of itself) and willingly places his instinctual nature at the disposal of the Self through his circumcision and integration into the Judaean community. He thus becomes a fully conscious shadow content/person at the fourth stage of consciousness. As has been demonstrated throughout my analysis of section II, all the events of section II may be and are related to him. This makes him the effective protagonist of section II.

Determining the Dilemma Facing the Effective Protagonist in Judith *8–16*

Since Achior is the effective protagonist of section II, which dilemma is he facing? Which challenges are implicit in this dilemma, and how does he meet them? I believe that the answers to these questions lie within the following considerations:

1) When Judith returns, it is still relatively dark so that the Bethulians have to light lamps by which to see her and her ἅβρα (13:13). This, as I have said, signifies that the people were still effectively steeped in the same measure of unconscious darkness that had beset their minds in section I. Since Achior is with them and is even 'residing' in Ozias' house (14:6)—that is his last textual 'address' (6:21)—the same may be said of him. I.e., he is still a partially integrated shadow content at the fourth stage of consciousness/Bethuliah. Being partially integrated means that he is both partially conscious and partially unconscious. The same applies to him as a person: he has partially acceded to the fourth stage of consciousness, but he is also partially outside of it. He is thus partially in darkness just as he is partially 'in the light'. Judith's arrival and the sequence of events that ensue ultimately lead him out of the 'darkness' of 'paganism' and into the 'light' of Judaism (cf. 14:10).
2) Achior is nowhere to be seen at Judith's return. In fact, we find that he is still in Ozias' house where the narrative left him at the end of section I (6:21 and 14:6). On a psychological level, this depicts the conscious stagnation that he finds himself in. I.e., he is still functioning out of his Deuteronomistically dominated mode of comprehending reality that has caused the Bethulians so much desperate depression (cf. 7:32). His behaviour—remaining in the house and not coming out to see Judith—is indicative of a deep depression and hopelessness that has set in and further immobilised him. (It is a well-known fact that people with depression 'remain indoors' and refuse to 'go out and face the music' for fear of failure, harm, death, etc. In other words, depressed people are often immobilised by the fear that both perpetuates and is perpetuated by the depressive cycle that they are in).
3) The terrible situation in which Achior finds himself, i.e., if Holofernes remains unbeaten then he (Achior) will definitely be destroyed along with the Bethulians (cf. 6:5–9)—and who knows what kind of torture this may involve—no doubt added the element of anxiety to his depression. It comes as no surprise, therefore, that he faints when he sees Holofernes' head being held in the hands of a single man (14:6). His fainting not only speaks of his spiritual

death and rebirth, or the fact that he is set up as a foil to Judith; it also speaks of the dissolution of the anxiety that he had been living in since Holofernes evicted him from the Assyrian camp and sealed his fate with that of the Bethulians (6:5–10). Moreover, I can imagine that his stress and anxiety level peaked to a frenzy when the Bethulians sat back and left a 'mere woman' (8:35–36; 9:9, 10; 13:14, 15; 16:5) to defeat an enemy that had left nothing but a path of cruel death and destruction in his wake. This no doubt compounded his stress/anxiety/depression and contributed to his fainting at the sight of Holofernes' severed head. (Achior's fainting is akin to the kind of exhaustion and the feeling of 'collapsing' that often settles in after one has suddenly ceased from lengthy periods of intense work).

4) It is only after Achior is raised to his feet and hears Judith's story that he believes in the Judaeans' God completely, with the result that he is circumcised and joined to the community of YHWH/becomes fully functional at the fourth stage of consciousness "unto this day" (14:7–10).

We see, then, that Achior's dilemma in section II is a terse extension of the dilemma that he experienced in section I. In the first section, his dilemma entailed freeing himself from the force of the negative Self *cum* power archetype that had ensnared him through the unconscious Shadow so that he could establish his own moral/ethical code (stage 3) and come to the realisation of social reality and so to his true self (stage 4). In section II, his dilemma may be described as follows: He must avoid falling back into the hands of the unconscious Shadow so that he may retain the conscious advances he has made and become fully integrated at the fourth stage of consciousness.

The challenges involved here may be described as follows:

i) Achior must find a way to surmount the fear, depression, and anxiety that has immobilised him into a position of complete passivity.
ii) He must trust God to save him and the Bethulians as, when, and by whom He chooses. This means that he must learn to:
   - Look at life and its realities from a perspective other than the Deuteronomistic one that he has been accustomed to.
   - Understand that YHWH often chooses the improbable to deal effectively with the impossible.
   - Have faith in and embrace the feminine aspect of the com-

munity and the feminine aspect of the divine, the anima, who is manifested in the guise of the warrior-woman-faithful-YHWH-devotee, Judith.

iii) He must willingly surrender his fearful, instinctual nature—which can keep him in the clutches of the unconscious Shadow—and his entire psyche to the workings of the Self.

iv) He must consciously integrate the *mana* that Judith brings and the anima that she represents in order to transcend his semi-conscious state and establish a better connection with the Self.

v) He must consciously and willingly align himself with the Bethulian community/people of YHWH. I.e., he must willingly become fully functional at the dominant stage of ego-consciousness, stage 4 (Bethuliah). Interestingly, Holofernes/the Shadow evicted him to the very threshold of this stage of conscious awareness; and yet it was the Self that directed this process as the entire psyche is encompassed by the Self and governed/ordered by it. The latter, in my opinion, is always concerned with evolving the psyche to higher and higher stages of consciousness, enabling deeper and deeper levels of integrating unconscious contents, withdrawing projections, and consciously re-uniting opposites. In short, this evolutionary process entails the greater and greater depth of individuation that the Self has destined for the human psyche.

These challenges are both similar to and an extension of those that Achior had to deal with in section I, so that resolving them would bring him to the ultimate aim of the dilemma facing him on both occasions, i.e., becoming a fully integrated psychological content/fully functional person at stage 4. This, as Jung has said, is the critical stage of the individuation cycle where one's projections about society are broken and one can become one's true self.

How, then, does Achior meet these challenges?

i) He comes out of Ozias' house when the Bethulians call him to verify that the severed head is indeed that of Holofernes (14:6). I.e., he allows himself to be drawn out of his conscious stagnation by not resisting the Bethulians' call.

ii) His anxiety is resolved when he sees Holofernes' severed head. This enables him to die to his old self and god-concept (he faints), and to arise with a new image of himself and the God of the Judaeans in his current situation. It also enables him to incorporate the *mana* of the unconscious Shadow and to realise the ascendancy of the Self over the Shadow (cf. further above and the ensuing point).

iii) His fear is finally abolished as the rebirth entailed in his fainting and revival enables his ears to open and hear what God has done (he asks Judith to recount the story of Holofernes' defeat—14:8). This, to my mind, entails a re-scription of the old Deuteronomistic lore according to which he had functioned, in the sense that he sees that God is not limited by it but rather transcends it.

iv) He realises that the Self works in mysterious ways as he praises Judith for her deeds (14:7). In so doing, he embraces not only her faith, but also the feminine aspect of the divinity and community that she represents. I.e., he is able to attain complete faith in God, and to accept and integrate the strength of the feminine aspect of Self and psyche.

v) He surrenders his old, fearful, instinctual nature to the Self as typified by his circumcision (see 14:10).

vi) He willingly aligns himself to YHWH and the community of YHWH by willingly and permanently converting to Judaism (14:10). This means that he has consciously (i.e., willingly) become a fully operational content/person at the fourth stage of individuation and that he has come far closer to the Self than he presumably ever has been (he converts from 'paganism' to Judaism).

vii) His 'mourning'/debilitating depression are transformed into energetic joy as he and the community praise God and Judith for their deeds (cf. 14:9).

Given the above, it would seem that Achior fares far better with meeting the challenges of his dilemma in section II than he did in section I. This is not surprising. It will be remembered that his partial integration in section I was almost solely directed by the Bethulians' deliverance and acceptance of him. By contrast, his integration in section II is the result of his own willing commitment to YHWH and the community of His people—although this commitment was facilitated by the Bethulians and Judith (the Bethulians call him out of Ozias' house at Judith's behest and this sets in motion the transformations in his character and psyche that we have noted above).

c. *Summary: Identifying the Effective Protagonist of the Entire Narrative and Determining the Dilemma Facing Him*

In the preceding subsections, we identified Achior as the effective protagonist of the first and second sections of *Judith*. He is thus unquestionably the effective protagonist of the entire narrative. Being an Ammonite, he begins *Judith* as a member of an outsider/outcast people, i.e., as part of the Judaeans' national shadow—albeit a more 'accessible' one (read: generally closer to the conscious threshold) by virtue of his ancestry. Although he functions primarily at the second stage of consciousness to begin with, a number of factors indicate that he was on his way to the third stage when the third wave of the unconscious attack subsumed him and brought him down to the realms of the unconscious Shadow. The fact that he retains some autonomy whilst he is there indicates that he is not completely subsumed by the unconscious psyche per se. This suggests that he has dropped down into the first stage of consciousness, which is still largely identified with the unconscious psyche, and not into the depths of the unconscious itself. There, he is assimilated as an advisor to Holofernes and as an ancillary to the Judaean national Shadow that is spearheading the attack. As a result of attempting to warn his 'lord' of the danger of attacking the Judaeans prior to determining their guilt or innocence before their Lord (5:5–20), he finds himself cast out to the foothills of his ancient relatives, the Bethulians-Judaeans (6:10–13). This, as I have previously stated, indicates the possibility of his entering an even higher level of consciousness than the one that he originally occupied as a person, and becoming integrated into consciousness as a psychological content. Here in Bethuliah, which represents the fourth stage of consciousness, he is received with open arms (cf. 6:14–16). After imparting valuable information concerning the plans of the unconscious forces (6:17), he proceeds to the house of Ozias for a banquet (6:21). The Bethulians' seven-step reception of this man is an indication that he has been partially accepted amongst them and partially integrated by consciousness.

In consideration of the above, we may formulate the dilemma facing Achior throughout *Judith* as follows: To transcend completely the partially unconscious stage into which he has fallen and become an integral, fully functional member/content at stage 4. In terms of Jung's stages of consciousness, this means that he must transcend the bounds of societal norms and values (stage 1), reclaim his otherness/

separate the ego from the shadow (stage 2), establish his own ethical-moral code (stage 3), break free from the bounds of society's norms and expectations and become who he really is (stage 4). His dilemma is therefore ultimately concerned with breaking free from society's fetters and becoming who he inherently is.

This is where the convergence we previously noted in terms of Achior's individuation process and that of the Bethulians comes into play. His complete integration at stage 4 brings about their stabilisation at the same level through their integration of the unconscious *mana* that Judith brings, his willing accession to stage 4, their complete acceptance/integration of him at that level, and the subsequent defeat of the enemy forces. It is thus not surprising to find that this is the point at which Achior is the most changed and, simultaneously, the point at which he effects the most change.

Thus, Achior has moved from the second stage of consciousness through to the unconscious realms (stage 1), to be finally integrated in the fourth. This is a total psychological change of four stages of consciousness—one descending (2→1) and three ascending (1→2; 2→3; 3→4). Four is also the square root of the sixteen steps Achior took to conversion. As four is the number of totality, this indicates the completeness of both his transcendence to the fourth stage of consciousness as a person and his conversion/integration into consciousness. In this way, Achior's link with the fate of the Bethulians, ironically initiated by Holofernes in section I, finds its full expression after the latter's death in section II. Achior is converted, circumcised, and becomes part of the Jewish community, an integrated (and thus valuable) shadow element at the fourth stage of consciousness "unto this day" (14:10).

C. *Analysing the Judithic Dream*

Having analysed both sections of *Judith* and identified Achior as the effective protagonist of the entire narrative, I am now able to apply Jung's twin method of dream analysis, namely the subjective and objective mode, to the Judithic dream. Before doing so, I should like to recall—as a point of reference—a number of interrelated aspects pertaining to Jungian dream analysis, Dawson's theories regarding the effective protagonist, Judith, and dreams in general that inform the theoretical/methodological background of this part of my book:

i) As indicated in chapter 2, a subjective dream analysis regards all the personalities and aspects of a particular dream as the unconscious manifestations of the dreamer's own fourfold personality (the ego, shadow, anima/animus, and the Self—Atkinson, op. cit., 85), her/his tendencies, components, and the forgotten, 'lost' and/or repressed aspects of her/his own psyche that require conscious (re)integration.

ii) According to Dawson, the effective protagonist of a narrative is a reflection of the dreamer's dominant unconscious personality. Since *Judith* may be regarded as a dream emanating from the collective Jewish psyche, relating the surface structure of this narrative, i.e., the story as it is told, to Achior would give us a clear indication of the state of the national Jewish psyche at the time in which the narrative was written.

iii) Relating the narrative's surface structure to Achior means that every aspect of the story is viewed in relation to him. The various components of *Judith*, i.e., its events as well as the reactions and characteristics of *all* the characters in it—including Judith, are treated as projections or reflections of various aspects of Achior's psyche, his fears, his desires, the implicit challenge/dilemma facing him and his individuation.

iv) Seeing that Achior is the dominant unconscious personality of the Jewish nation, what the unconscious tells the dreamer and the reader about him is what it 'intends' to communicate about the Jewish community as a whole. Similarly, the unconscious message is aimed both at Achior and the Jewish nation. Thus, reading the narrative from his point of view reveals not only the processes within the collective Jewish psyche as a whole, but also the dynamics within its community. Deducing these processes and dynamics will enable me to make certain inferences regarding the hypothetical context of the Judithic dream. This will, in turn, assist me to test my findings regarding the date and context of *Judith* as set out in chapter 1 and to conduct the objective dream analysis of this book.

v) The surface structure of *Judith* is divided into two sections. The first section, chapters 1–7, presents the reader with the surface structure problem/dilemma. It essentially explains how the Bethulians-Judaeans came to the point of desperation in which they find themselves at the end of *Judith* 7: having disobeyed Nebuchadnezzar's original call to battle, they find themselves at the mercy of his general, Holofernes. The latter effectively seals their fates by sealing the fountain that watered Bethuliah. As a result, they are ready to give in and become slaves to the Assyrians, even though Ozias manages to convince them to give God another five days in which to save them.

The second section, chapters 8–16, presents the surface structure solution to the problem/dilemma depicted in section I: Judith goes out and kills Holofernes. This empowers the Bethulians and the remaining Judaeans to route the Assyrian armies and 'live happily ever after', protected by Judith's valour and the memory of her deeds.

vi) In relation to the preceding point, I have previously indicated that dreams may have many functions: they may provide compensation for the dreamer's conscious state of mind or attitude, warn the dreamer, reveal the dreamer's conscious/ unconscious self-concept and attitudes, present a solution to a problem experienced in the conscious realm, and so forth. In addition, each dream may exhibit more than one or even all of these functions.

To my mind, the clear bipartite division of *Judith* suggests that each of its two sections has a different function/set of functions. Moreover, given that the surface structure of section I presents the problem while that of section II presents the solution, it is to be expected that the deep structure relationship between these two sections of *Judith* will be commensurate with that of the surface structure. This means that section I reveals the crisis in the dreamer's conscious state of mind and/or compensates for it, while section II reveals the solution to this crisis.

vii) According to Jung, it is very important to note when a particular character or event is introduced in a dream and how it is introduced. This means that any correspondences between Achior's psyche and the text of *Judith* must follow this text's contours. In my opinion, Craven's structural analysis of *Judith*, as depicted in chapter 1, provides an excellent guideline for analysing the text in this fashion. I will therefore follow her structural layout of the text when trying to discern the correspondences between the text of *Judith* and the psyche of the effective protagonist, Achior.

viii) Seeing that each character in *Judith* has been interpreted as a psychological construct and as a person, the same may be applied to my interpretation of these characters vis-à-vis Achior and the community from which he comes. In other words, each character can be interpreted as an aspect of Achior's/the community's psyche or as a characteristic of Achior/the community.

a. *A Subjective Analysis: The Surface-Structure Components of* Judith *as a Projection of Achior's Psyche*

To my mind, tabulation is the best way of presenting the correspondences between Achior's psyche (the subjective analysis) and the surface-structure components of *Judith* as this format readily allows for immediate comparisons. Keeping in mind that *Judith* 1–7 represents the crisis in Achior's psyche/society while *Judith* 8–16 represents the solution which the unconscious is putting forward to him/the dreamer, I should like to present these correspondences in the form of tables 12 and 13. The tabulations constitute the subjective analysis of *Judith*.

Table 12. The Correspondence between Achior's Psyche and the Surfce-Structure Components/Projections in *Judith* 1–7.

***Judith* 1–7**

I. Introduction to Nebuchadnezzar and his campaign against Arphaxad (1:1–16)

	Surface-Structure Component	Interpretation as a Projection of Achior's Psyche
1:1a	• It is the twelfth year of Nebuchadnezzar's reign in Nineveh. On a textual level, there is confusion regarding: – his national identity—Assyrian/Babylonian – the time in which he lived He has the name of the Babylonian king who exiled the Southern Kingdom in 586 B.C., but is called an Assyrian king. The Assyrians were responsible for the exile and complete assimilation of the Northern Kingdom in 721 B.C. • Nebuchadnezzar is the main thrust behind the unconscious forces attacking consciousness.	• The dream begins by depicting Achior's unconscious personality as a foreign, Assyrian *cum* Babylonian king. This indicates the essential conflict within him: he is unsure of who he is and with which 'nation'/faction in his society/himself he should identify. There is thus an element of self-alienation in his psyche. This internal conflict is also borne out by the fact that the dream identifies him with age-old enemies that alienated his people, the Israelites, from their land and forced them into exile. • Seeing that the Assyrians followed an assimilation policy with the exiles of the Northern Kingdom, there is an indication that at least a part of Achior feels assimilated—swamped and subsumed—by that which is 'other' within him and in his society.
1:1b–4	• Arphaxad embarks on extensive fortifications of Ecbatane, the city over which he reigns. • Even though there appears to be no immediate threat to warrant such fortifications, the syntactical juxtaposition of information regarding Arphaxad and Nebuchadnezzar suggests that these two kings may soon engage in conflict. Note the way in which information regarding Nebuchadnezzar (1:1a and 1:5.) encloses/frames the information regarding Arphaxad (1:1b–4). • Arphaxad's fortifications are indicative of a weak consciousness's fear of the unconscious.	• Achior's fear of the unconscious, the other within him, and/or the other in his society makes him set up protective walls to hold back its perceived destructiveness. • The textual framing described in the preceding panel (left) suggests that Achior is in danger of being completely subsumed by the unconscious other. The dream may therefore be warning Achior of this event/its potentiality.

1:5	• Nebuchadnezzar attacks Arphaxad seemingly without provocation. • Nebuchadnezzar is the negative Self/the Shadow and power archetype. • Arphaxad/Ecbatane represents the first stage of conscious development.	• Hidden contents arise from Achior's unconscious and take his conscious psyche by surprise, attacking it. More specifically, the negative Shadow contents of Achior's psyche arise and attack the first-level/weakest elements of his conscious psyche as his drive for power/supremacy over the other increases. • The element of 'foreignness' or 'otherness' is present once again. The fact that two 'foreign', non-Jewish, elements are at war with each other is a clear indication of the war that rages within Achior and his community or nation. It also attests to the presence of conflicting concepts of foreignness/conflicting foreign 'factions' within him. This observation applies to all the wars between Nebuchadnezzar-Holofernes and their enemies—particularly those who are 'foreign' to the Jewish nation—and will not be repeated.
1:6	• Arphaxad's eastern allies attempt to assist him against Nebuchadnezzar. • They too are elements of the first stage of conscious awareness although they represent a certain spirituality by virtue of their association with the East.	• The spiritual aspects of Achior's first-level conscious awareness (identity in itself) rally to the assistance of his conscious psyche.
1:7–11	• The western nations refuse Nebuchadnezzar's call for assistance, regarding him as "one man". Their refusal to respond to Nebuchadnezzar's call may be regarded as a derivative of their greater, though incomplete, conscious differentiation. • These nations—with the exception of the Judaeans—represent the second stage of conscious awareness.	• Achior's Shadow-side attempts to assimilate the second-stage and higher elements of his conscious psyche without success. In so doing it attempts to turn consciousness against itself. • Achior's consciousness foolishly ignores the Shadow's threat, which symbolises his repression of the rising Shadow contents

Table 12 (*cont.*)

	Surface-Structure Component	Interpretation as a Projection of Achior's Psyche
		This, in turn, signifies the false security of these conscious levels, i.e., the immaturity of Achior's second-stage and higher consciousness vis-à-vis the unconscious. This intimates that Achior is overly and falsely confident in his distinction from the other (stage 2), i.e., that he has become positively inflated; and the dream may be warning him of this.
1:12–16	• Nebuchadnezzar is severely angered, swears revenge upon the 'disobedient' nations and proceeds to annihilate Arphaxad and his allies. He then returns to Nineveh where he and his army feast together for 120 days. • Nebuchadnezzar is portrayed as a proud, power-wielding despot who expects all nations to do his bidding at the drop of a hat—irrespective of what it may cost them (loss of soldiers, depletion of finances, etc.). This is part of his 'divine profile' and a sign of the positive inflation out of which he acts.	• When ignored/repressed, the unconscious is stirred up in wrath, as Jung has indicated. The fury of Achior's rising Shadow contents explodes into a wholesale destruction of his first-stage elements. Having destroyed/subsumed them, the unconscious characteristically 'returns' to its 'abode' to replenish its strength and, presumably, to 'plan' the next phase of attack. • The Shadow-side of Achior's psyche is proud, selfish, inflated, and has a desire for godlike power. It requires unquestioning obedience.
	II. Nebuchadnezzar commissions Holofernes to take vengeance on the disobedient vassal nations (2:1–13)	
2:1–3	• In the eighteenth year of his reign, Nebuchadnezzar gathers his nobles to convey his secret will concerning the disobedient nations. Together, they seal these nations' destruction. • Despite his pride and apparent strength, Nebuchadnezzar requires his nobles to ratify his "will". This indicates that there is an element of insecurity within him arising from his positive inflation.	• At the same time, Achior's inflation and desire for godlike power (manifestations of the Shadow), are about to break through the next conscious threshold and attack the other levels of his consciousness. In other words, the Shadow is aiming to take over his conscious personality. • Even so, two inherent points defy his inflation: (i) There is an element of insecurity in his psyche. (ii) Part of him

	• Nebuchadnezzar's nobles represent those who often gather around someone functioning out of a positive inflation and may be seen as his disciples. They may also be regarded as weaker or attendant psychological contents that have constellated themselves around the dominant power archetype in the unconscious psyche.	wishes to be/regards himself as the disciple of someone great, perhaps even of God. The dream teaches that either or both of these points may lead to his redemption or his undoing—depending on how he handles them. If he becomes consciously aware of these points, realises his weakness, and changes his relation to others, then he will be 'saved' from the destructive effects of his inflation. If not, these weaker aspects of his psyche are likely to lead to his undoing as he tries to compensate for them by acting out more and more according to the inflated aspects of what is fast overriding his dominant conscious personality, i.e., his previously unconscious Shadow. • The dream may also be indicating that there is a certain weakness in the Shadow/within the shadow forces, which could jeopardise the success of its foray against consciousness.
2:4–13	• Nebuchadnezzar instructs Holofernes, his chief general and second-in-command, to execute his judgment upon the disobedient nations. This includes preparing earth and water for him, reserving those who yield for judgment, and having no mercy on rebels. • Nebuchadnezzar's god-complex and inflation manifest themselves most clearly in this passage. • Holofernes may be regarded as Nebuchadnezzar's choice disciple upon whom he has conferred an ego-conqueror function. • Holofernes may also be regarded as the shadow, a split-off of *the* Shadow or negative Self, and as a component of the power archetype.	• The Shadow tasks the psychological contents constellated most closely around it to subjugate Achior's consciousness. It purposes to suppress the resistant forces of consciousness and render them useless and ensure Achior's conscious functioning out of a Shadow-based identification. • Achior's shadow tendencies have now become completely aligned with the negative Self, which functions as its teacher and 'dispatcher' on a hero's quest. However, contrary to the hero's quest, the shadow does not go out to 'slay the dragon'/the unconscious on behalf of a beleaguered community/consciousness. Rather, it does so to destroy consciousness with each successful foray against it (please note: Nebuchadnezzar is convinced of his success against the Western nations—i.e., he is already successful from his point of view).

Table 12 (*cont.*)

	Surface-Structure Component	Interpretation as a Projection of Achior's Psyche
	III. Development **A. The campaign against the disobedient nations; the people surrender (2:14–3:10)**	
2:14–20	• Holofernes puts Assyria's forces into battle array and goes out to battle. He is accompanied by a numberless multitude that is likened to locusts and the sand of the earth. His vast army is accompanied by a host of beasts of burden, is well supplied in terms of rations, and also bears much gold and silver from Nebuchadnezzar's house. • Nebuchadnezzar exits as an active participant on the textual stage. While he sets the events of *Judith* 1–7 in motion, it is Holofernes who makes all the important decisions from this point forward.	• Achior's unconscious shadow prepares to cross over the threshold between the unconscious (Nineveh) and the second level of the conscious psyche (the non-Assyrian world—especially the western nations). It is well prepared and well equipped for its complete destruction of Achior's consciousness and the submission of the latter to the negative Self. • The unconscious shadow attack consists of hidden instinctual forces close to the threshold of consciousness; deeper contents that stem from pre-animal consciousness; and even deeper ones that hark back to the original chaos from which the world was made. Gold and silver, which symbolise transformation, are indicative of the transformative potential inherent in every archetype—even (or, rather, especially) the negative Self/the Shadow. • The negative Self transfers its power and authority to Achior's shadow. The latter takes over and carries out the Shadow's 'will' or 'intentions', presiding over all the unconscious incursions into consciousness from now on.
2:21–27	• Holofernes wreaks destruction throughout the Ancient Near Eastern, destroying high cities, burning sources of nutrition, and putting young men to the sword. • His separation from Nebuchadnezzar indicates that the shadow has become loosed from the deep recesses of the unconscious psyche.	• Achior's shadow is loosed from the recesses of the unconscious and completely subsumes the lower regions of the second level of his consciousness, i.e., the stage that signifies his separation from the other and his identity as seen in relation to an other/others.

	• These Ancient Near Eastern nations are seen as lower elements of the second stage of conscious awareness.	• Holofernes' actions signify the destruction of the lower regions of Achior's second stage of consciousness—particularly in terms of its conscious achievements, resources, and strength—in an attempt to render him incapable of striking back while it moves on to higher levels of conscious awareness.
2:28–3:10	• Fear falls upon the coastal dwellers and they attempt to sue for peace. They put themselves, their cities, and their resources completely at his disposal. They also receive him as though he were their own war hero. Even so, they are not spared—their boundaries are overthrown, their groves are burnt, and their young men are drafted into Holofernes' army. • Holofernes' mission to have Nebuchadnezzar worshipped as God alone is declared. • Holofernes encamps for a month before attacking Judaea. • The coastal nations represent the higher regions of the second stage of conscious awareness. • Holofernes' actions do not seem to accord with his mandate in *Judith* 2:10. His demand that Nebuchadnezzar be worshipped as god alone certainly seems to exceed this mandate. It symbolises both his growing identification with Nebuchadnezzar and his own desire to be worshipped/acknowledged as 'lord.' Once again, the latter points to the weakness of inflation that is compensated by means of self-aggrandisement.	• Fear grips Achior's consciousness as he has already 'lost' valuable first-and second-stage conscious resources to the Shadow and does not want to lose any more. In an attempt to ward off the attack, he foolishly gives in to suppressed shadow elements and suffers the consequences: – The boundaries of the second stage of his conscious awareness are overthrown (identity in relation to an other/others), giving the shadow access to the third stage of conscious awareness (moral/ethical differentiation). – He loses the higher regions and the strongest elements of his second-stage consciousness. – The shadow cleverly employs the conscious contents it has assimilated against the rest of Achior's consciousness. – His connection to the Self is dealt a severe blow as the shadow forces the second level of his consciousness to bow down completely to the negative Self. This threatens to topple his consciousness all the more into the realms of the unconscious and to sever the distinction between himself and the other (his shadow)/others around him. • Achior's shadow 'refuels' before continuing its attack. His attempt to placate it indicates that he has not yet integrated the tendencies/elements that it entails. As a result, he succumbs to its power at this level of conscious awareness, viz. he finds it difficult to separate himself from the other/others.

Table 12 (*cont.*)

	Surface-Structure Component	Interpretation as a Projection of Achior's Psyche
		• Achior's shadow increasingly behaves out of its negative Self empowerment. As this happens, its desire to control/destroy that which resists it in favour of the negative Self also increases. • The shadow becomes the dominant archetype and seeks to overtake Achior's conscious personality. • Holofernes' demand that all should worship Nebuchadnezzar reflects the rising shadow's inflation as well as the insecurity that it entails.
	B. Israel hears and is "greatly terrified"; Joachim orders war preparations (4:1–15)	
4:1–5	• Having heard of Holofernes' deeds, the Judaeans are terrified—particularly for the temple in Jerusalem as they had just come up from exile, reconstituted themselves in Judaea, and rededicated the temple, its vessels, and its altar after it had been profaned. They alert the surrounding towns, take charge of the high mountains, fortify the cities in them, and store up provisions for war. • The general Judaean populace represents the third stage of conscious awareness. • Jerusalem represents the innermost layer of central consciousness. • The temple represents the highest achievement/s of the conscious psyche and the central locus of ego-Self communication.	• Achior finally realises that the rising unconscious is not to be ignored or placated, but rather to be withstood. He therefore braces himself and prepares for the next phase of attack. Moreover, seeing that Achior is about to be attacked on a moral/ethical level—the third stage of conscious awareness—we may say that the fortification of the high cities in the text symbolises the moral and ethical fortification of his consciousness (see the panels below). • Having previously experienced the alienating and destructive force of the unconscious shadow on a large scale (the exile), and 'rebuilt' his psyche, Achior fears that this attack will allow the shadow finally to take over the innermost layer of his central ego-consciousness and destroy his highest conscious achievement/s and that which symbolises his connection to the Self (the temple).

4:6–7	• Joachim, the Jerusalemite high priest, writes to the villages near the mountain passes. He urges them to guard these passages as they are the entry points to Judaea and it would be easy to defend them against intruders owing to their extreme narrowness. • Joachim is interpreted as the highest element of the innermost layer of central consciousness (Jerusalem), which is situated at the fourth stage of conscious awareness.	• The highest (spiritual) elements in the innermost layer of Achior's central consciousness are activated, and so Achior begins fortifying the entry points (the weak points). These seem to be related to the moral/ethical dilemma represented by the Judaeans and the realisation of social reality/individual consciousness as symbolised by Joachim. I.e., the entry points are defined morally, ethically, and in terms of the development of individual consciousness. • The shadow is on the verge of attacking the most important stage in Achior's individuation, viz. stage 4. It aims to abort the individuation process at this stage and return Achior's consciousness to its grasp.
4:8–12	• The people obey Joachim and the *gerousiva*. Every living being—including the cattle and servants—humbles itself before YHWH in sackcloth, and they plead for deliverance. • The Judaean citizens represent the highest strata of third-stage consciousness, while the strangers, hirelings, and bought slaves represent the lowest strata. The animals, that represent the consciously integrated instinctual forces (they are part of the third stage), are referred to in between these two strata (4:10), indicating that instincts "are important to and hence tightly in the grip of consciousness". This, in turn, shows that the Judaeans may be/are cognisant of the instinctual nature of the unconscious attack and that they are willing to employ everything at their disposal in their intense attempt to elicit help from the Self [God] through a very deep self-humbling that extends to their very instincts, sacrifice, and prayer.	• Achior is now consciously aware of the instinctual nature of the shadow's attack and, having summoned all the strata of his third-stage consciousness, attempts to connect to the Self through a self-humbling that touches his very instinctual nature, self-sacrifice (the altar), and prayer. This may be seen as a type of *ekkenosis*—an emptying-out of the self and selfish constraints—for the greater good of his psyche and his people. It also intimates a break in his positive inflation. • Having realised the importance of the instinctual forces within his consciousness, Achior keeps a tight grip on them in the face of the attack. This is wise; acting out of the instinctual forces alone, irrespective of how conscious he may be of them, could well jeopardise his psyche's chances of overcoming the shadow—we all know that instincts often let us down in such tight situations if we do not temper them with sober rationality.

Table 12 (*cont.*)

	Surface-Structure Component	Interpretation as a Projection of Achior's Psyche
4:13a–b	• YHWH hears the nation's prayers and looks upon its afflictions. • YHWH is interpreted as the Self. Connections with Exodus indicate that salvation is imminent: when YHWH has heard and seen, YHWH has answered and delivered. • This portion constitutes privileged information that the reader/hearer is aware of but the characters in the story are not. • Furthermore, even though the Self has heard and seen, it chooses not to communicate this information to anyone.	• The highest and all-controlling element of Achior's psyche, the Self, becomes actively involved in the dilemma that Achior is facing. • Having heard and seen, the Self has already answered, despite the fact that Achior seems unaware of this. • The fact that the Self does not communicate with Achior (and that he is unaware of the Self's answer to his pleas) seems to indicate that all is not well in his ego-Self communication.
4:13c	• The nation continues fasting before YHWH's sanctuary in Jerusalem.	• Achior continues to practice *ekkenosis* in order to connect with the Self.
4:14–15	• Having their loins girt in sackcloth, Joachim and the Jerusalemite priests continue to offer "the continual burnt offerings and the vows and freewill offerings of the people" (4:14). This indicates that the possibility for ego-Self communication still exists. They put ashes on their mitres and pray to YHWH. • Loins represent the (sexual-)instinctual aspect of mankind, and the head represents mankind's intellect.	• Achior continues his attempt to establish communication with the Self at the highest level of his central consciousness. As he does so, he submits both his instincts and his intellect to the Self by means of traditional forms of *ekkenosis*. • The dream thus intimates that contact between the ego and the Self can (and will) be re-established.
	C. Holofernes talks with Achior; Achior is expelled from the Assyrian camp (5:1–6:11)	
5:1–4	• Terribly angered by the Judaeans' resistance, Holofernes enquires of his allies that are geographically closest to the Judaeans who they are, what their military strength is, who their leaders are, and why their resistance is greater than that of the other nations.	• Achior's shadow is angered by his conscious resistance and attempts to gauge the strength of his consciousness/conscious libido by turning to previously conscious shadow elements that have been subsumed into the unconscious. This aspect illustrates the potential and very real danger that previously

	• Holofernes' non-Assyrian advisors "represent conscious contents that have been subsumed by . . . the shadow/power archetype . . . Having fallen from consciousness, Holofernes' foreign advisors pose a threat to the Judaeans, who are still rooted in consciousness, and hence to the 'dreamer's' conscious psyche overall".	conscious contents hold for the conscious psyche. In this case, they threaten Achior's conscious-unconscious libido balance because they have been 'forgotten' or repressed at some point and have not been subsequently reintegrated. In Jungian terms, they have lost conscious libido and, as a result of their nonintegration, they have transferred their psychic libido to the unconscious where it remains to further the shadow's onslaught against consciousness.
5:5–21	• Achior, an Ammonite, responds willingly with a Deuteronomistically based narration of Israel's history on the basis of which he advises Holofernes first to ascertain the Judaeans' guilt or purity before YHWH so that he can avoid unnecessary loss of life: if the Judaeans have not sinned before YHWH, Holofernes should rather leave them alone as their God would vindicate them. • The speech reminds the Jewish audience of their heritage in divine-human interaction, apart from warning to Holofernes. • Apart from its Deuteronomistic perspective, Achior's speech contains a number of interesting factors: a) The Judaeans are said to have destroyed the Esebonites by their strength, ousted the inhabitants of Canaan, and taken the land (5:15–16). This is the only place in *Judith* where strength is accorded the Judaeans per se. Throughout the book, there is a strong visible contrast between those who trust in their own strength, such as Nebuchadnezzar-Holofernes and their forces, and the Jews whose strength lies in YHWH. These verses are flanked on either side by statements regarding YHWH's deliverance, etc. (5:10–14, 17–18).	• Achior's response to Holofernes indicates a contradictory identification with the 'Assyrians' *and* the Judeans/Bethulians. This means that the split in loyalties and identity, the self-alienation evinced at the outset of the book, has resurfaced once again. This is undoubtedly caused by the shadow's closeness to the centre of ego-consciousness. • The dream attempts to encourage Achior by reminding him of his spiritual *cum* psychological heritage vis-à-vis his ego's relation to the Self. It also admonishes him not to act outside of this spiritual-psychological heritage as this would jeopardise his ego-Self communication and the help that the Self can provide in the current circumstances. • Achior's espousal of Deuteronomistic lore: – Indicates that his psyche is nudging him to greater connection with the Self in the current situation so as to focus his thoughts on a particular conscious attitude and free himself from the shadow's clutches. – Illustrates the conflict within him: he identifies with traditional Israelite philosophy and the philosophy/ideology underlying the cause of the Assyrian enemy.

Table 12 (*cont.*)

Surface-Structure Component	Interpretation as a Projection of Achior's Psyche
b) Achior emphasises that the Jews have returned to their God, gathered together from the places that they were scattered (exiled), taken possession of Jerusalem where their sanctuary is, and dwell in the hill country which had been desolate. • Point b) is essentially a repetition of the narratorial comment in *Judith* 4:1, so that it 'confirms' the position of the Judaeans as described there. • The information in *Judith* 4:1 is framed by the Jews' return to their God and their dwelling in the hill country of the land. This underscores their dependence on YHWH. There is also a slight modification regarding the narrator's information about the sanctuary; it is said that they have taken possession of *their*—not YHWH's—sanctuary in Jerusalem. • Achior is interpreted as an erstwhile shadow content that has been subsumed into the unconscious but has nevertheless retained sufficient autonomy/libido to respond to Holofernes of his own free will. • The fact that Achior is able to stand out amongst his group of peers but still cling to the Deuteronomistic philosophy of retribution shows that he has reached a stage of consciousness in his personal capacity in which the 'ego' has separated itself from both the unconscious mass and its peers (stage 2) but has not quite distinguished itself from ancient norms and patterns of thought. In other words, it is not quite established at the third stage of conscious awareness, viz., the differentiation of his own moral properties.	– Shows that he as a person has not yet become established at the third stage of conscious awareness, the differentiation of moral/ethical properties. • The dream reminds Achior that he indeed has the strength to fight the shadow, and cautions that this strength is to be found in YHWH/the Self alone. It also reaffirms his ability to deal successfully with the shadow (Canaanites) by pointing back to his psychological heritage of doing so. • The dream further reminds Achior that: – His connection with YHWH/the Self is established and intact—despite the fact that something seems to have gone awry with it. – His conscious psyche and his identity are no longer 'scattered'/fragmented. He is still in possession of the centre of his ego-consciousness where his connection to the Self is situated. – He has reclaimed the psychological ground lost in previous sorties with the shadow/Shadow. This is at once an encouragement that he is 'OK' and has the power to succeed—in YHWH—against the shadow, as well as an admonishment not to give up hard-won conscious territory by giving in to the shadow's ploys. Perhaps this is reflected in the Deuteronomistic principle that he sets before Holofernes (5:21). • Seeing that Achior the psychological construct is the Jewish shadow and that it is this shadow that reminds Achior the effective protagonist of his psychological and spiritual heritage, we may deduce that Achior had relegated such mem-

ories of ego-Self communication to the background of his soul/psyche and that they are now a part of the positive personal shadow elements that can be called to the fore to assist him in the current situation.

- That the dream-character Achior represents an erstwhile conscious shadow element that has now been repressed to the realms of the unconscious, further points to the self-alienation that Achior the effective protagonist experiences. Not only is Achior a shadow of himself, as it were, but the unconscious also chooses to represent the effective protagonist in the guise of an impure Jewish relative/shadow, viz. an Ammonite, while the main ego-consciousness is actually Jewish (note the convergence between the fates of Achior and the Judaeans in the panels below).
- Furthermore, Achior's heightened libido indicates his desire to escape the clutches of the unconscious shadow. It also indicates that there is hope: if his consciousness could just give this erstwhile conscious shadow content a libido boost, then it will more than likely escape the clutches of the unconscious shadow. This means that the re-integration of this content at the conscious level that is about to be attacked is more than a mere possibility.
- The re-integration of this content/group of contents holds out the distinct hope that it will lead to an integration of other elements of the unconscious shadow attack and so halt its destructive forays against Achior's consciousness.

Table 12 (*cont.*)

	Surface-Structure Component	Interpretation as a Projection of Achior's Psyche
5:22–24	• Angered, the crowd surrounding Holofernes' tent call for Achior's death. They advise Holofernes to go up against the Judaeans without fear on the grounds of the latter's supposed militarily weakness. • The foreign advisors seem to have contracted Holofernes' inflation: they are far too confident of the (assumed) weakness of the Judaeans and their power. Without saying so, they regard the Judaeans as 'one man' that may easily be 'devoured'.	• This component once again illustrates the danger inherent to suppressing conscious contents. In this case, they fuel the shadow's drive to destroy/completely devour ego-consciousness as symbolised here by the effective protagonist, Achior. • The dream reflects the weakness inherent to inflation yet again. Whereas this weakness previously manifested itself as a form of insecurity (see column 3 relating to 2:28–3:10, above), it now manifests itself as overconfidence that has the potential to jeopardise the shadow's offensive. This may serve as an encouragement to Achior in that the dream may be indicating that the shadow will soon jeopardise its own operations.
6:1–10	• Incensed by Achior's words, Holofernes declares Nebuchadnezzar to be 'god' alone and 'prophesies' the victory of the Assyrian forces. He has Achior cast out to the foothills of Bethuliah (6:10), there to await the same disastrous fate that he (Holofernes) was sure to inflict on the Judaeans. • Bethuliah represents the outermost level of central consciousness that functions at the fourth stage of conscious awareness.	• Achior's shadow is completely confident of its victory over consciousness. • Simultaneously, something has given Achior the shadow content a libido boost that will free him from the unconscious shadow's realms. Achior's eviction from Holofernes' camp represents the first step in his rise to higher consciousness and so his first step to freedom from the unconscious as a shadow element. • The dream indicates that there is hope: something will happen to release Achior's consciousness from the grip of the unconscious shadow and lift him up to the fourth stage of consciousness, viz. the realisation of reality and individual identity.

6:11	• Holofernes' servants obediently take Achior out of the camp, through the plain, and to the foothills of Bethuliah. • They signify contents that occupy the lowest ranks of the psyche—the base instincts of mankind. Despite coming to the very boundary of higher consciousness, they do not traverse it, indicating that their libido infusion is temporary and controlled by the (shadow) archetype.	• Their actions represent the second, third, and fourth steps in Achior's rise to higher consciousness as a person, and his freedom from the unconscious as a psychological content. The conclusion of the fourth step symbolises the completeness of these processes. • The above shows that a libido burst has taken place that has withdrawn psychological energy from the unconscious and drawn it up to consciousness where it is most needed.

C'. Achior is received into Bethuliah; he talks with the people of Israel (6:12–21)

6:12–13	• The Bethulians sling stones at Holofernes' servants. The latter do not retaliate, demonstrating that they are weak elements of the unconscious that have been accorded no more libido than that which is necessary to perform *a* specific task only and that they have no psychic energy with which to actively engage with consciousness. They escape, leaving Achior bound at the bottom of the hill. • The Bethulians untie Achior and take him to their city elders. Achior relates all of Holofernes' plans, whereupon the people cry out to YHWH for deliverance. After they comfort Achior, Ozias invites him to a banquet where they pray all through the night. The Bethulians receive Achior, a (traditionally hated) Ammonite, with open arms—despite the Torah injunction preventing them from doing so. Their acceptance is rooted in their common ancestry and their common Deuteronomistic perception of the situation.	• Achior's stage 4 consciousness makes its first active resistance felt against the unconscious. • Achior has reached the threshold of a far higher consciousness as both a person and as a positive shadow content (the fourth) than that from which he originally came (the second). Even so, he has not yet been fully established/integrated there. • Achior's easy acceptance by the Bethulians shows that his conscious psyche recognises the validity and necessity of integrating this shadow element despite its (Deuteronomistic) predisposition of not doing so. This demonstrates Achior's greater maturity at this level. • The Bethulians' actions represent seven steps of greater conscious integration. As seven is not a complete multiple of four, it may be said that Achior has not become fully established at the fourth stage of consciousness as a person or

Table 12 (*cont.*)

	Surface-Structure Component	Interpretation as a Projection of Achior's
	• The Bethulians represent the fourth stage of conscious awareness. • Ozias and the elders symbolise the highest contents of consciousness at the outermost level of central consciousness.	a psychological content. Nevertheless, the fact that he has been integrated to the degree that he has shows his greater conscious differentiation as a person (the Bethulians' conscious differentiation increases because they have integrated him) and his accession to higher consciousness as a content.
B'. Holofernes orders war preparations; Israel sees and is "greatly terrified" (7:1–5)		
7:1–3	• The next day, Holofernes commands his armies to break camp and move against Bethuliah, which they do. The great multitude of men—more than 180,000—cover the length and breadth of the landscape all around Bethuliah.	• This aspect signifies the shadow's closing in on the outermost level of Achior's central consciousness, viz. Bethuliah (stage 4). • It also depicts the way that the unconscious can engulf consciousness in fear, leaving it with little or no libido to respond/fend for itself. • The magnitude and intensity of the attack is captured in he vast numbers of Holofernes' army.
7:4–5	• The Bethulians are greatly terrified of this numberless mass. Declaring that "neither the high mountains nor the valleys nor the hills will bear their weight" (7:4), they take up their weapons, light fires on the towers of Bethuliah, and stay up watching all night. • The high mountains, valleys, and hills signify various conscious strata at the fourth level of consciousness. • Fires represent the light of consciousness or the light of the Self. • The night represents the prime activity time of the unconscious.	• Achior's consternation increases along with his fear that his consciousness will never be able to survive the force of the unconscious shadow attack. This decreases his psychological libido/strength to deal with the situation. • Achior's conscious awareness of social reality and individual identity (stage 4) is destabilising, i.e., he is starting to lose his grip on social reality and his individual identity is severely challenged. • Achior finds himself in a very dangerous position: his shadow is about to take over his central consciousness or, at least, the outermost levels thereof, and his central consciousness is

		on the verge of bowing down to the shadow because of his negative attitude. Nevertheless, all is not lost. Central consciousness has the 'presence of mind' to light the fire of consciousness/of the Self at the prime time of unconscious activity against it. • The last point (above) also signifies Achior's attempt to bring the presence of YHWH/the Self into the forefront of the attack (as the ark of the covenant was carried before the Israelites in battles of old) in order to dispel the attack and ensure the victory of consciousness over the unconscious.

A'. The campaign against Bethuliah; the people want to surrender (7:6–32)

7:6–7	• Holofernes brings out his horsemen in full view of the Bethulians, reconnoitres the approaches to the city, sets garrisons over the water sources around Bethuliah, and returns to his (main) army. • Horses signify the instinctual forces, traditionally symbolising male sexuality in particular. • The approaches to the city represent the weak or entry points into the fourth stage of consciousness. • The water sources symbolise that which nourishes general consciousness (they are not *in* Bethuliah or directly responsible for its survival).	• The shadow tests the entry points into the fourth stage of Achior's conscious awareness by displaying the forces underlying the (male) sexual instincts. This suggests that unintegrated sexual instincts may be the weak or entry points into Achior's psyche at this stage. • The shadow takes charge of that which feeds Achior's general consciousness and impedes access to this life-giving force. • The shadow returns to those elements constellated most closely around it—its source of libido and nourishment—and waits for an opportune moment to strike.
7:8–15	• The foreign chiefs advise Holofernes to seize the spring at the foothill of Bethuliah in order to bring about a famine that will overthrow them. • These rulers represent previously conscious shadow elements that have been repressed and so re-incorporated into the unconscious realms.	• The unconscious psyche attempts to block that which is directly responsible for the nourishment/libido/strength of the outermost levels of Achior's central consciousness (stage 4). It withdraws libido from his concept of social reality and individual identity with the aim of causing his consciousness to capitulate to the will of the unconscious shadow.

Table 12 (*cont.*)

	Surface-Structure Component	Interpretation as a Projection of Achior's Psyche
	• The fountain of Bethuliah symbolises that which nourishes the central consciousness itself. Seeing that this fountain was not seized in the preceding exercise (7:6–7) we may safely surmise that it was hidden from Holofernes' view and/or that of his horsemen.	• Yet again, this component illustrates the danger of repressing conscious contents. They are far too 'knowledgeable' of the strengths and weaknesses of the consciousness from which they are 'banished'.
7:16–18	• Holofernes commands that this course of action is followed. The Assyrian forces cover "the whole face of the land" (7:18), forming a vast encampment with their tents and supplies.	• The shadow attack encroaches more and more upon the outermost level of Achior's conscious awareness. It seizes that which nourishes the outer levels of central consciousness and menacingly covers every sector of psychological 'space' surrounding it.
7:19-22	• The Bethulians quail at the sight of the Assyrian armies, knowing that they now have no way of escape. They cry out to YHWH in desperation for deliverance. After thirty-four days, their cisterns begin to run dry. Their children, women, and young men faint for thirst in the streets and at the city gates. They are without strength and in complete desperation.	• Achior turns to YHWH/the Self in fear and desperation as the outermost layer of his consciousness is completely ensnared by his unconscious shadow elements. Nevertheless, 'nothing' seems to happen. Moreover, his conscious libido is drying up at this level and he no longer has the strength to deal with the attack. As a result, he falls into a state of complete fear and desperation. This describes a state in which a great amount of libido has been diverted from his conscious psyche and transferred to the shadow that now has greater power over his consciousness than before.
7:23–28	• The Bethulians' fear of death causes them to lose faith in themselves and YHWH. They believe that God is not going	• The loss of conscious libido causes Achior to see himself in a very negative light as he adopts the negative aspect of

	to help them and that He is punishing them for their sins and those of their fathers. As a result, they berate Ozias and the elders for not having sued for peace with the Assyrians and demand that they hand the entire city over to Holofernes for plunder so that they may become his slaves and continue living.	Deuteronomistic philosophy. He is unsure of his conscious power and connection with the Self as a result, and a negative inflation takes hold of him. • He fears that his consciousness does not have the strength to fight against the shadow and believes that the Self has turned against him. Despairing of any assistance from the Self, Achior is prepared to give up and let his consciousness be assimilated by the shadow in an ironic attempt to survive.
7:29-32	• Ozias assures the Bethulians that YHWH would not abandon them and persuades them to give God another five days to act before he does as they desire. The men return to their stations and the women and children to their homes in great depression. • This component indicates clearly the people's dire need for a saviour at this point.	• Despite loss of faith, Achior is somehow recharged momentarily and believes in YHWH's benevolence once again. Nevertheless, his highly ambivalent attitude towards the Self and the current crisis cause him to be very cautious in his hope (cf. the five-day ultimatum) and bring him to a state of great depression/loss of conscious libido. • Achior's consciousness all but surrenders its libido and itself to the unconscious. The dream forespells that, should this happen, it would undoubtedly spell complete disaster in that Achior would now function completely out of his positive shadow inflation. He would lose conscious differentiation all the more until he becomes completely one with the unconscious/lets his consciousness be completely subsumed by the unconscious shadow. He would then effectively *become* his shadow. The highest elements at Achior's outermost level of central consciousness therefore call his consciousness back to faith in the Self. They broker peace between the lower elements of this conscious level and the Self—albeit for five days only. In this way, they thwart the shadow's attempt. • The dream indicates that Achior's consciousness is in dire need of a 'saviour' at this point who will have a fresh approach to the situation and secure his conscious survival.

Table 13. The Correspondence between Achior's Psyche and the Surfce-Structure Components/Projections in *Judith* 8–16.

***Judith* 8–16**

Aa. Introduction to Judith (8:1–8)

	Surface-Structure Component	Interpretation as a Projection of Achior's Psyche
8:1	• Judith hears of what has happened. There is a certain separatedness about her that points to her heightened level of consciousness (stage 5). • Her lineage is traced to the very founder of Israel and links her to Israel's major institutional and historical traditions. Her sixteen-tier genealogy indicates that she has reached 'perfection' at her level of individuation. She is a person/content with deep roots in the unconscious memories of the Jewish people. • Judith is interpreted both as the anima and the ego. She is also clearly the anticipated saviour.	• This component represents Achior's anima and the type of ego(-personality)/person that the dream is urging Achior to develop/become in order to succeed in his battle against the shadow. • Achior's anima is deeply rooted in his personal unconscious psyche and the collective unconscious psyche of his people, possibly indicating that she is deeply buried within the unconscious. Consequently, the dream may be encouraging Achior to let his anima emerge from the unconscious at this time. Alternatively, the dream may be showing him that he is well rooted and should therefore not fear being derailed by the unconscious. Naturally, both alternatives may be held simultaneously according to the text's multivalency. • The full depth of Achior's positive anima is evinced in Judith's genealogy: she is that which can lead him to a closer connection with the Self (Merari, Elijah), give him keen judgment/discernment (Gideon) in the current war situation, and deliver him from the bondage that he is in (Joseph).
8:2–3	• Judith's husband, Manasses, had died on his bed from heatstroke while overseeing sheave-binding and had been buried with his fathers. He gradually succumbed to inflation, lost conscious libido, and was consequently unable to withstand a small encounter with the unconscious that completely engulfed him.	• Manasses represents Achior's current strength of ego-consciousness and inflation. • The dream warns that Achior's ego-consciousness is weak and could easily be toppled by even the smallest unconscious attack. It intimates that he should strengthen his conscious psyche and counter his inflation in order to avoid losing

	• His consciousness is far weaker than Judith's as he depends on her at both a textual and an ancestral-psychological level. • Furthermore, his negative association with the Jonah story and the fact that he died a largely unfruitful person despite his wealth, indicates that his is an individuation drama that was never fulfilled. As such, he is a foil to both Judith and Achior whose individuation dramas were completed.	more conscious libido and functioning completely out of his unconscious shadow inflation. • The dream further warns that his current inflation could lead to rebellion against the Self and indicates that a lack of repentance in this respect would lead to his ego-Self communication being severed. It also intimates that, should this occur, he would be of no use to God/the Self any longer; his individuation cycle will be aborted; he will die at this level of conscious awareness and lose all the psychic riches that he has gained so far at the fourth stage of conscious awareness.
8:4–8	• Judith dwelt in a tent above her house, constantly praying since her husband's death. She wore sackcloth and widow's garments and followed an extensive fasting programme. She was also extremely beautiful, rich, wise, and blameless. • Judith's lives in continual ego-sacrifice as a person which facilitates her superlative communication with the Self and psychic wholeness. • Her intense integrity is the result of integrating unconscious contents and resolving of opposites, which also bears testimony to her high level of individuation.	• This aspect illustrates the anima's deep connection to the Self and her ability to lead Achior closer to the Self in the current situation. It also points to her integrative potential, i.e., that she can assist Achior to integrate opposites at a very high level in his conscious psyche/conscious awareness. • The dream emphasises Achior's need for psychic integration and the kind of *ekkenosis* that Judith models. I.e., part of the dream's solution for the current situation is that Achior should practice continual *ekkenosis* in his attempt to connect with the Self and that he should make every effort to achieve the psychic integration of opposites—as Judith has. • The dream promises that, should he be able to integrate opposites and follow Judith's model of continual sacrifice to the Self, he too will achieve the high level of individuation that she exemplifies.

Table 13 (*cont.*)

	Surface-Structure Component	Interpretation as a Projection of Achior's Psyche
	Bb. Judith plans to save Israel (8:9–10:9a)	
8:9-27	• Having heard of the people's "evil words" against Ozias and the five-day ultimatum that he had proposed, Judith sends her ἅβρα to bring the city's male leadership to her tent. They come immediately, indicating her higher level of authority and individuation. She replaces Ozias as the highest conscious factor at stage 4 as well as the Bethulian leadership from now on. • Judith addresses the Bethulian leadership, rectifying their concept of God (He is sovereign, impervious to manipulation; He is testing not abandoning them) and themselves (they are free from idolatry and sanctified by God). She encourages them to continue trusting God and alerts them to the broader ramifications of their defeat. • She is the only character who understands the nature of God and who is able to provide a different interpretation of His role in the current situation. She is also the only one who is able to look beyond Bethuliah's immediate need—surviving the thirst (cf. 7:22, 27; and 8:28–31)—to the fate of her fellow Judaeans and the temple. Her theology of divine testing frees both the Bethulians and God from the (human) constraints that the rigid application of Deuteronomistic principles impose upon them.	• The dream continues to indicate what Achior needs to become in order to succeed, viz. a person of authority and action who tackles issues head on. • Achior's feminine spirit/anima arises and draws his fearful, masculine aspects to herself. She becomes the highest form of authority in Achior's psyche. The dream could thereby be indicating that Achior needs to allow his anima or feminine side to lead his psyche from this point forwards. • Achior's anima attempts to correct his understanding of himself and the Self. She tries to divert his attention from himself and focus it onto the community from which he comes and his worship of/communion with the Self (cf. the mention of the temple). She also corrects Achior's understanding of himself, restoring a positive self-appraisal. • The anima further attempts to redirect Achior's attention from his own private battle with the unconscious to the suffering experienced by the heroes of his people's conscious existence. This is no doubt meant to encourage him to persevere and reap the rewards that they had reaped. She also encourages continued dependence upon the Self. • All the above represent the anima's attempt to boost Achior's conscious libido so that he can see the Self, himself, and the unconscious attack from the right perspective and

	• The above show that Judith has reached the most advanced stage of individuation, where one is freed from the collective unconscious—from the demands, opinions, etc. of one's 'herd' or group—and so empowered effectively to serve one's community. It bears clear testimony to her twofold connectedness to the Self and the community from which she comes.	overcome the shadow before it takes over his consciousness psyche. • The dream shows that Achior's dominant conscious mode of interpreting reality (the Deuteronomistic one), the Self, and his relation to these entities is incorrect and requires drastic revision. It also shows that Achior needs to see himself in a positive light and become far more community-orientated so as to overcome the shadow. It encourages Achior to trust the Self and endure the attack so as to overcome it. It effectively tells him that, when he does this, he will be as one of the heroes of his faith and reap the blessed rewards that they did. • The dream further warns Achior that, while this attack may be a personal one, his failure to overcome it and integrate the shadow will have dire consequences for his people and his relationship with the Self.
8:28–31	• Ozias confirms Judith's well-known wisdom and the correctness of what she has said. He avers that the people's thirst caused the leadership to offer the five day ultimatum and to take an oath upon it. Since this is an oath that they will not break, Ozias requests Judith to pray for rain on their behalf so that they can overcome the famine. • The male leadership represent the masculine aspects of Achior's psyche, viz. his (dominant) masculine side.	• The masculine elements of Achior's psyche resist the anima. Even though they are of the opinion that Achior's feminine side is correct and wise in her statements, they would prefer to see her wisdom restricted merely to her connection with the Self (prayer). • The masculine side of Achior's psyche will not give way to the wisdom of his feminine side at this stage. It is bent on continuing with its chosen course of action despite acknowledging the wisdom, correctness and godliness of his feminine side. Clearly, there is no conscious integration between Achior's male and female side at this stage.

Table 13 (*cont.*)

	Surface-Structure Component	Interpretation as a Projection of Achior's Psyche
8:32–36	• Judith declares that she will go down to the Assyrian camp with her stewardess to effect a secret plan by which God would deliver Israel. The leaders bid her well and return to their wards. • Judith is totally other to every character encountered so far. She is the only independent female actant in the book. • Her plan verifies that she has broken out of collective thinking, gendered expectations, and collective ideals. It also indicates that she has attained sufficient libido to break free from the collective unconscious of her people as a psychological content. This libido is sufficiently flexible to enable her to traverse the boundaries between the psychic realms. • Her wisdom shows that she has a high form of individuation and close ties with the Self.	• Judith's otherness is commensurate with that of the anima—from a male point of view. The secrecy of her plan shows that the anima is not yet consciously integrated. • Achior's anima is activated against the instinctual Shadow attack, and Achior's masculine side reluctantly gives her control of the counter-offensive. • The dream strongly encourages Achior to allow his anima to rule over the unconscious shadow's defeat. It also encourages him to adopt Judith's attitude of faith in the Self and himself for the resolution of the current crisis. It advocates that he should take responsibility for his 'fate' and actively engage/face his shadow. To do this, he needs to break out of "collective thinking, gendered expectations, and collective ideals." In other words, he should cease functioning according to the first stage of conscious awareness as affects his outlook on life and break free from his dominant interpretative philosophy, viz. the Deuteronomistic one. • Given the anima's psychological depth within Achior's psyche and the secrecy of her plan, we may further surmise that the dream is encouraging Achior not only to release the anima from the deep resources of his personal unconscious psyche, but also to look deep within himself for the resolution of the current crisis.

9:1–14	• Once the elders leave, Judith begins to pray. She falls on her face, puts ashes on her head, and dons sackcloth. By analogy, she places her entire being under the charge of the Self and all her 'weaponry' at its disposal. Her humility demonstrates a high level of individuation and psychological integration. • Judith's prayer draws a close analogy between the current situation and the rape of Dinah, i.e., between herself and Simeon and between Dinah and the temple. Simeon's vengeance is sanctified, which permits her to request for the same deceptive power by which she may defeat Holofernes. Her request is predicated upon the use of verbal and sexual deceit for its success, making them weapons of choice when dealing with rising unconscious shadow contents. Moreover, the use of this weaponry is directly attributed to God/the Self in that Judith sees Simeon's deceitful murder of the Shechemites as an action foreordained by God. The fact that her prayer offering coincides with the evening incense offering in Jerusalem signifies that God has indeed heard her prayer—inclusive of His association with verbal and sexual deception—and that He will grant her request. • The Shechem-Dinah analogy also indicates that Judith intends to plunder Holofernes' goods and nullify his power/the fear with which he holds her people captive. This intimates that Judith's action will break the power of the unconscious instinctual forces in the people's psyche. • Judith's prayer transforms her from a wise woman into a vengeful, bloodthirsty man like Simeon. It is the first step in	• Now that Achior's masculine elements are removed from the resolution of the problem, his anima is freed to connect his consciousness with the self. • Achior is encouraged humbly to submit all his plans and 'weaponry' to the Self and so put an end to the destructive force of his positive inflation. The dream promises that humility will re-establish his communication with the Self and allow the Self to assist him in salvaging his conscious psyche. • Judith's identification with Simeon, and her identification of the temple/connection with the Self with Dinah shows that some psychic integration is beginning to take place within Achior's conscious psyche. • The deceptive and sexual element of the counterattack confirms, once again, the instinctually deceptive and almost sexual nature of the unconscious attack. The dream therefore advocates that Achior should 'deceive' the unconscious by fighting fire with fire—i.e., that he should fight the shadow not with logic or reasoning, but with his own conscious instinctuality, while pretending to give in to its advances. (Exactly how this should be done is illustrated in the panels below). This strategy bodes well for Achior's deliverance from the shadow, in that the dream indicates that it carries the favour of the Self. • The dream indicates that, should Achior be able to prevail against the unconscious shadow, he will break the power of the unconscious shadow *cum* instinctual forces over his own conscious psyche and so that of his people too.

Table 13 (*cont.*)

	Surface-Structure Component	Interpretation as a Projection of Achior's Psyche
	the actualisation of a transformation process by which she becomes an active agent of the conscious psyche and sees to the conscious integration of shadow elements.	• Judith's transformation confirms that the first step in Achior's psychic integration of opposites has taken place and that he is well on his way to defeating the shadow attack and consciously integrating the shadow elements and the *mana* with which they are imbued. It also reaffirms that Achior needs to adopt a new, aggressive conscious attitude towards the shadow attack, and shows that allowing his anima to lead the counter offensive and integrating his masculine and feminine aspects neither precludes this transformation nor compromises Achior's masculine side in any way. Rather, it boosts its abilities or makes it stronger.
10:1–9a	• Having concluded her prayer, Judith calls her ἅβρα and descends to her house. She engages in an intense beautification process aimed at deceiving "the eyes of all men who might see her" 10:4). This process transforms her into a beautiful, operative seductress, and a 'transpsychic' content that is able to traverse the threshold conscious and enter the unconscious realm. • Judith packs a basket of kosher food and gives it to her ἅβρα. They set off to the city gate where Ozias and the elders are waiting. The men are completely astounded by Judith and pronounce a blessing upon all her endeavours to the glory of Israel. The men immediately obey her command to open the gate—a clear indication that her beauty-sexuality stratagem will work. • Judith's descent from her prayer tent symbolises the first phase of her descent from highest consciousness just as her	• Judith's beautification is symbolic of the anima's greater integration into Achior's consciousness, and so of his transformation through his feminine side. Judith's descent to her house then illustrates that the first step of this process has taken place—in as far as the progression of the dream is concerned. • The greater integration of the anima is further illustrated by the male leadership's reaction towards Judith: they recognise the transformation and bless her endeavours for the greater good of the nation (greater consciousness). This may indicate that the anima has succeeded in making Achior more community orientated. • The dream indicates that it is vital for Achior to take the first step in integrating his anima and effecting the necessary self-transformation. It intimates that such a self-transformation should not be limited to inward change, but should be

beautification externalises the internal transformation effected through her prayer. Her descent to the city gate then extends her physical transformation to the geographic and psychic arena. It also symbolises the completion of the second phase in her transformation.

• The ἅβρα represents Judith's consciously integrated shadow contents, which is why she follows her so closely throughout section II.

allowed to affect all his ways. The dream further intimates that transformation alone is insufficient. If the unconscious is to be stopped, then Achior must make provision to replenish his conscious strength from his own conscious resources while dealing with the shadow. In other words, he should not try to draw any psychic libido from the unconscious while dealing with it but continue to draw libido from his own consciousness. As food is also symbolic of the instinctual forces, the dream suggests that Achior will require the conscious reinforcement of his instinctual nature so that he is not waylaid by the instinctual forces that the shadow may deploy against him.

• Judith's ἅβρα is symbolic of the kind of attitude that Achior should adopt towards the anima, viz. he should follow her lead closely as she assists him to battle the shadow. This will also assist him to successfully complete the current 'leg' of his individuation cycle.

• Judith's effect on the Bethulian men intimates that Achior's mission against the unconscious shadow will be successful.

• Her descent to the gate symbolises the second step of Achior's anima integration.

Cc. Judith and her maid leave Bethuliah (10:9b–10)

10:9b-10 • The young men open the city gates for Judith and her ἅβρα. They represent the instinctual/sexual forces of the conscious realm, which makes it fitting that *they* should open the gates for Judith the sexual warrior.

• The men watch the two women go down the mountain alone, signifying their weakness as people and psychological

• The men's inertia shows the superiority of the anima vis-à-vis the masculine elements of Achior's consciousness. It also clearly indicates that the only way to wage this battle is through the anima. As the complete other—from a masculine point of view—the anima is ideally suited to fight the shadow-other.

Table 13 (*cont.*)

	Surface-Structure Component	Interpretation as a Projection of Achior's Psyche
	contents, and characterising them as Judith's foils. They represent an aspect of Judaean society that has reached the fourth stage of consciousness but lacks the libido to challenge the unconscious attack and move on to stage 5. • Judith's descent to the enemy camp clinches her functional transformation from a conscious content into an unconscious one.	• The anima traverses the liminal space between the outer layer of Achior's central consciousness and the current locus of the unconscious attack. As the anima prepares to do battle, the male (sexual) instincts (the young men and other men of Bethuliah; see the panels below) are held completely at bay, corroborating that this is the anima's battle and hers alone.
	D. Judith overcomes Holofernes (10:11–13:10a)	
10:11–17	• Judith and her ἅβρα head straight into the valley where they encounter an Assyrian border patrol. She convinces them that she has come at God's behest to tell Holofernes how he can succeed against the Jews. Captivated by her beauty, the soldiers detail one hundred men to escort her to Holofernes' tent. • Judith's descent to the enemy camp symbolises the third phase of her functional transformation into an unconscious content • The soldiers represent the unconscious instinctual forces and have a safeguarding function vis-à-vis the unconscious. Judith's arrival activates and focuses their instinctual nature, channelling it into a specifically sexual mode by which they are easily deceived and forsake their safeguarding function. By facilitating Judith's entry into the camp, they serve the ultimate end of the psyche, which is to stabilise consciousness at stage 4 and drive back the shadow attack. Their	• This aspect demonstrates the actualisation of Judith's deceptive strategy. The same applies to all of Judith's dealings with Holofernes and his forces. It also indicates the danger of anima projection and possession, and symbolises the third step in Achior's self-transformation vis-à-vis his anima-integration. • By fighting fire with fire, Achior's feminine side neutralises the shadow's first line of defence and so gains guided/protected/unhindered entrance to the unconscious shadow-realm. • Judith's descent to the Assyrian camp symbolises the third phase in Achior's integration of anima contents, by which the dream may be indicating the necessity of this step taking place now, i.e., at the time of the dream. • The dream indicates that Achior must be fearless when dealing with the shadow by illustrating the effectiveness of the strategy it has proposed.

	obsession with Judith and their resultant actions are a clear indication of unresolved group anima projection.	• Seeing that Judith and the soldiers are of different national origin, the dream may well be warning Achior that: i) He should not project his anima onto any foreign people—be they foreign by virtue of nationality, ideology, etc. ii) He should not permit himself to be ensnared or deceived by the allure of foreign elements (of whatever nature) during his battle with the shadow.
10:18–19	• There is great concourse throughout the camp as Judith is led to Holofernes' tent. Everyone admires her beauty and her people because of her, concurring that they should all be destroyed as they would otherwise be able to deceive the whole earth. • Judith's anima-magic continues to spellbind the Assyrians to the extent that they see the future, potential danger of her people but not the real danger that she poses right now.	• Achior's anima continues her defeat of the unconscious shadow elements constellated around the central shadow element, Holofernes. • The dream warns that not integrating the anima will blind Achior to the deceptiveness of his internal/external opponent in the here and now, so that he might focus his conscious libido on the future dangers that the shadow embodies and not the present ones.
10:20–11:23	• Holofernes meets Judith in the forecourt of his tent. In mock subservience and verbal irony she shamelessly flatters him and promises the victory of her "lord". Corroborating the verity of Achior's words she emphasises that she has fled the Judaeans because they had decided to sin against God. As a result, God had specifically sent her to assist Holofernes to set up his throne unresisted in Jerusalem. Holofernes and his officers marvel at her wise words and beauty. He promises, "if you do as you have said, your God shall be my God, and you shall live in the house of King Nebuchadnezzar and be renowned throughout the whole world." (11:23).	• This component illustrates the verbal aspect of the anima*'s* deceptive strategy. Note how she spins her deception around some aspect of truth (Achior's speech). Her strategy is so effective that she is able to neutralise the second level of elements constellated around the central shadow archetype. • Note how the shadow tries to play upon Achior's inflation by promising allegiance, position, and fame in exchange for compliance with its agenda. The dream may be warning Achior not to fall prey to his (internal and probable external) opponent's deceptiveness and promises of allegiance, position, and fame. This will only exacerbate his inflation and lead him straight

Table 13 (*cont.*)

	Surface-Structure Component	Interpretation as a Projection of Achior's Psyche
	• Judith's arrival at Holofernes' tent comprises the fourth phase of her descent and the fourth and final step in her transformation process. • Holofernes' officers represent his second line of defence. Being possessed of the anima, they too fail to recognise the true nature of Judith's mission as her verbal *cum* sexual strategy overcomes them. As a result, they temporarily disconnect themselves from Holofernes and constellate around the far stronger anima figure that Judith represents. • Holofernes' willingness to forsake his master and 'god', in favour of Judith and her God, illustrates, among others: i) The extremity of his anima possession. ii) His change in drive/focus. His inflation becomes channelled into possessing Judith/his anima, whereas it was previously focused into destroying the nations who had disobeyed Nebuchadnezzar. iii) The poor self-image that underlies all cases of positive inflation and the resultant destruction of feeding it (through flattery etc.).	into the unconscious shadow's embrace. He should also be very careful of those who claim to be speaking and acting on God/the Self's behalf but may not be. • Once again, since four is the number of completion, the fourth step of Judith's descent indicates the completion of Achior's self-transformation and anima integration. As these four steps follow each other in very quick succession, we may say that the dream presses the urgency of this complete (four-step) self-transformation through the conscious integration of anima contents. It warns that continually projecting his anima and permitting anima-possession, i.e., not consciously integrating his feminine aspect, will lead to: i) A case of *enantiodromia* where his inflation becomes manifest for what it is, viz. the outward manifestation of a weak conscious self-image. ii) A change in 'conscious allegiance'. In other words, it will lead to his consciousness being swallowed up by the unconscious/his 'changing gods'. iii) A loss of focus in his current battle against the shadow. iv) His own destruction, psychic and/or physical, etc.
12:1–9	• Blinded by Judith's beauty and his own self-assurance/pride, Holofernes grants her request to eat only of her own kosher food and commands his bodyguards not to hinder her from taking an evening bath at the spring outside the camp.	• The anima's verbal *cum* sexual strategy is so effective that it completely ensnares the central shadow element of the unconscious attack and immobilises the third (closer) level of elements that would be able to resist conscious intrusion.

	• Holofernes' bodyguards represent the shadow's third line of defence against consciousness. He effectively neutralises their function, thus disabling them. This points to the extremity of Holofernes' anima possession once again. • The spring represents that which feeds central consciousness.	• The anima's effectiveness is bolstered by her ability to draw upon conscious libido (the spring) while engaging with the shadow. • The dream warns Achior not to succumb to anima possession and so drop his guard against the shadow. It also reminds him to continue supplementing his conscious libido while dealing with the unconscious.
12:10–20	• Holofernes is overcome with lust and sends his eunuch, Bagoas, to call Judith to an exclusive banquet at which he hopes to seduce her on the fourth day of her sojourn in the Assyrian camp. Judith feigns exultation for this invitation in words full of deceit and irony. Her ἅβρα precedes her and lays out sheepskins upon which she reclines. Holofernes' heart beats wild with ecstasy as he enjoins her to partake in the feast. Judith, however, eats her own food while Holofernes drinks more than he had ever drunk before (12:19–20). • Banquets are often associated with fulfilling sexual desire and death: both eating and sex involve consumption of a desired object/the fulfilment of a basic need, etc., while death entails complete consumption. • The sheepskins represent tamed instinctuality as they are part of an animal that has been killed. • Bagoas represents Holofernes' unintegrated shadow elements, whereas the ἅβρα represents Judith's consciously integrated shadow elements. Bagoas also represents the weak	• The anima's strategy bears fruit 'in the fullness of time'—four being representative of wholeness/fullness. • The shadow prepares for a feast of sexual instinctuality by way of fantasy, food, and excessive drink. In other words, it launches an all-out sexually focused attack on Achior's psyche by which it hopes to 'consume' his consciousness. The dream warns of this and indicates that the only way of escape lies through practising tamed instinctuality, i.e., not giving in to the shadow's enticements, and continuing to feed his conscious libido. • The dream also warns of the danger that unintegrated shadow elements (Bagoas) pose to Achior's psyche at this time. It encourages him to integrate all known shadow elements so that they do not become a weak point in his psyche and let him down; they would be drawing on much-needed conscious libido at this time if unintegrated. • The unconscious shadow's fourth and last line of defence falls, leaving it unwittingly vulnerable to Achior's consciousness. Seeing that Bagoas lets Holofernes down on account of

Table 13 (*cont.*)

	Surface-Structure Component	Interpretation as a Projection of Achior's Psyche
	link in Holofernes' army—he is an instinctually deprived content in an instinctually based unconscious attack and the one closest to Holofernes. He is Holofernes' fourth and last line of defence. He lets his master down because of this loyalty, blindly obeying him with regard to Judith, whereas his deficient instinctuality should have enabled him to see through her schemes.	his (Bagoas') loyalty instinctual deprivation, the dream may be cautioning Achior that completely depriving his consciousness of instinctuality is just as dangerous as allowing it to be flooded by instinctuality. In the same breath, the dream may be warning Achior to rethink strategies and abilities that he may have come to rely on. It intimates that some of these may not be as helpful as he might have thought, and that they may, indeed, let him down at this crucial time in his battle with the unconscious shadow.
13:1–10a	• When evening comes, Holofernes' staff exit and Judith decapitates Holofernes with his own sword. She rolls his corpse off the bed, takes the canopy off the poles, and gives the severed head to her ἅβρα so that she can hide it in their food basket. The women wait a while and exit Holofernes' tent under the ruse of Judith's nightly ablutions. • The symbolic transformation entailed in Judith's initial prayer is actualised as she deactivates the chief shadow content/robs it of its *mana* just before it would have assimilated her completely. • Holofernes' decapitation symbolises the castrating potential of: (a) Women's sexuality. (b) *Anima* possession. (c) The protection that he and his army have lost, the deactivation (*mana* loss) of the sexually inclined forces of the instinctual attack, and the transference of power from the shadow to the anima.	• Achior's anima succeeds in deactivating the main element of shadow attack. She robs it of its *mana* and begins to process the *mana* into something useful for consciousness. • This aspect constitutes the first phase of: a) Reintegrating the shadow contents into the conscious psyche. b) Consciously integrating the *mana* of the unconscious shadow. • The dream indicates that conscious integration of the shadow's *mana* is the first step towards neutralising the unconscious shadow's power and making it useful for consciousness. It demonstrates that deactivating the main element of the unconscious attack will leave the unconscious defenceless against consciousness. It also indicates that integrating the *mana* of these neutralised instincts will bring about the rebirth of consciousness as symbolised by the regenerative potential of the basket/womb.

13:1–10a cont.	• The basket is symbolic of the womb, while Holofernes' head is symbolic of the penile head and so of the sexual instincts. At the same time, kosher food symbolises a source of conscious renewal as well as healthy, tamed instinctuality.	

Cc'. Judith and her maid return to Bethuliah (13:10b–11)

13:10b–11	• Judith and her ἅβρα exit the enemy camp and ascend to Bethuliah. She commands the gatekeepers to open the gate, declaring God's victory over the enemy. • Having deactivated the unconscious shadow and begun the process of integrating its *mana*, Judith is functionally transformed back into a conscious content and therefore ascends stage 4 once again.	Achior's anima rises out of the locus of the unconscious attack and returns to the (threshold of the) fourth stage of conscious awareness. • The dream indicates that Achior will begin the process of being re-established at stage 4 as he begins the process of consciously integrating shadow contents. It also indicates that the first step of reintegration is not the final one and that subsequent steps may require some effort—Judith reaches Bethuliah but must still wait for its gates to be opened so that she may enter the city. • In addition, the dream points out that the first step of integration will be of little or no benefit for Achior's greater psyche without further and complete conscious integration of the *mana*—the Bethulians will remain unaware of Judith's victory if they do not open the gates for her.

Bb'. Judith plans the destruction of Israel's enemy (13:12–16:20)

13:12–16	• The men hasten to open the gate and call the elders. The people run towards the two women, lighting fires by which better to see them. Judith triumphantly holds up Holofernes' head and canopy. She exults YHWH for his mercy, the victory that he has wrought through her hand, and the fact that he preserved her purity.	• Achior's consciousness, which had suffered from libido-deprivation while the anima battled with the shadow, rallies to embrace the triumphant anima. This begins the dissolution of his negative inflation. • The anima shows that Achior's relationship with the Self has never been severed. To the contrary, the Self has

Table 13 (*cont.*)

	Surface-Structure Component	Interpretation as a Projection of Achior's Psyche
	• Bethuliah's darkness symbolises the conscious darkness that Judith's absence has left, and the fact that consciousness has consequently slipped into a state of relative unconsciousness. • Judith's nightly return intimates that the unconscious has been thoroughly defeated on its own turf at its time of optimal functioning. Her arrival at the time in which night is transformed into day symbolises that: i) She is the bearer of consciousness who brings 'light' into the situation. ii) The Bethulians' state of consciousness/situation is about to change.	assisted her to rout Achior's unconscious adversary, the shadow, and restore libido to his consciousness that was in danger of being engulfed by the unconscious. This component illustrates the anima's ability to connect the ego with the Self. • The dream indicates that, having integrated the shadow in part, Achior's consciousness has been enlightened even though it had slipped into a relative state of unconsciousness as a result of his negative attitude (which had focused on the dark side of Deuteronomistic philosophy). At the same time, it indicates that integrating the shadow and the anima as fully as possible at this stage will restore his sense of social reality and individual identity (the fourth stage of consciousness from which he was 'falling'), as well as enabling him to become a light-bearer/saviour for his people.
13:17–20	• The people are elated by Judith's report and praise God, while Ozias pronounces a special blessing upon her—with their endorsement. This indicates a surge in conscious libido and the integration of the anima into the outer levels of central consciousness (Bethuliah). • Ozias, the elders, and the Bethulians readily receive the *mana* that Judith has secured and her leadership. This shows that they know and respect the power of a consciousness that is higher than their own, and that they do not impede it in any way.	• The integration of the anima causes a much-needed surge in Achior's conscious libido that lifts him out of his state of depression (see 7:32) and enables him to see the Self and the anima for who they are and praise them accordingly. I.e., Achior recognises the role that the Self and the anima have played in preventing him from succumbing to the unconscious shadow. • The dream advocates that Achior should adopt the Bethulians' attitude, i.e., that he should not hesitate to receive the unconscious shadow contents, their *mana*, and the anima's leadership so that he can become stabilised at the fourth stage of conscious awareness and so lay a solid foundation for acceding to the fifth and highest stage of consciousness.

14:1–5	• Judith commands the Bethulians to hang Holofernes' head on the city wall and details a battle strategy by which they may finally defeat the Assyrian army. She also commands that Achior is brought out to verify that the head is indeed that of Holofernes (14:5)—before her battle plans are executed. • Hanging Holofernes' severed head on the city wall signifies that the raw instinctuality of the unconscious has been tamed; its libido has been withdrawn and its *mana* is used to fortify the previously shadow-intimidated consciousness. • Achior the character represents the partially but not fully integrated shadow elements that were first released from the unconscious by the libido-infusion occasioned through the Bethulians'/Judaeans' prayers. Seeing that he has remained in Ozias' house for the duration of Judith's sojourn in the Assyrian camp, we may say that he remained a partially integrated psychological content, and that he had still not fully attained to stage 4 as a person.	• Having been consciously integrated, the anima takes charge of the battle against the unconscious from a conscious vantage point. • The dream is thus demonstrating the desirability of allowing the integrated anima control over the affairs of consciousness: the raw instinctuality of the unconscious is tamed; its libido is withdrawn and its *mana* is used to fortify the previously shadow-intimidated consciousness. • The dream points out that the time has come for Achior consciously to integrate all other partially integrated shadow elements and become stabilised at the fourth stage of conscious awareness, i.e., to see reality for what it truly is and grasp his individual identity with both hands. • The dream shows that recognising the impotence of the unconscious shadow vis-à-vis the supreme potency of the Self will be the final impetus to his complete and willing integration at stage 4.
14:6–10	• Achior is brought from Ozias' house and faints upon seeing the severed head. When the Bethulians revive him, he blesses Judith. Upon hearing her account, the crowd roars with great rejoicing and Achior converts to Judaism. • By recognising Holofernes' head, Achior recognises the Assyrian's impotence versus the omnipotence of YHWH. His fainting and revival signifies regeneration, while his circumcision signifies that he willingly sacrifices the old instinctual practices that may have thwarted his final integration. • When morning comes, the Bethulians follow Judith's commands. Bagoas discovers that his master is dead and alerts the others. Pandemonium breaks out and the Assyrian flee	• Achior willingly stabilises at stage 4 through nine steps that are discernable from the time that he comes out of Ozias' house to the time that he converts to Judaism and is circumcised—the tenth step. These nine steps complete a sixteen–step process begun in the first section of Judith and indicate the totality of his transformation ($16 = 4 \times 4$). As a result, he is regenerated and his negative inflation is nullified. • In the process, Achior willingly sacrifices his old instinctual nature to the self, gains a new understanding of the (divinity of the) Self and (of) the anima and is restored in his relationship with the Self. I.e., Achior's ego-Self communication is restored through the agency of the anima.

Table 13 *(cont.)*

Surface-Structure Component	Interpretation as a Projection of Achior's Psyche
in all directions. The Bethulians then rush upon them. Inspired by this news, the Jews from Jerusalem, Gilead, and Galilee join them at Ozias' behest and drive the Assyrians back beyond the borders of Damascus. The Judaeans then enrich themselves with the spoil from the Assyrian camp. • Fear represents a libido loss. • The Bethulians are transformed from the subjects of fear to its objects while the reverse takes place with the Assyrians, indicating a major transformation in the balance of power between consciousness and the unconscious. • The surrounding towns represent lower levels of consciousness while Jerusalem represents the innermost layer of central consciousness. • Of the Bethulian leadership, Ozias alone survives Judith's return, meaning that his form of consciousness is higher than that of his fellow magistrates. He also takes over Joachim's letter-writing role, signifying that Judith's feat has now enabled him to function at a slightly higher level of consciousness. • The remaining Judaeans join the battle almost at the very end, when the Bethulians have already won a sizeable victory over the Assyrians. This speaks of the general paralysis that all—bar Judith—had experienced in light of Holofernes' attack. Their contribution to consciousness' deliverance takes place in three phases, with the Assyrians being pushed back as far as Choba in phase one, and Damascus in phase three.	• This component illustrates the way that higher and lower levels of consciousness are able to influence one another positively to the ultimate benefit of consciousness as a whole once the unconscious *mana* and other unconscious (shadow) contents (Achior) have been assimilated. • The combined Bethulian-Judaean victory over the Assyrian forces depicts the cumulative effect that internalising unconscious contents at any conscious level has on the entire field of consciousness. • The force of the instinctual attack is scattered, i.e., loses its libidinous charge. Achior's consciousness absorbs this libidinous charge and is transformed so that it is now ruled by faith and positivity not fear and negativity. The outer layer of his central consciousness is empowered by this anima-inspired transformation to the extent that it is able to face the rest of the unconscious shadow-force and deal with it. This indicates that a major transformation has begun in the balance of power between consciousness and the unconscious. • The dream demonstrates that dealing effectively with the unconscious entails the principle of "strike the shepherd and scatter the sheep". • The dream holds out the promise that, having overcome the shadow in this manner, Achior will not only be able to establish his dominant consciousness at stage 4, but he will also have the potential to rise to an even higher conscious state. This is symbolised by the libidinous surge experienced by Ozias. He represents the most conscious element of the

		outermost layer of central consciousness, while the surge he experiences holds the promise that 'he' may be able to rise to the innermost level of central consciousness if consciousness provides 'him' with sufficient libido-bolstering.
14:11–15:7	• Judith's return, the *mana* that she internalised/shared with the Bethulians, and the final integration of the shadow-contents, represented by Achior, cause a libido surge that encompasses the highest contents of the outer levels of stage 4. The surge then spirals out to the surrounding towns/cities and influences the contents of central consciousness that, in turn, influence the lower levels of consciousness.	• Achior's psychic transformation at stage 4 enables other, weaker elements of his consciousness/society as well as the very centre of his consciousness to engage the shadow in battle and assist him to overcome the attack. In this way, the whole of consciousness is energised and its paralysis/severe state of libido withdrawal is reversed.
15:8–16:17	• Joachim and the Jerusalemite γερουσία come to bless Judith, establishing among others that: i) They acknowledge her as the highest form of consciousness in their society, eclipsed only by God/the Self. ii) Praising Judith is tantamount to praising the deity/the Self. • The people ravage the Assyrian camp and bring Judith the spoils from Holofernes' tent, indicating that: i) They recognise Judith's conscious ascendancy and that the *mana* of the unconscious's shadow and its treasures belong to her. iii) They willingly and actively enrich themselves with the libido that belonged to the various (lesser) aspects of the unconscious shadow.	• The actions of Jerusalem's leaders illustrate that: a) Achior's psyche is able to acknowledge the existence of a higher form of consciousness than its own. b) Achior realises that he is unable to save himself without the agency of the Self and the anima. c) The anima is the highest psychological component—with the exception of the Self. This points clearly to the anima's 'divine nature' and Achior's recognition of this nature. The above are clear indications that Achior's inflation is no longer operative; it has been 'cured' just before it could become a full-blown, ruinous psychological phenomenon. • All aspects of Achior's conscious psyche recognise the anima's ascendancy and her right to the *mana* of the unconscious's

Table 13 (*cont.*)

Surface-Structure Component	Interpretation as a Projection of Achior's Psyche
• Judith heaps the spoils onto her mules and chariots, after which all the women of Israel bless her and perform a dance to her honour. I.e., she accepts the people's homage and incorporates the libido entailed in these objects into her instinctual arsenal. • Judith distributes branches (θύρσος) amongst the women, they all don olive wreaths, and she leads them in dance with the men following. She leads the people in a triumphal song of exultation to YHWH until (?) they reach Jerusalem. The use of the θύρσος (Bacchic element) signifies that the instinctual shadow contents have been successfully assimilated into national consciousness and that they are put to the conscious service of the Self. Just before these 'Bacchic' activities begin, the women praise Judith as the shadow-destroying ego-conqueror. Their spontaneous praise is the first independent action accorded to a body of women in *Judith*, which indicates that her victory has raised their conscious (self-)awareness and enabled their conscious differentiation from societal norms and expectations. The women also represent previously undifferentiated multiple/collective anima figures that have become differentiated and consciously integrated as a result of Judith's victory. • Judith's success brings about a gender role reversal in cultic practice. The men accept this reversal, demonstrating (a) the greater maturity/conscious differentiation that they have achieved, and (b) that their conscious instincts have been subordinated to the anima in service of the Self/God. • The Jewish symbolism of the olive wreaths intimates that national life, joy, and peace lie ahead.	chief shadow element and so rightly 'pay her homage' or give her the place of honour in the psyche. • The dream indicates that incorporating the *mana* of the unconscious shadow and enriching all of consciousness with its libido takes the will actively to do so. • The dream indicates that incorporating the main anima component completely at stage 4 will: i) Bring about the incorporation of all the shadow elements of which Achior is consciously aware. ii) Cause these shadow elements and all of consciousness and instinctuality to be submitted to the Self and so benefit the greater psyche as a whole. iii) Bring about a libido-infusion in all of consciousness. iv) Ultimately cause life, joy, peace, and thanksgiving to abound in Achior's conscious psyche/that of his people. v) Give him victory in all matters pertaining to his growth and individuation at stage 4. vi) Enable Achior to take action that is free from the norms and expectations of his society, so that he may achieve greater conscious differentiation and grow as an individual. I.e., it will enable him to break free from a herd mentality and become a community-orientated (not community-bound) individual. vii) Facilitate the incorporation of other, previously suppressed elements related to the central anima component. viii) Lead him to accept and incorporate his feminine aspects and so function at a higher level of maturity.

ix) Submit his entire being to the Self so that he can collaborate with the Self to the greater good of his psyche and his community as a whole.

In other words, the dream indicates that Achior's attitude towards life, himself, and the Self will be transformed from negativity to positivity when the anima is completely incorporated at stage 4.

• The dream intimates that Achior's transformation has the potential to spread life, joy, and peace throughout his whole community.

16:18–20

• As soon as the people enter Jerusalem they worship YHWH, purify themselves, and offer sacrifices. Judith dedicates to YHWH all the spoils from Holofernes' camp as well as his canopy. The people feast for three months. Judith stays with them.

• The people's actions reflect the kind of *ekkenosis* that is necessary for healthy ego-Self communication. Judith's dedication of all the spoils of her success to YHWH proves that inflation has not been able to set in.

• Judith's victory and the people's acceptance and continuation of it takes the conscious awareness of the cultic community to a new level, the fifth and highest stage, albeit only for a short while—the celebrations in Jerusalem only last for three months.

• The women lead the procession to the innermost level of central consciousness, viz. Jerusalem. This too points to their heightened conscious awareness, and suggests that they have superseded the men's consciousness.

• Achior's anima components open the way for him to access the very centre of his conscious awareness where his relationship with the Self is re-established. Achior is now able to submit himself entirely before the Self (see the aspect of purification/*ekkenosis* in the panel to the left) and offer worship, sacrifices, and offerings that are commensurate with his new understanding of the Self.

• The fact that the anima figures lead shows that Achior has been able to accept the more feminine aspects of himself and follow their leading—a true sign of maturity in a man.

• As a result of integrating the anima and the shadow at stage 4, Achior achieves a higher state of conscious differentiation and is able to accede to and enjoy the benefits (feast) of stage 5, albeit temporarily.

• Achior's inflation is cured as a result of the completed anima and shadow incorporation.

Table 13 (*cont.*)

	Surface-Structure Component	Interpretation as a Projection of Achior's Psyche
	• Four months have passed since the people first spoiled the Assyrian camp—thirty days of spoiling the Assyrian camp plus three months of celebration in Jerusalem. This symbolises the complete assimilation of unconscious contents at stage 4 plus the resultant restoration of ego-Self communication.	
16:21–25	• Everyone returns to their abodes, and Judith to Bethuliah where she remains unmarried despite many suitors. She increases in honour and dies at the age of 105. Before her death, she frees her ἅβρα and bequeaths her goods amongst Manasses' family and her own. Her memory protects the Judaeans for a long time after her death. • These verses indicate clearly the blessing that surrender to the Self brings—for Judith and her community. • Judith's victory is achieved as a result of her engaging/re-entering her shadow side. This is not surprising as her victory entails a battle with the national Shadow in which the latter is defeated and its *mana* integrated into her consciousness and that of the people. Furthermore, Judith's victory has been facilitated by the partial integration of acceptable shadow elements that Achior represents and has, in turn, facilitated the full integration of the contents he represents. (Note too that Judith's descent into the unconscious was facilitated by Achior's ascent to consciousness). It has been accompanied by the integration of formerly suppressed anima contents, which has led to the integration of foreign/shadow elements into Judaean worship. It has also	• This component illustrates the good that comes from integrating the shadow and the anima, becoming established at a particular stage of consciousness, and surrendering to the Self. This benefits not only the individual in terms of her/his greater psychic integrity, improved ego-Self communication, and conscious differentiation, but also the community to which such an individual belongs. It is particularly significant that these processes occur here at stage 4 as this is the state where, having been freed from the bonds of society/the unconscious (stage 1) and self-identification in terms of contrast with an other/others (stage 2), and determined her/his own moral and ethical standards (stage 3), the person can finally see reality for what it is and begin to develop her/his own individual identity (stage 4). This enables the person to serve the community—to set the captives free, redistribute wealth, etc.—out of a genuine sense of camaraderie and a healthy self-sacrifice that is not complicated by the interference of unintegrated and uncontrolled instinctual drives (Judith remains unmarried). • This component clearly shows that there is a definite relationship between the shadow and the anima and that the

resulted in the release of Judith's shadow/ἅβρα and the distribution of her psychic wealth amongst her people and those of her husband subsequent to her death.

• Judith remains other till the end, indicating that the anima cannot be possessed.

integration of one—in whatever measure—facilitates the integration of the other.

• The dream hereby illustrates the interconnectedness of all psychic components and the desirability of achieving the type of psychic integrity it has demonstrated through the characters and story that it has put before Achior's mind. The dream also demonstrates the kind of fasting (Judith fasted excessively) that the Lord desires: the captives are set free, wealth is redistributed, etc. It thereby holds Judith up for emulation. I.e., it teaches that Achior must have Judith's attitude and extend his fasting into good deeds in order to please the Self, influence his community, and come to final rest in God.

b. *An Interim Situational Analysis*

In this subsection, I should like to extrapolate the insights gained from the preceding subsection onto *Judith's* most probable genetic context. It will therefore be helpful to summarise briefly the state of Achior's/the Jewish nation's psyche before proceeding to this interim situational analysis.

It is evident from the outset that Achior's/the nation's psyche (the terms will be used interchangeably from now on) is experiencing great turmoil on account of the shadow attack. The aim of the unconscious shadow is to engulf Achior's conscious psyche to the point that he identifies with the shadow and acts completely out of its instinctual nature and dictates. The battle is so severe that it is likened to the combined force of the most destructive full-blown shadow attacks that the nation had experienced: the Assyrian exile of the Northern Kingdom and the Babylonian exile of the Southern Kingdom (see 1:1).

The dream's portrayal of Achior as a Babylonian-Assyrian king indicates the strength of the self-alienation that the nation experiences: it is simultaneously portrayed as a foreign king and one who is a composite of all that is evil, proud, instinctually based, and 'inflated' in humankind, all that has alienated the nation from its land, split it, and alienated it from itself. The severity of the self-alienation is further illustrated by the portrayal of the effective protagonist as an Ammonite—a cursed nation according to the Deuteronomistic philosophy that the Bethulians and Achior espouse. This portrayal intimates that the nation's unconscious self-perception is that of being accursed—something which is corroborated by the Bethulians' negative self-image in *Judith* 7—while simultaneously warning the nation that it is not as 'pure' as it would like to imagine, that it has shadows that are close to the threshold of consciousness, and that these require re-integration if the Shadow/shadow is to be defeated. The fact that Bethuliah is an unknown/unidentified city furthers the picture of self-alienation, as does Achior's conscious identification that appears to be split between helping the Assyrians to conquer the Bethulians and adopting the Bethulians' chief form of conscious perception, viz. the Deuteronomistic philosophy. That all of these factors amount to a severe identity crisis requires little explanation. It is as though the nation no longer knows 'who' it is, where it is, and with whom to identify/'side'.

The self-alienation that the nation experiences is further complicated by the spiritual-religious, moral-ethical thrust of the unconscious shadow attack and the fact that the nation has succumbed to these aspects of the attack at the first two levels of conscious awareness. The complication is then intensified by what appears to be a definite break in the nation's relationship with YHWH and its increasing adoption of the negative aspect of Deuteronomistic philosophy: the people believe that the shadow attack is a punishment from YHWH against Whom they have sinned. This, as we have seen, leads to an increasing withdrawal of libido from consciousness and its transference to the unconscious psyche. Thus imbued and strengthened, the latter seizes upon the nation's escalating fear and attempts to 'devour' its consciousness altogether. It is not surprising, therefore, to find that the national consciousness is overcome with desperation to the extent that the nation would prefer to give in to the shadow attack and live rather than see itself further depleted of libido and robbed of all that it has accomplished. At this point, the nation seems blind to the fact that giving in to the shadow and becoming its slaves would mean a complete identification with the shadow and its agenda, which includes worshipping Nebuchadnezzar, the Shadow/negative Self, as god. That this would entail a complete reversal of the process by which a disparate group of people became a nation, the destruction of their conscious heritage, and a complete change in their conscious allegiance seems not to bother them at all in light of the terrible circumstances that they are enduring. In light of this, the dream makes it clear, that giving in to the unconscious shadow would achieve the very opposite of the survival they so desperately seek, i.e., they would be completely subsumed by the unconscious, and so the need for a saviour becomes all the more pressing.

In view of the surface-structure events described, their psychological significance, and the desired resolution of this national crisis, the dream introduces Judith as the ideal saviour/heroine in *Judith* 8. By means of her activities and character, the dream platforms its message of the first seven chapters, namely that the nation should withdraw its shadow projections and let go of its negative self-perception and the Deuteronomistic philosophy upon which it is founded in order to succeed against the shadow. Nevertheless, the dream clearly illustrates that none of this can be achieved without the agency of Judith who is both the nation's anima and the most individuated conscious ego in the dream-narrative. According to the dream, the nation must integrate its anima wholeheartedly, give her the acclaim due to her, and leave her to deal with the shadow in her own unconventional way. In this way, consciousness would be fighting fire with fire for, if the shadow is 'other', then the anima is the *altogether other*, consisting as it does "of psychic facts which have never before been in man's psychological possession; that hitherto were always to be found outside his consciousness in every possible form of projection" (Jung 1940:79):

The dream portrays Judith as a highly developed anima figure, one so close to the Self/God that her communication with Him seems to carry his prior sanction. She is effectively His second-in-command and, in so far as the narrative is concerned, the only one who can co-deliver the nation with YHWH and lead it into a closer relationship with Him. The dream avers that she alone can imbue the nation with sufficient *mana* to overcome the present crisis, i.e., to withdraw its shadow projections, come to a realisation of its own unique consciousness (stage 4), and so be well on the road of achieving an unshakable and indomitable national identity (stage 5).

To my mind, the subjective analysis summarised briefly above yields a number of clues as to the type of situation that underlies the Book of Judith. Once again, I should like to present the information in table form (table 14) for the sake of terse comparison.

Table 14. An Interim Situational Analysis.

	Key Insights, Aspects, and Events	Hypothetical Situation
1.	• Confusion of identity/identities and self-alienation/psychic splitting in Achior as seen in his psychic portrayal as a composite Babylonian-Assyrian foe and his identification with both the Assyrians and the Bethulians-Judaeans.	• This indicates that there are warring factions within the Jewish community itself. These factions appear to identify/side with different elements within their broader societal context and so threaten to split the nation/bring about national self-alienation.
2.	• The nation is under attack by the unconscious Shadow/negative Self and the shadow to which it has transferred its power. • The shadow is the chief element that is constellated around the Shadow. It takes on the role of the ego-conqueror, which has been conferred upon it by the negative Self; increasingly adopts the Shadow's inflation; and functions as its disciple. • The shadow also has elements of varying strength constellated around it that take on its inflation and function as its disciples.	• This indicates the presence of external and internal foes—both of which are shadows/'other' to what the dream regards as the 'real' national consciousness (henceforth, dominant consciousness). These enemies strike terror into the heart and soul of the nation/dominant consciousness. They seem to be possessed of great military power and prowess. • The main external-internal forces have deputised their power to ancillary forces. • It also seems that a clear alliance has been formed between external and internal forces and between similarly minded internal factions that oppose the dominant conscious psyche.
3.	• The unconscious shadow is power-hungry and instinctually motivated and suffers from positive inflation. • The shadow attack is aimed at completely assimilating consciousness on a moral-ethical and religious-spiritual level, and threatens to sever its relation to the Self. • More specifically, the shadow seeks to alter the dreamer's conscious allegiance from its own gods and ultimately the Self/YHWH to the negative Self, which would essentially entail the dissolution of the dreamer's conscious psyche.	• The internal-external forces (henceforth, the shadow forces)/their leaders are power-hungry, and instinctually motivated. They suffer from a god-complex/severe positive inflation to the extent that they may actually demand to be worshipped as gods. They attempt to assimilate the entire nation and make it conform to their 'otherness', viz. their moral values, customs and religious creed(s). • There seems to be a breakdown in traditional morality /morality according to the dominant consciousness as the instinctuality of these forces sweeps through the nation and

Table 14 (*cont.*)

	Key Insights, Aspects, and Events	Hypothetical Situation
		threatens to sever its connection with YHWH, disable its moral-ethical code, and dissolve its existence and/or identity as a nation. • This aspect may also signify a threat to the Jewish cultus.
4.	• The first two levels of consciousness are annihilated or suffer extensive damage in respect of their resources, achievements, and connection to the Self: i) The first stage of consciousness is destroyed in spite of extensive fortifications and a large degree of spiritual-religious assistance. ii) The second stage ignores the shadow at first, regarding it as 'one man'. As a result, much of it is destroyed. • Later on, higher-order second-stage elements attempt to escape destruction by submitting to the shadow. Nevertheless, they too suffer tremendous losses and the assimilation of their strongest elements into the unconscious shadow.	• The shadow forces succeed in assimilating the weakest aspects of the nation. The fact that a rather large component of spiritual-religious elements is placed at the first stage of consciousness may indicate the weakness of a great portion of Judaean spiritual-religious community vis-à-vis the dominant consciousness: they seem to resist at first but are assimilated without trace thereafter. It would also seem as though a certain sector of the community ignores the threat that the 'otherness' of the shadow forces poses, while another submits to this 'otherness' in order to survive. Nevertheless, both of these approaches lead to the complete assimilation of their proponents. • Seeing that the coastal dwellers' young men are drafted into Holofernes' army and used against the rest of the western nations, we may deduce that the shadow forces draft the nation's best men into their army and set them against 'dissident'/rebellious members of the Judaean community. Alternatively, we may deduce that they set various sectors of the Judaean community against one another.
5.	• The threat of the shadow touches the third stage of conscious awareness where it is translated into fear for the integrity of central consciousness and consciousness's highest achievement *cum* locus of ego-Self communication. This fear, which	• The nation has recently suffered a crushing defeat that is either akin to the Babylonian exile or may be equated with it. As a result, its core integrity, identity, and relationship with YHWH have been compromised and have, as yet, not been

	is rooted in a previous, harrowing experience with shadow forces, signifies that consciousness is still rather unstable vis-à-vis its central/core identity and relationship with the Self. This previous shadow-experience is represented by the exile in the surface structure of the text.	fully (re-) established. If we are to take the text at face value, then we are dealing with a period in which Jerusalem and its temple are once again under threat—after being rebuilt in the postexilic period. This implies that the Jewish cultus is also in danger of being demolished.
6.	• The highest (spiritual) elements in the innermost layer of Achior's central consciousness are activated. As a result, he begins fortifying the entry points (the weak points) into his consciousness. These seem to be defined morally, ethically, and in terms of the development of individual consciousness. • See further the surface-structure activities of Joachim and the people's self-humbling before YHWH, e.g., prayer and fasting.	• This component may reflect the intervention of an actual priestly person/spiritual leader of a dissident group or the intervention of a spiritual element/mass, or both. This person/element/group rallies the support of many like-minded people/elements and mobilises them for war. The war is characterised by a bid to save the nation from moral degradation and losing its sense of national identity/distinctiveness and relation with YHWH at a deep level of conscious awareness. • The textual reference to food preparations and the garrisoning of high cities may refer to such things literally. Alternatively, they may be interpreted figuratively as moral and spiritual fortifications. (Given the multivalency of the text, both interpretations may hold simultaneously). • The reference to mountains/mountain passes suggests that this particular dissident faction have taken refuge in the mountainous parts of Judaea. It could also reflect dominant consciousness's and/or unconsciousness's lofty perception about this group. • The dissidents follow the commands of their spiritual leadership. Realising the gravity of the situation, they attempt to restrain their instincts, i.e., to ensure that they do not act out of them alone. This may point to rigorous self-discipline in respect of abstaining from practices that do not conform with the dominant consciousness of this group and/or the rigorous practice of the dissidents' form of religion and way of life, etc.

Table 14. (*cont.*)

	Key Insights, Aspects, and Events	Hypothetical Situation
		• The dissidents follow the commands of their spiritual leadership. Realising the gravity of the situation, they attempt to restrain their instincts, i.e., to ensure that they do not act out of them alone. This may point to rigorous self-discipline in respect of abstaining from practices that do not conform with the dominant consciousness of this group and/or the rigorous practice of the dissidents' form of religion and way of life, etc. • The dissidents also attempt to connect to YHWH by means of self-sacrifice and prayer. They humble their entire society before YHWH, putting everyone and everything—including the cattle and the altar—at YHWH's mercy as they realise that the battle cannot be won without the assistance of YHWH. • The fact that the altar is mentioned may indicate that one or more members of this group (dissidents) have been sacrificed for the greater cause of rescuing the nation, its identity, and its ethical-moral link to YHWH. This implies if not presupposes the persecution of dissident factions. • The dream may also be reflecting a situation in which the dissidents and/or their spiritual leadership continue to serve YHWH in traditional ways despite opposition from the shadow forces and the sexual-instinctual *cum* intellectual bombardment that their otherness entails.
7.	• The unconscious shadow does not fold at the first sign of resistance. Rather, it consults erstwhile conscious contents in an attempt to determine the strength of consciousness so that it (the shadow) can take appropriate action against it. • Previously conscious elements that have been suppressed/relegated to the unconscious advise the shadow to block consciousness's access to its source of sustenance so as to cause a loss of conscious libido. This would enable the shadow to conquer consciousness more easily.	• The shadow forces are angered by the dissidents' resistance and try to determine their strength. In order to do so, they turn to those who were once close to them (the dissidents). This may indicate that certain persons have defected from the dissidents' camp and/or that some members of this camp have been incorporated into the opposing forces. • Judging from Holofernes' response, it is clear that that the shadow forces did not expect the dissidents to have the strength to resist them.

8.	• Achior, the effective protagonist, is portrayed as an Ammonite, i.e., as a shadow of the dominant Judaean consciousness. • Achior represents an erstwhile conscious shadow element that has been repressed to the realms of the unconscious. Nevertheless, his close 'familial' ties with the nation indicate that he is fairly close to the threshold of consciousness and that the latter may therefore more easily re-integrate him if it so wishes.	• This component also reflects the nation's split in identity by presenting Achior as an Ammonite/repressed Israelite shadow who identifies with an Israelite ideology as well as the cause/ideology of the Assyrian enemy. This indicates that there are various divisions in the nation itself and that each follows a different set of ideologies; one such set belongs to the shadow and the other to dominant consciousness. It is almost as though the nation has become a shadow of itself.
9.	• A libido burst causes erstwhile conscious contents to rise to the threshold of consciousness once again and be assimilated at a higher level of conscious awareness—stage 4, Bethuliah—where it is most needed.	Something appears to have stirred the dissidents' desire to re-integrate the shadow contents represented by Achior. This is translated into the psychic energy for doing so and may even reflect the dissidents'/nation's active attempt to incorporate/involve previously despised people/groups against the shadow forces.
10.	• The unconscious tries to block central consciousness from all possible resources of conscious renewal upon the advice of previously conscious contents. • The shadow specifically targets the outer layer of central consciousness—Bethuliah—and surrounds it with its instinctual forces.	• This component may reflect directly on an actual physical battle strategy aimed against a city on a high mountain/mountain pass, which could have been captured by or belonged to the dissidents. Alternatively, it may simply reflect a renewed attack against the nation as a whole. The instinctual aspect of the enemy attack may reflect renewed ideological attack in the form of attempts to 'proselytise' the nation/this specific group of people to the enemy's instinctually motivated religion/way of life. • Holofernes' blocking of springs may be interpreted literally. Alternatively, it may be interpreted as his wearing down of the Judaeans' strength and resistance.
11.	• Consciousness is fearful, loses much libido, and wishes to capitulate. However, it is temporarily prevented from doing so by the spiritual-religious elements at stage 4 that impose a five-day ultimatum on YHWH/the Self.	• The dissidents panic and want to give in to the shadow forces. They are prevented from doing so by their spiritual-religious leadership. Alternatively, this aspect could merely be reflecting the people's increasing loss of hope and strength.

Table 14 (*cont.*)

	Key Insights, Aspects, and Events	Hypothetical Situation
	• Bethuliah is situated on top of a mountain/ mountain pass. • The people despair on the basis of their Deuteronomistically informed negative self-image. • The need for a saviour becomes all the more clear at this point.	Naturally, both interpretations are equally and simultaneously applicable. • The people's desperation is intensified by their clinging to the negative aspect of Deuteronomistic philosophy. As a result of clinging to this negative viewpoint, they lose all hope in themselves and in YHWH's deliverance of them and are ready to yield to the enemy. This would entail a reversal of the process by which they became a nation and effectively see them worshipping another god. • The five-day ultimatum may directly reflect an actual ultimatum that was put before YHWH in a time of war. Alternatively, it may merely reflect the severity of the nation's desperation and loss of faith.
12.	• Judith/the national anima arises and delivers consciousness from the grip of the unconscious. a) She is highly individuated and has deep roots in the national unconscious psyche. b) She is simultaneously judge, prophet, priest, judge, etc. and has a high degree of community consciousness. c) She is very close to YHWH and is the only one who can offer the correct interpretation of the situation—one which counters the people's Deuteronomistic mindset. d) She plays the unconscious at its own game, targeting its weakest points (instinctuality and inflation). e) She uses unorthodox, deceptive means to destroy the chief shadow element and deliver the nation.	• This aspect probably represents the rise of a patriotic person/teacher in Israel who greatly influenced the self-perception, etc. of the Judaeans and led them to deliverance. It sketches/may sketch this person's actual qualities: integrity, strength of character, complete devotion to YHWH and her/his community, blamelessness, good lineage, full individuation, ability to act as ruler, prophet, judge, and deliverer, and use of unconventional methods to defeat the enemy. • Judith's repudiation of Deuteronomistic self-perception indicates a time in Israel's history when Deuteronomistic philosophy was being challenged and/or repudiated. • Judith's deceptiveness and seeming alliance with Holofernes may reflect a false (?) alliance/partnership forged between a

	f) She decapitates Holofernes by striking his neck twice with his own sword. g) She brings the nation back to YHWH and effects a host of transformations in her community. • Judith's success brings about a gender role reversal in cultic practice. It so terrifies the surrounding nations that they dare not attack the Jews for many years after her death. Judith dies at the age of 105, refusing all suitors who come her way.	specific section of the dissidents and the shadow forces, which ultimately led to the destruction of the latter/those to whom they had deputised their power. The fact that she decapitates Holofernes with two strikes of his own sword may indicate that the enemy is defeated twice at the height of his power, i.e., in two distinct battles. • The portrayal of the saviour as a woman may reflect: a) A real woman who saved the nation/a particular city and brought about widespread transformation within Judaean society. b) An unconventional male leader who saved the nation and brought about widespread transformation within Judaean society. c) A time of increased status for Judaean women and/or their increased participation in cultic worship. • Judith's longevity probably reflects the duration of a particular era/rule. Alternatively, it may simply be reflective of a time of stability within the nation. • Judith's 'protection' of her people, even after her death, probably reflects a time of prosperity and relative political peace for Israel. Similarly, her refusal of all suitors may indicate that Israel remained 'married to YHWH' during this time/after her defeat of Holofernes. Alternatively, it may be reflective of a desire for such peace, religious integrity, and prosperity.
13.	• Manasses had to die in order for the nation to be saved. He seems to have been a leader/ prominent figure in his community, and represents a weakened form of consciousness that succumbed to inflation, became rebellious, and was relegated to the realms of the unconscious that swallowed him up.	• This component represents the city (or national) leadership's current weakness in respect of dominant consciousness, their inflation, and their rebellion against YHWH. This profile stands diametrically opposed to that of Judith, the ideal hero(ine), that is held up for their emulation.

Table 14 (*cont.*)

	Key Insights, Aspects, and Events	Hypothetical Situation
14.	• The analysis has illustrated the interrelation between anima and shadow contents, particularly in terms of conscious integration and accession to higher levels of consciousness/maturity: a) Achior's partial integration facilitates the anima's release into the conscious realms and her deactivation of the main shadow element. b) The anima's victory facilitates: i) The integration of the main shadow element's *mana* into consciousness. ii) The complete integration of Achior. iii) The complete integration of the shadow elements represented by Holofernes' army. iv) The greater differentiation of anima contents and the greater integration of shadow elements into the worship of YHWH—note particularly the θύρσος and the wreaths used in the women's dance.	• This component may reflect the intervention of an actual priestly person/spiritual leader of a dissident group or the intervention of a spiritual element/mass, or both. This person/element/group rallies the support of many like-minded people/elements and mobilises them for war. The war is characterised by a bid to save the nation from moral degradation and losing its sense of national identity/distinctiveness and relation with YHWH at a deep level of conscious awareness. • The textual reference to food preparations and the garrisoning of high cities may refer to such things literally. Alternatively, they may be interpreted figuratively as moral and spiritual fortifications. (Given the multivalency of the text, both interpretations may hold simultaneously). • The reference to mountains/mountain passes suggests that this particular dissident faction have taken refuge in the mountainous parts of Judaea. It could also reflect dominant consciousness's and/or unconsciousness's lofty perception about this group. • The dissidents follow the commands of their spiritual leadership. Realising the gravity of the situation, they attempt to restrain their instincts, i.e., to ensure that they do not act out of them alone. This may point to rigorous self-discipline in respect of abstaining from practices that do not conform with the dominant consciousness of this group and/or the rigorous practice of the dissidents' form of religion and way of life, etc. • The dissidents also attempt to connect to YHWH by means of self-sacrifice and prayer. They humble their entire society

15.	• The interdependent integration of anima and shadow contents leads to the stabilisation of consciousness at the fourth stage of conscious awareness, and the restoration of ego-Self communication. It also leads to consciousness temporarily experiencing fifth-stage consciousness.	• This component may reflect the nation's collaboration with non-Judaean elements that assist it or hamper its progress towards 'self-identity'. • The people's stabilisation at stage 4 may reflect a time of (relative?) stability in the nation's constitution and identity. Their accession to stage 5 may reflect a time of temporary political and/or religious strength in respect of dominant consciousness (the people return to the homes from which they came after having feasted in Jerusalem).

c. *From Text to Context: An Objective Analysis of the Judithic Dream*

Insights Gained from the Interim Situational Analysis

The preceding interim situational analysis has yielded a number of insights regarding the context of *Judith* that may not have been obtained from a plain reading of its surface structure. These are enumerated below with the numbers in brackets reflecting the numbers in the first column of table 14.

1. *The shadow forces*:

   1a) These are comprised of internal and external forces both of which are shadows/'other' to the dominant consciousness of the Judithic dream (2, 10). They launch a military and ideological-religious-moral-ethical attack on the nation in general to begin with. They then focus their efforts on the dissident group(s) which resist(s) them. This attack is renewed/intensified at critical junctures of the battle (cf. 10) in an attempt to bring the nation/dissidents to its/their knees.

   1b) The shadow forces are power-hungry and largely instinctually based (3). They suffer from a god-complex or positive inflation to the extent that one may postulate that they/their leaders actually demand to be worshipped as gods (3). The same inflation leads them to impose 'other' gods onto the nation/dissidents (cf. 5, 14).

   1c) They attempt to assimilate the entire nation and make it conform to their 'otherness', viz. their moral values, customs, and religious creed(s) (3, cf. also 5, 14). In the process, they succeed in assimilating the weakest components of the national fabric (4). Surprisingly (?), this includes a relatively large number of the nation's spiritual-religious leadership (4). They also draft the nation's best men into their army, set them against 'dissident'/rebellious members of the Judaean community, and/or set various sectors of the Judaean community against one another (4).

   1d) In their attempt to assimilate the nation, the shadow forces often make use of defectors/those previously affiliated to the dissident forces (cf., e.g., 4, 7).

   1e) Their ferocity and military strength strikes fear into the hearts of the nation and the dissidents who oppose them, particularly those who appear to be holed up in 'Bethuliah' (2, 5, and 11).

1f) The main shadow forces deputise their power to ancillary forces (2)—either external or internal—empower them, and execute their will through them.
1g) An alliance has been formed between external and internal shadow forces and between similarly minded internal factions that oppose the dominant conscious psyche (2).
1h) A false (?) alliance/partnership has been forged between the dissidents and shadow forces, which ultimately leads to the destruction of the latter/those to whom they had deputised their power (12).
1i) The shadow forces oppress and persecute the dissidents—religiously and otherwise—in order to enforce their will (cf. 6 as well as 3, 5, and 14).

2. *The general Jewish community/the nation in general*:
2a) There are warring factions within the Jewish community itself that appear to identify/side with different elements within their broader sociopolitical environment (1, 5). Each follows a different ideology/set of ideologies, with one such set belonging to the shadow forces and the other to dominant consciousness (8). The identification of these groups with one side or the other is so strong that it threatens to split the nation politically and ideologically/bring about national self-alienation akin to the Assyrian and Babylonian exiles (1, 5). Furthermore, the shadow forces exacerbate the situation by setting various sectors of the Judaean community against one another and employing ex-dissidents or ex-dissident affiliates against the dissidents (4).
2b) There seems to be a breakdown in traditional morality, i.e., morality according to the dominant consciousness, as the instinctuality of these forces sweeps through the nation and threatens to sever its connection with YHWH, disable its moral-ethical code, and dissolve its existence and/or identity as a nation. (3). However, dissident spiritual forces intervene in an attempt to rout the shadow forces and fortify the nation on a spiritual-moral/ethical level (6).
2c) A certain sector of the community ignores the threat posed by the 'otherness' of the shadow forces, while another submits to this 'otherness' in order to survive. Nevertheless, both of these approaches lead to the complete assimilation of their proponents (4).

2d) According to the perspective of dominant consciousness, a great portion of the Judaean spiritual-religious community is weak in respect of the shadow forces—i.e., some resist them at first but are later assimilated without a trace, while others welcome them with open arms (4).

2e) The nation has recently suffered a crushing defeat that is either akin to the exile or may be equated with it. It has not yet been fully (re-)established (5) and suffers from identity dysfunction despite having been reconstituted.

2f) It is almost as though the nation has become a shadow of itself—i.e., it is identified with an impure Ammonite (8).

2g) Something appears to have stirred the dissidents' desire to reintegrate previously despised people/groups against the shadow forces (9, 15) and/or assimilate 'foreign' communities into the Judaean realm.

3. *The dissident forces/dominant consciousness*:

3a) The dissidents are led by a spiritual-political leadership (6). This person/element/group rallies the support of like-minded people/elements and mobilises them for war. The war is characterised by a bid to save the nation from moral degradation, the loss of its sense of national identity/distinctiveness, and its relation with YHWH at a deep level of conscious awareness.

3b) The dissidents are very devout to YHWH and continue to serve YHWH in traditional ways despite opposition from the shadow forces (6). It is even possible that one or more members of this group (dissidents) have been sacrificed/killed for the greater cause of rescuing the nation, its identity, and its ethical-moral link to YHWH (6).

3c) The dissidents/a particular faction of dissident forces have/has taken refuge in the mountainous parts of Judaea (6). They apply rigorous self-discipline, abstaining from practices that do not conform with dominant consciousness and/or their rigorous form of religion/way of life, etc. (6).

3d) The people's stabilisation at stage 4 may reflect a time of (relative?) stability in the nation's constitution and identity. The people's accession to stage 5 may reflect a time of temporary political and/or religious strength in respect of dominant consciousness (15).

4. *The unconventional saviour of the people*:
A patriotic person/teacher arises in Israel. This person greatly influences the self-perception of the Judaeans and leads them to deliverance by unconventional means. S/he is possessed of the following qualities: integrity, strength of character, complete devotion to YHWH and her/his community, fearlessness, and blamelessness. S/he is of good lineage, fully individuated, close to YHWH, and able to act as ruler, prophet, judge, and deliverer simultaneously. In short, this is a Moses *redevivus cum* Messianic leader and is hailed as such by the dissidents/broader Judaean populace.

5. *Other*:
5a) The deep-structure reading reflects a time in which women possibly enjoyed a higher status in Israel than is normally believed to have been the case. They may even have actively participated in cultic worship (12, 14).
5b) The women's incorporation of Hellenistic and Bacchic elements in their worship of YHWH could reflect the incorporation of shadow elements at a very deep level of the psyche. On a darker note, it may also reflect the kind of syncretism that the biblical authors have always frowned upon—i.e., the 'equation' of YHWH and other gods, etc. (5, 14).
5c) The political-religious leadership of the nation/dissidents is weak in respect of the dream's vision of dominant consciousness. They suffer from positive inflation and have rebelled against YHWH. This profile stands diametrically opposed to that of Judith/the unconventional saviour and is reflective of a time of weakened and/or demoralised dissident/national leadership (13). This intimates that the leadership may have to die/be deposed before the people can be saved (13).
5d) The nation's/dissidents' desperation is intensified by their clinging to the negative aspect of Deuteronomistic philosophy (11). As a result of this, they lose all hope in themselves and in YHWH's deliverance of them and are ready to yield to the enemy. They are blind to the fact that this would entail a reversal of the process by which they became a nation and effectively see them worshipping another god (11).
5e) Judith's repudiation of Deuteronomistic self-perception indicates a time in Israel's history when Deuteronomistic philosophy was being challenged and/or repudiated (12).

5f) The Jewish cultus may be in danger (3, 5).
5g) Other nations/foreigners are incorporated at various levels of Judaean/dissident society for different purposes (7, 10; see also 2, 12).

Application

When comparing the results of the interim situational analysis with events occurring in Judaea during the Hellenistic era, we see that the former fits well into the political-religious milieu of that time. Here, I should like to highlight key events. The numbers in brackets reflect the numbers accorded to particular insights in the preceding subsection.

- This was a time when the nation experienced a flood of Hellenistic ideology, culture, and religion under the enforced Hellenisation policies of the Hellenistic kings, particularly Antiochus IV and the various high priests to whom they effectively deputised their power (1a, 1f, 1g, 2c, 2d. Cf. also 1i). The latter, most notably Jason, Menelaus, and Alcimus, were ardent Hellenisers who, in their pride and greed for power and wealth (1b), attempted to turn most if not all of the age-old Judaean customs, beliefs, and practices on their head (1a, 1c, 2b, 2d, 2f, 5c), even stooping so low as to persecute their own people who 'rebelled' against/disobeyed them (1i, 2a, 2f, 3b.).
- Jerusalemite society became torn between the pro- and anti-Hellenisation factions (2a; cf. also 1g, 1c). Civil unrest was often the order of the day (cf. especially the rulership of Menelaus, Alcimus, and Jannaeus in this regard).
- Conservative Jews banded themselves under the name of *Hasidim* and continued to observe the Torah (3c) despite intense religious persecution from Hellenistic rulers such as Antiochus IV Epiphanes and even their own high priests (1i). At a later stage they retreated from active warfare, leaving this to Judas and his men (2a).
- Continuing unrest during Menelaus' time caused Antiochus IV to dispatch Apollonius, the Mysarch, to bring the situation under control (II Maccabees 5:21–26). The latter entered Jerusalem on a Sabbath and proceeded to massacre its inhabitants (1a, 1i). He tore down the walls of the city and erected a citadel, the Akra, in its midst. Antiochus began actively persecuting the Jews, enslaving and killing them in large numbers (1i). He plundered the

Jerusalemite temple—with the help of Menelaus—and turned it into a shrine for Zeus Baal Shamayim (1i, 2d, 5b, 5c, 5f). The latter was worshipped there with his consorts, 'Athena' and 'Dionysus' (1i, 5b, 5f). He set up an altar to Zeus in the Jerusalem temple and even sacrificed swine's flesh upon it (1i, 5b, 5c, 5f). The Jewish cultus came to an end at this time, with Menelaus and his priests ceasing to officiate in the temple (5f, 2f).

- Antiochus' edict proscribing Judaism in 167 B.C., and the intense persecutions which followed upon those who refused to abide by it (1i, 3c), were two of the main factors that led to the Maccabean revolt and the decapitation of Nicanor alluded to in *Judith* (see table 1). This revolt was carried out primarily in the form of guerrilla attacks launched from the mountainous areas under the leadership of the dissident priest Mattathias and his son and successor, Judas (2b, 3a, 3b, 3c, 4). Judas and his men also killed defectors, destroyed pagan altars, and circumcised the uncircumcised babies (2b, 3b, 4).
- Judas' defeat of Lysias, who came against Jerusalem with an army of 60,000 men and 5,000 cavalry, and his occupation of Jerusalem caused Antiochus IV to rescind his edict that had proscribed Judaism. This enabled Judas and his men to reconsecrate the temple on 25 Kislev 164 B.C. and offer up a sacrifice to YHWH on the altar—the first sacrifice to YHWH in three years (2b, 3c, 4, possibly 3d). Even so, they continued to be subjected to pogroms in areas where they were in the minority (1a, 1c, 1i, 2b, 3b).
- When Judas died in 161 B.C., his men chose Jonathan, his brother, as their new military leader. His defeat of Bacchides saw a five-year peace (158–153 B.C.) descend on the land (3d). Jonathan was a shrewd politician. He expertly manipulated the various contenders for the Seleucid throne, often switching sides between them and making himself militarily indispensable to those whom he favoured (1a, 1g, 1h). As a result, he wrested control of the Akra and had his brother, Simon, appointed commander of the coastal region from the Ladder of Tyre to the Egyptian border. Together, Jonathan and Simon expanded their territory to a great extent (1g, 4?). This came to include three toparchies (districts) in Samaria, Ascalon, Gaza, and the fortress of Beth-Zur (2g).
- After Jonathan fell prey to his own machinations, his brother Simon became head of state and high priest. He continued consolidating his power (2g) and made the Jews independent of the

Seleucids by forcing the capitulation of the Akra (possibly 3d). As a result, the grateful population met him "with thanksgiving, and branches of palm trees, and with harps, and cymbals, and with viols, and hymns, and songs" (I Maccabees 13:51). Some factions celebrated his reign as one of peace (3d) with near Messianic proportions (4).

- John Hyrcanus, his successor, found himself contending with Antiochus VII who was trying to re-establish Syrian control of the region. Antiochus devastated Judaea and besieged Hyrcanus in Jerusalem during a Sabbatical year. As there was little food in the city at that time, he was able slowly to starve out the residents and so forced Hyrcanus to sue for peace (1g, 1h). Nevertheless, the latter soon became the sovereign leader of Judaea as a result of Antiochus VII's death in 129 B.C. and the ensuing internal struggles for the Syrian throne. With the intent of restoring the dimensions of the Davidic kingdom, Hyrcanus conquered Madabe (northern Moab), Samaga, Shechem, Mt. Gerizim, Adora, and Marissa, destroyed the Samaritan temple on Mt. Gerizim, and forced circumcision upon the Idumaeans (1i, 2g). He used foreign mercenaries to achieve his territorial aims (1d, 5g). Exploiting the conflict between Antiochus VIII and IX, he next conquered and destroyed Samaria in 108–107 B.C. (2g). Even though his relations with the outside world were relatively good (cf., e.g., two treaties with Rome), Hyrcanus faced increasing opposition at home—primarily from the Pharisees—for his secularising policies (5c).
- During his brief reign, Aristobulus I expanded Judaea's territory to include areas of the Davidic Kingdom. He also enforced the Judaisation of large parts of Ituraea/Northern Galilee (1i, 2g).
- His brother, Alexander Jannaeus, claimed various cities in the rich commercial and agricultural areas east of the Sea of Galilee. He laid a bitter and protracted siege against the coastal city of Gaza, where he destroyed the town and many of its inhabitants for their resistance. His increasing despotism led to opposition from the Pharisees and a long and bitter civil war (2a). The turning point came when he massacred some 6,000 Jewish worshippers (1i) who pelted him with lemons and hurled insulting cries at him for his slovenly officiation at the Feast of Tabernacles (2b, 2d, 5c). This was followed by a six-year civil war (2a) during which some 50,000 Jews lost their lives. The leaders of the revolt called upon Demetrius

III Eukairos for assistance in c. 88 B.C. (1g). The latter marched through Galilee and into Samaria, adding dissident Jews to his ranks (1d). Even though he prevailed against Jannaeus' forces in a bloody battle near Shechem, he had to return home to face other problems. Some rebels changed heart and assisted Jannaeus to defeat the surviving rebels (1d). Many of the rebels were taken back to Jerusalem. There, Jannaeus crucified about 800 of them and murdered their wives and children before their helpless eyes while he watched, feasting with his concubines on the Baris, near the Temple (1i, 2b). Jannaeus also broke ties with the Pharisees for what he believed was their opposition to him (2a). He continued his expansionist policies so that, upon his death, his borders thus closely resembled those of David upon the accession of Solomon.

- Salome Alexandra (a model for Judith?) ruled wisely (5a) and restored ties with the Pharisees. Her reign was celebrated as a reign of peace (3d).
- After her death her sons Aristobulus II and Hyrcanus II vied against each other (2a) and for Pompey's support in an attempt to gain rulership of Judaea. Hyrcanus II made alliances with Antipater, an Idumaean, and Aretas, the Nabataean king (1g, 1h, 5g) to the same effect. Pompey's reticence to decide between Aristobulus and Hyrcanus saw the former trying to secure his rule with military arrangements. This made Pompey suspicious and he attacked Aristobulus and his men who were entrenched in Jerusalem (cf. 1e). He broke their resistance in 63 B.C. after besieging the city for three months and appointed Hyrcanus as high priest. He also entered the Holy of Holies, which sparked horror in the hearts of the devout. They believed that it was a sure sign of YHWH's judgment upon them for their sin (5d, 5e).

It is evident from the above that the events briefly listed here match almost perfectly with the insights gained from the interim situational analysis. Although the evidence adduced through a deep-structure analysis of *Judith* supports my hypothesis that the book was composed in c. 88 B.C., I find nothing to support my additional hypothesis that the book was edited c. 63 B.C. In other words, I find nothing to support my belief that *Judith* 16:23a–b is a gloss added to the text/basic story in c. 63 B.C. I also find no evidence, at a deep-structure level, to support multiple composition dates or a conflation of multiple narratives. To my mind, the book shows a unified deep structure, one that is supported by its surface structure. Since the events listed above, including Pompey's entrance into Jerusalem, find support in the interim situational analysis, I would like to emend my hypothesis as follows: *Judith* was composed as a whole shortly after Pompey entered Jerusalem in 63 B.C.

Interpretation/Analysis

Even though I have emended the second part of my hypothesis concerning *Judith's* date of composition, I have found the results of the analysis very gratifying as a researcher in the relatively untouched field of Jungian applications to the Book of Judith. My analysis has proved the versatility of a Jungian psychoanalytical/deep-structure analysis, helped to clarify *Judith's* date of composition, and corroborated its essential unity. Having completed the interim situational analysis, I now proceed to the objective analysis proper.

The dream occurs just after Pompey's entrance into Jerusalem in 63 B.C. The arrival and obvious military prowess of yet another world superpower (Nebuchadnezzar and his forces) strikes fear into the heart of the dreamer, who is a devout Jew and one who is committed to 'the old way of life'. It conjures up fears of the kind of apostasy, moral decay, national self-alienation—social-political and psychic—and political-religious domination/oppression and persecution that had occurred during the Hellenistic era (cf. Holofernes' dealings with the western nations). The dreamer's experiences of the events of that time rise up like spectres, reminding her/him of the cruelty of the Assyrian kingdom, as well as the national self-alienation and psychic torment caused by the Assyrians and the Babylonians through their exile of the Northern and Southern Kingdoms. Judaea's rulers had proved themselves weaklings, eager puppets of the Hellenistic rulers for the most part (cf. the various 'disciples' amongst the characters), proud, inflated people who had dared to arrogate to themselves dignities that did not properly belong to many of them (Holofernes, his 'people' and foreign advisors) and who had bought and sold the high priestly office, seen fit to desecrate the temple and/or permit the foreign rulers to do so, introduced the worship of foreign gods (Holofernes' dealings with the coastal dwellers), syncretised worship once again, and persecuted their own people most harshly for any form of resistance or rebellion (cf. Holofernes' mandate in 2:5–13). Even those alongside whom the dreamer had fought during the guerrilla freedom warfare initiated by Mattathias (Ozias), Judas (Judith), and his men eventually fell to the lure of power and became like their non-Hasmonean predecessors, persecuting the faithful, caring for nought but their own positions, the consolidation of their power and the extension of their territory (cf. the disposition of Nebuchadnezzar and Holofernes). For the dreamer, the nation has tragically become nothing but a shadow of its true self (Achior prior to his integration in Bethuliah), i.e., nothing but a shadow of the people called out and consecrated by YHWH. Would the advent of this new world power bring on more of the same, and who would save them this time? Recalling these events, the dreamer's psyche longs for the kind of peace that prevailed during the reign of Simon (Judith) and of Salome-Alexandra (the character Judith, and 16:25) and for a return to the land, with its traditions and religion that was facilitated by Cyrus, the Persian ruler, and the brave, messianic Judas Maccabeus. However, it all seems hopeless because the dreamer believes that the latest foreign inundation of the land and the horrific desecration of the temple by a Gentile (cf. the Judaeans' fears in 4:1–3) is nothing other than YHWH's judgment of His people for their sins (cf. 7:28).

It is within this context that the dream presents all these events, fears, and emotions, as a grand narrative of seeming hopelessness (*Judith* 1–7) contrasted with YHWH's salvation of His people (*Judith* 8–16, especially 13–16), whom he had neither abandoned nor punished, but saved by very decisive though unconventional means (8:18–20, 25–27, 32b–34 and Judith's dealings with Holofernes and his men). By means of Judith's speech to the elders (8:11c–27), the dream encourages the dreamer and the dissident forces (the Bethulians) not to engage in the kind of thinking spawned by their adherence to the negative side of Deuteronomistic thinking; it shows that this thinking is self-destructive, obsolete, and invalid. It will lead to the entire nation—not just the dissidents—being swallowed up by yet another foreign power, to further moral decay (cf. the results of the subjective analysis regarding this matter) and to more religious apostasy. It will prevent the dreamer (and her/his group) from experiencing the kind of clear thinking and deep connection to YHWH, the Self, that is necessary at this point in time. Such is the thinking, commitment, and piety of Judith. Once again, the dream reminds the dreamer that YHWH is indeed for and not against His people and will deliver them (4:13; cf. also 8:18–20, 33–34) through the hand of someone who is willing to trust Him, lean on His power alone, and follow His ways completely (Judith). It reminds her/him that YHWH is able "to console those who mourn . . . give them beauty for ashes, the oil of joy for mourning, the garment of praise for the spirit of heaviness" (Isaiah 61:3a–b. Cf. *Judith* 8–16 vs. *Judith* 1–7, especially 16 vs. 7 and 8) as He had done many times before (cf. Achior's speech in 5:5–22 that reminds the dreamer of her/his spiritual heritage and YHWH's salvific deeds towards His people). In fact, the dream asserts that YHWH is at the very point of delivering the nation from the clutches of the negative forces that constitute its shadow (see 4:13).

In compensation for the dreamer's feeling of impending doom, helplessness, and impurity, the dream offers her/him its portrait of Judith: priestess, prophetess, judge, wise woman and deliverer; an unconventional woman, yet one whom no one could fault (8:1; cf. also the meaning of Bethuliah that conjures up the imagery of the virgin daughter of Israel), one scrupulously, bravely, and wholeheartedly devoted to YHWH and His will, and one who remains pure to the end (13:16 and 16:22). This restores to the dreamer the image of the holy nation, called out by YHWH and consecrated to His will alone, and provides her/him hope about the strength that s/he has, while simultaneously affirming that this strength lies in YHWH alone.

The dream further admonishes the dreamer not to disregard the danger represented by the new foreign power (the western nations' initial response to Holofernes in 1:11), but also not to give in to it (the coastal dwellers' response in 3:28–4:4) or fear it (the Judaeans' response as well as that of the Bethulians in 4:2 and 7:19, 22ff.). It shows her/him that s/he must take decisive action along with prayer and cling fast to YHWH in order to rout the enemy. The dream also encourages the dreamer not to fear the enemy that is within, i.e., the Judaean political-spiritual leadership. It shows her/him that they are weaklings who had rebelled against YHWH and who would therefore not survive the 'heat' of His wrath (Manasses); that they would be defeated despite their seemingly strong position and allies from other parts of the world (Arphaxad's fortifications and eastern helpers); and that their pride and overconfidence in their own strength would soon lead to their own destruction (cf. Holofernes' attitude in this regard and the discussion of how the very instinctuality of his forces is what brought them down in the end). To drive the point home, the dream shows that they, like Manasses, are in fact already dead and therefore powerless to prevent the national freedom and rebirth that the dreamer longs for (the necessity of Manasses' death).

The dream therefore encourages the dreamer to fight fire with fire, to break down Rome's resistance systematically and relentlessly—as Judith disarmed those around Holofernes with her beauty and wisdom—so that they may defeat the enemy at 'his' own game and with 'his' own weapons (Judith took advantage of Holofernes' sexual-instinctual nature and pride and decapitated him with his own sword). This, the dream says, will cause a reversal in the balance of power in favour of the dissidents (the Bethulians) and the entire nation (the Judaeans) who will return to YHWH *en force* (everyone goes up to Jerusalem to worship; 15:12–13). In this way, the dissidents would prevent the nation from being swallowed up by the enemy, i.e., from going through yet another physical and/or moral-spiritual exile (cf. the self-alienation discussed in preceding subsections), and the desired reign of peace and joy would come (cf. the people's jubilation; 13:9, 15:12–13, 16:20 and 25).

According to the dream, however, there are some fundamental changes that need to be affected. As we have seen from the subjective analysis, the dreamer needs consciously to integrate the shadow and the anima. This is depicted primarily in the form of:

i) Achior's acceptance and integration into Bethulian society.
ii) The women's independent action in leading worship and the men following the women.
iii) Judith: her character, lineage, deeds, and incorporation of shadow elements in the form of her ἅβρα and the head of Holofernes.
iv) The incorporation of Hellenistic and Bacchic elements into the people's worship.
v) The location of Bethuliah in Samaria (see chapter 1).

These integrations teach the dreamer-dissidents a number of important lessons about their external world:

a) The essential oneness between themselves and the 'rebellious' Judaeans.
b) The essential oneness between themselves and the cast-out shadow races of Ammon, Moab etc.

c) The necessity of embracing those whom they had regarded as 'other', i.e., the impure Samaritans, Ammonites, etc., and the women of their own society.
d) The necessity of incorporating that which is good from Hellenistic/Roman society and throwing out, decapitating, and defeating that which is bad.
e) The necessity of getting in touch with and understanding their own shadow-side: they are not as pure as they think they are.
f) The necessity of getting in touch with their feminine, unconventional, truly spiritual side that connects them deeply and fundamentally with YHWH—more than sacrifices and rituals ever could (cf. sacrifices and fear vs. Judith's true piety?).

As we have seen from the subjective and interim situational analyses, the integration of the shadow and the anima is deeply intertwined, with the integration of the one facilitating the integration of the other. As we have also seen, integrating these 'others' is not only a necessary prerequisite for breaking out of collective patterns and ideals and achieving the desired state of individuation,—stage 4, but also the necessary outcome of the individuation process in that it enables one to get closer to YHWH and the community from which onestems.

The dream therefore advocates that the nation/dissidents must become more flexible in their approach to the current situation. I.e., they must break out of collective thinking, gendered beliefs and expectations, collective ideals, and traditional methods of dealing with the kind of problem that they are facing. It encourages them not to focus on their own suffering alone but to see the bigger picture: their failure to follow the dream's promptings will result in the destruction of the whole land (cf. 8:21–24).

In light of the oppression and persecution that they had gone through, the dream encourages the dissidents (and the nation) to emancipate the other and the anima, i.e., those 'other' to themselves, the foreigners and the women (cf. 14:10, 16:23c–24), and to seek reconciliation between themselves and these 'others' under the common goal of serving YHWH (not just with words or prayer but in heart and deed). That would bring about a true transformation of their society—one that comes from the inside out; and it would be a true reflection of their spiritual/psychological and salvific heritage, a true fast to YHWH—a true *ekkenosis*, true religion, and true worship. This is the will of YHWH, the Self, towards them, so says the dream.

D. *The Relation between the Subjective and Objective Analyses*—Judith's *Dominant Psychological Concern*

As indicated in chapter 4, "the text's dominant psychological concern is intimately connected to the self-awareness of the effective protagonist on the one hand, and the dilemma facing the author on the other. The correlation of these factors is to be expected as the effective protagonist symbolises the author's dominant unconscious personality". Throughout my work, I have treated *Judith* as a 'big dream' that was communicated to a devout Jew regarding the state of the Jewish nation c. 63 B.C. This means that *Judith's* dominant psychological concern may be established by correlating the self-awareness of the effective protagonist, Achior, and the dilemma facing the devout Jew whose dream this is. These aspects of the analysis are reviewed briefly below:

i) *Achior's Self-Awareness*:
When we first encounter Achior, he is in the process of exiting the second stage of conscious awareness, i.e., the separation from the other, and acceding to the third, the differentiation of moral properties. At this point, his ascent is thwarted by the third phase of Holofernes' attack, which throws him back to stage 1. A subsequent libido infusion causes him to escape this stage and rise to the fourth stage, viz. the realisation of social reality and individual consciousness. This stage is represented by Bethuliah and its people. At first, Achior seems rather reluctant to be completely integrated at stage 4, and his partial integration occurs only as a result of the Bethulians' embracing him. Later, however, once Judith has returned triumphant, he eagerly and willingly embraces all that a stage 4 consciousness entails (cf. his conversion) and becomes fully integrated there.

A large part of Achior's individuation depends upon his escaping from the shadow's clutches—i.e., integrating the shadow—and discarding the negative Deuteronomistic ideology that he clings to so that he can become fully integrated and fully functional at stage 4. As we have seen, this ideology is effectively the basis of the 'morality' upon which his society/community is founded. The dream calls upon him to discard it and frame his own moral/ethical code. This is a stage 3 activity—the differentiation of moral properties and, even though Achior finally accedes to stage 4 as part of the dream's solution to the problem, it places his overall self-awareness between stages 2 and 3.

ii) *The Dreamer-Author's Dilemma*

The devout dreamer-author's dilemma is closely related to the genetic context that has been established in the preceding subsection. As we have seen, the advent of the new world power, Rome, and Pompey's desecration of the temple resurrects the fears of persecution, moral decay, and spiritual apostasy that had prevailed during the Hellenistic era. Moreover, it brings upon the dreamer-author the conviction that this latest act of desecration is nothing other than YHWH's judgment of His people for their sins. In my opinion, this situation fosters a threefold dilemma in the dreamer's life:

a) Preserving the community of the devout, their traditions, morality, and relation to YHWH in the face of potentially new adversity. This relates to the community's survival in and of itself, the preservation of the 'old way of life' based on strict adherence to the Law, and the prevention of desertion amongst the ranks of the dissidents/devout Judaeans.
b) Preventing further moral decay and religious apostasy amongst the nation's leaders and the nation as a whole.
c) Bringing the nation back to YHWH.

As the objective analysis has indicated, the dreamer's threefold dilemma also requires rescuing the nation and possible deserters from the clutch of the shadow in respect of the three points above and discarding the negative self-perception associated with adhering to the negative aspect of Deuteronomistic philosophy in respect of point a) in particular. These requirements indicate that the dreamer-author's dilemma is related to Stages 2 and 3 of Jung's individuation cycle, which is where Achior's overall self-awareness is situated.

Given the exact correlation between Achior's self-awareness and the dreamer-author's dilemma, it is obvious that *Judith's* chief psychological concern lies between Stages 2 and 3, viz. separation from the shadow and the differentiation of moral properties. We may therefore say that *Judith* illustrates a phase in the evolution of consciousness prior to the differentiation of moral properties, stage 3. This assertion is further corroborated by the fact that the greater part of the nation, the Judaeans, is rather unstably situated at the third stage of conscious awareness for the first section of the narrative and stabilises at the same level towards the end of section II.

E. Judith *as an Individuation Drama*

I have expressed the opinion in chapter 1 and elsewhere throughout my thesis that *Judith* is an individuation drama. To this end, I have adduced the following evidence: "There is nothing haphazard about the composition of the book. Each of its two parts (*Judith* 1–7 and 8–16) is a palindrome that is reminiscent of the symbol of individuation—the mandala" (chapter 1). There is, however, more evidence that supports regarding *Judith* as an individuation drama, and I would like to discuss it below.

a. Judith *and the Hero Myth Patterns*

There are many parallels between *Judith* and both variations of the (sun) hero myth that Jung was so fond of. I should like to present these in the form of table 15 and table 16. The first column of each table is taken directly from my own discussion of these mythic patterns in chapter 2, whilst the second relates the various aspects of each pattern to *Judith*. Points of comparison are highlighted in both columns.

I should like to comment briefly as follows on the correspondences between *Judith* and the two Hero Myth patterns:

a) It is evident that there is a high degree of correlation between *Judith's* core events and scenarios and those typically found in both types of hero myth patterns. There are, however, some exceptions in which a particular aspect of the typical pattern is reversed or negated in *Judith*. This is the case with points F and G in table 15, and point V in table 16. Notably, these are the points that allude to the hero's marriage and some harm that has befallen him. (I say 'him' because both of these hero myth patterns are specifically male patterns of individuation). In *Judith*, both of these issues are related to Judith's (feminine) sexuality and her devotion to YHWH. The fact that she is a woman that is totally committed to YHWH and His ways protects her from harm (unlike the typical hero, point G in table 15, point V in table 16) and necessitates that she remains sexually 'pure' or unmarried (cf. 13:16;

16:22—*vs.* point F in table 15) because she is effectively married to Him. As Levine (1989:564) has indicated, "Judith remains a widow both because she had nothing to gain by marriage and because no man was worthy of her." By implication, therefore, YHWH is the only suitable 'husband' for Judith—which is why all other suitors are rejected (16:22).

b) Both hero myth patterns are specifically male individuation patterns. As Annis Pratt (1992a) has shown, these differ markedly from the individuation patterns of women that follow the Demeter-Kore myth (see my discussion of this in chapter 2). This brings me back to a point I made concerning the ἅβρα, namely, that she cannot be regarded as a goddess figure that assists women in their individuation process precisely because Judith manifests a distinctly male individuation pattern. In *Judith* we see a gender reversal, so that the male hero and male shadow are presented in female guise, i.e., as Judith and the ἅβρα (whereas the shadow in female individuation dramas is the animus/a male figure), and the monster that the hero battles—a traditionally female figure/ anima—is presented as a male enemy general, Holofernes. Interestingly, his shadow, Bagoas, is 'correctly' presented as male according to the male individuation pattern. Similarly, the male Achior is correctly depicted as a shadow to the predominantly male Bethulians and Holofernes, and *vice versa*. Why, then, does the narrative see fit to reverse gender in respect of Judith, her ἅβρα, and Holofernes? A number of different possibilities come to mind:

- The Judaean cultic community is predominantly male, which necessitates a male individuation pattern. However, the dream wishes to alert this community to the fact that they are not as weak as they think they are, and therefore presents the hero as a woman who conquers the enemy through her devotion, fearlessness, and obedience to YHWH. The ἅβρᾳ/hero(ine)'s shadow is then presented as a woman in parallel to the hero(ine)'s gender, and the 'dragon' is presented as a male to contrast the hero(ine)'s gender.
- Judith is essentially a personification of the Judaean community, which is often referred to as female vis-à-vis the male YHWH (*vide*, e.g., Ezekiel 16:1–43; Isaiah 62:11 and Jeremiah 4:31, 6:2; cf. also Isaiah 22:4, 37:22). Hence, the hero(ine) and her shadow must be female, and the aggressor-enemy must be male.

- Judith is both the community's anima and its ego. She must, therefore, be presented in female guise according to her anima status and follow a male pattern of individuation according to her status as the predominantly male cultic community's ego.
- The dream wishes to contrast the failed individuation of Holofernes, the conquered western nations, and Manasses with the successful individuation of Judith, Achior, the Bethulians, and the Judaeans. Whilst Holofernes succumbs to anima possession and dies, for example, the last three groups of predominantly male characters consciously integrate the anima and live. The dream underscores this difference by presenting the female Judith as the character to be emulated by all, particularly the devout dreamer and the Judaean community as a whole.
- Judith compares well to the wisdom figure that is also personified as female. See, e.g., the numerous references to her wisdom, her ability to teach her people the ways of YHWH and lead them closer to Him, and her dual chaste-vamp portrayal, all of which are features of the biblical and Sophia (primarily in Proverbs 1–9) and her many permutations in the later biblical and extra-biblical Judaeo-Christian literary tradition. The correspondence between these two figures renders Judith in female guise and underscores the foolishness of the male characters vis-à-vis her wisdom. It deepens and intensifies the message that the community should follow her example. (Unfortunately, spatial-temporal concerns prevent me from entering into a detailed discussion of this matter here. However, I hope to address it in a forthcoming article in the near future. For the time being, I should like to refer the reader to my 1995 conference paper, "Sexual Politics and the Power of Wisdom," Engelsman's 1994 monograph, Patai's *The Hebrew Goddess* [1990], and the comments in Alonso Schökel 1975a [chapter 3]).

I believe that the reasons mentioned above are interrelated, even though they differ from one another, and that they contribute jointly to the presentation of a female hero(ine) that exhibits a clearly male individuation pattern and her female shadow. (One may also conjecture that the dreamer-author could be male and therefore instinctively unfamiliar with a female individuation pattern, which leads to his presenting a female lead figure that exhibits a male individuation pattern).

Table 15. Judith and the General Patern of the (Sun) Hero Myth.

General Pattern of the Hero Myth	Judith
A. "Essentially, a **lack** or some kind of imbalance sets the hero on his quest to a **foreign country** or **up a difficult mountain** to find assistance or gain power to **solve the initial problem**".	The Assyrians surround Bethuliah. They block off the city's spring, which causes **great thirst and panic** to set in. Judith voluntarily sets off **down the mountain** to the **foreign enemy's camp** in order **to rectify the situation** (7:1–10:10).
B. "The hero sets off on his quest, and **arrives** at his point of destination after passing **many tests** and/or overcoming numerous monsters".	Judith descends to the foothills of Bethuliah where she encounters the Assyrian patrol at the outskirts of the **enemy camp**. She bluffs the patrol into thinking she is there to assist Holofernes (**test 1**), and is escorted to Holofernes by 100 Assyrian soldiers. Whilst all gather around her and clearly desire her, no one harms her (**test 2**). At Holofernes' tent she fools him and his entire entourage to the same effect (**test 3**), as a result of which she is granted safe passage in and out the camp 'to wash herself' (**test 4**). She resists the offer to eat nonkosher food (**test 5**) and also escapes Holofernes' intended seduction (**test 6**). Having killed Holofernes, she escapes undetected (**test 7**). (This portion may be found in 10:10– 13:10).
C. "[The Hero] is often **accompanied by a shadowy companion who seems to be his double** and **offered advice by various deities** and/or other magical creatures/people with magical powers (e.g., a magician, patron deity, old woman, or faithful *animal*)".	**Judith is accompanied by her** textually nameless, voiceless **ἅβρα/shadow** and is seemingly **offered advice by YHWH** himself. (Even though this is never directly indicated in the text itself, it is an underlying assumption throughout all her prayers. See 9:2–14; 12:5; 13:7). The kosher food (10:5; 12:1–4) and the food basket (13:10, 15), as well as her nightly wash at the spring (12:7), may be seen as demythologised magical elements which help her sustain her presence of mind etc. whilst she is in the enemy camp.
D. "[The hero's] **troubles are not over when he arrives at his destination**, as he usually **has to liberate a maiden**	**Having arrived at the camp, Judith has to make sure that she is not violated and that she kills Holofernes and flees**

and/or untold treasure from a dragon or other similar monster".	**undetected**. To this end, Judith liberates Holofernes of his **head and bed canopy** and flees undetected into the night with her ἅβρα (cf. especially 12:10–13:10).
E. "**He does so, with a little help from his magical friends, and returns to a hero's welcome** in the maiden's land and/or his own".	**Judith is assisted by her ἅβρα** and returns to Bethuliah (10:5–6; 12:15, 19; 13:3, 9–10). Even though the men are at first surprised to see her, she soon **receives a hero's welcome** to the extent that her people and the leaders of her society accord her the highest blessings/praise. The women welcome her as a conquering hero by performing a victory dance to her (and YHWH's?) honour, and the men follow. She leads a triumphal song in praise of YHWH and they all ascend to Jerusalem together (13:11–16:18).
F. "[The hero] **marries the maiden**—usually as a reward for his bravery—and **becomes a powerful leader who transforms his world and/or his vision of it**".	One may argue that the 3-month feast in Jerusalem (16:20) represents the people's remarriage (return) to YHWH. It is indicative that **Judith remains unmarried** despite many suitors (16:22). One may therefore also argue that YHWH is and remains her 'husband,' and that she is even more intimately 'married' to the deity after her return than she was before (cf. her complete surrender to Him). **Judith becomes a powerful leader** who leads her people to military victory over the Assyrians. Her fame keeps her people protected many years after her death. In the process of the entire narrative **she also transforms her society, her people's self-understanding, and their understanding of YHWH's nature and His role in their suffering**.
G. "Alternatively, **the hero is sometimes swallowed by the dragon he battles, but returns after slaying it from within**, with the rest [E. and F.] following".	**Judith** willingly **goes down to the enemy camp, slays Holofernes in his own tent and upon his own bed, and returns to Bethuliah** (cf. 8:32–34, 9:9; 10:10–13:10).

Table 16. Judith and the Pattern of the Alternative Hero Hero Myth/Night Sea Journey.

General Pattern of the Hero Myth	Judith
I. "**A hero is devoured by a water monster in the West**".	Judith is a member of one of the **western nations** who originally disparaged Nebuchadnezzar (see 1:9, 11). When the Assyrian army camps at the foothills of Bethuliah, **Judith** willingly **goes down into the enemy camp** to deal with the attack (8:32–34, 9:9; 10:10). One may therefore say that she allows herself to be swallowed by Holofernes and his forces.
II. "**The** animal **travels with him to the East** (sea journey), **usually in the night time**".	**Holofernes wishes to take Judith back to the East with him**, where she would become as one of the daughters who served Nebuchadnezzar (11:23; cf. also 12:13). **The central acts of section II take place primarily at night**: Judith arrives at Holofernes' tent in the night, goes out to wash at midnight, is invited to an evening banquet, kills Holofernes at night, and also makes good her escape at night.
III. "**Whilst in the monster's belly**, **the hero lights a fire and, feeling hungry, cuts himself a piece of the heart**".	**Judith eats her own** kosher **food whilst in the Assyrian camp** (12:1–4, 19). She decapitates Holofernes with his own sword and **places his severed head in her food basket** (13:6–10). In this way, she effectively cuts at the heart of the enemy camp, which is why the Assyrians panic and flee when they discover that Holofernes is dead and she is gone.
IV. "**The endangered monster soon glides to land and the hero escapes by cutting the animal open from within and slipping out**".	**Judith decapitates Holofernes and slips out of the enemy camp unnoticed** (13:6–10).
V. "One might find that [**the hero's**] **hair has fallen out** because the heat was so intense in the monster's belly. **Oftentimes, the hero simultaneously frees all those previously swallowed by the monster**".	**Judith** suffers no harm whatsoever and she **is not violated in any way**. In fact, she is adamant about that (13:16). **She liberates all those (her people) who were held fast in the clutches of fear and of the shadow** on account of Holofernes and his vast army (see 14:1–15:7).

b. Judith *and the Gnostic* Quaternios

At first glance, any correlation between *Judith* and Jung's Gnostic *quaternios* may seem spurious and ill-advanced. However, there are distinct correlations and I would like to present them here.

Before commencing, I should like to set out the following theoretical parameters that will facilitate our understanding of the correlations involved:

i) A *quaternio* represents the conjunction of the (pairs of) opposites that constitute it and depicts the fourfold basis of wholeness.
ii) Jung's *quaternios* depict the transformation of one substance, i.e., the fall of the *Anthropos* or Original Man into *physis* and her/his subsequent rise to spirituality.
iii) By virtue of the subjective analysis, all the characters in *Judith* may indeed represent (different aspects of) that one substance, viz. the effective protagonist who is the dominant unconscious personality of the author and the Jewish nation.
iv) *Judith* is a dream concerning national individuation.

Given the above, any correlations between *Judith* and Jung's *quaternios* must:

a) Identify the (pairs of) opposites that constitute the nation and relate to its wholeness.
b) Deal with the transformation of the nation.
c) Relate to the nation as a single entity or as a whole.
d) Elucidate the individuation process of the nation.

As we have seen, *Judith* consists of numerous opposites and pairs of opposites. For example, it is clear that YHWH and Nebuchadnezzar are opposites—the question in *Judith* is which one of the two characters will serve as God and, indeed, which one *is* God (cf., e.g., Hengel 1974:112). Similarly, Judith and Holofernes are opposites, not only in terms of their gender, but also as regards whom they serve and what their aims are vis-à-vis the Jewish nation, whilst Achior and the Judaeans-Bethulians are opposites regarding their ancestry and legal standing vis-à-vis the Deuteronomistic law that they both cling to. These six characters are central to the plot of *Judith*—the story simply could not be told without them—with Achior and Judith being the most central to a deep-structure analysis and the narrative's surface structure, respectively. In terms of the polarities that constitute Jung's vertical and uroboric arrangements (seen earlier in diagrams 5 and 6), the greatest polarity lies between YHWH-Judith and Nebuchadnezzar-Holofernes, whilst a lesser polarity exists between the Bethulians-Judaeans and Achior. This may be represented as follows (Jung's uroboric *quaternio* arrangement, diagram 6, is reproduced, for the sake of clarity):

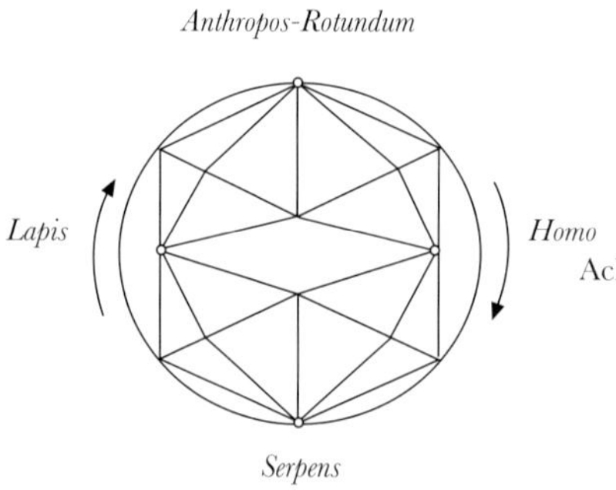

Diagram 6. The Uroboric Arrangements of Jung's *Quaternios*.

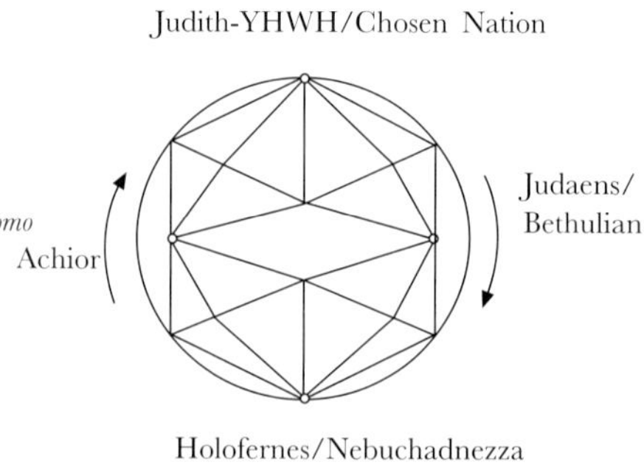

Diagram 12. Individuation in *Judith* According to the Uroboric Arrangement of Jung's *Quaternios*.

Diagram 12, above, sets out the individuation cycle of the Jewish nation as presented by the Book of Judith. The top-point of the uroboric arrangement is the "Chosen Nation", that entity which was called out by YHWH as His people to live according to His Law. The 'Chosen Nation' is necessarily a theoretical construct in that the Jews never reached the kind of perfection in their relation to YHWH and one another that His Law and representatives demanded. The perfection and 'purity' of this Chosen Nation corresponds to the perfection and purity of the *Anthropos*, the Original Man or First Adam, in diagram 6.

Seeing that all the characters in *Judith* represent the nation in terms of the subjective analysis, and Nebuchadnezzar and Holofernes are portrayed as the basest and most instinctual of these, we may say that these two characters represent the greatest distance from the ideal of the Chosen Nation (diagram 12). In this sense, therefore, they correspond to the serpent in diagram 6. This correspondence is further justified by my interpretation of Nebuchadnezzar and Holofernes as the Shadow/negative Self and shadow, respectively.

As indicated in chapter 2, the serpent is the shadow. It "foreshadows the possibility of a transformation towards light and wisdom, as well as a healing of the original . . . fall from grace [into *physis*] so that man may once again rise to her/his transcendent self . . . though now in a more conscious form (the snake introduces the original Edenic couple to consciousness)." The preceding analyses in chapter 5 have depicted this transformation process. More specifically, this process is inherent to the shadow in that Holofernes carries gold, the transformative alchemical symbol, from Nebuchadnezzar's house with him on his military expeditions. Moreover, the analyses have shown how the Book of Judith portrays Jung's belief that "that there can be no individuation without encountering the serpent, i.e., without experiencing the shadow and raising it to consciousness" (chapter 2).

The Judaeans-Bethulians (diagram 12) represent the first stage of the *Anthropos'* fall from grace/fall into *physis* in that *Judith* presents them as rather faithless, fearful individuals who would have given in to the shadow were it not for the book's obvious protagonist. They correspond to *homo* in diagram 6.

Being an Ammonite, Achior is also part of the Chosen Nation in that he is a descendant of Abraham via Lot. However, he is the produce of Lot and his daughters, and so part of a 'bastard' or shady (read: shadowy) race. This shadiness (read: shadowiness) is compounded by his accursed status according to the Deuteronomistic law. His ancestry and legal status therefore set him at variance with the Judaeans-Bethulians. Nevertheless, the tension between Achior on the one hand and the Judaeans-Bethulians on the other is not as great as the tension between Judith-YHWH-the Chosen Nation and Nebuchadnezzar-Holofernes who are outrightly other to them; Achior is far more 'palatable' to the Judaeans-Bethulians by virtue of their shared ancestry. Furthermore, prior to his conversion, Achior is a very unstable character that has one foot in the Assyrian camp and another in the Deuteronomistic philosophy. When he is expelled from the Assyrian camp, however, his instability makes him "a conductor for the tension which consciousness experiences regarding the Deuteronomistic philosophy, and the way is paved for a new interpretation of life to enter the conscious realm, resolve the tension within Achior/the Bethulian community, and facilitate the elimination of the crisis" (chapter 5). The elimination of the crisis aids in and results from the Judaeans-Bethulians' rise to higher consciousness.

These aspects of Achior's character and function lead to a correspondence between him (diagram 12) and the *lapis* (diagram 6), which "though decidedly of a material nature, is also a spiritual symbol" (chapter 2) in that it is situated on the ascending path to higher consciousness (diagram 6).

As we have seen, Judith has reached the fifth and highest stage of conscious awareness and is the highest form of consciousness next to YHWH (diagram 11). There is therefore a certain element of transcendence about her. She also stands in opposition to Holofernes just as YHWH and Nebuchadnezzar stand in opposition to each other. According to the preceding analyses in chapter 5, she is the goal of the individuation process in that she is perfectly individuated and the example that Section II continually holds up for emulation. She is also Sophia, the personification of wisdom, who is co-creatrix with YHWH according to various verses in Proverbs 1–9. Being a woman, Judith's primary symbolism is related to the circle/roundness (the ovum, the moon, etc.). According to alchemical teaching, the *rotundum* is round like the world soul. It "connotes a transcendent entity and the loftiest plane attainable" (chapter 2). Judith in diagram 12 thus clearly corresponds to the *rotundum* in diagram 6.

Taking all the above into consideration, we can see that diagram 12 portrays the nation's creation *cum* calling and subsequent fall into faithlessness, the way it is almost swallowed up by the serpent/shadow, and its rise through Achior's conversion towards the lofty position that Judith occupies in the Judithic dream. This depicts the individuation of the nation as a single entity according to the Book of Judith and satisfies the criteria of setting up correspondences between *Judith* and Jungian *quaternios* as outlined at the outset of this subsection.

c. *Judith, Achior, and the Judaeans-Bethulians vs. Manasses, the Conquered Western Nations, and Holofernes: Successful vs. Unsuccessful Individuation Cycles*

The preceding leaves us with no doubt that Judith's individuation cycle corresponds to the completed individuation pattern found in both forms of the hero myth, that she is the most individuated character in the book, and that her individuation cycle is complete and successful. Achior's individuation cycle is just as successful even though he does not achieve the same level of individuation that she does:

he reaches stage 4 whilst she is placed at stage 5 from the outset of section II. We have also noted that he is delivered from the unconscious in four steps, and that he accedes to and is fully integrated into the fourth stage of conscious awareness in sixteen steps, with sixteen being the square of four and the number of tiers in Judith's genealogy (8:1). We have further noted that Achior goes through "a total psychological change of four stages of consciousness—one descending (2 → 1) and three ascending (1 → 2; 2 → 3; 3 → 4)." As four is the number of totality and also the square root of the sixteen steps that he took to his conversion, we see indicated here "the completeness of both his transcendence to the fourth stage of consciousness as a person and his conversion/integration into consciousness" (chapter 5). Once again, there can be no doubt that his individuation cycle, like that of Judith, is complete.

The same may be said concerning the individuation cycle of the Judaean-Bethulians who represent the Jewish nation as a whole. Like Achior, they do not accede to the same level of consciousness as Judith. Unlike him, however, they do not go through any major psychological changes in terms of permanently transcending multiple stages of consciousness. The Bethulians, for example, begin at the fourth stage of consciousness and transcend temporarily to the fifth through their integration of the shadow and the anima. They become stabilised at stage 4 with the potential of acceding to the fifth through the extra libido they absorb in their temporary ascent to the fifth and final stage of conscious awareness. Similarly, the Judaeans return to and stabilise at the third stage of conscious awareness with the potential of acceding to the fourth after absorbing the extra libido that they acquired during their temporary ascent to the fifth stage of conscious awareness.

The correlation between Judith, Achior, and the Judaeans-Bethulians should come as no surprise: The identity between Judith and the Judaeans-Bethulians has been established psychologically and culturally in that she is their anima and ego as well as the personification of the nation. Similarly, the identification of Achior and the Judaeans-Bethulians has been established on the level of *Judith's* deep and surface structure: Achior is the effective protagonist to whom all the deep-structure events relate, the unconscious personality of the Jewish nation that is jointly represented by the Judaeans-Bethulians, as well as the character whose fate is most intimately linked to that of the Bethulians—narratively and psychologically.

The link between Judith and Achior is also narrative and psychological. It has been referred to in my discussion of Achior in chapter 1 and my evaluation of Roitman's work in chapter 3. As indicated in both these subsections, Roitman (1989 and 1992) proves that "there is an especially intriguing structural relationship and a subtle complementarity between Achior and Judith" (Roitman 1989:552) in terms of their respective functions. He traces this complementarity through five stages in each character's development and then 'summarises' his findings in tabular format (op. cit., 557–558). I reproduce this table at the end of this chapter, as table 18, to facilitate the discussion. Table 18 makes it clear that stage 1 (opposite roles and location) is characterised exclusively by difference, stage 2 (parallel roles and processes) is characterised exclusively by similarity, whilst stages 3–5 contain both differences and similarities. This complementarity, along with the relatively easy transition between Achior and Judith's words in the central stage (4), indicates to my mind that Achior is Judith's shadow or, as Roitman (op. cit., 558–559) puts it, her "double or 'alter ego'." (It will be remembered that Judith builds upon Achior's speech in order to deceive Holofernes). This interpretation of Achior is corroborated by at least two factors:

- Achior is the Judaeans-Bethulians' shadow and therefore necessarily Judith's shadow as she is a Judaean national who resides in Bethuliah.
- Achior is the Judaeans-Bethulians, shadow and therefore necessarily Judith's shadow as she is the personification of the cultically *male* nation.

The above, in combination with the strong interrelatedness between the Bethulians' assimilation of the benign shadow components represented by Achior and by Judith as anima, clearly demonstrate that there is a strong link between Judith and Achior. This means that all four characters/groups of characters who successfully complete their individuation cycles (Judith, Achior, the Bethulians, the Judaeans) are linked. These linkages form the four sides of a square, with four once again representing completeness and so corroborating the completeness of each character's/character group's individuation cycle:

In contradistinction to the completed individuation cycles of Judith, Achior, and the Judaeans-Bethulians, we find that the individuation cycles of Manasses, the vanquished western nations, and Holofernes remain incomplete in that they are interrupted and end midstream:

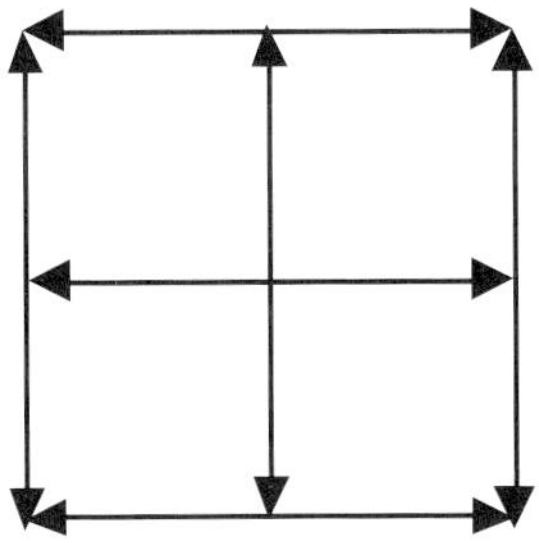

Diagram 13. The Fourfold Interrelation between Judith, Achior, the Bethulians, and the Judaeans.

- Manasses succumbs to inflation and dies, being killed by the wrath of the Self/YHWH as reflected in his death by the καύσων.
- The vanquished western nations are engulfed and destroyed by the shadow in the guise of Nebuchadnezzar-Holofernes.
- Holofernes succumbs to anima possession and is killed by his anima, Judith.

There is an interesting interrelationship between Manasses, Holofernes, and the vanquished western nations. There is also an interesting interrelationship between both sets of characters:

- Manasses prefigures Holofernes in dying upon his bed, and his pride/rebellion almost equates him with the haughty Assyrian general and his master.
- The western nations succumb to Holofernes' might. They either ignore the Assyrians and are destroyed or give themselves over to the Assyrians to suffer a similar fate.
- There is a certain similarity between Manasses and the conquered western nations, particularly the coastal dwellers. Both possess much property and livestock but carelessly give it up by succumbing to inflation and the shadow.
- The individuation cycles of Manasses, the conquered western nations, and Holofernes are interrupted as a result of their dealing carelessly with their unconscious psyche or an aspect thereof.
- Manasses is Judith's husband. He is completely opposite to her and has to die in order for Judith to be free to serve her God and her people as she does.

- The Judaeans-Bethulians, Achior, Judith, and Manasses are part of the western nations that had disparaged Nebuchadnezzar at the outset. The first three of these characters/groups overcome Holofernes, complete their individuation cycles, and live. The last two, however, are destroyed either indirectly (Manasses) or directly (the western nations) as a result of Holofernes' dealings with the people in the West.

F. *The Psychological Function of* Judith's *'Irregularities'*

The preceding subsections have demonstrated clearly that *Judith* is an individuation drama vis-à-vis its structural composition, its correlation to both versions of the hero myth and Jung's uroboric *quaternio* arrangement, as well as the way that the dreamer-author cleverly contrasts the successful individuation patterns of Judith, Achior, and the Judaeans-Bethulians on the one hand, and the unsuccessful individuation patterns of Holofernes, Manasses, and the conquered western nations on the other. I should now like to conclude chapter 5 by drawing together and summarising the psychological function of *Judith's* main irregularities vis-à-vis its dream nature as described in various subsections throughout chapter 5.

a. *The Conflation of Irregular Geographical and Anachronistic Historical Detail*

We have seen that the conflation of irregular geographical and anachronistic historical detail reflects the dreamer's anxiety about the new world power that is attacking the Holy City, Jerusalem, and desecrating its temple. The spiritual-psychological and political trauma of these events is so severe that it conjures up images of other groups that have ravaged the Jewish people, destroyed their lands, taken their people captive, and/or led their people astray by introducing new customs and religious beliefs and practices contrary to those that were received by means of tradition. So it is, for example, that the dissolution of national integrity embodied in both the Babylonian and Assyrian exiles is incarnated in Nebuchadnezzar, who is at once a Babylonian and an Assyrian king (1:1), and that exilic, pre-exilic and postexilic elements are mixed. There is also clear indication of the moral, political and religious devastation caused by the advent of the Hellenistic empire and the Jewish Hellenisers. The Hellenisers, as we have seen, attempted to turn all their people's received traditions, customs, and religious beliefs on their head in order to secure positions of power, curry favour with the Hellenistic lords, and see to their own prosperity. At the same time, the hope and desire for re-unification and national integrity stirs up the imagery of Cyrus allowing the Jewish people to return to their land, reconstitute themselves and rebuild their temple, while the desire for a redeemer sees Judith presented clearly as a Judas Maccabeus who is Moses revived, a prophet, judge, lawgiver, expounder of truth and defender of the faith/faithful all rolled into one.

The geographical irregularities, such as the vast distance covered by Holofernes' armies in three days and the seemingly circular, convoluted route they take to arrive at Judaea, are no errors. To my mind, it too reflects the traumatic events of the Judaeans' past as projected onto their present situation—the advent of the Roman power. It indicates how topsy-turvy the world has become for them, and also reflects the relative speed with which the Roman army descended upon Jerusalem.

The preceding subsections have also adduced a number of reasons for the mysterious identity of Bethuliah, the geographical location in *Judith*. One of these is linked to the possible meaning of the word, i.e., the virgin. This could depict the 'purity' of the dreamer-author and his people and provide them with the reassurance that YHWH would save them just as He had saved the Bethulians through Judith. Another reason is linked to the possibility of Bethuliah referring to the city of Shechem in Samaria. Making a Samaritan city the locus of YHWH and Judith's salvific action that extended to the rest of Judaea beautifully reflects *Judith's* passion for including the outcast and the previously despised, i.e., the shadow. It too reflects the necessity of assimilating the shadow as the rest of the narrative does.

b. *The Structure of the Book of Judith*

The preceding analyses have shown that there is nothing irregular about *Judith's* bipartite division, or the supposedly 'delayed' appearance of Judith the heroine (see comments to this effect by Alonso Schökel et al. in chapter 1). They have also proved that there is nothing at all inferior about the first seven chapters of the book, as some people have claimed (see e.g., Dancy in chapter 1). To the contrary, most of the important psychological events take place in the first section of the book (*Judith* 1–7) and find their denouement in section II (*Judith* 8–16). Furthermore, section I is vital in that it introduces the effective protagonist, Achior, about whose development the entire narrative is concerned on a psychological level. We have also seen that:

- Section I presents the problem, the magnitude of which necessitates the appearance of a hero at the end of chapter 7 when the Bethulians are ready to turn themselves over to the Assyrian enemy. This hero is then introduced at the outset of chapter 8 in the form of Judith.
- Section I establishes many of the opposites and pairs of opposites, whilst section II reflects the dissolution or integration of these opposites. For example, the shadow figure, Holofernes, is presented as the prime opposite to the Judaeans-Bethulians in section I and is integrated in section II. Similarly, Achior, a more benign shadow figure, is completely and willingly integrated in section II even though some integration took place during section I. The opposition in the book, Nebuchadnezzar and YHWH, is established in section I, where the main questions relate to which of the two the people will serve, whose strength will prevail, and which one is the one and true God. The answer is hinted at in section I (4:13) and triumphantly announced in section II through Judith's agency (see e.g., 13:11 and 16:2–17).
- According to the subjective analysis, section I reflects the dream's depiction of the problem or crisis in which the Judaeans find themselves, whilst section II reflects the solution that the dream proposes.
- The endless wars of Holofernes in section I are not vaguely superfluous as they not only set the scene for Judith's arrival in section II, but also reflect the psychological turmoil that the nation is in as a result of the unconscious shadow's attack.
- Similarly, the vast numbers of his forces are no mere theatrical exaggeration. They reflect the magnitude of the problem facing the devout dreamer-author and her/his community, as well as their feeling of being swamped by the 'evil forces' that they are facing.
- The relative monotony of section I reflects the dearth that the Judaean nation is undergoing. It is characterised by fear, just as

the second section is characterised by beauty and the revival that the community experiences through Judith.

There is thus a definite purpose to *Judith's* bipartite structure and the supposedly 'flatter' style of the first section as opposed to the 'fuller' style of the second.

c. *Judith's Dual Nature*

Judith's nature has been discussed at length in the various sections and subsections of chapter 5. Suffice it to say that she represents both the anima and the ego of the Jewish nation. As both these psychological entities are archetypes, they contain negative as well as positive features, 'divine' as well as mundane. The composite wholeness of the archetype then accounts for Judith's positive and negative aspects—her saintliness and vampishness—as well as their seemingly unconflicting side-by-side portrayal in the text. The same may be said of the way that she is both human and somehow paralleled to YHWH (see e.g., the statements concerning her state of individuation): as an archetype, she displays both numinous and non-numinous characteristics. The combined effect of these 'opposite' characteristics then leads to what might well be considered as a seriously misinformed request in dualistic western thinking: Judith asks for and receives divine assistance with and ratification for her verbal *cum* sexual deception of Holofernes.

When Judith is viewed through a Jungian lens, there is nothing immoral or ambiguous about her character, actions, and/or relation to YHWH and His people, as some authors like Bissel (1886) and Shumaker (1975) have supposed. Rather, we see that the dreamer-author has presented a composite picture of her that has not been divided into its dualistic aspects—i.e., she is not presented as saintly vs. 'unsaintly' or vampish; she is presented in a wholly Jungian way, one that makes it inappropriate to view anyone or anything according to the dualistic categories of western binarism.

d. *The Role and Relevance of Achior*

I have previously mentioned that Roitman (1989) is the only scholar who has elaborated upon Achior's relevance in *Judith*. As previously indicated, he has demonstrated the essential complementarity between

Achior and Judith and advanced the position that Achior is Judith's double or alter ego. Thus, he has built upon and expanded Moore's insight that Achior is essential to the plot of *Judith* in that he 'connects' the two sections of the book.

In my own study, I have shown that Achior is even more important than Roitman has imagined; I have shown him to be the unmistakeable effective protagonist of the entire *Judith* narrative. This means that Achior's function is far greater than merely connecting the two sections of the book; it means that he is the most important character of the book from a psychological point of view. Moreover, the preceding subsections of this chapter have shown that conducting the subjective analysis of the Judithic dream depends solely on him, whilst insights gained from the subjective analysis are vital to a credible objective analysis. Far from being a peripheral character, Achior is thus the most important character in *Judith*.

In conclusion to this subsection, we may therefore say that there is indeed a purpose behind the geographical, historical, and structural inconsistencies or irregularities of *Judith*, the 'contradictory' character of its eponymous heroine, and the inclusion of Achior in this masterful tale. All these aspects are vital to the deep structure of the text. They depict the anguish, hopes, fears, and aspirations of the nation's devout Jews and provide a purpose and a hope towards which they can strive.

Table 17. The Complementarity Between Judith and Achior According to Roitman 1989.

	Narrative	
Stage	**Achior**	**Judith**
1 Opposite Roles and Location	Man (5:5) Ammonite/enemy of Israel (5:5) Leader and soldier (5:5) Pagan Encampment of the Assyrians	Beautiful woman (8:7) Israelite (8:1) Secluded widow (8:4–6) Jewish (8:8) City of Bethuliah
2 Parallel Roles and Processes	Delivery of a speech to enemy of the Jews (5:5–21) – history of the Jews (5:6–19) – spiritual lesson (5:17–18ab) – suggestion/advice (5:20–21) – flattering words (5:5, 20–21) Anger as reaction (5:22; 6:2) Transformation into a 'Jew' (perceptual, from Holofernes' point of view)	Delivery of a speech to Jewish leaders of Bethuliah (8:11–27) – history of the Jews (8:18–19, 26–27) – spiritual lesson (8:20) – suggestion/recommendation (8:17, 24–25) – criticism (8:11–16) Wonder as reaction (8:28–29) Transformation into a 'heroine' (8:32–34) and a 'sensual woman' (10:3–4)
3 Change of Places	Expelled from the Assyrian encampment (6:7–13) Brought into Bethuliah by its citizens and taken into the presence of their city's rulers (6:14)	Voluntarily leaves Bethuliah (10:6–10) Brought into Holofernes' presence by his soldiers (10:11–23)
4 Change of Roles	Betrayer of Holofernes (perceptual from Holofernes' point of view; 6:17) Peaceful friend of the Jews (6:20–21)	Liar (e.g., 11:11–15), 'betrayer' (11:16–19), mistress (12:13–19) "Brave soldier" (13:6–8)
Function and Reactions	Disclosure of Holofernes' plans (6:17) Praised by the Bethulian people and brought to Ozias' house (6:20–21)	Disclosure of "Israel's plans" (11:11–14) Praised by the Assyrian 'people' and invited to stay at the encampment (12:5)
Speech	Achior/Holofernes A speech (5:5–21) in answer to Holofernes' questions (5:2–4) Opening words stressing truth (5:5) Truthful advice (5:20–21) Speech regarded as a prophecy (6:2) Negative reaction of Holofernes and his people (5:22; 6:2)	Judith/Holofernes A speech (11:5–19) in answer to Holofernes' question (11:3) Opening words stressing truth (11:5) Misleading advice (11:17–19) Judith as 'prophetess' (11:16–19) Positive reaction of Holofernes and his people (11:20–23)
5 Meeting and Transformation of the Characters	Meeting with Judith (14:6–10) Transformation into a civilian (14:6) and a Jew (14:10)	Commander role (14:1–4) Meeting with Achior (14:6–10) Transformation into a pious (15:14–16:19) and secluded widow (16:21–22).

CHAPTER SIX

CONCLUSION

In this chapter, I should like briefly to present the most salient points that have emerged from chapters 1–4 and reflect upon the extent they have been incorporated into my Jungian psychoanalytic approach to the Judithic dream. Given that I class myself amongst the demonstrably Jungian critics, i.e., those who acknowledge a strong Jungian influence upon their work and have applied Jung's theories to their lives, I begin my conclusion with a personal excursion.

A. *A Personal Excursion*

I have always maintained that no one writes a book or conducts any other such research for impersonal, 'purely scientific' reasons. Believing that research is intimately connected to the researcher's own journey through life, I found it hard to understand the personal reasons underlying my own research. It took me a very long time—chapter 5 was almost finished by then—to realise that I have been dealing primarily with my shadow-side for the last number of years and that it was this that (unconsciously) drove me to the study I have just completed. Having realised that, it took me a little while longer to realise with joy that dealing with the shadow involved withdrawing projections, accepting the shadow parts of oneself, and taking responsibility for them.

That it took so long to realise the above is evidence of the depth to which shadow contents and other elements of the unconscious are often buried within each one of us, the shrewdness of the unconscious mind in bringing things to the fore that one is not even aware of, and the sheer terror—perceived, not actual (in hindsight)—of dealing with oneself in a way that frees one from one's projections. While this is indeed a terrifying process to begin with, the rewards are immeasurable.

I have reaped tremendous personal benefit from this study and am a much better person as a result of it.

B. *An Evaluation of the Current Study*

a. *Jungian Theory and the Psyche*

Judith *and the 'Negative Criticism' of Jungian Thought*

While I found Jung's theories regarding the psyche, the archetypes, the individuation process and its various mythical precursors to be fascinating and valid indeed, I was particularly perturbed by how un(der)developed his thinking was in respect of the female contrasexual image, the animus, and its role in women's individuation *vs.* the intricate development of his anima theory. Seeing that Jung accorded great importance to the (male) individuation process and the role of the anima in it, I thought it very strange that he merely assumed that the anima function in men is the same as the animus function in women—and this despite his belief that the Demeter-Kore myth is of special and exclusive relevance to women and their individuation process. Further research showed that women's encounter of the animus is wholly different to men's encounter of the anima.

According to Pratt (1992a), the animus figure that women encountered during their quests/individuation dramas functioned as a shadow that alienated them from themselves and the society in which they lived. They were often driven to madness and/or suicide, which rendered their quests unsuccessful. Women's successful individuation dramas, on the other hand, were mediated by powerful, integrative goddess figures who also had the effect of alienating women from society even though they assisted them to achieve a greater sense of feminine wholeness within themselves. By contrast, in successful male individuation dramas, the dual mother (anima) re-integrates the man into society where he is welcomed as a hero. Based on Pratt's research and my own experience, I concluded, inter alia, that the function of the contrasexual images was different in men and women and, more importantly, that the integration of the feminine is fundamental for the success of male *and* female individuation dramas. This, to my mind, forms an important corrective to Jung's treatment and understanding of the animus.

In terms of the above, we have already noted that Judith's individuation cycle follows that of a man. It correlates exactly with both patterns of the hero myth—in contrast to what one might expect, seeing that Judith is a female character. We have also seen that the depiction of the hero-ego in female form within this male individuation pattern necessitates the reversal of gender for the other characters in the dream/individuation drama so that traditionally male figures are rendered female and *vice versa*. That is why Judith's shadow—the ἅβρα—is female, and the male Holofernes, whom she encounters at the nadir of her individuation cycle (her sojourn in the Assyrian camp), is her anima. The implications of this gender-reversal are rather disturbing for one like me who once thought that Judith could be used as a model for empowering women and/or the marginalized. The reason for my distress lies in the fact that, despite surface-structure appearances in which the hero(ine) is a strong female, the deep structure of the Judithic dream indicates that salvation is to be found through the enactment of the male individuation cycle. The book seems to be as androcentric as Schuller (1992) believes it to be. However, one cannot ignore the fact that Judith is a female character, as there is nothing accidental in dreams. Perhaps Judith's femininity and male individuation cycle transcend the issue of women's empowerment and depict something very close to Jung's heart, viz. the *hieros gamos* or marriage of the opposites—the ultimate aim of the individuation process. Perhaps this *hieros gamos* may also be seen in an earlier assertion of mine, namely that the human female Judith is a personification of the Judaean community who is perceived as YHWH's bride. This is certainly an area that requires further investigation and cannot be adequately addressed here. Suffice it to say, the investigation of the intricacies pertaining to Judith's gender and individuation pattern is further complicated by at least two other factors:

a) The analogy between Judith and the female wisdom figure Sophia, who is the female counterpart of the male Logos (see Engelsman, op. cit., 95–106).
b) The contrast that is set up between Judith as the Judaean people's anima and Holofernes as Judith's anima.

In my evaluation of Jung's theories, I also took issue with his conceptualisation of the archetypes, his interpretation of dream symbolism, and his 'unconscious' way of writing. While I no longer find the last aspect of Jungian thought problematic—it has become a point of rejoicing in me—I maintain my criticism of the first two. This is depicted most ably by the way in which Judith is able to function simultaneously as Holofernes' (negative) anima and the

Judaeans-Bethulians' ego and (positive) anima. Judith is not an archetype per se—she is a character—even though she functions primarily as an anima and an ego vis-à-vis the other characters in the text. Rather, she willingly takes on the ego function. For me, archetypes are neither transcendent nor unchanging in nature. Rather, they are dynamic, ever-changing, personal valuations that individual human beings/groups accord to various 'memories' at various times on behalf of their community and are imbued with archetypal anima qualities by the male characters in the text. Holofernes, as we have seen, projects his feminine soul-image/anima upon her and is destroyed (*i.a.*) as a result of not withdrawing his projection. His individuation is consequently stultified. By contrast, the Judaeans and the Bethulians integrate Judith as anima and are saved. They become stabilised at stages 3 and 4 with the distinct potential of rising to higher levels of consciousness in the future. Similarly, Holofernes acts as Judith's anima-shadow whilst he also functions as the Judaean-Bethulian national shadow.

In accordance with the findings of my analysis, I am therefore able to confirm my original agreement with Hillman's Archetypal School, namely that there is no archetype category per se, only that which is archetypal. I do, however, concur with Jung that 'archetypes'—or 'the archetypal' per Hillman—may and do affect the behaviour, emotions, and psyche of human beings. My analysis has illustrated the archetype's effect on humanity by demonstrating the effect that Judith as anima has on every male human character in the book from the men of her city to the Assyrian troops and Holofernes himself. (See also the effect that Holofernes as shadow has on the Judaeans-Bethulians throughout *Judith* prior to the heroine's defeat of him).

Having concluded my analysis of *Judith* as a dream and having analysed some of my own dreams, I now believe all the more in the important role that they and the unconscious play in a person's/group's individuation cycle. I am also convinced of the theoretical position that I expressed in chapter 2, namely that various occurrences of a particular symbol/group of symbols cannot be interpreted in the same way at every instance of their manifestation irrespective of the identity of the dreamer, the context of the dream, and the location of a particular symbol in it. Hence, in accordance with the proximity of Bethuliah's spring to the city in question and my understanding of the Bethulians as elements of consciousness, I have interpreted the said spring as that which feeds consciousness throughout my analysis. By contrast, Jung seems to regard all water bodies as symbols of the unconscious.

'Positive Criticism' and the Clarification of Various Aspects of Jungian Thought

The 'positive' contributions of Jungian theory have also found expression in my thesis, viz. Judith has shown that self-knowledge and Self-knowledge leads to a greater acceptance of the other/others. Similarly, my approach has illustrated a different and, dare I say, more creative approach to *Judith* than those that I have encountered. It has also afforded me a new appreciation of Judith as an ancient symbol of fortitude, piety, and divine providence. Furthermore, Judith's piety makes it obvious that her knowledge of YHWH and her understanding of His nature and the prevalent situation (the Assyrian attack against Bethuliah) stem from her experience with Him.

My analysis in chapter 5 has also clarified many other aspects of Jungian thought that I was uncertain about after having read Jung's momentous tomes. These are:

a) The relationship between the shadow and the anima
According to Jung, there is a correlation between the shadow and the anima in that both are forms of 'otherness' vis-à-vis the male psyche. However, I have found little in his writings to suggest whether and to what extent their integration is related apart from the fact that the shadow is usually encountered first because it is closer to the threshold of consciousness than the anima. My analysis has shown that the integration of the shadow and the anima is a codependant process: the Bethulians' partial integration of Achior as benign shadow enables Judith as ego to descend into the unconscious and destroy Holofernes in the guise of his negative anima. Judith's integration of the *mana* from the slain Holofernes as shadow then facilitates the complete integration of Achior, which leads to the greater integration/differentiation of the multiple anima in the form of the dancing women. This, in turn, leads to the integration of shadow elements into worship. From a slightly different perspective, we may also say that Judith's integration of Holofernes as anima enables the community to integrate Achior *and* Holofernes as shadows, which facilitates the integration of Judith as anima. As previously stated, the latter

integrations bring about the conscious differentiation of the multiple anima figures/dancing women and the integration of foreign/shadow elements into Judaean worship.

b) The Five Stages of Individuation
My analysis has illustrated Jung's assertion that a person may 'occupy' multiple levels of consciousness at any given time, even though s/he may function primarily at one of these. It has also illustrated how various contents of the psyche may lose or gain libido and consequently fall or rise to lower or higher levels of consciousness—an aspect of the individuation process that I have not directly encountered in the literature which I have read. Furthermore, my analysis has proved that one's unconscious personality is not necessarily at the same stage of development as one's conscious identity or persona. As we have seen, *Judith's* surface structure places the dominant form of consciousness at stage 4 (see diagram 13). By contrast, the conscious development of Achior, the effective protagonist, is situated between stages 2 and 3. Given the essential identity between Achior and the Bethulians, we may explain this discrepancy in their stages of individuation as follows: the Bethulians reflect the dreamer-author's conscious identity or persona, whereas Achior reflects the dreamer-author's unconscious identity that carries her/his actual stage of individuation.

c) Community and Transformation:
The analysis in chapter 5 has shown that community transformation must begin with a transformation of the individual: Judith's self-transformation is the starting point for the transformation of her community. My analysis has also demonstrated that transformation depends on withdrawing projections and consciously integrating various archetypal contents as they present themselves. Overcoming a particular archetypal content that is plaguing the community can only be achieved by means of someone who has already conquered that particular archetypal content within her/himself. Thus, Judith is able to conquer Holofernes the shadow because she is able to enter into *her* shadow-side as a result of already having integrated her shadow, the ἅβρα.

Furthermore, the objective analysis has indicated that identifying with women and the 'other' elements of society as well as their suffering is a necessary part of integrating the archetypal contents that they signify and bringing about the desired transformation.

d) Positive and Negative Inflation
My analysis of *Judith* has shown that at least four characters and/or groups of characters suffer from various forms of inflation: Nebuchadnezzar, Holofernes, the Judaeans-Bethulians, and Achior as the unconscious representation of the collective Jewish psyche. Intertextual parallels have also strongly suggested that Manasses was cast out of the conscious realms because he succumbed to positive inflation and rebelled against the Self/YHWH. As affects the other characters that I have referred to, we have seen that Nebuchadnezzar and Holofernes suffer from positive inflation as people. Nebuchadnezzar's inflation may be ascribed to his self-assigned ego-conqueror function and his complete identification with the negative Self/Shadow (he *is* the Shadow on an archetypal level); Holofernes' inflation, on the other hand, is derivative from that of his master: it takes hold of him as the result of the ego-conqueror function that Nebuchadnezzar confers upon him and his (Holofernes') identification with him (Nebuchadnezzar) as his disciple. Both men continuously act out of their positive inflation, with Holofernes' inflation mounting as the narrative events unfold. Both men also show signs of the reverse of their positive inflation, i.e., insecurity: Nebuchadnezzar needs to have his will ratified by his nobles, and Holofernes' insecurity as a man causes him to fall prey to the wiles of a beautiful woman. As neither men deal with their inflation, it finally leads to their downfall: Holofernes is beheaded by Judith, which effectively brings Nebuchadnezzar's expansionist drive to an end.

By contrast, the Judaeans and the Bethulians are afflicted with negative inflation almost immediately upon their encounter with Holofernes as shadow. It will be remembered that the Judaeans' panic when they hear of what Holofernes has done to the other nations, and that their desperation increases as time progresses. The Bethulians come to a place where they are willing to give in to the enemy completely as they believe that YHWH has abandoned them because of their sin. Their negative inflation is broken by Judith's restoration of their identity in *Judith* 8 and, more especially, by her victory that proved that YHWH had not abandoned His people. As a result, they are empowered to fight the enemy, deplete its store of power, and defeat it.

Interestingly, the subjective analysis has shown that Achior, as the unconscious representation of the collective Jewish psyche, also suffers from positive inflation to begin with, and that his inflation is akin to that of Nebuchadnezzar and Holofernes (see my discussion of his inflation on 1:7–11, 12–16, 2:1–3, and 2:28–3:10 in table 13). His positive inflation is broken through self-abnegation, but quickly turns to negative inflation as the situation worsens and YHWH's assistance seems to be lagging (see discussion on 4:8–12, 13c, 14–15, 7:23–28 in table 13). As with the Judaeans and the Bethulians, his negative inflation is broken when Judith returns victorious (see discussion of 13:12–16 in table 14). As a result, he converts and comes to his true self (14:6–10 in table 14).

It may be seen from the above that my analysis has given credence to my criticism against Jung's theories regarding the nature of the archetypes, the role of the animus in women's individuation cycles, and the interpretation of dream symbols. It has highlighted various aspects of the characters that demonstrate the positive aspects of Jung's theories as I see them, and elucidated certain aspects about which I was not completely certain prior to my analysis. In the process, I have also learned to rejoice in Jung's unconscious mode of writing, and so that 'negative' criticism of his work has fallen away.

b. *Identifying a Jungian Approach to* Judith

In this subsection, I would like to define how I developed a Jungian approach that would be suitable to *Judith*. I would then like to continue evaluating my analysis in terms of this approach in the following subsection.

When I began my studies, I was particularly interested in the psychological structure of *Judith*. I was particularly drawn to the text's use of archetypes, its compensatory aspects, its psychological structure, its depiction of the individuation process, its mythopoeic qualities, and the psychology of its characters. More particularly, I was interested in testing my hypothesis that *Judith* could be interpreted as a national dream that reflected the Jewish nation's stage of individuation at the time in which the book was written. I could, therefore, have applied Jung's subjective and objective method of dream analysis to the book. However, I was dealing with a text not a person; and there was therefore no dreaming subject to interrogate. Moreover, the date of *Judith's* composition has never been certain, and so I could not follow Jung's guidance for interpreting a dream in the context in which it occurs.

That is why I found Dawson's method of discerning a narrative's effective protagonist the most promising of all the approaches that I had encountered. Not only was it based on Jung's concept of the dream ego, but it provided me with a 'subject' whose dream I could analyse—the effective protagonist—and the possibility of being able to move from text to context in order to conduct the objective analysis. I therefore decided to combine Jung's dream analysis and Dawson's theories when analysing the Book of Judith, and developed a methodology that may be summarised briefly as follows:

a) I must first identify the effective protagonist by analysing each character/group of characters in the book according to Jungian categories and determining which character had changed the most.
b) In the absence of a dreaming subject, I reasoned that relating each aspect of *Judith* to the effective protagonist would enable me to conduct a subjective analysis of the Judithic dream.
c) Seeing that the date of Judith is not known with any degree of certainty, I further reasoned that the results of the subjective analysis would provide me with important clues regarding the dreamer's context. I could use these clues to establish a hypothetical context for the Judithic dream—the interim situational analysis—that could be extrapolated onto the obviously Hellenistic background of the book in order better to determine its context. This would, in turn, enable me to test my hypothesis regarding *Judith's* date and composition that had been established in chapter 1. Determining the text's date would then assist me to conduct the objective analysis and so complete my study on *Judith* as a dream.
d) I would then be able to comment meaningfully on the text's dominant psychological concern and examine my hypothesis that: a) *Judith* is an individuation drama and b) the book's inconsistencies have a psychological function that points beyond the narrow concerns of those who have discarded it to its essential and functional integrity.

c. *The Application of Jung and Dawson's Theories to* Judith

Keeping the above in mind and wishing to retain the text's bipartite structure, I applied Jungian categories to every character/group of characters in order of their appearance in the first section of *Judith*. I then determined the effective protagonist of that section and the dilemma facing him. I proceeded in the same manner with section II and concluded that Achior is the effective protagonist of both sections of *Judith*.

Achior's dilemma throughout the Judithic dream was then expressed as follows: To transcend completely the partially unconscious stage into which he has fallen and become an integral, fully functional member/content at stage 4. . . . this means that he must transcend the bounds of societal norms and values (stage 1), reclaim his otherness/separate the ego from the shadow (stage 2), establish his own ethical-moral code (stage 3), and break free from the bounds of society's norms and expectations [see the Deuteronomistic philosophy to which he and the Bethulians adhere] and become who he really is (stage 4). His dilemma is therefore ultimately concerned with breaking free from society's fetters and becoming who he inherently is.

The insights gained from this analysis were then used to conduct the subjective analysis and extrapolated onto a hypothetical context to yield the interim situational analysis. The results of the latter were used to test my hypothesis regarding the book's dating and composition namely that *Judith* was composed soon after Demetrius III's attack on Jannaeus in 88 B.C., with the gloss in *Judith* 16:23a–b added—and the book possibly 'reviewed'—shortly after Pompey's attack on Jerusalem in 63 B.C. Having completed my analysis of *Judith*, I then determined the text's dominant psychological concern, explored *Judith* as an individuation drama, and outlined the role of its inconsistencies as indicated throughout the analysis in chapter 5. I have therefore followed my proposed methodological approach very closely indeed. The outcome of the resultant analysis may be summarised briefly as follows:

a) *Subjective Analysis*

Achior's/the nation's psyche (the terms are interchangeable) is experiencing great turmoil on account of the unconscious shadow attack. It is in danger of being engulfed by the shadow to the point that it identifies with it and acts completely out of its instinctual nature and dictates. The nation also experiences an identity crisis that is exacerbated by the spiritual-religious, moral-ethical thrust of the unconscious shadow attack, the fact that some parts of the nation's psyche have already succumbed to these aspects of the attack, and the nation's conscious perception of life through the eyes of the Deuteronomistic philosophy of retribution. The dream's solution to this problem is that the nation should withdraw its shadow projections and consciously integrate its own shadows—people/groups with opposing viewpoints, etc.—through the agency of its anima. This would lead the nation closer to YHWH, enable it to realise its own unique consciousness (stage 4) and so be well on the way of achieving an unshakable and indomitable national identity (stage 5).

b) *Interim Situational Analysis*

The shadow forces are military-political entities that oppose the dominant consciousness. The latter are identified as dissidents vis-à-vis the former, whilst the former consist of external and internal elements vis-à-vis the nation. The shadow forces launch a military and ideological-religious-moral-ethical attack on the nation, attempting to assimilate it and make it conform to their 'otherness'. At the same time, the warring factions within the nation adhere to different ideologies and attitudes regarding religion, received tradition, and life in general. Their warring threatens to split the nation politically and ideologically and bring about national self-alienation akin to that experienced in the Assyrian and Babylonian exiles. According to the dissidents, there seems to be a breakdown in the nation's relationship with YHWH and the traditional morality to which it is intimately connected. The dissidents, being very devout to YHWH, step in to rescue the nation, its identity, and its ethical-moral link to YHWH. They continue to serve YHWH in traditional ways despite being opposed and possibly martyred by the shadow forces. They take refuge in the mountainous parts of Judaea and follow a spiritual-military leader. A patriotic teacher and warrior arises amongst them who greatly influences the self-perception etc. of the Judaeans/dissidents, leads them to deliverance by unconventional means and reinstates traditional worship in Israel. This counters the syncretism of the time. It is also possible that women may have enjoyed a higher status at this time.

c) *Objective Analysis*
A comparison between the results of the interim situational analysis and events occurring in Judaea during the Hellenistic era revealed a close correspondence that supports my original hypothesis concerning the book's composition in c. 88 B.C. Nevertheless, I found nothing to support my additional hypotheses that (a) *Judith* 16:23a–b is a gloss added to the basic story in c. 63 B.C. and (b) the book was also edited at that time. I also found no evidence of multiple composition dates or a conflation of multiple narratives. My hypothesis concerning the book's composition and date was consequently emended as follows: *Judith* was composed as a whole shortly after Pompey entered Jerusalem in 63 B.C.

The preceding context led to the following conclusions in respect of the objective analysis:

> For the devout dreamer, Pompey's entrance into Jerusalem and his desecration of the temple entails nothing other than YHWH's judgment of His people for their sins. It also conjures up the spectre of apostasy, moral decay, and national self-alienation that had occurred during the Hellenistic era. In light of this, the dream encourages the dreamer to lay aside her/his negative perception that is informed by Deuteronomistic philosophy, as engaging in this kind of thinking would only incapacitate her/him and finally lead to the complete assimilation of the entire nation in the Greco-Roman otherness. In compensation, the dream alerts the dreamer that YHWH is about to deliver the nation and offers her/him its portrait of Judith for emulation. Furthermore, the dream encourages the dreamer not to disregard the Roman power, but also not to fear either it or the internal forces that may or may not collude with it, as their pride and disobedience towards YHWH would bring about their own demise. Instead, it admonishes the dreamer to integrate the shadow and the anima by changing her/his views of and behaviour towards the 'others' in her/his midst—the women, the non-Judaeans, and the opposing Judaean factions—and to trust in YHWH's strength alone. This, the dream says, will cause a reversal in the balance of power in favour of the dissidents and the entire nation that will return to YHWH *en force*. This would bring about a true transformation of Judaean society—one that comes from the inside out; and it would also

be a true reflection of their spiritual/psychological and salvific heritage, a true fast to YHWH—a true *ekkenosis*, true religion, and true worship in accordance with YHWH's will. Then the desired reign of peace and joy would come.

d) *The Text's Dominant Psychological Concern*
This was established by correlating the self-awareness of the effective protagonist, Achior, and the dilemma facing the devout Jew whose dream this is. It was discovered that the dreamer-author's dilemma is related to stages 2 and 3 of Jung's individuation cycle, which is where Achior's overall self-awareness is situated. Given the exact correlation between these two factors, it became obvious that *Judith's* chief psychological concern lies between stages 2 & 3, viz. separation from the shadow and the differentiation of moral properties. Hence, it was concluded that *Judith* illustrates a phase in the evolution of consciousness prior to the differentiation of moral properties.

e) *Judith as an Individuation Drama*
It was discovered that there is a keen correlation between *Judith* and both forms of the hero myth pattern, proving that Judith's individuation pattern is male vs. that of a woman. The latter involves, inter alia, the intervention of a powerful goddess figure. In turn, this finding (Judith's male individuation pattern) corroborated my earlier suggestion that Judith's male individuation pattern is offset by the author's according the female hero/protagonist a female shadow—the ἅβρα.

It was further shown that the individuation of the Judaean nation, as presented by the Book of Judith, may be explained by means of Jung's uroboric quaternio arrangement, and that the individuation cycles of Judith, Achior, and the Judaeans-Bethulians are successful vs. those of Manasses, the conquered western nations, and Holofernes which are unsuccessful.

The above corroborated my belief that *Judith* is an individuation drama, as expressed in chapter 1.

f) *The Psychological Function of* Judith's *irregularities*
The irregularities singled out for attention in chapter 1 were discussed on the basis of insights gained from the preceding aspects of my analysis:

- Judith's historical inconsistencies reflect the turmoil experienced by the dreamer-author's psyche that regards the Roman invasion as a combination of the terror involved in the country's Assyrian and Babylonian exiles. Similarly, the geographical inconsistencies reflect how topsy-turvy the world had become in the dreamer-author's eyes.
- It is shown that the book's structure is by no means haphazard or unbalanced: the second section provides the denouement for the first on both the surface- and the deep-structure level. Moreover, the first section of the Judithic dream reflects the most important psychological events that are occurring in the dreamer's psyche, while the second provides the dream's solution for the dilemma(s) that the dreamer faces in the first. Following on from this, the 'flatter' style of Section I reflects the dearth that the dreamer's psyche experiences whilst the livelier style of Section II reflects the hope that the dream holds out to her/him should s/he follow its admonitions.
- The duality of Judith's character in terms of spirituality *vs.* carnality, masculine vs. feminine aspects, is explained according to her psychological function in the text: Judith is both anima and ego for the Jewish nation. This means that she carries the unsplit aspects of these archetypes within her—the 'good' and the 'bad'—and is presented as such.
- Far from being a marginal character that merely connects the two sections of *Judith*, Achior is central to the understanding of the narrative on a psychological level as he is its effective protagonist and so the unconscious reflection of the dreamer-author's psyche. He is also Judith's alter ego or shadow. Moreover, all the aspects of the dream analysis are completely dependant on him as the effective protagonist. The narrative would therefore be incomplete without him, making him an integral part of *Judith's* psychological functioning and integrity, as is the case with the rest of the supposed inconsistencies that have been discussed in my thesis.

It is evident from the above that I have followed my proposed methodological course exactly in analysing *Judith* as a national dream according to Jung's dream analysis and Dawson's theory concerning the effective protagonist. The analysis has not only corroborated my theoretical criticism of Jung's work and deepened my understanding of his psychoanalytic theories, it has also afforded me a far deeper insight into the complicated psychological and textual dynamics underlying *Judith*. To the best of my knowledge, my thesis is the first-ever Jungian psychoanalytic reading of *Judith* in its entirety. It is also the first study to analyse *Judith* as a dream by means of Jungian dream analysis and Dawson's method of discerning the effective protagonist. The combination of these methods has brought the text's multivalency to the fore in that it has enabled me to view each character simultaneously as a person (Judaean and/or non-Judaean), a psychological content, and an aspect of Achior's psyche.

The analysis has shown that Achior is the most important character in the book from a psychological point of view. Achior is not only Judith's shadow or alter ego (Roitman 1989/1992), but also the book's effective protagonist upon whom the entire dream analysis and the discernment of the text's time of writing depends. He is thus even more important to the unfolding of the story than Roitman imagined him to be.

Seeing Achior as the effective protagonist of the tale radically transforms the way we read it. At a deep-structure level, *Judith* becomes a story about him and his individuation, even though it is outwardly concerned with Judith's/the Bethulian-Judaean victory over Holofernes. The events of *Judith* as well as the reactions and characteristics of the characters in it are seen as projections/aspects of Achior's psyche, his fears, his desires and the implicit challenge/dilemma facing him.

The analysis has further given the lie to those who have disregarded *Judith* on account of its historical, geographical, and structural inconsistencies and the supposedly questionable, dual character of its eponymous heroine. It has been shown that the book's historical and geographical inconsistencies are an integral part of the narrative; its integrity, as defined by its psychological functioning, has been proven; and the importance of the first section of *Judith* and the structural integrity of the book as a whole has been vindicated (see Craven 1977 and 1983a) and elaborated upon. Judith's integrity has also been restored in that she is regarded as the anima and ego, i.e., as the expression of two archetypes that retain the 'bad' and the 'good' within themselves without conflict.

In my opinion, my analysis has also demonstrated that *Judith* may indeed be classed amongst Jung's visionary works. These, we may recall, are drawn from mankind's collective unconscious and call for psychological elucidation as they do not present their characters in a psychological light. Furthermore, the artist who produces a visionary work is the tool of the collective unconscious. S/he unconsciously chooses to use those archetypal ideas that are best suited to coping with the conscious conditions of her/his time, with the result that her/his work represents a process of self-regulation in the life of nations and various periods in time.

As we have seen, *Judith* possesses mythopoeic qualities that reflect how the dreamer-author was carried along by the wave of the unconscious psyche to produce a dream-like narrative that compensates, warns, and guides the entire nation through the dreamer. In this way, the Judithic dream performs a self-regulatory function in respect of the national psyche.

Furthermore, my analysis has proved that Jungian theory can provide a holistic lens through which to view all aspects of the text and demonstrated the compatibility between Jungian analysis and the biblical texts.

C. *Suggestions for Further Study*

The current study has evoked many questions—almost as many as it has answered. I should like to present these here as suggestions for further study and address some in academic articles at a later point in time:

i) *Judith*/Judith and Society

As we have seen in chapter 3, authors like Narito (1992), Craghan (1982a), Lacocque (1990), and Newsome (1992) acclaim *Judith* for its subversive-liberative potential, particularly for women and the marginalized. However, one has to wonder whether and to what extent *Judith* may be acclaimed as such in the face of the following:

- The obvious protagonist/hero of the tale is the female Judith. Nevertheless, this female character is the personification of an essentially male cultic community and her character follows an exclusively male individuation pattern.
- The effective protagonist is the male Achior.

Further study could investigate the extent to which the above points affect the liberative potential of the book and its heroine, taking into consideration the assertions of authors like Levine (1989) and Schuller (1992) who find that Judith is subverted through her metaphorisation and that *Judith* is an androcentrically orientated document. These factors could then be examined against the backdrop of inter alia:

- The book's insistence on the assimilation of the shadow and the anima.
- The necessity of self-transformation and the transformation of consciousness for 'salvation'.
- The fact that Judith's actions lead to the conscious differentiation of the anima figures represented by the dancing women and the greater independence of the latter in the text.
- Achior's easy acceptance into the Bethulian community and his conversion.
- Judith's freeing of her ἅβρα and distribution of her wealth to Manasses' relatives and her own (were they rich or poor?).
- The identification of Judith/the anima with YHWH.
- The objective analysis of *Judith* which has shown that identification with women and their suffering, as well as the suffering of the weaker elements in society, is a necessity as this will begin the process of integrating the feminine aspects of the national psyche, the anima.
- possible ways that Judith, as an inspiration to women and the marginalized, can be related to the fact that Judith follows a male individuation drama.

ii) *The Intertext of* Judith

Whilst many of the works examined in chapter 3 featured the text's intertextuality, it is my opinion that more in-depth intertextual analyses could be conducted that would build upon the fine works that were referred to in chapter 3. For example, one could examine in detail Judith's relation with the wisdom figure and the strange woman/adulterous woman in Proverbs. Such an analysis could throw more light on the way that Judith embodies the anima archetype in unsplit format. The results of such a study could then lead to a better understanding of the role and position of women at the time in which *Judith* was written—particularly if *Judith's* chronological location amongst the other wisdom writings is established. One could then use the findings to address broader issues such as the way that a text is influenced by the societal conditions of its time.

iii) *Judith and Jungian* Quaternios
My brief discussion on the relation of the individuation drama in *Judith* to Jung's *quaternios*, especially Jung's uroboric *quaternio* arrangement, requires further investigation, particularly in terms of correlating the events and characters of the book to each of Jung's four *quaternios* and determining Achior's/the nation's individuation exactly according to his *quaternio* equation.

iv) *Self-transformation, the Text, and the Reader*
In terms of reader response, one could examine whether and to what extent self-transformation occurs in the reader of the Judithic tale and how the reader's transformation relates to the self-transformation in Judith/the self-transformation patterns/models in *Judith*.

v) *Nonacademic Community Interpretations*
In my opinion, it would be very interesting to compare prescientific approaches to *Judith*—i.e., those of the 'ordinary' or nonacademic reader—and more critical approaches to the text. If Judith functions inspirationally for 'ordinary' people and women in particular (see, e.g., the examples in Stocker's 1998 monograph as indicated in chapter 1), how does this inspiration relate to Judith's male individuation pattern? Such a study could also benefit from an investigation of the interrelation of *Judith's* surface and deep structure in respect of the book's usability for empowering women and the marginalized.

vi) *Judith as a Folktale*
In chapter 3, I discussed Coote's 1975 article that refers to *Judith* as a folktale of the type AT 888, The Faithful Wife: Enslaved Husband is Rescued by his Wife in Disguise as a Man. In my opinion, it would be very rewarding to elaborate upon Coote's study and compare the results with those gained from subjecting *Judith* to Vladimir Propp's categories. According to Propp (1968:21–24), fairy tales exhibit thirty-one stock functions that may be applied to seven characters/*dramatis personae*: the villain, donor, helper, sought-for person/its father, dispatcher, hero (seeker or victim), and false hero. These functions are understood as "an act of a character, defined from the point of view of its significance for the [fairy tale's] course of action" (see also op. cit., 25–70 and 79–83). They are constant elements independent of who

fulfils them, and their sequence is identical even though some elements may be omitted in particular tales. To my mind, it would be profitable to determine which of these functions are present in *Judith* and how the various primal characters (i.e., the characters whose actions are central to the development of the plot) change roles. The results of this analysis could then be compared with the transformations that *Judith's* primal characters go through and the various psychological functions assigned to them in my analysis. Such a comparison would enrich a Jungian analysis of *Judith* and significantly augment our understanding of the book's psychological function and dynamics. It could also help us better to understand how and why the *Judith mythos* was altered (see Elder 1994).

In terms of Propp's morphology of the folktale, it is interesting to note that, contrary to the typical fairy-/folktale, *Judith* does not end in the wedding of the heroine/hero. As indicated in chapter 5, Judith's singleness at the end of the narrative is one of the important differences between *Judith* and the first pattern of the hero myth.

As a final note, I have been pleasantly surprised by the outcome of my study. When I began reading *Judith* with Dawson's categories in mind, I was under the impression that Holofernes would be the effective protagonist. This has not been the case. As we have seen, this role is played by Achior. This discovery in itself has been very gratifying for me as a young researcher in the relatively untouched field of *Judith* studies in general and psychoanalytic approaches to *Judith* in particular. Holofernes' function has been elucidated, the integrity of the book and its heroine have been proven, and I trust that *Judith* has been better understood.

BIBLIOGRAPHY

Ackerman, S. 1998. *Warrior, Dancer, Seductress, Queen. Women in Judges and Biblical Israel.* New York: Doubleday.

Adams, M. V. 1997. The Archetypal School, in Young-Eisendrath, P., & Dawson, T. (eds.) 1997, 101–118.

Alonso-Schökel, L. S. J. 1975. *Narrative Structures in the Book of Judith. Protocol of the Eleventh Colloquy: 27 January 1975.* Berkeley, Cal.: Center for Hermeneutical Studies in Hellenistic and Modern Culture.

——. 1975a. Narrative Structures in the Book of Judith, in Alonso-Schökel 1975, 1–20.

Aschkenasy, N. 1986. *Eve's Journey: Feminine Images in Hebraic Literary Tradition.* Philadelphia: University of Philadelphia Press.

Atkinson, M. 1992a. Robert Bly's *Sleepers Joining Hands*: Shadow and Self, in Sugg, R. P. (ed.) 1992, 83–102.

——. 1992b. Type and Text in *A Study in Scarlet*: Repression and the Textual Unconscious, in Sugg, R. P. (ed.) 1992, 328–342.

Bade, P. 1979. *Femme Fatale. Images of Evil and Fascinating Women.* New York: Mayflower Books.

Baird, J. 1992. "Preface" to *Ishmael.* Jungian Psychology in Criticism: Some Theoretical Problems, in Sugg, R. P. (ed.) 1992, 38–53.

Bal, M. 1995. Head-Hunting: 'Judith' on the Cutting Edge of Knowledge, in Brenner, A. (ed.) 1995, 253–285.

Brenner, A. 1995 (ed.). *A Feminist Companion to Esther, Judith and Susanna.* The Feminist Companion to the Bible, 7. Sheffield, U.K.: Sheffield Academic Press.

—— & Van Dijk-Hemmes, F. 1993. *On Gendering Texts: Female and Male Voices in the Hebrew Bible.* Biblical Interpretation Series, Volume I. Leiden: E. J. Brill.

Brown, J. A. C. 1961. *Freud and the Post-Freudians.* Baltimore: Penguin Books.

Bruns, J. E. 1956. The Genealogy of Judith, *Catholic Biblical Quarterly*, 18:19–22.

Campbell, J. 1992. The Fashioning of Living Myths, in Sugg, R. P. (ed.) 1992, 75–82.

Caponigro, M. S. 1992. Judith, Holding the Tale of Herodotus, in VanderKam, J. C. (ed.), 1992, 47–60.

Coote, M. P. 1975. Comment on "Narrative Structures in the Book of Judith," in Alonso-Schökel 1975, 21–26.

Craghan, J. 1982a. *Esther, Judith, Tobit, Jonah, Ruth.* Old Testament Message, A Biblical-Theological Commentary, 16. Wilmington, Del.: Michael Glazier, Inc.

——. 1982b. Esther, Judith and Ruth: Paradigms for Human Liberation, *Biblical Theological Bulletin* 12:1, 11–19.

Craven, T. 1977. Artistry and Faith in the Book of Judith, *Semeia* 8:75–101.

——. 1983a. *Artistry and Faith in the Book of Judith.* Society of Biblical Literature Dissertation Series, 70. Chico, Cal.: Scholars Press.

——. 1983b. Tradition and Convention in the Book of Judith, *Semeia* 28:49–61.

——. 1995. Judith Prays for Help (Judith 9:1–14); Prayer from Alexander to Constantine: a Critical Anthology, in Lovering, E. H. (ed.) 1995. *Society of Biblical Literature 1995. Seminar Papers.* Atlanta, Ga.: Scholars Press, 208–212.

Dawson, T. 1997. Jung, Literature, and Literary Criticism, in Young-Eisendrath, P. & Dawson, T. (eds.) 1997, 255–280.

Drew, E. 1992. T. S. Eliot: The Mythical Vision, in Sugg, R. P. (ed.) 1992, 9–20.

Dundes, A. 1975. Comment on "Narrative Structures in the Book of Judith," in Alonso-Schökel 1975, 27–29.

Edinger, E. F. 1986. *The Bible and the Psyche: Individuation Symbolism in the Old Testament.* Studies in Jungian Psychology by Jungian Analysts. Toronto, Canada: Inner City Books.

Efthimiadis, H. 1995. Sexual Politics and the Power of Wisdom, unpublished paper presented at the Annual Congress of the Old Testament Society of Southern Africa (September 1995, University of Port Elizabeth, South Africa).

Efthimiadis-Keith, H. 1999a. Judith: Lorena Bobbit of Yesteryear? A Psychoanalytic Perspective on the Book of Judith according to the Castration Complex, *Scriptura* 70:3, 211–228.

——. 1999b. The Dream of *Judith*: A Jungian Psychoanalytic Approach, *Journal of Northwest Semitic Languages* 25:2, 151–169.

——. 1999c. Is There a Place for Women in the Theology of the Psalms? Part I: An Investigation into the Female Imagery of the Ancient Hebrew Psalter, *Old Testament Essays* 12:1, 33–56.

Elder, L. B. 1994. Judith, in Schüssler Fiorenza, E. (ed.) 1994. *Searching the Scriptures. Volume Two: A Feminist Commentary.* New York: Crossroad, 455–469.

Engelsman, J. C. 1994. *The Feminine Dimension of the Divine. A Study of Sophia and Feminine Images in Religion*, revised edition. Wilmette, Ill.: Chiron Publications.

Enslin, M. S. 1972. *The Book of Judith: Greek Text with an English Translation, Commentary and Critical Notes.* Edited with a General Introduction and Appendices by Solomon Zeitlin. Jewish Apocryphal Literature Series. Leiden: E. J. Brill for Dropsie University, Philadelphia.

Fontaine, C. 1988. "The Deceptive Goddess in Ancient Near Eastern Myth: Inanna and Inaras, in Exum," in "Reasoning with the Foxes. Female Wit in a World of Male Power," ed. J. C. & Bos. J. W. H., special issue, *Semeia* 42. Atlanta, Georgia: Scholars Press, 84–102.

Fontana, D. 1993. *The Secret Language of Symbols: A Visual Key to Symbols and Their Meanings.* (Illustrations by Hanna Firmin). London: Pavillion Books Ltd.

Freeman, J. 1964. Introduction, in Jung, C. G. & M.-L. von Franz (eds.) 1964, 9–15.

Friedman, M. 1998. Why Joseph Campbell's Psychologizing of Myth Precludes the Holocaust as Touchstone of Reality, *Journal of the American Academy of Religion* 66:2, 385–401.

Frye, N. 1992. The Archetypes of Literature. "Forming Fours," "Expanding Eyes," in Sugg, R. P. (ed.) 1992, 21–37.

Gelpi, A. 1992. Emily Dickinson and the Deerslayer: The Dilemma of the Woman Poet in America, in Sugg, R. P. 1992 (ed.), 103–117.

Goldenberg, N. R. 1977. Jung after Feminism, in Gross, R. M. (ed.) 1977. *Beyond Androcentrism. New Essays on Women and Religion.* AAR Aids for the Study of Religion, 6. Missoula, Mont.: Scholars Press, 53–66.

Gowan, D. E. 1986. *Bridge between the Testaments: A Reappraisal of Judaism from the Exile to the Birth of Christianity*, third edition, revised. Pittsburgh Theological Monograph Series 14. Alison Park, Pa.: Pickwick Publications.

Hall, J. A. 1989. *Hypnosis: A Jungian Perspective.* Guilford Clinical and Experimental Hypnosis Series. New York: Guilford Press.

Hambidge, J. 1989. *Psigoanalise en lees.* UNIN: J. & J.

Harrington, D. J. 1999. *Invitation to the Apocrypha.* Grand Rapids, Mich.: W. B. Eerdmans Pub. Co.

Hart, D. L. 1997. The Classical Jungian School, in Young-Eisendrath, P. & Dawson, T. (eds.) 1997, 89–100.

Henderson, J. L. 1964. Ancient Myths and Modern Man, in Jung, C. G. and M.-L. von Franz (eds.) 1964, 104–157.

Hengel, M. 1974. *Judaism and Hellenism: Studies in their Encounter in Palestine during the Early Hellenistic Period. Volume One*. London: SCM Press.

Hillman, J. 1992. Healing Fiction, in Sugg, R. P. (ed.) 1992, 129–138.

Hinz, E. J. & Teunissen, J. J. 1992. War, Love and Industrialism: The Ares/Aphrodite/Hephaestus Complex in *Lady Chatterley's Lover*, in Sugg, R. P. (ed.) 1992, 139–152.

Hudson, L. & Jacot, B. 1991. *The Way Men Think: Intellect, Intimacy and the Erotic Imagination*. New Haven & London: Yale University Press.

Jacobi, J. 1942 (fifth edition 1951). *The Psychology of C. G. Jung. An Introduction with Illustrations*, translated by K. W. Bash. London: Routledge & Kegan Paul.

——. 1959. *Complex/Archetype/Symbol in the Psychology of Jung*. Translated from the German by R. Manheim. London: Routledge & Kegan Paul.

Jacoby, M. 1992. The Analytical Psychology of C. G. Jung and the Problem of Literary Evaluation, in Sugg, R. P. (ed.) 1992, 59–74.

Jung, C. G. 1933. *Modern Man in Search of a Soul* (Reprinted 1973). London: Routledge & Kegan Paul.

——. 1940 (eighth impression 1956). *The Integration of the Personality*. Translated by S. Dell. London: Routledge and Kegan Paul.

——. 1953a (second edition, revised and augmented 1966; second printing 1970). *Two Essays on Analytical Psychology*. The Collected Works of C. G. Jung, 7. Translated by R. F. C. Hull. London: Routledge & Kegan Paul.

——. 1953b. (second edition, completely revised 1968; third printing 1974). *Psychology and Alchemy*. The Collected Works of C. G. Jung, 12. Translated by R. F. C. Hull. London: Routledge & Kegan Paul.

——. 1956a (second edition, with corrections 1967; second printing, with corrections 1970). *Symbols of Transformation. An Analysis of the Prelude to a Case of Schizophrenia*. The Collected Works of C. G. Jung, 5. Translated by R. F. C. Hull. London: Routledge & Kegan Paul.

——. 1956b. *Two Essays on Analytical Psychology*, translated by R. F. C. Hull. New York: Meridian Books.

——. 1958a (second edition 1969; fourth impression 1973). *Psychology and Religion: West and East*. The Collected Works of C. G. Jung, 9:1. Translated by R. F. C. Hull. London: Routledge & Kegan Paul.

——. 1959a (second edition 1968; fourth impression 1975). *The Archetypes and the Collective Unconscious*. The Collected Works of C. G. Jung, 9:1. Translated by R. F. C. Hull. London: Routledge & Kegan Paul.

——. 1959b. *Aion. Researches into the Phenomenology of the Self*. The Collected Works of C. G. Jung, 9:2; second edition. Translated by R. F. C. Hull. London: Routledge & Kegan Paul.

——. 1964a. Approaching the Unconscious, in Jung, C. G. and M.-L. von Franz (eds.) 1964, 18–103.

——. 1966. *The Spirit in Man, Art and Literature*. The Collected Works of C. G. Jung, 15. Translated by R. F. C. Hull. London: Routledge & Kegan Paul.

——. 1986. *Jung: Selected Writings*. Introduced by Anthony Storr. Fontana Pocket Readers. Hammersmith, London: Fontana Press.

Jung, C. G. and M.-L. von Franz (eds.) 1964. *Man and His Symbols*. Introduction by J. Freeman (coordinating editor) and Conclusion by M.-L. von Franz. London: Aldus Books.

Kerbelker, M. 1997. Jung's Concept of the Shadow as Portrayed in Three English Novels, unpublished study project submitted in partial fulfillment of the requirements for the degree of master of education (Educational Psychology: Internship) at the University of Stellenbosch, South Africa.

Kikawada, I. 1975. A Comment on Irony: observations on Louis Alonso-Schökel's "Narrative Structures in the Book of Judith," in Alonso-Schökel 1975, 38–39.

Kille, D. A. 1995. Jacob—A Study in Individuation, in Miller, D. L. (ed.) 1995, 40–54.

The King James Version Apocrypha. 1995. Oak Harbor, Wash.: Logos Research Systems Inc.

Koester, H. 1995. *History, Culture, and Religion of the Hellenistic Age*. Volume One: Introduction to the New Testament, second edition. New York: Walter de Gruyter.

Kolenkow, A. B. 1975. Response to Professor Alonso-Schökel's Paper, in Alonso-Schökel 1975, 40–42.

Lacocque, A. 1990. *The Feminine Unconventional. Four Subversive Figures in Israel's Tradition*. Overtures to Biblical Theology. Minneapolis: Fortress Press.

Levine, A.-J. 1989. Character Construction and Community Formation in the Book of Judith, in Lull, D. J. (ed.) 1989, 561–569.

——. 1992. Sacrifice and Salvation: Otherness and Domestication in the Book of Judith, in VanderKam, J. C. (ed.) 1992, 17–30.

——. 1995. Sacrifice and Salvation: Otherness and Domestication in the Book of Judith, in Brenner, A. (ed.) 1995, 208–223.

Liddell and Scott's Greek-English Lexicon, 1983. Abridged Version. Oxford: Clarendon Press.

Lohse E. 1976. *The New Testament Environment*. London: SCM Press Ltd.

Lull, E. D. J. (ed.) 1989. *Society of Biblical Literature 1989 Seminar Papers*. SBL Seminar Paper Series, 28. Atlanta, Ga.; Scholars Press.

Lundbom, J. R. 1975. Response to Louis Alonso-Schökel's Paper "Narrative Structures in the Book of Judith," in Alonso-Schökel 1975, 36–37.

Meredith, B. 1989. Desire and Danger: The Drama of Betrayal, in Bal, M. (ed.) 1989. *Anti-covenant: Counterreading Women's Lives in the Hebrew Bible*. Journal for the Study of the Old Testament Seminar Series, 81. Bible and Literature Series, 22. Sheffield, U.K.: Almond Press, 63–78.

Miller, D. L. (ed.) 1995. *Jung and the Interpretation of the Bible*. N.Y.: Continuum.

Monick, E. 1991. *Castration and Male Rage: The Phallic Wound*. Toronto, Canada: Inner City Books.

Moore, C. A. 1985. *Judith. A New Translation with Introduction and Commentary*. Garden City, N.Y.: Doubleday & Company, Inc.

——. 1989. Why Wasn't the Book of Judith Included in the Hebrew Bible? in Lull, D. J. (ed.) 1989, 579–587.

——. 1992. Why Wasn't the Book of Judith Included in the Hebrew Bible? in VanderKam, J. C. (ed.) 1992, 61–72.

Narito, Z. C. 1992. The Book of Judith, in Lee, O. C. et al. (eds.) 1992. *Women of Courage. Asian Women Reading the Bible*. Asian Women's Resource Centre for Culture and Theology. Seoul, Korea: SaDang Publishing House.

Nelson, M. 1991. *Judith, Juliana, and Elene. Three Fighting Saints*. American University Studies Series IV. English Language and Literature, vol. 135. New York: Peter Lang.

Newsome, J. D. 1992. *Greeks, Romans, Jews: Currents of Culture and Belief in the New Testament World*. Philadelphia: Trinity Press International.

Nickelsburg, G. W. E. 1981. *Jewish Literature Between the Bible and the Mishnah. A Historical and Literary Introduction*. London: SCM Press.

Otzen, B. 2002. *Tobit and Judith* (Guides to Epigrapha and Pseudepigrapha). London: Continuum Sheffield Academic Press.

Patai, R. (ed.) 1990. *The Hebrew Goddess*; third enlarged edition. Detroit, Mich.: Wayne State University Press.

Perry, C. 1997. Transference and Counter-Transference, in Young-Eisendrath, P. & Dawson, T. (eds.) 1997, 141–163.

Peterson, W. H. 1975. Observations on Luis Alonso-Schokel's "Narrative Structures in the Book of Judith" in Alonso-Schökel 1975, 34–35.

Pfeiffer, R. H. 1949. *History of New Testament Times with an Introduction to the Apocrypha*, 1963 edition. London: Adam and Charles Black.
Phipps, W. E. 1992. Assertive Biblical Women. Contributions in Women's Studies, Number 128. Westport, Conn.: Greenwood Press.
Pratt, A. V. 1992a. Spinning among Fields: Jung, Frye, Levi-Strauss, and Feminist Archetypal Theory, in Sugg, R. P. (ed.) 1992, 153–166.
——. 1992b. Archetypal Patterns in Women's Fiction, in Sugg, R. P. (ed.) 1992, 367–375.
Propp, V. 1968. *Morphology of the Folktale*. Austin and London: University of Texas Press.
Raine, K. 1992. C. G. Jung: A Debt Acknowledged, in Sugg, R. P. (ed.) 1992, 167–176.
Roitman, A. D. 1989. The Function and Meaning of Achior in the Book of Judith, in Lull, D. J. (ed.) 1989, 540–549.
——. 1992. Achior in the Book of Judith: His Role and Significance, in VanderKam, J. C. (ed.) 1992, 31–46.
Rollins, W. G. 1983. *Jung and the Bible*. Atlanta, Ga.: John Knox Press.
——. 1995. Psychology, Hermeneutics, and the Bible, in Miller, D. L. (ed.) 1995, 9–39.
——. 1999. *Soul and Psyche. The Bible in Psychological Perspective*. Minneapolis: Fortress Press.
Russo, J. 1997. A Jungian Analysis of Homer's Odysseus, in Young-Eisendrath, P., & Dawson, T. (eds.) 1997, 240–254.
Samuels, A. 1985. *Jung and the Post-Jungians*. London: Routledge & Kegan Paul.
Schäfer, P. 1995. *History of the Jews in Antiquity: Jews of Palestine from Alexander the Great to the Arab Conquest*, translated by D. Chawcat. Luxembourg: Harwood Academic Publishers.
Schuller, E. M. 1992. Apocriefen, in Newson, C. A. & Ringe, S. H. (red.) 1992. *Met Eigen Ogen: Commentaar op de Bijbel vanuit her Perspectief van Vrouwen*. Zoetermeer, The Netherlands: Meinema, 301–311.
Segal, R. A. 1999. Joseph Campbell as Antisemite and as Theorist of Myth: A Response to Maurice Friedman, *Journal of the American Academy of Religion* 67:2, 461–467.
Septuaginta. Deutsche Bibelgesellschaft Stuttgart. 1979. Logos Library Services 2.1.
Shumaker, W. 1975. Critique of Luis Alonso-Schökel on Judith, in Alonso-Schökel 1975, 30–33.
Skehan, P. W. 1963. By the Hand of Judith. *Catholic Biblical Quarterly* 25: 94–110.
Sölle, D., Kirchberger, J. H. & Haag, H. 1994. *Great Women of the Bible in Art and Literature*. Grand Rapids, Mich.: W. B. Eerdmans Pub. Co.
Solomon, H. M. 1997. The Developmental School, in Young-Eisendrath, P., & Dawson, T. (eds.) 1997, 119–140.
Stocker, M. 1998. *Judith: Sexual Warrior. Women and Power in Western Culture*. New Haven & London: Yale University Press.
Stone, N. 1992. Judith and Holofernes: Some Observations on the Development of the Scene in Art, in VanderKam, J. C. (ed.) 1992, 73–94.
Sugg, R. P. (ed.) 1992. *Jungian Literary Criticism*. Evanston, Ill.: Northwestern University Press.
——. 1992a. Introduction to the Selections, in Sugg, R. P. (ed.) 1992, 1–6.
Ulanov, A. 1997. Jung and Religion: The Opposing Self, in Young-Eisendrath, P., & Dawson, T. (eds.) 1997, 296–313.
Van Dijk-Hemmes, F. (ed.) 1986. *'t Is kwaad Gerucht, als Zij niet Binnen Blijft. Vrouwen in Oude Culturen* (esp. 123–147). Utrecht: Hes Uitgevers.
Van Henten, J. W. 1994. Judith as Female Moses: Judith 7–13 in the Light of Exodus 17, Numbers 20, and Deuteronomy 33:8–11, in Van Dijk-Hemmes, F.,

& Brenner, A. (eds.) 1994. *Reflection on Theology and Gender*. Kampen, Netherlands: Kok Pharos Publishing House, 33–48.

——. 1995. Judith as Alternative Leader: A Rereading of Judith 7–13, in Brenner, A. (ed.) 1995, 224–252.

VanderKam, J. C. 1992 (ed.). *"No-one Spoke Ill of Her." Essays on Judith*. Atlanta, Ga.: Scholars Press.

Von Franz, M.-L. 1964. The Process of Individuation, in Jung, C. G. and M.-L. von Franz (eds.) 1964, 158–229.

Watt, T. 1995. Joseph's Dreams, in Miller, D. L. 1995 (ed.), 55–70.

White, S. A. 1989. In the Steps of Jael and Deborah: Judith as Heroine, in Lull, D. J. (ed.) 1989, 570–578.

——. 1992. In the Steps of Jael and Deborah: Judith as Heroine, in VanderKam, J. C. (ed.) 1992, 5–16.

Williams, J. G. 1982. *Women Recounted: Narrative Thinking and the God of Israel*. Bible and Literature Series 6. Sheffield: Almond Press.

Wright, E. 1998. *Psychoanalytic Criticism. A Reappraisal*, second edition. Cambridge, U.K.: Polity Press.

Wuellner, W. (ed.) 1975. Minutes of the Colloquy of March 11, 1975, in Alonso-Shökel 1975, 45–69.

Young-Eisendrath, P. 1997a. Gender and Contrasexuality: Jung's Contribution and Beyond, in Young-Eisendrath, P., & Dawson, T. (eds.) 1997, 223–239.

Young-Eisendrath, P., & Dawson, T. (eds.) 1997. *The Cambridge Companion to Jung*. Cambridge U.K.: Cambridge University Press.

Zeitlin, S. 1972. The Books of Esther and Judith: A Parallel. Introduction, in Enslin, M. S. 1972: 1–37.

Zeligs, D. F. 1974. *Psychoanalysis and the Bible. A Study in Depth of Seven Leaders*. New York: Human Sciences Press, Inc.

INDEX OF BIBLICAL SOURCES

INDEX OF EXTRA-BIBLICAL SOURCES

INDEX OF MODERN AUTHORS